NELSON'S LETTERS TO HIS WIFE
AND OTHER DOCUMENTS
1785–1831

Miniature portrait in water-colour of Lady Nelson, painted by Daniel Orme in 1798, when she was about forty.

NELSON'S
LETTERS TO
HIS WIFE

AND OTHER DOCUMENTS
1785–1831

Edited by

GEORGE P. B. NAISH

F.S.A.

Published in conjunction with
the Navy Records Society by

ROUTLEDGE AND KEGAN PAUL

First published 1958
by Routledge & Kegan Paul Ltd.
(in conjunction with Navy Records Society)

PRINTED IN GREAT BRITAIN BY
SPOTTISWOODE, BALLANTYNE AND CO. LTD.
LONDON AND COLCHESTER

CONTENTS

FACSIMILES

FAMILY TREES

LIST OF ILLUSTRATIONS

PLATES

PREFACE

The editing of this work has taken much time and trouble, and the editor could not have attempted it without the steady, informed and enthusiastic help of Miss Katherine Lindsay-MacDougall, the custodian of MSS. on the staff of the National Maritime Museum. That museum possesses a valuable collection of Nelson MSS., as was first shown at 'The Little Admiral' special exhibition arranged at Greenwich in 1955 in honour of the hundred and fiftieth anniversary of Nelson's death. It was then that we first realized the amount of new material on Nelson which had come to Greenwich from various sources since the war.

We wish to thank the authorities at Monmouth, and the Trustees of the British Museum and of the National Maritime Museum, for permission to use material in their charge. And we are also deeply indebted to Viscount Hood and Viscount Bridport, who have graciously deposited family MSS. on loan in the National Maritime Museum for the use of students. Indeed, we venture to claim that this volume makes a useful appendage to the seven volumes of Nicolas, who in 1846 published the *Dispatches and Letters of Lord Nelson*, the backbone of all subsequent lives of Nelson.

GEORGE NAISH.

NATIONAL MARITIME MUSEUM,
GREENWICH.
March 1958.

GENERAL INTRODUCTION

'In lapidary inscriptions a man is not upon oath', says Dr. Johnson. Yet Richard Brinsley Sheridan seems to have hit the chisel fairly and squarely on the head when composing the epitaph to Nelson's monument in the Guildhall, London, which he finished with the words: 'The period of Nelson's fame can only be the end of time.' Nelson's fame, on the two-hundredth anniversary of his birth, is now safely enshrined in the affections of the British peoples. And the Nelson they chiefly remember is the little, one-armed, one-eyed admiral who hated the French, and who being at heart a simple sailor, was quickly entrapped when he met on shore a beautiful and designing woman. And indeed the contrast between the brilliant, fighting seaman, the idol of his brave tars, sharing his Emma with her elderly ambassador at Naples or Merton has been a subject inviting fantasy and even ribaldry. A contemporary caricature by Gillray, the picture of a large Emma as Dido in despair as her Aeneas sails away, has under it the verse:

'Ah, where, and ah where, is my gallant Sailor gone?
He's gone to fight the Frenchman, for George upon the Throne.
He's gone to fight the Frenchman, t'lose t'other Arm and Eye,
And left me with the old Antique, to lay me down and Cry.'

Nelson's poor wife usually receives but frigid respect. Yet Nelson remained devoted to her for thirteen years, during six of which he lived at home in retirement as a country gentleman. For the remainder he was absent and very active, afloat, only returning for six months to England to recover from the loss of his arm. The mass of his correspondence with her has fortunately survived, extending from his love-letters to a young widow Nisbet in 1785 to his final letter of dismissal to Lady Nelson in 1801. The letters of Nelson to his wife have been edited and published, for the first time in their entirety, in 1958 in memory and honour of the two-hundredth anniversary of the Admiral's birth at Burnham Thorpe on September 29, 1758. This is also the hundredth volume to be published by the Navy Records Society, established in 1893 for the purpose of rendering accessible the sources of our naval history. The other ninety-nine volumes publish, usually for the first time, personal letters, official despatches, instructions and memoranda, autobiographical materials, in fact the sinews from which naval history can be written. This is the first time that a whole volume has been devoted to Nelson.

The reason why the Society has not previously devoted a whole volume to Nelson is not far to seek. The seven volumes of *The Dispatches and Letters of Vice-Admiral Lord Viscount Nelson*, with notes by Sir Nicholas Harris Nicolas, G.C.M.G., have rightly been considered almost complete and has properly formed the backbone of most biographies. Whenever possible, Nicolas transcribed the original manuscript, but this was not possible in certain cases. For example, he could not get access to Nelson's letters to his wife and had to reprint the version given by Clarke and M'Arthur in their *Life and Services of Admiral Lord Nelson*, published in 1809, although he rightly suspected them to have been guilty of most of the editorial faults, such as omissions, alterations, joining up of letters and misdatings. Fortunately the originals, many of which Lady Nelson had withheld from Clarke and M'Arthur in the first place, have been discovered as will be described later, since Nicolas published his monumental work in 1846. Carola Oman consulted them before writing her biography of Nelson published in 1947, and quoted some new extracts, but gave no complete transcripts. They are now being published in full with the generous permission and co-operation of the Monmouth Borough Council.

In these letters there is a great deal of fresh information about Nelson's service in the West Indies and Mediterranean as a captain. New light is thrown by the letters on Nelson's character, his thoughts and daily habits, and on his relations with his stepson Josiah Nisbet and the other youngsters he took to sea with him and brought up to be naval officers. His letters help to explain his happy memories of his long commission in command of the *Agamemnon*. Nelson's letters during this period provide an interesting study of the life of a zealous naval officer during an important period of our naval history, which becomes of particular interest when that officer is Horatio Nelson.

Nelson's letters to his wife divide naturally into three periods afloat. Some thirty letters are written from the *Boreas* in the West Indies, mostly during his courtship of the 'widow Nisbet'. Nelson has been quarrelling with the local island administrations over the illegal activities of the American traders, and conducting Prince William on a round of good-will visits to the islands. He marries Fanny in March 1787 and Prince William gives the bride away. They return to England in May 1787.

After some six years ashore, Nelson joins the *Agamemnon* in 1793, his first ship of the line, and proceeds to the Mediterranean with Lord Hood's flag. One hundred and twenty-three letters from this period, 1793–7, were written from the *Agamemnon*, and another forty-one from the *Captain*, *La Minerve*, *Irresistible*, and *Theseus*. In August 1797 he sails home, having lost his right arm and the sight of his right eye. The occupation of Toulon, the sieges of Bastia and Calvi, the blockade of Cadiz, the victory off Cape St. Vincent and the failure off Santa Cruz are all described. The consul at Leghorn referred to Captain Nelson in 1794 as 'the most active of his Majesty's commanders in these seas, where none are idle'. Nelson's letters testify to the truth of this remark, which he epitomized to his wife 'active service or none'. His advice was freely given to, and often accepted by, Lord Hood and Lord St. Vincent. His conception of combined operations by land and sea was both novel and successful in Corsica.

The last forty letters cover the Nile campaign and Nelson's sojourn at the Neapolitan court from 1798 to 1800. There is little new here, for some of the Nile letters are probably missing, and his extravagant descriptions of Neapolitan hospitality and the Hamiltons' many kindnesses are well known, but there are some interesting details about his 'Mediterranean fag' in the years which followed his great victory of August 1, 1798.

Sixty-four letters from his wife to Nelson, now in the British Museum, belonging to the years 1794 and 1797–1800, give the other side of the picture. She deserves the reader's sympathy. Nelson is always imploring her to buy a suitable residence in England for their future retirement together. He is always coming home, and so seldom comes. His fondness for Josiah turns to impatient criticism which can only wound a mother's heart, the consolation offered being that perhaps Lady Hamilton, and she alone, can reform his errant stepson, with his 'warm disposition'. Little attention has been paid to these letters. Lady Nelson is too easily written off as a worried, neurotic woman, occupied with trifles and incapable of understanding the importance of her husband's achievements, only lamenting his prolonged absences. Her letters give a different impression. She tells her husband the naval gossip of the day from Bath and London, where she spent the greater part of his absence with his father, the Reverend Edmund Nelson. Family news fills a large part of her paper. She welcomes returning naval officers, who come to visit her with the latest information about her husband's health, and her son's progress. She rejoices in his promotions. She settles into the house they bought together in his short time in England when he returned to recover his health in September 1797, before returning for his victorious campaign in the summer of 1798, and has a constant stream of his relations to stay. Unfortunately the last of her letters for this period which has survived was written in April 1800 and there are only seven short letters from Nelson to her for the whole of 1800. It is not therefore possible from their correspondence to trace any lessening of affection or confidence, before Nelson returned to England in November 1800.

The final separation between Lord and Lady Nelson in 1801 was mainly due to his infatuation for Lady Hamilton, but contributory causes were his dissatisfaction with her son's conduct as a naval officer and her own lack of appreciation of the value of his services to his country.

SOURCES

(a) NELSON'S LETTERS TO HIS WIFE

1785–1800

This collection of 251 letters written by Nelson to his wife over a period of fifteen years has been compiled almost entirely from the original letters now preserved in the Nelson Museum at Monmouth, only nineteen letters being taken from other sources. The collection does not claim to represent the full extent of Nelson's correspondence with his wife during that time. Although he used all means of conveyance to ensure the safe arrival of his letters, sending some by the regular postal service, which he thought most reliable, others under Admiralty cover, by officers returning to England, and through members of his family holding official positions, and stated more than once that he was convinced that most of his letters arrived eventually, it is clear that some were lost. Others have escaped from the main series. Both Nicolas and Pettigrew, when compiling their works on Nelson in the 1840's, found a few letters for the years 1798, 1799 and 1801 which had not been quoted by Clarke and M'Arthur. A story is current among the descendants of Lady Nelson that in the middle of the last century, a fit of tidiness led to a moth-eaten hat of Nelson's being burnt, together with some letters to his wife which were found in the same hat-box. Six are in the Huntington Library in California.

Until now the only version of these letters which has been available has been that given by Clarke and M'Arthur in their standard life of Lord Nelson published in 1809. Since their biography concentrated on Nelson's public life, little real use was made of this material. The reference made in the advertisement to the correspondence indicates Lady Nelson's attitude to the publication of the letters, and may explain why only short extracts, often of an impersonal nature, are all that has been taken from long letters. 'The very interesting correspondence with Lady Nelson that marks through a long interval the private character and feelings of her husband in the vicissitudes and various professional incidents of his life, were kindly though reluctantly granted.' The unreliability of Clarke and M'Arthur's transcripts is well known. Nicolas wrote of them in scathing terms. 'Dr. Clarke and Dr. M'Arthur seem to have been actuated by the same love of improving the letters which fell into their hands, as their predecessor Mr. Charnock; and though they, like him, thereby disregarded the first principle of editorship, they are rarely open to the suspicion of having made the alterations from a worse motive than the desire to exhibit Nelson's production in what they considered a fitting epistolary state; as if a hero could never think, write or speak naturally, but must always appear in full dress. Be the motive, however, what it might, the effect is that no reliance can be placed on the literal fidelity of any one extract printed in their voluminous work.' The extracts of Nelson's letters to his wife which they quoted are not only edited in this way, but are confused, several letters of different dates being made to appear as one letter. Very few letters are given in full, and about half the series has not been used. Since Nicolas's *Dispatches and Letters of Lord Nelson*, is the standard work of reference for Nelson's correspondence, references have been given to his quotations which are exact copies of Clarke and M'Arthur's.

The history of these letters is rather obscure. When Lady Nelson died in 1831 no mention of the disposal of her papers was made in her will. Her first husband's cousin, Mrs. Francklyn, who had been living with her for some years, seems to have taken charge of them. In spite of his well-advertised efforts Nicolas was unable to bring the collection to light when preparing the text of his monumental work. The Rev. J. S. Clarke had died some years previously, and the executors of Dr. M'Arthur, who died in 1840, were chary of admitting that they still had any papers in their possession. Lord Hood, one of the many who had lent documents for publication in their life of Nelson, had after much perseverance been able to get only one bundle of letters returned in 1840, although he knew the M'Arthur family still had others in their possession.

It was the end of the century before the collection came to light again. In 1898 Mr. Thomas Case, President of Corpus Christi College, Oxford, and a keen Nelson collector, discovered sixty letters from Nelson to his wife in the possession of Mrs. Francklyn's son, Alexander, who had taken his mother's maiden name of Webbe. Further search revealed another 172 letters and their publication was discussed. The project did not come to anything, apart from a series of articles which appeared in *Literature* in 1898 written by Case, based on the first batch of letters which he had found. After Mr. Webbe's death, the collection, which included other Nelson family letters, pamphlets and contemporary documents, was auctioned by

b

Messrs. Christie, Manson and Woods on July 14, 1914. The whole collection was bought by Messrs. Quaritch, from whom it was purchased by Lady Llangattock, who presented it to the Nelson Museum at Monmouth.

Nelson's letters to his wife are now preserved in three elaborately bound volumes, with Lady Nelson's wedding-ring bound into the cover of the first volume. The other letters and papers have been made into two more volumes bound in similar style. All the letters quoted by Clarke and M'Arthur are now in the Monmouth collection, with two exceptions. A copy of one short and relatively unimportant letter (No. 83, August 11, 1794) has been bound up with the original letters, and one letter (No. 12, August 19, 1786) is only known from Clarke and M'Arthur's version. Of the 131 letters which were quoted by Clarke and M'Arthur, considerably less than half the full text has been given, and 102 letters have not been published even in extract. Some explanatory notes have been added by Lady Nelson, and notes made by Clarke in pencil occur on several of the letters, doubtful dates being queried. The present arrangement of the letters is the work of Mr. Case, and a few notes written in 1904 are probably his.

In the text now given, the letters have been arranged in strict chronological order, and spelling and punctuation have been modernized, except for proper names. Additions of words which have been lost owing to the tearing of the paper where the letter was sealed, or which seem necessary to the sense, have been shown in brackets. Nelson's style is sometimes involved and there are places where the meaning is clearer than the grammar.

(b) LADY NELSON'S LETTERS TO HER HUSBAND

1794, 1797–1801

The basis of this collection of seventy-four letters from Lady Nelson to her husband is the series of sixty-four letters preserved among the Nelson MSS. at the British Museum bought from Lord Bridport in 1895 (Add. MSS. 34988). The other ten letters have been added from various sources: two from the original documents, two from Lady Nelson's drafts, and six from printed sources. Although a disappointingly small collection, it is remarkable that any of Nelson's letters from his wife have survived at all, since his policy was to destroy all such personal letters. According to Clarke and M'Arthur, when Nelson was preparing for the attack on Santa Cruz in July 1797, he called his stepson Josiah to his cabin 'that he might assist in arranging and burning his mother's letters'. If this is true, only one small batch of letters written in the last quarter of 1794, and the letters he had received in the last few months, twenty-five of them written between February and May 1797, then escaped destruction. The letters covering the last three years of their correspondence which have survived are far from being a full record. The problems of maintaining communication between England and the Mediterranean in time of war, combined with the uncertainty of Nelson's movements, made the arrival of letters a matter of chance, and, in spite of his optimism that the letters which did not arrive had probably never been written, even Nelson admitted that some of his letters had been lost. After Nelson's separation from his wife in 1801 no further interest can have been taken in preserving these letters.

Nicolas wrote of them with some appreciation as being 'in their style perfectly simple and unaffected, filled with expressions of warm attachment to her husband, great anxiety for his safety and lively interest in his fame and entire submission to his wishes', but he only quoted four short extracts as footnotes to Nelson's letters.

(c) MSS. MATERIAL RELATING TO NELSON'S SERVICES

1785–1800

In order to supplement the correspondence between Nelson and his wife, use has been made of several other collections of documents, found in the various collections of Nelson papers and in those of his colleagues. These papers have been printed in the appendices to the six chapters into which Nelson's letters have been divided, and in the last chapter, which forms the epilogue.

Some of these documents have been taken from the Monmouth collection, which includes several letters between members of the Nelson family, as well as Nelson's journals of the siege of Bastia and Calvi, looked for in vain by Nicolas. A few have been taken from the Bridport papers, now at the British Museum (Add. MSS. 34902–34992), but as these papers have always been available to students, their contents are generally well known through the work of Sir Harris Nicolas and Nelson's biographers. The other collections which have been used are in the National Maritime Museum. The most important of these is the Croker collection, which now forms part of the papers of Sir Thomas Phillipps of Middle Hill, the eccentric nineteenth-century collector, who died in 1872. John Wilson Croker, secretary to the Admiralty from 1809 to 1830, acquired a valuable section of Nelson's papers in 1817, which had come indirectly from Lady Hamilton. It included a very large number of letters received by Nelson, some drafts of his correspondence, his sea journal, kept almost daily from June 1793 till February 1794, and a series of his letters to Lady Hamilton. A small selection of these papers was lent by Croker to Sir Harris Nicolas, but some of the longer items, notably the journal, were not printed. After Croker's death in 1857, his collection was acquired by Sir Thomas Phillipps, and it was bought with his other naval manuscripts by the National Maritime Museum in 1946.

Other collections which have been used include some Nelson family letters found in the residue of the Bridport papers, which did not go through the sale-room, in the Girdlestone papers, which came from the descendants of Mrs. Bolton, Nelson's elder sister, and in the Nelson-Ward Collection. The personal papers of Lord Hood, Lord Minto, Lord St. Vincent and Lord Keith have also been used. Two valuable groups of Hamilton papers, a series of letters from Sir William Hamilton to Sir John Acton, prime minister of Naples, and the letters received by Sir William during the last ten years of his time as ambassador at Naples, together with his draft replies, add considerably to the unravelling of Neapolitan diplomacy.

Among the letters now in the Autograph collection at the National Maritime Museum are twenty-seven from Nelson to the Duke of Clarence, a series which Sir Harris Nicolas looked for in vain in 1844. Among them are a number which were not used by Clarke and M'Arthur. Some important Nelson letters which have been separated from their original groups, and become collectors' gems, have also found their way to the National Maritime Museum. One such letter, from Nelson to St. Vincent, was in fact deposited in the Museum while this book was in the press (p. 380).

PRINTED SOURCES

The following books containing original material have been used and quoted:

The Life of Admiral Lord Nelson K.B. from his lordship's manuscripts. The Rev. James Stanier Clarke, F.R.S., and John M'Arthur, LL.D. (2 vols. London, 1809.)

Clarke and M'Arthur relied principally on the very large collection of MSS. inherited from his brother by the first Earl Nelson, which is now in the British Museum and known as the Bridport collection. They also borrowed a good many letters from Nelson's better-known correspondents, such as the Duke of Clarence and Lord Hood, and from Lady Nelson.

The Dispatches and Letters of Vice-Admiral Lord Viscount Nelson, with notes. Sir Nicholas Harris Nicolas. (7 vols. London, 1844–6.)

> Where possible, Nicolas made his transcripts from original sources, but in some cases, particularly for Nelson's letters to his wife, and to the Duke of Clarence, Nicolas was forced to rely on the extracts given by Clarke and M'Arthur.

Memoirs of the life of Vice-Admiral Lord Viscount Nelson, derived principally from his private correspondence, hitherto unpublished. Thomas Joseph Pettigrew, F.R.S., F.S.A. (2 vols. London, 1849.)

> Pettigrew bought a large mass of Nelson papers from the creditors of Lady Hamilton, including some private as well as official correspondence, which he used as the basis for this work. Some further manuscripts from Lady Hamilton's collection were acquired by John Wilson Croker, secretary to the Admiralty, in 1817. These are now in the National Maritime Museum among the Phillipps papers and have been extensively used in preparing this text. They have not been previously published.

The collection of autograph letters and historical documents formed by Alfred Morrison: *The Hamilton and Nelson Papers.* (2 vols. Printed for private circulation 1893.)

> Morrison, a well-known collector, bought many of the papers which had been in the possession of Sir William Hamilton's heirs, as well as a large number of those which Thomas Pettigrew had collected and partially used for his memoirs of Lord Nelson.

The Wynne Diaries. Edited by Anne Fremantle. (2 vols. Oxford University Press, 1937.)

> The diaries of Betsy Wynne, who married Captain, later Sir, Thomas Fremantle.

Publications of the Navy Records Society:

> Volume XXV. *Nelson and the Neapolitan Jacobins.* Edited by H. C. Gutteridge. (1903.)
>
> Volume XC. *The Keith Papers*, vol. II. Edited by C. Lloyd. (1950.)
>
> Volume XCII. *The Naval Miscellany*, vol. IV (1952):
>
> No. V. 'Prince William and Lieut. Schomberg.' Edited by B. Ranft.
>
> No. VII. 'Corsica, 1794.' Edited by Admiral J. H. Godfrey.

The Huntington Library Quarterly. Volume XI (1947). 'Lord and Lady Nelson: some unpublished letters.' By Hardin Craig, junior.

FACSIMILES

1. Nelson to his wife, from London, on his way to Chatham to commission the *Agamemnon*, March 4, 1793.

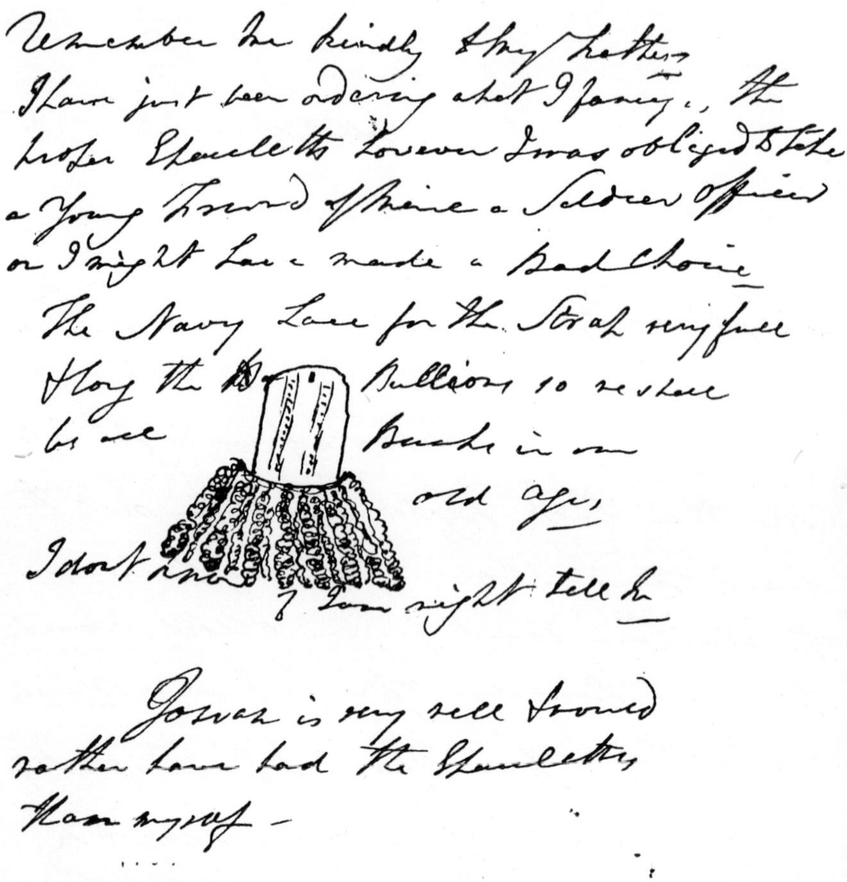
Remember me kindly to my Father
I have just been ordering what I fancy is the
proper Epaulette however I was obliged to take
a Young Friend of mine a Soldier Officer
or I might have made a Bad Choice
The Navy Lace for the Strap very full
& long the [illegible] Bullions so as to stand
[illegible] all Brushes in our
old age,
I don't know [illegible]
you might tell him
Josiah is very well & would
rather have had the Epaulettes
than myself —

2. Nelson's sketch of a naval epaulette, July 18, 1795 (see p. 217).

3. Nelson to his wife after the battle of Cape St. Vincent, February 16, 1797
(see p. 314).

to the first Order of Chivalry in Christendom — such at least "was my aim in the indication

N B

The thip: shold have 13 fingers or sprigs instead is The 13 thips Taken —

4. Description and sketch of the chelengk, the Turkish decoration given to Nelson after the Battle of the Nile (see p. 405).

5. Nelson's draft of his last letter to Lady Nelson, March 4, 1801 (see p. 580).

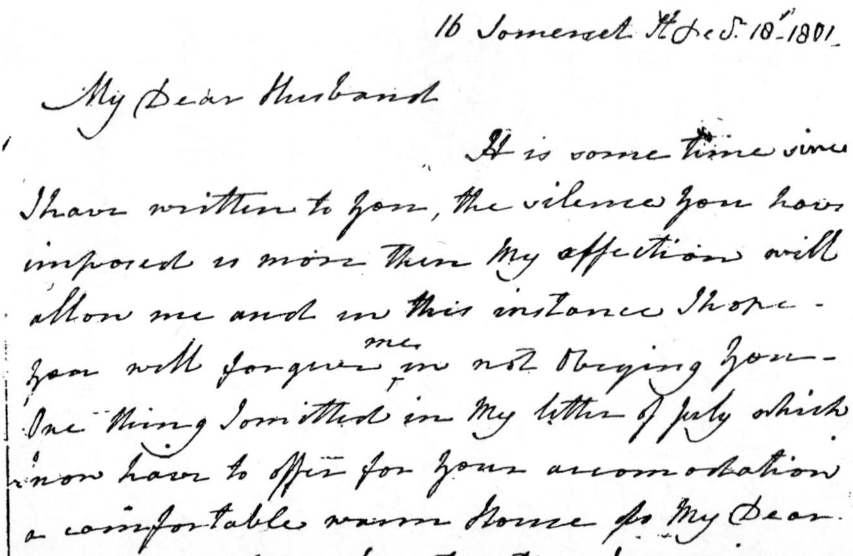

16 Somerset St Decr 18th 1801

My Dear Husband

It is some time since I have written to you, the silence you have imposed is more than my affection will allow me and in this instance I hope you will forgive me in not obeying you — One thing I omitted in my letter of July which I now have to offer for your accommodation a comfortable warm House. Do My Dear Husband let us live together I can never be happy till such an event takes place. I assure you again I have but one wish in the World, To please you — let every thing be buried in Oblivion it will pass away like a dream I can now only intreat you to believe I am most sincerely & affectionately

Your Wife
Frances H Nelson

6. Lady Nelson's last letter to Nelson, December 18, 1801.

7. Endorsement on the outer cover of Letter No. 6 by Mr. Alexander Davison (see p. 596).

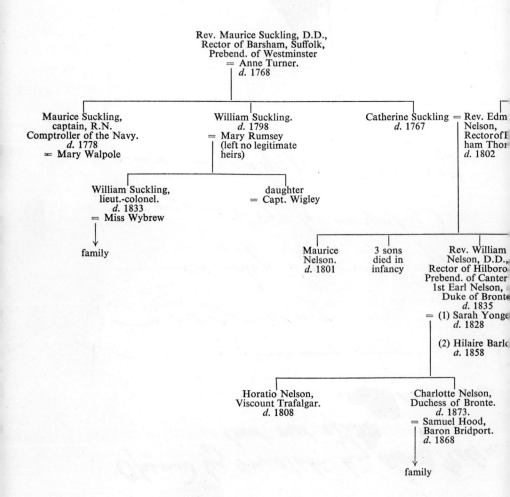

Rev. Maurice Suckling, D.D.,
Rector of Barsham, Suffolk,
Prebend. of Westminster
= Anne Turner.
d. 1768

Maurice Suckling,
captain, R.N.
Comptroller of the Navy.
d. 1778
= Mary Walpole

William Suckling.
d. 1798
= Mary Rumsey
(left no legitimate
heirs)

Catherine Suckling = Rev. Edm
d. 1767   Nelson,
                    Rector of F
                    ham Thor
                    d. 1802

William Suckling,
lieut.-colonel.
d. 1833
= Miss Wybrew

daughter
= Capt. Wigley

family

Maurice
Nelson.
d. 1801

3 sons
died in
infancy

Rev. William
Nelson, D.D.,
Rector of Hilboro
Prebend. of Canter
1st Earl Nelson,
Duke of Bronte
d. 1835
= (1) Sarah Yonge
d. 1828

(2) Hilaire Barlo
d. 1858

Horatio Nelson,
Viscount Trafalgar.
d. 1808

Charlotte Nelson,
Duchess of Bronte.
d. 1873.
= Samuel Hood,
Baron Bridport.
d. 1868

family

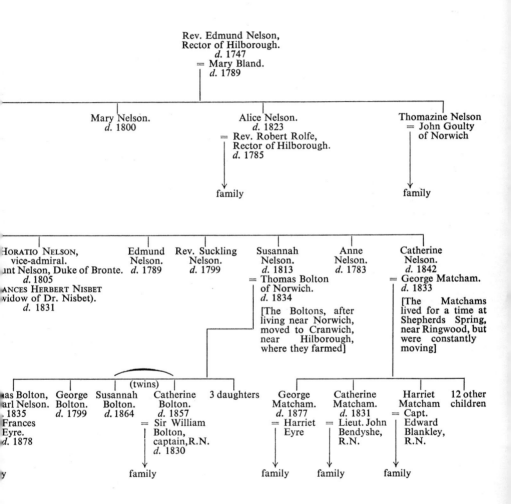

Rev. Edmund Nelson,
Rector of Hilborough.
d. 1747
= Mary Bland.
d. 1789

Mary Nelson.
d. 1800

Alice Nelson.
d. 1823
= Rev. Robert Rolfe,
Rector of Hilborough.
d. 1785

family

Thomazine Nelson
= John Goulty
of Norwich

family

HORATIO NELSON,
vice-admiral.
d. 1805
Viscount Nelson, Duke of Bronte.
FRANCES HERBERT NISBET
(widow of Dr. Nisbet).
d. 1831

Edmund
Nelson.
d. 1789

Rev. Suckling
Nelson.
d. 1799

Susannah
Nelson.
d. 1813
= Thomas Bolton
of Norwich.
d. 1834

[The Boltons, after
living near Norwich,
moved to Cranwich,
near Hilborough,
where they farmed]

Anne
Nelson.
d. 1783

Catherine
Nelson.
d. 1842
= George Matcham.
d. 1833

[The Matchams
lived for a time at
Shepherds Spring,
near Ringwood, but
were constantly
moving]

(twins)

Thomas Bolton,
Earl Nelson.
, 1835
Frances
Eyre.
d. 1878

George
Bolton.
d. 1799

Susannah
Bolton.
d. 1864

Catherine
Bolton.
d. 1857
= Sir William
Bolton,
captain, R.N.
d. 1830

3 daughters

George
Matcham.
d. 1877
= Harriet
Eyre

Catherine
Matcham.
d. 1831
= Lieut. John
Bendyshe,
R.N.

Harriet
Matcham
= Capt.
Edward
Blankley,
R.N.

12 other
children

family

family

family

family

The HERBERTS of NEVIS

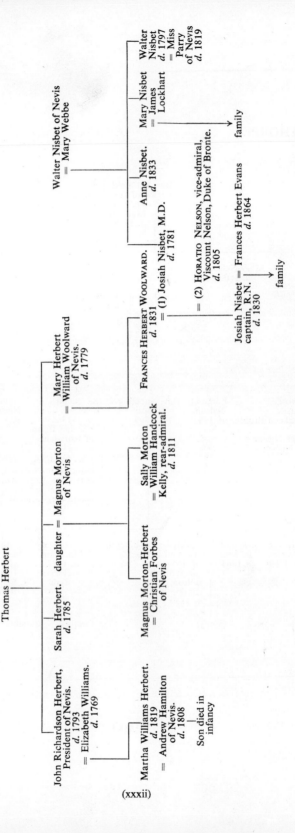

Thomas Herbert

John Richardson Herbert, President of Nevis. *d.* 1793 = Elizabeth Williams. *d.* 1769

Sarah Herbert. *d.* 1785

daughter = Magnus Morton of Nevis

Mary Herbert = William Woolward of Nevis. *d.* 1779

Walter Nisbet of Nevis = Mary Webbe

Martha Williams Herbert. *d.* 1819 = Andrew Hamilton of Nevis. *d.* 1808

Son died in infancy

Magnus Morton-Herbert = Christian Forbes of Nevis

Sally Morton = William Handcock Kelly, rear-admiral. *d.* 1811

FRANCES HERBERT WOOLWARD. *d.* 1831 = (1) Josiah Nisbet, M.D. *d.* 1781

= (2) HORATIO NELSON, vice-admiral, Viscount Nelson, Duke of Bronte. *d.* 1805

Josiah Nisbet = Frances Herbert Evans captain, R.N. *d.* 1864 *d.* 1830

family →

Anne Nisbet. *d.* 1833

Mary Nisbet = James Lockhart

Walter Nisbet *d.* 1797 = Miss Parry of Nevis *d.* 1819

family →

Chapter 1

THE LITTLE CAPTAIN OF THE BOREAS
1785–1792

Introduction

What manner of man was this Captain Nelson of the *Boreas*, who proposed to the widow Nisbet on the island of Nevis in 1785? Much has been written of Vice-Admiral Lord Nelson, the darling of the nation, whose remains, in great pomp and with real sorrow, were deposited in St. Paul's Cathedral. It is worth while to try and distinguish the younger man before his great fame had crystallized him into a public figure. Nelson's own sketch of his early career, which he wrote for the editors of *The Naval Chronicle*, tells us what he thought noteworthy in it, and a shorter version, which stops when he assumes command of the *Agamemnon* in 1793, is printed here in the Appendix to Chapter 1.

In 1785 he was already distinguished as an active officer with an exceptional knowledge of all the aspects of his profession. He prided himself on being a seaman, a disciplinarian, a tactician, a diplomat and a soldier. That he held a command in times of peace was as much a tribute to his own energy, efficiency and winning graces, as it was to the original patronage of his uncle, Captain Maurice Suckling, who had first taken his nephew to sea in 1771, and looked after his interests until his sudden death in 1778. When he died Captain Suckling was Comptroller of the Navy and head of the Navy Board. But his death did not leave the young officer without friends, and Nelson became a post captain at the earliest opportunity, even before the regulation age of twenty-one. And this early promotion was very important because the step to flag rank depended on seniority and a captain's position on the list. He had always kept in touch with and honoured the memory of all his early captains and admirals.

The shortest sketch of Nelson's service career before 1785 brings out the variety of his service, and the zeal which had carried him forward, despite ill health. Nelson was only twelve years old when in 1771 he joined as a midshipman his maternal uncle's ship the *Raisonable*, 64 guns, lying in the Medway. We are told his uncle was not on board; no one was expecting the lad, and it was some time before he could attract anyone's notice. There was a threat of war with Spain, but the war-clouds dispersed and his uncle sent the boy to learn to be a sailor in a merchant ship, afterwards receiving him back again as a midshipman into his next command, the *Triumph*, guard-ship at Chatham. There was reason in this, because, to pass as a lieutenant, among other things the candidate had to have served six years at sea, two of them as a midshipman in one of his Majesty's ships. In 1773 the influence of his uncle enabled Nelson to volunteer successfully to serve, although under age, in a voyage of discovery towards the North Pole, promoted by the philosophers of the Royal Society, and to be undertaken by two ships, specially strengthened bomb vessels, the *Racehorse*, Captain Constantine Phipps, later Lord Mulgrave, and the *Carcass*, Captain Skeffington Lutwidge. Nelson served as a coxswain of the captain's barge in the *Carcass*. Nothing much was accomplished, but the two ships were beset in the ice and were in danger of being crushed and wrecked when a change of wind shifted the ice-pack and released the ships. On this voyage, the young Nelson disappeared over the ice one night with a friend, and attacked a polar bear with a musket which misfired. He wanted a hearth-rug for his father. He failed to get his bear, but his high spirits impressed his captain in his favour despite his disobedience to orders. Nelson's next service was the very opposite, for he sailed to the East Indies in the *Seahorse*, frigate, Captain Farmer, and in the course of duty visited the ports from the Bay of Bengal to the Persian Gulf, taking care to make himself a pilot for these seas, for in those days, when charts were poor and uncorrected or even non-existent, local knowledge was of greater importance to an officer than it is today. Unhappily Nelson's health gave way and his kind friend and commander-in-chief, Commodore Sir Edward Hughes, sent him home in the *Dolphin*, Captain Pigot. In 1776 he was made an acting lieutenant in the *Worcester*, Captain Mark Robinson, of whom Nelson was wont to remark proudly, 'he felt as easy when I was upon deck, as any officer in the ship'. Nelson passed as a lieutenant on April 8, 1777. He was in fact too young, because he would not be twenty years of age until the next year, but this was quite often overlooked. His uncle, now Comptroller of the Navy, was the senior of the examining captains, but concealed their relationship until the candidate had passed with credit.

Nelson was soon commissioned as second lieutenant of the *Lowestoffe*, frigate, Captain William Locker, who was to become Lieutenant-Governor at Greenwich and one of Nelson's dearest friends. Cruising on the Jamaican station they made a prize of an American privateer. In a gale of wind the first lieutenant failed to get on board to take possession and the master of the *Lowestoffe* stepped forward to take his place. But Nelson stopped him, saying, 'It is my turn now, if I come back it will be yours.' Needless to say, Nelson boarded the prize. His zeal on service, and courage and capable seamanship, as usual so impressed his shipmates that they remembered the incident.

In 1778 Admiral Sir Peter Parker took him into the flagship as third lieutenant of the *Bristol*. This was a usual way of bringing forward exceptional or favoured officers, and rising by rotation to become first lieutenant Nelson was soon given the command of the *Badger*, sloop of war. On June 10, 1779, Nelson was made a post captain and appointed to command the *Hinchingbrooke*, 20 guns. An expedition was planned against the Spanish settlements on the river San Juan, now the border between Nicaragua and Costa Rica, with the intention of seizing Lake Nicaragua and so severing Spanish America in two. Captain Nelson was given the naval command: he was to take the troops there and land them. There was a river to ascend, guns to get on shore, batteries to erect, and many other difficulties to contend with which could better be overcome with help from the sailors. So Nelson volunteered for service with the army, and with a small party of seamen materially assisted at the capture of Fort San Juan and other enterprises. Captain John Polson, commanding the land forces, spoke very highly of Captain Nelson, 'the first on every service, whether by day or night; and there was scarcely a gun fired, but what was pointed by him, or Lieutenant Despard, chief engineer.' This was a very difficult operation and the climate claimed very many victims, including at last Nelson. His devoted nurses included Lady Parker, his admiral's wife, whom he never forgot. He returned to England in the *Lion*, Captain Cornwallis, and retired to Bath to try and recover his health. A portrait by Rigaud, in the National Maritime Museum, shows him at this time, aged twenty-three, standing in a post captain's full-dress uniform with the fort at San Juan in the background. He gave this portrait to Captain Locker, whose son sold it to the third Earl Nelson, from whose descendants it came to Greenwich. It used to hang in Captain Locker's residence at Greenwich.

As soon as he thought his health was restored, as usual Nelson applied for a ship and was given the *Albemarle*, a frigate of 28 guns. In her he first served a winter in the North Sea, taking a convoy to the Baltic, and in the spring he was ordered with another convoy to Newfoundland. He thought the climate in the wintertime would kill him, but would not seek a change. At Quebec that winter he made friends with Alexander Davison, who later became his business agent and lifelong friend. At Quebec, before he left for Sandy Hook, Davison persuaded him against marrying an amiable American lady who had attracted his fancy. Nelson knew he would, at

Sandy Hook, meet Lord Hood, who was second-in-command to Admiral
Pigot in the West Indies, and he hoped to serve under him, although Rear-
Admiral the Hon. Robert Digby commanded the North American Station
based on New York. The *Albemarle* arrived at New York on November 13,
1782. Rear-Admiral Lord Hood's flagship, the *Barfleur*, lay off Staten
Island, and a midshipman, Prince William Henry, had the watch on deck
'when Captain Nelson of the *Albemarle* came in his barge alongside, who
appeared to be the merest boy of a captain I ever beheld; and his dress was
worthy of attention. He had on a full laced uniform; his lank unpowdered
hair was tied in a stiff Hessian tail of an extraordinary length; the old
fashioned flaps of his waistcoat added to the general quaintness of his
figure, and produced an appearance which particularly attracted my
notice; for I had never seen anything like it before, nor could I imagine
who he was or what he came about. My doubts were, however, removed
when Lord Hood introduced me to him. There was something irresistibly
pleasing in his address and conversation; and an enthusiasm, when speaking on professional subjects, that showed he was no common being.' The
Duke of Clarence dictated these memories to Nelson's biographer in 1806,
but they give a picture of the young Nelson which agrees well with the
Rigaud portrait.

Captain Samuel Hood had returned from North America in 1771 to
command the *Royal William*, guardship in Portsmouth harbour. In 1778
he became Commissioner at Portsmouth, and remained so until he obtained
flag rank in 1780 and was made second-in-command to Rodney. Therefore
it is not surprising that Nelson already knew him. He went out of his way
to call on Lord Hood, and incidentally be introduced to Prince William
Henry, before putting himself under the orders of Admiral Digby.
Bromwich, then the first lieutenant of the *Albemarle*, describes this
meeting. 'You are come upon a fine station for making prize money,' said
the admiral. 'Yes, sir,' replied Nelson, 'but the West Indies is the station
for honour.' Nelson was quite determined to serve under Hood, who had
been a friend of Captain Suckling's, and had recently been made an Irish
peer, being second-in-command to Rodney at the battle of the Saints on
April 12 last, when by the defeat of the French Admiral de Grasse, the
West Indian islands, and in particular Jamaica, had been saved from the
fate which had so recently overcome the English forces at Yorktown in
1781.

Lord Hood's official business with Digby was difficult, probably
because Digby lacked energy, whereas Hood was a brilliant, if a sometimes
impetuous and overbearing officer. As second-in-command to Lord
Rodney during a famous victory, he had afterwards unmercifully criticized

his chief for incompetence and hanging back from a vigorous chase so as to lose the chances of making the victory complete. Hood proved himself an able fleet commander and so far in his service career Nelson had had but little experience of fleet work. Lord Hood sailed with a squadron at the end of 1782 to get information of the state of the enemy at Le Cap François in Hispaniola, and on November 13, 1782, he requested Rear-Admiral Digby, the Commander-in-Chief, to direct the *Albemarle* to accompany him, excusing his request because he would require frigates to dispatch with any information to Jamaica and the Windward Islands, and also because the *Albemarle* did not belong properly to the North American station. Digby permitted Hood to detach any frigate he chose, taking care that the captain of this frigate waited upon Digby before he proceeded to sea. On November 18 Hood complained to Digby that Captain Nelson 'was under sail to come to me on the 16th and stopped by your order, which is matter of the greatest surprise to me, as you have *twice* assured me from under your hand, that the *Albemarle* should certainly join me the moment she was ready.' Digby directed the commander of the *Albemarle* to follow Hood's orders. Hood reported to his chief, Admiral Pigot, that the *Albemarle* had joined him on November 20, after his 'pressing very strongly for her, again and again'. Nelson was delighted, and wrote to Locker: 'My situation in Lord Hood's fleet must be in the highest degree flattering to any young man: he treats me as if I were his son, and will, I am convinced, give me anything I can ask of him. Nor is my situation with Prince William less flattering: Lord Hood was so kind as to tell him (indeed I cannot make use of expressions strong enough to describe what I felt) that if he wished to ask questions relative to naval tactics, I could give him as much information as any officer in the fleet. He will be, I am certain, an ornament to our service. He is a seaman, which you could hardly suppose: every other qualification you may expect from him: but he will be a disciplinarian and a strong one.'

Nelson's friendship with Prince William Henry, the third son of George III, who became Duke of Clarence and William IV, commenced in 1782 and continued throughout his life. William, born in 1765, was sent to sea as a midshipman by his father in June 1779. Sir Samuel Hood, then Commissioner at Portsmouth Dockyard, advised on his outfit, and he joined the *Prince George*, the flagship of Rear-Admiral the Hon. Robert Digby. His father hoped the young midshipman would be received 'without the smallest marks of parade', but this was scarcely possible. In 1779 Britain's naval might was not very impressive, and there is something rather fine and trusting in the King sending his young hopeful to sea when the wearisome courts martial which had followed the indecisive action

against the French off Ushant were only just over, and when Admiral
Keppel, the victor of the courts martial, if not of the battle against the
French fleet, had resigned his command in the Channel, in disgust with
Lord Sandwich's conduct as First Lord of the Admiralty, and had been succeeded by a dug-out veteran admiral, Sir Charles Hardy. Prince William
was popular in the midshipmen's berth and he continued to enjoy such
high spirits and horseplay all his life. He was early noticed as having the
makings of a fine seaman and good officer. He remained with Digby,
seeing active service on occasions until after the fall of Yorktown, which
found him at New York, generally living ashore with the admiral and
rather idle. After which, on his father's orders, he was taken into Lord
Hood's flagship and became his signal midshipman. This was a busy
occupation, as a sight of his log-books, preserved at Greenwich, show.
The fleet was constantly being exercised and the frigates, including the
Albemarle, sent in chase of the many strange sails. Lord Hood's letter-
books, from which we have quoted, include his energetic cruise off Le
Cap François on the north shore of Hispaniola, and it is noticeable that
Nelson's name is the only one amongst his captains which is remarked
upon with commendation to their Lordships of the Admiralty. The
Albemarle was kept very busy by her captain. On one occasion, in March
1783, Nelson made an unsuccessful surprise attack without orders on
Turk's Island, which the French had just captured. For this, the Duke of
Clarence remembered, he was severely lectured by Lord Hood. But Hood
did not pass on his strictures, as he did for other officers on what might
seem lesser occasions.

On the peace of Versailles, Lord Hood returned home, turning aside
to let Prince William visit Havannah in the *Fortunee*, where the Spaniards
entertained him royally. At the Prince's request, Nelson accompanied him.
Home again, Lord Hood took his young protégé Nelson to a levee at St.
James's. After this levee, we are told, Nelson dined with his friend Davison
and borrowed a dressing-gown so that he might take off what he called his
'iron bound coat' and spend the evening in comfort. He had worn his full-
dress coat, similar to that which Rigaud has painted for us, and which was
uniform for levees and for calling upon admirals. The *Albemarle* was paid
off at Portsmouth and when in London Nelson attempted to get the wages
due to his ship's company for various ships they had served in during the
war. 'The disgust of the seamen to the navy,' he wrote to Captain Locker
'is all owing to the infernal plan of turning them over from ship to ship;
so that men cannot be attached to their officers, nor their officers care the
least about the men.' Yet in his case, the whole ship's company of the
Albemarle offered, if he could get a ship, to enter for her immediately.

When Nelson had paid off the *Albemarle* he wrote to Captain Locker that he had no thoughts of going to sea again, for he could not afford it, presumably because he considered it was necessary to have private means to keep up the state of a naval captain afloat in peacetime. So he travelled in France with a brother officer, Captain Macnamara, meaning to learn the language. Instead he fell in love again, with an English girl, the daughter of a clergyman, and in January 1784 returned to London alone and unexpectedly. He later took her brother, George Andrews, to sea with him. He returned to look into his accounts, probably some matter connected with the paying off of the *Albemarle*, and he called on Lord Howe, the First Lord of the Admiralty, who offered him a ship, which he promptly accepted. He also waited on Lord Hood, who invited him to call as often as he liked. And his published correspondence shows the great interest he took in the political situation, now complicated and bitter.

Lord North's administration, through which the King had ruled since 1770, had not been able to withstand the clamour of indignation aroused by disasters in America, culminating in the surrender of a well-entrenched English army to the rebels at Yorktown in 1781. This unexpected and severe military defeat had been the direct result of the Navy's failure to stop the French fleet from blockading and investing the place. But Rodney's victory of the Saints the next year had quickly restored the Navy's self-confidence, though it had not restored confidence in the Government, which fell. The new Whig administration, nominally headed by Lord Rockingham, the First Lord of the Treasury, was dominated by Lord Shelburne and Charles James Fox, the two Secretaries of State who dealt with colonial and foreign affairs respectively. The King supported Shelburne's plan of making peace with France part and parcel of Britain's acceptance and public acknowledgment of American independence. Fox wished to grant the independence outright and then to treat separately with the French and Spanish coalition, clear of the entanglement with the Americans. Rockingham died suddenly in 1782, and when the King asked Shelburne to form a ministry, Fox angrily resigned and was followed by his political friends, the Rockingham Whigs. The young Pitt stood by Shelburne, and so did Admiral Lord Keppel, the First Lord of the Admiralty, but only for a while.

The new ministry pressed on eagerly with the peace, and the Treaty of Versailles in 1783 frankly recognized the sovereignty and independence of the United States and agreed to an exchange of conquests with France and Spain. Pitt in the Commons and Lord Howe, the First Lord, in the Lords compared the relative strengths of the navies of Britain and France and Spain and declared that if the war had continued the country stood to have lost more than it had gained by the peace. This was hotly denied by Keppel in the Lords, and the Government was defeated in the Commons too and resigned. Perhaps the worst thing about the treaty was that the rights of the American loyalists had been left undefined and those who did not fly to Canada were harshly used by Congress. The Duke of Portland now became the nominal head of an administration in which Fox and the discredited Lord North were the principal Secretaries of State. Amongst other reforms, Fox introduced an India Bill which his enemies reckoned was calculated to place the impressive patronage that great Company wielded into the hands of Fox and his friends. In December 1783 the King hurriedly dismissed his two Secretaries of State, without a personal interview. The weather was wet and boisterous and the unruffled Lord North is said to have exclaimed, 'What! Turn us out in such a night as this!' William Pitt, aged twenty-four, now became Prime Minister and Lord Howe relieved Keppel once again as First Lord of the Admiralty. The Duke of Portland later made his peace with Pitt and was Home Secretary under him 1794–1801. This is worth noting because in 1795 Nelson declared himself to be a follower of the Portland Whigs.

Pitt and the King were aware that a party must be in office for a few months before it could hope to manage to win an election, using the patronage which the combined control of the Treasury, friendship of the King and the aid of the outraged East India Company could bring together. A general election of unprecedented bitterness between the rival parties was fought in the spring of 1784. Lord Hood, at the desire of his friends Mr. Pitt, Lord Buckingham and Lord Grenville, stood for Westminster, a constituency with two members, against Fox. Hood ranged some three hundred sailors against Fox's bodyguard of chairmen and duchesses. The Irish chairmen are said to have routed the sailors. Hood was elected although second to Fox on the poll.

After his election the Prince of Wales dined Fox at Carlton House, whereas Hood wrote an account of the fortunes of this 'tedious' contest to Prince William Henry, at his studies in Germany. As Nelson had been taken to a levee by Hood and had bade the Prince farewell on his departure from England and accepted the command of the frigate *Boreas* from Lord Howe, he must have been considered a friend of the present administration. A ship in peacetime was not easy to get and his brother William expressed surprise. Nelson wrote back: 'You ask, by what interest did I get a ship? I answer, having served with credit was my recommendation to Lord Howe, First Lord of the Admiralty. Anything in reason that I can ask, I am sure of obtaining from his justice.' Brother William had determined to sail in the *Boreas* as a Chaplain. 'Come when you please,' Nelson wrote.

'I shall be ready to receive you. Bring your canonicals and sermons. Do not bring any Burnham servants.' The frigate was destined for service on the Leeward Islands station and Nelson consented to carry out as passengers the Admiral's wife, Lady Hughes, and daughter, although he would have preferred to have been spared the inconvenience and expense. He also carried a number of young midshipmen, thirty of them, according to Lady Hughes. The ship was crowded and Nelson noted the officers and passengers 'walking the *Boreas*' quarter-deck on the 30th May, 1784, at 7 in the evening,' thirty-three of them, and three of them women, Lady Hughes and her daughter and Mrs. Peers, the Purser's wife. Nelson did not like Lady Hughes, but it is her reminiscences, in a letter to George Matcham, Nelson's brother-in-law, which record for us his kindness to the young gentlemen who sailed with him, how he would race them aloft, to accustom their dizzy fears to a frigate's taut spars, and how he would take them ashore with him when he dined out of the ship, so as to accustom them to polite society. His first lieutenant in the *Boreas*, James Wallis, describes how Nelson waited on the Governor of Madeira, on the voyage out, taking ten of his midshipmen with him, as well as every other officer who could be spared from the ship.

The West Indian islands in the British Commonwealth today have not the same importance in the economy of the British Isles as they had as the rich sugar islands in the eighteenth century when the *Boreas* slowly sailed towards them across the wide Atlantic. Then, as now, the islands were governed indiscriminately by many masters, in particular the English, French, Dutch and Spanish. Some islands were divided between two masters. The most important British possessions were Jamaica, the Windward Islands, Barbados, and a compact group known as the Leeward Islands, because they lay to the leeward of Barbados, the trade wind always blowing from the east. The four chief settlements of the Leeward Islands were Antigua, Montserrat, St. Kitts and Nevis. The last is the smallest, about fifty square miles in extent, or rather more than a third the size of the Isle of Wight, a volcanic mountain, separated from St. Kitts by a Narrows some two miles broad. The one great crop of Nevis was sugar, grown on plantations worked by slaves. The population was then estimated as 1,500 whites and 8,000 slaves. The West Indian islands were ruled by a Governor and Council appointed by the Crown, and an elected legislative Assembly. The Governor's salary was voted by the Assembly on his appointment. In the case of the Leeward Islands the Governor or Captain-General of the Forces usually resided at Antigua; there was a Lieutenant-Governor on St. Kitts, and a President of the Council on Nevis. The Governor was also Commander-in-Chief and commissioned the officers of the militia, and President Herbert of Nevis had only recently, in 1782, capitulated to the French and been allowed to remain in the island on his estates, as a neutral, until the island was restored to Britain by the Treaty of Versailles. In those days, the life of a planter was one full of anxiety. He feared not only capture, and Lord Rodney had set a bad example to Britain's enemies when, in 1781, he plundered the Dutch island of St. Eustatius, but also bad crops and bad markets. And he was often severely handicapped by the oppressive trade laws deemed necessary by the mother-country.

Colonies, or plantations, in the eighteenth-century sense, were supposed to exist for the benefit of the mother-country and were jealously watched so as to preserve their usefulness. The Navigation Acts, dating from Charles II's reign, with later modifications, were designed to prevent all commerce between a British colony and any part of Europe except Great Britain, unless in cases specially allowed. In the case of a West Indian island, according to the Act, no goods might be imported into or exported out of a British island but in a ship either belonging to subjects of 'England, Ireland, Wales or Berwick' or in such as belonged to that island, and had a master and three-fourths of the crew English subjects, 'on pain of forfeiture of ship and cargo; and all admirals and commanders of King's ships are authorized to make seizure of ships offending herein'. Before the war the British islands had exported sugar, molasses and rum to London or Bristol in return for manufactured goods. And their surplus sugar and rum had been exchanged with the New England colonies in New England ships for timber and food, particularly fish, flour and grain. It was claimed that to this neighbourly intercourse, over more than a century, was due, in great part, the prosperity of the islands. During the American War of Independence, naturally the trade had stopped. At the peace the Americans became foreigners and the old trade was forbidden by the Navigation Acts. At the time of the Treaty of Versailles Pitt had been working on a commercial treaty with the United States which would have restored, in an amicable settlement, some of the former trade which neither the British Isles nor Canada could supply. Not only did the West Indian islands lack timber and foodstuffs but also they had lost an important market for their surplus rum. The islands were faced with famine, and a limited trade with the United States, but only in the islanders' own ships, was allowed, to stave off this serious consequence. When Pitt became Prime Minister in 1784 a commission considered the case which before, in 1782, Pitt had proposed remedying in a Bill 'for the purpose of revising the beneficial intercourse that existed before the late American War, between the United States and the British Sugar Islands'. Perhaps unfortunately, opinions had hardened between 1782 and 1784, and the commission decided otherwise and the

Navigation Acts were retained and dealt hardly with the sugar islands however justly they might be thought to treat the late rebels.

The *Boreas* sailed from Spithead on May 17, 1784, and arrived at Barbados on June 26. Here Rear-Admiral Sir Richard Hughes, the Commander-in-Chief of the Leeward Islands station, having been saluted with fifteen guns, came off to fetch ashore his wife and daughter. At the end of July his little squadron assembled in English Harbour, Antigua, and took measures to shelter there during the hurricane months. In the interval between the beginning of August and the end of October, 'those dreadful visitations of the Almighty', the hurricanes, were apprehended. Brother William sailed home on account of ill health at the end of September. On November 1, Nelson sailed out of English Harbour and returned to Barbados. The ships of the squadron were next ordered to visit the islands and examine the anchorages and see which had facilities for the provision of wood and water for the ships. It was then that Nelson and his friend Cuthbert Collingwood, captain of the *Mediator*, expostulated to the Admiral about his failure to order his captains to enforce the Navigation Act against the American traders, for, as Nelson wrote to Locker, 'the rebel Americans at this time filled our ports.' They did this with the connivance of the British authorities, civil and military. When Nelson and Collingwood pointed out his duty forcefully to the Admiral he gave way. But Nelson also had trouble with the Captain-General of the islands, Governor Shirley, and with the Custom House officials and with the law as interpreted by the American traders and their friends in the islands. Nelson did not acquiesce but wrote home copiously to everyone interested, including the King. In 1786 the Treasury transmitted their thanks to Admiral Hughes for his activity and zeal in protecting the commerce of Great Britain. But it was President Herbert of Nevis who offered in court to become Nelson's bail for £10,000 if he chose to suffer the arrest which the merchants were demanding on account of the several writs issued against him. Herbert's housekeeper was his niece, an attractive young widow, with a dear little boy, and Nelson, although he had dismissed Lady Hughes as a 'fine talkative lady' and 'a clack', liked quiet sensible women and children.

Nelson's zeal in this matter of enforcing the Navigation laws is very noticeable and he had the support of both Cuthbert Collingwood, who soon sailed for home, and his brother Wilfred, captain of the *Rattler*. Indeed, it was probably the Collingwoods who advised Nelson what was going on and encouraged him to help them put a stop to it. In their eyes the Americans were rebels and carrying on a trade contrary both to the law and inimical to the lawful trade of the Canadians and Nova Scotians,

who had given refuge to the American loyalists. And they considered that
the island planters were rebels at heart too! The support given Nelson by
Governor Herbert perhaps goes to show that he did not consider that the
planters were trading with the Americans only because they were otherwise faced with starvation, as had certainly been the case on occasions during
the duration of the American war.

Nelson's next act, in contravention of his admiral's orders, is less easy
to justify. He sailed into English Harbour on February 7, 1785, and found
a junior captain, Sandys of the *Latona*, flying the broad pendant, by order
of the Admiral, of the resident Commissioner Moutray. Nelson ordered
Sandys to haul it down, and carried the news ashore to the Commissioner
himself, whose wife was a dear friend of his and Collingwood's. Whilst the
Admiralty supported his contention that the Commissioner was a civil
officer at the time and could not hold rank afloat, yet, in view of his own
senior officer's order, they thought Nelson should have referred the matter
back to Admiral Hughes in the first place. As Nelson was recognized as
senior captain and second-in-command on the Station, he was certainly
justified in objecting to the flying of this unauthorized broad pendant at
English Harbour.

James Wallis, first of the *Boreas*, remembered later how they never
remained longer than three or four days at any island at a time. The
frigate 'was always on the wing, and when it happened that any of the
other ships were in company, he was always forming the line, exercising,
chasing, etc.' This was just like Lord Hood's energetic cruise, remembered
so well by Prince William, with the fleet off Le Cap François at the end of
the American war. And during the hurricane months, Wallis tells us, 'he
encouraged music, dancing, and cudgeling, etc., and the Young Gentlemen
acted plays which kept up their spirits and kept their minds employed,
which is of the utmost utility in preserving health in these climates.'

From the log of the *Boreas* it can easily be calculated that in the 300-
odd days separating the hurricane months he may have spent as many as
sixty within sight of St. Kitts or Nevis, of which Bryan Edwards writes:
'This beautiful little spot is nothing more than a single mountain, rising
like a cone in an easy ascent from the sea.' Nelson's biographers, Clarke
and M'Arthur, quote from a letter from a female friend of Mrs. Fanny
Nisbet on St. Kitts who was visited by Nelson, they say, in 1784. The
movements of the *Boreas* suggest rather the January of 1785.

'We have at last seen the little captain of the *Boreas*, of whom so much
has been said. He came up just before dinner, much heated and was very
silent: yet seemed, according to the old adage, to think the more. He
declined drinking any wine: but after dinner, when the president, as usual,

gave the three following toasts, the King, the Queen and Royal Family, and Lord Hood, this strange man regularly filled his glass, and observed, that those were always bumper toasts with him; which having drank, he uniformly passed the bottle, and relapsed into his former taciturnity. It was impossible, during this visit, for any of us to make out his real character; there was such a reserve and sternness in his behaviour, with occasional sallies, though very transient, of a superior mind. Being placed by him, I endeavoured to rouse his attention by showing him all the civilities in my power; but I drew out little more than yes and no. If you, Fanny, had been there, we think you would have made something of him; for you have been in the habit of attending to these odd sort of people.' According to Nelson's biographers, the president in this letter is Mr. Herbert, and Nelson did not see him again for six months, on which occasion the President hurried out of his room, half-dressed, and returned to his toilet, exclaiming: 'Good God! If I did not find that great little man, of whom everybody is so afraid, playing in the next room, under the dining table, with Mrs. Nisbet's child.' Even now, according to his biographers, Nelson was not to meet Mrs. Nisbet until a few days after, when she thanked him in person for the great partiality he had shown her little boy. After which they became great friends, 'and she was soon informed by his friend Captain Collingwood, of the conquest she had made.'

The first of Nelson's letters to the widow Nisbet which survives is dated August 19, 1785, and he had arrived at English Harbour on the 10th. All is arranged between them, and he is only awaiting a favourable reply from Mr. Herbert. Nelson's use of a code for a short, very harmless sentence, suggests a previous correspondence conducted with delicious secrecy, and cunningly arranged trysts, justifying the use of a simple code, a jumble of figures, letters and signs against the alphabet, for which Mrs. Nisbet must have held the key, judging from the difficulty of breaking it down without one. There is no reason to suppose that Nelson's love-making in the President's house and garden was so utterly cold-hearted as some of his biographers, wise after the event, have confidently suggested.

Nelson cannot have been a very contented man at the commencement of his time in the West Indies, although he had on occasions the company of the Collingwoods and his own fine frigate was well manned and officered. Neither he nor Cuthbert Collingwood had any use for the Admiral, whom they regarded, with some justification it would seem, as a time-server. They both wrote home seeing if they could be moved elsewhere, Nelson writing to his old friend Cornwallis. But while the peace lasted, there was little chance of anything better. The seizing of the Americans should have brought some reward, but it resulted only in expenses. Nelson was very sad, as was Collingwood, at the departure for England of the Commissioner Moutray and his delightful wife, who had given them a glimpse of some home comforts. The little captain who dined on St. Kitts with Mrs. Nisbet's friends does not give the impression of being a happy man. And James Wallis records a bitter comment by Nelson when offered pity by a sympathizer at his persecution by the planters and American traders: 'I hate pity. I shall live to be envied and to that point I shall always direct my course.' It is very obvious that his friendship with a young widow was most likely to lead to marriage, especially as Nelson was a naval officer who struck most people as possessing exceptional merit and Mrs. Nisbet was both young and attractive where English women were scarce, and possessed not only obvious charms of her person but also had some of the attributes of an heiress. Indeed, it is only fair to her uncle to suggest that she might have done better out of him if only he had not made other arrangements later. His instinctive attachment to Nelson is shown by his generous offer to stand bail to the sum of £10,000.

On October 17, 1785, the *Boreas* left English Harbour, the hurricane season being over, and her first call was at Nevis, where she ran ashore and had to be hove off with the aid of a stream anchor and cable astern. Nelson was busy as usual, examining American traders and effecting repairs to his frigate and visiting the islands and spending a good while between St. Kitts and Nevis. On August 1, 1786, the Admiral sailed for England and Nelson was left as senior officer on the station. Another hurricane season was passed in English Harbour and Collingwood promised to keep him 'very orderly', presumably in the captain's mess, and Mrs. Nisbet was assured that in this case she had no need to worry about the possible truth of salt water and absence washing away love.

At the end of 1786, the appearance of Prince William Henry as captain of the *Pegasus* led Nelson, his admirer and senior officer, into a round of festivities that make the reader feel tired even to read about them. The lively, fine young man, who had acted as a midshipman, and done his duty strictly night and day, had been regularly passed as a lieutenant and then rather rapidly advanced to a post captain and sent on a cruise to Newfoundland and the West Indies under strict instructions from his father to which he does not appear to have paid much attention. Nelson's own account of his meeting with the Prince will be found in the Appendix. It will be noticed that Nelson is immediately on his guard against allowing the Prince to disregard the King's orders and is quite satisfied with the conduct of his own officers before he learns that the Prince is dissatisfied with his. Colonel the Honourable Stephen Digby told Fanny Burney, when they were in attendance at court together, that there was something in the violence of all the King's sons' animal spirits that would make him accept no post and no pay to live with them. 'Their very voices', he said, 'had a loudness and force that wore him.' This seems to describe Prince William. His quarter-deck manner was well known at Kew and Windsor. Fanny Burney, as the sister of a naval officer, was in favour with him, and as she had no love for her superior, Mrs. Schwellenberg, she may well have been highly delighted when Prince William, on hearing the elder woman speaking disrespectfully of the Duke of York, sharply threatened her with 'a stinging dozen before all the pages of the back stairs'.

The Prince, after Nelson's death, told the Rev. J. S. Clarke that he lived constantly with Captain Nelson, dining alternately with each other from their meeting on December 2, 1786, until he sailed for Jamaica the following summer. 'During this interval the Prince discerned the seeds of greatness in his friend.' His admiration of Nelson was genuine. And writing to Lord Hood he gives an interesting picture of 'poor Nelson' being 'head over ears in love' with 'a pretty and a sensible woman' who 'may have a great deal of money if her uncle, Mr. Herbert, thinks proper'. Meanwhile Nelson's health was not at all good, so that the Prince remarks, 'he is more in need of a nurse than a wife'.

Nelson's ill health, his worry over the Navigation Act and its observance, his responsibility as the senior naval officer and his pleasure and gratitude at the Prince's attentions must all be taken into account before judging some of Nelson's later actions during the Prince's stay too harshly. In the affair of Lieutenant Schomberg, that officer misjudged Nelson as much as he misjudged the Prince. Later, after he had through the kindness of Lord Hood become a post captain, he was sent home by Cornwallis for behaving in an arrogant, overbearing fashion which one feels he can have only learnt from Prince William himself. In the quarrel with the Naval Storekeeper at Antigua Yard over a muster-book, Nelson supported the Prince in his contention that he was not bound to provide such a muster, yet Nelson continued to obey the instructions himself as the Admiralty later pointed out to him. Altogether, despite his early warning that the Prince was going to be difficult, Nelson did not manage too well, and the Prince can be said to have twisted Nelson round his little finger. The Prince, by his insistence on giving the bride away, did hurry up the marriage. When he sailed away, in an attempt to get poor Schomberg court-martialled, he left Nelson with a new crop of worries and soon to be in disfavour with both Lord Howe and Lord Hood, who, to do them justice, probably had not intended to have tried Nelson so severely as to have given him the responsibility of looking after a Prince already well known as being much addicted to his own pleasures, as well as having a high sense of what became a Prince and of the customs and discipline of the Service, which could always and only be disregarded with his royal approval.

For some reason not immediately explicable, Captain Pringle, an old friend of both Nelson and Mrs. Nisbet, remarked to James Wallis after the wedding: 'The Navy lost yesterday its greatest ornament by Nelson's marriage. It's a national loss that such an officer should marry. Had it not been for that circumstance I foresee he would be the greatest officer in the Service.' The only possible comment seems to be that he was right in the sense that marriage and a career for Nelson were not compatible, only it was the marriage that broke up, not the career of naval greatness.

Nelson and Mrs. Nisbet were married on March 11, 1787. The marriage certificate is printed in the Appendix. He sailed for home on June 7. His wife, with her uncle and family, took passage in a merchant ship. Nelson anchored at Spithead on July 4. The *Boreas* was sent round to the Nore, and, to Nelson's intense annoyance, the ship was not immediately paid off, but employed on the impress service. The *Boreas* was finally paid off at the end of November, by which time Nelson even talked of joining the Russian service, so disgusted was he with his own. He decided to visit France and learn the language with his wife's help, but his father's desire for his company made him change his mind and the young married couple settled at Burnham Thorpe.

No. 1

Boreas, English Harbour,[1]
August 19, 1785

MY DEAR MRS. NISBET,—To say how anxious I have been and am to receive a line from Mr. Herbert [2] would be far beyond the descriptive powers of my pen. Most fervently do I hope his answer will be of such a tendency, as to convey real pleasure not only to myself, but also to you, for most sincerely do I love you and I trust that my affection is not only founded upon the principles of reason but also upon the basis of mutual attachment, indeed my charming Fanny did [I] possess a million my greatest pride and pleasure would be to share it with you; and, as I am, to live in a cottage with you I should esteem superior to living in a palace with any other I have yet met with.

My age is enough to make me seriously reflect upon what I have offered and common sense tells me what a good choice I have made. The

[1] Antigua.
[2] Mrs. Nisbet's uncle, John Richardson Herbert, President of Nevis.

more I weigh you in my mind the more reason I find to admire both your head and heart. But come, don't say: 'What a vain young man is this, 'tis a modest way of telling me I have given a proof of my sense by accepting him.' No, to your heart do I own myself most indebted, yet I trust you approved of me for this obvious reason. 'He esteems me, therefore he is the person I ought to expect most happiness from by return of affection, if there is nothing in his character or situation that renders it improper.'

My temper you know as well as myself, for by longer acquaintance you will find I possess not the art of concealing it. My situation and family I have not endeavoured to conceal. Don't think me rude by thus entering into a correspondence with you, consider that separation from the objects we esteem lose some of its pangs by a mutual unreserved correspondence. Therefore if you think it right let me now and then be favoured with a few lines. The pleasure I shall receive them with, you will give me credit for.

We arrived here on the Wednesday at breakfast and found the Admiral[1] not overpleased at the ships staying 48 hours. He did not make the most civil speech to Mr. Stanley,[2] he will tell you when you see him. The Admiral is in high spirits at having left her Ladyship at Barbados. He is every day expressing his happiness. He was much disappointed at not receiving one line from his fair correspondent, but he trusts that a moment will sometime be found to spare, in order to write to him. Entre nous the A. makes quite a —— of himself in this business. I should suppose him a bachelor instead of a married man with a family.

Kelly[3] I could and would tell you a long history of was I sure this would come safe to your hands, all I shall say is I hope he is constant.[4]

Little Sandys[5] has received two dismissions since he arrived here, but he has so fixed his (affections) I can't call them upon the object that will take no denial. How weak a man must be to expect happiness in being united with a person who absolutely dislikes, and almost I may say hates him.

Although you probably know of Miss Whitehead's desertion from her father's house in St. John's to St. Christopher's, yet as you may not have heard the story I will tell it you. Why do you not keep Capt. Sutherland at the islands to Leeward? I hear you are to be indicted for letting him run about these islands doing mischief. Captain Acres and Miss came out by the same ship a few weeks ago. Upon their arrival the gentleman made some offers to Mr. W. for his permission to pay his addresses to Miss.

---

[1] Sir Richard Hughes, Commander-in-Chief of the Leeward Islands 1784–6.
[2] John Stanley, Attorney-General of Nevis and Judge of the Vice-Admiralty Court, Leeward Islands.
[3] Captain William Kelly; died 1811, a rear-admiral.
[4] The words 'I hope he is constant' are written in code.
[5] Captain Charles Sandys, commanded the *Latona* and died 1814 a rear-admiral.

C

His letter was not noticed and Miss was desired to know no more of him. How weak must they be who endeavour to control love they may advise but can never restrain. Captain A. went to St. Chris: (and the young lady appeared quite reconciled to his absence) where he met your shoe friend Captain S. a gentleman well versed in the business of carrying off young ladies. Capt. S. arrives here the Prince of Wales' birthday with a vessel prepared for the purpose, sees Miss at the ball, fixes every matter with her and is seen no more. On Tuesday evening Miss was singing and playing on the harpiscord to her mother and a Dr. Merchant. After two or three tunes she gets up, walks out of the room, down stairs through yard into the bathing house and out of the window into Captain S. arms. She was not suspected, for till Dr. M. went away and desired his compliments to Miss W. which brought on an enquiry where she was, when *Lo* the bathing house was found open, and the vessel appeared sailing out of the harbour. They sent to the Fort but too late—Set them merry. I hope they will never be anxious to run from each other.

My letters from England which I found here upon my arrival are all comfort. My dear father, brothers and sisters are all well. By the death of an uncle who possessed a family living, my brother [1] who came out with me has got a living of £700 a year. Miss S. is mentioned as wonderful being yet single, but the father will not let any man come into his house—strange oddity. She will run away with somebody by and by. I had a long letter from my good Mrs. Moutray [2] who is well thank God. A more amiable woman can hardly exist. I wish you knew her. Your minds and manners are so congenial that you must have pleasure in the acquaintance.

I have been three days on the other side the Island with Mr. Stanley, but I caught a slight fever by my journey there. It was on the Saturday you had so much rain: care however has quite set me up again. Pray present my best compliments to your aunt,[3] although I have not the pleasure of much personal knowledge I must esteem her, by having heard every individual sound her praises. To Miss Herbert also good wishes,[4] to our little Sally everything. May all blessings be showered upon her head. I am certain she deserves them and don't forget me to Mr. and Mrs. Morton.[5]

For a short time fare well and let me assure you with what truth I am your affectionate sincere HORATIO NELSON

---

[1] The Rev. William Nelson, first Earl Nelson, died 1835. He inherited the living of Hilborough, Norfolk, from his uncle, the Rev. Robert Rolfe. He had come out in the *Boreas* with Nelson, as the ship's chaplain, but returned to England owing to ill health.

[2] Wife of John Moutray, Commissioner at Antigua, and a great friend of Nelson and Collingwood. She and her husband had returned to England in March 1785.

[3] Miss Sarah Herbert, the President's sister.

[4] Martha Herbert, daughter of the President. His wife had died in 1769.

[5] Mrs. Morton, sister of the President, had two children, Magnus and Sally.

No. 2
[Nicolas I, p. 139]

Boreas, English Harbour,
September 11, 1785.

Indeed, my dear Fanny I had buoyed myself up with hopes that the Admiral's schooner [1] would have brought me a line from you, but the tidings she brought of the release of poor Mrs. Herbert [2] from this world, sufficiently apologises for your not thinking of an absentee; but this believe, from my heart, that I readily partake of all the sorrows you undergo. But I comfort myself that however great your grief at this moment may be, at losing a person who was so deservedly dear to you as you good aunt, yet, when reason takes place, you must rather have pleasure in knowing she is released from those torments she had undergone for months past. Time ever has and in the present instance I trust will soften grief into a pleasing remembrance, and her unspotted character will then afford you real comfort. Call religion to your aid, and it will convince you, that her conduct in this world was such as will insure everlasting happiness in that which is to come.

I have received a letter from Mr. Herbert in answer to that which I left at Nevis for him. Probably he has shewn it to you; if not it is deferring saying much upon the subject till we have a conversation, and expressive of his regard. My greatest wish is to be united to you, and that foundation of happiness, real love and esteem, is I trust what you believe I possess in the strongest degree towards you. If the return is mutual (for there can be no love without it), I have that good opinion of Mr. Herbert, which convinces me he will say or propose nothing upon this matter, that I must not think open and right. And I believe he loves you too well, not to let you marry the man of your choice although he may not be so rich as some others, provided his character and situation in life renders such a union eligible. I declare solemnly that did I not conceive I had the full possession of your heart no consideration should make me accept your hand. We know that riches do not always insure happiness, and the world knows I am superior to pecuniary considerations in both my public and private life, as in both instances I might have been rich, but I will have done leaving all my present feelings to operate in your breast, only of this truth be convinced that I am your affectionate HORATIO NELSON.

Do I ask too much when I venture to hope for a line, or otherwise I may suppose my letters may be looked upon as troublesome.

To Mrs. J. Nisbet.

[1] The *Berbice*.   [2] Miss Sarah Herbert died on September 5, 1785.

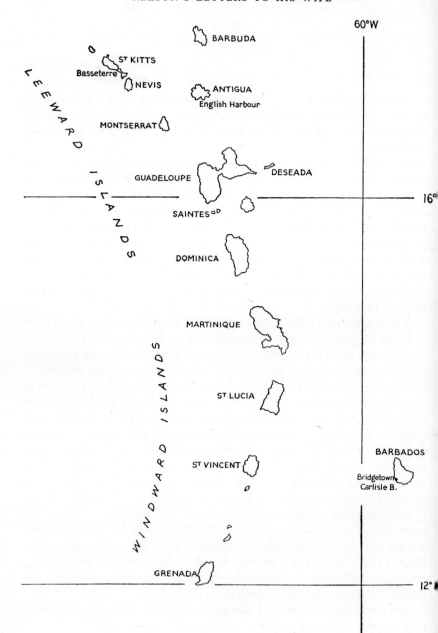

THE WEST INDIES

No. 3

Boreas, English Harbour,
December 13, 1785

MY GOOD FANNY,—Most sincerely do I regret that I am not safe moored by thee instead of being in this vile place. Although even this place is being in paradise after the very bad weather we have experienced since our departure from Nevis. Such weather I never saw in the West Indies; even in Europe we could not have had worse.

The main mast is so badly sprung that there was great danger of our losing it and our sails and rigging are tore to pieces. The carpenters of the Dock Yard say it is not safe to carry us to Barbadoes but I have determined to try, as soon as the weather moderates, for well we know that if a person does not perform what he promises, the world is very apt to say he never did intend to do it. Therefore I will get up and bring down Mrs. Parry [1] at all risks.

You have had a merry time I hope with your gay company and the rain you have had cannot have allowed them to leave you, therefore pray make my remembrances to them.

A servant is going to St. John's to ask Lady Hughes' commands to Sir Richard, therefore as we are 12 miles from it I must give over writing. Only of this truth be assured, that I am ever yours most affectionately
HORATIO NELSON.

Pray my best respects to Mr. Herbert and Miss Herbert.

To Mrs. J. Nisbet.

No. 4

[Nicolas I, p. 154, part]

Boreas, English Harbour,
25 February 1786

MY DEAR FANNY,—Mr. Adye [2] we landed yesterday afternoon at St. John's and after a disagreeable night here we arrived this morning. Captain Collingwood [3] is gone into the country, therefore from this I sail at daylight tomorrow morning.

News is as scarce here as anywhere, therefore but little you will get. The Admiral sailed on Thursday, ill with the gout and not overpleased

[1] Wife of David Parry, Governor of Barbados.
[2] A. C. Adye, Crown lawyer and deputy registrar of the Vice-Admiralty Court, Leeward Islands.
[3] Captain Wilfred Collingwood, in command of the *Rattler,* died in March 1787.

with the Major's [1] proceedings in his regiment. I hear of none of that beating which the malicious impute to him and from what is told me I think he will come off well, considering how many invidious people are attacking him. His temper is warm which lays him open to his enemies, but he may be good at bottom, which I hope he is for his wife's sake. The mail is arrived and my servant carries this to St. John's 12 miles from hence, therefore you must forgive the shortness of it. And be assured it is sorry to me to be obliged to desist from writing to my affectionate Fanny.

You are too good and indulgent I know and feel it, but my whole life shall ever be attempting to make you completely happy, whatever whims sometimes take me. We are none of us perfect and myself probably much less so than you deserve.

Give my compliments to Miss Herbert. Most likely the Admiral has told her much more news than it is in my power to send. Josiah [2] I dare say makes a wonderful progress in his book. The greatest favour you can at present grant me is to learn him to read. Give my kind love to him and do rest assured my excellent ——, fill up the blank, that I am with the purest affection your HORATIO NELSON.

To Mrs. J. Nisbet.

No. 5

[Nicolas I, pp. 154-5, part]

Boreas, 10 leagues ESE. off the Island of Desiade,
Friday morning 9 o'clock, March 3, 1786

Separated from my dearest what pleasure can I feel? None! Be assured all my happiness is centred with thee and where thou art not there I am not happy. Every day, hour and act convinces me of it. With my heart filled with the purest and most tender affection do I write this, for was it not so you know me well enough to be certain that even at this moment I would tell you of it. I daily thank God who ordained that I should be attached to you. He has I firmly believe intended it as a blessing to me, and I am well convinced you will not disappoint His beneficent intentions. Fortune—that is money—is the only thing I regret the want of, and that only for the sake of my affectionate Fanny. But the Almighty who brings us together, will I doubt not, take ample care of us, and prosper all our undertakings. No dangers shall deter me from pursuing every honourable

---

[1] Major John Brown had married Rose Mary Hughes, the Admiral's youngest daughter, in September 1785.
[2] Mrs. Nisbet's son, born in 1780. His father, Dr. Josiah Nisbet, had died in 1781.

means of providing handsomely for you and yours, and again let me repeat that my dear Josiah shall ever be considered by me as one of my own. That Omnipotent Being who sees and knows what passes in all hearts knows what I have written to be my undisguised sentiments towards the little fellow.

I am uneasy but not unwell. Mr. Kelly of his great goodness has suffered my letters to remain at the post office Antigua, although he knew I was coming up to Barbadoes to suit his convenience, and the Post master at St. John's sent them down to St. Christopher's the day I reached St. John's. Therefore not a scrap of a pen have I received by this packet. It is in my opinion an unpardonable neglect and inattention to a friend. Nothing but the Admiral's orders to be at Barbadoes at a given time hindered me from coming down after them (for I have no consideration for Mr. Kelly nor shall I forget the civility for some time to come). Sir Richard Hughes I am certain would have overlooked my disobedience to his orders and have thought I had served Mr. K. very properly, but I can't bear the idea of disobeying orders. I should not like to have mine disobeyed, therefore I came on, but it was a toss up I assure you. I shall tell the Admiral the circumstances as soon as I arrive but when that will be I can't possibly guess.

We sailed on Sunday morning at daylight from English Harbour, since which time the weather has been so calm that we are scarcely 30 leagues from Antigua. We have just got a little breeze and if it holds we may arrive on Sunday or Monday. I shall not be surprised to find the *Adamant* sailed as I hear the *Latona* is at Barbadoes. If W. K. [1] is kept till my arrival I shall be mischievous enough to think it only a just punishment for his inattention to me who never deserved it at his hands. And as the sea is as smooth as glass, if I am to return to my dearest Fanny the last of March I am perfectly satisfied in spending a great part of the time at sea instead of Carlisle Bay.

March 9: At last we are arrived and as we came into the Bay on one side the *Adamant* made her appearance on the other; Capt. Kelly has brought me one letter from Antigua for which one although I know there are more I retract my mischievous wishes and I have received several at this place from my sister and brother. The former from Bath where my old friend Scrivener desires to be kindly remembered to me. His daughter is still Miss.[2] Nor do I hear of any likelihood of her changing her name. It is wonderful such an immense fortune should lay so long upon hands. I don't think my dear Kate [3] knows of my intentions of altering my

---

[1] Captain William Kelly, commanded the *Adamant*, Sir Richard Hughes's flagship.
[2] Dorothea Scrivener, daughter and heiress of Mr. Scrivener of Sibton Park, Suffolk.
[3] Nelson's youngest sister, Catherine, married to George Matcham in 1787.

situation or she would have mentioned it. Mrs. Moutray is still there but I have not a line from her, it is wonderful and I can't account for it. I know myself to be so steady in my friendships that I can't bear the least coolness or inattention in others. My brother takes it for granted I am a married man, and in consequence desires his love. From my uncle Mr. Suckling[1] I have a very kind letter saying he will do everything in his power to add to my felicity and that if I should want it that he will give me pecuniary assistance, but at the same time he says and very justly that Mr. Herbert should consider you properly and that I should well consider my situation in life and that in my present bachelor situation I am quite an independent man with a sufficient income to keep me so. It is a disagreeable task but I must either write to Herbert or speak to him when I come down, for it is strongly reported that we are to sail from this country in June next. If that is to be the case my time is short. All this, my dearest, gets hold of my spirits and will not allow me to feel so pleasant as I wish and makes me more regret I had not paid more attention to getting money, but I will have done this subject.

Captain Sandys quitted the *Latona* yesterday. Captain Berkeley has got her and Captain Gregory is appointed to the *Falcon*. The Admiral I know nothing off. I hear he expects to remain here another year. He has taken a small house he says in Bridgtown but where it is none of the squadron I believe know yet. As I must answer my English letters by the *Adamant* to reach the packet at St. Kitts, I must be short but believe that I am with the tenderest love and affection ever your

HORATIO NELSON.

Give my compliments to Miss Herbert. I believe I shall inclose a line in this for Stanley. If I do, you are to read it and give it him or not as you please. You can judge of that matter perhaps better than myself.

2 p.m. Well in the course of the morning I have wrote to Mr. Herbert and have touched in as handsome a manner as I was able about you. *I fear* but hope it will have that effect I wish it. I am going to dine at Pilgrim.[2] I wish dinner was over for I am miserably low spirited.

March 10: I have been to the Admiral's house, but although only ½ past 8 I find he is gone to Miss Daniels, therefore cannot ask him about the harpiscord strings. Kelly I find is not to sail from Nevis till 8 April and as there is to be some courts martial after his arrival most likely I shall not see Nevis till near or quite May day. I am truly vexed but I can't help myself. You must write often and long letters. Give my kind love to Josiah

---

[1] William Suckling, Collector of Customs, the brother of Nelson's mother, to whom he had appealed for financial help (see Appendix, p. 53).
[2] The Governor's house, Barbadoes.

and tell me all about Mr. Herbert; he will I take for granted show you the letter.

Heavens bless my dearest Fanny.

To Mrs. J. Nisbet, Nevis.

No. 6

[Nicolas I, p. 163, part]

Boreas, Carlisle Bay,[1]
March 25, 1786

MY DEAREST FANNY,—Most probably when the packet arrives the Admiral's schooner will be so soon hurried away that I shall not have a moment's time to write, for Sir Richard has already all his letters for Antigua on board her. I fear he will not allow her to come to Leeward. I have hinted his promise of forwarding the mail but he says it will get down as soon nearly from Antigua and he wants the vessel for other purposes. However this will come with the mail and although I shall not have the felicity of getting a line yet it will serve to convince you of my inviolable affection.

The inhabitants here are heartily tired of my company. I am ready to give them my room, and they may assure themselves I will not trouble them one moment longer than I can help, for although my person is amongst them, my heart, thoughts and affections are far off. Upwards of a month from Nevis, when I sailed I hoped by this time to have been there again but how uncertain are human expectations, and how vain the idea of fixing periods for happiness.

I am anxious yet sometimes fear receiving Mr. Herbert's answer to my letter. Yet why I should fear I know not for I conceive I have wrote nothing but what was proper and right. What signifies professions of friendship if they are never to be put to the test. You my dear Fanny is all I care about. If you are satisfied you will readily believe me when I say I shall. But I shall give up this subject and hope the best.

The Admiral lives very retired. I have twice dined with him. We are very good friends, nor do I think I should very soon disagree with him. He seems ready to do everything I can wish him and only wants to be well informed. The world says he is for ever with a Miss——, her character is much hurt I hear. Many people do not, from her intimacy with Sir Richard, invite her as they had been used to do, and she is often at his house for a

[1] Barbadoes.

whole day. There may be nothing criminal after all is said, but when a gentleman goes beyond what is deemed common civilities and reaches particularities the world is fond of believing any story which is current.

The Governor and Mrs. Parry are very civil, have given me a general invitation and always appear glad to see me. Mrs. P. still remains very lame and always will; for contractions seldom give way after 50. For this last week a French man-of-war has been here, and going about with them so much in the sun has given me violent headaches, but a little rest will I trust remove it again.

Tell Miss Herbert my endeavours for a red bird have hitherto been fruitless but I shall always remain upon the look-out till I get one. The strings I have got, but the hat and ribbon is not at present in this town.

March 26: The Admiral has just sent to tell me as the packet is not arrived he shall send the schooner to Antigua tomorrow as he has many things to send Lady Hughes for her passage home. You know most likely both she and Mrs. Brown go in the storeship, at least so they have wrote Sir Richard. He does not intend to go to Antigua to visit them before they embark. What a blessed couple. Common decency ought to have induced such a *polite* man as Sir Richard to have gone down but his time is taken up here and he minds but little else. The schooner likewise goes to Nevis and St. Kitts with a letter for Mr. Stanley, therefore I shall expect you will have the goodness to send me a long epistle and tell me everything which has passed concerning me since my departure.

March 29: Every day I may go on, the Admiral is not fixed about anything. The schooner now sails he says tomorrow, but whether she reaches Nevis is uncerrtain. He says if possible he shall visit her Ladyship before she sails.

I am involved in law that you will conclude and have Custom House etc., etc., upon me, but I fear not, being conscious of the rectitude of my intentions. The Admiral is highly pleased with my conduct here, as you will believe by sending me such fine lines with a white hat. I well know I am not of abilities to deserve what he has said of me, but I take it as they are meant to show his regard for me and his politeness and attention to me is great, nor shall I forget it. I like the Man although not all his acts. If you should show them to any person, I desire it may not be to any part of the squadron who is with you as the compliment is paid me at their expence. You will understand this as meant to extend to the very near relations of the parties. Indeed I do not wish to have them shown to anyone. How is my dear Josiah. Pray give him a kiss for me. To Miss Herbert I beg you will say everything that's handsome, to the Morton family compliments. If Stanley is with you remember me to him.

Bless you my dearest and believe that I am with the purest affection yours most sincerely, HORATIO NELSON.

No. 7

Boreas,
April 2, 1786

MY DEAR FANNY,—The packet arrived here yesterday but my letters except from my brother are in the Antigua mail. Reports are strong we are all to return to England this summer, but still I think the *Boreas* will stay here till 1787 although I am prepared for either and am perfectly indifferent about it. A few months sooner or later is a matter of no consequence.

I hope everything relative to you is fixed in Mr. Herbert's mind. Let things be as they may they are firmly fixed in mine. Whatever I have is yours and I can only regret for your sake that I have not more to offer. But my exertions shall never cease until I have everything you can wish for. I have not time to say much but you will give me I am sure ample credit for what passes in my mind and know as well as myself what that is.

I think it is possible these letters will find Mr. Herbert at Antigua, therefore I shall tell you for Miss Herbert's information that Sir Richard has great hopes of remaining here, as no one is appointed for this station and some gentlemen who have asked have been told by Lord Howe [1] that the arrangement was fixed. Present my compliments to Miss Herbert and Stanley if he is with you and remember me, if they ask after me, to the family at Hardtimes. Kiss my dear Josiah for me and rest assured that I am yours most affectionately, HORATIO NELSON.

P.S. I have a most affectionate letter from my father in which you are much concerned. I shall shew it you when I come down, and you will regard the writer of it I am certain.

Capt. Gregory is here and desires his compliments.

To Mrs. J. Nisbet, Nevis.

No. 8
[Nicolas I, p. 166, part]

Boreas, Carlisle Bay,
April 17, 1786.

MY DEAREST FANNY,—I have been looking out anxiously for some time past for the *Adamant* and *Berbice* making sure of the pleasure of receiving

[1] Lord Howe was First Lord of the Admiralty 1783–8.

a letter, but it is not to happen, therefore I must write what I know and not answer to what you say.

My letters from my sister and brother are very kind and from the former filled with every sentiment of affection for you. I will not say more but you shall see the letters when I come down. But when that is to be God knows. I am in law and although everything will go as I wish it, yet I fear it will keep me this fortnight. I shall wish the vessels at the Devil and the whole continent to boot. Sir Richard Hughes is in hopes to remain here another year as no person is as yet appointed and they are to all the other stations. But Lord Howe says nothing has never said he shall, therefore after all these hopes which the Admiral is cherishing he may be disappointed at last.[1]

The under-secretary of the Admiralty has wrote to Capt. Sterling or told his friends in England that all the ships were to be relieved this Summer, but it is still my opinion that *Boreas* will remain till next year. However, we are always ready for England as for the next island. The Storeship which came up here for Lady Hughes is sailed on her way to Antigua. I should not like to go home in her, for the company are thirsty souls, and I think she will either be lost or burned before she gets to England.

I have a letter from my amiable Mrs. Moutray, she is full of affliction and woe: she is upon the eve of going to France with her family as it was the plan of her late husband.[2] The Duchess of Richmond carried her to court to present her petition for the Commissioner's pension, and both King and Queen were very kind to her and said they had no doubt but she would get the pension, but that hard-hearted Lord Howe in Council opposed the measure as a bad precedent, therefore she has not got it. I hope the King will yet give her something from the privy purse. And this is not all her affliction. Mr. Moutray's agent has stopped payment and near £2,000 is lost by this event. What has this poor dear soul undergone in one twelve months. Lost father, mother, husband and part of her fortune and left with two children. The most unfeeling heart must, I should have hoped, relented and endeavoured to give ease to the wound affliction had made. Lord Howe if he does not take care will get the character of a brute. Dear soul, she desires I will say everything to you for her. Her kind wishes for our happiness equal to what she enjoyed but *far, far* more lasting. Indeed my dearest I can't express what I feel for her and your good heart I am sure will sympathize with mine. What is so truly affecting

---

[1] Nelson was right—Sir Richard Bickerton was appointed Commander-in-Chief of the Leeward Islands in the summer.

[2] Captain John Moutray died suddenly at Bath, shortly after returning to England

as a virtuous woman in distress. But if partaking of grief is an alleviation
to the sufferings of that all amiable woman she has many sharers. When
you know her you must love her.

Lord Hood has the command at Portsmouth.[1] I had a letter from him
by the packet. I am all anxiety to hear and know what I have to hope for
from Leeward. We have not even heard of Kelly's marriage or of him
since he sailed. Pringle [2] I take for granted is with you. He has been
scolding me most wonderfully I am only glad I do not deserve it at his
hands. To Miss Herbert make my best compliments and good wishes.
The Morton family as they enquire after me. My dear little Josiah you will
be convinced how well I like him and I hope he will be able to read most
charmingly to me when I come. Sir Richard is taken up more than I can
tell you by a letter: I have got a young grey parrot but am unable to get a
red bird. I am sorry for it as I wish much to get something to present to
her. The hat I can't get. When I ask, they tell me ladies do not ride in this
country. Adieu bless you and believe me to be yours most affectionately,
HORATIO NELSON.

12 o'clock: I think it possible Mr. Herbert may be at Antigua, therefore
I send this under cover to Mr. Bannatyne, St. Kitts. An account is just
arrived that the storeship is cast away but I am in hopes the people are
saved. Lady Hughes I think I told you in some former letter was to have
gone home in her. All her stock was on board. Captain Sandys, a parson
and many others were in her.

Remember me to Stanley and all who ask after me. I have a great
bundle of newspaper from the sitting of Parliament to 4th March. I wish
Miss Herbert had them.

Lady Hughes goes home in the *Unicorn* [3] who sails in three days for
Antigua and England. Once more adieu for a week after you get this. I
have wrote to Mr. Herbert by this same conveyance and hope he will get
it as soon as this, but in case he should be at Antigua have directed the
person in the brig to enquire.

To Mrs. J. Nisbet, Nevis.

Endorsed: 'Came to hand this instant and forwarded by her most obedient
humble servant, Thomas Pringle, who wishes much to be
informed if there is anything new relative to the motions of the
squadron.'

[1] Lord Hood was Commander-in-Chief at Portsmouth 1786–8.
[2] Captain Thomas Pringle; died 1803, a vice-admiral.
[3] Captain Charles Stirling.

No. 9
[Nicolas I, p. 166, part, under date April 17]

Boreas, Carlisle Bay,
April 23, 1786

MY DEAREST FANNY,—I will not begin by scolding you although you really deserve it for sending me such a letter. Had I not known the warmth of your heart, by the epistle I might have judged you had never seen me. However as I have fixed my resolve of not saying more I have done. You will not send me such another I am certain.

All the squadron are now here holding courts martial which will finish tomorrow when they all go to their respective stations except poor me, who am kept to take care of two Yankees. I wish they were a 100 fathoms under water, and when I am likely to be released, I have not the smallest idea. Captain Kelly arrived here the 20th. Mrs. K.[1] had been seasick nearly the whole passage. They are now at Pilgrim where they have taken up their abode till Tuesday or Wednesday when the *Adamant* sails for Antigua with Sir Richard. The trip will not be very agreeable for Mrs. Kelly: so much for flag ship. I should be sorry to have one, a Captain in her is never his own master.

I am so much out of temper with this island that I would rather sacrifice anything than stay. Unpleasantly enough 4 navy captains of which I am one have had a little difference with Governor Parry on the 21st. Therefore unless he makes a very handsome apology I never set foot in his house more. It makes this island more disagreeable than ever, for now I know nobody in it.

The Admiral's schooner sails this day for Nevis to bring up Mr. Stanley if he wants a conveyance. I am much obliged by his very kind answer to my letter. Kelly had been here near two days before I knew he had it. Why would you not tell me you had given it to Stanley? But at this moment I am sorry for what I began the letter with, therefore forgive me and I will never scold more, but trust everything to your good heart.

Kelly and the Admiral have had a little difference. Mr. K. had the modesty to ask the Admiral to give up entirely the ship which is appointed for his convenience from home, and to go into a frigate. The Admiral very properly refused him for which Mr. K. is very angry and will not speak to the Admiral. Although the *Adamant's* stay may only be two months longer yet it may be made very disagreeable to Kelly. Sir Richard has done everything I am told he could to please Capt. K. and because he will not do a

[1] Sally Morton married Captain Kelly in March 1786.

thing which no man would do, or, if he did, he would be very wrong, he is to be upbraided of doing uncivil things. I have been upon the best terms with the Admiral and I declare I think I could ever remain so. I am often sorry to hear of his private history but he is always remarkably kind and civil to every one. When he told me about Kelly I told him that everybody would think he was very kind but you, and I hoped you would be very angry with him for keeping me away so very long. Whenever I can settle about my prizes here, I shall sail directly for Nevis.

How is my little Josiah? Give him a kind kiss for me and pray present my best compliments to Miss Herbert. The red bird I fear is past my power to get. Three letters, besides this one, by *Adamant* and *Berbice* are on their way. I hope you have received them but if not you must give me credit for writing. I have missed no opportunity or ever will. This must be a very short and a very dull letter for I have a violent headache. Having been sitting day after day for near a week at Courts Martial we are now trying Lt. Johnson for the loss of the storeship but I hope it will be finished tomorrow or Tuesday at farthest.

Farewell for a little time and bless you with all my heart and soul and do believe and never doubt but that I am with the most sincere affection, ever your HORATIO NELSON.

P.S. I sent yesterday the moment the Admiral told me the schooner was going to Nevis, for nobody but myself knew it, as polite a note as I was able to tell Mrs. Kelly (for Kelly was not at Pilgrim) of the opportunity that offered of sending anything she pleased to Nevis. The servant brought word back—there was no answer, not even: 'Much obliged, thank you,' or any other word, but what I have told you. I may be uncivilly treated once and then it is my misfortune, but if I put it in any person's power to be so a second time, it's my fault. But the next note I write her, if head does not act till then, she will long remain without. I do not know very well whether the first part of my letter has not got a little of the anger she ought to have.

No. 10

[Nicolas I, p. 167, part]

Boreas, Barbarous Island,
May 4, 1786

MY DEAREST FANNY,—Never, never, do I believe shall I get away from this detestable spot. Had I taken your advice and not seized any American I should now have been with you, but I should have neglected my duty which I think your regard for me is too great for you to have wished me to do. Duty is the great business of a sea officer. All private considerations must give way to it however painful it is. But I trust that time will not have lessened me in the opinion of her, who it shall be business of my future life to make happy. I trust you believe me, therefore I will say no more upon the subject at present.

When the Admiral comes up I will get him to release me. Nothing from England. I have prepared all my matters for going home in case we should be ordered, therefore I am ready to go or stay and it is a matter of very little importance to me which happens. It is you are the only person who I care about. The vessel which this line goes by is only laying too in the bay, therefore I can say no more than God bless you and believe to be ever with the greatest affection your HORATIO NELSON.

Present my compliments to Miss Herbert and don't forget me to my good little fellow. He reads I take for granted quite masterly. I am sure he ought under such a tutor. Bless you, bless you.

[Address torn away.]

(*Some notes on the back by Mrs. Nisbet:* 'Mulattoe Nanny, Black Hannah, Romeo, Cook, Mary came afterwards.')

No. 11

Boreas, English Harbour,
August 6, 1786

MY DEAR FANNY,—Having only this moment heard from General Shirley [1] that the packet sails tomorrow from this island, tomorrow noon, you must not expect much from me, for my English letters are hardly begun and you know I have been sadly negligent in that respect, let this plead for me. I have letters from my father [2] and uncle, both kind and good towards you. May all men be so is my sincere prayer. You well deserve it without a compliment. Indeed, you know I am not famous for giving them.

I don't think but I am better.[3] A pint of goat's milk every morning and

---

[1] General Sir Thomas Shirley, Governor of the Leeward Islands, died at Bath, 1800.
[2] The Reverend Edmund Nelson, Rector of Burnham Thorpe, Norfolk, died April 1802.
[3] On July 21, 1786, Dr. Sholto Archbald wrote to Nelson: 'Dear Sir, The judicious plan on which you have been treated by my friend Dr. Graham leaves very little room to expect much from medicine—I am therefore clearly of opinion that an immediate removal to another climate is highly necessary—The situation of English Harbour is so badly adapted to complaints like yours that a continuance there for any time may not improbably be attended with serious consequences' (B.M. Add. MSS. 34903—Bridport Papers).

PLATE I. Portrait in oils of Captain Horatio Nelson by John Francis Rigaud, R.A., dated 1781, when Nelson was aged twenty-three.

beef tea will make me what I wish to be for your sake, for indeed I am with the most ardent affection, ever your HORATIO NELSON.

Turn over:

Pray remember me most kindly to Miss Herbert. My best wishes ever attend her. I would send the newspapers but I don't know whether the packet will take them, but at an enormous price. Kind love to Josiah. I wish he could read, try and learn him. It is the greatest favour you can confer upon me.

Captain Collingwood desires his best respects to you and Miss Herbert. He desires me to say he shall keep me very orderly. I ought to write a line to Ward.[1] But if you see him tell him the reason I could not and give him my compliments.

To Mrs. J. Nisbet.

No. 12[2]

[Nicolas, I, p. 187]

Boreas, English Harbour,
August 19, 1786

MY DEAREST FANNY,—Having seen in this day's newspaper that a vessel cleared out from St. John's to Nevis a few days ago, I feel vexed not to have had a letter in the office for you: however, if I can help it, I will not be behindhand again. To write letters to you is the next greatest pleasure I feel to receiving them from you. What I experience when I read such as I am sure are the pure sentiments of your heart, my poor pen cannot express, nor indeed would I give much for any pen or head that could describe feelings of that kind: they are worth but little when that can happen. My heart yearns to you, it is with you, my mind dwells upon nought else but you. Absent from you, I feel no pleasure: it is you, my dearest Fanny, who are everything to me. Without you I care not for this world; for I have found lately nothing in it but vexation and trouble.

These you are well convinced are my present sentiments: God Almighty grant they may never change. Nor do I think they will: indeed there is, as far as human knowledge can judge a moral certainty they cannot: for it must be real affection that brings us together, not interest or compulsion which make so many unhappy.

---

[1] John Ward, Judge of the Vice-Admiralty Court of Nevis.
[2] As the original MS. is not now with the rest of the series, this letter has been quoted from Nicolas.

D

I have not been able to get even a cottage upon a hill, notwithstanding my utmost endeavours: and therefore have been kept here most woefully pinched by mosquitoes, for my sins perhaps, so the generous inhabitants of Antigua think, I suppose; not one of whom has been here, or has asked me to leave English Harbour: but I give them credit for not paying attention to me, to another cause, that I am a faithful servant to that country which most of them detest, and to which all their actions are inimical: I wish not for a better proof from them of my having done my duty. These gentlemen I shall in my mind hold very cheap in future: but I will have done with such trash. I am not that jolly fellow who for a feast and plenty of wine, would sacrifice the dearest interests of his Country: they are fond of those gentry.

Leave all Antigua by itself, tis not fit company for the other parts of the letter.

Monday, seven in the evening: As you begin to know something about sailors, have you not often heard that salt water and absence always wash away love? Now I am such a heretic as not to believe that faith: for behold every morning since my arrival, I have had six pails of salt water at day-light poured upon my head, and instead of finding what the seamen say to be true, I perceive the contrary effect: and if it goes on so contrary to the prescription, you must see me before my fixed time. At first I bore absence tolerably, but now it is almost insupportable; and by and by I expect it will be quite so. But patience is a virtue; and I must exercise it upon this occasion, whatever it costs my feelings. I am alone in the Commanding Officer's house, while my ship is fitting; and from sun-set until bed time I have not a human creature to speak to: you will feel a little for me I think. I did not use to be over fond of sitting alone. The moment old *Boreas* is habitable in my cabin, I shall fly to it, to avoid mosquitoes and melancholies. Hundreds of the former are now devouring me through all my clothes. You will, however, find I am better: though when you see me I shall be like an Egyptian mummy, for the heat is intolerable. But I walk a mile out at night without fatigue, and all day I am housed. A quart of goat's milk is also taken every day, and I enjoy English sleep, always barring mosquitoes; which all Frank's [1] care with my net cannot keep out at present. What nonsense I am sending you. But I flatter myself the most trivial article concerning me, you feel interested in. I judge from myself; and I would rather have what passes in your mind, than all the news you could tell me, which did not concern you. Mr. Horsford our neighbour came to visit me, making many apologies for his neglect, and pressing me much to come to his house, which has *Boreas* in

[1] Frank Lepée, Nelson's servant.

view. Also the Comptroller of the Customs with fine speeches: he may go back whistling if he pleases. I cannot add any thing further, for I do not know if you would read more than a sheet full.

August 23: At any rate I will shew some mercy. *Berbice* arrived yesterday. All at home are well. I am still apt to suppose this winter will carry me to England. Pringle has been at Portsmouth, so says Lord Hood; he longs to see you. May every blessing attend my far better half and may I soon be with you, is the sincere wish of your most affectionate HORATIO NELSON.

No. 13

[Nicolas I, p. 193]

Boreas, English Harbour,

August 31,

½ past 7 in the evening

MY DEAREST FANNY,—What can I say? Nothing if I speak of the pleasure I felt at receiving your kind and affectionate letter. My thoughts are too big for utterance; you must imagine everything that is tender, kind and truly affectionate has possession of my whole frame. Words are not capable of conveying an idea of my feelings, nothing but reciprocity is equal to it. I flatter myself it is so.

I must get into something from what I have been writing or I should be a fool. I left off a dozen times and found I did not know one word from another. Well on the Saturday morning after *Berbice* left me Mr. Lightfoot came and paid me a visit with an apology of his having been confined to his house or he would have done it before, that not writing he meant as a mark of attention. He prevailed upon me to sleep at his house on Monday last, the day I dined with Sir Thomas Shirley. His great attention at his house made amends for his long neglect and I forgot all anger. I can forgive sometimes you will allow. And I only came from thence this morning, it is nine mile and with writing ever since my arrival I feel a little tired, therefore expect nothing but sheer stupidity. I have also seen the great Mr. Martin; he says he understood and believed I was gone to England. *Whistle.*

The country air has certainly done me service. I am not getting very fat, my make will not allow it, but I can tell you and I know your tender heart will rejoice that I have no more complaint in my lungs than Capt. Maynard and not the least pain in my breast.

I wish Mr. Herbert would come to Antigua but I have nothing of my own to offer him; if *Boreas* could be got ready I would fetch him, but that's impossible. Pray present my best respects to Dr. Jeffreys; I am very much flattered indeed by his good opinion.

September 1: Although I am just from salt water, yet as I am in a hurry to get the *Berbice* away that she may reach Nevis by the evening I must finish this thing, for letter I can't call it. I have a news-paper for Miss Herbert; it is all I have to offer which is worth her acceptance and I know she is as fond of a bit of news as myself. Pray my compliments to her and love to Josiah. If he can't read, I shall have exercise for my patience, therefore agreeable to your desire I have kept a little for future occasions.

Heavens bless you and believe me ever your affectionate HORATIO NELSON.

To Mrs. J. Nisbet, Nevis. By favour Lt. Dent.[1]

No. 14
[Nicolas I, p. 194, part]

Boreas, English Harbour,
September 23, 1786

MY DEAR FANNY,—Although when you wrote me last Montpeliri[2] was an infirmary, ere this I hope it has resumed its antient name, for the time thank God draws near when I shall visit it and you know I never liked it as an infirmary. It is certainly too fine a house to be sick in.

On the 9th October barring something extraordinary you certainly see H. N. again and I need not say if it is possible with a stronger affection than he left you. I have been a day or two at a Mr. Horsford's who was very kind and attentive.

If you want anything from Antigua for yourself, Jiah or any of your friends, send me word and I will get them. Tell Miss Herbert any commands likewise of hers I shall be happy to execute. I have sent all my collection of newspapers.

My letter is short but my mind could say the paperful, therefore don't let that be a reason for your writing either a short letter or making the lines very far from each other. I want to know but everything which concerns you. You are certain the letter will come safe and unopened. Apropos did you ever receive a letter I sent you by a vessel two or three days after my arrival here. I sent it under cover to Frazer and Bannytine merchants in Basseterre. And I sent one to Mr. Herbert about 10 days ago under cover to Mr. Adye.

My best compliments attend Miss Herbert and believe my dearest that I am ever the same HORATIO.

To Mrs. J. Nisbet, Nevis. By favour Lt. Dent.

---

[1] Digby Dent, a lieutenant in the *Boreas*.
[2] The house built by Mr. Herbert, usually spelt Montpelier.

No. 15

Boreas, English Harbour,
November 27, 1786

MY DEAR FANNY,—I don't think this will reach you as soon as the one I purpose sending by the *Berbice* when she arrives, but as I am writing to Mr. Herbert I can't resist the inclination to say How do ——

This Prince hunting [1] is but a bad sort of business. I had much rather be quiet at Montpeliri. I have seen Mr. Burke [2] and have done what was proper to retain him should the business be obliged to come before the Chancellor. You will see what I have said to Mr. Herbert. I am anxiously looking out for the *Berbice* that I may know where to find the Royal sailor.

What signifies my saying much? This may never reach you, but I shall send it under cover to Mr. Wm. Priddie. Give my best compliments to Miss Herbert and love to Jiah. Should any kind mortal enquire after me, pray give them my compliments. For a short time farewell, and believe I am with the most pure affection ever your sincere HORATIO NELSON.

To Mrs. J. Nisbet, Nevis.

No. 16

Boreas, English Harbour,
December 1

MY DEAR FANNY,—I wrote you a few days ago from St. John's but perhaps you have not received that letter. You will believe I lost no time in seeing Mr. Burke and have secured him for your cause.[3] He says the business cannot be settled but by Chancery. The *Berbice* is this moment arrived from Barbadoes and I am now going out of the harbour to join Prince William at Dominica. On the 6th I expect to have him here, from whence I will write Mr. Herbert, when he may expect him. Mr. Andrews [4] will tell you all the parade concerning him. I can only repeat what you well know, that you are my best beloved and that I believe it to be reciprocal. Ever your affectionate HORATIO NELSON.

[1] Prince William Henry, who Nelson had first met in 1782 when he was a midshipman, came to visit the Leeward Islands in November in the *Pegasus*. Sir Richard Hughes had sailed for England in August, leaving Nelson the senior officer on the station.
[2] John Burke, Crown lawyer for the Leeward Islands and Solicitor-General of Antigua.
[3] Settling the affairs of Dr. Josiah Nisbet, who had died intestate in England in 1781.
[4] George Andrews, a midshipman in the *Boreas*, and lieutenant in the *Agamemnon*, died a captain in 1810.

Love to Jiah. I hope he is better. I have sent for shoes but purser and them will be left behind I fancy. Sir Richard Bickerton [1] does not sail till the middle of November.

To Mrs. J. Nisbet, Nevis.

No. 17
[Nicolas, I, p. 203, part]

Boreas, off Antigua,
December 12, 1786

MY DEAREST FANNY,—It is an age since we parted and is likely to be much longer before we meet again, unless good fortune should induce the Commodore [2] to come down to English Harbour then perhaps we may come first to Leeward.

Our young Prince [3] is a gallant man. Some ladies at Dominica seemed very much charmed by him. He is volatile but always with great good nature. There were two balls during his stay and some of the old ladies were mortified that His Royal Highness would not dance with them, but he says he is determined to enjoy the privilege of all other men, that of asking any lady he pleases. Mrs. Parry dined at table the first day at the Government House, but afterwards never appeared at dinner, nor were any ladies at Governor Orde's [4] dinner.

The *Berbice* will bring this line and although I may not see her this fortnight, yet I should like to know what Mr. Adye has done in your business, for Capt. Holloway [5] says I may expect to be relieved when Sir Richard Bickerton arrives, but I don't think such a thing is likely to happen.

Wednesday: We arrived in here this morning at daylight and my friend Sir Thomas never cut a worse figure. He was in such a tremor that he could scarce articulate a word and I was glad to get him on board the *Boreas* to relieve both him and the Prince. His Royal Highness dined with me and, of course, the governor, but I believe never was man more relieved than him when he got away from such company. He muttered something about Clark's Hill but what it was none have been able to find out.

[1] Sir Richard Hughes's successor as Commander-in-Chief.
[2] Captain Alan Gardner was commander-in-chief on the Jamaica Station with the temporary rank of commodore. He died, Admiral Lord Gardner, in 1809.
[3] Prince William met Nelson at Dominica on December 2 (see Appendix, p. 56).
[4] Captain John Orde, later Admiral Sir John Orde, was appointed Governor of Dominica in 1783.
[5] Captain John Holloway of the *Solebay*, a friend of Prince William, was promoted Admiral of the White in 1810.

I can tell you a piece of news which is that he is fully determined and has made me promise him that he shall be at my wedding and says he will give you to me. He has never yet been in a private house to visit and is determined never to do it except in this instance. We shall not sail from here these fourteen days at least and should Sir Richard Bickerton come here probably we shall continue the tour to Leeward and if he does not arrive within that time we shall sail for Barbadoes where a foolish female is ready to resign herself to His Royal Highness. Vanity what obstacles thou removest.

Adieu my dearest and believe me to be your affectionate HORATIO NELSON.

I have said nothing to Dent. He dined in company with the Prince yesterday so of course it is a certainty I have looked over his absenting himself from his duty. He is ruined I fear past redemption but he shall never hear of his misfortunes from me. It is enough to have them.

Kind love to Jiah and best compliments to Miss Herbert; not looking at the signature of the letter wrote by Miss Herbert I thought myself honoured by one from her, but how short is human felicity, after having began an answer I saw Mr. Herbert's name at the end.

No. 18
[Nicolas I, p. 203, under date December 12]

English Harbour,
December 24, 1786

MY DEAR FANNY,—We returned last night from St. John's and I fancy many people were as happy to see His Royal Highness quit as they were to see him enter St. John's for another day or two's racquet would have knocked some of the fair sex up. Three nights' dancing was too much and never broke up till near day. Miss Athill [1] is the belle of the Island and of course attracted His Royal Highness's attention. I will tell you much when we meet, for you know the danger of putting too much upon paper. I could not have supposed there had been near the number of females on this island as appeared at the balls, and all being in their best clothes made them look tolerably well.

You will wonder I have been able to get through all this fatigue. I have not more than twice or thrice been in bed till morning and have rode a

[1] Anne Athill, daughter of Dr. James Athill, married Captain Richard Bickerton, son of Sir Richard Bickerton, in 1788.

great deal in the day, but so far from doing me harm everybody tells me they never saw me look so well. I am reconciled to the business as I really love to honour the Prince, otherwise I could not have gone through it.

You know I will ever strive to bear that character which will not discredit any man from taking notice of me. I know of no action of my life that I do not honour. I am more happy at this time on that account for I would if possible or in my power have no man be near the Prince who can have the smallest impeachment as to his character for as an individual I love him, as a Prince I honour and revere him. Telling you this history is as to myself, but my thoughts on all subjects are not kept from you.

We shall go to Barbadoes certainly from this place and when I shall see you 'tis not possible for me to guess. So much for marrying a sailor. We are often separated but I trust our affections are not by any means diminished by that circumstance. Our country has the first demand for our services, and private convenience or happiness must ever give way to the public good. I have sent the *Berbice* to carry Mrs. Menzies down. I hope by her to have a long letter and I hope to hear from Stanley. I send Miss Herbert the newspapers, pray present my best compliments to her, and give my love to Jiah.

Heavens bless and return you safe to your most affectionate HORATIO NELSON.

No. 19

[Nicolas I, p. 206, part]

English Harbour,
January 1, 1787

MY DEAR FANNY,—Your truly affectionate letter by the *Berbice* I received with much pleasure. How vain are human hopes. I was in hopes to have been quiet all this week. Today we dine with Sir Thomas, tomorrow the Prince has a party, on Wednesday he gives a dinner in St. John's to the regiment, in the evening is a mulatto ball, on Thursday a cock fight dine at Col. Crosbie's brother's and a ball, on Friday somewhere but I forget, on Saturday at Mr. Byam's [1] the President. If we get well through all this I shall be fit for anything, but I hope most sincerely the Commodore will arrive before all this is carried into execution. In many instances it is better to serve than command and this is one of them.

I would have got almonds with pleasure but sweet almonds I don't understand and I thought they could not be got in this island more than

---

[1] Edward Byam, President of the Council at Antigua and Judge of the Vice-Admiralty Court.

at St. Kitts. Mr. Adye only got my letter of November 28th, the 27th December. Yours arrived at the same time I take for granted. He promises me he will come to Nevis immediately after the Christmas holidays and that your business shall not be delayed. I have had no opportunity of speaking more to Mr. Burke than I did at first for he knows nothing of the business. I sent yesterday to St. John's for two pair of shoes and behold they have sent two pair of dancing pumps.

A happy New Year and many, many of them attend you is the most fervent wish of your affectionate HORATIO NELSON.

Pray present the compliments of the season to Miss Herbert and if any other honour me with an enquiry, pray do not forget remembering me.

No. 20

[Nicolas, I, p. 206, part, under date of January 1]

Boreas,
January 13, 1787

MY DEAR FANNY,—When I wrote by Dr. Archibald I little thought of having an opportunity of sending another letter from this vile place,[1] but if the Commodore does not come down and relieve me I think it likely we shall remain here all this month at least, for the *Pegasus's* ship's company are all sick and I cannot with propriety leave him by himself. Should Sir Richard Bickerton come down, for I think he must be at Barbadoes, and send me to Nevis I will bless him, and I shall not feel very pleasant if he does not. But I would sooner die than ask any favour. If he is polite he will do it without. If not, he will not perhaps do it with asking, and I should not like the mortification of being refused.

What is it to attend on Princes, let me attend on you and I am satisfied. Some are born for attendants on great men, I rather think that is not my particular province. His Royal Highness often tells me he believes I am married for he says he never saw a lover so easy or say so little of the object he has regard for. When I tell him I certainly am not he says then he is sure I must have a great esteem for you and that it is not what is (vulgarly) no I wont make use of that word commonly called love. He is right, my love is founded on esteem the only foundation that can make love last. I need not tell you what you so well know that I wish I had a fortune to settle on you but I trust I have a good name and that certain events will bring the other thing about. It is my misfortune not my fault. You can marry me only from a sincere affection therefore I ought to make

[1] Antigua.

you a good husband and I hope it will turn out that I shall. I believe few men before marriage or even after often say as much as I do, but I have not a thought that I wish to conceal from you. If it is possible absence increases my affection. You are never absent from my mind in any place or company. I have wrote Mr. Herbert about going home in the *Boreas*,[1] but I don't think Miss Herbert will like it, for what reason I know not. It is certainly as clean as a sugar loaded ship, although accommodation may not be so elegantly fitted up.

I may be relieved when Sir Richard arrives, but I am inclined to believe it will not be till May or June. Bold *Rattler* sailed this morning for Barbadoes and if the Commodore is arrived we shall have them all down next week for we cannot come to him. I have requested the General will allow his brigadier to send this letter on shore at Nevis. Give my compliments to Miss Herbert and kind love to Jiah and be assured that I am my dearest Fanny ever your most affectionate HORATIO NELSON.

To Mrs. J. Nisbet.

No. 21

Antigua,
February 5,
Monday: Noon

MY DEAREST FANNY,—I am exceedingly sorry to tell you that Mr. Herbert was taken with a fever yesterday noon, which has not yet left him. Our scheme of visiting Monseratt this day is of course at an end and all Mr. Herbert's wishes centre in getting into his own bed. Indeed I wish he was there at this moment, but I hope the fever will soon go off and then some of his spirits will return. At sea he has been uniformly well but when ever he reaches the shore the vile fever never fails taking hold of him and he is worse by his constant wishes to be at home. The wish is natural but should not be indulged. I shall be most sincerely happy when we reach Nevis, and never again do I wish to be separated from the object of my heart. 'Tis that separation which makes me unwell with incidents which you are acquainted with. Heavens bless my dearest and let her be assured that I am her affectionate HORATIO NELSON.

Pray my best compliments to Miss Herbert and love to Jiah. Whilst I have been writing this letter I have the pleasure to say Mr. Herbert has dropped asleep and a most profuse perspiration has come upon him, which there is no doubt will entirely carry off the fever.

[1] Mr. Herbert and his daughter returned to England with Nelson's wife in the *Roehampton*, a merchant ship, in the summer.

No. 22

[Nicolas, I, p. 215, part]

Boreas, Monseratt,
February 11, 1787

MY DEAR FANNY,—We are out of English Harbour thank God, and so far on my way to be with you. I anticipate with pleasure our meeting for never do I feel truly happy when separated from you. The time of our acquaintance gives me fresh proof of my unalterable affection and of your worth. Length of time often, too often gives proof of the failings of human nature and how difficult it is to be perfect. You have given me a proof that your goodness increases by time. These I trust will ever be my sentiments; if they are not I do verily believe it will be my folly that occasions it. You I know esteem and regard me. It is not cast away. But one proof is worth all protestations and when we are one I trust you will find the proof equal to your expectations.

Mr. Mead was the first of Monseratt on board the *Boreas* where I had the honour of presenting him to the Prince who dines with him on Tuesday and on Wednesday evening I hope to be at Nevis. Whether I shall see you that night is uncertain. It depends upon His Royal Highness, for unless he desires me I shall not presume to leave him. Adye has talked with Burke about your business and I have done that for Mr. Adye with His Royal Highness, that there is no doubt but he will be anxious to return the favour which it is impossible he can do more pleasantly than by attending to that business. Pray present my best compliments to Miss Herbert. I have sent her an Antigua newspaper. Kind love to Jiah and never think otherwise than that I am in the fullest sense of the word most affectionately your HORATIO NELSON.

If any good people enquire for me pray give my compliments. I have a letter from Stanley. He desires his love. You may send a line back by the bearer.

No. 23

Boreas,
Friday Morn, [23 February]

MY DEAR FANNY,—That anything new should turn up since we parted [1] is hardly possible, yet I write as I believe that you will receive pleasure in seeing a letter from me. In this respect I feel as I should in having one from you.

[1] Nelson was at Nevis from February 15 to 22, when he sailed from St. Kitts.

This business of Mr. Forbes's [1] seems in some measure a mistake throughout for I have talked to His Royal Highness upon the subject as much as an humble individual could to a person in his elevated situation. It appears upon the whole clear to me that Mr. F. asked Mr. Herbert without thinking and when His Royal Highness desired that nobody might be there he came to tell Mr. Herbert of it, but he might certainly have done in a better way. I told the Prince that Mr. Herbert was fearful he had done something that was displeasing. He said by no means and that it was impossible he could be uncivil to a person who had wished to shew him every attention. But that he desired to be alone at Forbes's that they might talk over old stories. I then mentioned Mr. Nisbet's being there as also Capt. Goldfrap. He told me it was not his intention to have had Mr. Nisbet but he had rode to town with him in the morning had attended him to the race course and that as he could not at that late hour get home that he could not do otherwise than ask him. That Capt. Goldfrap he knew nothing about him, but he understood he was some relation of Mr. Forbes's. He said many handsome things of Mr. Herbert that he had always heard him well spoken of etc. but that it was natural he should like Mr. Forbes his old acquaintance and wish to be much with him. This most probably is all I shall ever hear of the story. If you think Mr. Herbert would like to know it you will tell it, if not keep it to yourself. Tell me a little on that head. If this letter comes safe and you think there is no danger of their miscarrying I shall perhaps say much. If there is, I shall write less.

Governor Woodley [2] dined on board the Prince yesterday. Today we dine with him, tomorrow the Prince dines here and goes to a dance at Mr. Woodley's [3] in the evening.

Bless you my dearest Fanny and believe me ever your affectionate HORATIO NELSON.

Pray give my kind compliments to Mr. and Miss Herbert. Don't you forget to write.

No. 24

Boreas,[4]

Saturday 1 o'clock, [24 February]

MY DEAR FANNY,—The packet is just come down and has brought me your letter which is so very full of news I can't read it at present. However

[1] George Forbes, of Bush Hill.
[2] William Woodley, Governor of St. Kitts.
[3] Samuel Woodley, probably a younger brother of the Governor, died 1795.
[4] The *Boreas* was anchored in Basseterre Road, St. Kitts, from February 23 to March 3.

I hope Mr. Herbert is better and that nothing is amiss with you for that would give me pain indeed.

All the news I shall tell you is that a man is cracking my head with tuning your pianoforte. However be assured there is nothing in this world I would not bear with to please my dearest Fanny.

I shall send Frank up with it when it is done. Heavens preserve you and believe me to be ever your HORATIO NELSON.

Compliments to Miss Herbert and love to Jiah.

No. 25

Boreas,

Sunday 6 o'clock. p.m., [February 25, 1787]

MY DEAREST FANNY, for such indeed you are to me, when present I am too apt to talk lightly of what is to me the most painful of all things, when I am absent viz. your not being with me.

I have been so unwell this day that I am not able to attend the Prince on shore. You and you only are the cause. For my health's sake I wish he was out of the country much as he honours me. Then I should be restored to you, and health and all other blessings, I doubt not would attend me. This I purpose sending up by Frank with the pianoforte which I hope will arrive safe and well tuned. Therefore I shall not be so very cautious in what I write.

Has Mr. Herbert said anything to you about myself? If he has not, you will know that I asked him when he thought I ought to be married. His answer was that he regarded me more and more every day he knew me, and that I might be united to you when I thought it most convenient or let it alone till we got to England. I objected to the latter for many reasons for the ill natured part of these islands would say that I had only been playing the fool with you. Nothing else passed but I dare say Mr. Herbert will do everything which is handsome upon the occasion. I hope he will for your sake for it would make me unhappy to think I had taken you from a state of affluence to a small pittance. I never wished for riches but to give them to you and my small share shall be yours to the extreme. I little thought once that even you could make me ill by absence but it's too true.

I can't write Mr. Herbert about the Prince since you have not told me what to do about it. He certainly told Mr. Forbes that he would not have anybody there and Mr. F. to please him thought fit to offend Mr. Herbert and yet its possible the latter was not intended. The great man told Captain

Holloway that he saw I was very much hurt and had said much to him about Mr. Herbert and that he saw my displeasure by my rising from table when he was sitting without speaking to him as I had always done before, that he was vastly sorry to see me hurt, but that he certainly told Forbes not to have anybody there, but had not the most distant intention of offending anybody. That he had the highest esteem for Mr. Forbes and should be much with him when ever he came to Nevis (*that man has been given histories*). Captain Holloway will anchor at Nevis on his way to Antigua and dine with Mr. Herbert if he will send a horse to town when he sees the ship coming into the roads. On Thursday or Friday he will be up and will carry Mr. Herbert to Antigua if he wishes and is able to go up.

Monday evening: I am just come from the great dinner but have escaped Woodley's ball. I shall not get to Nevis God knows when. Words can't express what my feelings are at not being with you and united never more to part. I shall say something about both young and old Woodley when we meet but shall not put it to paper. May heavens preserve my best, and I believe I may say with truth, my only, love is the most fervent prayer of HORATIO.

No. 26

Boreas,
Tuesday noon, [February 27]

MY DEAR FANNY,—I must write a line before I dress for Mr. Adye's dinner or you will accuse me of neglect, indeed to tell you the truth I should feel uneasy did I not do it for by writing you are in imagination brought closer to my thoughts. Indeed you are never very far from them.

His Royal Highness is this moment come from me, and tells me he had a very pleasant ball at Mr. Woodley's, that the women got well routed by Mr. Woodley and he improved vastly under his tuition. I told him he never appeared to me to want an instructor in that business. He spoke most kindly of you and we talked of Mr. Herbert his health, going home etc. and amongst other things saying that here Mr. Priddie advanced money to the country and at Nevis he knew he could not have been entertained if Mr. Herbert had not given security for the money. He has never shewn by any word or action that he had the most distant cause not to like Mr. Herbert, indeed I do believe he likes his character, but that Mr. Forbes etc. are far more convenient companions in certain offices. He could not so long have kept it concealed but I must have found out something. And should I, my regard for Mr. Herbert would instantly (if he was a King instead of a Prince and I was dependent on him for bread) tell him of it. I don't think the Prince ever understood that Mr. Herbert was actually invited. Miss Parsons is liked. The Prince danced with her and Miss Thompson last night. Tonight I have to fag at the public ball. Oh how I wish it over and that I was returned on board the *Boreas*.

Heavens preserve and protect you is the constant wish of, my dearest Fanny, your affectionate HORATIO NELSON.

You tell me you write every day. I have received only one letter. Number them. No. (4).

To Mrs. Josiah Nisbet, Nevis.

No. 27
[Nicolas, I, p. 216, part]
Boreas,
February 28, 1787, 2 p.m.

MY DEAR FANNY,—I have this moment your letter of this morning and received it as I do everything which comes from you with the sincerest pleasure, indeed I am not well enough to write much and I have much fag before me. Captain Holloway is gone from us, Captain Newcome is laid up, therefore I must be worked and I am the more mortified as I purposed when the Prince went over to the other side the island to have escaped that trip, and have got a few hours up to see you, but that is all over. It is possible His Royal Highness may stop at Nevis on his way up from Tortola. This however shall be his own act and not mine. Adye was to go up tomorrow about my business in the Admiralty and I dare say will call upon Mr. Herbert.

I saw Mr. Parsons last night with Miss Parsons who made kind enquiries after you, she looked vastly well. The Prince danced with her and Miss Thompson not a beauty but something very pleasant about her. Mrs Adye is quite in love with the Prince. Today we dine with the merchants. I wish it over. Tomorrow a large party at Nicholas Town, and on Friday in town here—Saturday sail for Old Road. Sunday dine on Brimstone Hill [1]—Monday Mr. Georges [2] at Sandy Point and in the evening the Free Masons give a ball. Tuesday please God we sail.

[1] The fortress at Brimstone Hill, St. Kitts, 700 feet high, was considered one of the strongest posts in the West Indies.
[2] W. P. Georges, chief justice of the Leeward Islands and St. Kitts, and colony agent of St. Kitts.

The *Berbice* arrived last night but the Governor of Barbadoes would not let the Captain of the packet put the Leewards mails into her they were put on board a small boat which sailed 9 days ago from Barbadoes and has not yet been heard of.

Nothing very particular and nothing about Mr. Herbert or family was mentioned all the time I was at Mr. F. but I did not like the cast of the day and I can't carry two faces. I will write Mr. Herbert tonight if I am able, pray tell him so, for it does not want 10 minutes of 3 and I have not begun to dress. Farewell till tomorrow and be assured I am ever your faithful HORATIO NELSON.

No. (5).
To Mrs. Josiah Nisbet, Nevis.

No. 28
[Nicolas, I, p. 217, part]

Boreas,
March 3, 1787

MY DEAR FANNY,—Your letter dated Charlestown [1] I conclude was wrote on Wednesday. I received yesterday noon at Mr. Woodley's. I was in hopes to have heard from you upon my getting on board last night of what Captain Holloway had said but I shall leave a boat here to wait the arrival of the packet and to follow me to Old Road. My journey to Nicholas Town was too great a fag in the highth of the sun, I was very ill after it and nothing but His Royal Highness's attention and condescension could or should make me go through it. However I am quite well this morning and as we shall be pretty quiet today, I hope to be able to bear tomorrow and Monday tolerably well. I wish for poor Jiah's sake you may be able to settle with Ward and Nisbet. The latter you never can without a Chancery suit. We shall most likely be at Nevis about the 18th but keep this to yourself for I never wish, although you may know everything, that you should appear to know anything of our movements. I am just going to send to the office to examine if there are any letters for Mr. Herbert or yourself.

There cannot be a word of truth about Mr. Wallis.[2] I don't believe he has any intention of marrying that person, I have never heard a syllable

[1] The capital of Nevis.
[2] James Wallis, first lieutenant of the *Boreas*, was given command of the *Rattler* after Captain Wilfred Collingwood's death.

PLATE II. Water-colour, painted by Nicholas Pocock in 1810, of the frigate *Boreas* off the island of Nevis.

about the other lady. I rather think you had better not write me any more letters as they may not come to my hands, unless you direct them under cover to Mr. Adye and he will let his boy bring them to Old Road.

The boat is returned and there are no letters for any person but Miss Herbert. Adieu. Heavens preserve and give you safe to your ever affectionate HORATIO NELSON.

Love to Jiah and compliments to Miss Herbert. You can send a line on Monday under cover to Mr. Adye and desire him to forward it.

To Mrs. Josiah Nisbet, Nevis.

No. 29

Boreas, Old Road,[1]
Sunday morn.
[March 4, 1787]

MY DEAR FANNY,—Never was poor mortal more disappointed than myself yesterday at not receiving a letter. I had left the boat at Basseterre to follow me to this place, but behold the boat returned and reported no letter for me. Indeed perhaps it is wrong to set our hearts upon anything too much in this world. However, I forgive you in hopes it is owing to being a little lazy. Did I think, which I sometimes fear, it was occasioned by illness, it would make me miserable. Indeed my dear Fanny no person but yourself can tell what my feelings are. You I hope can because I believe they are reciprocal.

This most probably will be the last letter I can send you from this island. We have nothing new here but as the Prince dines on the top of Brimstone Hill I shall not close my letter till night. I wished much to know what Captain Holloway has said but unless I hear from you tomorrow want must be my master.

10 at night: We are just returned from the Hill and Adye is on board with me. I am not pleased too much with this day. I wish every day more and more I was out of this country.

Pray give my kind compliments to Mr. Herbert I hope he is better. Pray heavens protect you and be assured I am as ever your affectionate HORATIO NELSON.

To Mrs. Josiah Nisbet, Nevis.

[1] The *Boreas* was anchored in Old Road, St. Kitts, from midday, Saturday, March 3, till 11 a.m. on Sunday, when she proceeded to Sandy Point in company with the *Maidstone* and *Pegasus*.

E

No. 30
[Nicolas, I, p. 218, part]
Boreas, Sandy Point,
March 6, 1787

MY DEAR FANNY,—Your kind letter of Friday night I received yesterday having sent Frank to Basseterre to wait the arrival of the packet.

How uncertain are the movements of us sailors. His Royal Highness is rather unwell therefore I have given up the idea of visiting Tortola for the present. Today we dine with Georges at his country house. The Prince admires Mrs. G. very much. I have had a severe scolding from her but as you was the cause I felt perfectly easy. A neglected female does not easily forgive.

I am glad Mr. Forbes has explained everything to Mr. Herbert's satisfaction. The message he delivered must not be too much trusted to as to the complimentary part. Men make those things as they please and we are all fond of flattery. Adye will deliver this letter. I wish Mr. Herbert would let him settle the business with Nisbet for poor Jiah's sake, although he may have stated the business home pretty accurately yet he will not tell the opinion of the lawyers he has employed if it should be against himself.

I am now feeling most awkward. His Royal Highness has been with me all this morning and has told me that as things have changed if I am not married this time we go to Nevis it is hardly probable he should see me there again, that I had promised him not to be married unless he was present and that he did it to show his esteem for me and should be much mortified if any impediments were thrown in the way to hinder his being present. He intends it as a mark of honour to me as such I wish to receive it. Indeed his behaviour to me has ever been that of a friend instead of a person so elevated above me. He told me this morning that since he has been under my command he has been happy, and have given me to understand that there is no doubt whenever he may be placed in a high situation that I will find him sincere in his friendship. By keeping in his esteem there is no doubt but I shall have my right in the service if nothing more.[1]

I hope Mr. Herbert can have no objection, especially if he considers how much it is my interest to be well with the Prince. I beg you will show him this letter and assure him that in this as well as in other matters I

[1] Nelson married Mrs. Nisbet on March 11. Prince William gave the bride away and signed the register. (See Appendix, p. 55, for the marriage certificate.)

leave it to him persuaded that he will do everything which is right and proper on the occasion. You may think this an awkward way of speaking to Mr. Herbert thro' you. But I am convinced you are perfectly assured of my affection and that I have no thought which is concealed from you. In this I believe as in our affection we are reciprocal. No sinister views can be in the way.

Heavens bless you and I need scarcely say how much I am your affectionate HORATIO NELSON.

No. 31

[Nicolas, I, p. 276, part]

August 26, 1788, [London]

MY DEAREST FANNY,—Last night Mr. H. and self went over to Mr. Hamilton where I heard nothing but flattery and fulsome discourse till 11 o'clock. Mrs. Mills and myself could not keep from laughing. Poor Mr. Huggins is quite in disgrace and is to be turned out very shortly. Mrs. Hamilton [1] is to take possession of Montpelier if their house is not ready, and now she is learning to ride that she may never be absent a day from the dear father. In short such stuff and to his face I never heard.

I saw Lord Hood this morning. He made many enquiries after you. He was very civil but harped about P. W.[2] I said nothing about him. He agreed with me that a ship in peaceable times was not desirable; but that should a disturbance take place I need not fear having a good ship. Lady H. is at Portsmouth.

I saw my brother [3] who went with me to the Custom House. I really wonder all my things are not lost, they lay in such a place. My brother is very sorry to part with polly. Captain Locker [4] I find has been very unwell. I shall breakfast with him tomorrow. I saw Mr. and Mrs. Thomas and sat half an hour with them.

God bless you and believe me most affectionately your husband H. N.

Mr. Herbert certainly goes out in the spring.

To Mrs. Nelson, at Thomas Bolton [5] Esq., Norwich, Norfolk.

[1] Martha Herbert had married Andrew Hamilton of Nevis in May 1787. She had returned to England with her father, the President of Nevis, and Mrs. Nelson.
[2] Prince William, Nelson's handling of the case between the Prince and Schomberg, his lieutenant, had roused much criticism. (See Appendix, p. 59, for Prince William's letter to Nelson, December 3, 1787.)
[3] Maurice Nelson, employed in the Navy Office.
[4] Captain William Locker, Nelson's captain in the *Lowestoffe* and friend.
[5] Nelson's sister Susannah married Thomas Bolton, a merchant of Norwich, in 1780.

APPENDIX

Nelson's Memorandum of his services to 1796.[1]

Horatio Nelson son of the Rev. Edmund Nelson and of Catherine (his wife) Suckling sister Maurice Suckling Esqr. late Comptroller of the Navy was born at Burnham Thorpe in the county of Norfolk on the 29th day of September 1759,[2] was educated at the free school in Norwich and at North Walsham in the same county. He first went to sea with his uncle on the 1st of January 1771 in the *Raisonable* of 64 guns, on the appearance of a war with Spain relative to Falkland Islands. Captain Suckling being appointed to the *Triumph* a guardship in the Medway he sent H. N. a voyage to the West Indies in a West Indiaman with Mr. Rathbone who had been a mate in the former war in the *Dreadnought*. On his return he remained in the *Triumph* till the expedition under Lord Mulgrave in 1773 was fitting for a voyage towards the North Pole when he was sent in the *Carcass* bomb under the protection of that good man Captain now Admiral Lutwidge. Being paid off at Deptford on the 15th of October he immediately embarked on board the *Seahorse* Captain George Farmer and sailed for the East Indies on November 20th 1773 where he served till March 1776 when from ill health he returned in the *Dolphin* of 20 guns with Captain now Admiral Pigot. Being paid off at Woolwich in September 1776 he was appointed by Admiral Sir James Douglas to act as 4th Lieutenant of the *Worcester* 64 Captain M. Robinson, who was on the point of sailing with a convoy to Gibraltar. On his return from Gibraltar in April 1777 having served his time and passed for a lieutenant he received a commission for the *Lowestoffe* frigate Captain William Locker then fitting out at Sheerness for the Jamaica station in which ship he served as 2nd lieutenant till Admiral Sir Peter Parker then commander-in-chief took him in June 1778 into the flag ship where he served till December 1778 when he was made a Master and Commander into the *Badger* brig and was employed in the Mosquito shore and in protecting the North side of Jamaica from the depredation of privateers.

On the 11th June 1779 he was promoted by the same Admiral to be a post Captain and appointed to the *Hinchinbroke* of 28 guns. In this ship he was sent to co-operate with Captain now Major Polson in an expedition against fort St. Juans and the Spanish settlements on the lake of Nicaragua. The fleet arrived at the harbour of St. Juans on the 28th March 1780

---

[1] N.M.M., M.44, from the Bridport collection; sold at Sotheby's 1933.
[2] Nelson was inaccurate over dates. He was born in 1758.

when there not being a man who had ever been up the river or had any idea of the distance of any fortification from its mouth, Captain Nelson manned several of the Mosquito shore craft and two of the *Hinchinbroke* boats and carried the soldiers up to the castle of St. Juan storming the lookout and fighting the batteries till it surrendered April 29th 1780. Captain Nelson was then appointed to command the *Janus* of 44 guns which ship he was obliged to leave from exceeding ill health contracted on the late expedition. In August 1781 Captain Nelson was appointed to the *Albemarle* frigate in which ship he served in the North Sea, Canada, New York and the West Indies during the remainder of the war and was paid off in her at Portsmouth July 3rd 1783.

In March 1784 Captain Nelson was commissioned for the *Boreas* frigate ready to sail for the Leeward Island station, during his service on this station he prevented, by an activity never exceeded, the contraband trade carried with American vessels to the great prejudice of British shipping. Captain Nelson had also the opportunity of discovering great frauds in the expenditure of public money and as the Naval Storekeeper is punished by fine and imprisonment it is to be hoped a strain by his means be put to farther embezzlement. Being paid off November 30th 1787, he remained on shore till January 31st 1793, when he was appointed to the *Agamemnon* of 64 guns. Whilst belonging to that ship fought four sea actions and upwards of 100 days actually in battle against the French.

Nelson to Mr. William Suckling [1]
[Nicolas, I, p. 144]

Boreas, Nevis,
November 14, 1785

MY DEAR SIR,—Not a scrap of a pen have I by the last packet from any relations in England but however you see I don't think I am forgot; more especially when I open a business which perhaps you will smile at in the first instance and say this Horatio is for ever in love. My present attachment is of pretty long standing, but I was determined to be fixed before I broke this matter to any person.

The lady is a Mrs. Nisbet widow of a Dr. Nisbet who died 18 months after her marriage and has left her with a son. From her infancy (for her father and mother died when she was only two years of age),[2] she has been

---

[1] Monmouth MSS., Nelson autograph collection.
[2] Nelson's facts are inaccurate. Fanny Herbert Woolward was born in 1758; her mother died while she was a child, her father, William Woolward, senior judge of Nevis, in 1779.

brought up by her mother's brother, Mr. Herbert president of Nevis, a gentleman whose fortune and character must be well known to all the West India merchants therefore I shall say nothing upon that head. Her age is twenty-two and her personal accomplishments you will suppose *I think* equal to any persons I ever saw, but without vanity her mental accomplishments are superior to most peoples of either sex and we shall come together as two persons most sincerely attached to each other from friendship. Her son is under her guardianship but totally independent of her. But I must describe Herbert to you that you may know exactly how I stand for when we apply for advice we must tell all circumstances. Herbert is very rich and very proud. He has an only daughter and this niece, who he looks upon in the same light if not higher. I have lived at his house when at Nevis since June last and am a great favourite of his. I have told him I am as poor as Job but he tells me he likes me and I am descended from a good family which his pride likes. But he also says 'Nelson, I am proud and I must live myself, therefore I can't do much in my lifetime, when I die she shall have twenty thousand pounds, and if my daughter dies before me she shall possess the major part of my property. I intend going to England in 1787 and remain there my life, therefore if you two can live happily together till that event takes place you have my consent.' This is exactly my situation with him and I know the way to get him to give me most is not to appear to want it. Thus circumstanced who can I apply to but you? The regard you have ever expressed for me leads me to hope you will do something, my future happiness I give you my honour is now in your power. If you cannot afford to give me anything for ever you will I am sure trust to me that if I ever can afford it I will return it to some part of your family. I think Herbert will be brought to give her two or three hundred a year during his life and if you will either, give me I will call it for I think you will do it, either one hundred a year for a few years or a thousand pounds, how happy you will make a couple who will pray for you for ever. Don't disappoint me or my heart will brake, trust to my honour to do a good turn for some other person if it is in my power.

I can say no more but trust implicitly to your goodness and pray let me know of your generous action by the first packet. . . . [Nelson continues with some queries about the legal rights of seizing vessels to the King's use under the Navigation laws.]

Best wishes for the happiness of every part of your family and may they enjoy the happiness 'tis so much in your power to give me but in every occasion believe that I your most affectionate HORATIO NELSON.

William Suckling Esq.

Nelson's Marriage Certificate [1]

Nevis

I, William Jones, Clerk, rector of the parishes of St. John and St. Thomas in the said island do hereby certify that Horatio Nelson Esq. Captain of His Majesty's Ship the *Boreas* and Frances Herbert Nisbet Widow, were married this eleventh day of March in the year of Our Lord 1787 according to the canons and constitutions of the Church of England at the dwelling house of the Honourable John Richardson Herbert (President of His Majesty's Council and deputy ordinary of the said island) in the aforesaid parish of St. John. Given under my hand the day and year above written.

WILL. JONES

This marriage was solemnized between us
in the presence of   HORATIO NELSON
    WILLIAM   FRANCES HERBERT NISBET

Nelson's Will [2]

14 April 1787

This is the last will and testament of me Horatio Nelson commander of His Majestys Ship *Boreas* I give and bequeath unto my dearly beloved wife Frances Herbert Nelson if I have no children at the time of my death all my estate or estates both real and personal of whatever kind or nature and wheresoever to her and her heirs absolutely for ever and I hereby appoint my beloved uncle William Suckling Esqr. of the Custom House London my sole executor of this my will hereby revoking all former and other wills or will made by me.

And declaring this only my last will and testament in witness whereof I have hereunto set my hand and seal this fourteenth day of April in the year of Our Lord one thousand seven hundred and eighty seven.

This will is wrote with my own hand.

HORATIO NELSON.

Signed sealed published and declared by the said Horatio Nelson as and for his last will and testament in the presence of us who in his presence and at his request and in the presence of each other have subscribed our names as witness thereunto.

JAMES JAMESON. [3]

Witnesses.

JAMES WALLIS. [4]

[1] B.M. Add. MSS. 28,333: a small collection of legal documents relating to Nelson.
[2] Monmouth MSS., Nelson papers, vol. I.
[3] James Jameson, Master of the *Boreas*.
[4] James Wallis, first lieutenant of the *Boreas*.

Nelson's Draft Account of his Meeting with Prince William in
December 1786 [1]

On Saturday the 2nd December 1786 I joined the *Pegasus* commanded by His Royal Highness Prince William Henry at Roiseau in the Island of Dominica. A few hours after my anchoring P. W. came on board and after having delivered me a packet from My Lords Commissioners of the Admiralty he requested to see it, and as I knew P. W. had a copy of it, I made no scruple of shewing it, and took the liberty of telling His Royal Highness that as he had seen them I hoped that nothing would happen that could possibly induce me to deviate in the smallest article from them, that he knew as well as myself they were drawn up by His Majesty's approbation, and that I should take every measure to carry them rigidly into effect. H.R.H. assured me that I should find every good wish from him and was pleased to say that he was happy at being placed under my command. At this time he produced his orders from Commodore Sawyer which were that H.R.H. was to come to the West Indies and to visit such islands in His Majesty's possession as he thought fit and to return to Halifax by the middle of June. He said that Commodore Sawyer considered the *Pegasus* as belonging to his station. I told H.R.H. that I must attend to the orders of the Admiralty, and could not consider Commodore Sawyer as having any force, although I should pay them every attention which lay in my power. Why replied P. W. don't you see the difference of the Admiralty's and his orders about my coming on the coast of America, I told him I did but that at present I ought only to think of those I received from the Admiralty. He enquired how I was officered and having told him very well, he said I wish I could say so, for although I think mine know their duty yet that they give themselves such airs that he could not bear them. Do you know that they would not go to the ball which Governor Parry gave me at Barbados, which I think a mark of great contempt to me. I told H.R.H. that I could not suppose they could mean anything disrespectful to him, that every other consideration out of the question it was too much their interest to wish to disoblige him. He said that it was so. However he should keep a sharp look out and there is your friend Schomberg as he calls himself, but I don't believe you know much of him. I told H.R.H. that I had a great opinion of Mr. S. This was all that passed that evening.

On the next day Sunday a French frigate having come in with compliments from the French governor of Martinique, the P. I suppose had ordered his people to be in their blue jackets, for when I went on board the

[1] B.M. Add. MSS. 34,902, Bridport papers.

Pegasus, after H.R.H. has spoken to me he turned to Mr. S. and said Sir, I ordered the ship's company to have their uniform jackets on. Mr. S. said he thought that cloth was too warm for this country but that if H.R.H. chose he would order them to be put on directly. The manner in which this was spoke made a much greater impression upon me than all that happened afterwards for I plainly saw all was not right.

The next day Capt. Brown of the *Amphion* told me he saw that Schomberg and the Prince would not long be friends, and hoped that I would endeavour to prevent a court martial from happening in the *Pegasus*, that he feared I should have a disagreeable time of it. From that time I was perfectly on my guard, and what I did afterwards was the effect of deliberation and not hastiness and what I trust will be found to have been unavoidable.

On our arrival in English Harbour the *Pegasus* was ordered to the careening wharf. I offered H.R.H. the commanding officer's house and he did me the honour to ask me to stay in it with him, and said he did not wish to ask any officers of the squadron to dine except Captain N., and that his lieutenant could not be spared from the duty of the ship. The lieutenants of the *Pegasus* I saw were displeased with me and the officers of the *Boreas* told me that they attributed H.R.H. change of conduct to me.

(*Unsigned and undated: but in Nelson's hand and with many corrections.*)

Prince William to Lord Hood [1]

A

Carlisle Bay,
December 1, 1786

MY LORD,—Since I last wrote many things have happened from the various situations I have been in and now to recapitulate them. . . .

On the 9th November I arrived at St. Vincent having missed Barbadoes in the night: here I stayed till the arrival of the packet, which came in the 19th: my stay was too short to be able to give your Lordship my ideas about these islands, which in the course of time I hope to do. On the 20th I sailed, and on the 25th arrived at Barbadoes: the *Amphion* and *Solebay* were arrived the night before in Carlisle Bay from England and last from Jamaica. Holloway delivered me your Lordship's letters, by which I was at last made happy.

We stayed at Barbadoes till the 30th. The inhabitants treated me with singular marks of respect and esteem and presented me with a sword worth 300 guineas. The entertainments and balls were magnificent. They

[1] Extracts from N.M.M. 50 MS. 0096, Hood papers. Prince William, who had served with Lord Hood as a midshipman, kept up a frequent correspondence with him.

individually and collectively strove to show their loyalty. It gave me great satisfaction to hear the manner they speak of your Lordship. The island is in a most prosperous and flourishing situation; fine crops and great prospects of prodigious advantage to be gained by the culture of cotton. On the 30th of November I sailed for Dominique in company with the *Amphion, Solebay*, and *Rattler* Sloop and arrived in the evening of the 1st December; I must now end as the packet is under weigh.

I am my Lord yours sincerely, WILLIAM.

B

Nevis,
March 15, 1787

MY LORD,— . . . On the 12th of February the *Boreas, Solebay* and *Pegasus* sailed for Mountserrat, where we stayed three days to visit that romantic island. From thence we all proceeded to Nevis. Here we remained a week. Nelson introduced me to his bride. She is a pretty and a sensible woman and may have a great deal of money if her uncle Mr. Herbert thinks proper. Poor Nelson is over head and ears in love. I frequently laugh at him about it. However seriously, my Lord, he is in more need of a nurse than a wife. I do not really think he can live long. During our stay at Nevis Newcome in the *Maidstone* arrived. We then proceeded to Basse Terre and St. Kitts. In this island we remained some time. As I found myself heated by the exercise I was obliged to take in that island, by my desire Nelson returned to Nevis before we should proceed to Tortola. He married Mrs. Nisbet on the 12th of March,[1] and I had, my Lord, the honour of giving her away. He is now in for it. I wish him well and happy and that he may not repent the step he has taken.

I beg my best compliments to Lady Hood, and assure her how sensible I am of her goodness in not forgetting me, and ever believe me yours sincerely, WILLIAM.

C

English Harbour,
April 18, 1787

MY LORD,— . . . I have not yet had one man desert from the *Pegasus*. She is at present complete in her numbers, healthy and manned with able bodied and thorough bred seamen, people inclined to do their duty with obedience, alacrity and cheerfulness. Since this affair of Schomberg, I allow nothing to be done but with my previous approbation. Everything going through me, I have an opportunity of seeing the disposition of the ship's company. I see with pleasure that by my having been very severe

[1] The marriage took place on March 11.

at first and by my constant attention to my own conduct on board, I am respected and feared, which is the situation every officer ought to put himself in with his officers and men. The officers upon my first arrival in the West Indies ran away with the foolish notion that it was Nelson who advised me to keep them at the proper distance. They are now convinced of their error and Schomberg would be very happy to have everything forgot. However it is now, my Lord, too late, he must suffer for his impropriety of conduct. . . .

Tomorrow I sail with Holloway for the Granada Islands, so that till the next opportunity I must take my leave. My best wishes and compliments always attend Lady Hood and all your worthy family. I am my Lord, Yours sincerely, WILLIAM.

Prince William to Nelson [1]

Pegasus,
December 3, 1787

MY DEAR NELSON,—Since I left you at Nevis last May I have received three letters from you, two from the West Indies and one from Portsmouth: in which you write about the propriety of Captain's refusing complete books to the muster master, the Lords of the Admiralty being displeased with you for sending the *Pegasus* and *Rattler* to Jamaica, your wish about Schomberg and desiring me to give Hope a certificate, all of which I shall endeavour to answer in a clear manner.

Upon my arrival at Jamaica the storekeeper applied to my clerk for a perfect book and being referred to me received for answer he should have a proper book. Commodore Gardner was angry with him for applying for any book and ordered me to give none upon which he produced a letter to the Commodore from the Admiralty lodged in his office requiring all captains to give perfect muster books; however the Commodore again ordered me to give none. At Halifax I found a letter from their Lordships *requesting* as they termed it that I would for the future furnish the muster master with such a book as is specified in the 10 and 11 articles of the Captains' instructions and more particularly described in the 30 article of Purser's instruction: and since that a duplicate: I accordingly supplied the Muster Master with such a book at Halifax, which he said was not proper and that he would not muster my ship's company. I immediately went to Commodore Sawyer and he read him the Admiralty letter and the heads of the book: he approved of my proceedings; and wherever I go Purser was not to give in any other book without positive orders from the Admiralty or written order from my commander-in-chief.

[1] N.M.M. 37 MS. 1625, Autograph collection.

In my opinion Nelson we were both to blame; you in sending the *Pegasus* and *Rattler* down to Jamaica and me in asking and proposing it. I was greatly surprised to see the matter taken up so seriously and severely by the Admiralty but we both know who is at the bottom of the whole. Your observation is just, it is sufficient for a man either to be respected in his profession by me or to be my friend to be disliked by Lord Howe. Were you in a similar situation again you had better not do it.

With respect to Schomberg I must confess myself surprised that you should recommend him after what I have so often said and in what we do both agree, namely, the never forgiving an officer for disrespect: rest assured I never shall and particularly Schomberg after the fair chance he had when he was released the first time. I am by no means of a revengeful temper: what I did, I did for the good of His Majesty's service and most certainly shall do again, but this affair has so stamped my character in the service that I trust and hope this will be the only act of severity I shall ever be under the disagreeable necessity of performing:

With respect to Hope I shall send him his certificate; but I must observe that the determination of the Admiralty in the business has given me uneasiness. Their lordships acknowledge that an officer cannot receive his pay without the usual certificate from his captain and yet that the captain cannot refuse the certificate: if a man is authorized to certify, I conceive he is to certify to the best of his judgment, otherwise the certificate is nothing. The Admiralty in this instance have not thought proper to support the Commanding Officer, by which the King's service will be hurt: my consolation is my own conscience and the approbation of my brother officers: there is a good lesson for me in future how to act and I shall take care not to be caught again.

Wallis will inform you of Commodore Gardiner's sentiments on the subject: Commodore Sawyer approves of my conduct, but wishes I had brought Schomberg to America, for he would certainly have held a Court Martial on him. The Commodore has shewn me letters from Captain Hope who with all his family are exceedingly angry with Lieutenant Hope: through his uncle General Hope I have offered a mediation which I trust the young man will accept. He has in his excuse inexperience in the service and world and the fire of youth, but the other has no excuse: let me know how Hope behaved on board the *Boreas*.

In my own ship I go on pretty well: I have had two Courts Martial one on the Master at Arms, who was broke and received 100 lashes and the other on a seaman who received 50 lashes on board his own ship. Church is confined; with him I have had some unpleasant work and I am afraid he is of a sulky disposition. Upon the whole we reckon well enough:

Hargood is a diligent attentive officer, in short I can rely in him: My health thank God is perfectly recovered: I never was better in my life. Fidge quitted me through ill health upon my arrival at Halifax and Commodore Sawyer appointed my Surgeon's mate to the vacancy which the Navy Board have approved of: One of the gentlemen Mainwaring I desired the Commodore to appoint as third Lieutenant which the Admiralty did not approve of: they have appointed Church third, and Lord Howe my particular and obliging friend has wrote out to know who I could wish to have appointed as second: Sir William Young's grandson is arrived and appears to be as extraordinary a mortal as the facetious baronet: if you have not been able to provide for young Andrews, I shall be happy to enlist him under my banner as well as any other young man you may recommend. Believe me dear Nelson, yours sincerely, WILLIAM.

To Horatio Nelson Esq.
H.R.H. P.W.

Lady Nelson's Memorandum [1]

When we went to Burnham Thorpe we had no thought of residing with Mr. Nelson as it was only to make him a visit preparatory to our going to France as Captain Nelson had experienced the great inconvenience of not speaking or understanding the French language a very useful and necessary part of a sailor's education; and at that time I was in the habit of speaking French as it always fell to my lot to entertain the French officers who came recommended by the Governor of the French islands to my uncle, whose ancestors had so great a dislike to the French, that they would not allow their children to learn the language least they should have any communication with them.

Mr. Nelson's joy at seeing this best and most affectionate of sons was so great that he told us that we had given him new life or some such expression, and that we had better not have come to him, than to have cheered and then to leave him and that he was sure a little native air would do much for Horatio. In short this good old man seemed to suffer much at the thought of our leaving him, saying his age and infirmities were increasing and that he could not last long which made us give up entirely our former plan. Then we agreed to live together. A great comfort to Mr. N. and some convenience to all parties.

The first writ was served on me from the circumstance of Captain Nelson's going to a fair to buy a Galway or small horse and just before the time came for his arrest he wrote to the Treasury saying if a satisfactory

---

[1] Monmouth MSS., Nelson papers, Vol. V. Written for the Rev. J. Clarke, c. 1806.

answer was not sent him by return of post he should be immediately off to France (by return of post an answer came) and it was settled his brother Maurice was to have accompanied me there in ten days after he went.

He once talked of the Russian service—in short he was so dissatisfied at the ill usage particularly when at *the Nore* that I am certain he never would have gone to sea if he had had a fortune.

The Rev. Edmund Nelson to Nelson [1]

October 11, 1790

MY DEAR H.,—From the contents of those letters which your good wife has communicated to me; it seems necessary to call forth all your prudence and mature deliberation, how to act at this critical juncture so as to justify your own character and give no offence to either party. It ought certainly to be made known at least to particular persons, why you are so marked as to render any application fruitless, viz. merely for supporting the dignity and character of a person whose rank and situation as well as some testimony of his regard had attached you to him, for which you are now as it were persecuted, tho' an ill natured world may attribute to other causes your being unemployed. What passed between you, and the Irish peer,[2] (if confidential friendship is not broke thro') ought to be by yourself, or the medium of a friend to be told to W. C.[3] Nay I think if it can be, you should either ask an audience at C. house,[4] or if etiquette will allow it, visit there and introduce a subject where you own interest is so immediately concerned, tho' I have no doubt but on the issue, all will come about, still as you smart, they, who are the sine qua non for the lashes given, ought to feel a part.

God bless you, you will do what is right. It is Monday morn, indeed the Sabbaths return too quick for my strength.

Mrs. N. will write tomorrow; the letter of attorney I sent to Suckling and desired it might be returned to the Navy Office directly. Yours etc., EDMUND NELSON.

If a war I am inclined to think the commanding officer you dined with will take all the merit of anything that is done for you entirely upon his own consequence at the Admiralty.

To Captain Nelson.

[1] N.M.M. MS. 9292, Bridport papers.
[2] Lord Hood, who had been appointed one of the Lords Commissioners of the Admiralty in January 1790.
[3] Captain the Hon. William Cornwallis, a friend of Nelson. Admiral Sir William Cornwallis died in 1819.
[4] Carlton House, the residence of the Prince of Wales.

Nelson to Mr. Thomas Bolton, his brother-in-law [1]

A

Burnham,
December 14, 1789

MY DEAR SIR,—At 1 o'clock I received your letter: my father and myself are sorry that matters are so arranged that the funeral [2] must take place tomorrow at 11 o'clock. I shall as I am sure both you and my sister would wish that everything handsome and proper should be done, tell you our plan for conducting this last sad scene. Poor fellow thank God he went off perfectly in his senses, which for the last week were more collected than at any other period since his being here. He sent for my father on the day before his death to ask where he was to be buried and on my father telling him somewhere near where he should one day be laid he answered he hoped so, and then told my father two or three things which he wished you to do and which he had omitted to tell you. All his other wishes he said he had told you.

Inside the railing next George [3] is his grave near seven feet deep in which is built a vault which will not be filled up after the coffin is placed in it and a stone laid over the coffin about 4 or 5 inches from it, on which is inscribed his name and the year. About 4 feet of earth will be laid over, and the chancel is going to be boarded. His body is laid in a shell which is inclosed in a strong oak coffin quite plain. A hearse is to come from Fakenham at 10 o'clock to receive the body which will be met at the church gate by Mr. Crowe who is ordered a scarf, hat band and gloves. The body to be carried by six the oldest parishoners who are to receive a crown a piece after the funeral and instead of gloves each man is to have a hand-kerchief for their wives of the same price. This with a few pairs of gloves is I think the whole of the funeral expenses. My father dear good man has not suffered me to pay a farthing everything which I bought he instantly paid for but more of this when we meet. I am sorry so is my father that he should take anything of you, but demands will never cease coming on him. Since poor Edmund's death, Maurice has made some which with all my partiality for him he ought to be ashamed of having done.

We shall be happy to see you whenever it is convenient and have pro-cured a bed well aired and prepared for your reception at our neighbours. Mrs. Nelson I am sure with pleasure performed her kind offices. They are what one day we shall all want. My father is tolerable and with Mrs.

[1] N.M.M. MS. 9590, Girdlestone papers.
[2] Of his brother, Edmund Nelson.
[3] A brother who died in infancy.

Nelson joins me in all kind wishes to my sister and yourself and little ones and believe me your most affectionate HORATIO NELSON.

To Mr. Thomas Bolton, Merchant in Norwich.

B

Burnham,
December 11, 1791

MY DEAR SIR,—When a journey is once deferred the time is hardly ever to be recalled so it is with me. By not coming to see my sister at the time fixed circumstances so alter as almost to put it out of my power. We were at Wolterton a few days and intended to have rode to Norwich last Sunday but the day was so very rainy that I could not move.

I am always troubling you with my commissions which I would not do if I could execute them here. My friend Capt. Locker has requested me to send him to make presents three very fine large Norfolk turkeys also sausages sufficient to eat with them. Let the turkeys be ready for the spit sewed up in separate cloths and securely packed up in a basket. If sausage meat is more convenient let it be put into a jar and sent with them. I cannot get a turkey, such as is wanted, in this neighbourhood, therefore will you have the goodness to get them from some of your market acquaintances and direct the basket as on the other side. Will you also choose me a good Gloucester cheese and send it by the carrier. Please to send me the account of what I am in your debt I had much rather pay it than let it remain unsettled therefore pray send it.

Please to order the turkeys to be in London by Wednesday the 21st, if they are brought to you on the Saturday this weather will keep them much longer than Christmas Day. I am sorry you have lost Lord Orford. How he disposed of his affairs you are more likely to know than myself. I hear he has left the Wolterton family something handsome. Mrs. Nelson desires to be kindly remembered to my sister, yourself, Miss Bolton and family.

Believe me your most affectionate HORATIO NELSON.

Josiah came home yesterday just in time to be shut up.

The basket to be directed for Mr. Townsend, No. 13 Ludgate Hill, London.

To Mr. Thomas Bolton, Merchant, Norwich.

C

Burnham,
April 23, 1792

MY DEAR SIR,—I thank you for your information about the horses and as I should not wish knowingly to throw away my money on horse flesh I will thank you to attend to every particular about him. The owner must warrant him sound in every respect. I wish his feet to be examined and that his shoes are not kicked out at the toes, for really I am so much afraid of getting another daisy cutter that if you have any doubts about him, will with pleasure pay Stephenson or any other farrier you may wish to examine him. You will of course find out if he is starter, or has any vicious tricks. I hope you will excuse my being so particular for really I am afraid to buy a horse off any body. My father is pretty tolerable. Mrs. Nelson joins me in kindest remembrances and believe me yours most affectionately, HORATIO NELSON.

If you purchase the horse let me know and I will send William over for him. With the amount in the receipt let the words 'Warranted sound in every respect' be inserted. The horse must be fourteen hands high at least or I would not choose to have him. Brown by his forgetfulness at Fakenham lost the pointer and all my endeavours cannot hear of him. Pray do not send me another I will certainly not take out a shooting licence. To Mr. Thomas Bolton, Merchant in Norwich, Norfolk.

D

Burnham,
April 30, 1792

MY DEAR SIR,—Mr. Bretts' horse which I intended to try is too small therefore I have said nothing about him, therefore if the mare has all the qualifications which I want in a horse you will please to receive her for me and I will send William by Brown next Monday to bring her home if you can take care of her at Thorpe till he arrives. In the receipt have inserted 'warranted sound in every respect'. I hope Mr. Robinson's liking the mare is not to enhance her price. Has Mr. R. tried her? 23 guineas I think you said was the price. I would certainly not give more for I can make a shift with the black mare for a little time. The pointer arrived last Saturday I sent William to Fakenham for her. I suppose the finder took the collar from her more especially as the direction I take for granted was tied to it, and as that was on her, the collar must, but it is not arrived. She was apparently half starved. She seems poor animal very happy. At all events she shall be well taken care of. Mrs. Nelson desires her kindest remembrances to Mrs. Bolton and family. Believe me dear sir your obliged HORATIO NELSON.

To Mr. Thomas Bolton, Merchant, Norwich.

Capt. Nelson requests Mr. Bolton to order him a piece of good old Gloucester cheese.

F

Chapter 2

HONOUR AND SALT BEEF
1793–1794

Introduction

Captain Nelson had been on shore and unemployed for over five years when, at long last, as it seemed to him, he was promised a ship by Lord Hood, a Lord Commissioner of the Admiralty on a Board presided over by Lord Chatham, the elder brother of the Prime Minister. On February 7, 1793, Nelson commissioned the *Agamemnon* 64 guns, lying without her masts in her, at Chatham, where she had been laid up 'in ordinary' for the past ten years. The *Agamemnon* had been launched in 1781 from a private yard in the New Forest at Buckler's Hard, on the Beaulieu river, and had been built by Mr. Adams of that place. The site of the dock in which she was built is still pointed out to visitors. She was mostly built of English oak, and the length of her gun-deck was 160 feet. Nelson was pleased to fit out at Chatham, because his old captain, William Locker, was the Commodore at Sheerness and was able to help in getting the *Agamemnon* ready for sea, and particularly in collecting her ship's company, which in those days was very much the concern of the captain and his officers. The day Nelson left Burnham Thorpe, February 4, his father wrote to his sister, Mrs. Matcham: 'If you can send him any good sailors, they will be acceptable. Several men in and about the Burnhams are entered for him. Indeed his character commands respect and esteem wherever it is known. A son of Mr. Hoste the clergyman, another of Mr. Weatherhead's and ditto of W. Bolton's goes with him as midshipman. He has been lucky in securing his old servant Frank.' Nelson had already written to Commodore Locker to request that men raised for the *Agamemnon* should be taken care of on board the *Sandwich*, and stating that he had sent out a lieutenant and four midshipmen to get men at every sea-port in Norfolk and to forward them to Lynn and Yarmouth. His friends in Yorkshire and the north would send what men they could lay hands on to the Regulating Captains at Whitby and Yarmouth. His bills, inviting men to enter the *Agamemnon*, were dispersed over Norfolk, but were not shown in London until his commission as her captain had been signed on January 31 by four

Lords of the Admiralty, including Lord Hood. Nelson found his lordship once again very civil indeed. With a real prospect of war, the long-drawn-out and official disfavour with which Nelson thought he had been treated by Lord Howe and Lord Hood had evaporated. Amongst his ship's company Nelson received twenty boys from the Marine Society. On February 19 he took eight boys, of ages between thirteen and nineteen years, and entered them as captains' servants. These boys came on board supplied with a sea kit and a bible from the Society, but few of them had had any experience at sea. Their trade varied from errand-boy to drawer of beer, shoemaker, tailor and plasterer.

A new ship's company was busily employed rigging the ship with help from the dockyard. Masts were stepped, the rigging made up, put over, set up and rattled down. The sails were finished off and bent to the yards. Meanwhile, as the carpenters and joiners, shipwrights and riggers, made the ship ready for sea, at the same time the stores and provisions were being stowed away. The scene must have been one of great confusion to Josiah, who had joined with his stepfather, and the young lads recruited from the Norfolk clergy. But the fitting out of a man-of-war was a business well understood and co-ordinated between the ship's company and the shore authorities.

On March 23 the ship was ready to be moved down the river. The captain read the Articles of War to the ship's company, a monthly duty, and was receiving on board water, beer and spirits. On April 1 the main yard was rigged to hoist the guns on board, and on April 7 the powder hoy came alongside. The powder magazines were a danger to a ship at all times, and the gunpowder was always taken on board last. The *Agamemnon* was ready for service and sailed round to the Nore and then to the Downs on April 24, where she awaited a convoy.

Although the outbreak of the French Revolution had probably made war between France and England inevitable, Pitt delayed the crisis until the execution of Louis XVI and the threat to Antwerp shocked the public conscience and commercial interests alike. Despite the gloomy lessons of the American Revolution, the nine years of peace with which Pitt's period as Prime Minister had opened had been remarkably prosperous. In 1789 the agriculturist Arthur Young, travelling in France, was told how the American Revolution had brought a French one in its train. He was able to point out how different was the case in his own country, although he admitted it was almost unbelievable 'for a people to lose an empire, thirteen provinces, and to *gain* by that *loss* an increase of wealth, felicity and power.' The cause of this prosperity in time of peace has been ascribed to the extension of trade brought about by the increased production due to the Industrial Revolution, and certainly the French threat to Antwerp resulted in a stoppage of the introduction into Europe of goods turned out in English factories. When France at last declared war on England and Holland on February 1, 1793, the challenge was eagerly taken up by George III and his countrymen. Pitt planned military intervention on the continent, both in Holland to free the Scheldt and in Brittany to help the French royalists. He must also defend Ireland.

Nelson was destined to join a strong fleet, commanded by Lord Hood, bound for the Mediterranean, to join the fleet of our Spanish allies, and operate off the shores of the Maritime Alps and Genoese Riviera in support of the Austrian army. In return for subsidies paid in hard cash, the kingdoms of Sardinia and Naples would place troops under British command. Naturally, with England receiving French refugees, and the tales of the reign of terror and of the factions amongst those who inspired the terror filling the newspapers, nobody considered that the war could last long. The forces of reaction, from which Britain had held back as long as possible, were too ruthless and powerful to be withstood by a country disorganized and torn with internal dissensions.

Nelson, who considered the navy a worthwhile profession only in wartime, thought Josiah had best be introduced to a profession ashore, if only his mother could interest his relations in him. The legacy which he had been left by his grandfather, President Herbert, altered the situation and Nelson agreed to take the boy with him. To do so in the way Josiah did seems to have been the ideal way of joining the navy in those days. He was now twelve years old, the same age Nelson had been when he had joined the *Raisonable* one winter's day when his uncle was not on board and he had not been expected. Josiah experienced none of this, and in addition he had the companionship of the young sons of Norfolk clergymen, William Hoste, John Weatherhead and William Bolton, all of whom Nelson treated as his family. Later in the Mediterranean a schoolmaster joined, and Josiah was soon 'in fractions, preparing to learn navigation'. But for a time life on board must have been very exciting and very strange in a man-of-war, filled with men under a strict discipline, working hard, and soon eagerly counting up the prospects of prize money, the constant theme of conversation in the officers' and Jack-tars' messes alike.

On April 28 the *Agamemnon* left the Downs with seventeen sail of merchantmen in company and anchored at Spithead on the 29th. The next day a captain, lieutenant and thirty-one privates of the 69th Regiment joined in lieu of marines. On May 2, with three reefs in her topsails, the *Agamemnon* left Spithead on a Channel cruise, and sighting some French ships in the bay of La Hogue, Nelson summoned a pilot out of Alderney,

but he was 'not capable of taking charge of the ship'. After this disappointment, Nelson returned to Spithead. On May 7 Lord Hood hoisted
his flag on board the *Victory*, and it is noteworthy that this ship, alone of
all the many hundreds which passed before the eyes of Nelson and his
tars, survives today, carefully preserved as she appeared when Nelson
last served in her at Trafalgar. Then, with the fleet exercising on all
occasions, Hood made his way to Gibraltar, Nelson being one of the
squadron which called in at Cadiz on the way out, where he saw his new
allies, the Spanish fleet which was to operate in the Mediterranean.
Nelson's own journal of his operations after reaching Gibraltar, recently
discovered, is printed for the first time in the Appendix.

It will be noticed that as a Mediterranean captain Nelson was never
idle. Mrs. Nelson was asked to address her letters to the care of John
Udney, Esq., His Britannic Majesty's Consul at Leghorn. The consul was
soon to write to an unknown correspondent of 'Captain Nelson of His
Majesty's Ship *Agamemnon*, the most active of His Majesty's commanders
in these seas where none are idle.' 'All we get', was Nelson's comment to
his wife, 'is honour and salt beef.'

The British effort in the Mediterranean was planned to be a naval
demonstration until an opportunity occurred of supporting the Austrian
army, and Lord Hood took the Ministry by surprise when he accepted the
custody of Toulon at the invitation of the local French royalists in August
1793. The occupation was carried out without much difficulty, and Lord
Hood's natural distrust of the army was increased when a garrison of
50,000 men was considered necessary for its defence, this being rather
larger than the whole British Army on its present footing. The Austrian
court, to whom Hood looked for reinforcements, proved a broken reed,
but he raised some 17,000 troops, of whom only 12,000 were fit for duty,
2,000 of them British, and the remainder Spaniards, Neapolitans, Sardinians and French royalists. Nelson in the *Agamemnon* did not enter Toulon
with the fleet. The *Agamemnon* was noted as a fast sailer and Nelson was
immediately sent off to obtain the promised, subsidised troops from
Sardinia and Naples. He reached Naples on September 11 and was
immediately in conclave with Sir William Hamilton, Sir John Acton and
the King, a foretaste of things to come. The King of Naples' gracious
letter to Lord Hood, begged from him by Nelson, is given in the Appendix.
Nelson certainly hurried up the provision of troops and left in a characteristic flurry, when, regardless of a party on board for the ladies, he landed
his guests and sailed away without full supplies, on the news sent on
board by Acton that a French corvette with English prizes was in the
vicinity. By way of Genoa he sailed back to Toulon with the news of re-

inforcements, where 'The lord is wonderfully pleased with us.' 'The lord is quite as he used to be, "his dear Nelson" etc.' But all was not well at Toulon. The ministry in England did not realize the task that faced the defenders. Toulon might have been held for the French Crown if re-inforcements had been sent in time, but the perimeter of the defences was too great for the forces available. Lord Hood was constrained to give up valuable outposts. In the fighting the Spaniards, with the most soldiers, claimed the right to command. Meanwhile Carnot, the French War Minister, sent a young artillery officer from Marseilles, named Bonaparte, to reorganize the artillery bombardment. By seizing certain heights it was possible to deny Toulon harbour to ships-of-war. Soon, despite determined defences of untenable forts, Bonaparte had mounted his batteries and the position in Toulon was desperate. The allies cleared out in a hurry. Eighteen French warships were brought away and twenty-seven left behind damaged, of which eleven were soon repaired. The French royalists were removed in part, and the remainder were butchered with the new ferocity of the Jacobins. With the fall of Toulon, what had seemed a major triumph, a prelude to victory and peace, became a failure, with a loss of prestige to the allies and particularly to the French royalist cause. General O'Hara had been captured while gallantly leading a sortie, and his successor was David Dundas, who quarrelled bitterly with Lord Hood. Nelson was away with a squadron under Commodore Linzee (Hood's brother-in-law) when the end came. He sent a covering note of warning to his brother Maurice that rumours were grave. He did not blame Lord Hood. 'The lord put himself at the head of flying troops and was the admiration of all but the torrent was too strong.'

Nelson rejoined the fleet and was immediately sent away with a squadron of frigates to drive the French out of Corsica. Now he first met Sir Gilbert Elliot, later Lord Minto, who was to become his lifelong friend. Elliot had been sent out as Governor of Toulon, and being in Hood's confidence, was transferred to be Viceroy of Corsica, offered to the British Crown by the patriots led by Boswell's friend, the great Corsican guerilla leader and patriot, Paoli.

In February 1794, with ten frigates and the backing of Lord Hood, Nelson commenced the siege of Bastia. Lord Hood 'says he comes to make the army active'. Certainly the bad feeling between the army and navy was then lamentable and both Hood and Dundas were to blame. Elliot, friend to both parties, did his best to intervene, but without avail, as will be seen in the extracts from his journal printed in the Appendix. General Dundas resigned his command and General Stuart took his place. Nelson supported his admiral, but seems as usual to have retained the army's respect, although he did not spare their feelings. Of course, with his experience of the San Juan campaign behind him, he regarded himself as knowing all about soldiers and their business. With his own type of modesty he wrote home to his wife from Bastia on March 4, 'My seamen are now what British seamen ought to be. To you I may say it almost invincible. They really mind shot no more than peas.' And on May 4: 'The expedition is almost a child [of] my own, and I have no fears about the final issue, it will be victory, Bastia will be ours.' And on May 22: 'Josiah came to me and has been with me at the head of the British Grenadiers.' The army was now advancing and Bastia surrendered.

Lord Hood was delighted with Nelson's conduct before Bastia, which had thoroughly discomfited the pessimistic judgement of the army, and had, too, helped him to regain his own self-confidence after the Toulon disappointment, but his official dispatches made slight reference to it. This Nelson regarded as a deliberate slight. There was the chance of a brush with a French fleet, and Nelson wrote a solemn letter home on June 7, but no engagement took place. Then Nelson embarked the troops from Bastia into transports and was soon investing Calvi. General Stuart sailed in the *Agamemnon*. He remained Nelson's friend although he supported the army viewpoint. The troops were landed before Calvi. It was the seamen's work to haul 24-pounders and mortars and howitzers up to the top of hills to form the batteries. Getting cannon up mountains suited Nelson. He writes on July 8: 'I am so busy but I own in all my glory, that, except with you, I would not be anywhere but where I am for any consideration.' On July 10 Nelson, busy in a battery, was struck severely on the face and breast by splinters of stone and he never recovered the sight of his right eye, although he could distinguish light from darkness. Calvi surrendered on August 10.

Despite his wound, Nelson remained healthy, but his ship's company was very sickly, and indeed worn out. Unhappily General Stuart and Lord Hood were as far asunder as ever general had been from admiral. Nelson wrote of the soldiers, 'They hate us sailors, we are too active for them. We accomplish our business sooner than they like.' On August 18 the *Agamemnon* was at Leghorn and her company had an opportunity to refit and recuperate. They were very sickly indeed. Lord Hood said he was going home, and Nelson hoped he might accompany him, but did not. He was, however, able to live ashore, having his first rest after eighteen months' continuous and arduous service.

Meanwhile, in England, Mrs. Nelson travelled on a round of visits between her father-in-law at Burnham Thorpe, her brother-in-law, the Reverend William Nelson at Hilborough, Nelson's uncle, Mr. William

Suckling, at Kentish Town, his sister at Ringwood, and her friends at Bristol. None of her letters to Nelson seem to have survived from this period, but a few letters from Nelson's father printed in the Appendix give us some glimpses of her 'in her widowhood.'

No. 32

[Nicolas, I, p. 297, part]

[London]
January 7, 1793

My dear Fanny,—*Post Nubila Phoebus*—your son will explain the motto—after clouds come sunshine. The Admiralty so smile upon me that really I am as much surprised as when they frowned. Lord Chatham [1] yesterday made many apologies for not having given me a ship before this time, but that if I chose to take a 64-gun ship to begin with I should be appointed to one as soon as she was ready, and that I should as soon as in his power be removed into a 74. Lord Hood has sent for me to nominate the 1st lieutenant [2] and that probably my ship would either be the *St. Albans* or *Intrepid*—one at Portsmouth, other at Plymouth. I want one at Chatham, as it would be convenient on every account and I have just been with the Comptroller [3] to try and get one ordered at Chatham which I hope to be able to accomplish.

As the Duke of Clarence [4] wished to know what passed about me at the Admiralty I cannot leave town before Thursday or Friday. Perhaps this ship will not be ready before the end of the month. Everything looks war. One of our ships looking into Brest has been fired into. The shot is now at the Admiralty.

Tell my father I had not forgot his hat, it is ordered. You will write him my news, which I am sure will please him. Adair is not come to town if he comes I will certainly see him.

Love to Josiah and believe me your most affectionate Horatio Nelson.

To Mrs. Nelson, Burnham,[5] Norfolk.

[1] Lord Chatham was First Lord of the Admiralty from 1788 to 1794.
[2] Nelson chose Martin Hinton, who had served with him in the *Albemarle*.
[3] Sir Henry Martin, Comptroller of the Navy, 1790–94.
[4] Prince William Henry was created Duke of Clarence in 1789.
[5] Nelson and his wife had been living at Burnham Thorpe with his father, while he was unemployed.

No. 33

London,
March 4, 1793

MY DEAR FANNY,—Never a finer night was seen than last night and I am not the least tired.

I have taken my place in the Chatham coach for one o'clock.[1] I write this in Mr. Rumsey's office.

Have not seen my brother.

Yours most affectionately HORATIO NELSON.

To Mrs. Nelson, Hilborough,[2] Brandon, Norfolk.

No. 34

[London,]
March 12, 1793

MY DEAR FANNY,—I received your letter yesterday. I went out to dinner with Mr. Suckling [3] where I met the Matchams.[4] My sister enquired if you had got a letter from her a month ago. Mr. Suckling's house is clear and he desired me to say that he shall be glad to see you for a month or six weeks or as long as shall be agreeable to you. I have talked a good deal about your matters, perhaps it would be better to come to Kentish town for a week or two. The Matchams go out of town next week they say, and as they have their children with them, it would be impossible to go down with them, if you are inclined to make them a visit, which I don't believe would be over pleasant.

Mr. Suckling thinks that it would take our whole income to keep him [5] at the Temple, and I suppose we must think of some other walk of life for him. My objection to the Navy now he will be certain of a small fortune is in some measure done away. You must think of this. Would you like to bring him up with you? For if he is to go, he must go with me.

[1] Nelson commissioned the *Agamemnon* at Chatham on February 7. He spent the next month fitting out the ship.
[2] Nelson's brother, the Rev. William Nelson, who had married Miss Sarah Yonge in 1786, lived at Hilborough, where he had the living.
[3] Nelson's uncle, William Suckling, who married Miss Rumsey in 1786, lived in Kentish Town.
[4] The Matchams, who lived in Hampshire, were on a visit to London.
[5] Josiah Nisbet.

I called at Frasers this morning, they had not opened the copy of the will [1] but they are to send me word if there is anything in it which I don't know. The £100 they don't think can be paid. Have you got Mr. Herbert's letter to me wherein he promised the £100 a year if you have, bring it up. Mr. Suckling will pay the £100 this year, but I don't think any longer,[2] therefore whenever the legacy is paid our income will be lessened instead of increased.

I called on Mr. Thomas. Every body knows the amount of the legacy. Mr. Maynard and Mr. Brown told Mr. Thomas that the estate is only entailed to Mr. Morton,[3] therefore in fact he has given his whole property to the Mortons, except the few legacies, but never mind it. Mr. Suckling says we are lucky to get so much, for he did not expect it. The will is to be proved in the Commons.

God bless you, yours affectionately H. NELSON.

You ought not I think to come up in the day coach, you will be tired to death. If you liked it I dare say the Rector [4] would come up with you. Sleep at Hockeril. If I stay in town, I shall write you tomorrow. Most likely I shall not be in town for this fortnight to come, therefore you need not hurry. Think about Josiah.

To Mrs. Nelson, Hilborough, Brandon, Norfolk.

No. 35
[Nicolas, I, p. 301, part]

Chatham,
March 15, 1793

MY DEAR FANNY,—If the wind is to the northward of west, we go down the river tomorrow, and are ordered to proceed to Spithead with all possible dispatch as we are wanted Lord Hood [5] writes me for immediate service, and hints that we are to go a cruise and join his fleet at Gibraltar. This is what I understand by his letter, so very desirable a service is not to be neglected therefore I am anxious to get to Spithead. I hope to be able to see you at Mr. Suckling's for a day or two notwithstanding. My things from Norfolk are not yet I fear sailed from Wells. I shall write to my father

[1] Mr. Herbert had died January 18, 1793. By his will he left £4,000 to Nelson and £500 to Josiah. Mr. Fraser was one of his trustees and executors in England.
[2] See Chapter 1, Appendix, p. 54.
[3] Magnus Morton, Mrs. Nelson's cousin.
[4] Nelson's usual way of referring to his brother William.
[5] Lord Hood, while retaining his appointment as one of the Lords Commissioners of the Admiralty, was given the command of the Mediterranean fleet.

today to say if the vessel does not sail in a few days, some of them must be sent by land and so to Portsmouth.

I never was in better health. And now you will recollect that a handsome fortune for Josiah depends on your surviving Mrs. Hamilton,[1] I hope you intend a new lease of your life. The not tying up any of the money he left you I consider as a confidence reposed in me and I shall take care that it is not misplaced. He was engaged to marry Miss Fraser till last autumn when they let him off. That house is failed for £400,000 as is Mr. Willock for near that sum.

I have not yet bought glass, tea cups or a single article. I looked at shirts at Mrs. Blunt's Charing Cross where I shall buy them. If the wind is to the westward direct for me at Sheerness, if not gone by Sunday can't go for 10 days. Love to all. The Matchams were very kind in their wishes for your going into Hampshire for a month or two, you would like to go. H. N.

I wrote what I thought about the visit the day before, I rather think otherwise now, the change of air will do you good. Have not heard from Josiah which I am sorry for. Tell him to write to me and inclose it to my brother. My father wrote me he had not heard from you.

To Mrs. Nelson, Hilborough, Brandon, Norfolk.

No. 36

Agamemnon,[2]
April 5, 1793

MY DEAR FANNY,—Josiah and myself came down very comfortably yesterday morning and he seems quite settled, we slept on board last night and are now at home. The Admiral has orders to man us in preference to any ship here. Therefore we go out to the Nore on Monday morning, and I suppose shall sail in the course of next week for Portsmouth, but I would have my things sent down here, and I will request some of my brother officers to bring them round for me. Indeed as they are directed here, I don't think it would be an easy matter to have the direction altered. Josiah seems to like his situation very much.

With best respects to Mr. Suckling and family. Believe me yours most affectionately HORATIO NELSON.

To Mrs. Nelson, at Mr. Sucklings, Kentish Town.

[1] Mrs. Nelson's cousin, the daughter of Mr. Herbert.
[2] The *Agamemnon* was moored at Blackstakes, March 23–April 16.

No. 37

Sheerness,
April 9, 1793

MY DEAR FANNY,—You forgot to send my things from Mr. Thomas's by the Sheerness boat, but I have wrote to Mr. Thomas that if not sent to go by the Chatham coach. I have got a keg of tongues which I suppose you ordered, and also a trunk from Wells, Norfolk and a hamper of 3 hams, a breast of bacon, and a face, not very well packed, there being no straw between them and the motion of the waggon has rubbed them very much. However they will do. My things sailed from Wells, March 30th, therefore hope they are on board the Sheerness boat. Even should I be sailed, I would wish them to come to Sheerness and some of my brother officers will take them on board for me. They come from Wells in the *Supply*, Robert Franklin, Master.

Josiah seems very happy on board and has little or no cough. I shall be glad to have the schoolmaster on board. I have got Mr. Gordon's goat and a very civil letter with it.

Pray remember me kindly to Mr. Suckling and Mrs. Suckling and family. I have wrote to Captain Suckling[1] and hope to see him. Believe me yours most affectionately, HORATIO NELSON.

Will you write a line to my father? Josiah desires his love. My things in the hamper are arrived since writing the letter.

To Mrs. Nelson, Kentish Town.

No. 38
[Nicolas, I, p. 302, part]

Sheerness,
April 14, 1793

MY DEAR FANNY,—Although I have not been out of the ship since I wrote you last yet I know you wish to hear frequently from me. The wind is now got to the westward and we are unmooring to go out to the Nore where I suppose our stay will be very short. All my things from Norfolk are safe arrived, but the key of my drawers to the bureau is not come. However I can break them open without much difficulty.

I have this day wrote to the book keeper of Archers waggon desiring him to send the trunk and box with Josiah's cloaths to Mr. Thomas's and don't send them till I write where they are to come to.

---

[1] The eldest son of William Suckling; later a colonel in the Dragoons.

I had a visit from the Admiral yesterday to examine my ship and I can say with truth she is getting into high order. Although we are upwards of 100 short of complement, yet I think we shall be far from ill manned, even if the rest are not so good as they ought to be. The surgeon[1] seems to be a very good sort of man; indeed I have reason to be satisfied at present with every officer in the ship. Josiah is in high glee to think we are going to sail, and says he has not time to write to you just yet. I shall send the boat on shore for the post and expect to hear from you.

Have you heard anything more of Mr. Brounker. I don't know as you, when asked, you could do otherwise than offer my services but I hope he will not come nor anyone else. I shall not put myself to the expense of carrying passengers if I can help it. Believe me yours most affectionately, HORATIO NELSON.

Best respects to Mr. Suckling. Have not seen the schoolmaster which I am very sorry for.

To Mrs. Nelson, at Mr. Suckling's, Kentish Town.

No. 39

Nore,

April 18

MY DEAR FANNY,—We came out here on Monday morning,[2] have not had a boat out since it blowing a strong gale. Yesterday Josiah was a little sea-sick. I thank you for your letter and most likely I shall be able to go over to see you at Mr. Matcham's for a few days, which will give your son as well as myself great pleasure.

My ship appears to sail very fast indeed and every day puts us in higher order, in short we are well officered and manned, the greatest comfort a captain can have. My orders are not yet on board but I expect them every day and when they come I shall not be an hour longer at this place but shall sail for the Downs.

I am sorry my father sent Josiah's cloaths to Portsmouth but it can't be helped now. Best compliments where you are and believe me your most affectionate, HORATIO NELSON.

You have done well about Mr. Brounker. I am sorry I wrote so much about him before as you certainly could not offer less.

To Mrs. Nelson, at Mr. Suckling's, Kentish Town.

[1] Michael Jefferson, who served with Nelson until his return to England in September 1797.   [2] April 15.

No. 40

Nore,
April 23, 1793

MY DEAR FANNY,—Why we are not sailed I can't tell you, but think our orders will be down this day, as we are perfectly ready for any service. I wrote to Mr. Brounker as you desired but as you did not send me his direction was obliged to inclose it to my brother. As it is now certain I am going with Lord Hood I will write him word when we are likely to sail, for if we are to wait till the number of his Lordship's fleet is completed, it will be some time before we leave Portsmouth,[1] and if you are at Mr. Matcham's I shall certainly go over for a few days, or if it is likely we should stay a few weeks at Portsmouth and take lodgings there. What can I do with Mr. Brounker? The writing to me here must be very uncertain.

I had a letter from Mrs. Bolton[2] yesterday in which she says you are going to see Mrs. Matcham, that she has wrote you 2 or 3 letters but have not heard from you. Pray write to her. Josiah and myself have had colds these nasty easterly winds but are getting the better of them. Indeed my ship's company nobody can be sick with, they are as fair a set of young *[page torn—part of the letter missing]* me most kindly to Mr. Suckling and family. Do you ever write to Hilborough? you must correspond with my father for me. Believe me your most affectionate HORATIO NELSON.

Josiah desires to be remembered.

Have you brought me any towels? If not I can buy them at Portsmouth.

To Mrs. Nelson.

No. 41
[Nicolas, I, p. 304, part]

Spithead,
April 29, 1793

MY DEAR FANNY,—We arrived at Spithead[3] last night, and this morning have got my orders to go to sea till the 4th of May when I shall be at Portsmouth. Lord Hood will then be at Portsmouth. If you and my sister

---

[1] Lord Hood's fleet was assembled in four divisions. The *Agamemnon* formed part of the third division.

[2] Nelson's sister, Susannah.

[3] Nelson completed his ship's company at Spithead by embarking soldiers of the 69th Regiment in lieu of Marines.

wish to come, shall be glad to see you, but do as you like. Mr. Brounker is gone to sea with Captain Woodley for Gibraltar.

We are all well. God bless you, love to my sister. Believe me ever affectionately yours, HORATIO NELSON.

Don't mind what newspapers may say about us.
Can't hear of Josiah's things—write about them.

No. 42

[Nicolas, I, p. 305, under date of April 29]

Spithead,
April 30, 1793

MY DEAR FANNY,—We should have gone to sea yesterday but it blew so strong we could not get our anchors, and today unless the wind changes in the afternoon we shall not get out to sea,[1] which is a great mortification to me, for something might be done if we were at sea and I fear orders may come to stop us. I must be here on Sunday at the farthest as Lord Hood sails, if the wind is fair, on Thursday, May 9th. You will, if you come to Portsmouth, put up at the George.[2] This Miss Palmers keep it still, their father you may remember is dead. Love to my sister. Maurice[3] arrived yesterday evening on board and I was concerned to find you had like to have been hurt by your overturn. He slept on board. God bless you, yours most affectionately, HORATIO NELSON.

To Mrs. Nelson, George Matcham's Esq., Ringwood, Hants.

No. 43

[Nicolas, I, p. 305]

Spithead,
May 6, 1793

MY DEAR FANNY,—I arrived here last night and rather expected to have seen you here but Mr. Matcham's said true, there is no certainty in winds and waves. We had some blowing weather but nothing for *Agamemnon* to mind. Your son was a little seasick for a day or two but soon got over it.

[1] Nelson got to sea the next day, May 1.
[2] The well-known inn where Nelson spent his last night in England in September 1805; it was destroyed in 1941.
[3] Nelson's elder brother had joined the Navy Office when their uncle, Captain Suckling, was Comptroller.

We fell in with two French frigates and two armed vessels but they got into La Hogue harbour where we could not follow for want of a pilot.[1] I was again ordered for sea this morning but am now stopped, as my ship wants many things before she sails for Mediterranean.

Lord Hood comes down tonight. Shall be glad to see you when convenient to Mr. Matcham. Maurice came to me and it blew so hard I could not land him, he consequently went to sea with me. He was in London at 6 o'clock this morning.

Give my love to my sister and respects to Mr. Matcham, believe me most affectionately yours, HORATIO NELSON.

My things and Josiah's trunk are arrived.

To Mrs. Nelson, at George Matcham's Esqr., Ringwood, Hants.

No. 44

St. Helens,
Noon Saturday, [May 11, 1793]

MY DEAR FANNY,—I hope you all got home safe you had a fine day. We got out here with the squadron last night and sail at 4 o'clock this afternoon. You shall hear by every opportunity from me. God bless you believe me your most affectionate HORATIO NELSON.

Josiah is in high spirits. You may write to my father to say we are gone and pray write Mrs. Bolton. I write the names that you may know when any of us come into port.

Britannia,[2] *Courageux, Colossus, Fortitude, Agamemnon, Lowestoffe, Meleager.*

To Mrs. Nelson, George Matcham's Esqr., Ringwood, Hants.

No. 45

[Nicolas, I, p. 306, part]

Agamemnon, 12 leagues NW. of the island of Guernsey
18 May, 1793

MY DEAR FANNY,—We have done nothing or are intended I may venture to say. Indeed I believe we are sent out for no other purpose than to amuse the people of England by having a fleet at sea, for where we are placed the

[1] A pilot from Alderney was taken on board on May 3 but he proved incapable of taking charge of the ship.
[2] Vice-Admiral William Hotham, with his flag in the *Britannia,* commanded the third division of the fleet ordered to the Mediterranean.

French it is not likely will have a fleet. The English are hum'd and the Fleet made fools off. We can do nothing, no not even protect our trade for no privateers ever cruised in this place to intercept it. The King may be told that his fleet is at sea and the French are not to be found. The Minister may stop the mouths of the opposition by saying the same thing. This is not the first squadron sent out to do nothing and worse than nothing. I suppose we are to stay here till Lord Hood comes out which I think will not be this week to come. We have spoke many neutral vessels from the French ports who tells us that Nantes, Bordeaux and L'Orient are filled with English prizes to the French privateers and frigates, this information makes us feel more uneasy.

My ship sails very well and I have every reason to be satisfied with her. We are all well. I write this for our week's work. Shall send it when opportunity offers.

May 19, 10 leagues off the Lizard: The Admiral has just told me that he shall have an opportunity of sending our letters on shore tomorrow at Falmouth where we are going for farther orders.

Best love to my sister and regards to Mr. Matcham. I think we shall see Torbay before we leave England. Believe me yours most affectionately, HORATIO NELSON.

Will you write a line to my father.

[Postscript by Josiah]

DEAR MAMMA,—We [have] taken nothing at present nor are not likely to take any thing. I am very well at present and hope you are the same.

JOSIAH NISBET.

To Mrs. Nelson, George Matcham Esq., Ringwood, Hants.

No. 46

[Nicolas, I, p. 307, part, under wrong date, June 5]

SW. 16 leagues of Scilly,
June 6, 1793

MY DEAR FANNY,—So many vessels have been spoke to by our fleet that I cannot but be truly sorry not to have had it in my power to send a letter, but my station being in the rear of the fleet and lee division that very seldom any opportunity will offer at sea of getting a letter on board such vessels. What the fleet is doing here I can't guess. I hope for some good purpose but it appears by our not having seen a single Frenchman to be our endeavour to avoid them. I own I expected when Lord Hood[1] joined that we

[1] Lord Hood, in the *Victory*, joined Hotham's squadron on May 25.

G

should have gone for Gibraltar but what his intentions or orders are I cannot guess. I have not seen Lord Hood since he joined us a fortnight tomorrow or had even a boat hoisted out. Our weather although not bad has been very unpleasant. Foggy with drizzling rain. I have not left off my fire. Josiah is very well and as a schoolmaster joined us in the *Victory*, we now go on very well. Now Josiah has got the better of sea sickness I think he gets stout.

My ship sails very well indeed. We think better than any ship in the fleet. Our force is 11 sail of the line frigates etc. and in very tolerable order. We have had some naval evolutions when the weather would permit. I shall pay the Lord a visit whenever an opportunity offers and leave this letter with Captain Knight.[1] Therefore you must not be surprised at not receiving a letter from me although many vessels may have spoke us.

June 7th: Have just fell in with a large convoy. Shall try and get this letter on board one of them. Hope this is the fleet we have been looking out for and that we shall shift our station. This has been a very barren one. Love to all with you. Let my father know where we are. Josiah is well and a good boy. God bless you and believe your most affectionate HORATIO NELSON.

Hope when you travel you will not trust yourself in a stage.

To Mrs. Nelson, George Matcham's Esqr., Ringwood, Hants.

No. 47

[Nicolas, I, p. 308, part only]

Agamemnon, off Cape St. Vincent,
June 14, 1793

MY DEAR FANNY,—I wrote you a few lines by a vessel in a convoy we spoke this day week off Scilly, and which turned out to be the fleet we were waiting to protect, and the East Indiamen passing us the same evening relieved us from a very unpleasant station. We have had the finest passage and weather possible but have seen nothing but one poor miserable National brig, which one of the ships took. I paid Lord Hood a visit a few days back and found him very civil. I dare say we shall be good friends again. Six sail of the line under Captain Elphinstone[2] have just parted company going to Cadiz to water, one of which number is *Agamemnon*. We shall be in Cadiz tomorrow at 12 o'clock as will Lord Hood at Gibraltar.

[1] Captain John Knight, Hood's flag-captain.
[2] Captain George Elphinstone, later Admiral Lord Keith.

The Lord has just sent me a civil note to say he had ordered one of his small vessels to go in with us to take our letters, and bring them to Gibraltar as he should send a vessel for England within 24 hours after his arrival.

We are all well, my ship remarkably healthy. Give my love where you are. Shall inclose this letter to Mr. Suckling. Believe me your most affectionate husband, HORATIO NELSON.

Letters put in the post Office directed for Gibraltar will find their way, but I am not sure whether the postage must not be paid as foreign letters.

No. 48
[Nicolas, I, p. 309]

Agamemnon, at Sea,
10 o'clock Sunday, June 23, 1793

MY DEAR FANNY,—The wind having continued to the westward since Lord Hood's arrival at Gibraltar last Wednesday I think none of his frigates have been able to turn out of the straits, and that therefore this letter will go by the same conveyance as the one I began to you off Cape St. Vincent and finished in Cadiz.

We came out this morning having completed our ship with everything except wine, which is to be done at Gibraltar. The Spaniards have been very civil to us. More in my opinion than we deserved. For to my surprise Elphinstone our commodore has amazingly neglected those etiquettes which at all times I should consider necessary in a foreign port, and more particularly so in our new alliance with Spain.[1]

We dined on board the *Conception* of 112 guns with Admiral Langara and all restraints of going into their arsenals, dockyards were removed. They have four first rates in commission at Cadiz and very fine ships but shockingly manned. If those 21 sail of the line which we are to join in the Mediterranean are not better manned they can't be of much use. I am certain if our six barges' crews (which are picked men) had got on board one of their first rates they would have taken her. Therefore in vain may the Dons make fine ships, they cannot however make men. What our plan of operations is to be in the Mediterranean I can't guess but the Lord is in a hurry. He wrote Capt. E. to hurry his sailing from Cadiz as he wished to get from Gibraltar as today. I think we shall not get into Gibraltar before the morning we are parading when we should be crowding sail. However

[1] Spain had joined the coalition formed against France after the declaration of war in March 1793.

be careful of what opinion I may give of officers, and Elphinstone is very civil to me.

Agamemnon is very healthy. Josiah is well and a good boy which I know will give you pleasure. Our weather is very fine, and fruits etc. we have had in the greatest abundance. I shall not close this till we get to Gibraltar. A bull feast (for which the Spaniards are famous and for their dexterity in attacking and killing of which the ladies choose their husbands) was exhibited in which we English had certainly to regret the want of humanity in the Dons and Donnas. The amphitheatre will hold 16,000 people, about 12,000 were present. 10 bulls were selected and one brought out at a time. 3 cavaliers on horseback and footmen with flags were the combatants. We had what is called a fine feast for 5 horses were killed and 2 men very much hurt. Had they been killed it would have been quite complete. We felt for the bulls and horses and I own it would not have displeased me to have had some of the Dons tossed by the enraged animal. How women can even sit much more applaud such sights is astonishing. It even turned us sick, and we could hardly sit it out. The dead mangled horses with their entrails tore out, the bulls covered with blood, was too much. However we have seen one and agree that nothing shall tempt us to see another. The better sort of people never miss a feast, if within reach of them, and the lowest will sell his jacket or go without his victuals rather than be absent.

Gibraltar, June 24th: I find the vessel has not sailed for England. We arrived here last night and in a few days' time we are to sail up the Mediterranean.[1] God bless and preserve you is the sincere wish of your affectionate HORATIO NELSON.

To Mrs. Nelson.

No. 49
[Nicolas, I, p. 315, part]

Gulf of Lyons,
July 15, 1793

MY DEAR FANNY,—The Admiral has just sent us word that he shall very soon send a frigate to Genoa and Leghorn, who will take our letters, therefore I take the pen to say we are all well. We have had a very long and tedious passage from Gibraltar (which we left on the 27th June) owing to the very little winds which blow here at this season of the year. I hope we shall get off Toulon tomorrow when we may stand a chance to see something like an enemy. There seems to be no French ships at sea, at least we

[1] Nelson's sea journal (printed in the Appendix, pp. 128–154) begins when he sailed from Gibraltar on June 27.

have seen nothing like one. We fell in with the Spanish fleet a week ago returning into port I believe glad we are arrived. And they mean to leave us the honour of keeping the French in order. I really expect never to see them out again.

I can hardly guess where this letter will find you but I hope you will get comfortable somewhere. Have you made a visit to Lady Walpole? I shall like you to do it. The Lord Hood is tolerable good friends with me. I shall not finish this letter till we look into Toulon when something may occur. Josiah is a very good boy and grown very much. He tells me he shall write you a letter. He is now in fractions, preparing to learn navigation.

Perhaps Hoste[1] may not have an opportunity of writing a letter. If he has not, send a note to his father to say he is well and a good boy.

18th: The frigates are sent to Genoa and Leghorn without my having an opportunity of sending a letter but a brig is standing into the fleet which may be bound to England therefore I shall finish this letter. We have not yet looked into Toulon. Two of our ships fell in with 3 French frigates and after firing at each other a short time the frigates got away. The Lord is I fancy very much dissatisfied. God bless you and believe me your most affectionate HORATIO NELSON.

We have just got a French sloop of war of 18 guns bound to Toulon. You will remember most kindly to our good father.

2 p.m. The above brig is a prize from Marseilles. Don't think I shall make a fortune by these gentry, £20 is the utmost I shall get for them.

26th July, all well.

[Postscript by Josiah]
I am well at present and hope you are the same.

JOSIAH NISBET.

To Mrs. Nelson.

No. 50
[Nicolas, I, p. 316]

Off Toulon,
August 4

MY DEAREST FANNY,—The Admiral has just sent us word that the *Aquillon* will proceed to England with Prince Augustus,[2] therefore I send this letter

---

[1] William Hoste, one of the Norfolk boys Nelson took as a midshipman, son of the Rev. Dixon Hoste, rector of Tittleshall, Norfolk. He had a distinguished naval career. Captain Sir William Hoste died in 1828.
[2] Prince Frederick Augustus, Duke of Sussex, sixth son of George III, returned to England in the autumn of 1793 after a year in Italy.

on board him in case *Agamemnon* should be on the look out, for as we sail fast we are always employed. Whether the French intend to come out seems uncertain, they have a force equal to us. Our jacks would be very happy to see them, and as our fleet is in the fullest health I dare say we should give a good account of them.

I hardly think this war can last, for what are we at war about? Next winter I think will send us home. How I long to have a letter from you. Next to being with you, it is the greatest pleasure I can receive. I shall rejoice to be with you again. Indeed I look back as to the happiest period of my life the being united to such a good woman, and as I cannot show here my affection to you, I do it doubly to Josiah who deserves it as well on his own account as on yours, for he is a real good boy and most affection-ately loves me. He tells me he intends to write you all the news. Captains Lutwidge[1] and Man[2] have been very ill. The Lord has sent to offer me a 74 but I have declined it. As the Admiralty chose to put me into a 64 there I stay.[3] I cannot give up my officers. The Lord approved of my reasons. So far well, as to my health I never was better. God bless you and believe me ever your most affectionate husband, HORATIO NELSON.

If I have not an opportunity of writing to my good father, send my kindest remembrances to him.

To Mrs. Nelson.

No. 51

[Nicolas, I, p. 318 part; order transposed]

Agamemnon, off Nice,
August 8, 1793

MY DEAREST FANNY,—Leghorn is to be the place where letters are more likely to get to us than to any other place, therefore direct my letters— Captain N. *Agamemnon* to the care of John Udney Esqr. His Britannic Majesty's Consul at Leghorn. The foreign postage must be paid or they will not be sent, 18 days is the time of the post from London to Leghorn.

The French here are in a wretched state of confusion. An army is marched from Marseilles to Paris and a civil war seems inevitable. I have

---

[1] Nelson's captain in the *Carcass* in 1773; he was promoted Rear-Admiral in April 1794.
[2] Captain Robert Man, died 1813, an admiral.
[3] Nelson remained in the *Agamemnon* until June 1796.

now a letter for you on board the *Victory* but write to say where letters will find us.

We are all well. God bless you and believe me your most affectionate husband, HORATIO NELSON.

The *Aquillon* is just joining the fleet by whom I hope to send this letter. To Mrs. Nelson, Swaffam, Norfolk.[1]

No. 52

Agamemnon, off Toulon,
August 17, 1793

MY DEAR FANNY,—We stopped a vessel yesterday from Marseilles bound to Smyrna. The cargo we believe to be French. Elphinstone is going to send her into Leghorn. I do not think it will be condemned for the chest is too well covered for us to get at, however this line is only to say we are all well.

The Lord left *Robust* and *Colossus* with ourselves and a frigate off Toulon. He is gone off Genoa to scold the Genoese for sending corn to the French.

God bless you and believe me your most affectionate HORATIO NELSON.

To Mrs. Nelson.

No. 53

[Nicolas, I, p. 318, part, under date August 8th]

Off Toulon,
August 20, 1793

MY DEAR FANNY,—The convoy for England is just in sight, therefore I shall not miss the opportunity of saying we are all well. I wrote you a line by Leghorn the other day.

No event has occurred indeed since our arrival worth mentioning, the use of sending for parade seems nonsensical.

Marseilles I am sure would almost be put into our hands if we acted against it. They generally wish for nothing more than our possessing it when they would get something to eat. They are now almost starving, only six days' provisions in the place.

Monsieur Egalité[2] is still in the prison with his daughter. They wish for

---

[1] Mrs. Nelson took lodgings at Swaffham for the summer.
[2] Philippe, duc d'Orléans, who had voted in favour of the King's execution and assumed the surname of Egalité, was himself put to death during the reign of terror in November 1793.

peace and are you know at war with the Parisians with whom they have lately had an action. The Convention has denounced the Marseillesois as traitors. If Toulon joins them they propose I hear offering themselves to our protection.

We hear of Lady Spencer[1] and her family at Lucca about 30 miles from Pisa living I fancy in style. Send to our good father that I am well and kindest remembrances to him. I wish much to hear you are fixed at some place to your satisfaction. Believe me, your most affectionate HORATIO NELSON.

To Mrs. Nelson.

Josiah Nisbet to Mrs. Nelson[2]

Off Toulon,
August 20, 1793

DEAR MAMMA,—Since I wrote to you last Lord Hood with most of the fleet is gone to water at Port Especia 12 leagues from Leghorn. We have seized a brig[3] valued at 10 or 12 thousand pounds and have sent her to Leghorn, but do not know whether she will be condemned. Mr. Suckling[4] is gone as prize master in her with a midshipman and eight men. We heard that the French had only six days' provision in Marseilles and the people say if the French do not make peace with us before the winter comes on they will set fire to the fleet at Toulon. The Duke of Orleans is in prison at Marseilles. We thought we should have taken something yesterday but could not. I am your affectionate son, JOSIAH NISBET.

[Addressed, by Nelson, to Mrs. Nelson]

No. 54

Agamemnon, August 31, 1793

MY DEAR FANNY,—We are all well. You will hear of our success[5] which it would not be proper to write.

God bless you and believe me yours most affectionately, HORATIO NELSON.

To Mrs. H. Nelson, at the Rev. Mr. Nelson, Hilbro', near Brandon, Norfolk.

[1] The dowager Lady Spencer, who had been travelling on the Continent for a year with her family, returned to England in October 1793. She was known to the Nelson family as she had Norfolk connections.
[2] Monmouth MSS., Nelson papers, vol. IV.
[3] A brig from Marseilles bound for Smyrna under Ragusa colours was taken on August 16.
[4] Maurice William Suckling, a connection of Nelson's, who had been a midshipman with him in the *Boreas*.
[5] The surrender of Toulon.

No. 55

[Nicolas, I, p. 323]

Begun off the Island of Sardinia, September 7,
finished at anchor off Naples, September 11, 1793

MY DEAR FANNY,—I wrote you a line by Lord Conway[1] who is gone home
with Lord Hood's dispatches. As soon as the treaty was concluded
Agamemnon as being a fast sailer was sent off with dispatches to the courts
of Turin and Naples for ten thousand troops to secure our possession. I
should have liked to have stayed one day longer with the fleet when they
entered the harbour but service could not be neglected for any private
gratification. I have only to hope I shall succeed with the King of Naples.
The last visit he had was from a French Grenadier belonging to Mons.
Truguet's[2] fleet, how different he must feel.

What an event this has been for Lord Hood. Such a one as History
cannot produce its equal. That the strongest place in Europe and twenty-
two sail of the line etc. should be given up without firing a shot, it is not to
be credited. On Sunday August 25th a party deposed Admiral Trogoff[3] and
placed St. Julien[4] at the head of the fleet manned sixteen sail of the line and
were determined to come out and fight us who were only 12 sail, Lord
Hood having sent away the other part of his fleet to give them the option.
The fleet regret they did not. The issue we should, I doubt not, have liked
better than laying them up dismantled. The perseverance of our fleet has
been great and to that only can be attributed our unexampled success.
Not even a boat could get into Marseilles or Toulon or on the coast with
provisions; and the old saying that hunger will tame a lion was never
stronger exemplified. The Spanish fleet arrived as ours was sailing into the
harbour and joined in the general joy which this event must give to all
Europe. St. Julien with about 4,000 men left the fleet as ours entered,
and joined General Corteau who I think it probable by this time has
attacked Toulon with the Parisian army. They have made sad work with
the Marseillois who were in treaty with us. I hope to God our success may
be so used as to give peace to that unhappy distracted country. Nice, Ville
Franche, Monaco and Menton which were taken from the King of Sardinia must fall again to him, so soon as our fleet can be liberated from

[1] Lord Hugh Seymour Conway, captain of the *Leviathan*, died a vice-admiral in
1801.
[2] Admiral Truguet commanded the Republican fleet; he died in 1839.
[3] Rear-Admiral Trogoff, with his flag in the *Commerce de Marseilles*, had been in
command at Toulon, but retired owing to ill health.
[4] Trogoff's successor; he was unable to control his men when Toulon surrendered
to the English.

Toulon. No conquests of importance I believe the world is convinced of, can be made without us, and yet as soon as we have accomplished the service we are ordered on, we are neglected. If Parliament do not grant something to this fleet our jacks will grumble, for here there is no prize money to soften our hardships. All we get is honour and salt beef. My poor fellows have not had a morsel of fresh meat or vegetables for near nineteen weeks and in that time I have only had my foot twice on shore at Cadiz. We are absolutely getting sick from fatigue. No fleet I am satisfied ever served their country with greater zeal than this has done from the Admiral to the lowest sailor.

Admiral Goodall[1] is governor of Toulon, Elphinstone commander of the grand batteries at the harbour's mouth. I may have lost an appointment by being sent off. Not that I wish to be employed out of my ship. I have sent in a ship from Smyrna bound to Marseilles and I think it probable she will be condemned worth about £10,000. I hope she may it will add something to our comforts. Josiah is well and a good boy. He has got a Turkish sabre of which he is not a little proud. I have inclosed this letter to Mr. Suckling but have not mentioned to him my having sent in any vessel. If she is condemned your knowing it is quite sufficient except my good father for many reasons which you know as well as myself, and if she is not the least that is said about her the better.

We are now in sight of Mount Vesuvius which shows a fine light to us in Naples Bay where we are laying too for the night and hope to anchor early tomorrow. Shall take this letter on shore with me in case the post goes out directly.

You will write to my father to say where we are and my kindest remembrances to him and remember me to all those who wish to hear of me. We were in the Bay all night becalmed and nothing could be finer than the views of Mount Vesuvius. Believe me your most affectionate husband, HORATIO NELSON.

To Mrs. Nelson.

No. 56

[Nicolas, I, p. 326]

Naples, September, 14, 1793

MY DEAR FANNY,—My other letter you will receive with this. Our news was received here with the greatest satisfaction. The King has twice sent for me and I dine with him tomorrow after he has made me a visit which he is to do on board *Agamemnon*. We are called by him the saviours of

---

[1] Samuel Cranston Goodall was third in command in the Mediterranean.

Italy and of his dominions in particular. I have acted for my Lord Hood in such a manner that no one could exceed and am to carry from the King the handsomest letter in his own handwriting which could be penned.[1] This I got done through Sir William Hamilton[2] and the Prime Minister[3] who is an Englishman, knowing how much it would please the Lord. He will get soon also I think a handsome present. Lady Hamilton[4] has been wonderfully kind and good to Josiah. She is a young woman of amiable manners and who does honour to the station to which she is raised.

Remember me to my dear father. Also to the Lord and Lady Walpole etc. Believe me your most affectionate husband, HORATIO NELSON.

I am to carry the Lord six thousand troops from hence, to help to take care of our possession the whole of which is absolutely ours if Louis xvii is not re-established.

Shall write you a line before I sail.

To Mrs. Nelson.

No. 57

[Nicolas, I, p. 329]

Leghorn,
September 27, 1793

MY DEAR FANNY,—'Tis a sad thing not to know where to direct to you.[5] I hope to hear from you today when the post arrives. I am sorry to tell you the vessel I sent in here is cleared so all my hopes (which I own were not very sanguine) are gone. Prizes are not to be met with but so covered by neutral papers that you may send in fifty and not one turn out good.

I was hurried from Naples by information of a French ship of war and 3 vessels under her convoy being off. I had nothing left but to get to sea which I did in two hours. Fortune has not crowned my endeavours with success. Have seen nothing of them. I am here plagued with a French 40-gun frigate who was to have sailed the day I arrived, and will take the first dark moment to get out. I am determined in my own mind to pursue

---

[1] This letter, written in French, is preserved among the Hood papers now at the N.M.M. (see Appendix, p. 150).

[2] Sir William Hamilton, ambassador at Naples 1764–1800.

[3] Sir John Acton, Minister to the King of Naples, had joined the Tuscan fleet in 1779. He was asked to reorganize the Neapolitan navy by the Queen of Naples, mother of the Empress of Austria, with whose support he became Chief Minister. He died in 1811.

[4] Emma Hart, who married Sir William as his second wife in 1791.

[5] Mrs. Nelson spent the year in a round of visits. She had no fixed address until the end of 1794 when she settled in Bath with Nelson's father.

him, the measure may not be quite regular, however I will if possible take him and leave the two courts to settle the propriety of the measure. This makes this place no place of rest for us. I hope to sail tomorrow if this gentleman does not and shall lay in his route to intercept him if he sails.

I have just heard that last night the crew of my neighbour deposed their Captain, made the Lieutenant of Marines Captain of the ship, the sergeant of marines Lieutenant of Marines and their former Captain sergeant of Marines. What a state. They are mad enough for any undertaking. They say as they have 500 men on board they will go to sea this night in spite of me. I shall be surprised at nothing they may attempt.

The English post is not arrived and the mail does not come in till Sunday next. I was in hopes to have heard from you. I dined with the King of Naples the day before I sailed and was placed at his right hand and every attention paid me. He was to have visited my ship the day I sailed but I was hurried away so unexpectedly. Direct my letters for Mr. Udney consul at Leghorn and the postage must, I suppose, be in part paid. I shall not finish this till tomorrow.

We have been looking out all night for our neighbour cutting his cables as it has blown a gale of wind and rain all night but he lay in such a position that he could not cast his ship without getting on board us which he did not chuse to risk. I shall sail tomorrow for Toulon. God bless you and believe me your most affectionate husband, HORATIO NELSON.

To Mrs. Nelson.

No. 58

[Nicolas, I, p. 331, part]

Agamemnon, Toulon,
October 7, 1793

MY DEAR FANNY,—As I never omit an opportunity of writing I shall not let a ship sail for Leghorn without a letter. I came here 2 days past and sail on a cruise tomorrow. The Lord is wonderfully pleased with me. Suckling is on board his ship [1] in the list for promotion and he assures me he shall have a fair chance for promotion and he shall be glad of the opportunity. The moment I asked he granted in the handsomest manner. Our situation here is wonderful. The hills are occupied by the enemy who are erecting works for mortars and cannons. Whether we shall be able to maintain our

[1] The *Victory*. Suckling was promoted lieutenant in March 1794.

most extraordinary situation, time only can determine. However one hour will burn the whole French fleet.

Josiah is well and in high spirits. God bless you and believe me your most affectionate HORATIO NELSON.

You will not forget me to my father and the other parts of my family in the different counties. Have not yet received a *line*.

To Mrs. Nelson.

No. 59

[Nicolas, I, p. 333]

Agamemnon,
October 12, 1793

MY DEAR FANNY,—I received a letter from Mr. Suckling yesterday by a ship I spoke from Gibraltar dated July 26th, the only one I have yet got since I left England. I was indeed truly sorry to hear you were not perfectly well. Why should you fret yourself? I am well, your son is well and we are as comfortable in every respect as the nature of our service will admit. I am now going where if any prizes are to be taken (which I doubt) it is likely I shall fall in them. The Lord is now quite as he used to be, his dear Nelson etc. He is so good an officer that every body must respect him. All the foreigners at Toulon absolutely worship him. Was any accident to happen to him I am sure no person in our fleet could supply his place, but I never saw him in better health or spirits.

I daresay I have letters from you at Leghorn, which I may get in time. What a loss Robert Rolfe [1] has had in not coming out with me. I have seen and am likely to see more of the Mediterranean than any ship in the fleet. The Bishop of Winchester [2] asked one of the officers how it came I had not a chaplain and he told him the story. The Bishop thought my relation was wrong every way for the opportunity was never to be regained. However Robert Rolfe never goes to sea with me let his inclination be ever so much for it.

Every day at Toulon has hitherto afforded some brilliant action on shore in which the sea officers have cut a very conspicuous figure, Elphinstone in particular who is a good officer and gallant man. I have only been a spectator, but had we remained I should certainly have

[1] Nelson's cousin, son of the late Rev. Robert Rolfe, also a clergyman. Nelson later appointed him as his personal chaplain.
[2] The Right Rev. Brownlow North, Bishop of Winchester, was one of the visitors to Nelson's ship while he was at Naples.

desired to be landed. Some of our ships have been pegged pretty hand-somely but such is the force of habit that we seem to feel no danger. The other day we sat at a court martial on board Admiral Hotham, when *Princess Royal*, a French 74 (our friend), 3 frigates and 4 mortar boats were firing at a battery for four hours, the shot and shells going over us, but extraordinary as it may seem it made no difference. The *Victory* lays within reach of the enemy, goes on the same as if 100 leagues off.

Linzee,[1] who you know, is made a Commodore with a Captain under him and was sent to attack Corsica. He went against a battery with his squadron but was obliged to retreat with some loss. The *Ardent*, Captain Robert Manners Sutton, brother to the Bishop,[2] was much cut up after behaving with the greatest gallantry and good conduct. Near 30 of his men were either killed or are since dead of their wounds. Indeed wherever our ships or sea officers have had an opportunity (except one instance) they have all behaved well.

Say everything for me. God bless you. Your most affectionate husband, HORATIO NELSON.

To Mrs. Nelson.

[Letter from Josiah on the back.]

DEAR MOTHER,—I have been very well since I wrote to you last and hope you have been so. I hope Mr. Nelson is very well. I still like being at sea and think I always shall. We have been at Toulon which I think a very strong place. The Spaniards have ran away every time they have engaged the French and have behaved with the utmost barbarity to all those who laid down their arms and also the Neapolitans have behaved very cruelly in some cases. JOSIAH NISBET.

No. 60

Off Sardinia,
December 1

It is impossible my dearest Fanny to say the pleasure I felt in receiving your letter of September 16th, the only one I have received from you since I left England, although you have wrote me, but now if you direct them under cover to Mr. Udney at Leghorn, I shall get them to a certainty, you paying foreign postage.

I wrote Maurice a line from Tunis where I have been with a squadron under the command of Commodore Linzee to negotiate for or take a

[1] Robert Linzee, Lord Hood's brother-in-law. Died, Admiral of the Blue, in 1804.
[2] The Right Rev. Charles Manners-Sutton, Bishop of Norwich, who became Arch-bishop of Canterbury in 1805.

French convoy under an eighty-gun ship and a corvette. We negotiated
so long that the Bey of Tunis would not give us leave to take them, which
if we had done afterwards our trade would have suffered by these Barbary
pirates, and by not suffering the French to be taken he has had very great
presents, and bought a great many of their cargoes for one third of their
value. My opinion in a council of war you will readily guess—was to take
the men of war and the whole convoy and then to begin negotiating. We
could I am satisfied have then with ease bribed him to keep the peace, or
had he not, have knocked the Goletta and Porto Farino about his ears.
He would soon have come to his senses. However thank God Lord Hood
has taken me from under his command and given me one of my own in a
very handsome manner: as follows:—

You may have heard of our little brush with a French squadron of
frigates. I had every disadvantage but in the zeal and gallantry of my
officers and ship's company. In them had the enemy fought me fairly I
had the firmest reliance and trust I should not have been disappointed.
Their force united was 170 guns 1600 men superior to *Agamemnon* 106
guns 1255 men. Had they been English a 64 never could not have got from
them. Linzee went out to look for them but did not go far enough or he
would have fallen in with them with our squadron. They are got into
Saint Fiorenza in Corsica where they cannot unfortunately be got at.
The Lord has wrote me a handsome letter, and given me the command of a
squadron of frigates to watch them which is the strongest proof of his
approbation of my conduct on every occasion, when there are still so
many older captains in the squadron.

I am now at sea making the best of my way to look at them, but shall
send a ship into Leghorn with my letters. Admiral Gell with Captains
Pole, Conway and another ship are sent to the West Indies. Had I been at
Toulon I should have been a candidate, for I think our sea war is almost
over in these seas. The land one is only beginning and Toulon will be
warmly attacked this winter.

I rejoice to hear you are well. Mr. Suckling's letter did not give so good
an account of you as I sincerely wished. I assure you it cannot give you
more pleasure than it will me, for us to be settled again at Burnham and I
sincerely hope our father will not part with the house to any one so as to
prevent our getting into it again. I am glad you are improving in your
music and you must have a good instrument, we can afford that I am sure.

Has Fraser etc. paid you or how will that be settled now that they are
bankrupt? As to Mrs. Hamilton I am not surprised at her conduct: it is all
of a piece. I think before many months are over we shall have peace.
Those wretches in France must be got to the pinnacle of wickedness and a

fury some day will destroy the convention and put the King on his throne. I got your letter in Tunis bay by a frigate which our Commodore sent to Toulon for orders how to act. From Mrs. Bolton and Maurice I had letters of October 16th a month after yours. I had also a letter from the Duke of Clarence, I am sorry he is not employed. What does it matter to him whether the war is right or wrong? As an officer who I would wish to see rise in the esteem of his country, I wish he was at sea where I am sure he would acquire honour.

December 8th: we are all well, Josiah a very good boy.

Believe me your most affectionate husband, HORATIO NELSON *[part of the signature torn away]*.

Remember me at Hilborough—me to my aunt.[1]

To Mrs. Nelson, Swaffham, Norfolk, Angleterre.

Cover to No. 61: Nelson to Maurice Nelson

Leghorn,
December 23, 1793

MY DEAR BROTHER,—Be so good as to send the inclosed. Report has just arrived of Toulon being destroyed by 60,000 convention troops and Lord Hood retreating in the best manner from Fort Le Malque. Our people are said to have burned the Arsenal and French fleet. A man running away makes things worse probably than they are, but something very bad has taken place.

Mrs. Nelson I expect is at Wolterton. Your affectionate H.N.

To Mr. M. Nelson, Navy Office, London.

No. 61

Leghorn,
December 23, 1793

MY DEAR FANNY,—We are well and just arrived here for provisions. A very bad report is just arrived about Toulon, viz, that on the 13th the Convention army was increased to 60,000 men, that on the 16th they carried many of our outposts, on the 17th the mob in Toulon set the town on fire and began plundering, our people set fire to the Arsenal and fleet in it, that the troops and families were embarking in the greatest confusion. In short that Lord Hood was getting clear of the place as well as he could, keeping fort Le Malque to retreat from.

[1] His father's sister, Mary Nelson, who also lived at Hilborough.

PLATE III (b). Captain Horatio Nelson, aged thirty-six, painted by a Leghorn miniaturist (see p. 191: Nelson's letter to his wife, December 12, 1794).

PLATE III (a). Captain Horatio Nelson drawn by his friend Captain Cuthbert Collingwood at Antigua c. 1784.

I do not vouch this is all true, but that something serious has certainly happened. As to giving up Toulon I shall rejoice at it, wish it had been done long ago. The expense of keeping it hitherto has been enormous, and our loss of brave Englishmen has been too great. This account comes by a vessel who says he escaped and several families are on board from Toulon embarked expecting the attack and which the Master declares took place as I mentioned before. 100 sail he says he saw out of the harbour.

How this event will elevate the French and it is impossible to conceive how the people are depressed here. I have just been with the governor who is frighted to pieces, expects the French at Leghorn for the Grand Duke has been, not in a very handsome manner in my opinion, been drawn into the war. I am glad to hear you are at Wolterton and hope this will find you there, where pray make my best respects.

The post is just going out have only time to thank you for your various letters down to the 17th November. God bless you and believe me your most affectionate husband, HORATIO NELSON.

To Mrs. Nelson, at Lord Walpole's, Wolterton, Norfolk.

No. 62

[Nicolas, I, p. 345, part]

Agamemnon,
December 27, 1793

MY DEAR FANNY,—Your letters of August 21st, Sept. 18th, 26th, Nov. 17th, Dec. 2nd, October 14th have all been received, as will those by the *Gorgon* when we meet. I wrote you last post of our evacuation of Toulon. It is all true. Everything which domestic wars produce usually are multiplied at Toulon. Fathers are here without families, families without fathers. In short all is horror which we hear. The Lord put himself at the head of the flying troops and was the admiration of all but the torrent was too strong. Many of our posts were carried without resistance. At others, where the English were, everybody perished. I cannot write all, my mind is truly impressed with grief. Each teller makes the scene more horrible. Even at this moment I don't know whether fort Le Malque is blown up and the fleet left Toulon. Each is so occupied with his own misery, that no thought was given to the public. The Lord is the same collected good officer which he always was. I have wrote to Lady Hood to say he is well, she must be very uneasy.

As you desire my opinion about Bath etc., I have only to *order* that

H

you do what you like and give you full power to give my assent to your own wishes, that is settled. I cannot write much for this is post day and I am writing to the Duke of Clarence, to the Admiralty, and amongst others to the Rector of Hilborough. Nothing official from Lord Hood has come here which I am surprised at.

Pray remember me in the kindest manner to Lady Walpole, Lord Walpole, Miss Walpole, Mr. and Mrs. Hussey, and do not omit to every one of the family.

I have only time to say I will write you on Monday more particulars. God bless you and believe me your most affectionate husband, HORATIO NELSON.

I have the Count de Grasse [1] under my command in a French frigate his wife and family at Toulon. Josiah is very well, as is Hoste and Bolton [2] good boys.

To Mrs. Nelson, Right Honble. Lord Walpole, Aylsham, Norfolk, Angleterre.

No. 63

Josiah Nisbet to Mrs. Nelson

[December 30, 1793]

We are now at Leghorn and have just heard of Toulon's being evacuated by Lord Hood. He burnt fifteen sail of the line and carried out with him the *Commerce of Marseilles* [3] and two ships of the line and seven frigates. Lord Hood is laying at anchor with nine miles of Toulon.

I heard we had very few killed, we had not time to blow up La Malque. The *Scipion* a French ship of the line blew up on 23rd of November in this road supposed to set on fire wilfully. We did not even take one vessel at Turin, although we anchored close to the *Duquesne*. We have since seen those frigates we fired at in Fiorenzo laying close under the batteries we were not more than three miles from them. We think the *Melpomene* is sunk. We heard at Corsica that one of them had half her men killed and her hull very much shattered.

[1] Nephew of the Comte de Grasse, defeated by Rodney at the battle of the Saints in 1782, he had commanded the French fleet at Toulon jointly with Trogoff, but declared against the Republicans and joined Lord Hood's forces.
[2] William Bolton, one of Nelson's midshipmen, son of the Rev. William Bolton, and related to Nelson's brother-in-law, Mr. Thomas Bolton. He continued under Nelson's patronage; died Captain Sir William Bolton in 1830.
[3] Flag-ship of Admiral Trogoff.

[Postscript added by Nelson]

December 30, 1793

I had letters from Lord Hood last night to announce the leaving Toulon and that he had burned 15 sail of the line, the arsenal and all the great store houses. The fleet is in Hieres Bay. I am going to sea directly [1] and made your son stop writing. Best compliments where you are, yours most affectionately, HORATIO NELSON.

To Mrs. Nelson, Right Honourable Lord Walpole, Aylsham, Norfolk, Angleterre.

No. 64

[Nicolas, I, p. 345, part, under date January 6]

Agamemnon, off Calvi,
January 16, 1794

MY DEAR FANNY,—I left Leghorn on the 3rd and got very soon off here, since which time have had nothing but hard gales of wind and the heaviest rains I almost ever met with. I am waiting anxiously for troops from Lord Hood to take St. Fiorenzo and the frigates which will fall in a few hours after their arrival. I was most unfortunately drove a few miles to leeward two days ago in the height of the gale and a frigate took that opportunity of getting from St. Fiorenzo to Calvi with provisions. One of my frigates exchanged a few shots with her but at too great a distance to prevent her getting in. I had so closely blockaded Calvi that they must have surrendered to me at discretion. Not a vessel before got in for the 6 weeks I have been stationed here. This supply will keep them a week or two longer.

We now know from a deserter that it was the *Melpomene,* 44 guns, 400 men who got the dressing from us. She had 24 men killed 50 wounded and the ship so much damaged as to be laid up dismantled in St. Fiorenzo. She would have struck long before we parted but for the gunner who opposed it, and the colours were ordered to be struck by general consent when we run into a calm whilst the other ships came up with a fresh breeze and joined their consort. She is allowed, Admiral Trogolphe tells me, to be the finest frigate out of France and the fastest sailer, we were unlucky to select her, the others we could outsize. Had she struck I don't think the others would have come down and I should have had great credit in taking her from such a superior force. Now of course nothing can

[1] Nelson sailed for Elba on January 2.

be known of that business and I have to look out for another opportunity which are very scarce here.

I have just received the handsomest letters from Lord Hood. He looks upon these frigates as certain trusting to my zeal and activity. He knows if it is in the power of man to have them I will secure them. I have just got your letter of October 1st and November 4th but nothing by the *Gorgon*. I suppose I shall when I see her. Linzee was to have been here for this service and to settle plans with General Paoli [1] the chief of the Corsicans relative to landing the troops etc. Andrews [2] is my ambassador. This matter going through my hands is a proof of Lord Hood's confidence in me, and that I shall pledge myself for nothing which will not be acceptable to him. Suckling is not made yet, but, if he does not ride resty, he will I have no doubt. I sometimes fear his spirit may get the better of his prudence if so he is upset in the *Victory*. Linzee has gone to Malta to perform quarantine a very pleasant place.

I have kept the sea, but I have promised my people as soon as we have taken Corsica, I will ask for a month's rest for them and indeed all our hard work will be done in this country. Except to get provisions I have not been one hour at anchor for pleasure since April 23rd, but I can assure you I never was better in health as is Josiah. On Sunday I expect Lord Hood and the troops. A week or two will I think take Corsica, certainly long before you get this letter it will be ours. I hear the *Commerce de Marseilles* will be sent home in the spring. She is the largest ship I ever beheld, our 1st rates are nothing to her, 28 feet longer than the *Victory* and four feet wider.

I am glad the Hostes seem sensible of my attention to their son, but he is indeed a most exceeding good boy, and will shine in our service. He will tell them there is a wide difference between shooting French men and shooting partridges, but we shall talk these matters over again in a winter's evening. I think if the Lockharts [3] will get Josiah a good place he has sense enough to give up the sea, although he is already a good seaman. He desires his love. Believe me your most affectionate HORATIO NELSON.

January 18th: You will not I am sure forget me to my father. If this finds you at Bath don't forget my kind remembrances to Mr. and Mrs. Scrivener. You will also see Admiral Robinson [4] my old Captain with a wooden leg.

To Mrs. Nelson.

[1] The Corsican patriot, who rallied partisans against the French.
[2] Lieutenant George Andrews, who had been in the *Boreas* with Nelson.
[3] Dr. Nisbet's sister Mary, married James Lockhart, who lived near Glasgow, where he had some property.
[4] Nelson's captain in the *Worcester* 1776–7. He died in 1799.

No. 65

[Nicolas, I, p. 349, part]

Leghorn,
January 30, 1794

MY DEAR FANNY,—I was unfortunately drove from my station with the whole squadron on the 28th by the hardest gale of wind almost ever remembered here. The *Agamemnon* did well but lost every sail in her. Lord Hood had joined me off Corsica the day before and would have landed the troops but the gale has dispersed them over the face of the waters. The *Victory* was very near lost, however we are safe. A number of transports are missing. I am fearful the enemy will get their troops from France before I can return to my station which will be a vexing thing after my two months' hard fag. I hope to get my ship to sea tomorrow.

I received some of your letters and others you mention I have not got but they will come forth in time. I also received my dear father's letter of October 17th yesterday and today his of January 1st for which I thank him. I am glad to hear such good accounts of Suckling [1] and of the Baronet's [2] family at Burnham. I direct this to Bath where I desire you will not want for anything. My expenses are by no means great, therefore don't be afraid of money. Only don't let my father pay anything for you.

A thing happened a few days past which gave me great satisfaction. The 21st January the French had their store house of flour near a water mill close to St. Fiorenzo, I seized a happy moment, landed 60 soldiers and seamen. In spite of opposition at landing the sailors threw all the flour into the sea, burned the mill the only one they have, and returned on board without the loss of a man. The French sent 1,000 men at least against them and gunboats etc., but as the French shot went over them they were just within reach of my guns. It has pleased the Lord, if this dreadful gale has not blown it out of his memory.

I had a kind letter from Mr. Scrivener. Pray write him it gave me pleasure to hear from him. I will write very soon but am full of business. I wish Maurice may have exchanged his place for a better but am fearful these temporary appointments are not of much use, but if he had made himself useful to Mr. Davison [3] he can do something for him. Josiah is with me and desires his love. Remember me to all friends who you see at Ringwood, etc. Believe me yours most affectionately, HORATIO NELSON.

[1] His younger brother, studying for Holy Orders at Cambridge.
[2] Sir Morduant Martin, Bart., who had settled in Burnham when he returned to England from Jamaica.
[3] Alexander Davison, merchant contractor and agent, first met Nelson at Quebec in 1782, and remained a lifelong friend.

Three boxes are got on board *Agamemnon* for me but have not yet seen them. Write to Suckling and remember me to him.

[Postscript added by Josiah Nisbet]

I am much obliged to you for your remembrance to me. I am glad to hear the hobby is well. I will thank you to remember me to Mr. Nelson. JOSIAH NISBET.

To Mrs. Nelson, Bath, via London, Angleterre.

No. 66

[Nicolas, I, p. 354, part]

Agamemnon, at sea,
February 13, 1794

MY DEAR FANNY,—I am just going to Leghorn to get a little water, therefore write a line to say I am well. Our troops are now landed on Corsica which I hope will fall in due time. Our weather begins to get much better. Commodore Linzee has the command of the sea business. Although Lord Hood lays off with 3 admirals [1] close to him, it is intended to give Linzee the éclat of taking St. Fiorenzo, where he was once beat off.[2] On the 9th he sent *Fortitude* 74 Captain Young against a fort. She got 56 men killed and wounded and did no good whatever. I am glad Lord Hood did not leave me under his command. I had the pleasure to fulfil in every respect the service I was upon before leaving Tunis, neither to allow provisions or troops to get into Corsica or the frigates to get out. I am, after getting a little water at Leghorn going to cruise off Bastia to prevent succours getting in there. Corsica is a wonderful fine island.

I expect to have the pleasure of hearing from you when we anchor and hope you are feeling comfortable. I take for granted you will pay a visit at Bristol.[3] I desire you will make my remembrances to the old lady and Mr. Tobin's family. We are anxious to hear how Parliament likes the war. I am still of opinion it cannot last much longer, not by the French having an absolute monarchy again, but by our leaving them alone, perhaps the wisest method we can follow. This is post day, therefore have only time to

[1] Vice-Admiral Hotham, Rear-Admiral Hyde Parker, Rear-Admiral Goodall.
[2] See letter No. 59.
[3] There was steady trade between Bristol and Nevis, and many of the West Indian trading families had personal connections with Bristol.

say God bless you and believe me your most affectionate husband HORATIO NELSON.

You will remember me in the kindest manner to my father. Josiah is very well and a good boy.

To Mrs. Nelson, Bath, via London, Angleterre.

No. 67
[Nicolas, I, p. 361, part]

Agamemnon, off Bastia,
February 28, 1794

MY DEAR FANNY,—I don't know when I shall have an opportunity of sending this letter but not being willing to miss any opportunity I write literally to say I am well, never better, and in active service which I love. Lord Hood expresses himself on every occasion well pleased with my conduct. He is come on this side himself but would not bring an older captain than myself therefore the sea part of Bastia is under my direction (under his Lordship). He says he comes to make the army active. I have now six frigates with me.

Our little brush last Sunday happened at the moment our army made their appearance on the hills over Bastia, they having marched overland from St. Fiorenza which is only 12 miles distant. The General [1] sent an express to Lord Hood at Fiorenza to tell him of it. What a noble sight it must have been. Indeed on board it was the grandest thing I ever saw. If I had with me 500 troops to a certainty I would have stormed the town and believe it might have been carried. Army go so slow that seamen think they never mean to get forward, but I dare say they act on a surer principle, although we seldom fail. St. Fiorenza at last was carried by the seamen but being out of proper form has given great offence to the army, the colours being carried to Lord Hood. You can't think how pleased the Lord was with my attack, or rather repelling of an attack which the enemy made on me. He said he was glad it had happened and no damage done us but that he would not send us against the walls for the army were fully equal to take it and if they wanted assistance on shore he would send it them. Lord Hood is gone to Porto Ferraio for some supplies but will return in two days. I am to anchor to have communication with the army.

[1] General Dundas and some of the army officers held different views from Hood and Nelson on the wisdom of attacking Bastia (see Appendix, p. 151, Sir Gilbert Elliot's Journal).

Bastia is a large town, populous, having 10,000 inhabitants and a fine mole for shipping. If we take Corsica of which I have not the smallest doubt I hope we shall keep it. The natives love us, hate the French and are a brave people and free. It is wonderful the attachment of the Corsicans to General Paoli. When I took Miomo near Bastia, the Corsicans all declared for the English. A gentleman came down and said he could now venture to say how attached he was to Paoli and pulled a picture of him from his bosom kissed it, and immediately hundreds begged to kiss it down on their knees. This is pure affection. Paoli has nothing to give them, no honours to bestow, it is the tribute of a generous people to a chief who had sacrificed everything for their benefit. I hope he will live to see the Corsicans truly free. The island is fine, well cultivated but has been kept under by numerous bodies of French soldiers. The produce of wines interfered with those of France the exportation was almost prohibited. If it belongs to us it will soon be a rich country and hurt the Italian powers very much.

Captain Lutwidge is at Leghorn wishing he was made an Admiral when I believe he would very gladly go on shore. As to Lord Hood he is as active as a man of forty, writes all his own orders and correspondences with all the Italian states.[1] The army etc., is absolutely under his direction. His business is enough for three common heads but to him it is easy.

I expected to hear from you since your arrival at Bath but think you have wrote before this time. Nothing can give me so much pleasure as frequent letters. When you go to Bristol remember me to Mrs. Webb and Mrs. Tobin [2] and family. I hope Mr. Baillie has done matters to your satisfaction but you can always write to Marsh and Creed [3] for whatever you want. I wish Mr. Lockhart could get Josiah a good place on shore I am sure I don't like his going to sea if he can be better provided for, and I am certain Josiah would give up the sea for anything we can wish him to do.

March 1st: Lord Hood has been blown off in a gale last night. It will probably be some days before he returns. Myself and one frigate are the only ships who kept their station. Give my kindest remembrances to my father and compliments to those who may enquire after me. Believe me your most affectionate husband, HORATIO NELSON.

Josiah writes you. He is a very good boy and much grown.
To Mrs. Nelson, Bath, Angleterre.

[1] Lord Hood at this time was seventy.
[2] Friends from the West Indies.
[3] Nelson's agents.

No. 68
[Nicolas, I, p. 367, part]
Agamemnon, off Bastia,
March 4, 1794

MY DEAR FANNY,—My letter of the 1st was hardly gone not out of sight before I received yours of February 3rd which gave me great pleasure. I believe there was no occasion to write to my agents but I have done it for form's sake. I am glad to hear you are so well. I am glad Mrs. Kelly is coming to join the party, I know your fondness for her. You will remember me kindly to her. I dare say you will manage matters very well with Mr. Baillie. I don't like to write to those in the West Indies. Mrs. Hamilton never answered my letter. I don't understand your story about my brother and Peggy etc. I never heard of any story, nor about a group of persons, what is it all?

You will be surprised to hear that the English General Dundas [1] has retired from before Bastia without making an attack. God knows what it all means. Lord Hood is gone to Fiorenza to the army to get them forward again. 1,000 men would to a certainty take Bastia. With 500 and *Agamemnon* I would attempt it, Lord Hood said publicly that if he thought it proper to give me three sail of the line and 500 men, he is sure I would take the town although probably not the heights. But the Lord will not sacrifice his seamen and ships in doing what the finest army of its size that ever walked could and wish to do with ease. General Paoli has told them that if they don't keep my force low I shall take Bastia before they pitch their tents in Fiorenza. However, those are only civil speeches, but we now know that I was very near getting possession. On Sunday the 23rd, Lacombe St. Michel, the National Commissioner, was obliged to hide himself or he would have been massacred and then the town would have surrendered. On Tuesday the 25th by myself I did them great damage, and if I had force to go again and cannonade it, I believe I should yet get it. My seamen are now what British seamen ought to be, to you I may say it, almost invincible. They really mind shot no more than peas.

The Lord has just got account that Calvi, one of the ports I blockaded so long, is relieved, two French frigates getting in, in spite of our cruisers, who by not attending closely left a passage. Lord Hood yesterday offered me the *Courageux* 74 supposing Waldegrave does not come out. I declined it, if *Agamemnon* sticks by me I will do the same by her. Josiah is very well. Pray remember me kindly to our father and compliments to Mr. and

[1] General D'Aubant succeeded Dundas in command of the military forces on March 12.

Mrs. Lockhart and Miss Nisbet,[1] we may perhaps one day be known to each other. God bless you and believe me your most affectionate HORATIO NELSON.

To Mrs. Nelson, No. 13, New King Street, Bath, Angleterre.

No. 69

Agamemnon, St. Fiorenza,
March 22

MY DEAR FANNY,—I wrote my father the moment I anchored here. Nothing relative to myself has happened since. We have been getting provisions, water and stores and are to proceed to sea tomorrow to my station off Bastia. However, I write literally to say that nothing.

Like almost all our joint expeditions with the army I find we are at variance. The army say we cannot attack Bastia, it is too strong and defended by too many French troops. Lord Hood and those in whom he is pleased to place confidence are of opinion that Bastia may possibly be taken, but certainly ought to be attacked. The army will give us nothing which they can keep from us. Lord Hood has this day made a requisition for artillery and artillery officers and engineers being determined to attack the place himself. Many think the General will refuse Lord Hood his requisition. I can hardly think it, for that would really be the dog in the manger. What are we come too that 1,500 or 2,000 British troops, and as good as ever marched, are not thought able to attack under 1,000 French? But where am I getting you?—into batteries etc. I hope all will end for the honour and glory of my dear country.

You will be glad to hear Suckling is made a lieutenant. In a very few days he will be 5th lieutenant of *Agamemnon*.[2] The Lord is very civil and attentive. We are I believe better friends than ever. This place now we have it has no inducements to tempt us to remain at anchor, at sea is much wholesomer and pleasanter. We are to go to Naples to refit when the proper time arrives but continue to direct to Leghorn. A vessel is just arrived from Leghorn, not a single letter for me by her.

If you take a trip into the west you will probably call at Exmouth. Remember me to Mrs. Kelly. Wallis who was in the *Boreas* is now Captain of the *Gorgon* a storeship made 4 months ago by Lord Hood. It is said that part of our fleet here will be reduced. Some of the Admirals going home.

---

[1] Anne Nisbet, sister of Dr. Josiah Nisbet and Mrs. Lockhart, died in 1833.
[2] Nelson had a vacancy, as his third lieutenant, Thomas Edmunds, was sick, and likely to be invalided.

Remember me kindly to my father and believe me your most affectionate husband, HORATIO NELSON.

You will say I have told you nothing new, we have nothing and the ground here as barren as our news.

I assure you I please myself much with the hopes of hearing you play on the pianoforte when we are snug at Burnham. Josiah is very well and desires his love. He will begin a letter to you very shortly and make it a *very* little longer.

March 24th: Am now at sea making the best of my way off Bastia. All well. Compliments to the Lockharts.

To Mrs. Nelson, No. 13, New King Street, Bath, Angleterre.

[Forwarded in another hand to:] At John Pinney's Esqr., George Street, Bristol.

No. 70
[Nicolas, I, p. 381, part]

Near Bastia,
April 6, 1794

MY DEAR FANNY,—I have received yours of March 3rd and since that of January 15th. You think I do not receive your letters but I believe I have at last got nearly all them, and believe that nothing gives me a pleasure equal to them.

We are in high health and spirits besieging Bastia,[1] the final event I have little doubt of it will be conquest. Lord Hood is now at anchor near Bastia and our troops are active. Having only just heard of the opportunity for England I have only time to say your son is well. And God bless you and believe me your most faithful and affectionate husband, HORATIO NELSON.

To Mrs. Nelson, Bath.

No. 71
[Nicolas, I, p. 371, part, under date April 6th]

April 16, 1794

MY DEAR FANNY,—A vessel is just going to Leghorn by whom I write a line to say we are all well. Our batteries opened against Bastia on the 11th and apparently have done great execution. Time I hope indeed have no

[1] The siege of Bastia began on April 4 when seamen were landed under Nelson's command (see Appendix, p. 155, for his Journal).

doubt will crown our zealous endeavours with success. We are but few, but of the right sort, our general at Fiorenza not giving us one of the five regiments he has there laying idle.

Josiah is very well. God bless you and believe me your most affectionate husband, HORATIO NELSON.

Remember me kindly to my father and all our friends.

To Mrs. Nelson.

No. 72
[Nicolas, I, p. 385, part]

April 22, 1794

MY DEAREST FANNY,—Your letters of March 17th and 25th reached me a few days past, and I don't believe that any of your letters miscarry, sometimes the late ones come before others of a prior date. I thank you for them, they are proofs of your affection for the many proofs of which I have reason to be thankful to that Being who has ever protected me in a most wonderful manner, in none more than since my landing here. If it is his good pleasure nothing can rejoice me so much as being once more by your side when we shall talk over all these stories and laugh at them.

We are here with a force not equal to our wishes or wants, not near half the force at present in this island, but General D'Aubant will not attack an enemy with two thousand as fine troops as ever marched while we are here beating them from post to post with 1,000. I have no scruple in saying the heads at Fiorenza deserve to be exalted above the people for their conduct, but it is thus our country is sacrificed. This island is to belong to England. Reinforcements are expected and our generals will I am sure be ordered to act.

If you can get your legacy remitted to England, I think you will be perfectly right, suppose you write to Stanley. You know my wish is to have it settled as you like, therefore make use of my name as you please. I have not a thought separate from your interest. Your trip to Plymouth I hope will be pleasant and I know your regard for Mrs. Kelly.

My ship lays on the north side the town with some frigates and Lord Hood on the south side. It is a very hard service for my poor seamen, dragging guns up such heights as are scarcely credible. The town and citadel is most amazingly battered and many of their batteries ruined. The loss of the enemy we know has been very great, stated so far as 500 killed and wounded and ours is not more than 20, the *Agamemnon* has to number five amongst them. They are not the men to keep out of the way. A vessel

is just going to Leghorn therefore must finish. Josiah is very well. Remember me kindly to all our friends and believe me your affectionate husband,
HORATIO NELSON.

This campaign finishes the war.

To Mrs. H. Nelson, at Kelly's Esqr., Great George Street, Plymouth.

No. 73

[Nicolas, I, p. 391]

May 1–May 4, 1794

MY DEAREST FANNY,—I need not I am sure say that all my joy is placed in you, I have none separated from you, you are present, my imagination be where I will. Every action of my life I know you must feel for, all my joys of victory are two fold to me knowing how you must partake of them, only recollect a brave man dies but once, a coward all his life long. We cannot escape death, and should it happen to me in this place, recollect it is the will of Him in whose hands are the issues of life and death. As to my health it was never better, seldom so well.

The expedition is almost a child my own, and I have no fears about the final issue, it will be victory, Bastia will be ours. If so it will be an event which the history of England can hardly boast its equal. Time will show the enemy's force. If it is small, the Fiorenzo *heroes* ought to be broke, if it is large they deserve to be shot for allowing a handful of brave men to be on service unsupported. My only fears are that these gentlemen will advance when Bastia is about to surrender and deprive us of part of our glory. The King we trust will draw the line of deserts. Bastia is a most beautiful place and the environs of it delightful with the most romantic views I ever beheld. This island is to belong to England, to be governed by its own laws as Ireland, and a viceroy placed here with free ports. Italy and Spain are jealous of our taking this island it will command the Mediterranean. I shall most probably be in England in August if Lord Hood has a proper opportunity of sending me. I shall ask him and I am sure he will not deny me anything in reason.

You may have heard rumours of the loss of the *Ardent*. She was commanded by the Bishop of Norwich's brother, a gallant good officer.[1] Miss Day's brother was a lieutenant in her. Lord Hood has just wrote me he fears there are no hopes of her being safe. How such an accident as blowing up could happen to her, I cannot conceive for it is the most

[1] Captain Robert Manners-Sutton.

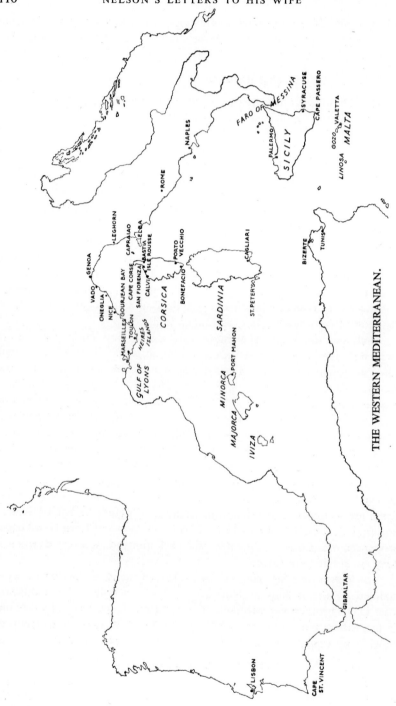

THE WESTERN MEDITERRANEAN.

unlikely of all things to happen. I will tell you as a secret, Bastia will be ours between the 20th and 24th of this month if succours do not get in. Our ships are moored across the harbour's mouth and 3 boats row guard every night from each ship. Lord Hood is as anxious as myself for that event. Our loss has been very trifling, the enemy's very great. Only think of a beautiful town being bombarded and cannonaded for a month what knocks it has had. It is said a Mid. of mine (a Norfolk lad) is deserted to the enemy, I do not believe it. If he is, to a certainty he will be hanged. We have many deserters from Bastia who paint the horrid situation they are in but they have behaved so ill to the Corsicans that they are afraid to surrender.

Josiah is very well. I have not seen him these 10 days, have wrote him to invite him and Hoste to dinner. Apropos I had a letter from Hoste's father yesterday expressive of his gratitude. The lad is a charming good boy. You will write my father I am well. Remember me to all our friends. Believe me your most affectionate husband, HORATIO NELSON.

If you write to Miss Walpole I desire you will remember me to all that good family. I must enclose this letter to Mr. Suckling I am afraid it is very troublesome to him. If I knew where to write Maurice I would like to write him. Josiah is just gone off, he dined with me.

To Mrs. Nelson, Captain Kelly's, Great George Street, Plymouth.

No. 74

[Nicolas, I, p. 397, part]

Camp,
May 20, 1794

MY DEAREST FANNY,—Your letter of April 14th I received today's post for which I sincerely thank you, you know the pleasure they give me, and before any great length of time I hope to thank you in person, for if Lord Hood goes to England which is strong in report, I shall certainly be a candidate for going with him.

I have the pleasure to tell you that yesterday afternoon the enemy sent off a flag of truce to Lord Hood. The truce still continues, and I hope there will be a surrender of the town in consequence of it. Our Fiorenza army hearing what was going on here, most meanly have marched to the top of the heights to rob us of the very little merit we may expect. I always was of opinion have ever acted up to it, and never have had reason to alter it that *one Englishman* was equal to three *Frenchman*. Had this been an English town, I am sure it would not have been taken by them. They have allowed us to batter them without once making an effort to drive us away. I may say with truth that this has been a naval expedition, our boats preventing anything from getting in from the sea and our seamen in getting up great guns and fighting them on shore. All the hurt the enemy have received has been from seamen, not a soldier has fired a musquet. I don't mean they were not ready and willing if it had been wanted. We shall take we expect 1,000 regulars, 1,500 National Guards and a large party of Corsican troops, 4,000 in the whole. These will I hope lay down their arms to 1,000 British and 200 seamen. There is some difficulty about the terms and hostilities may commence for a day or two longer, but they must submit. To this day we have fired 20,000 shot and shells in the town and citadel. I shall not write more till I see how this ends.

May 22nd: Josiah came to me and has been with me at the head of the British Grenadiers, taking possession of forts and posts sufficient to have prevented our success had they been fought well. 1,200 men quitted the first post we went too. Lord Hood has gained the greatest credit for his perseverance and I dare say he will not forget that it was due to myself in a great measure this glorious expedition was undertaken. Tomorrow morning we take possession of the citadel. When I reflect on what we have achieved I am all astonishment. God Almighty has ever been good to me and my protection from the many perils incident to my situation here. How I shall rejoice to see you.

God bless you; Josiah tells me he will write. Andrews has been slightly wounded. Your affectionate husband, HORATIO NELSON.

Our killed and wounded is only 48. Theirs above 500.

To Mrs. Nelson, at Captain Kelly's, Plymouth.

No. 75

Agamemnon,
May 30, 1794

MY DEAREST FANNY,—I am got safe on board again having (to you I may say it) acquitted myself through this expedition in a way which has gained the esteem of all parties, no very easy task, when the Navy and Army seem to wish each other at the devil. Lord Hood's thanks to me both public and private are the handsomest that man can pen. Having ever since our leaving England been in the habit of getting thanks and applauses, I look for them as a matter of course.

I have just got your letter of last December which came in a box Maurice sent me of newspapers. The *Agamemnon* is now taking on board the needful for Calvi, the last remnant the French have got in this island. When taken we are to go to Gibraltar get something done to us and then

PLATE IV. Oil painting, by J. Pocock, of the Parsonage House, Burnham Thorpe, where Nelson was born. He lived here with his wife and father from 1787 to 1793, while he was on half pay.

I hope proceed to England to get well fitted. You may direct a few letters to Gibraltar, I shall certainly be there in a few weeks.

We have taken and destroyed 3 of the frigates I fell in with, the remainder are at Calvi, and I hope to have them, so we get these at last. My ship is full of the officers and crews. The officers blame the crews, the people their officers for not coming down to us after we were disabled.

I direct this to Plymouth. Remember me to Mr. Kelly and believe me your most affectionate husband, HORATIO NELSON.

Josiah is very well.

To Mrs. Nelson, Captain Kelly R.N., Plymouth, Devon, Angleterre.

No. 76
[Nicolas, I, p. 404, without date]

Agamemnon, at Sea
June 7, 1794

MY DEAREST FANNY,—We are just got to sea after the French fleet, who we hear are out of Toulon, and our squadron after them steering for Calvi which I fear they will get to in spite of Admiral Hotham's endeavours. The enemy are nine sail of the line, Admiral Hotham seven, two will join him from Fiorenza and Lord goes with six of us. If we have but the good fortune to catch them at sea we shall I am sure give a good account of them. Lord Hood only got the account last night at eleven o'clock and by seven this morning we were all under sail. The *Agamemnon* had two hundred tons of ordnance stores to get out, and Lord Hood had given me orders to follow him as fast as possible, but I was enabled to sail in half an hour after him and are now alongside the *Victory*. I pray God we may meet this fleet who I have no doubt we shall give a glorious account of.

If any accident should happen to me I am sure my conduct will be such as will entitle you to the Royal favour, not that I have the least idea but I shall return safe to you full of honour, if not the Lord's will be done. My name shall never be a disgrace to those who may belong to me. The little I have you know, except a small annuity I have given to you. I wish it was more, but I never have got a farthing dishonestly. It descends with clean hands. Whatever fate awaits me, I pray God to bless you and preserve you for your son's sake. I think always in the most affectionate manner of my father. Tell him so and ever believe me your most affectionate husband, HORATIO NELSON.

To Mrs. Nelson, George Matcham Esqr., Ringwood, Hants., Angleterre.

I

No. 77

June 10, 6 o'clock evening

My DEAR FANNY,—I was in the greatest hopes when I wrote you on the 7th that we should have fallen in with the French fleet. The wind failed us on the 7th at night or we should; and had little wind all day the 8th in the night we joined Admiral Hotham who had left the enemy on the 6th at night soon after they came out of Toulon. On the 9th in the morning I was on board Lord Hood and he was giving me directions to go to Bastia to take the troops and proceed to Calvi or Fiorenza as the General wished, the flag captain came down and said a frigate on the look out had made the signal for the enemy fleet, you will believe I did not stay to receive more orders but got on board with the signal for a general chase, which continued the whole day and night without our getting sight of them. I have the pleasure to say *Agamemnon* was the headmost ship but one and the headmost from the general chase. The frigate who joined us had left the fleet off St. Margaret on the coast of Provence on the night of the 8th laying too with their heads to the southward. Lord Hood being off that place this day at noon, and seeing nothing of the fleet, ordered me to proceed to Bastia and to convoy round the transports with the troops etc., to Fiorenza and to wait there till I heard from his Lordship.

Bastia, June 12th: I arrived here this morning and tomorrow embark the troops and sail, I hope for Fiorenza. I never had better health than since my being in this country. Remember me kindly where you are, and be assured I am your most affectionate husband, HORATIO NELSON.

Josiah is very well and a good boy, grown very much.

To Mrs. Nelson, George Matcham's Esqr., Ringwood, Hants, Angleterre.

No. 78

[Nicolas, I, p. 418]

Camp near Calvi,
June 27, 1794

My DEAR FANNY,—I wrote you a few lines just as we landed [1] since which nothing particular has occurred. Dragging cannon up steep mountains and carrying shot and shells has been our constant employment. Josiah is very well, amazingly grown and will be a handsome young man and I have no fears but he will be a good one. He is affectionate but warm in his

---

[1] Nelson landed 250 seamen for the siege of Calvi on June 19.

disposition which nothing can cool so well as being at sea where nobody have entirely their own way. I was happy to receive your letter of May 18th; I am not sorry to find others get rich it does not make us one bit the poorer. Corsica in the prize way produces nothing but honour, far above the consideration of wealth. Not that I dislike riches, quite the contrary but would not sacrifice a good name to obtain them. The only treasure to you I shall expect to bring back is Josiah and myself.

The French here do not know what to make of us. They know we have landed, yet have not seen us, nor have they any idea about our batteries, which when they open will be heavy on them. That we shall take Calvi in due time I have no manner of doubt. You will know probably that George 3rd is King of Corsica,[1] chosen by the unanimous consent of the people themselves the best of all titles. They are now our fellow subjects. The first resolution of the Parliament of Corsica was to declare they were Englishmen, they might have been mistaken for Irishmen by their *Bull*.

Write often. Your letters afford me the highest gratification. It is probable I shall not get to Gibraltar very soon. You will hear Lord Hood fell in with the French fleet on the 11th but they were too near the shore to prevent them getting into port. The Lord wished to attack them, but a council of flag officers prevented him, but he will either take or destroy them you may be assured, but I trust not before Calvi is taken, when I shall immediately join the fleet. Be so good as to write a line to my father to say I am well never better, also to Mrs. Bol[ton] shall write soon myself, God bless and believe [me] your most affectionate HORATIO NELSON.

I expect this will find you at Ringwood—remember me kindly.

To Mrs. Nelson, George Matcham's Esqr., Ringwood, Hants., Angleterre.

No. 79
[Nicolas, I, p. 418, under date of June 27]
June 28, 1794 [2]

MY DEAR FANNY,—Although I wrote yesterday yet I cannot allow a vessel to go to Leghorn without writing a line to acknowledge the receipt of your letter of June 1st (by mistake dated May 1st). I am sorry Stanley did not

[1] Corsica was ceded to Great Britain on June 19, Sir Gilbert Elliot being appointed Viceroy.
[2] This letter was written on board the *Victory*.

answer your letter but hope he will. We know he can be a warm friend or a bitter enemy. Why should Captain Suckling stay at home? As his friends and himself chose the life of a soldier he ought to go out and I think he will acquit himself well. How you are to travel from Plymouth to Ringwood I cannot tell, not alone I hope. Maurice ought to go for you. Those people who so liberally abuse every body but themselves, are probably the very people who deserve abuse. Sir J. Jervis [1] I dare say would not tell an untruth, although I can readily believe his wish to push forward a Lord. I hope those people who are to get so much money will make a proper use of it, had I attended to the service of my country less than I have I might have made some too. However I trust my name will stand on record when the money makers will be forgot.

I am with Lord Hood. I dare say high in his esteem. He writes and tells me much. I am honoured with the apparent friendship of Sir Gilbert Elliot and General Stuart [2] who commands the troops; their acquaintance can do me no harm, may one day or other be useful. We go on well here.

Best love to my sister and Mr. Matcham and believe me, Your most affectionate HORATIO NELSON.

Josiah is very well.

To Mrs. Nelson, George Matcham's Esqr., Ringwood, Hants, Angleterre.

No. 80
[Nicolas, I, p. 427, part]

Camp,
July 8, 1794

MY DEAR FANNY,—I long to hear from you, for a post has arrive without a letter. Although I ought to thank you for so many proofs of your kindness in writing me, yet I am always wishing for letters. Therefore 'tis in letters as in money the more a person has the more he wishes for.

Our batteries opened yesterday and it is possible you may have heard that a Captain of Navy got his head knocked off! [3] To assure you it is not me I write a few lines, for if such a report should get about I well know your anxiety of mind. We shall take Calvi in due time and I hope without much loss of men.

---

[1] Vice-Admiral Sir John Jervis commanded the expedition sent to the West Indies late in 1793.
[2] General Charles Stuart commanded the military operations against Calvi.
[3] Captain Walter Serocold; killed by grape-shot on July 7.

I am so busy but I own in all my glory that except with you I would not be any where but where I am for any consideration. I am well aware my poor services will not be noticed. I have no interest and when I read a letter about Bastia [1] that a gentleman [2] fought the battery who scarcely ever saw them, and that my merit was landing cannon and stores, which I declare I never did, every body here are thunder struck at the letter. But however services may be received, it is not right in any officer to slacken his zeal for his country. I only wish Lord Hood had never mentioned my name. I should have felt more pleasure than in a general way which he has done. More specially as the officer mentioned before me would to a certainty have quitted the situation if it had not been for myself. However the Lord and myself are good friends. I have not seen him since I have the letter.

God bless you. Josiah is well, dined with me today. Your most affectionate husband, HORATIO NELSON.

To Mrs. Nelson, George Matcham's Esqr., Ringwood, Hants., Angleterre.

No. 81
[Nicolas, I, p. 439, part]

Camp before Calvi,
July 14, 1794

MY DEAR FANNY,—Although but little have occurred since I wrote last, yet as I never miss an opportunity I take up the pen to say I am well, that our batteries have been as successful as we could wish and that our loss of men has been remarkably small. A fortnight will, I have no doubt, give us Calvi but our efforts here are at such a distance and so eclipsed by Lord Howe's great successes at home [3] that I dare say we are not thought off. However we must exert ourselves. Josiah is very well now sitting by me. Wrote you a letter which I sent off yesterday.

Best regards and love where you are and believe me, your most affectionate husband, HORATIO NELSON.

To Mrs. Nelson, George Matcham's Esqr., Ringwood, Hants., Angleterre.

[1] In his dispatches after the surrender of Bastia, Lord Hood referred to the services of Captain Nelson 'who had the command and directions of the seamen in landing the guns, mortars and stores and Captain Hunt who commanded at the batteries very ably assisted by Captain Bullen and Captain Serocold . . .'.
[2] Captain Anthony Hunt.
[3] The battle of the Glorious First of June.

No. 82

[Nicolas, I, p. 468, part under date August 4]

Camp,
August 1, 1794

MY DEAREST FANNY,—As a messenger is going home I have requested Lord Hood to forward this letter by him, as our communication is stopped by way of Flanders. I continue as well as usual and, except a very slight scratch towards my right eye which has not been the smallest inconvenience, have received no hurt whatever.[1] Indeed our losses have been very trifling. We shall have this town in due time. The out posts are all Ours. Lord Hood is cruising off the port and *Agamemnon* lays under my tent, so you see I am not far from home.

Josiah is very well. Little Hoste has been unwell but is better. Reports are so various about Lord Hood going home that I cannot say how it is. All I hope is that if he goes he will not leave me behind him.

Remember me kindly to my sister and Mr. Matcham and believe me your most affectionate husband, HORATIO NELSON.

August 4th: At a specified time this town will be ours,[2] no more firing will take place, so you see I am not the worse for campaigning, but I cannot say I have any wish to go on with it. This day I have been four months landed (except a few days we were after the French fleet) and feel almost qualified to pass my examination as a besieging general. It blows a strong gale and Lord Hood *Agamemnon* etc., are all gone to Fiorenza. Your son came to dine with me and is on shore. I suppose his letter will tell you all the news. He is a very good boy. Much grown.

No. 83[3]

[Nicolas, I, p. 482, part]

Victory,
August 11, 1794

MY DEAR FANNY,—I have only time to say I am perfectly well, as is Josiah, and that this day I go on board *Agamemnon* again and am going so soon as I get our guns etc., landed on board again to Leghorn to refit my ship's

---

[1] On July 12 Nelson wrote to Lord Hood: 'I got a little hurt this morning, not much as you may judge by my writing.' This wound, in fact, led to the loss of the sight of his right eye.

[2] A truce was granted on August 1 for ten days. Calvi surrendered on August 10.

[3] A copy, but bound up with the rest of the series. This letter was written on board the *Victory* to go home with Lord Hood's dispatches.

company who are all worn out, as is this whole army except myself. Nothing hurts me.

God bless you and believe me, your most affectionate HORATIO NELSON.

To Mrs. Nelson, George Matcham Esqr., Ringwood, Hants.

No. 84

[Nicolas, I, p. 484, part]

Agamemnon, off Leghorn,
August 18, 1794

MY DEAR FANNY,—I wrote you a line by the officer who carries home Lord Hood's dispatches and a letter a few days before, but which I find probably went by the same conveyance.

I left Calvi on the 15th I hope never to be in it again. I was yesterday in Fiorenza and today shall be safe moored I expect in Leghorn, where I am to remain and recruit a worn out ship's company. Since the ship has been commissioned this is the first resting time we have had. You may hear, therefore as it is all past I may tell you that on the 10th of July [1] last a shot having struck our battery the splinters of stones from it struck me most severely in the face and breast. Although the blow was so severe as to occasion a great flow of blood from my head, yet I most fortunately escaped by only having my right eye nearly deprived of its sight. It was cut down, but is as far recovered as to be able to distinguish light from darkness, but as to all the purpose of use it is gone. However the blemish is nothing, not to be perceived unless told. The pupil is nearly the size of the blue part, I don't know the name. At Bastia I got a sharp cut in the back.

But what degree of credit may be given to my services I cannot say. General Stuart and Lord Hood are as far asunder as the other generals. They hate us sailors, we are too active for them. We accomplish our business sooner than they like. We throw them and I hope ever shall both at sea and on shore in the back ground. Lord Hood has been very ill and no doubt has applied for leave to go home. I hope he will take me with him.

You must not think that my hurts confined me. *No*—nothing but the loss of a limb should have kept me from my duty and I believe it to have conduced to my keeping up in the general mortality. Mrs. Moutray's

[1] In his Journal and in his letter to Lord Hood, Nelson says he was wounded on the 12th.

son [1] who was on shore with me I am fearful will fall a sacrifice to the climate. He is a lieutenant of the *Victory* a very fine young man who I have a great regard for. Lord Hood is quite distressed about him. Poor little Hoste is also so extremely ill that I have great fears about him. Bolton very ill, Suckling that giant knocked up and 150 of my people in their beds. Never say I have not a good constitution. Of 2,000 men I am the healthiest. I have been disappointed in not getting a letter but perhaps it is my fault in desiring you to direct to Gibraltar, but I hope to get some letters here.

I see by the papers the death of a Captain Kelly, I hope most sincerely it is not our friend. I have I assure you done with campaigning, it was in some measure forced upon me I never solicited it. Josiah is very well and a clever smart young man so I must call him his sense demands it. As I only expect barely to save post, I leave the saying I am well to my father for you to say. Believe me your most affectionate husband, HORATIO NELSON.

To Mrs. Nelson, George Matcham's Esqr., Ringwood, Hants., Angleterre.

No. 85

Leghorn,
August 25, 1794

MY DEAREST FANNY,—I think that my not having lately received a letter from you is owing to myself having desired you to direct you for Gibraltar, where it was intended the *Agamemnon* should have gone to refit but the melancholy state of my ship's company made it necessary to come here as the nearest port. We are recovering although as yet but slowly. Hoste and Bolton are well. Suckling has been exceedingly ill but is at present out of danger. Josiah is never sick. As to my health it never was better. You will expect me to say something of my eye. It is no blemish so my *beauty* is saved. As to the other part if the sand (which turned the shot) had not come in my face the shot would, therefore I hope I am thankful. I can distinguish light from darkness but no object distinctly.

I am sorry to say that Lord Hood and General Stuart are not better friends than the others but the General has imbibed the army notions against the Navy. I may perhaps suffer by it. Lord Hood, every body says, goes home. If so, I hope he will take me with him. I am a candidate as well as many others. Lord Hood has done a handsome thing in taking my first lieutenant into the *Victory* to promote him. What may be done for me time only can show.

[1] Lieutenant James Moutray.

We expect the Lord here every day and great preparations are making for him. No officer's character can stand higher than Lord Hood's in this country of which he is certainly the saviour for could the French get their fleet in to Italy their army could follow and it is gone, for it is not all the Pope's anathemas would make them retreat. But whilst we keep masters of the sea no harm can happen to them and they know it.

Josiah, myself and Hoste go tomorrow to Pisa for to spend a day.

Remember me kindly to my sister and Mr. Matcham and children and believe me my dearest Fanny, your most affectionate husband, HORATIO NELSON.

[Part of the last page is missing]

To Mrs. Nelson, George Matcham's Esqr., Ringwood, Hants., Angleterre.

No. 86

Leghorn,
September 1, 1794

MY DEAR FANNY,—I yesterday received your letter of August 4th which I sincerely thank you for. The uncertainty of a ship's destination you are now aware off therefore pray continue to direct here. If I should be so happy as to go home I shall leave directions for my letters to be sent to Marsh and Creed. I hope you will apply to them for whatever money you may want, it would indeed grieve me if I thought you wanted for anything. I shall not be in their debt therefore do not be afraid to call on them. Indeed my dear Fanny my love, regard and esteem for you cannot I think be exceeded by any man whatever.

Lord Hood is something better but when he goes home or who goes with him is still uncertain. I think if he can with propriety take me I shall be one of the ships. He has been grievously thwarted in this country by envious people which has added to the load he has had on his mind.

You will be sorry to hear young Moutray is dead.[1] I wrote you he was ill with the Calvi fever. He was 2nd lieutenant of the *Victory* and at this moment would have been a Captain. What a shock it must be to his poor mother who was all expectation of hearing of his promotion when a very different account will be told her. His own amiable disposition will never be forgot by all who knew him. Lord Hood was his godfather and feels much for the loss of him. Suckling has been very ill but is out of danger.

---

[1] Nelson placed an inscription to Lieutenant James Moutray in the church at St. Fiorenzo: 'This stone is erected by an affectionate friend, who well knew his worth as an officer and his accomplished manners as a gentleman.'

Bolton, Hoste and Weatherhead [1] are recovered. My ship's company are not yet much better but time I hope will restore us. As to my health it never was better. My constitution is absolutely the wonder of the fleet. Nothing hurts it. I have been 5 nights without sleep (at work) and never felt an inconvenience. Josiah has as good health as myself. He is a very good boy and will be an excellent officer. Captain Valiant's son [2] is on board the *Victory* and will soon be made a lieutenant. I have not yet seen him.

I have had a letter from our father who seems pretty well. I hope we shall meet him before the year expires at Burnham but that pleasure I cannot much build upon. From your not mentioning Kelly I hope no accident has happened. I suppose for the same reason you never hear from the West Indies.

The French squadron are still in Gourjourn Bay blocked up by us and the Spaniards but another month must liberate them and they will get I dare say to Toulon. The opportunity was lost by Admirals of fighting them, and it is a thousand to one if we ever have so fair an opportunity. Equal numbers and the British fleet declined battle. Had Lord Hood been there, I am sure he would have given a good account of them. We sailed from Bastia with only 5 sail of the line in search of them and should most certainly have brought them to action had fortune favoured us. Best love where you are. Your most affectionate H. N.

To Mrs. Nelson, George Matcham's Esqr., Ringwood, Hants., Angleterre.

No. 87

[Nicolas, I, p. 487, part]

Leghorn,
September 12, 1794

MY DEAREST FANNY,—I had the happiness of receiving your letter of August 18th yesterday and do most truly rejoice that your mind did not take alarm at Captain Serocold's death, which I feared might have found its way to newspapers without a name. I ever feel the protecting hand of Providence covering me and when it shall be His good will that I am to leave this world I trust I shall leave a fair name behind me. I hope to see you in the fall of the year. Lord Hood's inclination I believe leads him to take me with him if the service will admit of it, and although I shall not

---

[1] John Weatherhead, midshipman, son of the rector of Sedgeford, Norfolk. Promoted lieutenant, he died of wounds at Santa Cruz, July 1797.
[2] Paul Valiant, son of Captain Isaac Valiant.

bring with me either riches or honours, yet I flatter myself I shall bring a sound constitution and an unblemished character. My ship's company are better but still in a very weak state.[1]

The French are getting on at Toulon rather faster than was expected. They have now 11 sail of the line ready for sea and in a few days will have two more, therefore my going must depend on Elphinstone's reinforcement of ships. It always rejoices me to hear you are comfortable and that my friends are attentive to you. I hope we shall find some snug cottage whenever we may be obliged to quit the Parsonage.

It is probable we shall get to sea in about 3 days from hence with Lord Hood in the *Victory* to Genoa, Port Especia and Vado Bay then off Gourgian Bay, Toulon and I hope to Gibraltar and England. When Lord Hood quits I should be truly sorry to remain.[2] He is the greatest sea officer I ever knew and what can be said against him I cannot conceive. It can only be envy. It is better to be envied than pitied, but it comes from the Army who have also poisoned some of our minds. The taking of Bastia contrary to all military judgement is such an attack on the understandings of these gentry that it is never to be forgiven and the mind to recover itself flies to revenge. General Stuart I am sorry to say has most deeply inbibed this diabolical leven.

Remember me kindly to my sister and Mr. Matcham and to other parts of my family when you write and believe me your most affectionate husband, HORATIO NELSON.

Josiah is very well.

To Mrs. Nelson, George Matcham's Esqr., Ringwood, Hants., Angleterre.

No. 88

[Nicolas, I, p. 490, part]

Agamemnon, Genoa Mole,
September 20, 1794

MY DEAR FANNY,—You will see by the date of my letter where *Agamemnon* is got too. We are too active to remain long in one place. Lord Hood and Admiral Hotham are gone to Port Especia in the Genoese territories not choosing to trust themselves here after what has happened with this republic. You know that the last ship here was Admiral Gell's squadron

---

[1] Nelson recorded in his log on September 9: 'The Physician of the fleet came on board and surveyed the ship's company, and found them in a very weak state.' Fresh meat, milk, bread and wine were supplied for the sick, but several died.
[2] Lord Hood was granted leave to return to England to recover his health.

when they broke the neutrality of the port by taking the *Modeste* French frigate and that Genoa has been blockaded ever since, to the detriment of none but the English for not [an] article was dearer on that account and all ships who were prevented from coming here by our cruisers sent their cargoes in small vessels which the insurers were obliged to pay for, but our minister [1] was too hasty and now he is obliged to recant. He is not arrived although he ought to have been here a week ago, but I suppose he waited to see how an English man of war would be received, which has been very well. This city is without exception the most magnificent I ever saw superior in many respects to Naples. If not quite so magnificent from the sea, yet on shore it is much superior. All are palaces on the grandest scale. However I trust we shall soon quit these grand scenes and return to England where all my charms are placed.

Lord Hood is inclined to take me with him and if it is proper I am sure of going with him or the convoy, and if I do not shall rest satisfied it was not in his power. Josiah is very well as he may tell you himself. Remember me kindly to my sister and Mr. Matcham and believe me your most affectionate husband, HORATIO NELSON.

[Postscript by Josiah Nisbet]

I hope you are well. We are now at anchor in Genoa mole; we expect to come home shortly with the *Victory* or with the convoy. I am your dutiful son, JOSIAH NISBET.

To Mrs. Nelson, George Matcham's Esqr., Ringwood, Hants., Angleterre.
[*Forwarded in another hand to:* Wm. Suckling Esq., Kentish Town, London.]

No. 89

[Nicolas, I, p. 491, part]

Agamemnon, Genoa,
September 27, 1794

MY DEAR FANNY,—We are just going to sea with Lord Hood and Admiral Hotham who came in here 4 days ago. We are going off Gourgen to look at the French ships, from thence off Toulon where the enemy have 6 sail ready for sea and most probably will soon make an effort to join their other ships. The French have taken possession of Vado Bay in the Genoa territories and of course will prevent our ships from anchoring and I have

---

[1] There was usually only a consul at Genoa, at this time John Brame. Francis Drake was minister of Turin.

little doubt but if the enemy turn their thoughts to the invasion of Italy but that next spring they will do it. The allied powers seem jealous of each other and none but England are hearty in the cause.

Lord Hood goes from the fleet to Corsica from whence he sails for England. I do not now think we have any chance of going with him. The fleet here cannot be lessened. Admiral Hotham [1] thinks we are too few, therefore I stand no chance of seeing you at present but let's hope whatever is is best. Many here are using their interest to go home when Elphinstone arrives therefore I have not nor do I build too much on my prospect of seeing you till the spring, by which time I hope the war will be over and we shall get to the farm again.

Remember me kindly where you are and believe me your most affectionate husband, HORATIO NELSON.

Josiah is very well 5 feet high he says he is 5 feet 1 inch. I have not wrote my father from hence.

To Mrs. Nelson, George Matcham's Esqr., Ringwood, Hants., Angleterre.

[*Forward in another hand to:* William Suckling Esq., Kentish Town, London.]

No. 90

[Nicolas, I, p. 493 part]

Agamemnon, off Gourgean,
October 3, 1794

MY DEAR FANNY,—I wrote you twice during my stay at Genoa. Lord Hood is gone to Leghorn to receive his dispatches by a messenger arrived there from England, and most probably we shall only see him to take leave before his departure for England where I have no chance of going at present. I give up all thoughts of it, for the French are now equal to us, Admiral Hotham will be commander-in-chief and with new men *new* measures are generally adopted, therefore I can at present say nothing about myself only that I am in most perfect health as is Josiah. To tell you this is the whole purport of a letter if it was to fill a sheet of paper. Let me hear often from you that is my greatest pleasure.

We are here 11 sail of the line the enemy have 14, 7 here 7 at Toulon. They will probably before the winter expires effect a junction when our

[1] Vice-Admiral William Hotham was senior officer in the Mediterranean in the interim period between Lord Hood's return to England and the appointment of Sir John Jervis at the end of 1795.

fleet will be kept together but whenever they choose to give us a meeting the event I have no doubt will be such as every English man has a right to expect.

Remember me kindly to my sister and Mr. Matcham, and believe me your most affectionate husband, HORATIO NELSON.

To Mrs. Nelson, George Matcham's Esqr., Ringwood, Hants., Angleterre.

No. 91

[Nicolas, I, p. 494, part, under date October 2]

Agamemnon, off Gourgean,
October 10, 1794

MY DEAR FANNY,—I am disappointed by not hearing from you this day when a ship from Leghorn has joined the fleet. I got a letter of September 1st from my good father and one from Captain Locker.[1] Lord Hood is to join us in a few days but I fear I have no chance whatever of going home. My ship's company are by no means recovered but we are destined to keep the seas till ship and crew are all rendered unfit for service.

Pray let me hear often from you, it is my greatest comfort. The enemy are in the same state as usual and we cannot get to them or our fag would soon be over. God bless you and believe me your most affectionate husband, HORATIO NELSON.

Josiah is very well. I scrawl this on board the *Britannia*.[2]

To Mrs. Nelson, George Matcham's Esqr., Ringwood, Hants., Angleterre.

No. 92

[Nicolas, I, p. 494, part, under earlier date]

Agamemnon, off Gourgean,
October 12, 1794

MY DEAR FANNY,—Lord Hood left us yesterday therefore all hopes of my going home at present are at an end. However we must not repine, it may turn out for the best. At all events I shall cheat the winter and as I under-

---

[1] Captain Locker had been appointed Lieutenant-Governor of Greenwich Hospital in 1793. He died in 1800.
[2] The flag-ship.

stand I am to have a cruise it may possibly be advantageous. I believe Lord Hood is very well inclined towards me to do civil things but the service must ever supersede all private consideration, so far about myself.

Now, how do you intend to spend the winter? Does Norfolk take up any part of it? I hope you will spend it cheerfully. All I beg is that you will not travel in a stage coach, this I insist upon. Perhaps if my father goes to Bath you will spend part of it with him. The Wolterton family I am sure will be happy to receive you for as long a time as you please. All I have to beg is that you will not repine at my not coming. I am sure Lord Hood will get *Agamemnon* ordered to England as soon as circumstances will admit of it.

When you go to London I beg you will call on Lady Hood and perhaps you will see the Lord. Before spring I hope we shall have peace when we must look out for some little cottage. I shall return to the plough with redoubled glee I assure you. I hope you are not sparing in sending to Marsh and Creed for money. I have never drawn on them since I have been in the Mediterranean. Do you get the interest of the legacy regularly paid? I hope you do, keep it yourself and don't trust any merchants with your little property. I had got several little matters which I wished to send home but the *Victory's* stay was only 2 hours with us therefore I lost the opportunity.

Josiah is very well and a good boy. Remember me kindly to Mr. Matcham and my sister and to those who enquire after me wherever you go.

God bless you and believe me your most affectionate HORATIO NELSON.

Two of my opponents which I fell in with last year about this time are now or near it in England *St Fiorenza* (late *La Minerve*) and *La Melpomene* both of 40 guns—18 pounders, two as fine frigates as are in the world. I have been fortunate in being present at the taking and destroying of that whole squadron and which but for our disabling them were intended for France, but being forced into Corsica are better disposed of. I wish you could think of some little matter which you think could be agreeable to send to my Aunt Mary, perhaps a little tea and sugar, a dozen of the best mountain wine, these I have heard her say are better than fine clothes. Get Mr. Thomas to do it and pay the carriage down to Hilborough.

October 15: Your last letter is dated August 18th—Letters are in the fleet to September 12th but a ship is now in sight hope she brings me some.

To Mrs. Nelson, George Matcham's Esqr., Ringwood, Hants., Angleterre.

APPENDIX

Nelson's Sea Journal [1]

June 27, 1793, to April 1, 1794

June 27th: Sailed from Gibraltar with 19 sail of the line, and a convoy of merchantships under *St. Albans.*

June 30th: Off Cape De Gatte *Iris* and *Tisiphone* were sent to Tripoli and Tunis, *L'Aigle* to Barcelona with letters for the Spanish Admiral. Parted from the convoy.

From July 1st to 7th: Spoke many neutral vessels from Marseilles who informed us that the French had 30 sail of the line ready for sea and that 3 Spanish frigates had been carried into Toulon. This information we did not believe and now know it to be absolutely false.

July 7th: In the evening off Alicante saw a large fleet lay too all night between that place and Irica. At daylight on the 8th formed our line of battle a head. Found them to be the Spanish fleet 24 sail of the line. The Dons attempted to form a line for 4 hours but not succeeding sent a frigate to Lord Hood to say they were very sickly and going into port. The Captain of the frigate told his Lordship it was no wonder they were sickly for they had been 60 days at sea. It appeared rather extraordinary to me that no salutes whatever took place.

July 9th: Leda sent to Barcelona.

July 13th: L'Aigle and *Leda* joined, the news they bring is that the French are preparing their ships with forges for shot, this information if true I humbly think would have been as well kept secret, but we must take care to get so close that the shot may go through both sides when it will not matter whether they are hot or cold.

July 14th: Received orders to consider Marseilles and Toulon as invested and to take all vessels bound into those ports. This order may induce these red hot gentlemen to come out.

July 16th: Made Cape Sicie about 5 miles from Toulon; in the afternoon saw 3 sail to leeward. *Leda* and *Illustrious* were sent in chase. Between 9 and 10 a firing was heard for half an hour, when I believe every person in the fleet expected to have seen some of the enemy's ships brought in.

July 17th: The above ships joined us with a corvette they had taken

[1] N.M.M., M.S. 9960: Croker Collection in the Phillipps papers, June 27, 1793–February 23, 1794. The continuation is in B.M. Add. MS. 34,902.

that morning. The ships they fired at were 3 French frigates who after giving and receiving fire got away. The account we have hitherto heard has only been from a disappointed flag ship. The following are allowed to be facts, that our ships got near enough to hail them, had some men killed (Master of the *Illustrious* one of them), that it was a bright moon till 12 o'clock and all night very light airs of wind.

July 19th: Close off Toulon saw several ships in the outer road with sails bent, a flag of truce was sent in to propose an exchange of prisoners. Till the 23rd we had a very heavy gale of wind from the N.W. *Berwick* parted company and from her signals of distress are much alarmed for her. *Leda* lost her main mast and went for Leghorn with the *Romney.* *Meleager* was ordered to attend *Berwick* but unfortunately missed her.

July 25th: The flag of truce joined us from Toulon. It is uncertain whether the French will exchange prisoners with us. They have 16 sail of the line in the outer road of Toulon ready for sea and five sail fitting. The *Commerce of Marseilles* carries 136 guns and 1,800 men (having guns on her gangways). The prisoners we have, believe her sides are so thick that our shot will not go through them, and that she can with ease take the *Victory.* We have our opinions whether they will come out or not. In my opinion when they have 21 sail ready and we under 20 they will come out, the people will force them to it.

July 26: *Ardent* sent to Leghorn. Our fleet only 17 sail of the line.

August 5th: Laying off Toulon from the 26th ult. Yesterday *Alcide* and 2 frigates sent to Genoa. Our fleet only 16 sail of the line. An express from Capt. Inglefield that on his attempting to come out of Genoa two French frigates showed every movement that they would not regard the neutrality of the port, but should come out with him. They hauled on board *L'Aigie* hoisted up their yards and showed him every insult.

August 6th: *Illustrious* sent down to Barcelona and Gibraltar with French prisoners.

August 7th: Fleet steering to the eastward going off Villa Franca and Nice.

August 8th: Prince Augustus Frederic joined the fleet in the *Aquillon* attended by *Romney.* The *Victory* hoisted the standard and Lord Hood shifted his flag to the *Egmont.* The *Aquillon* and *Romney* parted in the evening. *Meleager* sent to reconnoitre 3 sail standing down.

August 9th: Ordered to put myself under Roberts orders with *Colossus* and *Romulus.* The fleet standing to the eastward.

August 10th: Chased and spoke a ship from Toulon. The French fleet 17 sail of the line ready for sea, saw our fleet to the eastward. The French by this ship in no want of provisions.

K

August 11th: After a long chase spoke two Spanish smugglers and a Dutch vessel from Toulon who had been detained since last January. The French have 17 sail of the line ready for sea, but no discipline. The people ordered for the defence of Toulon (300 guns) had all gone to Marseilles.

August 12th: Colossus joined having chased since the 11th in the forenoon a French frigate, also joined the *Mermaid* frigate sent from off Tunis by Capt. Lumsdain to say the French fleet was there one 80 gun ship five frigates etc., and convoy.

August 13th: Calm all day. A Hanoverian who left Toulon in a Genoese boat Sunday last says that every day the number of ships seen from the signal house is published on board the Admiral's ship and at the Grand Place the numbers made for the populace are sometimes 60 sail of the line. Has been as high as 85 sail consisting of English, Spanish and Dutch fleet which is the reason they are told their fleet does not come out. That the red hot shot are kept ready from the time of our fleet's first appearance: that a rostrum is erected in the Grand Place where on extraordinary news it is proclaimed. The battle of the frigates and our ships was spoke of in the highest terms of applause: that our ships were a 74 and 60 gun ship, that the 60 would certainly have been taken but for the proximity of the English fleet. He says two sorts of people are seen, one all fear and horror, the other mad and drunk. That a tail block is commonly in the crowd, and any person who a single one of the nobility does not like is instantly hung up or guillotined if they choose to take the trouble to carry them so far, and that no enquiry or punishment is inflicted: that hardly a day passes without some murders.

August 14th: Saw a sail to the Southward. *Robust* and ourselves chased for 30 hours when we spoke her found her to be a Spanish privateer of 18 nine pounders 120 men: out 4 months spoke nothing.

August 16th: Stopped a Ragusa snow from Marseilles to Smyrna richly laden, intend sending her to Leghorn.

From August 16th to 18th: Nothing particular. On the 18th in the afternoon saw two ships armed steering close alongshore; gave chase fired two shot at them when they hauled under a French battery and hoisted Genoese colours. On getting within gun shot the battery fired at us but not a shot took place, ours hit the battery, blocked up the vessels all night.

August 19th: In the morning stopped a Genoese brig sent her in to say that if the ships were Genoese to come out, for if they did not I should consider them as French and as soon as the sea breeze set in should run in and burn them. On this message being delivered every vessel came out and although they were loaded with French property yet their papers were so clear that I was obliged to let them go. Found we had struck the battery several times and that a man had lost his arm.

August 20th: Joined Lord Hood with the convoy (under *St. Alban, Castor,* and *Bulldog*) from England consisting of 97 sail. From the observations I have been able to make it appears that the French have very little provisions at either Marseilles or Toulon and that they would gladly make peace with us on almost any terms.

August 23rd: This morning three commissioners came off from Marseilles to say that they had only 11 days provisions and to request that Lord Hood would either go and take possession of Marseilles or allow them to receive provisions from the neutral ports and that the Prussian army was very near and that they must either be starved or put to the sword, that Commissioners were coming from Toulon with similar offers. Lord Hood made the signal for all flag officers. I hope he will not accept anything from the Marseillois unless Toulon and the French fleet is delivered up to us as security for their good behaviour.

From the 23rd to 26th: The negotiation still going on. The following are the circumstances of this very extraordinary negotiation. A number of people belonging to the municipality of Toulon are on board Lord Hood wishing to acknowledge Louis XVII as their sovereign agreeable to the constitution of 1789. The fleet is in the utmost disorder. Many of the Captains and officers willing to deliver up their ships and some of the crews are of the same way of thinking. Others are for coming out to fight us and are known by the denomination of Clubbists. Time and famine may do much for us. The government of Hières has offered Hières bay for the fleet to anchor in and the men are withdrawn from the forts on the islands. At Marseilles Louis XVII is proclaimed. Lord Hood however cannot take possession of Marseilles. We have no troops for the defence of an almost open town. Toulon is the only object for us to get hold of, and to destroy their fleet. This is certainly a most extraordinary situation for an Admiral to be placed in and if Lord Hood brings it to an happy issue he will deserve every honour which his country can bestow, as will all his fleet, for it is by their indefatigable perseverance night and day that the enemy have not been able to get supplied with provisions and are reduced to the humble necessity of treating. *Who* could have thought the proud Marseillois would have been so soon tamed? *But hunger will tame a Lion, so says Josiah.*

On the 27th: The Committee from Toulon came off to Lord Hood with such terms as he has thought proper to accept, viz: that their fleet shall be laid up and the colours and constitution accepted by Louis XVI should be in force. I was immediately sent off with dispatches for the courts of

Turin and Naples with a requisition for 4,000 troops from Sardinia and 6,000 troops from Naples. When I had got a few miles from the fleet a Sardinian frigate joined and I was called back and ordered to see her safe clear of Corsica.

On the 31st: spoke the *Tartar* who informed us that on the 28th our troops took possession of the batteries at the harbour mouth and that on the 29th our fleet and that of Spain who just arrived sailed into the harbour of Toulon, the French fleet being previously moved into the inner port, Admiral St. Julien with about 300 men left their ships and are gone to join General Corteau who took Marseilles on the 28th and crushed the party who were in treaty with us.

In the evening of the 31st: landed my dispatches at Oneglia and got off some fresh meat for the ship's company.

September 1st: This day the Sardinian frigate took on board £100,000 for the payment of the troops in Sardinia. This frigate although very handsome sails intolerably ill and detains us very much indeed.

September 3rd: Close in with Corsica very little winds southerly, the Sardinian cannot move.

September 4th: Off Bastia sent a letter on shore to General Paoli to acquaint him that Toulon is in our possession.

September 5th: Spoke a ship from Scio with corn was in great hopes she had been a French frigate, also a Turkish ship from Constantinople with corn.

September 7th: Parted from the Sardinian frigate. Spoke a ship from Cyprus under Ragusa colours richly laden. At even spoke a Ragusa brig from Genoa bound to Malta, kept her all night examined her very strictly.

September 8th: Took possession of a Ragusa brig 10 guns from Smyrna bound to Marseilles, sent her into Leghorn with Mr. Andrews.

September 9th: Spoke the *Speedy* brig from Naples to Leghorn four days out. Sent our great news to Mons. Calvonne who was on board.

September 10th: Made the Islands of Pounce, steering for the Bay of Naples which we entered in the night. The throws of fire from Mount Vesuvius were grand.

September 11th: At 2 o'clock anchored in the Bay of Naples. The King sent and ordered us pratique and an officer from the Admiral with compliments and to say the King was on board his ship. I immediately went on board to pay my duty. I found the news of Toulon having been taken had reached Naples on the 6th September and that it was reported by the Castilian sent to Leghorn that it was taken by the Spanish and English fleets. I took the liberty to inform his Majesty of the truth and that the treaty was signed and ratified before the Spanish fleet hove in sight. The King seemed surprised but said he was glad to hear it and that the Spaniard had *Trompe Trompe.* I presented his Majesty with a list of the French fleet and said what Lord Hood wanted now was troops to secure our possession. I told him that to my Lord Hood's perseverance only was to attributed our success. The King replied that no person had a higher opinion of Lord Hood than he had and was sensible that to his Lordship and his fleet was Italy indebted for security, that we were the saviours of Italy and of his Kingdom in particular.

Went on shore to Sir William Hamilton our ambassador and delivered Lord Hood's dispatches and communicated all the information I had got respecting Toulon and Lord Hood's wishes about the troops. We went immediately to Sir John Acton Baronet, the Prime Minister, who appointed at 9 o'clock in the evening to be at his office. We accordingly went and his Excellency communicated the King's pleasure in the following words as far as I recollect: 'The King is highly sensible of the magnitude of the success of the English fleet of the necessity of securing Toulon, that Lord Hood's wishes communicated by Captain Nelson to your excellency shall be immediately complied with, but this point is to be considered: Lord Hood's fleet is short of provisions, at Toulon they are not to be expected to be obtained, therefore whether it would not be better to wait a few days and to carry provisions with them, than to go and be a trouble to Lord Hood instead of a service.'

Sir William replied that if only 2,000 men could sail in 3 or 4 days it would perhaps be of more service than the six thousand might if kept back for a fortnight. Sir John said then that shall be done, 2,000 shall be ready with provisions in 4 days and that the others should be ready as soon as possible. His Excellency expressed the highest respect for Lord Hood and thought the Spaniard had not done handsomely in propagating a report which had no truth in it.

September 12th: Requested to dine with Sir John Acton. Before dinner he informed Sir William and myself that the necessary orders had been given to hasten the embarkation of the troops that he hoped they would embark on Sunday and be ready to sail on Monday. After dinner I mentioned to Sir William Hamilton that the King had been pleased to express himself in the handsomest manner of Lord Hood's services as had also his Excellency Sir John Acton, that words might be misunderstood and that if it could be brought about I should like the King to write to Lord Hood. Sir William immediately informed the Minister of my wishes and conversing on the subject I mentioned the Emperor Charles as having wrote to Sir George Byng on his success against the Spanish fleet. Sir John said he would speak to the King about it and let us know his pleasure. His

Excellency then took occasion to say that the troops were considered as only under Lord Hood, that the treaty was only between England and Naples and hoped they would not be put under Spanish generals or Sardinians, that wherever Lord Hood wished them to serve there they would always be ready. At night sent to acquaint Sir William that the King would write a letter with his own hand.

September 13th: The Minister sent to Sir William and myself to come to him and acquainted Sir William that the King would write a letter to Lord Hood with his own hand and showed Sir William the copy of the letter and that the King desired me to go to Portici at 8 o'clock. The Spanish frigate who went to Leghorn arrived in the bay.

At 8 o'clock went with Sir William to Portici. The King was attentive. Spoke in the handsomest manner of Lord Hood and his fleet and told me he should come on board to see the ship on Sunday and desired me to dine with him afterwards at the Cassern. The Queen being 8 months with child I was not presented to her.

September 14th: Received a note from Sir John Acton to dine with him. Was obliged to stop our watering and prepare the ship for the reception of the King. It begins to blow a strong sirroc wind. At dinner before the Spanish ambassador and Captain and a great company His Excellency came to me in the middle of the room and expressed himself in the following terms:—

'Inclosed in a letter to you is a letter from His Sicilian Majesty wrote with his own hand for my Lord Hood which the King desires you will present to him at your first meeting.'[1]

After dinner he desired Sir William and myself to stay after the company were gone and showed me his most magnificent house and said something besides a letter might be thought of for my Lord Hood. In the evening the Princess of Belle Mont came to Lady Hamilton to be introduced to me and to say that Her Majesty was sorry she could not see me, and that the Princess would come on board on Monday to see my ship. This lady is first lady of the chamber to the Queen.

September 15th: Sir William Hamilton and myself went on board at 8 o'clock the King having wrote to Sir John Acton that he should be on board his own ship at ½ past 8 in the morning. There was a very great swell. At ½ past an officer came from the King to say the swell was too great for him to come afloat. At 1 o'clock went to dinner where the King placed me at his right hand. He said every handsome about not having come on board but that he certainly would come before I sailed. His Majesty told Sir William Hamilton that he wished I would look at his

_____
[1] See Appendix, p. 150.

troops in the morning at 6 o'clock when he should be at their head marching into town and that they would embark about noon and the ships sail Tuesday morning, with 2,000 and that the frigates should go to Sayette for the other 2,000 at the same time. The King told me to tell Lord Hood that he should be glad to see him at Naples and that if he would come the Queen would go on board and dine with him. In speaking of the troops he desired me to tell Lord Hood that the troops on board ship as Marines were Albanese–Macedonians, that they were good cannoniers and handled the broad sword well and to take them out of the ships if you wanted them therefore 5,000 troops would be sent off within the week.

September 16th: Went to see the King at the head of the Grenadiers, who as we went a little on the road to be out of the crowd, His Majesty as soon as he saw us made his troops halt and dressed them before they marched by us, went on board with Lady Hamilton etc., to breakfast and hoped to have got a good quantity of water on board. An noon an extract came from Sir John Acton to inform me through Sir William Hamilton that there was anchored off the south end of Sardinia one French corvette with a small English ship her prize and two ships under her convoy from Smyrna bound to Leghorn. That they would have sent but they were otherwise employed. Although my ship was almost without water, casks on shore for wine etc., yet I considered that the city of Naples looked what an English man of war would do, I ordered my barge to be manned, sent the ladies on shore and in two hours my ship was under sail, all our boats etc., hoisted in. God send us good success. I believe we carry with us the good wishes of Naples and of Sir William Hamilton and Lady Hamilton in particular which I esteem more than all the rest. Farewell Naples. May those who were kind to me be repaid ten fold. If I am successful I return, if otherwise go to Toulon.

I should be wanting did I not say how active Sir William Hamilton has been in getting these troops sent off, for left to themselves I am sure they would not have sailed these 3 weeks. The vanity of the —— of Naples is such that he wished to cut a great figure by sending his stipulated force all at the same time and to that vanity are we now indebted for the 4,000 instead of the 2,000 at first promised.

September 17th: Saw a sail at 4 o'clock to windward coming down before the wind. When she got within 4 leagues she hauled her wind for the Neapolitan shore; I don't think she was French. Saw the Neapolitan squadron to leeward. At night spoke an English ship from Leghorn bound to Smyrna who had been plundered the day before by a galley in company with a small ship. He supposed them Algerines.

September 18th: The Neapolitan squadron in sight at 3 p.m. saw 2 sail bearing down. After dark the two vessels steering for us. At 10 o'clock they hoisted lights to each other the galley first. At 11 o'clock one steering for our bow the other for our quarter. At ½ past 11 the ship hauled for our quarter, fired a shot over them. They immediately hauled on a wind to the southward. Fired a 2nd shot when the galley towed her head round and stood to the northward. Saw two large boats out, fired 4 shot at the ship and finding her lay quiet sent a boat on board who found no creature a board her. The galley standing on a wind to the northward wore after the galley fired a number of shot and grape at her, on her not bearing down concluded the people had left her. Stopped firing and sent a boat who found her deserted. They appear to be Genoese vessels, bound for Palermo and from thence to Marseilles. They could hardly have taken us for Algerines, as they altered their course after dark to speak us. Found they mounted four guns each 6 swivels and plenty of small arms all loaded and matches a light. Suspect they are the vessels who boarded the English ship, sent them to Leghorn.

18th: Fine weather: from that to the 22nd hard gales from the westward and a heavy sea.

23rd: Of Cape Corse saw nothing.

24th: Not seeing anything in the morning made sail for Leghorn not having either water or provisions on board. In the evening anchored in the road. Found here a French frigate *L'Imperieuse* ready for sea.

From 24th to 30th: Gales of wind easterly employed getting provisions and water on board, and watching the French frigate who would certainly have put to sea if I gave him any opportunity.

On the 30th: At 4 in the morning sailed, hope to catch the French man. Providence will put me one time or other I hope in the way to take a French man of war.

1st October: Saw a fleet in the S.W. bore away and spoke them. The Neapolitan fleet of transports under two frigates and two brigs. In the afternoon took a Genoese boat laden with bale goods to Corsica. Sent her to Leghorn.

2nd: Looking out for the frigate. Spoke some boat from Leghorn who inform us the French frigate is not coming out for 4 or 5 days. Saw a ship of war in the N.W. could not get to her being calm. All night a gale of wind from the S.W.

3rd: Spoke a brig from Barcelona to Genoa. At 3 o'clock saw three ships of war in the S.W. made sail and gave chase. Found them in a Spanish first rate one of 74, one 50 gun ship, made the private signal. Blowing a gale of wind all night.

N.B. at sun set saw 7 sail of the line supposed Spanish.

4th: In the morning calm saw two sail in shore and 16 sail in the offing. In the afternoon took a small French boat with wine for Corsica.

5th: Arrived in Toulon harbour.

6th: 7th: and 8th: Employed fitting my ship for sea, shot and shells are throwing about us every hour, but such is the force of habit we seem to feel perfectly safe. The enemy have many strong posts on the hills which are daily augmented with men.

9th: At 3 o'clock this morning a party of English under Lt. Sericold and a party of Spaniards to the amount of 450 made a sortie to an advanced work of the enemy's. The guide got them so close that the sentinel had not time to fire his piece and only said 'Pardieu La troops Anglois.' He was instantly bayonetted and our troops got into the enemy's mortar battery before they were seen, when trusting entirely to the bayonet the French run for their gun battery our people followed them into it, drove them a heap and turned their own guns against them. The mortars, guns and battery was entirely destroyed. One Lt. Colonel an officer and 20 men were brought in and 150 left killed and wounded. Our loss 3 killed 7 wounded. The Spaniards behaved infamously deserting the English, being only intent on plunder.

In the evening I sailed under secret orders.

10th and 11th: Turning to the eastward.

12th: Saw a fleet which proved to be *Fortitude* with a convoy from Toulon for Marseilles.

13th: Turning up the east side of Corsica saw a French frigate in Calvi ready for sea, to the

16th: Calms and beating to the N.E. at day light took a French transport from Bastia to Antibes with troops going to join the army before Toulon. In the afternoon spoke *Colossus* who took her under protection for Leghorn.

17th: Spoke a number of neutral vessels off Bastia, in the afternoon saw a small vessel which by the report of the vessels spoke this morning I took to be French privateer. Sent a boat manned and armed in pursuit of her. She got into Cabreea. The officer landed and went to the Governor to know if he had any objection to our taking her out. He said no, on the contrary she was a nuisance to the place and had taken a Spanish brig the day before and chased an English one into Leghorn. On hearing this report sent 3 boats armed with 1st lieutenant in search of her. He could not find her, but the officer of the guard came on board our boat, showed us a French boat which he said we might take out of the harbour, between 2 and 300 people assisted the lieutenant in moving her clear of the vessels.

Found her from Bastia, the cargo admitted to be French but the bottom said to be Genoese. In the afternoon stood under Planosa where we thought by information to have found some French privateers.

From 18th to 21st: Making the best of our way to Cagliari. In the night of the 21st fell in with 5 sail of French men of war, four frigates and a brig. Brought one of the frigates to action but a calm prevented our capturing her. The other frigates (I fancy found enough to do to take care of their consort who appeared well hided) declined bringing us again to battle although with such a superiority they ought to have taken us. Each had more men than the *Agamemnon* had on board, the remainder of our complement being landed at Toulon. Their force united was as follows:—

            70 . . . nine pounders
            16 . . . twelve pounders
            56 . . . eighteen pounders
            28 . . . thirty-six pounders
            ———
            170 guns–1,600 men.

Agamemnon:—   12 . . . nine pounders
            26 . . . eighteen pounders
            26 . . . twenty-four pounders
            ———
            64 guns–345 men.

The enemy superior to us:—

            106 guns–1,255 men.

How thankful ought I to be and I hope am for the mercies of Almighty God manifested to me this day. We lost only one man killed and six wounded, although my ship was cut to pieces, being obliged to receive the enemy's fire under every disadvantage believing for a long time one of the enemy to have been of the line.

My thanks and offerings to the Almighty have been nearly in the same words and certainly with the same meaning as those so inimitably wrote in the *Spectator:*—[1]

'When I lay me down to sleep I recommend myself to the care of Almighty God, when I awake I give myself up to his direction, amidst all the evils that threaten me, I will look up to him for help, and

[1] Addison's *Spectator*, No. 7, March 8, 1711, closing sentences.

question not but he will either avert them, or turn them to my advantage, though I know neither the time nor the manner of my death, I am not at all solicitous about it, because I am sure that He knows them both, and that he will not fail to support and comfort me under them.'

Arrived at Cagliari on the 24th in the morning where the Commodore did not think it right to give us the least assistance, but sent to me to give my reasons if I could not go to sea with him the next morning totally unfit as my ship was which he knew I would not say *Agamemnon* was ever unable to go in search of an enemy. We worked all night fishing our masts and yards and stopping shot holes, mending sails and splicing our rigging.

25th: At daylight sailed with *Alcide, Berwick, Illustrious, Lowestoffe,* and *Nemesis* under Commodore Linzee in search of the enemy till the 28th going along Sardinia when we got a fair wind gave over the pursuit when I think it probable that the enemy were either at Port Vecchio or Bonafacio in Corsica within 12 leagues of us.

29th: Finished fishing our masts and repairing our sails. To my very great joy in the evening got a strong wind from the N.W.

31st: At daylight saw the Barbary coast working in for Tunis bay all the day. At 7 o'clock in the evening anchored in Tunis Bay. Run *Agamemnon* between a line of battle ship and a frigate which I take to be the *Duquesne* and a 40 gun frigate in a most glorious situation for service which if it pleases God to spare my life I will most effectually perform.

November 1st: A handful of wind all day *La Duquesne* and a corvette are the only French ships of war here and a few merchantmen. The Commodore does not choose to act against them till he has seen the Consul.

From November 1st to the 6th: Carrying on a damned palaver with the Bey. We are negotiating when in my opinion we ought to have been acting. Whoever yet heard of an Englishman's succeeding in a negotiation against the French. *Never, never, never.* How much better could we have negotiated with a French 80 gun ship and a corvette, and merchandise to the value of £300,000 in our possession. My spirits are low, we shall do nothing, and of course be laughed at.

November 7th: The Commodore went to Tunis to talk with the Bey. Have no great idea we shall improve English negotiation here.

November 10th: Commodore made the signal for all captains, and informed us that he had an audience of the Bey, who had refused us leave to attack the French men, that he had sent the *Nemesis* to Toulon for Lord Hood's further orders, during which time he had promised the Bey not to attack the French men. He wished to know our opinion of what was now to be done should the *Duquesne* attempt to get under the Moorish forts, as he considered himself bound only as she lay fast.

My opinion was this. That as I should have thought it right to have taken all the French men in the first instance without asking the Bey's leave, therefore as Commodore had pledged himself not to attack the *Duquesne* till he heard from Lord Hood unless she moved, it was my opinion that she would take the first opportunity of moving nigher under the forts, and that if she made such an attempt, to take her. This seemed the general opinion when I left them, and orders were given for moving our ships within her, but the Commodore has altered his mind I suppose, for no signal has yet been made and the enemy may move when ever he pleases. My spirits are low indeed. Had I been Commodore most likely I should have been broke by this time, for certainly I should have taken every French man here without negotiating, even had negotiations taken place, I would have had the French men of war and believe that the people of England will never blame an officer for taking a French line of battle ship.

November 11th: Arrived a French vessel with provisions etc., for *Le Duquesne.*

November 12th: Lowestoffe ordered to sea. We are shutting the stable door now the steed is stolen.

Till November 16th: Doing nothing. On that day went to sea where I stayed till November 26th in one continued gale of wind, lightning and rain. Chased the French gun boat but she got into Buserte.

November 29th: Received orders from Lord Hood to take *Lowestoffe* with me and go off Corsica and look for some French frigates and to take all the frigates stationed there under my command. Sailed in the evening *Lowestoffe* in company.

November 30th: A fine breeze got round Cape Carbonarre at noon, in the evening thunder, lightning and rain. Spoke a brig from Boston bound to Naples.

Till December 4th: When we got off Cape Corse chased a Neapolitan convoy. Nothing particular till December 8th when we got a fine wind and run into St. Fiorenzo. Saw four frigates at anchor close under the batteries, the wind will never allow us to get at them, *Melpomene, Minerva, Fortunee* and *Minion.*

From 5th to 14th: Continued gales of westerly winds. On the 14th took a French gun boat going to St. Fiorenzo. The crew got on shore.

December 15th: A French Polacco brig attempted to get to sea from St. Fiorenzo. We had very near caught her; all the afternoon within 3 miles of the enemy's squadron with our colours flying daring them to come out, a French 64 dared not treat an English squadron with such contempt.

December 16th: All day close to the French squadron with our colours hoisted, nothing I believe will tempt them to come out.

December 17th: Sent our boat on shore to Isle Rousse where we learnt that the French squadron had got into St. Fiorenzo on November 5th two frigates, and a corvette, that the Calvi frigate had joined them a few days after their arrival, that they were in the greatest distress for provisions and got none but what they nightly plundered, that the frigate we fired at October 21st was much shattered in her hull and masts and lost above half her men. In the night fell in with the *Lowestoffe, Meleager* and *Amphitrite*.

December 18th: Sent *Meleager* and *Amphitrite* to Leghorn for provisions.

December 19th: Lowestoffe took a Genoese brig from St. Fiorenzo who had been supplying the French with necessaries. In the night fell in with a Neapolitan convoy under two frigates from Naples bound to Toulon, could not get them to bring too.

December 20th: Cruising off Cabrera *Lowestoffe* sent a Dane ship into Leghorn.

December 21st: Sent a boat on shore to Cabrera where they gave us pratique, parted from *Lowestoffe*.

December 22nd: Got into Leghorn where we remained till the 2nd of January. The Consul's people are the slowest at getting water etc., for a ship that ever I saw and at Leghorn they all seem to wish to keep the English men of war in port. Sent *Meleager* and *Amphitrite* to cruise off St. Fiorenzo.

On the 25th: Leda and *Lowestoffe* to join them.

On the 31st: Lowestoffe to proceed on secret service.

January 1st (1794): Getting all on board ready for sea, sent an officer and 30 seamen to take care of *Topaze* French frigate.

January 2nd: Sailed with *Topaze* for Porto Ferraio in the Isle of Elbe. Arrived the 3rd, found here the *Britannia*, Admiral Hotham, *Windsor Castle*, Admiral Cosby, *Commerce de Marseilles*, Admiral Trogulf. 3 ships 3 admirals.

January 4th: Getting water on board and repairing our rigging.

Sunday 5th: At daylight got under way running all day for Cape Corse.

January 6th: All day strong breezes bore away for St. Fiorenzo. At noon within 2 miles of the French squadron hoisted our colours, Fort Mortello fired one shot at us and hoisted national colours. Three frigates ready for sea one dismantled. A gale of wind all night.

January 7th: Joined *Leda, Meleager* and *Amphitrite,* Captain Campbell acquainted me that one of the frigates had been out twice, once on the 3rd and again on the 5th, that a deserter had come off to the *Lowestoffe,* who told them they were very much distressed for provisions, and that one of the frigates was dismantled and her guns landed, that each ship had 300 men on board.

January 8th: Hard gales and heavy rains close off St. Fiorenzo.

January 9th: 10th: 11th: Hard gales and a heavy sea and constant torrent of rain. 50 men in the sick list.

January 12th: In the morning strong gales, at noon saw a firing between *Leda* and *Meleager* and two French frigates, who got into Calvi. They in hopes from the excessive bad weather we were drove off our station attempted to get to sea notwithstand we made all sail in standing in shore we got light winds variable and a heavy sea, we could get nearer them than 6 or 7 miles. Had the wind stood to a certainty we had cut them off from Calvi. How unfortunate to us, but on the other hand how fortunate for the service that we were enabled by the closest attention to keep on our station, it has fagged us all very much. At night a gale of wind from the N.W.

January 13th: Westerly gale all day and heavy rain.

January 14th: A most beautiful day. Captain Campbell came to inform me of his damages which are considerable in his masts, but fortunately not a man killed and only 9 wounded. The French had 8 killed 5 wounded. Sent *Meleager* and *Amphitrite* off Calvi.

January 15th: Saw only two ships in St. Fiorenzo. Sent a boat on shore with a letter for General Paoli and an officer to go to him. Sent *Amphitrite* to look for a Genoese brig said to be at anchor about 7 miles to leeward of Calvi. Took my station off Calvi, sent *Lowestoffe* to lay off St. Fiorenzo, ordered *Meleager* to join her. The French ships ready for sea.

January 16th: Close to Calvi all day. It appears pretty strong. Fresh breezes.

January 17th: Saw a ship and galley standing for Calvi. Sent *Leda* and *Amphitrite* after them, it falling calm the galley rowed away from *Leda* but *Amphitrite* drove the ship on shore and totally destroyed her by fire. She was a National ship of war called *L'armee de Italie,* 10 guns 8 swivels and full of men, loaded with flour for Calvi.

January 18th: Close off Calvi all day.

January 19th: *Juno* frigate joined me from Lord Hood.

Monday 20th: Received a letter from the Commandant of Isle Rousse that the enemy had 400 sacks of flour in a mill near St. Fiorenzo and that it would be of the greatest consequence if I could destroy it, as not only the loss of the flour, but that there was no mill nearer than Bastia. I determined to attempt destroying it and getting a person from Isle Rousse to show us the place, bore away and made all sail in the evening and all night becalmed in the gulf, expecting my ship to be drove on shore every minute. A heavy sea and no possibility of anchoring.

January 21st: Getting my ship within two gun shots of the landing place I landed 60 soldiers and 60 seamen under cover of a gun boat. They met with some opposition but landed, hove all the flour and corn into the sea, and burned the water mill, the moment the people in St. Fiorenzo saw what we were after they sent down 3 gun boats and five launches full of troops to oppose us or cut off the retreat, but the officers employed much to their credit, so well managed the business that every thing was effectually completed and the troops under cover of my guns by the time the enemy's gun boats opened their fire. Their shot fell short, the shot from our gun boat went over them. This little matter will give the Corsicans confidence which I find it is necessary to do. Took two Tartans with provisions for the frigates and garrison.

January 22nd: Sent a boat on shore at Isle Rousse. The prisoners gave us information that 8,000 troops were embarked on board eleven sail of transports under convoy of one frigate 36 guns one 24, two gabars 24 guns each, one brig 16 guns one zebeck. Detained the *Juno*, placed *Leda*, *Juno*, and *Meleager* off Calvi. *Billet* who just joined with information from Commodore Linzee that the enemy intended to land 12,000 men at Bastia and to recommend my sending ships to prevent them. My opinion of this officer has been long formed and I never have had reason to alter it. Ordered *Billet* to lay off Isle Rousse, to repeat signals between the two squadrons about 7 or 8 leagues asunder. *Agamemnon* and *Lowestoffe* to be between Cape Corse and St. Fiorenzo. I trust with this disposition it will be almost impossible for the enemy to land troops without our intercepting them. Sent *Amphitrite* away with Sir G. Elliot.

January 23rd: Off Cape Corse sent *Lowestoffe* in chase, saw about noon a large smoke near *Leda* and *Juno* which I take to be a vessel on fire.

January 24th: *Lowestoffe* took a Genoese boat which was cast away in the gale of the 26th and 27th.

January 25th: Fresh gales all day, in the evening saw 6 sail to the westward. In the night spoke several vessels under Lord Hood's convoy.

January 26th: Strong gales saw the *Victory* went on board her, Lord Hood not being able to land the troops, bore away for Port Ferraio; [1] all night hard gales.

[1] In Elba.

January 27th: Very heavy gales all day. *Leda* made signal of distress and parted company. In the afternoon every appearance of a storm. Made the ship as snug as possible all night it blew such a gale as is very seldom felt, neither canvas or rope could stand it. All our sails blew in pieces. Made a great deal of water. A most amazing heavy sea. The ship under bare poles.

January 28th: Anchored in Leghorn roads with *Lowestoffe, Juno* and *Meleager.*

January 29th and 30th: Strong gales.

January 31st: Moderate weather made the signal to weigh not one of the squadron was able to put to sea but myself.

February 1st: Got on my station fine weather. *Dido* in company.

February 2nd: Joined *Le Bilette* who brought me letters from Lord Hood with 3 gun boats, found to my great joy that the French had not landed in Corsica, or the frigates sailed, that 12,000 men are embarked at Nice under convoy of *Le Duquesne* 80 guns, 8 frigates and four corvettes. Yet if they come I think we shall give a good account of them.

February 3rd: Lowestoffe, June, Meleager, and *Romulus* joined. Send *Juno, Meleager* and *Dido* with a gun boat to lay off Calvi.

February 4th: Off St. Fiorenzo fine weather. Wish Lord Hood would arrive, the enemy hard at work on the batterys at Fiorenzo.

February 5th: L'Aigle joined with letters from Lord Hood to say he would sail the first moment he could get to sea. Having received information that at the little port of Centuri the enemy had seized our prize who was blown on the coast, and that they had several vessels loaded with wine for Fiorenzo, I determined to destroy the vessels and ordered Captain Wolseley of the *Lowestoffe* to perform that service but on no account to fire or plunder the village. Landed under cover of the *Lowestoffe* the marines of *Lowestoffe* and *Romulus* with but little opposition and totally destroyed four vessels loaded with 150 tons of wine with the loss of only one man wounded. Several of the enemy fell. The inhabitants came to the officers on shore to thank them for their humanity in sparing the village from fire and plunder. This service was accomplished much to the credit of Capt. Wolseley and the officers landed as well the men and to my entire satisfaction.

February 6th: Vanneau joined with letters from Lord Hood to say he could not get out yesterday to his very great disappointment but that Commodore Linzee with some of the transports were at sea and would join me during the day. At noon Commodore Linzee joined till night laying too. In my humble opinion the troops might with ease have been landed tonight. Beware of dilatoriness. Expedition ought to be the universal word and deed.

February 7th: Joined Lord Hood who expressed himself very much satisfied with my service and gave me the choice to take the command of the ship off the port of Calvi or to command the ship off the port of Bastia. I chose the latter and in the evening joined the ship off Bastia. Found the Ragusa ship had been unloaded and got into Bastia. Intend tomorrow to land at Ragliani or Porto Nova and take the vessels, they having the insolence to hoist national colours to me.

February 8th: At 8 anchored off the mole head sent a boat on shore with a flag of truce to say I was come to deliver them from the republicans, but that if a musket was fired on the troops I would burn the town, but that I wished to be received as friends. Saw vast quantities of flour carrying out of the town from daylight.

I gave the Governor five minutes to answer my summons which he did in the following words viz:—

> 'Nous sommes republicains: ce mot seul doit suffice. Ce n'est point au Maginiaggio, lieu sans defence, a qui il faut vous adresser. Allez a St. Florent, Bastia a Calvi et l'on vous repondra selon vous desirez. Pour la trouppee que je commande, elle est prête à vous montrer qu'elle est composé de soldat française.'

The moment I received this answer I landed, went instantly to an old castle where the national colours were flying and struck them with my own hand, the Governor not choosing to stay with his soldats français but running off as fast as his legs could carry him, posted himself on a hill about 2 miles off, with national colours and paraded the whole day leaving us to do what we pleased.

I destroyed about 500 tons of wine burned 8 vessels and brought two away and re-embarked without the loss of a man.

Took a Tartan from Leghorn to Ragliani laden with corn, flour and a bag of Republican crowns.

February 9th: Took a boat belonging to Corsica from Leghorn laden corn, flour, bread and a bag of republican crowns, in the evening anchored in Caprera, wished myself out again, not room for the ship to swing, wind right in. The Governor would not give me leave to search any of the vessels for French property, but assured me on his honour that there was no privateer there or vessel under French colours.

February 10th: Got to sea again. This day and the 11th saw several vessels under Corsican colours enter Caprera but could not get at them.

February 12th: Sent Lieutenant Andrews to see if he could cut off any

L

vessel from getting to the Island and to order the gun boat to keep much nearer in shore. As the boat was rowing past a cove where a very small vessel was laying without the least previous warning they received a heavy fire of musketry from the shore from people who were placed behind rocks and not seen. One man was badly wounded and the boat and oars damaged. Mr. Andrews very properly came on board to acquaint me of the circumstance. I immediately ordered the *Fox* cutter to attend me, took 40 troops and our boats and went to the place. When the enemy fired on us, we attempted to dislodge them by grape shot from the cutter, but that was impossible, or for the troops to land, it being steep cliffs. The vessel made fast by a rope to her mast head, finding nothing could be done this way I resolved to board her and put the troops in the boats to keep the enemy in check. We instantly carried the vessel and killed several of the French an officer amongst them. We had six men wounded, found the vessel was a French courier boat from Bastia to Antibes but during the day had hoisted no colours which were bent to the ensign staff.

February 13th: Joined Lord Hood. *Victory* made my signal to chase east, in the evening brought too a Genoese which carried us in sight of Leghorn.

February 14th: Anchored in Leghorn roads.

February 15th and 16th: Employed in getting water and some provisions.

February 17th: At daylight sailed from Leghorn.

February 18th: Joined the *Tartar* frigate.

February 19th: At 10 a.m. landed 60 troops at L'Avisena but found the valuable cargo of the *Ragusa* deposited there had been removed to Bastia on our taking Ragliani. Was joined by about 100 Corsicans armed who said they had declared for us on our taking Ragliani and were our good friends. Marched to a place which they said belonged to the French which we entered without the smallest opposition. By this time the inhabitants of this place joined us in arms, said they were our friends. We were now within 3 miles of Bastia from whence a party was marching towards us, surrounded by 200 Corsican friends, most of whom half an hour before were our declared enemies and if we might judge from their appearance would join against us if a strong party came out from Bastia. Under these circumstances of distrust I judged it proper to order the troops to be reimbarked. Find from all accounts of these people that there is not more 400 regulars in Bastia, and about 2,000 in the whole capable of carrying a musket. Went with my ship close under Bastia, find they have about 20 guns to the sea, and six out posts with cannon to the land 4 of which posts are regular store works.

February 20th: Went over to Planosa to look if any of the enemy's privateers where they landed on the island but none were there.

February 21st: Received letters from Lord Hood to tell me St. Fiorenzo was taken and that he had sent 400 stand of arms and ammunition for the inhabitants of Cape Corse. At night anchored in Maginaggio.

February 22nd: Working up for Bastia in the evening the Mayor of Arbalanga came off to say that in consequence of our landing on the 19th all the people up to the walls of Bastia had declared for us and that from our landing, the French were prevented from coming with their gun boats and troops and burning all the revolted villages.

February 23rd: Got to the southward of Bastia and determined to examine the enemy's works closely, but not to fire unless fired upon. *Romulus* and *Tartar* frigates with me. The wind was fair, the water smooth. We soon got within reach of a battery newly erected about 1 mile to the southward of the town of six guns. They begun to fire on us and as soon as my ship was in a good situation I opened on them and soon drove them out of the battery and they run into the town, unfortunately I had no troops or I would have destroyed it. We then went on towards the town which as soon as we got within reach began on us with shot and shells. Backed the maintopsail and was one-hour-and-a-half in passing it. Our fire was well directed not ten shot were fired by us which did not do service, the enemy's fire was ill directed. The ship were struck but not a man killed or wounded. An explosion of powder took place on the south-east battery which set on fire the fascines which they had placed inside the wall and it was sometime before it was extinguished.[1]

[2]*February 24th:* The enemy came out and carried off the guns from the work we fired on yesterday. A Ragusa ship came out of the mole who informed us that our shot had done much damage and killed several gunners.

February 25th: Lord Hood with 5 sail in sight to leeward. Two Corsican boats came off to tell me our troops were on the hills (believe we see them) and to beg ammunition. Saw the French attack the Corsicans and carry a village which they burned to the ground, at ½ past noon we being within shot of the town, they fired on us with both shot and shells, did not return a single gun, many went over us and all round us but not one struck the ship. The bursting of one shell shook the ship very much. The enemy have begun a new work just to the southward of the town. In the afternoon at 4 o'clock bore down to the enemy's new work and began to cannonade it, but it falling calm could not perceive we did the enemy much

---

[1] End of the MS. at the N.M.M. This part has not previously been printed. The last part was printed by Nicolas, Vol. I, p. 348, Journal B.
[2] B.M. Add. MS. 34,902. Although now in different collections the journal continues without a break.

harm hauled off. Being within shot of the town they fired on us with both shot and shells, returned the fire and did good service.

February 26th: Joined Lord Hood.

February 27th: The fleet blown off in a gale of wind none but *Agamemnon* able to keep her station.

February 28th: Off Bastia Lord Hood not in sight.

March 1st: Off Bastia.

March 2nd: Lord Hood in sight.

March 3rd: Lord Hood made my signal and acquainted me of the retreat of our troops from the heights and of their return to St. Fiorenza. Saw General Dundas's letter to Lord Hood as also Paoli's, what the General could have seen to have made a retreat necessary I cannot conceive, the enemy's force is 1,000 regulars and 1,000 or 1,500 irregulars. I wish not to be thought arrogant or presumptiously sure of my own judgement but it is my firm opinion that the *Agamemnon* with only the frigates now here laying against the town for a few hours, with 500 troops ready to land when he had battered down the sea wall would to a certainty carry the place. I presumed to propose it to Lord Hood and his Lordship agreed with me, but that he should go to Fiorenza and hear what the General had to say, and that it would not be proper to risk having our ships crippled without a co-operation of the army which consists of 1,600 regulars and 180 artillery men, all in good health and as good troops as ever marched. We now know from 3 Ragusa ships and one Dane that our cannonade on Sunday the 23rd February, threw the town into the greatest consternation that it almost produced an insurrection, that La Combe St. Michel the Commissioner from the convention was obliged to hide himself for had he been found and massacred, to a certainty the town would have been surrendered to me. But St. Michel having declared he would blow up the citadel with himself was the only thing which prevented a boat coming off to us with offers. A magazine blew up and the people believe we fired nothing but hot shot. The French shot were all hot. That by our cannonade on Tuesday afternoon the 25th February the camp was so much annoyed that the French ran, and in the town they so fully expected I should land that St. Michel sent orders for the *Le Fleche* to be burnt but it falling calm I could not lay near enough the town to do good service. Many people were killed and wounded, and the master of the *Ragusa* who has been on board me, had a piece shot out of his leg, and the man next him killed. I lament that several women were killed and a most beautiful girl of 17. Such are the horrors of war.

My ship's company behaved most amazingly well, they begin to look upon themselves as invincible almost invulnerable, believe they would fight a good battle with any ship of two decks out of France. Lord Hood offered me the *Courageux* 74 but I declined it, shall stay by *Agamemnon*.

March 4th: Close off Bastia. *Romney* joined.

March 6th: Close off Bastia, the enemy adding strong posts for the defence of the place. At this moment Bastia is stronger than when our troops retired from it, how that has hurt me. Received a letter from Monsr. J. Defridiani to request an interview, provisions, powder shot, flints and if possible two cannon. Sent an officer over land to Lord Hood with my opinion that it was yet possible to take Bastia with 500 Regulars and two or three ships. Received a letter from Lord Hood to say he would send me two gunboats according to my desire, when I get them the inhabitants of Bastia sleep no more. Sent the *Romney* to Lord Hood.

March 7th: Close off Bastia.

March 8th: Close off Bastia.

March 9th: Went on shore to Erbalunga and from thence to the Corsican camp. Had a good view of all the enemy's posts and the town. I am yet of opinion that Bastia may be taken by our troops although it is certainly stronger than when our troops retired and every day adds strength to the place.

March 10th: Got to my ship.

March 11th: *Romney* joined me from Lord Hood brought me letters to say that General Dundas was going home and that he hoped and trusted the troops would once more move over the hill. Sent the *Rose* cutter to lay off Caprera for a day or two.

March 12th: Off Erbalunga 5 miles from Bastia getting off a little water. We are absolutely without water, provisions, or stores of any kind, not a piece of canvas, rope, twine or a nail in the ship, but we cheerfully submit to it all, if it turns out for the advantage and credit of our country.

March 13th: Blowing strong the whole day. The *Vigilant* Gun boat joined me.

March 14th: A strong gale all day with thick weather with difficulty cleared the shore towards Cape Corse.

March 15th: More moderate got up with Cape Corse.

March 16th: Got off Bastia. Found that one small boat with 56 sacks of corn had got in, that the inhabitants were in the greatest distress for provisions, a small loaf selling for 3 livres. The *Petit Victoire* having started a plank was obliged to run on shore and is hauled up. The *Vigilant* and *Fortunee* gun boats not joined. The *Romney, Tartar, Vanneau, Fox* & *Rose* Cutter with me. Sent off an express to Lord Hood to tell him we have nothing to eat.

March 17th: Lieut. Duncan of the Artillery and a Mr. Debats engineer came over to examine the ground I had thought eligible for erecting batteries to bombard the citadel.

March 18th: Went on shore with Lieut. D. and Mr. D. to examine the ground, they both thought it an eligible situation for erecting a mortar battery found a most convenient place for landing cannon and stores. At noon the officers returned to St. Fiorenzo. At 4 p.m. received a letter from Lord Hood desiring me to come to Fiorenzo. Left the command with Capt. Paget.

March 19th: At 8 a.m. got into Fiorenza. Gave Lord Hood my free opinion that 800 troops with 400 seamen would take Bastia and that not attacking it I could not but consider as a national disgrace. Found all the army against an attack and declaring the impossibility of taking Bastia even if all the force was united. Getting water, provisions and stores on board.

March 20th: 21st: 22nd: 23rd: 24th:—ditto employed. The General absolutely refused to attack Bastia but wonderful to tell he refused Lord Hood a single soldier, cannon or stores to assist in the siege.

March 25th: Sailed from St. Fiorenza with Lt. Duncan R.A.

March 27th: At daylight got off Bastia. Sent the *Romney* to Naples for mortars, shells, field pieces and stores. Anchored the *Tartar* 4 miles to the southward of Bastia, and the *Scout* off the Tower of Miomo 3 miles to the northward of Bastia.

March 28th: 29th: 30th: 31st: Close off Bastia our boats rowing guard off the Mole and town every night, sent the gun boats to cannonade the town.

April 1st: [*No entry and end of journal*].

The King of Naples to Lord Hood [1]

MILORD,—Receves les complimens sinceres et empressée que je me fais un plaisir de vous addresser sur la reddition de Toulon. Le service important que vous venes de rendre à la cause comune et sourtout à l'Italie entiére n'a du qu'aux soins infatigables et energiques que vous aves employés. Il vous donne Milord un titre inefacable à notre reconoissance.

Je partage ce sentiment avec tous ceux qui vous le doivent si justement, mais éprouve une particuliere satisfaction à vous temoigner combien il me penetre, je faus exercer Milord tous les moyens, que la promptitude et la circonstances permettent d'employer pour concourir aux souhaits que vous aves fait parvenir à mon connoissance. It sera consolant pour moy de pouvoir au moins vous aider à conserver une aussy belle acquisition et

[1] N.M.M. 50 MS. 0096, Hood papers. Spelling as in original.

à en tirer le pratique le bien general va devoir à vos soins, vos vues et votre experience.

La division de Marine et de troupes que je suis empressée de voir sous vos ordres tachera Milord de meriter votre aprobation. Ils sont flattés de suivre la carriere glorieuse ou vous les introduires, sous un aussy digne chef. Puissent vos succes être bientot couronnes par l'accomplissement des voeux que nous formons tous pour le bien et la tranquillité genèrale.

Je desire que les circostances me procurent la satisfaction Milord de vous assurer de vive voix de l'estime, et de la confiance que vous m'aves inspirée. FERDINAND B.

Napola le 15 7bre. 1793.

[*Endorsed by Hood:* 'The King of Naples 15 Septr. recd. Octr. 5th.']

Extracts from Sir Gilbert Elliot's Journal,[1] March 1794

March 9th: Came on shore. Some letters passed between Lord Hood and General Dundas. They were both in the habit of shewing me their correspondence and I saw the letters of each on this occasion even before they were sent. But they were written and determined on before I saw them, and I not only had no share in advising either, but it was evidently too late to attempt the alteration of any thing they communicated to me. My situation has been unpleasant throughout this affair. For they were both in some degree right and in some wrong, and they are both men deserving of respect and esteem, so that it was difficult to profess with perfect justice to take a decided part either way. If the case had been cleared it would have been still highly improper for me to become a partisan in this difference. Whatever chance I had of doing good depended entirely on my preserving the confidence which both have always placed in me, and that was sure to be withdrawn by him against whom I should declare myself.

I endeavoured as far as I was able to soften the conduct or language of each to other; but I was obliged to hear on both sides much mutual crimination and abuse, and that circumstance was what rendered my position most unpleasant.

The dispute now turned on two points. First the attack of Bastia which Lord Hood pressed and which General Dundas declined. Secondly the extent of their powers as commanders-in-chief. Lord Hood told General Dundas in his letter of this date that he considered all his authority and command to have ceased on his quitting Toulon. General Dundas determined on the receipt of that letter to quit the command and go home. He intimated this intention to Lord Hood on this day and said he should

---

[1] N.M.M. MS. 9217, Minto Papers. The journal starts on March 4 when Minto sailed from Porto Ferraio on board the *Britannia*, Admiral Hotham, for St. Fiorenzo, Corsica.

be ready to sail on the 11th. On the question of command Lord Hood seems to have been drawn further in the warmth of this correspondence than he originally claimed or than he proposes at present to assert in practice. For he did not before claim any authority over the troops after they were on shore and he does not mean now to attempt the exercise of any such authority. I know however that he has always had some notion that the command of the troops belonged to him, except in so far as it was given by an express commission to a commander-in-chief, as was the case with General O'Hara and with General Dundas at Toulon. But when this commission ceased to operate by the evacuation of Toulon he seemed to think the whole command military as well as naval devolved on him. Yet he does not appear to me to have had any intention of attempting to exercise this authority in the present case, and he was I believe drawn into something like an assertion of this claim, first by the course of altercation and secondly and chiefly by thinking that there would be no other way to get the service forward, for I am convinced that if General Dundas had been willing to go on, as Lord Hood thought he ought, he never would have thought of disputing his command with him, or had even an inclination to interfere with it, but would on the contrary have co-operated with him and supported him in every possible way.

[General D'Aubant succeeded Dundas in the command on March 12.]

March 16th: [The coast to the north of Bastia was reconnoitred:] This was proposed by Lord Hood at Capt. Nelson's suggestion of the *Agamemnon*.

March 19th: Lieut. Duncan and Mr. de Butts made their report of the coast to the Northward of Bastia, Capt. Nelson of the *Agamemnon* attended them. This report is extremely favourable. I saw all three on board the *Victory* and they say in the strongest and clearest terms that Bastia and its citadel may be taken from that quarter, and that the other out posts must fall also.

March 30th: Col. Wemyss has reconnoitred twice since the Council of War and is thoroughly convinced that Bastia may be attacked successfully from the mountain. He has offered to General D'Aubant if he will trust him with 400 men to give him the possession of Guardida (the fourth post below the summit of the mountain) in one night. Major Smith accompanied him the second time (yesterday and the day before) and is entirely of his opinion. They also agree entirely with Lieutenant Duncan in the security of the post which Lord Hood proposes first to occupy on the north of Bastia and of the practicability of annoying the enemy from thence.

Several days have now been passed in debating and deliberating and intriguing for and against co-operating with Lord Hood's expedition, by making a combined movement from hence. But yesterday General

D'Aubant wrote to Lord Hood to say that: 'He could not promise any active operation, but should lose no fit opportunity of promoting the King's service.' If this oracular answer means any thing it is a refusal to concert or combine any measure with Lord Hood, and a determination to keep secret at least from one half of our force what the other half may do.

Sir James St. Clair has from the beginning done an infinite deal of mischief and intrigues as hard to prevent the taking of Bastia as if he had an interest that way. Koehler has been very fluctuating and equivocal in this discussion. He is afraid of Sir James St. Clair on one hand and of me on the other. They all join however in abusing General D'Aubant and treating him as a fool, and he has fully justified that imputation. It is impossible for any man to have behaved worse than D'Aubant and Sir James St. Clair. Probably both from the same cause, extreme folly, at the same time the part of Sir James St. Clair is very unlike the spirit natural to a young officer, who has a very fine regiment of his own within call. D'Aubant in the meanwhile is making way by fortifying the neighbourhood of St. Fiorenzo.

I have desired Lord Hood to let me go round in the *Victory* in order to witness the expedition which he is about to make.

I have dined twice with Col. Moore at his camp. He puts his promised difficulty concerning the attack of Bastia on the absurdity of D'Aubant who he says would probably order something that must ruin the undertaking and perhaps destroy those engaged in it. Major Koehler says exactly the same thing, and grounds the opinions he has given against the attack entirely on that consideration.

March 31st: General D'Aubant in conversation with me told me of Col. Wemyss' proposal to attack Guardiola with 400 men; and said that eventually, as Col. Wemyss proposed to conduct the attack himself and it might lead to requiring the rest of the troops to act, it would amount to putting the *whole army* under Col. Wemyss' command; and he censured Col. W. for having made any offer on the occasion as contrary to the discipline of the army. He said that it was the consequence of consulting the officers at all, and that such things ought to be discountenanced and discouraged. I mentioned in conversation to General D'Aubant that as Lord Hood was going to act on the north of Bastia circumstances might occur which would render it adviseable for him (the General) to take some measure on this side, and that it might be convenient for that purpose if some mode of regular or expeditious communication were preconcerted between them. General D'Aubant after repeating the old abuse of Lord Hood and his expedition said: 'He was determined not to interfere himself with any co-operation,' on which I said: 'That is to say a predetermination not to give him any assistance.' He replied angrily: 'That is not what I said Sir.' I repeated his words and begged if I mistook him that he would state it in his own way. Being interrupted nothing more passed. I collected however that he would not assent to Colonel Wemyss' proposal, and that he was determined not to act against Bastia, or at all events that if he should act at all it should not be in the way of co-operation with Lord Hood, with whom he refused any sort of concert.

I saw Paoli on the same day, who told me that Major Koehler and Col. Wemyss had been with him, I think the evening before, to desire that he would furnish them with a body of Corsicans in order to make an attack on the enemy's posts on the hills. If they had any authority from General D'Aubant to do this, it would appear that notwithstanding his conversation with me he does propose to act, and only wishes to avoid concerting his measures with the other half of the King's forces. But I am satisfied that Koehler and Wemyss acted entirely of their own head in demanding aid from Paoli and that General D'Aubant has no intention to do anything. It is remarkable that to this day he has never yet seen anything on the other side of the hill with his own eyes. In the meanwhile he is making fortification on a rising ground to the eastward of St. Fiorenzo and he has begun to trench garden ground, as if we were to remain here a considerable time.

I said to John Erskine, commissary general, today, amongst other things, that if D'Aubant should see Lord Hood's expedition and attack on Bastia go on, without taking any step to co-operate with him from St. Fiorenzo, I thought the public could attribute such extraordinary conduct only to one of two motives, either that he was a coward, or that he was bribed by Le Combe St. Michel. Erskine, without assenting to this strong expression, said however, that since I spoke so freely to him he would say on the article of corruption that General D'Aubant had pretty plainly proposed to him that they should cheat government to a very great amount together, and divide the profits.

I came on board the *Victory* this evening with my baggage, secretary and servants to accompany Lord Hood on his expedition against Bastia.

A Journal of Occurrences which took place between April 4th and the 23rd day of May when the English got full possession of Bastia in the Island of Corsica, kept by Captain Horatio Nelson, who commanded the seamen landed on the service of carrying on the siege of Bastia, 1794.[1]

[1] Monmouth MSS., Nelson papers, Vol. V. This Journal was quoted by Clarke and taken from him by Nicolas, who described it as 'Journal C.' (Vol. I, p. 348). It has not been printed in full or consecutively before.

On April 4th: At 10 a.m. the troops consisting Artillery and Gunners 66—11th Regt., 257—25th Regt., 123—30th Regt., 146—69th Regt., 261—Marines 218—Chasseurs 112. Total 1,183. Seamen 250 under the command of Lieut. Colonel Villettes and Capt. Nelson of the Navy landed at the tower of Miomo three miles to the northward of Bastia. At noon the troops encamped about 2,500 yards from the citadel of Bastia, near a high rock. All night the seamen and carpenters were employed in cutting down to form an abatis and also to clear the ground towards the tower of Torga from when the access to our camp was by no means difficult. A Captain's picket was always mounted at Torga and the sentry about 100 yards in front of it.

From April 4th to the 10th: All the seamen were employed in making batteries, and roads, getting up guns, mortars, platforms, and ammunition, works of great labour for so small a number of men, but which was performed with an activity and zeal seldom exceeded. On the 9th about 11 o'clock at night the enemy opened a very heavy fire upon our camp from mortars and guns, the alarm was beat and we fully expected an attack. This firing lasted till daylight. Extraordinary not a single man was hurt. The tents were much damaged but from the troops being under arms they escaped.

April 11th: Lord Hood send in a flag of truce at 7 o'clock in the morning in the *Victory's* boat. The officer when landed was grossly abused till the arrival of Le Combe St. Michel the commissioner from the convention when the mob were quiet. Having offered his letters to St. Michel, he told him that he could not receive Lord Hood's summons, that he had hot shot for our ships, and bayonets for our troops, that when two thirds of his troops were killed he should then trust to the generosity of the English. On the officer's return on board Lord Hood hoisted a red flag at the main topgallantmast head of the *Victory*, when our batteries opened on the town, citadel and redoubt of Camponella, (first hoisting English colours on the rock over my tent and every man giving three strenuous cheers). Our battery were two 13 inch mortars, two 10 inch mortars one 8 inch howitzer, five twenty-four pounders, two 18 pounders carronades, three 12 pounders, one four pounder field piece distant from the redoubt of Camponella 800 yards, from the town battery 1,800 yards, and from the centre of the citadel 2,300 yards. The enemy returned a heavy fire during the whole day.

The *Proselyte* frigate anchored off the Tower of Torga about 1,200 yards from the town battery, and I learn from Capt. Serocold that she was on fire from red hot shot, and finding the impossibility of getting the ship off the shore, he thought it right to set her on fire, and she was burned to the water's edge.

April 12th: A heavy fire was kept up by us during the whole of last night and this day and apparently with good effect, the enemy keeping a continual fire upon. In the afternoon went with Colonel Villettes, Lt. Duncan, Royal Artillery, and Captain Clerke Brigade Major, with a Corsican guide to examine a ridge about 1,000 yards nearer the town than our present position, and on which the Corsicans keep a strong guard every night. The enemy kept a continued fire of musketry and grape on us during the whole evening, unfortunately by the last shot they fired from Camponella, killed the Corsican our guide who was standing behind Clerke, and shot off Clerke's right arm and a part of his right side. Clerke was looking over my right shoulder at Camponella from which we were distant about 250 yards.

April 13th: Began a battery for three twenty-four pounders close to Torga Tower which stands on the sea side 1,230 yards from the town battery and 1,600 from the citadel, about 150 yards to the right of Torga battery and a little in the rear, a battery for two twenty-four pounders, a mortar battery for one 14 inch Neapolitan mortar, and for the two 10 inch mortars which are to be removed from the upper battery. Employed getting up the guns, mortars, shells, shot, powder platforms and making the batteries till the 21st as also a breast work to cover 100 men in case of an attack.

April 21st: The Torga batteries opened at daylight on the town battery and Camponella and apparently with good effect. The enemy kept a most heavy fire on us the whole day with shells, and shot from the citadel, town, Stafforella, Camponella, a square tower and the two batteries newly erected under Stafforella, Brigadier General D'Aubant came on the heights from Fiorenza with all the staff, and field officers of that army, and a guard of 50 Corsicans.

April 22nd: The enemy hard at work on the heights strengthening all their posts the natural consequences of the parade of reconnoitring yesterday. A constant firing kept up night and day. By several deserters we are informed that our batteries have done great damage and killed and wounded a great number of the enemy. Our batteries have twice totally demolished the town battery, and very much damaged Camponella but from our not having a sufficiency of men to take advantage of the success of our batteries the enemy are enabled to repair them and indeed make them stronger than ever. This night and the night of the 23rd the Corsicans made two false attacks on the upper posts and those to the southward, which must harrass the enemy a good deal. On the night of the 25th Le Combe St. Michel quitted the town and embarked in a felucca for Caprera and although chased by the lugger got in, with him went Monsieur Rochon the Commander in chief of the troops and some of our deserters.

April 27th: Began a battery on the ridge for two 18 pounders carronades and one 12 pounder on the spot where Capt. Clerke was shot, 250 yards from Camponella, 900 yards from the citadel, 700 yards from the town. The work of getting up guns to this battery was a work of the greatest difficulty and which never in my opinion would have been accomplished by any other than British seamen.

May 1st: The new battery opened, the 11th Regiment and Chasseurs were removed to the ridge for the protection of the battery and the post strengthened with an additional number of Corsicans, 45 seamen under Lieutenant Andrews were also appointed to fight the battery.

May 3rd: Began a battery for one 24 pounder and a 10 inch howitzer which was finished on the seventh at night. The enemy from the 1st of the month showed several dispositions as if they meant to attack this post, but they for some cause never came on. Five four pound field pieces with good abatis would in my opinion if the post had been well defended, prevented them making any impression on it. The seamen always slept on the battery with their pikes and cutlasses.

May 8th: At 8 o'clock Lord Hood sent in another flag of truce which was refused, the Mayor telling the officer that they would return bomb for bomb and shot for shot. Opened the 24 pounder and howitzer with the greatest good effect nor could every effort of the enemy knock down our works. A continued and unceasing fire was kept up on the town and out-works.

May 12th: In the night a large boat came out of Bastia. She was closely pursued by our guard boats and taken. In the boat were 3 deserters, Capt. of *Le Fortunee* frigate, 12 seamen, 8 Corsicans and 30 wounded soldiers going to Capraia. Her dispatches were thrown overboard. In the morning of the 13th at daylight Lieut. Suckling of the *St. Croix* Schooner saw a packet floating on the water which he took up and brought to me. The weight which had been tied to them had slipped out of the string, from probably the swing of throwing them over board. They were all letters from Gertilly the commander-in-chief of Bastia saying how much they had been annoyed by our fire which had been open on them near forty days and that if succours did not arrive by the 29th of the month, they must look upon the town as lost to the Republic. The letters were to Salicetti, Le Combe St. Michel, and Santelli.

Lord Hood sent in the boat with her crew and wounded men, with a week's provisions. Got a nine pounder on the ridge.

May 14th: The enemy showed a picture on Camponella the whole day, they did not treat it with insult and I think it was intended for Lord Hood. Our battery constantly firing many deserters coming to us who all agree in the great damage we have done them and also of their loss of men.

May 15th: In the night the guard boats took a boat from Capraia with gun powder bound to Bastia, Gagliazini the Mayor's brother was in her. No dispatches could be found. Firing as usual the enemy preparing Sardiola for a mortar.

May 16th: The enemy got up a 13 inch mortar to Sardiola which kept a constant fire in the night. It blowing strong from the northward 3 boats attempted to get into the town with powder and provisions. Two were taken but one got in. The enemy from this day to the 19th fired more than usual night and day. We had often five shells in the air at once all going to Bastia.

On the 18th: Some means were taken to convey a message to Lord Hood that if he would condescend to send a boat with a flag, a negotiation would be entered into for the surrender of the town and its dependencies.

May 19th: At 4 o'clock this afternoon a flag of truce was hoisted on board the *Victory* and a boat went from the *Victory* and one went from the town to the *Victory*. The enemy from Camponella without arms, and our officers advanced, shook hands and were good friends. They said it was all over Bastia was ours. So many interests were to be consulted that it was the 22nd in the evening before our troops could take possession of the outposts.

On the 19th: In the evening our troops from Fiorenzo made their first appearance on the hills. On the 20th General D'Aubant and the whole Fiorenzo army consisting of the 18th Regiment, 50 and 51st Regiments, 12 Regiment Dragoons with 100 artillery came on the hills to take Bastia.

May 22nd: At 6 o'clock this evening our troops marched from their posts, the band playing God Save the King, and the Grenadiers' March. At 7 the French colours were struck upon Camponella, Stafforella, Croix de Capuchin, Monseratto Rock, Fort St. Mary's and all the other outposts, and the British colours hoisted under three cheers from every seaman and soldier. The French troops all retired to the town and citadel.

May 23rd: At 8 o'clock this morning the British Grenadiers took possession of the town, gates and gate of the citadel, the French troops all retiring to the citadel.

May 24th: At daylight this morning the most glorious sight which an Englishman and which I believe none but an Englishman could experience was to be seen, four-thousand-five-hundred men laying down their arms to less than 1,000 English soldiers. Our loss of men in taking this town containing upwards of 14,000 inhabitants, and fully inhabited would contain 25,000 was the smallest possible to be conceived.

Seamen killed and died of their wounds   . 12
Seamen wounded   14
Soldiers killed and died of their wounds   .   7
Soldiers wounded   23
Total: Killed . . . 19. Wounded. .. 37

Capt., Clerke 68th Regt. Wounded.
Lieutenant Andrews *Agamemnon.*
Capt., Rudsdale 11th Regt.

Desertion: 2 seamen, 4 soldiers.

By the most accurate account we can get of the enemy's killed and wounded it is about:—

Killed   .   . 203
Wounded .   . 540 Most of whom are dead.

Account of the shot and shells fired by us during the seige:

Powder barrels   .   .   . 1,058
Shot 26 and 24 pounder   . 9,566
Shot 18 pounder   .   . 1,081
Shot 12 pounder .   .   .   927
Shot 9 pounder .   .   .   349 Total 11,923 shot.

Shells 12 and 14 inch   . 2,552
Shells 10 inch   .   .   . 1,210
Shells 8 inch   .   .   . 1,611
Shells 5 inch   .   .   . 2,000 Total 7,373 shells.

———

Nelson to Sir William Hamilton [1]

Bastia,
May 24, 1794

MY DEAR SIR,—Will you have the goodness to forward the enclosed to Mr. Brand and to present my letter to Lady Hamilton.

Every lover of his country will rejoice in our great and almost unexampled success to the honour of my Lord Hood and to the shame of those who opposed his endeavours to serve his country. General Stewart I am happy in saying is just arrived. We shall now join heart and hand against Calvi, when conquered I shall hope to pay my respects to your Excellency at

[1] N.M.M. MS. 9960; Croker Collection in the Phillipps papers.

Naples which will give real pleasure to your very faithful and obliged
HORATIO NELSON.

Sir William Hamilton.

A Journal of the Siege of Calvi, from June 10th, when the 'Agamemnon'
left Lord Hood at sea, to the 10th August, when the English took possession
of the town, by Captain Horatio Nelson, who commanded the seamen
employed on the expedition.[1]

On the 10th of June 1794: At 2 o'clock parted from Lord Hood and
steered for Cape Corse.

June 11th: All day little wind, in the night got a fine breeze from the
Northward running alongshore.

June 12th: At 8 o'clock anchored off the Town of Bastia, went on
shore to General Stuart and settled that all the troops for the expedition
against Calvi should be embarked the next morning at 6 o'clock. Ordered
every transport and victualler to be ready to sail with me. Ordered a ship
to be loaded with empty casks.

June 13th: By 8 o'clock every soldier was embarked in the different
transports, 1,450 men exclusive of officers. At noon made the signal to
unmoor. At 4 the signal to weigh, made sail in company H.M. Ship
Dolphin and 22 sail.

June 14th: Little wind all day and night.

June 15th: At 7 o'clock in the evening anchored in Mortella Bay,
General Stuart came on board and as he seemed anxious to go on to the
attack of Calvi, if I thought it right to go with the shipping which I
certainly did placing the firmest reliance we should be perfectly safe under
Lord Hood's protection who would take care that the French fleet should
not molest us. I therefore gave the necessary orders for the fleet to be
ready to sail on the next day as also H.M. Ship *Lutine*.

June 16th: Raised 110 volunteers from the transports and took 30
seamen from the *Inflexible*. At ½ past 5 in the evening sailed from Mortella
Bay with the *Dolphin*, *Lutine* and 16 sail of transports, victuallers and
storeships. Little wind all night.

June 17th: Very little wind all day. It was 10 o'clock at night before
any of the ships could get to an anchor on the coast about 4 miles to the
westward of Cape Revalata, the bottom rocky and very deep water, the
Agamemnon laying in 53 fathoms one mile from the shore opposite a
little inlet called Port Agra. This coast is so rocky that a boat cannot land
except in the inlet.

[1] Monmouth MSS., Nelson papers, Vol. V. In the same notebook as the Journal of
the siege of Bastia.

PLATE V (*a*). The *Agamemnon* cutting out French vessels at Oneglia, August 25, 1795 (see p. 221: Nelson's letter to his wife, September 1, 1795).

PLATE V (*b*). The *Agamemnon* capturing *Ca Ira*, March 14, 1795 (see p. 200: Nelson's letter to his wife of that date).

June 18th: In the morning at ½ past 3 o'clock went on shore with General Stuart to examine the coast for a proper landing place which we both agreed must be at the inlet called Port Agra, by no means a convenient place for landing guns or stores as sunken rocks lay 20 feet from the shore with deep water between them and with a common sea breeze such a swell sets in as to prevent boats landing. This inlet is 3½ miles from the town of Calvi. Examined the enemy outposts and found them as follows:—

Monachessco about 2,200 yards from the town on the S.W. side of it. The Mozelle fort about 650 yards, the Fountain battery in a shoulder of a hill between Mozelle and San Francesco which last stands on a rock on the north side the Peninsular and is washed by the sea.

Monan Bessco has one eighteen pounder and 3 or 4 other guns 6 and 8 pounders.

Mozelle a star stone fort with a Cavaliere in the centre mounting 10 guns 18 and 8 pounders with a bomb proof under the cavaliere.

Fountain battery 6 18 pounders landed from the *Melpomene* a fascine work defended by seamen who had a camp behind it.

At the old tower the enemy had a small entrenchment and an howitzer.

San Francesco two brass 18 pounders and one iron.

The town apparently well fortified but without any ditch.

June 19th: By 7 o'clock in the morning all the troops were landed under the direction of Captain Cooke with 6 field pieces which the seamen dragged up the hills. Landed in the afternoon with 250 seamen, encamped on the beach, landing baggage and provisions for the army. By the General's desire sent the *Fox* cutter with directions for 180 Royal Louis the 18th Regiment and 100 of the 69th Regiment to join as soon as possible. In the night landed from *Lutine* 4 26 pounders.

June 20th and 21st: It blew so strong with a heavy sea as to preclude all intercourse with the shipping. By morning of the 21st every ship had put to sea. We were employed in making roads for our guns and getting up 3 26 pounders to the Madona about 2½ miles from the landing place. The road for the first ¾ of a mile is up a steep mountain and the other part not very easy in the heavy rains with much thunder and lightning.

June 22nd: More moderate got off boats to such ships as got back again. Employed landing provisions, powder, shot, gun, carriages. Of the first article we were much in want. The *Fox* returned with 180 Royal Louis. Got one 26 pounder up the hill. Still a great deal of surf. A serjeant deserted from Calvi. At night got 2 26 pounder from the Madona to the place intended for the battery against Monachessco from which it is distant 850 yards. A working party of soldiers filling sand bags.

M

June 23rd: The water pretty smooth. Landed two 26 pounders, a great quantity of provisions shot etc. At night got one 26 pounder from the Madona to the intended battery against Monachessco and mounted the 3 guns.

June 24th: Landed one 26 pounder, 2 24 pounders and 2 18 pounders. A very fine day. Capt. Hollowell and Capt. Serocold joined with 50 seamen from the *Victory.* Got 2 24 pounders to the top of the hill.

June 25th: Captain Cooke left me. Got up one 26 pounder and 2 18 pounders to the top of the hill. Employed making a road to carry on the guns towards the Mozelle. The *Agamemnon* and the transports returned from Fiorenza.

June 26th: Got up 2 26 pounders, 2 12 inch mortars, 1 8 inch howitzer to the top of the hill. The 18th Regiment and flank company of the 69th Regiment arrived. Our force exclusive of seamen 2,000 men.

June 27th: Got up 2 10 inch howitzers. Employed carrying forward about ¾ of a mile the heavy guns and carriages. All the day a gale of wind. All intercourse with the shipping cut off. At 2 o'clock in the afternoon the French came out and made an attempt to turn both flanks of the Corsicans and a gun boat came out to fire in the rear of the Corsicans, and under cover of a heavy cannonade the enemy advanced. The light corps were under arms, ready to support the Corsicans if necessary. Seamen got down two field pieces and fired at the gun boat who instantly retired. The enemy rather forced the Corsicans to retire. Went with General Stuart to the Corsicans who kept a smart firing of musketry and regained their post. Colonel Sabbatini their commandant was killed with 2 or 3 others, and 5 or 6 wounded. The enemy retired about 4 o'clock, believe they have not the smallest idea of our intentions of bringing cannon over the mountains. The *Victory* in sight from the hills.

June 28th: The boats were with difficulty enabled to get off to the ships. Employed carrying forward the guns and mortars and making a road nearer Calvi. Went on board the *Victory.* Landed 4 18 pounders.

June 29th: Shifted the seamen's camp to the top of the hill. Landed 2 26 pounders, got them up a hill to the left of the Madona 1,500 yards west of the Mozelle and 1,000 yards N.W. of Monachessco. This is called Hill Battery.

June 30th: Got 2 12 pounders on the point inside Cape Revalata and 1 12 pounder on the pitch of the cape, also 1 12 inch mortar on the Hill Battery.

July 1st: Went on board the *Victory.* Landed inside Cape Revalata. All night employed in moving the guns, mortars, and howitzers to within 450 yards of the intended battery.

July 2nd: Made two trips to the landing place for stores. At night got two mortars to their battery carrying platforms etc., till 2 in the morning.

July 3rd: Employed 6 hours bringing up stores from the landing place. At night carrying casks, sand bags and platforms towards the intended battery. The French cannoniers and Royal Louis made a 3 gun battery against Monachessco. The French are to have the fighting of this battery.

July 4th: The Royal Louis battery opened at 5 o'clock on Monachessco which did considerable damage to the enemy's works. By evening, it being the General's intention to make our advanced battery this night against the Mozelle, he judged it proper to endeavour to draw off the enemy's attention from that place, by a show of an attack on Monachessco. In the evening the Royal Irish marched from the right, while the Light Corps moved to the left. The Corsicans as soon as it was dark began a firing which the enemy thinking an attack on Monachessco began to fire in all directions, not only from Monachessco but from the Mozelle Fountain Battery and the Town. In a short time the enemy thinking I suppose that we were in possession of Monachessco directed their cannon against it. Their musketry was fired entirely across the isthmus, doubtless apprehending a general attack. It was General Stuart's orders for the working parties to move forward with sand bags, casks and platforms and as soon as they were got forward, I was to move with the guns. At ½ past 10 o'clock not an engineer had gone forward, and when the General returned an attempt was made to erect the battery but it was too late, and all the bags etc., were obliged to be brought back again.

July 5th: Carrying junk for mortar platforms and placing the mortars on their beds all night. 100 seamen employed in getting forward things for the advanced battery. Lieut. Moutray made a battery for 2 18 pounders inside Revalata with 25 men.

July 6th: Getting some planks and preparing everything to be ready to get on brisk in the evening. At ½ past 9 o'clock in the evening a feint of an attack was carried on against Monachessco and the enemy turned their fire during the whole night towards that post which they supposed was attacked. By excessive labour in every department the battery was erected by day light on the 7th and the guns brought close to it.

July 7th: It was impossible to get the guns on their platforms before 6 o'clock which exposed us to a heavy fire of grape shot, but the seamen did their duty as became them, and 4 26 pounders and 2 24 pounders were mounted in spite of all opposition. Amongst those who fell was to be regretted Captain Walter Serocold of the Navy, Mr. Corney mate of a transport and one seaman belonging to the *Agamemnon*. Several soldiers were killed and wounded in the rear of the battery. At 10 o'clock the battery was opened on the Mozelle 6 gun fascine battery and San Francesco. Very much silenced before night the enemy's fire at the fascine battery and Mozelle which latter is much damaged. Our distance from Mozelle 750 yards. Seamen fight this battery one artillery man to each gun.

July 8th: The enemy repaired much of their fascine battery during the night and during the whole day they kept up a constant heavy fire of shot and shells on our battery. They destroyed two of our guns and much damaged another and the works. One shell burst in the centre of our battery amongst the General, myself and at least 100 of us, but wonderful not a man was hurt, although it blew up our battery magazine. The Mozelle is a good deal battered but if any of their guns are disabled, they have others to supply the place. Got 2 guns to replace the damaged ones. 2 seamen killed 3 soldiers wounded.

July 9th: The enemy during the night repaired much of their fascine battery and the Mozelle with sand bags. By 10 o'clock we got the superiority of fire and before night dismounted every gun in the fascine battery and Mozelle, but the guns on San Francesco annoyed us very much being so much on our left flank cannot get our guns to bear on it. In the night mounted a 10 inch howitzer which fired on the enemy as the battery did every three minutes to prevent their working. Landed shot and shells in Port Vaccaja between Revalata and Calvi. Found in this bay a small cove where I think guns may be landed. 1 soldier killed 1 wounded 2 seamen wounded.

July 10th: At daylight opened our fire on the Mozelle and occasionally a gun on the Fountain battery. Found the enemy had not done any work on this battery during the night. At the Mozelle's they had laid great numbers of sand bags to prevent our shot hitting under the arches of the bomb proof of the Cavaliere, which we did yesterday by beating down the marlins of the lower work. By 7 o'clock all the bags were knocked down and our fire went on without any opposition. By evening the Mozelle was much shaken and I am sure a practicable breach may be made when ever the General thinks it right to turn his attention to it. To the honour of General Stuart he is not sparing of himself on any occasion. He every night sleeps in the advanced battery. Landed 2 36 pounders this night in the cove I examined yesterday. 1 artillery man killed.

July 11th: Our fire constant on the Mozelle. Fired some hot shot at the fascine battery which set the marlins on fire, but they had put too much sand with the fascines for us to effectually destroy the battery. At 10 o'clock saw the enemy carry off their field pieces and howitzer and totally abandon the work, which was no sooner done than they opened their fire from the bastions of the town, firing over their old battery and over the Mozelle, and although they could not see our battery from the bastions yet great numbers of their shot struck it and killed an additional gunner. At night a large breach was made in the lower work of the Mozelle. At 10 o'clock got up 2 36 pounders and one 26 pounder to the rear of the battery. Lieut. Moutray joined me with 25 seamen.

July 12th: The enemy opened a heavy fire at daylight from the town and San Francesco seldom (very extraordinary) missing our battery. At 7 o'clock C. N. was much bruised in the face and eyes by sand from the works struck by shot. 2 26 pounders were dismounted by evening. The Mozelle much breached at night. Replaced the guns destroyed, fired a gun and mortar every three minutes. At $\frac{1}{2}$ past 12 the town was on fire and burnt for three hours.

2 seamen and 3 soldiers wounded.

July 13th: The enemy kept up a constant fire all day from the town and dismounted another 26 pounder. This is the 5th gun disabled since the 7th when our battery opened and having only 6 guns in it, 'tis wonderful. At night landed 4 18 pounders with a quantity of shot and shells in Port Vaccaja. Employed getting them up to the rear of our battery. I must here acknowledge the indefatigable zeal, activity and ability of Captain Hollowell and of the great readiness he ever shews to give me assistance in the laborious duties entrusted to us. To this night by computation we may be supposed to have dragged one 26 pounder with its ammunition and every requisite for making a battery upwards of 80 miles, 17 of which up a very steep mountain.

1 soldier killed.

July 14th: Firing all day at Mozelle the General not thinking the breaches sufficiently practicable. At night landed 3 26 pounders 1 24 pounder 1 13 inch mortar 1 10 inch mortar and a great quantity of shot and shells. The enemy laid a great quantity of sand bags in the breach.

July 15th: Landed scaling ladders, the General thinking the breaches would be practicable in the evening, but it seems they were not thought so. Got up from the beach to the rear of the battery the guns and mortars landed last night. The enemy fired a good deal during the night but without doing any damage.

July 16th: The enemy have fired much this day and have fixed the range of their guns to the Mozelle and the height between it and the old tower. At night landed 2 howitzers and carriages. Went with General Stuart to examine the ground for a battery against the Mozelle or Town.

3 seamen 3 soldiers blown up with gunpowder.

July 17th: The enemy got clear 2 or 3 guns in the Fountain battery and laid them to fire on our approach to the Mozelle. The breaches very large, every thing ready to go forward but from some cause the attack is deferred for this night.

1 additional gunner killed.

July 18th: Getting everything ready to proceed. The 50th Regt. to assist in making a battery for the 3 26 pounders to the right of the Mozelle and about 300 yards distant. The seamen to carry forward the guns and mount them, also 1 13 inch mortar. 60 seamen under Lieut. Edmonds and Lieut. Harrison to carry forward the field pieces.

The disposition of the troops were as follows:—

Colonel Wemyss with the 18th Regt. to proceed by the left of our 6 gun battery with two field pieces drawn by seamen commanded by Lieut. Edmonds of the *Agamemnon* and with fixed bayonets to take possession of the Fountain Battery which when he had got possession of he was if San Francesco fired to direct his fire against it, when the troops under Colonel Moore with two field pieces drawn by seamen commanded by Lieut. Harrison of the Navy were to move forward under cover of the 3 gun battery. Carpenters under Lt. St. George to go before and to cut down the pallisadoes. A party under Major Brereton to go by the right of the Mozelle to cut off the enemy's retreat from the town. Colonel Moore's party to be supported by the 51st Regt. The 50th Regt. after work to remain under arms. All night hard at work. The troops to move forward laying on their arms. Landed 112 seamen in addition from the *Agamemnon* under Lieut. Suckling.

July 19th: At 3 o'clock a smart firing of musketry opened on the 18th Regt., who marched into the Fountain battery without firing a shot although the Mozelle fired grape on them. The enemy abandoned the work and trench behind it and fled into the town. The 3 gun battery began to fire at the Mozelle as did the field pieces under Lieut. Harrison into the breach. The Royal Irish giving an huzza the Pioneers pushed forward cut down the pallisadoes and the troops under Colonel Moore giving an huzza were in the breach. The enemy only firing a few musketry were panic-struck and fled except a very few who threw down two large shells one of which burst. One or two of the enemy were bayonetted in the Mozelle and two taken prisoners, but so fast did they fly that Major Brereton with the light infantry had not time to get between the Mozelle and the town before they all escaped. Capt. McDonald led up one breach, Lieut. McDonald up the other, both were slightly wounded. Thus fell the Mozelle; it cost us 4 men killed and 7 wounded.

The Royal Irish employed from the moment they got into the Fountain battery in throwing up an intrenchment being within grape shot of the town. At daylight the enemy opened a heavy fire of shot and shells from every part of the town on the Royal Irish and the 3 gun battery and this regiment not being well under cover before 11 o'clock suffered accordingly 6 killed 12 wounded. The Mozelle is an absolute heap of ruins. In the afternoon the General sent a flag of truce to the town to know if they had any terms to propose. Their answer was the motto of the town: 'Civitas Calvis semper fidelis.'

Capt. McKenzie wounded.

July 20th: Not a gun fired on either side since the flag of truce. All night seamen employed in carrying forward from the 6 gun battery to the rear of the Mozelle, 2 36 pounders 3 26 pounders 1 24 pounder 2 12 inch mortars 1 13 inch mortar 1 10 inch mortar 1 10 inch howitzer 8 gun carriages 2 mortar beds 1 howitzer carriage 1,500 shot 36 pounders and 26 pounders, 500 8 inch shells. 700 seamen at work, the whole of this night and no one else.

July 21st: Resting part of this day, the remainder carrying shot and shells to the rear of the Mozelle. Every seaman continued at work till 2 o'clock in the morning. Carried to the rear of the Mozelle 1 26 pounder 1 20 inch howitzer 1 8 inch howitzer 2 mortar beds for 12 inch mortars. None but seamen and mules at work.

July 22nd: The enemy at work changing their light guns for heavy ones, filling the embrasures and mounting their guns on Dumourier carriages. Seamen employed carrying shot and shells and 4 26 pounders and one howitzer to the battery on the left of the Mozelle, a working party making batteries all day.

July 23rd: At night removed all the mortars from the right to the left of the Mozelle. Removed 3 18 pounders from the 6 gun battery to the 3 gun battery and changed them. 3 26 pounders which we carried to the Fountain battery. A working party making batteries.

July 24th: Not a gun fired since the 19th. The enemy hard at work as well as ourselves. Mules and seamen carrying shot and shells.

July 25th: Mounted all the mortars, howitzers and 7 gun battery with 26 pounders. At night attempted to remove the Royal Louis battery, broke the devil carts, only got one gun half way down the mountain.

July 26th: Seamen employed all day carrying shot and shells from the beach to the batteries.

July 27th: Not a gun fired. Landed 2 32 pounders. At night mounted 2 36 pounders 1 26 pounder and 4 18 pounders, all ready to open before day light on the 28th. Our batteries as follows:—

From the left: 1 26 pounder 1 10 inch howitzer 1 24 pounder 6 26 pounders 1 10 inch howitzer 3 13 inch mortars 3 18 pounders 1 8 inch howitzer 1 5½ inch howitzer 1 10 inch mortar 1 18 pounder 2 36 pounders 1 26 pounder—all these within 600 yards of the town wall.

To the right: 900 yards distant 2 26 pounders besides our 3 gun battery and the hill battery.

July 28th: At 7 the General sent in a letter to say he should not fire at their black flags (hospitals) according to their desire. The Governor sent an answer that he would send a letter in the course of the day. At ½ past 5 a flag came out with two officers and a letter, which was to say that if no succours arrived in 25 days that they would then enter upon terms for the surrender of the town.

July 29th: The truce still continues. At 10 o'clock the General went on board Lord Hood and it was determined to give the garrison to the 10th August when if no succours arrived we were to be put in full possession of the town. In the night four small vessels got in. The garrison gave three cheers which will probably end our negotiation. The seamen (except one artillery man to each gun to point it) manned the whole of these batteries as they did every other, except the Royal Louis battery. The greatest merit is due to every lieutenant landed from the fleet for their constant assiduity and attention, as I must also say to the seamen, only 2 have been punished since our first landing. Lieutenants Edmunds, Ferrier, and Morgan were constantly with the seamen who fought the 6 gun and 3 gun battery. At the near batteries they were assisted by Lieutenants Moutray, Hoye and Suckling, assisted by Mr. William Harrington Master of the *Williamson* Transport, Lieutenant Harrison agent for Transports who volunteered this service with us, was alert and assiduous in every duty he was desired to perform. Our troops and seamen getting sickly.

July 30th: At noon a flag sent in with our final determination. At 1 he returned the enemy having rejected our terms. Got everything ready to commence hostilities. At 5 o'clock opened our fire, the enemy began also firing, but very soon run from their guns. By dark 3 or 4 guns were dismounted and the enemy only now and then fired a gun at us. Lieut. Byron 18th Reg., Ensign Boogus 51st Regt., killed. Lieut. Livingstone 30th Regt., and one seaman *Agamemnon* wounded. At 9 o'clock the town was on fire in five places from our shells which fired incessantly the whole night.

July 31st: Our fire kept up very brisk during the whole day. The enemy seldom firing, and only one gun from the left and one howitzer to their right, by sun set nearly all the enemy's guns seemed disabled, a great part of the parapet wall beat down, and three fires burning. At 5 o'clock a flag came out to say 2 men had been killed in the hospital.

Mr. Banks midshipman killed. 1 additional gunner killed.

August 1st: Our fire kept up till 11 o'clock when the enemy hung out a flag of truce and demanded the same time 10th August, which General Stuart thought proper to grant without consulting Lord Hood, and granted the enemy such terms as he thought proper, or even sending to Lord Hood to sign the capitulation.

To the 10th: Every hour our troops and seamen falling ill and dying. On that day not 400 soldiers were fit for duty.

August 10th: At 9 o'clock about 300 troops a party of seamen, some Royal Louis and some Corsicans were drawn up opposite the Great Gate to receive the garrison who at 10 o'clock marched out with two pieces of cannon and the honours of war and laid down their arms, in the whole 300 troops and 247 armed Corsicans. Sent Lieut. Moutray and a party of seamen to take possession of the frigates, gun boats and merchant vessels in the harbour. Ordered six transports into the harbour. Employed all day embarking the garrison, sick and such inhabitants as chose to return to France. The enemy had out of their armed men 313 sick in the hospital.

SHIPS TAKEN	GUNS
Melpomene . . .	40
Mignonne . . .	32
Ca Ira Gun Boat.	
Two Merchant Brigs and some small craft.	

A list of killed and wounded officers and seamen:—

	KILLED	WOUNDED	MISSING	TOTAL
Victory	1	2	0	3
Agamemnon	1	2	1	4
Transports	4	2	0	6
Inflexible	0	0	1	1
Total:	6	6	2	14

Captain Serocold	.	killed
Mr. Banks . .	.	killed
Mr. Corney	.	killed

Nelson to Lord Hood [1]

Camp,
August 10, 1794

MY LORD,—Having transmitted my journal of what the seamen have been employed upon during the whole siege, I have now only to acquaint

[1] Nelson wrote this copy of his letter at the end of his Journal.

your Lordship of the highly meritorious conduct of every officer and seaman landed under my command, to express my sincere acknowledgements for the very effectual support and assistance I have received from the ability, zeal and activity of Captain Hollowell, and that Lieutenants Edmunds, Morgan and Ferrier were constantly with the seamen fighting the batteries to which were joined on the last batteries Lieutenants Moutray, Hoye, and Suckling. I must not also omit to acquaint your Lordship that seamen being wanted for this service on our first landing, the agents for Transports raised 110 volunteers from the transports, and that Lieutenant Harrison one of the agents, and Mr. William Harrington, Master of the *Willington* transport came on shore and served with great credit during the whole siege.

Herewith I transmit a list of killed and wounded seamen. I am etc., etc., H. N.

Powder, shot & shells expended during the siege of Calvi		Remains after the siege of Calvi	
Powder Barrels	. . 1,340	Powder	. . 760
Shot 26 & 24 pounders	. 7,175	Shot	. . . 6825
Shot 18 pounders	. . 3,800	Shot	. . . 2,200
Shot 36 pounders	. . 300	Shot	. . . 2,100
Shells 12 & 13 inch .	. 1,350	Shells	. . . 1,157
Shells 10 inch .	. . 821	Shells	. . . 1,935
Shells 8 inch .	. . 400	Shells	. . . 1,453
Shells 5½ inch .	. . 182	Shells	. . . 3,818
(Shot 11,275. Shells 2,753)			

Letters received by Sir Gilbert Elliot, Viceroy of Corsica [1]

FROM GENERAL STUART BEFORE CALVI

June 24, 1794

. . . I have had my men working like slaves to get up the guns while they should have been securing the avenues to the post I had taken and ought to maintain; in short other objects have attracted his lordship's [Hood's] attention than the reduction of Calvi, and unless he gives very good reason for a proceeding that has greatly augmented the strength of the enemy's posts and must consequently occasion the loss of many brave men, I shall quit an army which must always be ill treated when his personal vanity is not concerned. I shall be happy in finding myself wrong and

[1] N.M.M. MS. 9217, Minto papers.

wish that in your political arrangement you may not have reason to complain of his deserting you as he has done me at the only time he could have been of any material assistance. Captain Nelson with 150 men has certainly exerted himself and Capt. —— who two days ago [only] brought fifty men from the *Victory*. I write with much hurry as my whole attention is given up to facilitate the business which I have undertaken. . . . CHARLES STUART.

FROM LORD HOOD

A

Victory, Martello Bay,
June, 25, 1794

. . . I am preparing to go to Vice-Admiral Hotham off the Bay of Gourjean with all the strength I can collect to prevent a junction of the enemy's ships if possible, but I am apprehensive the first division is now arrived at Toulon and have no clue by which I can judge of its number and force. This is a very mortifying circumstance, particularly as it must prevent my giving that attention and support to General Stuart my inclinations strongly lead me to and I fear he will find the reduction of Calvi a more arduous business than he first imagined. The moment the weather would permit, after my return from seeking the French fleet, I sent Capt. Hollowell and Capt. Serocold with some active officers and fifty men to assist in getting up the ordnance and stores and shall take care to forward whatever he may want. I propose to have some communication with him if I cannot see him in my way across, and hope to move from hence tomorrow; I wait only for the ships to get some provisions and water. . . .

B

Victory, off Calvi,
July 3, 1794

. . . I had reason to expect from the account I had from the camp some little time ago, that the batteries would open against the enemy this morning, but Capt. Knight who saw the General yesterday evening has reported to me that it will be two if not three days before they will be ready. The labour is immense in dragging up the cannon near three miles, but all are in the highest spirits and there is the most cordial and animated exertion in the whole. General Stuart most fortunately is not only a very able officer but most amiable man, but he is without real assistance. Such a miserable staff I believe no General ever had upon service. Happily he has great abilities and judgement, with a will of his own and am confident he will succeed most honourably. . . .

C

Victory, off Calvi,
July 15, 1794

. . . I confess I am greatly at a loss to conceive upon what ground you could imagine that because I had ordered two fireships to be prepared to act against the enemy, whenever a favourable opportunity should offer, for using them, and they had sailed from Fiorenzo, that they were to divert me from Calvi. I am here stationary until the place is reduced. So soon as that event takes place I shall repair to the coast of Italy but not till then, as the army make daily demands from the *Victory* and cannot be supplied elsewhere. . . . I have heard nothing from the shore since yesterday when I was told the Morelle Fort was pretty well pounded, and that the General will soon be in it, probably this night. Capt. Nelson has received a hurt in the face by the contents of a sandbag which had large pebbles in it: he speaks lightly of it, but I wish he may not lose the sight of an eye.

D

July 29, 1794

Lieut. General Stuart came on board the *Victory* this morning to say, that an amnesty or truce, had been proposed by the French for 25 days, after that, in case they were not relieved they would be disposed to enter upon terms for capitulating. The General had limited the amnesty or truce to six days, which had been refused, so the matter stood when the General came on board.

Admiral Hotham and I were of opinion to stick to the six days, or at least not to extend the truce beyond ten. It seems the garrison can muster provisions for 25 days, and are afraid of the guillotine if they surrender before. The General left the *Victory* a little before three. He says he has not powder and shot for more than seven days. Admiral Hotham and I thought he might as well try three day's fire, he might then remain where he was if the enemy still holds out, and no further supplies of ammunition could be given him. What he will do. I cannot venture to say, but think it probable he will propose to extend the truce to 12 days. . . .

E

Victory, Martello Bay,
August 4

[After repeating the proposal of a truce, Hood continues:]
. . . The General said he had but seven days' firing. That in my opinion could not justify a truce for 25 days and was of opinion that if our batteries

were opened for three days, the enemy would submit but my health being very much impaired and should probably be soon incapable of any part of my duty; I judged it expedient to desire the favour of Admiral Hotham to come on board who after reading the correspondence General Stuart delivered was decidedly of opinion with me, that a truce for 25 days was inadmissible, and wished the effects of a few days' firing to be tried, but before the General went on shore it was submitted to his judgement whether under all the existing circumstances the truce might not be extended to ten days. Whether an attempt was made for it I do not know, having not heard a word of what has since passed between the General and the garrisons, until between eleven and twelve o'clock at night on the 2nd when Sir James St. Clair Erskine brought, of which I send you a copy. But I was happy to see that after two days' firing the enemy threw out the white flag. When Sir James Erskine came, I was too ill to get out of my bed but saw him, and desired he would acquaint General Stuart that I would order a sufficient number of transports to carry off the garrison, and such of the inhabitants as were inclined to leave the island.

Between 12 and 1 o'clock Sir James Erskine, much inclined to stay on board until daylight, was put on shore, as the weather looked suspicious and before daylight the *Victory* and *Britannia* were put by to many of their sails, that they lost ground upon every tack, and in the afternoon the *Agamemnon* parted her cable. . . .

The Rev. Edmund Nelson to Nelson [1]

March 12, [1793]

MY DEAR H.,—I thank you for the early intelligence of what has happened at Nevis.[2] After the first agitation which such an event must occasion both Mrs. Nelson and yourself will be perfectly reconciled. You are freed from a state of anxiety and dependance upon the caprice of another. Your measures will be concerted and your future plans formed upon a more durable basis than heretofore. Since Mrs. N. left me she has not wrote. Her health and spirits were improving and I hope a little cheerful society may establish both. Your naval preparations seem to go forward with as much alacrity as you can expect. Pray God they may be successful in restoring public tranquillity as well make some return for your prudent and invariable attention to professional duties.

---

[1] Monmouth MSS., Nelson papers, Vol. IV.
[2] The death of Mr. Herbert.

A party of the Yorkshire militia are here with two Lieutenants, the one a Sir Griffith Boynton, a married man, the other a bachelor, not young nor rich. Our Baronet and family are wonderfully pleased with the new acquaintance. He asked me to let them go into the Parsonage. I begged to be excused. They lodge at Bretts. Mr. Rolfe of Hitcham has wrote to our Baronet desiring he would visit him no more. It has cut him down much. Crowe has notice to quit the Hall. He is mighty civil to me, has secured the Overy curacy.

You may recollect that by some accident you was in the house of a Mr. Stevens, a clergyman. That poor man is in very great distress by ill-health and low circumstances. I find he is brother to the Chaplain at Plymouth Dock and relation to Stevens at the Admiralty. If it falls in your way, enquire how it is that the one brother is so rich, the other poor, and that he is not in some measure relieved.

What wind gets you down the river I know not. Here is the sharpest N.E. we have felt this season.

At Thorpe all is as usual. Poor Nobbs cannot make good all his penitential promises.

Your sister Matcham is in London but the direction I have entirely forgot.

Am glad your boys are good. God prosper you. Adieu. EDM. NELSON.

To Mr. Maurice Nelson, Navy Office, London.
[*With note:* 'This is for Captain Nelson.']

The Rev. E. Nelson to Mrs. Nelson [1]

A

[May 14, 1793]

MY GOOD MADAM,—At this time, I feel myself from motives of true affection and concern called upon to give every proof in my power that in the absence of your dear husband you will find in me a readiness to show those several acts of friendly attention which at any time you may have occasion to look for. From me particulars I neither can or need to offer as your own prudence and understanding will suggest what is fittest, and most likely to make you happy.

The fleet I presume is sailed, God prosper it as well for the public weal as for our own private interest. Lord Hood is come about and a steady perseverance in what is right will always subdue every obstacle and

---

[1] Monmouth MSS., Nelson papers, Vol. IV. Selected from the series of nineteen letters preserved in that collection, except that of 13 December, 1793.

generally obtain our wish. This maxim is well rooted in the principles which steer the conduct of our friend.

The plan and prospect for your son is founded upon judgement and good policy and will succeed. Your own handsome independency must free you from abundance of anxiety which there was room for before the event of Mr. Herbert's death happened.

If I have any chat it shall be reserved for my next and will now detain you only with an adieu God bless you. EDMUND NELSON.

Bett Thurlow is waiting your commands with eager expectation. The boxes are still at Hilborough with all her paraphernalia.

To Mrs. Nelson, at George Matcham's Esq., Ringwood, Hampshire.

B

June 9, 1793

DEAR MADAM,—From Hilborough intelligence as well as your last favour to me, it is I find determined that Swafham shall be your head quarters and that apartments are engaged for midsummer the 24th instant. Upon this Bett Thurlow desires me to say she shall be ready to attend you whenever required. She seems pleased at the hope of being in your service, and her luggage remains at Hilborough. I see no symptoms of a consumption.

When Fame gets up any report there is no saying how far she may carry it. Therefore it is as well to get the start of her and tell you last Sunday I had a fall from the pony, which happening near the church, it made some bustle. But thank God nothing more than bruises and strains happened. I am now upon my legs and have sent the hobby to Thurlows. It will come to be useful by and by, for this we know what it is a gentleman has to sell no body wants or will give a price.

We that is those afar off, not privately connected, as well those whose hearts beat warmer are in the pleasing expectation that the naval force now in the Mediterranean is sufficient for every purpose it has in commission.

As private stations seldom has wherewithal to make up any thing beyond a sailor's letter: 'How do ye etc.?' and my good wishes are ever the same and long details of anecdotes are tedious, give me leave to say only pray God bless you all. EDMUND NELSON.

To Mrs. Nelson, Ringwood, Hampshire.

C

Friday, December 13, 1793[1]

MY DEAR,—I have only this moment, been able to speak upon the subject you mention, to J. Thurlow. Mary is sixteen years of age, is a spruce girl, and knows as much as her years and education will allow of, is willing to take Bett's situation, if you approve it. Respecting Bett, John talks like a kind father. When she returns to him, he will do all that is within his power to recover her, and will take her at any time you shall wish it, and if the younger daughter is approved will bring her, when Bett leaves you. All this is teasing, yet still, not an object to make yourself uneasy. Bob Wilson has offered his daughter Mary, whom you know and Carter, the school master, has a young woman they would gladly get from home, not the London daughter.

I am indeed vexed your health is so precarious, and your resolution not equal I fear, to the trials you meet with, your own good understanding is a much better source of comfort, than anything that can be offered by me, or any of those who have great respect towards you, my only fear respecting myself is that any thing should be left undone, by me, or that you will not, through kindness to me, be explicit enough to give me a hint of. Swaffham, you are not perfectly pleased with; can you fancy any other place? Spending the winter months with me at Bath, you have said no word about it.

To leave you in an unpleasant or unsettled state I shall regret, though my intention is to leave Burnham early in the next month, yet to accommodate you in any way that scheme shall be altered, and if you can put yourself under my protection a poor substitute, all shall be done that can be. Don't at this time consider the expense. It can, it shall, be made easy, sure I am our dear friend would have it so, and to look no farther why might not the summer be past away at the Parsonage? Be assured if I omit anything, it is for want of judgment. Do you like to come here?

I am in all situations, yours affectionately, EDM. NELSON.

D

December 1793

MY DEAR,—I do most heartily join with you in humble thanks to divine providence who has protected our dear friend from the danger of such a severe engagement as your good boy describes. Angels and those ministering spirits sent from the great Jehovah's throng are the guardians of the

[1] N.M.M. 36 MS. 0826, Autograph collection.

PLATE VI. Oil painting, by Daniel Orme, of Commodore Nelson receiving the sword of the dying Spanish admiral on the quarter-deck of the captured *San Josef* on February 14, 1797.

good. Pray God continue his care of them for the future felicity of their friends.

I don't know whether my last letter was explicit enough as to myself. I mean nothing intervening to leave Burnham on the 2nd January lest bad weather should set in, take my route by Lynn and get over the journey as quick as my powers of travelling will allow. Perhaps 2 or 3 months hence you will follow me. I wish I knew your real inclinations. Don't shorten your visit in so good a family. Write me as much as often as you can.

Adieu, EDMUND NELSON.

Saturday evening—yours just arrived.

I admire your injunction of secrecy to me who am not very loquacious and have nobody to speak to except the Widow Gab once in 5 or 6 days.

Kate and her son Edmund are well. The first compliment of that kind I have received.

[*Note by Mrs. Nelson:* December '93. I was then at Lord Walpole's.]

To Mrs. Nelson.

E

July 29, 1794

MY DEAR,—The letter from our dear Hor. is very full and communicative as to the operations as far as the 23rd of June and what followed if we judge from probabilities was I hope successful, and that his steady perseverance in what is right will one day terminate as we wish. Your kindness in remembering my anxiety to hear from him I thank you for and shall rejoice to know when there may be any well founded expectation of seeing him. But for that pleasure we must wait till he himself knows and feels it to be right and proper. In the meantime we are to rejoice that his health is good, his person unhurt and his character unblemished.

Your first letter from Ringwood gave me pleasure, having been in some pain about your health and difficulty of removing. You are now stationary it may be presumed for this campaign, and whenever inclination or the season of the year induce you to a change, I shall obey your summons. Am glad my name's sake is of so placid a temper. Although a good natured man is not the first character in life, yet it has many advantages to itself and society. G's son George is no doubt very polite in his attention. Tell him I am perfectly at peace with him.

Our harvest is beginning. Suckling has visited at Hilborough, all well and jolly. He returned upon your husband's mare. She is improved and fit for actual service. Pony is at Thurlow's. Poll is well—in the straw.

N

Our Burnham gazette has acquainted us that Miss Kitty Crow is to be married by and by to a Mr. Helsham, a young man of reputable parents, good circumstances and brought up in the physical line. His father lives at Stoke, in the smart house the man told you was Sallop Hall. When you have returned me a counter part to all this chat, I shall be at liberty to return an acknowledgment to Kitty for her letter to me, but as I have nothing to say, and both you have much matter for my information and amusement, you will now and then indulge me.

Suckling has seen the two Aylsham relations they are to be country neighbours. We hear two of the Miss Sucklings of Norwich are married. The Boltons are I hear got to schools but indeed she is very slow in writing to me.

The widow has buried her father, is going into Suffolk for a visit, is still my best and only chatty neighbour. Mrs. Barnard is come for the summer.

God bless you all and prosper the improvements at Shepherd's Spring. Adieu, EDMUND NELSON.

Suckling desires love. He dines with me every day. Indeed being much alone does not agree with me, as my years allow no amusement.

To Mrs. Nelson, G. Matcham, Esq., Ringwood, Hampshire.

Chapter 3

THE INVINCIBLE AGAMEMNON
1794–1795

Introduction

When Lord Hood sailed for England in the *Victory* on October 11, 1794, Nelson would have liked to have accompanied him in the *Agamemnon*. Not only was the sixty-four worn out, but the same arduous service had sent a hundred and fifty men to hospital, of whom fifty were to die. Lord Hood had not hauled down his flag, but returned to England to recover his health, intending to take up his Mediterranean command again in the spring. He was still a member of the Board of Admiralty, and was reappointed under a new First Lord, Lord Spencer, in December. Nelson would have chosen to have sailed home with him and, with Hood's good graces, to have turned over the remains of his tried ship's company into a new 74-gun ship. But this did not come about. Instead, Nelson remained on in the Mediterranean, hoping for Hood's return, and in the meantime under the uninspiring if worthy command of Vice-Admiral William Hotham in the *Britannia*. Nelson suffered another disappointment when it became obvious Hood was not going to return. He was seventy years of age, and even as a younger man had never suffered fools gladly. On March 7, 1795, his name was omitted from the reconstituted Board of Admiralty, with Lord Spencer at its head. Hood wished to take reinforcements back to the Mediterranean with him and, after Hotham's indecisive action with the French off Genoa in March, increased his demands in a tactless manner. He was ordered to haul down his flag at the moment of sailing. 'Oh, miserable Board of Admiralty,' wrote Nelson to his brother William, 'they have forced the first officer in our service from our command.' But in face of the old man's overbearing arrogance and refusal to work harmoniously with army officers, it is difficult to blame Lord Spencer for his decision. In 1796 Hood was made Governor of Greenwich Hospital, where, between long spells at Bath, he spent the remaining twenty years of his life, dying in 1816, and being buried in the vaults of the hospital cemetery.

On October 24, 1794, Nelson was at Leghorn and still had seventy of his people sick. The French armament at Toulon was suspected by Hotham of designing an attempt to recapture Corsica, where Sir Gilbert Elliot was having a troublesome time as viceroy. The *Agamemnon* was sent to reconnoitre Toulon, and Nelson took her in so close in his determination to count and distinguish the men-of-war in the inner and outer roads that a report was circulated that he had been captured. This rumour made him most indignant. '*Agamemnon* is not to be taken easily. Not any two-decked ship in the world is able, we flatter ourselves, to do it.' Back from counting the French fleet in Toulon, the *Agamemnon* was due for a complete refit alow and aloft at Leghorn. All her masts were taken out and a new mainmast out of store stepped. Nelson lived ashore, fretful lest the French be tempted out of Toulon to engage Hotham's blockading fleet whilst the *Agamemnon* was absent refitting. He had engaged a French master for himself, Josiah and Hoste, and wrote fairly frequently to Hoste's father. Josiah, now aged fourteen, he thought 'quite a man'. Whilst at Leghorn Nelson had a miniature painted of himself, which he sent home to his wife, care of his brother Maurice. If this is the miniature which came to the third Earl Nelson from Lady Nelson's family and is now at Greenwich, it is an indifferent production; Nelson, wearing a captain's undress uniform, is expressionless. Unfortunately, if the promised portrait of Josiah was ever painted, its existence has not been publicized. On June 22, 1795, his stepfather writes it is not done, and adds that Josiah, 'a great stout boy', was always busy and seldom ashore.

On December 19 the *Agamemnon* was in order and ready to sail on the morrow. Her trained, but ailing ship's company, in five weeks of hard toil, had carried out the many and disciplined acts of brute strength, mechanical skill and improvization needed to get out and in the masts of a 64-gun ship. The year 1795 opened with any hopes of a quick victory dulled. French armies had won sixteen pitched battles in 1794 and had established the French frontiers on the Rhine, occupied the Netherlands and invaded Spain. Britain's allies in the coalition were suspected of seeking peace. And our own operations on land since the war began, whether in Belgium or Brittany or at Toulon, had been uniformly unsuccessful. Only at sea had there been any successes and the navy had secured some credit, notably by Lord Howe's victory. Secure of Lord Hood's approval, Nelson had worn out self, company and ship and had performed prodigies of valour of which only Lord Hood, who had gone home, had taken notice. In Nelson's eyes, the future lacked promise.

At sea again, the *Agamemnon* spent a tiring time, racked by gales with the fleet off Toulon between December 21 and January 9, 1795, after which a month was spent at anchor in Mortello and St. Fiorenzo bays, Corsica. Then they were at sea again between February 7 and 25, when they anchored at Leghorn. Nelson hated the idleness he experienced during the long periods in harbour, and hoped to be sent off again with a squadron of frigates as in Lord Hood's time. His ship was very short of men, but otherwise in good order, and he considered there were but few ships equal to her. The French fleet in Toulon was about equal in strength to the British, fourteen sail of the line. But the British fleet was now under-manned and the discipline in some of the ships was not too good. The successes of the French army had called attention to the inaction of their fleet. A convoy with reinforcements was expected from England. The French fleet put to sea determined to force an action. News reached Hotham from Genoa. His opportunity had come. All officers were ordered to repair on board their respective ships on March 6 and he put to sea at dawn on the 9th. The rival fleets sighted each other in the neigh-bourhood of Genoa but there was little wind and a heavy swell from the south-west. The French were inshore and not anxious to engage immedi-ately. Hotham ordered a general chase, but retained his line of battle. The fleets lost sight of each other and were not in contact again until March 12, when there was a chance of the French cutting off the *Agamemnon* and *Princess Royal*, separated from their friends. On the 13th the French were discovered far to windward, but the 80-gun *Ca Ira* had been dismasted through carrying a press of sail, for it was now blowing very fresh and squally. A frigate was trying to take her in tow. Nelson describes vividly to his wife how her escape was delayed by the gallant action of Captain Fremantle in the *Inconstant*, frigate, which received a broadside. Nelson, coming up in the *Agamemnon*, kept the heavily armed French ship's stern onto him, so that her broadside would not bear. Finally, her consorts supported her, and the *Ca Ira* escaped that day. At daybreak on the 14th, with light airs again, the *Ca Ira*, 80 guns, was discovered in tow of the *Censeur*, 74 guns, and the two French ships were cut off by the British line of battle, but gave a good account of themselves before hauling down their flags as the *Agamemnon* came up and took possession. In a brush with the main French force, two English ships of the line were dismasted and another badly cut up. Captain Nelson went on board the *Britannia* and besought Hotham to pursue the enemy with his undamaged ships. Despite the entreaties of both Captain Nelson and Admiral Goodall, his second, Hotham was affable but determined. Thanks to Nelson's graphic reporting, his words, 'We have done very well. We must be contented', have sealed his character as that of a half-hearted commander-in-chief. That is the penalty for the honour of having had the active Nelson as a captain serving under one. Nevertheless, Parliament voted him their thanks, and his victory was later included in a public service of thanksgiving at St. Paul's. Nelson's letter to his wife of April 1, in which he aspires to become a flag-officer, has often been quoted with approval, but from the version given by Clarke and M'Arthur. This is the first time it has been printed as he wrote it.

The little boys, in their first fleet action, which, by the way, was also Nelson's first fleet action, behaved uncommonly well. We have already been told Josiah was 'every inch a seaman'; now in battle, 'Josiah and Hoste with Bolton were my aide-de-camps and behaved with great courage, and Josiah thinks there is no great danger from a Frenchman's shot.' After the battle the *Agamemnon* took the *Censeur* in tow. Strong gales on March 18 tested Nelson's seamanship as the two damaged ships struggled on. The damaged *Illustrious* was indeed driven ashore and had to be burnt. Some parts of her were saved and the *Agamemnon* was later fitted with her capstan in place of one shot to pieces. On March 19 the two ships made Port Especia and were followed in by the whole fleet.

On March 25 the fleet changed its anchorage to St. Fiorenzo Bay, Corsica, put to sea again on April 18, and was in Leghorn between April 27 and May 9. Then followed a period at sea until June 30, when the fleet returned to St. Fiorenzo Bay. On July 5 Nelson was sent away with three frigates and a cutter to co-operate with the Austrian general in the recovery of the Genoese Riviera. But falling in with the French fleet supposed to be in Toulon, the squadron was chased for 24 hours back to St. Fiorenzo, an exciting chase: twenty-three sail of the enemy in sight and a fresh breeze in which the English squadron was favoured by superior seamanship. Hotham got his fleet under way, but could not get to sea because the wind had fallen light. Hotham did not again discover the French fleet until July 13, when he ordered a general chase. The French escaped with the loss of one of their rear ships, the *Alcide*, 74 guns, which ship unfortunately blew up before possession had been taken. Nelson, who had joined in the chase, and had forced the *Agamemnon*, a fast ship, well ahead as usual, was disappointed by a shift of wind in engaging his chosen opponent. Once again Hotham is blamed for his excessive caution.

Nelson was sent away again with a more powerful squadron, five frigates and a brig, to aid the Austrian general, de Vins. It is interesting to find Nelson on his own once more, for he had never been happy tied to Admiral Hotham's apron-strings and it is worth considering whether his continued complaints were really justified. In numbers the opposing fleets were evenly matched, but the English ships were worn out and undermanned. On the other hand, the English crews were experienced. Yet naval battles were not won by pitched contests between fleets of equal force. Hotham strove to cut off portions of the enemy's fleet. And the vagaries of the wind seem to have defeated his efforts. Although as critical as ever of Hotham's orders and opinions, Nelson seems to have cheered up considerably on having once again an independent command and was immediately planning with Mr. Drake, British minister at Genoa, to alter and enlarge his orders and responsibilities. He was also greatly encouraged by his promotion to being a Colonel of Marines. Four of these appointments were kept to reward naval officers, senior captains, standing at the top of the list for promotion. They gave up the rank and its emoluments when themselves promoted to flag rank. He was also interested in the new uniform regulations, which changed the lapels of his full-dress coat to blue, instead of white, and gave him plain gold epaulettes with bullion, such as British naval officers had never worn before, although common to army officers and foreign naval officers. Without patterns, the regulations left room for variety of interpretation and Nelson called in to advise him both Josiah and a military officer to ensure he appeared suitably dressed. Josiah wished for some epaulettes for himself.

The captain of the *Agamemnon* was full of confidence and enthusiasm when with his squadron of frigates and minor war vessels he established contact with General de Vins and the Austrian army which had driven the French from Vado Bay and was now contemplating a further advance towards Nice. Nelson considered himself a proved diplomat and soldier and he was ready to strain every nerve to push forward 'the common cause '. He confided to his wife, characteristically, 'Hotham has no political courage, which is in an officer abroad as highly necessary as battle courage.' Although pleased at being made a Colonel of Marines, Nelson was indignant Hotham had not given him a distinguishing pendant as a commodore, which would have added ten shillings a day to his emoluments, and given him an increased prestige, useful for impressing neutral powers and half-hearted allies.

At first victory once again seemed just round the corner. Soon, he thought, the French royalists would once again hand over Toulon. And there was a wonderfully rich prize waiting to be condemned and sold for his squadron's benefit. This was on August 2. But on August 25 Nelson was inactive, dreaming of his English cottage and home life, disgusted with Hotham and the British fleet 'rollicking their time' at Leghorn, and de Vins getting nowhere but awaiting his subsidy from the English Government. Josiah, his mother must have been pleased to hear, enjoyed excellent health. 'Josiah will be a good officer I have no doubt, but I fear will never be troubled with the graces.' Nelson thought Hoste 'without exception one of the finest boys I ever met with.'

On September 1 he was able to report the capture of a French corvette, but no great sum must be expected in prize money because too many shared in the capture. An unfortunate action with Turkish craft led to regrettable casualties; 'however, those who play at bowls must expect rubbers.' Nelson really wanted to inspire the Austrian offensive. He wished to transport some troops by sea, but Hotham would not help. By September 15 he had decided that the Austrian general was as sleepy and inactive as his own admiral. All his diplomacy could not rouse them; neither seemed to understand Nelson's doctrine of urging forward 'the common cause.' Nelson was gratified by the Duke of Clarence's continued notice, especially with the Duke's declaration, 'I never part with a letter of yours. They are to me highly valuable.' Nelson commented to his wife, 'One day or other he may be useful to me', and he wrote at length to the Duke and gave his 'campaign' a narrative.

Even his usual activities were curtailed when Hotham had reduced his force, and some French warships he had been watching in Genoa escaped. Yet his admiral remained 'frolicking' at Leghorn. His pleasure was in his friends, especially the arrival of Collingwood in the Mediterranean, 'a great comfort, a very old acquaintance'. By December Hotham had struck his flag and gone home, leaving Sir Hyde Parker in command. It was known, however, that Sir John Jervis was coming out 'to the great joy of some and sorrow of others in the fleet.' But in Nelson's opinion it was owing to Hotham's carefulness and laziness, and lack of energy, that the Austrian army had been thrown out of Vado by the French, a young army almost naked, as a boat's crew captured from his own ship reported to him. Nelson withdrew to Leghorn to refit. Honours had not come his way, but once again he had worked hard, and he could recollect with pride that two of his first lieutenants, Hinton and Andrews, were now captains, and all from the fame gained by the *Agamemnon*, in which crippled ship he soon hoped to sail home. He was convinced the name *Agamemnon* was as well known and admired by both friend and foe, as his own.

Nelson's letters home are long and frequent in this time of inactivity. Josiah noticed it. 'He says he will one day write but I write so often he is sure there is no occasion for him.' In January 1796 a truce between France and Austria made Nelson think a peace was inevitable. He sailed from Leghorn to St. Fiorenzo Bay in Corsica and there on January 15, 1796, met his new commander-in-chief, Sir John Jervis.

The documents printed in the Appendix concerning Nelson's Vado Bay command have mostly been printed by Nicolas, but not together, as intended by Nelson for Jervis's edification. They explain Nelson's actions and motives, as do his letters to the Duke of Clarence. The eleven letters written to Nelson by his wife during the last months of 1794 show her anxious fears for the safety of her husband and son, and her constant expectation of their early return to England. Having finished the round of visits with which she passed the first eighteen months of Nelson's absence, she was now living in Bath with Nelson's father. There she often met Nelson's service friends, and their old West Indian friends too. There she saw Lord Hood on his return, who 'received me with every mark of affection and said all that would gratify an affectionate wife.' He also assured her that three months would see her husband in England, so that she wrote out asking for some trifles to be brought home, adding with restraint, 'but pray don't load yourself with presents thank you.' By the end of 1794 her optimism, never very conspicuous, was wearing thin. 'I am hurt and think it very hard you are not ordered home.' She was doomed to be sadly disappointed on many occasions. Nelson's father was more encouraging, and wrote of the conversations they had of the future, when 'we often are fixing the cottage retirement you are looking forward to.' He found Bath kept 'Mrs. F. H. N.' cheerful, and as his son, Suckling, could now be left in charge of the parish at Burnham Thorpe, in accordance with Nelson's wishes, he rented a house in Bath for three years.

No. 93

[Nicolas, I, p. 497, part]

Leghorn,
October 24, 1794

MY DEAREST FANNY,—What changes our life is subject too. The other day when I wrote you I was going up the Levant, now that is gone by and I am under other orders. I received your letter of September 15th the day I wrote you last. It gave me real pleasure. I yet don't think I shall be very long before I see England. Other ships must soon arrive and *Agamemnon* must be one of the first ships home, if attention is paid to the state of the ships. We came in here to get a few refreshments for my people 70 of whom are still very ill and I go to sea on the 26th to join the fleet again, which cannot I should suppose remain more than one month longer at sea.

As to these West India people I put no confidence in them. I hope we shall get the legacy paid in due time and then I shall not care about them. I have many little things for you which I wish you had but fear no mode can be fallen upon for them to reach you in safety.

We have but little news here. The French have retreated from Piedmont but whether it is only to come again stronger who can say. A number have been put to death within this month both at Marseilles and Toulon and some people think we may make a peace with them. I wish we could on any fair terms, for poor England will be drained of her riches to maintain her allies who will not fight for themselves.

Josiah is very well. I met him, Hoste and Bolton as I was coming off this morning and asked them where they were going. The answer was on leave to spend the day on shore that a good dinner, wine etc. and come on board at sunset. Remember me kindly to every one where ever you may be and be assured I am as ever your most affectionate HORATIO NELSON.

To Mrs. Nelson, George Matcham's Esqr., Ringwood, Hants. Angleterre.

No. 94

[Nicolas, I, p. 497, part, under date October 24]

Agamemnon, Leghorn,
October 31, 1794

MY DEAR FANNY,—It is an ill wind that blows nobody good. Being obliged by a gale of wind to put back last night in consequence I received your letter of September 30th [1] this morning, which gave me infinite pleasure. Why you should be uneasy about me so as to make yourself ill I know not. I feel a confident protection in whatever service I may be employed upon. As to my health I don't know I ever was so truly well. I have no doubt but this climate has done much good for me. I fancy myself grown quite stout. Although *Agamemnon* did not go home with Lord Hood, yet home she must go before long.

My ship and ship's company are not half the strength as when I left Spithead. Several of my guns being landed in Corsica were destroyed which has also diminished our force. Yet I am sure this ship's company feel themselves equal to go alongside any 74 out of France. Every man has seen so many shot fired that they are very superior to those who have not been in action. We had the report here about the King. I hope the villians will be hanged.

You tell me news about Miss S. [2] I hope sincerely she will get well married. I have not forgot her, let *Agamemnon* sail for England tomorrow. I love and respect Mr. Suckling never having found his want of kindness.

---

[1] See Appendix. A short series of Mrs. Nelson's letters from September to December 1794 have been preserved, pp. 252–267.
[2] Miss Suckling.

I am glad you intend to call on Lady Hood. Do so after the Lord's arrival and enquire after him. He will be pleased to know it although most probably you will not see him. He says he shall come out here again. I own I don't think it, although he retains the chief command. It rejoices me to hear Maurice is so well off. I hope he will remember peace will one day come and that he should take care and lay up a little. Has this yellow fever reached Nevis? I hope not by your not mentioning it.

Admiral Hotham cannot keep the sea much longer. The fleet must return in to some port. We have had 3 gales of wind in 13 days all very strong. Neither sails, ships or men can stand it. In the Channel the fleet goes instantly into Torbay here we always keep the sea. Josiah is very well as is Hoste. Write his father a line to say so etc. both very amiable good boys. I am sorry to tell you that Frank [1] is now so continually subject to those epileptic fits, that his mind is evidently deranged . . . [*Part of letter missing*] . . . believe me your most affectionate husband, HORATIO NELSON.

Love to Maurice if you see him. I don't know how to direct to him I never hear from him.

[*Part of the last page missing*]

To Mrs. Nelson, Bath.

No. 95
[*Nicolas, I, 504, part*]

Agamemnon, St. Fiorenzo,
November 12, 1794

MY DEAR FANNY,—I have since I wrote you last been sent to look after the French fleet who had again given Admiral Hotham the slip. I found them in Toulon 16 sail of the line and several frigates. Our fleet had gone to Fiorenzo to refit and be prepared for any movement of the enemy. I came in here two days ago, and found a most unpleasant circumstance a mutiny on board the *Windsor Castle*, Admiral Linzee's ship. The crew wishing to change their captain [2] and 1st lieutenant, the officers have been tried at their own requests and most honourably acquitted but the Admiral notwithstanding has removed them and forgiven the ship's company who richly deserved a halter. I am of opinion 'tis mistaken lenity and will be the cause of present innocent people being hanged. I wish Lord Hood was

---

[1] Frank Lepee, Nelson's coxswain.
[2] Captain William Shield. Hotham's leniency on this occasion roused a good deal of criticism.

either here or I was in England with him. The French say they will have Corsica again and we have croakers who believe them. I am of a totally different opinion and have no doubt that the enemy will in the first instance not make any attempt and in the next that should they come out, we shall beat them if our Admiral will give us leave, which many doubt so much do characters alter. There has been a most diabolical report here of our being captured and carried into Toulon (owing to my running into the harbour's mouth) I hope it has not reached England. Never believe anything you may see in the papers about us and rest assured that *Agamemnon* is not to be taken easily. Not any two decked ship in the world is able, we flatter ourselves, to do it.

Josiah tells me he will write you on Monday when the post next goes to England. I am now at Leghorn to get new masts and to endeavour to restore my worn out ship and ship's company. God bless you and believe me your most affectionate HORATIO NELSON.

I don't know I ever had such good health as since I have been in Italy, not one day's illness. Josiah is quite a man. I am now getting a French master to him, Hoste and myself. Best love and remembrances to Mrs. Suckling, Miss Suckling and Mr. Ramsey.

To Mrs. Nelson, Bath.

No. 96

[Nicolas, I, p. 504, part, under date November 12]

Leghorn,[1]
November 15, 1794

MY DEAR FANNY,—I received your letter from Gibraltar yesterday evening for which I sincerely thank you.

Agamemnon begins to look miserably without a mizen mast and will soon be without a main mast. Lord Hood should had he considered our very hard service have taken us home with him. Sure I am we are not fit to remain out here. What can be expected from a worn out ship and ship's company? Notwithstanding I am in the best possible health, yet I don't like to be any longer kicked about. I am tired. Now service is over at least I believe for the present, I have more time to think and believe that no person has been treated so ill as myself. I now think knowing to be true that I was the humble instrument of Corsica's being taken, the active

---

[1] The *Agamemnon* refitted at Leghorn, November 14–December 21.

instrument for Bastia's being attacked by the English and without vanity all agree (except Lord Hood and Captain Hunt I suppose who never was on a battery when a gun was fired, the former never was within shot of the place) that I was the cause of 4500 French troops laying down their arms to 1000 English marines and seamen, but it is forgot. I have just received a letter from the Vice Roy of Corsica [1] in which are the following expressions. As they are flattering to me I know they will give you pleasure. It was on the subject of Corsica being attacked: 'I know that you who have had such an honourable share in this acquisition will not be indifferent to the prosperity of the country which you have so much assisted to place under His Majesty's Government.' All equally flattering, whether they are words of course and to be forgot I know not, they are pleasant for the time however.

I wish most devoutly Lord Hood may get me sent home, I am tired, not of the country which is fine in the extreme, but of our present conduct and situation. Remember me kindly to all where you are and believe me, your most affectionate husband, HORATIO NELSON.

To Mrs. Nelson, 17 New King Street, Bath.

No. 97

Leghorn,
November 28, 1794

MY DEAR FANNY,—I have not heard from you since your first arrival at Kentish Town October 5th especially as I know your punctuality in writing and we have letters to the 1st of November.

Our fleet is gone to sea and report says the French fleet have left Toulon. Should that be the case I shall be truly unfortunate, but I sincerely hope they will remain in port till *Agamemnon* is ready. It would go nigh to break my heart, but I will hope the best. We are in a miserable plight and God knows when we shall be better. If the fleets do not meet the Admiral will very soon be here and I hope will give us some help to get on with. The laying in port is misery to me. I have little to say. Josiah is very well and a good young man.

Believe me ever your most affectionate HORATIO NELSON.

To Mrs. H. Nelson, Bath.

[1] Sir Gilbert Elliot.

No. 98

[Nicolas, I, p. 509, part, given without date]

Leghorn,
December 5, 1794

MY DEAR FANNY,—I have just got your letter of November 2nd and as I do not know your lodgings or arrival at Bath shall send this under cover to Mr. Suckling.

Agamemnon is in her worst state and any alteration must be for the better. We are without masts or yards. In about a fortnight I hope we shall get in order again. We have not heard of our fleet since their departure the 25th of last month. I only hope they have not fallen in with the enemy's fleet, if not they will be here very soon. We have some fears for two frigates of ours on the coast of Barbary. One is arrived who escaped from six frigates and we have not heard of the other two. The French have sent over as a present to the Bey of Tunis a zebec completely armed. Thus by trifling presents they keep up their weight whilst England sends nothing. Of course they are the well wishers of one and dislike the other. They give the enemy every information of our cruisers whilst we are in total ignorance.

I am sorry to tell you that poor Frank is better in health but that there are no hopes the surgeon tells me of his judgements returning, at least not for a certainty. I really am distressed to know what to do with him and have now no servant. Porter turned out so infamous that I was obliged to dismiss him in disgrace, and have now only a Norfolk ploughman. I have lodging on shore during the refitment of my ship and a French master, which with the amusements of the place fully occupy my time.

My health is extraordinary good and I feel myself 7 years younger than when I left England. It is extraordinary the interests of the legacy is not paid. They ought to be the first. I suppose I shall soon be home and something must be done. You will of course see Mr. Baillie at Bristol before long and will talk to him on the subject. I certainly wish the legacy was paid and placed in his hands. The interest he will I hope pay you up to the present time and the arrears.

I wrote my father a line last post to Burnham you will remember me kindly to him and also to our Bristol friends when you see them. Josiah is very well and very good. Believe me ever your most affectionate husband, HORATIO NELSON.

To Mrs. H. Nelson, No. 17 New King Street, Bath.

No. 99

Leghorn,
December 12, 1794

MY DEAR FANNY,—Our fleet is arrived and I shall be ready to go to sea with them again. Our frigates on the coast of Barbary must continue blocked up, for the Admiral will not part with a single ship of the line to relieve them.

I have sent to Mr. Suckling a miniature of myself.[1] I don't know it is a strong likeness but I know it will be acceptable. I shall take another opportunity to send Josiah's who is very well and says the picture is not the least like me. Every body else says it is, but I believe he is right.

With kind remembrances to our father believe me ever your most affectionate husband, HORATIO NELSON.

To Mrs. Nelson, Bath.

No. 100

[Nicolas I, p. 509, part, under earlier date]

Leghorn,
December 19, 1794

MY DEAR FANNY,—I have this moment your letter of the 17th November.[2] I really do not think that one letter of yours has miscarried since I came to this country. Those by shipping and to Gibraltar have been late in coming to hand.

The fleet is here and we sail tomorrow for a cruise and I have no doubt but good fortune will attend us, therefore I only scribble a line to say I never was better nor Josiah. *Agamemnon* is got once more in order as far as masts and yards. We hope Lord Hood[3] is safe arrived and I have no doubts but *Agamemnon* will be one of the first ships relieved and early in the spring we shall be in England, and I really believe Peace is not far distant.

At this moment I have much to do. Just come from a court martial which has lasted 2 days. God bless you and give us a happy meeting says your most affectionate husband, HORATIO NELSON.

Say everything which is kind to my father.

To Mrs. Nelson, Bath, Angleterre.

[1] The miniature painted at Leghorn, now in the National Maritime Museum, is often described as being commissioned by Nelson's wife, but her letter asking him to be painted is dated December 16, 1794 (see Appendix, p. 263).
[2] See Appendix, p. 258.
[3] Lord Hood arrived in England on November 21. Mrs. Nelson called on him in Bath on December 4.

No. 101

[Nicolas, II, p. 1, part]

Agamemnon, St. Fiorenzo,
January 17, 1795

MY DEAREST FANNY,—I wrote you a few days past, since which we have had nothing but gales of wind and a heavy sea, so much so that one of the ships lost all her masts last night. In *Agamemnon* we mind nothing. She is the finest ship I ever sailed in and was she a 74 nothing should induce me to leave her whilst the war lasted. I understand Admiral Hotham will not part with a ship till Lord Hood's arrival which I own much disembarrasses me, for my hopes were to be in England whilst Lord Hood was at home and being put into a good 74 with my ship's company that I might be ready for service early in the spring for not an hour this war will I, if possible, be out of active service. My hopes were originally to have gone home with Lord Hood, to have been placed in a 74, to have got two months' leave of absence and to have my ship ready for sea in March or April, but this plan is all over and I must wait patiently till Lord Hood's arrival, when I shall hear what he says and be guided accordingly. Much as I shall regret being so long parted from you, still we must look beyond the present day, and two or three months may make the difference of every comfort or otherwise in our income. I hope we have many happy years to live together and if we can bring £2000 round I am determined to purchase some neat cottage, when we shall never have occasion to change. As for Josiah I have no doubts but he will be a comfort to both of us. His understanding is excellent and his disposition really good. He is a seaman, every inch of him.

The fleet is on the eve of going to sea again to cover our reinforcements and although we have lost the use of one 74 still I have no doubts of our superiority over the French fleet, should they give an opportunity of meeting at sea. In three days I dare say we shall sail.

I have really nothing to tell you, not having been but once out of my ship but that I am in most perfect health and ever my dearest Fanny, your most affectionate husband, HORATIO NELSON.

Remember me kindly to my father. Did you send something to my Aunt Mary? I find the letters I wrote you some days past are in quarantine and will be so smoked and dried that probably you will hardly be able to read them.

To Mrs. Nelson, No. 17 New King St., Bath, Angleterre.

No. 102

Agamemnon, Fiorenzo,
January 23, 1795

MY DEAREST FANNY,—Two letters, I think, are now in the packet I have on the table ready to go to Leghorn but as I never omit an opportunity of writing I am preparing another although but little has occurred without I I have not mentioned the *Berwick* 74 having lost her masts, as the admiral thinks through carelessness and for which we are now trying the captain [1] of her and the 1st Lieutenant and master. We have sat four long days and I fear it will last full a week longer. It is a sad part of our duty but must be got through. I much fear the captain is in a very unpleasant scrape and I am rather of opinion, poor young man, that he will not be able to clear himself from the charge of negligence. If not, he will certainly be severely punished. We all feel for his unhappy situation; a very young man and the first ship of the Post kind he ever commanded.

So soon as this trial is over we go to sea for a month and return to Leghorn, at least the fleet. Probably I shall be left with a squadron of frigates. I hope so for I hate laying idle. Nothing can give me more satisfaction than continuing to serve under Lord Hood as circumstances are I shall be guided by his advice. My ship is got once more in good order, only very short of men, and there are but very few equal to her.

January 24th: We have just got account of the change in the admiralty.[2] How it may affect me God knows, if Lord Hood gets the command of the channel fleet, I hope to God I shall be ordered home in that case. I am tired of this country but I see no prospect of the reinforcements. I see by papers of January 1st that they had not left England. If the French send ships from Brest, which I believe they will, we are so indolent, what a fine scrape we shall be in. Our admiral must *jump about.*

Poor Captain Smith's trial is over, unfavourable for him. The first Lieutenant and Master's comes on on Monday and will probably last a week.

This goes by a messenger. I see the great polite Captain Bowater has stood before a court martial.

Josiah is perfectly well and sends his love. Remember me most kindly to our father and believe me ever your most affectionate husband, HORATIO NELSON.

To Mrs. Nelson, No. 17 New King Street, Bath.

[1] Captain William Smith was dismissed his ship for neglect of duty. The Master and first lieutenant were also found guilty of negligence.
[2] Lord Spencer replaced Lord Chatham as First Lord of the Admiralty on December 19, 1794.

o

No. 103
[Nicolas, II, p. 2, part]

Agamemnon, Fiorenzo,
January 31, 1795

MY DEAREST FANNY,—It is with inexpressible pleasure I have received within these two days past your letters of December 16–17th up to 24th and 28th, with our father's of January 1st. I rejoice that my conduct gives you pleasure and I trust that I shall never do anything which will bring a blush on your face or on that of any of my friends. It is very true I have ever served faithfully and ever my fate to be neglected but it is no reason I should be negligent of my duty. I have pride in doing my duty well, and a self approbation, which if not so lucrative yet perhaps give more pleasing sensations—but I trust the time will come when I may be rewarded but really I don't flatter it is near. General Stuart's anger to me arises from no cause but hatred to my Lord Hood, hatred founded on the most diabolical principles, because and because only Lord Hood took Bastia against all army opinions and never gave the army or General one opportunity of complaining of his neglect of them at the siege of Calvi. The refusal of one gun would have been the greatest satisfaction to the General, much more than supplying 700 men to do nothing which had been required. I parted from the General on the best terms possible but my journal of the siege, sent home by Lord Hood, showed what the General must from his conduct wished concealed, that all the heavy work and every gun which was fired, was done by seamen and sea officers. This is my crime and I suppose the Scotchman will do all he can to injure me, so far as not saying anything for me, or any other way I defy his malice.

I have got *Agamemnon* into high order again and was I full manned, think her equal to any service whatever, and I believe my ship's company are attached to me. Had she 10 more guns nothing should tempt me to part with her.

I think Lord Hood told me that my loss of an eye should be represented to the King. Many have for much less losses handsome pensions. That I do not expect, it would be too good luck for me. However they ought to give me an equivalent. Lord Chatham carried my papers [1] (so Lord Hood tells me but this is secret) to the King. Now he is out all those hopes will

---

[1] Before Lord Hood left the fleet, Nelson gave him certificates testifying to the loss of the sight of his right eye, signed by the surgeon-general of the forces, the physician of the fleet and the surgeon on shore at Calvi.

be done away. I ought to have the Colonel of Marines or King's Yacht, neither of which I expect, or £200 a year pension. My eye as you may conceive is now grown worse and is almost total darkness and very painful at times. But never mind. I can see very well with the other.

I have wrote to Mr. Bailey and Mr. Stanley. Hope you have got the letters and that they will have the desired effect. Get hold of the money or any part of it, if you can. It is very cruel to keep us out of it, particularly the interest of ours and Josiah's. Lord Hood has so many particular friends to serve that I depend but little from that quarter, except public declaration in my favour as an officer. I believe I shall write Lord Hood what I never told him yet, that after everything was fixed for the attack of Bastia, that I had information given me of the enormous number of troops we had to oppose us, but my honour, Lord Hood's honour, and the honour of our country must have all been sacrificed had I told what I knew; therefore you will believe what must have been my feelings during the whole siege, when often I had proposals made to me, by men *now rewarded*, to write to Lord Hood to raise the siege.

I had improved a good deal in French at Leghorn and brought with me an Italian Frenchman but he is no use to me whatever and I shall return him to the shore again as soon as I go to Leghorn.

Captain Inglefield's [1] is a good place, certainly equal to £1000 a year but I have no desire to be a commissioner.

I thank you for sending the things to Aunt Mary. We must not neglect her.

Feb. 1st: The fleet goes to sea on the 3rd, to parade off Toulon, where the Spanish fleet are at present, and if the French will not come out to fight them it is not very likely they will come out to us. I am afraid I shall not make prize money enough to make any purchases out of it.

Remember [me] kindly to our friends at Bristol. I shall write to my father whilst we are at sea. Josiah is very well and a very good young man. Hoste tells me he writes sometimes to his father but if you write say he is very well and what is true as amiable a young man as ever lived. Weatherhead has just heard of the death of his brother.[2] Believe me ever my dear Fanny, Your most affectionate husband, HORATIO NELSON.

I beg my best respects at Wolterton. *Feb. 3rd:* All well.

To Mrs. Nelson, No. 17 New King St., Bath, Angleterre.

---

[1] Captain John Inglefield was Commissioner at Corsica 1794–6.
[2] In the expedition to the West Indies under Sir John Jervis (see p. 259, Mrs. Nelson's letter of November 17).

No. 104
[Nicolas, II, p. 7, part]

Agamemnon, Fiorenzo,
February 7, 1795

MY DEAR FANNY,—This day twelve months our troops landed at this place to attempt the conquest of the Island, at least of those parts which the French were in possession of; and, however lightly the acquisition of Corsica may be desired by many in England, yet I take upon me to say, it was a measure founded in great wisdom, and during the war must be ever of the most essential service to us and detriment to our enemies. After the evacuation of Toulon we had no place whatever of our own for the fleet to anchor in; Tuscany was wavering and although since declared for us yet we are not certain of her alliance with us from one day to the other. The French Consul at Leghorn, although not received officially, has never quitted Leghorn, and we know the attempts which have been made to get Tuscany again acknowledged by the French as a neutral power, in which case what security have we for our fleet and the numerous victuallers and storeships attendant on it. Corsica ever has supplied Toulon with all the strait timbers, beams, decks and sides for their ships—they are now deprived of that supply which would have enabled them by this time to have built a little fleet, and the Corsican tar and hemp was by no means an inconsiderable supply for the dockyard at Toulon. And further, all our trade and of our allies must ever make the coasts of this island, and the ports would have been so full of row galleys that no trade could have been carried on, nor could our men-of-war have prevented the evil, for half the 24 hours is calm, when these vessels would take the merchant men, was the whole British navy in sight. So much for the value of Corsica at present, which is enough to justify the measure of taking it, and I see no reason it may not be just as valuable as any other part of the King's dominions. But I have done, the recollection of one short year brings it to my mind. It was Lord Hood's plan and it was accomplished chiefly by seamen. We are in expectation every hour of going to sea and believe our next return to port . . . *[Part of letter missing.]*

The Lord certainly never did my conduct justice although ever attentive to me. From our leaving England to the taking of Calvi his silence about my conduct at Naples, which enabled us to hold Toulon, has never been known, or in the affair of the frigates 170 guns and 1200 or 1500 men against me was never publicly noticed, nor my various landings in Corsica and by managing the Corsicans driving the French into the city of Bastia, my blocking up St. Fiorenzo and Calvi that neither supplies of men or provisions could be introduced during a whole winter are not even mentioned although I see others commended for the same service in the summer at Calvi, my close blockade of Bastia that for two months before we landed only 50 sacks of flour was thrown into the town consisting of 18000 or 20000 souls. My heavy fag ashore in which Hunt did very little. Totally neglected I must and do feel but I expect no reward. Had I been done justice to in all these points besides other services and skirmishes in which my ship and person have been risked, I believe the King would not have thought any honour too great for me.

God bless you. Josiah is well. Your most affectionate HORATIO NELSON.

To Mrs. Nelson, No. 17, New King Street, Bath.

No. 105

[Nicolas, II, p. 8, part]

Leghorn,
February 25, 1795

MY DEAR FANNY,—We arrived at Leghorn last night after a very bad cruise. We have had no mails from England for nine weeks past and when we may expect any God only knows; all the ways seem stopped up. This country, I understand, will in a very few days declare its neutrality. Therefore, as all powers give up the contest, for what has England to fight? I wish most heartily we had peace or that all our troops were drawn from the continent, and only a naval war carried on, the only war where England can cut a figure, but I have done and have only to wish to be in England. I have only to say God bless you and believe me ever your most affectionate HORATIO NELSON.

A courier is just going to England by whom I write this letter. I am well as is Josiah. You will not forget me to my father. I never forget you or him. Once more God bless you.

To Mrs. Nelson, Bath, Angleterre.

No. 106

[Nicolas, II, p. 8, part, under date February 25]

Leghorn,
March 2, 1795

MY DEAR FANNY,—I wrote you a few lines by the last messenger three days past but as another is going to England this night I cannot allow him to go off without another line from me to say we are still here with the signal out to prepare to sail, but I don't think we shall go this week to come. Whether the French mean to come out seems uncertain from all the accounts we hear; some say their destination with their troops is for Italy, they having 124 transports full of troops, others that Barcelona in Spain is their object, something they certainly mean to attempt. Tuscany has just concluded a peace and this port is now open to the French as well as ourselves. The *Berwick* [1] is refitted so we are again 14 sail of the line and one Neapolitan [2] ship of the line is joined to us so we are strong. Josiah is very well, just buying a jacket and complains things are very dear.

I received your letter of January 5th, the day after I wrote you, it having been a voyage to sea in search of me. I own I see at present but little prospect of leaving this country but we must have peace after this campaign. I wish Lord Hood would make haste out to us. We want his headpiece.

Give my best remembrances to my father and believe me ever your most affectionate husband, HORATIO NELSON.

To Mrs. Nelson, Bath, Angleterre.

No. 107
[Nicolas, II, p. 8, part, under date February 25th]

Leghorn,
March 6, 1795

MY DEAREST FANNY,—The Admiral has just got some information which has induced him to go to sea immediately. I sincerely hope it is for a good purpose. We are taken rather suddenly but we got off pretty tolerable as to order. My health is perfectly good as is Josiah's. That I know to you is everything. Remember me to my good father. I have only to pray God to bless you.

Believe me ever your most affectionate husband, HORATIO NELSON.

To Mrs. Nelson, No. 17, New King Street, Bath.

[1] Under the command of Captain Littlejohn.
[2] The *Tancredi*, 74 guns, commanded by Captain Francesco Caracciolo.

No. 108

[Nicolas, II, p. 17, part]

Agamemnon, at Sea,
March 10, 1795

MY DEAREST FANNY,—I shall commence a letter at this moment to assure you, although I flatter myself that no assurance is necessary, of my constant love and affection. We are just in sight of the French fleet and a signal out for a general chase. We have but little wind and unfortunately the enemy are in-shore of us, however I hope the Admiral will allow us to go on, and if the French do not skulk under their battery, I trust we shall give a good account of them. Whatever may be my fate, I have no doubt in my own mind but that my conduct will be such as will not bring a blush on the face of my friends. The lives of all are in the hands of Him who knows best whether to preserve it or no, and to His will do I resign myself. My character and good name is in my own keeping. Life with disgrace is dreadful. A glorious death is to be envied, and, if anything happens to me, recollect death is a debt we must all pay, and whether now or in a few years hence can be but of little consequence.

March 11th: did not get sight of the French fleet this morning. I suppose they stood to the westward all night. The Admiral has just got information that the French fleet sailed from Toulon on the 1st March and on the 8th off Cape Corse took the *Berwick* [1] of 74 guns. They are certainly out looking for our convoy every moment expected from England.

March 12th: the French are now within 4 miles of *Agamemnon* and *Princess Royal*, our fleet 10 miles from us, we standing towards our fleet, the enemy attempting to cut us off. God bless you and believe ever your most faithful and affectionate husband, HORATIO NELSON.

To Mrs. Nelson, Bath, Angleterre.

No. 109

Agamemnon,
March 14, 1795,
½ past 8 at night

MY DEAREST FANNY,—I wrote you a line on the 12th which I would not send to anyone but my better half as it might appear a boasting letter but I flatter myself it will appear from my conduct these two last days to be no boast. Yesterday morning at daylight, the French fleet being very far

---

[1] Captain Littlejohn was killed while defending his ship.

to windward, the Admiral made the signal for a general chase. By carrying a press of sail one of their ships carried away her main and fore top mast, which enabled us to get up with her although a French frigate took her in tow. The *Inconstant*, Capt. Fremantle gave her in her distress a broadside but the firing killed him 4 men and obliged him tack off. *Agamemnon* being very far to windward of the English fleet at ¼ before 11 o'clock got within shot of him, the *Ca Ira*—late *Couronne* of 84 guns, now 92, and 1300 men. By management I kept clear of his broadside and only received a few broadsides, the other being his stern-chasers. In two hours the French fleet bore down and obliged me to quit him. It appears by the French Captain's account to Admiral Goodall [1] and myself this day that we killed 110 men and so cut him up that he was unable to refit his ship which was the cause of his not being able to join his own fleet. A French 74 took him in tow. Extraordinary, although we were a good deal chipped about the sails and rigging and masts, yet only 7 men were wounded. The *Sans Culotte* in my retreat honoured me with a broadside but as it did not reach halfway to us we did not mind. By 8 o'clock we were refitted. We had only 344 men at Quarters. Providence certainly protects me and all who sail with me.

March 14th: at daylight the *Ca Ira* and *Censeur* who had her in tow were about 4 miles from us, and we, getting a fair wind, stood in line of battle between the two ships and their fleet but it getting calm as they drew with them they cut them up most amazingly. The *Illustrious* and *Courageux* are entirely dismasted and *Captain* very much cut up. These three ships [2] behaved like gallant officers. Then came Admiral Goodall and *Agamemnon*, fighting both sides to their assistance. When getting alongside the *Ca Ira* and *Censeur* they struck and my first lieutenant Lt. George Andrews as gallant an officer as ever stepped took possession of them, most extraordinary the *Ca Ira* had 400 men killed and wounded and the *Censeur* 300, both dismasted. The rest of the fleet kept at such an awful distance that no good came by firing and yet they damaged our ships whilst our shot hardly reached. Admiral Hotham seems to have given the business up and thinks we have done enough, whilst Goodall and myself think we have done nothing in comparison to what we might, would the Admiral have pursued our victory, which as it turns out is a very dear bought one, but we want Lord Hood to command us, we should have had a glorious victory. We had only 5 or 6 men wounded today.[3]

---

[1] Vice-Admiral Goodall, second-in-command, had his flag in the *Princess Royal*.
[2] The *Illustrious*, Captain Frederick, the *Courageux*, Captain Montgomery, and the *Captain*, Captain Reeve, were all 74-gun ships.
[3] The Master, John Wilson, and six men were officially reported as wounded in this engagement.

Josiah and Hoste with Bolton were my aide-de-camps and behaved with great courage, and Josiah thinks there is no great danger from a Frenchman's shot. Write a line to Hoste's and Bolton's father to say they are well. *Agamemnon* was very much cut up today but at this moment we are again ready for action, would the Admiral but give us an opportunity. The action lasted from van to rear, firing I ought rather to say with most of the ships about 6 or 7 hours. These two French ships behaved amazingly well but their fleet in general most shamefully. They were bound against Corsica. We have taken their battering train and their expedition is spoiled.

God almighty bless you and believe me ever your most affectionate H. N.

March 15th: The French fleet out of sight. We shall have no more fighting at present. They came out with orders to take our fleet or at least defeat us and then retake Corsica. I suppose we stand to the westward after today to protect convoy which may yet be in danger. H. N.

Kind remembrances to my father.

To Mrs. Nelson, No. 17, New King Street, Bath.

No. 110

Agamemnon,
March 15, 1795

MY DEAREST FANNY,—You may have heard of our little brush with the French fleet. Therefore I only write a line to say we are all well, with best remembrances.

Believe me ever your most affectionate husband, HORATIO NELSON.

This goes by the Admiral's dispatches. I shall write you further particulars very soon by post.

Hoste, Josiah, Bolton etc. all well.

To Mrs. Nelson, No. 17, New King Street, Bath.

No. 111

Porto Esperia,
March 23, 1795

MY DEAREST FANNY,—I wrote a line which went with the Admiral's dispatches since which I have wrote you more fully. I have now little to add. We are refitted and ready to sail for Corsica. The French fleet are in

Vado except the *Sans Culotte* who is in Genoa Mole. I never had better health in my life. This is the last campaign and I shall have great pleasure in turning my sword into the ploughshare. We have now the upper hand in these seas and without the people at home are very negligent of us, we must keep it. Josiah still threatens to write you but when his threats are to be put into execution I cannot say. With best and kindest remembrances to my father, believe me, your most affectionate husband, HORATIO NELSON.

To Mrs. H. Nelson, Bath.

No. 112

Agamemnon, St Fiorenzo,
March 28, 1795

MY DEAR FANNY,—I have received your letter of January 20th, inclosed in one from Lord Hood. We have 16 mails due, therefore your others are on the way. I have no reason to suppose that any one letter has miscarried. Yours of the 16th October last directed to Gibraltar I have just received. We shall soon meet and be a long while before we again separate. We got in here yesterday with our prizes who have been much more trouble to me since their capture than before. Two of the French ships are dismantled, therefore it must be very uncertain when they can get to sea again and if any reinforcements soon come out I think they never will attempt it. We shall get to sea in about a fortnight but as the weather is now set in very fine our hard service is over for some time to come. The *Blenheim* [1] and *Bombay Castle* [2] have joined us from England which makes up for the *Courageux* and *Illustrious* who will be a long time before they can join us, indeed the latter is not yet got off the shore, but I hope she will. I hope Lord Hood will make haste out. Had he been with us I am sure we should have done much more but having beat the enemy I don't think we made the most of our victory. The French admiral is to be tried and some of the Captains are under arrest.

I was sorry to hear of poor Mrs. Scrivener's death. I have not heard from Mr. S. this very long time and now I know not where to direct to him. Josiah is very busy at this moment in watering the ship but the wars will all be over long before he has served his time and then he must wait a long time for promotion.

---

[1] The *Blenheim*, 90 guns, Captain John Bazeley: promoted rear-admiral 1795, died 1809, admiral.

[2] The *Bombay Castle*, 74 guns, Captain Charles Chamberlayne: promoted rear-admiral 1795, died 1810, admiral.

At this Island they were very much alarmed by the appearance of the enemy's fleet and only began to put their forts into any sort of repair, and so sure were the French of defeating our fleet that the Mayor and all the Municipality of Bastia were on board *Sans Culotte* to resume their stations but we see the battle is not always to the strong nor the race to the swift, for they were far superior to us and sailed much better. I have only to thank God that next to the wind, which carried away the *Ca Ira's* topmast, the success of our action chiefly rested on the conduct of the *Agamemnon* and as all allow it I feel proud on the occasion. I have just seen Captain Chamberlayne and thanked him for his civilities at Plymouth. He said Mrs. Kelly would not let you come out enough. I don't think she is much liked. C. C. said as much as that she was odd.

March 30th: This goes by a messenger who the Viceroy is just sending to England. We are looking anxiously for Lord Hood and reinforcements. With kindest remembrances to my father, believe me ever your most affectionate husband, HORATIO NELSON.

To Mrs. Nelson, No. 17, New King Street, Bath.

No. 113

[Nicolas, II, p. 25, part]

Fiorenzo,
April 1, 1795

MY DEAREST FANNY,—I have just received your letters of January 15th, 22nd, 28th and February 20th, the last of which is a scolding one but I dare say long before this you will know that I have not been negligent in writing. All the letters at one period came back from Hamburgh to Florence, nor can I conceive that general letters ever came from the fleet, some few might as the Admiral has dispatched ships without all the fleet's knowing it. However, I will not argue that point, but assure yourself, my dear Fanny, that you are never absent from my thoughts, no, not for a minute. Therefore rest assured I always write. I don't know when you are to hear from Josiah. He is a bad hand at writing letters. I hope you will have a delightful spring to make up for the badness of the winter which has been very severe even in these mild climates.

I wish from my heart Lord Hood was arrived. We make but a bad hand of managing our fleet. I am absolutely at this moment in the horrors, fearing, from our idling here, that our active enemy may send out 2 or 3 sail of the line and some frigates to intercept our convoy which is momently expected and which, if taken, would ruin all our affairs in this country, but we are idle and lay in port when we ought to be at sea. In short I wish to be an admiral and in the command of the English fleet. I should very soon either do much or be ruined. My disposition can't bear tame and slow measures. Sure I am, had I commanded our fleet on the 14th, that either the whole French fleet would have graced my triumph, or I should have been in a confounded scrape. I went on board Hotham so soon as our firing grew slack in the van, and the *Ca Ira* and *Censeur* struck, to propose to him leaving our two crippled ships, the two prizes, and four frigates, to themselves, and to pursue the enemy, but he is much cooler than myself and said 'We must be contented. We have done very well', but had we taken 10 sail and allowed the 11th to have escaped if possible to have been got at, I could never call it well *done*. Goodall backed me. I got him to write to the Admiral, but it would not do. We should have had such a day as I believe the annals of England never produced but it can't be helped. The *Illustrious* [1] is lost, and *Berwick* taken, oh dear, oh dear, but now I verily believe, if the Admiral can get hold of them once more but we shall do better, and if he does but get us close, we will have the whole fleet. Nothing can stop the courage of English seamen.

I may venture to tell you, but as a secret, that I have a Mistress given to me, no less a personage than the Goddess Bellona; so say the French verses made on me, and in them I am so covered with laurels that you will hardly find my little face. At one period I am 'the dear Nelson', 'the amiable Nelson', 'the fiery Nelson'. However nonsensical these things are, they are better than censure and we are all subject and open to flattery. I am writing a long letter literally about nothing for nothing I have to say but you desire me to fill my paper. The French Admiral St. Martin has shot himself, the Captain of the *Sans Culotte* run away, and many others will be done for. The Toulonese will not allow the French fleet to enter the Port of Toulon but make them remain in Hieres Bay telling them to get out and execute their former mission or they shall never enter the ports of the republic.

I hope and feel I have now a right to the Marines and if Lord Spencer does not give it to me he is an unjust man for no man can since Lord Howe's action claim equal to me but I don't expect any favours. I have been infamously treated. What must Lord Hood feel in having left this station and what must I have felt had I gone with him. You will agree with me it is better as it is. Let what will happen, I will not stay out longer than this summer. Can the *Ca Ira* be fitted out I shall take her certainly, but not in her present state. She is the largest two decked ship in the world,

---

[1] While being towed the *Illustrious* broke loose and was driven on-shore in a gale. As he could not get her off, Captain Frederick set her on fire.

superior to those taken by Lord Howe. Her force is superior to *Agamemnon* if all her lower deck guns which are 42 pounders were taken out of her. Our admiral is now afraid of ordering a good price to be given for these. I much fear I shall not during the whole station get prize money enough to bear my expenses. I have had my share of fag and no profit.

I never hear from the Matchams. Indeed I have no right as I do not write except you and my dear Father it is the same therefore perhaps I am in his debt many letters. God bless you. I shall not seal my letter till the last moment. Hotham has made 5 post captains besides Masters and Commanders since he has had the command, but he has offered nothing to *Agamemnon*.

With kindest remembrances to my father, believe me ever your most affectionate husband, HORATIO NELSON.

Captain Chamberlayne desires his compliments.

To Mrs. Nelson, No. 17, New King Street, Bath.

No. 114
[Nicolas, II, p. 28, part]

St. Fiorenzo,
April 12, 1795

MY DEAREST FANNY,—I have just received your two letters of March 5th and 9th and am glad to find my letters came to hand as nearly all do which are wrote. Perhaps a mail or two may have been lost both outward and homeward bound by the State of Holland. The letters which came from the fleet went by Major Smith. I did not know of his going or perhaps I should have wrote a line by him although I much disapprove of sending letters by private hands where a post is regular. At that time for a wonder letters by Major Smith got home whilst ours by post were either lost in Holland and several mails returned again into Italy, which accounts for the long distance of time in getting letters. Rest assured I always write and that you are never, my dear Fanny, absent from my thoughts.

If the folks will give me the Colonel of Marines I shall be satisfied, but I fear my interest is not equal to get it, although I will never allow that any man whatever has a claim superior to myself.

We have just got the thanks of the Corsican Parliament and Viceroy for our gallant and good conduct on the 13th and 14th day of March, which they say, and truly, has saved them from an invasion. The Viceroy's private letter to me has a very flattering compliment which cannot but be pleasing to you viz. 'I certainly consider the business of the 13th March as a very capital feature in the late successful contest with the French fleet, and the part which the *Agamemnon* had in it must be felt by everyone to be one of the circumstances which gave lustre to this event and rendered it not only useful but peculiarly honourable to the British arms. I need not assure you of the pleasure with which I so constantly see your name foremost in everything that is creditable and serviceable, nor of the sincere regard and affection with which I ever am etc. G. E.'

So far as all hands agree in giving me these praises, which cannot but be comfortable to me to the last moment of my life, the time I may call well spent by being left by Lord Hood out here. How mortified should I have been to have been absent on this occasion and what has happened perhaps may never happen to anyone again, that only one Ship of the Line out of 14 should get into action with the French fleet, and for so long a time as $2\frac{1}{2}$ hours, and with such a ship as the *Ca Ira*, but had I been supported I should certainly have brought the *Sans Culotte* to battle, a most glorious prospect. A brave man runs no more risk than a coward, and *Agamemnon* to a miracle has suffered scarcely anything. Three or four of our wounded are dead, the others in a fair way of doing well. We have got accounts of the French fleet, the troops landed and their expedition given up. The ships have suffered much, many at this time are shifting their masts. Our fleet was never in better order and I only want Lord Hood to make haste out to us. If I think nothing is to be done here I shall be a candidate for home, but to arrive at Spithead, have all my men taken away and I perhaps to fit out another ship is too much fag. It is better to stay here till October and then rest in England in the winter. I believe you will think so, but many things may turn up which may make it necessary to alter my opinion. I shall hear what Lord Hood says and then form a judgement. Reports say the fleet is going to Leghorn to see our homeward-bound convoy to the westward of Toulon and then some ships will take them to Gibralter.

Josiah is very well and a very good boy. I beg my kindest remembrances to my father and believe me ever, my dear Fanny, your most affectionate husband, HORATIO NELSON.

To Mrs. Nelson, No. 17, New King Street, Bath, Angleterre.

No. 115

April 16, 1795

MY DEAR FANNY,—Although I have a letter by me to send by this vessel yet as it is wrote a day or two ago I will not let the last moment go by without saying I am well never better. We are in momentary expectation of Lord Hood and a squadron which, although I don't believe we want, yet may not altogether be unacceptable. Our fleet is in very high order and healthy. God bless you for ever and ever and believe me, your most affectionate husband, HORATIO NELSON.

Josiah is very well.

To Mrs. Nelson, No. 17, New King Street, Bath, Angleterre.

No. 116
[Nicolas, II, p. 34, extract only]

Leghorn,
April 28, 1795
(arrived too late for post)
May 1

MY DEAREST FANNY,—Although I wrote my Father a very few days past and I know the letter cannot be gone from Leghorn and of course both will arrive at the same time yet I never miss *knowingly* the latest opportunity. Don't laugh at my dash as some letters came formerly from some in the fleet by a private hand Major Smith.

We have been trying these 10 days past to get to the westward to join our expected reinforcements from England, but the winds have been so contrary that we have every day lost ground. Yesterday, to our surprise, our storeships and victuallers from Gibralter arrived in the fleet. Their escape from the enemy has been wonderful for had we lost them our game was up here. This I suppose has induced the Admiral to bear up for this place and by it we shall get the *Courageux* ready for sea when we shall be 14 English Sail of the Line, 2 Neapolitans, and 2 44-gunships, English, a force sufficient at any time to fight 20 French ships of war, and should they venture out, which I sometimes doubt, we shall certainly beat them back again for, thank God, however much our armies may have failed, yet our seamen are as superior to the French as ever during this war. We have never once failed, neither in single action nor in a fleet.

May 1st 1795: I have sent my agents for a wonder a bill for £500 which as it is the first I daresay will be the last I shall send them this war for I shall think myself a very fortunate man if I can be set on shore preserving my pay which will be £1000, for living here is as in all other places very expensive. Reports from Genoa this day tell us that the preliminaries of peace between France, Spain and Naples are signed. If so, we shall lose the use of the 2 Naples 74s, which will make us anxious for Lord Hood's arrival.

We sail on the 4th for Fiorenzo, then to proceed to the westward to look for our reinforcements who I hope will be with us before we sail. Lord Hood must be anxious to get to us and I for one am very anxious to join him for we get on but very so, so.

Josiah has not yet sat for his picture for the Admiral harries us so about nothing that we are not a moment which we can call our own.

With kindest remembrances to my Father, believe me ever your most faithful and affectionate husband, HORATIO NELSON.

To Mrs. Nelson, 17, New King Street, Bath, Angleterre.

No. 117

Leghorn,
May 7, 1795

MY DEAREST FANNY,—We have just got accounts of the honours which are paid to Admiral Hotham [1] in England for the victory obtained over the French on the 14th March, and I hope if justice is done that I shall have the Marines. Sure I am none in the British fleet has worked harder for them. We sail tomorrow morning to endeavour to join Lord Hood, who must be in the Mediterranean, and whose *Nose* I consider as at least equal to four sail of the line.

I have by post also received your letter of March 31st and wonder I have not some of later, as my letters went by the same opportunity as the Admiral's dispatches but which perhaps you have not received. It would I assure my dear Fanny, give me infinite pleasure to return to England but it is necessary to look beyond the present moment. The *Agamemnon* comes to Spithead, all her people are turned over to other ships and I may have, if I have interest, a ship just put in commission which will never be manned for the whole campaign. This would hurt me much more than staying here till October next, when I have no doubt but peace will take place and I shall look out for a peaceful cottage in Norfolk.

May 8th: The signal is just made for sailing and I must conclude with saying myself and Josiah are most perfectly well. Believe me ever my dear Fanny, your most faithful and affectionate husband, HORATIO NELSON.

To Mrs. Nelson, Bath, Angleterre.

[1] Vice-admiral Hotham received the thanks of both Houses of Parliament and was promoted admiral.

No. 118

Agamemnon, off the Isle of Minorca,
May 22, 1795

MY DEAR FANNY,—I have two days past received your letter of April 9th by a frigate who joined us from Leghorn, to which place the Admiral has just made the Signal that he shall send a frigate. I sent by the messenger who carried Admiral Hotham's dispatches 3 letters for you which you ought to have had on the 8th of April but I suppose they will be forthcoming. Many in the fleet have had letters of the 20th of April but I suppose you have sent by my Lord Hood but no way is so good and certain as by post. We sailed from Leghorn on the 8th of May and are here cruising in anxious expectation of Lord Hood's arrival and we cannot conceive the reason of his being so long on his passage. Luckily for us we have no accounts of the enemy's having sailed from Toulon but if Lord Hood does not quickly arrive they will be out and invade Italy or Corsica and we shall have all our work to do over again. I shall certainly either change my ship or go home as Lord Hood may think best. I should like to save myself much trouble to have a ship here till October next. I am tired of *Agamemnon.* Allison [1] is so much given to liquor and then behaves so ill that I have enough to do to refrain from bringing him to a court martial. I have ever heartily repented taking him. I ought to have known enough of him before. He only with one other will be the cause of my leaving the ship but my mind is made up and I shall not alter it. I think Andrews will go into the *Victory* and sooner than have Allison 1st Lt. I would quit the ship and go home by land. However he does not know my intentions or anyone else. He will soon be broke when left to himself.

I am always glad when my conduct gives pleasure to you and my dear Father. I assure you no small part of the pleasure I had when by myself in action was knowing that you and my Father must partake of it. The Admiral's is not a first rate letter but I have no great cause to complain. The world will know what ship I engaged and our escape has been wonderful.

We have now the finest weather in the world and my health never was better. Josiah is also as well as ever, grown very tall and stout. I need not tell you to remember me kindly to all who enquire after me, nor not to be afraid to call on Marsh and Creed for whatever you may want. We suppose Admiral Hotham and Linzee will go home the moment Lord Hood arrives. I have not time to write to any one else. Therefore you must say all that is

[1] Lieutenant Wenman Allison.

P

necessary for me, and believe me ever my dear Fanny, your most affectionate husband, HORATIO NELSON.

To Mrs. H. Nelson, Bath.

No. 119

[Nicolas, II, p. 39, part]

Agamemnon, off Minorque,

May 29, 1795

MY DEAR FANNY,—A frigate came into the fleet two days ago but the weather has been so very bad that none of the fleet have had any communication with her, yet the Admiral has made the signal that she is going to Leghorn. If she goes before we get our letters by her we shall not be pleased with him.

We are in daily, almost hourly, expectation of seeing Lord Hood but as yet we have no accounts of his having actually sailed from St. Helens, and what the people can mean by sending him with only five sail of the line is truly astonishing but all men are alike and we in this country don't find any amendment or alteration from the old Board of Admiralty. They ought to know that half the ships in this fleet ought to go to England and long ago they ought to have reinforced us. At this moment our operations in this country are at a stand for want of ships to support the Austrians in getting possession of the sea coast of the King of Sardinia, and behold our Admiral does not feel himself equal to show himself much less to give assistance in their operations. Indeed my dear Fanny I have nothing to tell you. My boat has not been hoisted out since I wrote you last, therefore for the present you must be content to hear I am well. Josiah is well, and believe me ever your most faithful and affectionate husband, HORATIO NELSON.

You will remember me kindly to my father. If I get any letters I will write another but I am not willing to miss this opportunity.

To Mrs. Nelson, No. 17, New King Street, Bath, Angleterre.

No. 120

[Nicolas, II, p. 39, part, under date May 31]

Agamemnon, off Minorque,

June 7, 1795

MY DEAREST FANNY,—Our new Commander in Chief[1] never gives us many minutes' notice of his intentions to send a ship into port, not but it is

[1] Hotham was now given the command, it being known that Lord Hood was not returning

sufficient for me or any one to say all that is necessary. I am well. As to news we can have none. We have been off here a month very near expecting, first Lord Hood, then Admiral Dickson but the latter has not made his appearance, which makes some of us think that either further alterations are taking place or he is very dilatory in making his passage. Our Commander is elated with his appointment. It is more than most of his fleet are for we have made a sad change, Holloway [1] is to be first Captain of the fleet, both certainly good as men but very unfit for such appointments. We have lost much by Lord Hood's going to England, and much more probably by his not returning. Was he here at this moment with the same force as we have at present, instead of skulking here we should be off Toulon but Admiral Hotham has had as yet most extraordinary good luck. It was the 18th of April we sailed from Fiorenzo with the avowed intention of running away from the French fleet, although he couched under the words of avoiding an action with them. The French fleet had not sailed on the 30th of May most likely never believing such to be our intentions, and as they had only 19 sail of the line. Rome, Corsica and Naples would all have fallen, had they come out with their transports. We are tired and fatigued with our laying off here doing nothing, every moment expecting our ships, till even expectation is wore out. I hope I shall be ordered home but at present I see no prospect of it. I am tired of this business, however I hope peace will very soon come and send us all to our cottages again. Josiah is very well but with myself most heartily sick of this cruise. With kindest remembrances to my father, believe me ever your most faithful and affectionate husband, HORATIO NELSON.

To Mrs. H. Nelson, Bath.

No. 121

[Nicolas, II, p. 39, part, under May 31]

Agamemnon, off Minorca,
June 15, 1795

MY DEAREST FANNY,—Yesterday Admiral Man [2] joined us with the squadron but by some mistake not a letter from you or my father are yet come to my hands nor can I hear any tidings of them. So much for writing

---

[1] Captain John Holloway, who had been in the West Indies with Nelson, had served with Hotham as a junior officer.
[2] Rear-Admiral Robert Man came out in the *Victory* with a squadron of seven sail of the line.

by private persons when there is a regular post. Lord Hood writes me he gave them to Admiral Dickson who going ill on shore very probably left them in his trunk. Whichever way they are gone. I never expect to see them. His Lordship also enclosed me a copy of a letter from Lord Spencer about me, acknowledging my pretensions to favour and distinction but what is all this polite words, 'when proper opportunities offer' (his Lordship's expression), they may never offer for rewarding me. This letter is wrote before the account of our action that may throw an additional weight into the scale for me. I know nothing at present, not having been on board the Admiral since the fleet joined. *Agamemnon* is not, I fancy, ordered home with this convoy and perhaps the Admiralty will commission me for one of the vacant ships here when promotion of Admirals takes place, and if they give me the Marines I shall be satisfied.

I have this moment received from the *Britannia* your letters of February 12th, April 16th and 24th and my father's of March 28th. I hope you will be able to settle with Bailey. It must rest with him. We have nothing to do with Mr. Hamilton nor has he the charge of payment of the legacy, or interest of them. Whenever I can get home I will have those matters settled and regularly paid. As to living, it is expensive everywhere and perhaps as much so here as any place for the sea officers spend in eating much more than is right but all must be nearly in the same way of living. However I hope to save my pay which with a little addition will buy us a very little cottage where I shall be as happy as in a house as large as Holkham.[1] I think I shall get the Marines or a yacht. My services seem pretty well understood. I wrote to my father a few days past and though it is not gone from the fleet—I shall not recall it. Shall not close this till the signal is made for a vessel going in to port. The French fleet will not come out again. Linzee goes home in the *Bedford*.

June 20th: A vessel just going for Leghorn. No convoy but expect them every moment. Josiah etc. all well. Ever my dear Fanny your affectionate husband, HORATIO NELSON.

To Mrs. H. Nelson, Bath.

No. 122

Off Minorca,
June 22

MY DEAR FANNY,—My letters sent off two days past by a ship for Leghorn are this morning returned into the fleet, she having got accounts that the

---

[1] The residence of Thomas Coke, first Earl of Leicester (1752–1842).

French have a squadron at sea and as the Admiral has made her signal to return again I write a line to say I have just by another ship from Leghorn got your letter of 12 and 13 May. I did not know you had scolded me, therefore did not feel on the occasion. I have no thoughts of the *Ca Ira* at present, she would require too long a time to repair for my active mind. No, I shall remain here unless the Admiralty change me. Some say I am to have my flag, some say the Marines, the latter I hope, the former will half ruin me, going home by land and most probably be unemployed, or if not, the war I hope is so near an end that all would be expense and no chance of profit. I don't know what papers you allude to to be copied for Lord Spencer, however he does not want or probably wish for my correspondence or knowledge. I believe Mr. Andrews has a great disappointment in Lord Hood's not coming out. I wrote to Lord Howe about him but his letter was a jumble of nonsense, *his little influence* necessarily directed to the Channel fleet knew of no way but has taken a commission for the *Queen Charlotte*, the vacancies there very uncertain, and he was to consider whether it was better to give up his prospects with me, in short nothing that any young man could with propriety build upon. Had Lord Howe said half as much before he left England, Andrews would have been a captain but these great men have neither gratitude nor regards.

Josiah's picture is not done. We have so much in hand when we are at Leghorn that time flies away and he is but very little on shore. He will brag himself a great stout boy. If you see Captain Trigge make my compliments to him. He bears a good character but is very infirm. Josiah's teeth are good, his cough as usual but I believe it is a great deal habit. It neither affects his eating, sleeping or growth. I am glad to hear poor Mrs. Matcham [1] is well. She should leave off having any more children. I had letters from Mr. & Mrs. Bolton. We are all well. Remember me kindly to my father and our friends at Bristol. Bailey must do something. Can it be expected we can live on air? They have no authority to give up any part of the produce of the estate till our legacies and interests are paid. I hope Mr. Pinney will be able to put you in the proper way.

With kindest remembrances to my father, believe me, ever your most affectionate husband, HORATIO NELSON.

To Mrs. Nelson, New King Street, Bath, Angleterre.

---

[1] Mrs. Matcham had her fifth child in May 1795; she had six more.

No. 123

[Nicolas, II, p. 48, part]

St. Fiorenzo,
July 1, 1795

MY DEAR FANNY,—Our convoy having joined us on the 22nd we made sail for this port and arrived all safe on the 29th. So far we are fortunate. The French fleet 17 sail of the line are out but only to exercise their men, at least our Admiral says so. However they may make a dash and pick up something. We have *Zealous* 74 and three ordnance ships expected daily from Gibraltar. I hope they will not look out for them but our good Admiral trusts all to chance. Two French frigates were for 10 days very near us as we learnt by neutral vessels. I requested the Admiral to let me to go after them but he would not part with a ship of the line. When the fleet bore away for this place he sent two small frigates, *Dido* and *Lowestoffe*, to look into Toulon. The day after their parting from us they fell in with the two frigates of the enemy, the *Minerva* of 40 guns 18 pounders they took, the other of 36 guns 12 pounders got away. It is a very handsome done thing in the Captains who are Towry and Middleton, and much credit must be due to these officers and ships company. Thank God the superiority of the British Navy remains and I hope ever will. I feel quite delighted at the event. Had our present fleet but one good chance at the enemy, on my conscience, without exaggeration, I believe if the Admiral would let us pursue but we would take them all.

I am sorry to tell you that Allison [1] is just invalided from extreme bad health but I do not think he will ever live to see England, all brought on by his own intemperance. What is to become of me? I know not whether I am to change my ship or what. I have made up my mind to do what the Admiralty wish me. If they give me the Marines and appoint me to a ship here, I shall take her. If they order *Agamemnon* home I shall wish not to leave her but I leave it to them, and if they behave well to me they will always find me ready to meet their wishes. Josiah is very well but not very fond of writing. We are in daily expectation of a promotion of flags when four of our captains go home and of course as many will come out, fish by land carriage.

With kindest remembrances, believe me ever your most affectionate husband, HORATIO NELSON.

---

[1] Nelson filled the vacancy by promoting James Summers, a protégé of Captain Locker.

Have just received your kind letter of May 25th St. Fiorenzo July 2nd 1795.

To Mrs. Nelson, New King Street, Bath, Angleterre.

No. 124

Off Cape Corse,
July 9

MY DEAR FANNY,—The Admiral having sent me to assist the Austrian general [1] in driving the French out of the Riviere of Genoa and from the sea coast of Piedmont with a few frigates, the French fleet to prevent such a design came on the coast with 17 sail of line and 6 frigates. The pursuit of us lasted 24 hours and at times we were hard pressed. 7 hours our fleet in Fiorenzo were spectators of our apparently inevitable fate but the wind was in such contradiction that I could neither get to them nor they get to us. It required all my knowledge to manage my ship. However, thank God, the enemy at last gave me up as a bad job. They are neither seamen nor officers. Our fleet came out yesterday morning but the *Sans Culotte* having a fine breeze and we becalmed they are over on their own coast and I have but little hopes we shall get at them. If we do, the campaign will be over at sea in this country for besides our great superiority a finer fleet never graced the ocean.

I have parted with Mr. Allison but by drinking, his health is so much injured that I doubt much if he ever recovers from the complaints it has brought on. I shall keep this letter open till an opportunity offers of sending it to Leghorn.

July 10th: no enemy in sight off Ville Franche, fear they will get into port.

July 14th: yesterday morning we got sight of the French fleet and had the wind lasted I verily believe the whole fleet would have been captured. Six or seven of our ships only got into action and that at a great distance. Had the wind lasted us only 10 minutes, six of us under Admiral Man would have had each one his ship. I was certain in appearance of getting alongside an 80 gun ship with a flag but the wind changing gave them the weather gage and enabled them to reach their own coast, from which they were only a few miles distant. We were just getting up with them again being within reach of grape shot, when Admiral Hotham made the

[1] General de Vins. Nelson wrote a short account of his proceedings, known as his Vado Campaign, for the information of Sir John Jervis when he arrived to take over command in the Mediterranean in November (see Appendix, pp. 241–252).

signal to discontinue the action. The risk might have been great but so was the object. Had Lord Hood been here he would never have called us out of action but Hotham leaves nothing to chance. The van of the English might now have been covered with glory. Troubridge of the *Culloden* lost his main topmast and *Victory* was a good deal cut up about her rigging, the enemy firing to dismast us. We have lost but few men, *Agamemnon* none killed and only one badly wounded. Our sail and rigging have suffered and some bad shot under water but all are now nearly repaired. We are now steering for St. Fiorenzo.

With kindest regards for my father, believe me ever your affectionate HORATIO NELSON.

Victory, Captain, Agamemnon, Defence, Culloden, Cumberland, Blenheim latterly *Audacious* might have fired a few shot but I did not see her. Josiah and Hoste are both well.

To Mrs. Nelson, New King Street, Bath, Angleterre.

No. 125

Genoa Mole,
July 18, 1795

MY DEAR FANNY,—I arrived here yesterday and active as I am I have still to regret not being more so, at least that other people were not as active as self. The Admiral keeping me for 24 hours in St. Fiorenzo prevented my falling in with two French frigates and two brigs who only arrived here 16 hours before me. I sail tomorrow to co-operate with the Austrian General in driving the French out of the Riviera of Genoa. My Admiral has given me such orders as to be useless to the common cause and I must run some pecuniary hazard to serve my country. I have determined in concert with His Majesty's Minister here, Mr. Drake, to stop all Genoese vessels bound to France. An express will go to England for the approbation of Government so soon as I can get answers to mine and Mr. Drake's letters going to Admiral Hotham. I just see in the paper my Marine appointment [1] although I dare say they will not allow me to hold it long yet the appointment is both honourable and pleasant. God bless you my dear Fanny and believe me ever your most affectionate husband, HORATIO NELSON.

Remember me kindly to my father. I have just been ordering what I fancy is the proper epaulettes. However, I was obliged to take a young

[1] Nelson was commissioned colonel in the marine forces on June 1, 1795, when there was a vacancy owing to the promotion of flag-officers.

friend of mine, a soldier officer, or I might have made a bad choice. The navy lace for the strap very full and long the bullions so we shall all be bucks in our old age.[1]

I don't know if I am right, tell me. *[A sketch follows.]*

Josiah is very well and would rather have had the epaulettes than myself.

To Mrs. Nelson, New King Street, Bath.

No. 126
[Nicolas, II, p. 59, part]

Agamemnon, off Vado Bay,
July 24, 1795

MY DEAREST FANNY,—What changes in my life of activity, here I am, commenced a co-operation with an old Austrian General, almost fancying myself charging at the head of a troop of horse. As nothing will be wanting on my part towards the success of the common cause I have no doubt but you will hear by autumn that we are in possession of 60 miles of sea coast, including the towns of Monarco and Nice. I have 8 sail of frigates under my command. The service I have to perform is important and, as I wrote you a few days ago from Genoa, I am acting not only without the orders of my commander in chief but in some measure contrary to them. However, I have not only the support and countenance of His Majesty's Ministers both at Turin [and] at Genoa but a consciousness that I am doing what is right and proper for our King and Country's service. Hotham has no political courage which is in an officer abroad as highly necessary as battle courage.

We took three days ago, that is the squadron, a vessel from Marseilles bound to Genoa, deserted when near the shore by the master and crew, who certainly carried off with them great riches. What they left we know not. She is said to be valued when she sailed from Marseilles at the enormous sum of £160,000 sterling. However, we must expect nearly all the money is gone. I have got one large chest of silver, some lumps of gold, 7 and 8 lbs. in the lump, with a great number of diamond rings, loose diamonds and other valuables on board *Agamemnon*, besides a rich cargo of silks,

---

[1] New uniform regulations were issued on June 1, 1795. Post-captains of three years' standing were to wear the following full-dress: 'Blue coat with blue lapels and long slash sleeves as formerly worn: the lapels to have one row of gold lace and the cuffs and pockets two: two plain gold epaulettes: white lining: white waistcoat and breeches: gold laced hat.' Officers were allowed to wear their old uniforms for one year from the date of the order. Epaulettes, now introduced for the first time, were only worn by senior officers.

spices etc. However some may value her, if she gives me 1000 or 1500 pounds I shall be well satisfied. I have information of three others but the knowledge of my activity is gone forth and I do not expect much more success. The Ministers want the Admiral to give me an order to wear a distinguishing pendant. Lord Hood would in the present situation of affairs at once order it—No expense but honorary. The Austrian army is composed of 32,000 the finest troops I ever saw, and the General when he gets Nice will have the baton of a Marshal. What shall I get? However, this I can say, that what I have got I owe to myself and to no one else. To you I may say my character stands high almost with Europe, even the Austrians knew my name perfectly. When I get through this campaign I think myself I ought to rest.[1] I hope to God the war will be over and that I may return to you in peace and quietness. A little farm and my good name is all my wants or wishes.

Josiah is very well and a good boy. With kindest remembrances to my father, believe me ever your affectionate HORATIO NELSON.

July 27, Leghorn.

Blown in here in a gale of wind. Now fine weather. Hope to get to sea this night. All my letters gone to the fleet and to Genoa. God bless you. HORATIO NELSON.

To Mrs. Nelson, New King Street, Bath, Angleterre.

No. 127

[Nicolas, II, p. 65, part, and order transposed]

Vado Bay,
August 2, 1795

MY DEAR FANNY,—We returned here the day before yesterday and I was happy to find that no event had happened which caused me to regret my absence. I expect in a few days this army will get farther westward.

August 3rd: Last night I received your two letters of June 11th and 22nd. I do not see myself how I can with any degree of propriety quit a situation of much credit immediately as the Admiralty have done the handsomest possible thing by me. As I told Admiral Hotham some time ago that if the Admiralty gave me the Marines I should certainly do whatever they appeared to wish me. Such I think highly proper but I really believe *Agamemnon* will be ordered home this autumn for we cannot

---

[1] Writing to Sir Gilbert Elliot on July 17, Nelson said: 'I find my exertions have been beyond my strength. I have a complaint in my breast which will probably bear me down; but please God if I see this campaign out, if *Agamemnon* does not go to England, I must, the medical people tell me, be on shore for a month or two without the thoughts of service.'

want so great a fleet in the Mediterranean, therefore unless the Admiralty actually send me out a commission for another ship I shall certainly remain in the *Agamemnon*. The fighting part of our business is over and we have all play before us, and I really believe the English fleet will again enter the harbour of Toulon. We want Lord Hood's head for at the time we got possession before, the Royalists were by no means so strong at Toulon as at this moment.

Allison is gone home very ill. His heart is good but when in liquor he is mad. Suckling has at times been rather troublesome but that is I hope all over. He is a very attentive, good officer and will if he pleases do credit to the service.

My dear Fanny, I cannot bear the thought of your being expensive to my father. Why not draw for £200? and my father and myself can settle our accounts when we meet. At present I believe I am the richer man and should our prize be condemned I shall be quite rich, therefore I desire you will give my dear father that money. At all events it is better in his hands than in my agents. Josiah is very well. I wish he had served his time for till then nothing can be done. Young Hammond had I will venture to say served 10 years but I was too scrupulous. However, a few years will soon slip away and he is young enough. At present he is signed midshipman. I do not believe he is the least altered in countenance, at least I do not perceive it, except the enlargement of his features.

I had a long letter of congratulation from the Rector of Hilborough. He seems, and is I am sure, pleased with my preferment. He seems to think it necessary he should take his Doctor's degree.[1] His son Horace [2] has some thoughts of going to sea. I [am] sure I would not recommend it. The living of Hilborough is a much better thing.

Josiah intends to write you soon and desires his love. Believe me ever, my dear Fanny, with the greatest affection. Your most faithful husband, HORATIO NELSON.

Remember me to our friends at Bristol and to any naval friends who may enquire after me. I have been very negligent in not writing to my father which I rest assured he knows I would have done long ago, had you not been under the same roof. At present I do not write less than 10 or 20 letters a day which, with Austrian Generals and Aide-de-Camp and my own little squadron, fully employ my time, which I like, active service or none.

To Mrs. Nelson, New King Street, Bath, Angleterre.

[1] The Rev. William Nelson took his doctor's degree in 1802.
[2] Horatio Nelson, born in 1788, was sent to Eton. He became Viscount Merton in 1805, but the title was afterwards changed to Viscount Trafalgar. He died in 1808. Following family tradition, he was called Horace in the home circle.

No. 128

Vado Bay,
August 25, 1795

MY DEAREST FANNY,—I have been some time in answering your three last letters but as I wrote to my good father it was pretty nearly the same thing. We are doing nothing here. The Austrians cannot get over the mountains and I cannot get the Admiral to come here to give us his assistance in carrying a part of the army a small distance by water, but Hotham will not entangle himself with any co-operation. I may do what I please with my small force but he will not give me either help or countenance. The whole fleet is now at Leghorn idling their time. I am now on shore waiting for a conference with General de Vins, to know what he will do. I cannot bear this life of inactivity. So much for public affairs.

Yesterday I received your letter of July 27th and was both surprised and sorry to hear of poor Mr. Rolfe's death. No *age*, no *profession* is exempt from death and the apparent dangers we go through are nothing in reality. Under God's protection it matters not how we are employed. I think it most probable *Agamemnon* will be one of the first ships ordered home. I shall certainly follow her fate unless the Admiralty absolutely commission me for another ship, which is not likely, but to give up a ship to go home would subject me to disgrace which I am sure you would not wish. Probably I should never be employed again. Time will come round and we shall certainly get the cottage. I shall be glad to hear Stanley is arrived and I beg you will write to him and request his interference that the legacy may be paid. It is scandalous to withhold the scanty pittance from you. As to Mrs. Hamilton I am not surprised at any part of her conduct or young Morton, who is a blockhead. Your letters, my dear Fanny, are not only affectionate but full of news. You used to say you could not write letters but very few people write so well, this without flattery. My situation here is rather pleasant than otherwise but at the same time I am sorry to say, more expensive. In former times a distinguishing pendant was always here and I ought to have it, which would give me 10 shillings a day extra pay, half my table. Lord Hood would have done it as it is right but our present Admiral will do nothing. He is alarmed at everything and dreads doing wrong, which makes him err 20 times in a month.

Josiah will be a good officer I have no doubt, but I fear will never be troubled with the graces. He is the same disposition as when an infant. However he has many good points about him. He is in extraordinary good health, never sick. With best regards to my father, believe me ever your most affectionate husband, HORATIO NELSON.

To Mrs. Nelson, Bath, Angleterre.

No. 129
[Nicolas, II, p. 79, part]

Vado Bay,
September 1, 1795

MY DEAREST FANNY,—We have made a small expedition with the squadron and taken a French corvette and some other vessels but of little value to such numbers as share for them. In this expedition I lost no men but since I have not been so successful. Sending Mr. Andrews to cut off a ship from Oneglia, on his passage he fell in with three Turkish vessels as it has since turned out, who killed and wounded 17 of my poor fellows. Seven are already dead and more must be lost by the badness of their wounds, and I am sorry to say the Turks got into Genoa with six millions of livres hard cash. However, they who play at bowls must expect rubbers, and the worse success now, the better I hope another time.[1] Our fleet is still at Leghorn as idle as is possible to conceive. Collingwood [2] I hear is arrived in the *Excellent* 74 with the convoy from England. I am almost afraid from the inactivity of our Admiral that the campaign in this country will end in a very different manner to what might have been expected. It is almost in vain my shutting up one door when the Admiral allows half a dozen to be open, but I will do my best till the campaign finishes. Had proper assistance been given and which I had every reason to expect, I would have had this army in Nice and my squadron in Ville Franche, good winter quarters.

September 3rd: Tomorrow morning I am going a little cruise for I cannot bear an idle life and hope to be successful. Nothing has sailed from Genoa for France since the 18th July. Of course the French are a little angry with me. We have reports that another promotion of flags is shortly to take place. I sincerely hope it is not true. A voyage home by land would be very disagreeable to me in the winter months.

I am sorry to tell you poor little Hoste has very near broke his leg but it is in a fair way of being very soon well. He was prize master of a vessel and fell down a scuttle. Josiah is as well as usual.

[1] See Appendix for Hotham's letter to Nelson, p. 236.
[2] Captain Cuthbert Collingwood, Nelson's close friend.

With kindest remembrances to my father, believe me my dear Fanny, your most affectionate HORATIO NELSON.

To Mrs. Nelson, Bath, Angleterre.   Via London.

No. 130

[Nicolas, II, p. 82, part]

Vado Bay,
September 15, 1795

MY DEAR FANNY,—Although I have received no letter from you since I wrote last, yet as I know your great anxiety for letters I write merely to say we are all well and that I am not quite so well pleased as I expected with this army, who are slow beyond all description, and I begin to believe the Emperor is anxious to touch another four million of English money. As for the German generals, war is their trade and peace is ruin to them, therefore we cannot expect they have any wish to finish the war. I have just made some propositions to the Austrian general to spur him on, which I believe he would have been full as well pleased had I omitted. In short I can hardly believe he means to go any farther this winter. I am now under sail on my way to Genoa to talk with our Minister on the inactivity of the Austrians, and he must take some steps to urge these people forward.

Our fleet is just passed with the Neapolitans, 23 sails of the line. The enemy have no ships ready for sea nor do I believe they will come out very soon. The small flotilla from Naples has just joined but the season is almost too late for their acting. However, if they will act, I can find them plenty of employment but I doubt their inclination.

I hope my dear father is as well as I sincerely pray he is. Believe me ever your most affectionate husband, HORATIO NELSON.

Going into Genoa Mole.

To Mrs. Nelson, Bath, Angleterre.

No. 131

[Nicolas, II, p. 86, part]

Agamemnon, at Sea,
September 21, 1795

MY DEAR FANNY,—I have not received a letter from you later then the end of July which I cannot account for as our posts are regular, but at present I believe the fault must lay with the people at Leghorn not forwarding my letters, although several ships have joined me from thence. I have had a long letter from Suckling [1] telling me all the Burnham news, which is all new to me and very pleasant to hear. For the moment I fancy myself at the old parsonage. I have been in concert with His Majesty's Minister very hard at work in pushing the Austrian general forward and yesterday morning got them to make an attack which has been successful, and they have carried the centre post on the ridge of mountains occupied by the French troops. The action lasted 10 hours, and if the General will carry one other point we shall gain 33 miles of country. Another is in agitation which, if the Admiral will give me transports to carry a certain number of troops, will astonish the French and perhaps the English. The General, if he can be brought to move, is of great abilities, but generally the politics of his Court so ties his hands that he cannot always do what he thinks proper. However, if this army does not move, the Minister who is fixed at head-quarters, will endeavour to withhold the remainder of the Emperor's loan—say gift. This is an all powerful motive with a German Court and for which the lives of their subjects are held in no estimation. I shall now become a politician almost fit to enter the diplomatic line, for the tricks of each Court are so mean that if a private man was to act so, he would be scouted. The common cause has no weight with anyone. England wants to rule all the Courts and by her money does much. They dislike it and take every opportunity of thwarting the schemes proposed by our Ministry.

I am now on my way to Leghorn to get some provisions, where I shall finish my letter. Josiah is very well. Hoste quite recovered and not the worse for his accident. He is without exception one of the finest boys I ever met with.

September 24th, Leghorn: I am just arrived and received your letters of August 16th, 20th and 27th. I build little on prize money. When it is paid it is time enough to reckon on it. What is to turn up, who can say, but I believe *Agamemnon* cannot much longer be kept on here.

I have just received the most handsome testimony transmitted to our Minister which he has sent home of my conduct from the Austrian General. Much has not been in my power but I have done my all to serve the cause.

I have letters from Lord Hood whose loss we feel every day and should a Spanish war take place Hotham must give up the command.

I will write to our father very soon. I have received his letter. Believe me my dear Fanny, your most affectionate husband, HORATIO NELSON.

To Mrs. Nelson, Bath, Angleterre.

[1] Suckling Nelson had taken holy orders, and was doing duty at Burnham Thorpe for his father.

No. 132

[Nicolas, II, p. 91, part]

Vado Bay,
October 5, 1795

MY DEAR FANNY,—Since I wrote you last nothing has occurred except the sailing of the French squadron from Genoa who, so soon as they knew of my absence, made a push and I fear are all got off. Two of our frigates were seen firing at them but indeed I have not much expectation of their success. It was a near touch for I came back in the morning after they sailed the evening before. I am vexed and disappointed but the best laid schemes, if obliged to be trusted to others, will sometimes fail, but I must submit and hope for better luck another time, but a squadron of French ships would have so graced my triumph. I never hear nor know anything of our fleet. Here I am—left to do as I please. My squadron have, in the opinion of the Genoese, that it almost appears a trial between us, who will first be tired, they of complaining, or me of answering them. However, my mind is fixed. Nothing they can say will make me alter my conduct towards them.

Report says Hotham is going home but in this country we know nothing about it. How different would our situation have been if that great officer Lord Hood [had] been out here. I am almost certain we should at this moment have possessed all Provence.

Our army here are very close to the French. Every hour I expect an attack from the French for the General from some cause does not seem just now in the humour for to attack them.

God knows what is intended for *Agamemnon*. I hear nothing of her going home and yet I cannot bring myself to believe she can be kept out much longer, but I hope whatever is is best. If she does not sail this month I hope she will not be sent in the winter.

I have just received a very affectionate letter from the Duke of Clarence and he seems to remember our long acquaintance with much seeming satisfaction. One expression 'I never part with a letter of yours. They are to me highly valuable.' God knows what may ever arise from this acquaintance. However, we are certain no harm can come from it. He finds me unalterable, which he has never, I fancy, found in any of those he has given the preference. One day or other he may be useful to me.

With kindest affection to my father, believe me, your most affectionate husband, HORATIO NELSON.

Josiah is very well, but I cannot get him to write letters.

To Mrs. Nelson, Bath, Angleterre.

PLATE VII. Rear-Admiral Horatio Nelson wounded at the landing at Santa Cruz, July 24, 1797, supported by Josiah Nisbet (see p. 374: Lady Nelson's memorandum of events). One of a series of paintings by Richard Westall, R.A., engraved for Clarke and M'Arthur's life of Nelson in 1809.

No. 133

Leghorn,
October 19, 1795

MY DEAREST FANNY,—I came in here two days ago having searched St. Fiorenzo in search of the Admiral who I found was got here frolicking. Having got the few stores I wanted for the present, I sail for Vado tomorrow morning and hope to get some success in the prize way now winter is approaching as I shall get some of my squadron off Marseilles and Toulon.

I received with infinite pleasure your two letters of Sept. 7th and 17th and agree with poor Chamberlayne that I hope not to be made an Admiral, to take a land voyage. It must be terrible in the winter months, but I fear every post to hear I am made an Admiral. I understand many of our fleet go home in the spring and most probably *Agamemnon* will be one of the number. Sure I am, she ought to be sent home, but this I shall always say, that my health has been much better in the Mediterranean than in any other country I ever saw. Collingwood is here. I see him for a day, a great comfort, a very old acquaintance. In short having the good opinion of my Commander-in-Chief and the friendship of my brother officers, I am as happy, separated from you, as I could wish.

You don't tell me that Mr. Bayley has paid any part of the legacy. I wish most heartily he would pay the interest at least. If the Royalists fail in their attempt we must have peace and if they succeed it must very soon arrive. If Maurice retains his half pay I shall be glad to hear he is again in the Navy Office. It is what he has been used to and I daresay regrets the leaving it.

I cannot write a long letter for my time is full. What an odd animal Scrivener must be. I have never heard from him since he lost his wife. Josiah is very well but cannot be brought to write letters.

Believe me ever, your most affectionate HORATIO NELSON.

To Mrs. Nelson, Bath, Angleterre.

No. 134

Agamemnon, at Sea,
November 2, 1795

MY DEAR FANNY,—Since I wrote you from Leghorn I have been at Vado and from thence into the Bay of Marseilles and off Toulon but I am sorry to say without any success to signify, only a small vessel with flour and

Q

stopped another which I fear will not be a prize. I have had many fishermen and people on board from the coast of the Gulf and all agree that
France is by no means in distress for want of provisions. On the contrary
in these parts they have plenty and by no means very dear. Certainly
inland they may not have it so cheap but they have had a very good harvest
of corn, although not so good for wine and oil. In short from all I see and
learn the resources of France will continue so long as the confiscated
estates remains in the hands of the nation. As in America, they regard
not the depression of their paper currency, it answers the purpose for the
moment, and by allowing the depression, hard money which was probably
hid begins to make its appearance and a tradesman so much if hard money,
so much if paper, makes no scruple of demanding for his goods. The army
which they had against Spain is now divided, 20,000 gone to the Northern
Army and 20,000 against the Austrians at Vado, and what is extraordinary,
near Avignon they have prepared barracks for 80,000 men. These are now
collecting from the country to form a new army which is to be drilled and
made fit for service against next spring. These movements do not look like
fear in the Convention. The people say the Army is true to the Convention
and they do not think the Comte D'Artois [1] will be successful. If he is to
be, I pray God it may be soon and let us have peace. I assure you I begin
to be tired of the *Agamemnon* and do not much like the prospect of any
winter's campaign. However my health is perfectly good and I shall do
full as well as my neighbours. I prepare to send this letter away by the
first vessel which offers for Leghorn, therefore I cannot tell you what the
Austrians have been after since my departure a fortnight ago but I expect
to find them as I left them. This Italian campaign has certainly been a
most useless and most expensive one. I know of no good it has done.
Each ally lays the fault on the other. But I verily believe the Court of
Vienna has no sincerity or good will to finish the war. Certain it is the
interest of their generals to prolong it, more especially if we pay them.
Had they pleased, I am sure, Nice might long ago have been in our
possession.

Josiah is most perfectly well but as I have often told you not very fond
of letter writing.

November 6th, Vado Bay: The night after I wrote the above we took a
ship loaded with corn for France. I hope the cargoe will be a prize and
would do very well did we not share with all the squadron—*Agamemnon*
fags and others are idle—therefore my share will not be much, 50 pounds
perhaps instead of £700 but I cannot help it.

---

[1] The Comte d'Artois, who had emigrated from France, was trying to raise a royalist
revolt at La Vendée.

I got last night your letter of Sept. 24th. God bless you. I am writing to Ministers, Admirals, Generals, etc., therefore must leave off by begging my kindest love to my father and that you will believe me ever your most affectionate husband, HORATIO NELSON.

To Mrs. Nelson, Bath, Angleterre.

No. 135

Genoa Mole,
November 13

MY DEAREST FANNY,—I have received your letter of Oct. 11th and my father's of the 5th. I am always glad to find that my conduct is approved of by my superiors but very few I assure you work so hard for a few compliments as myself. God knows if any real benefit will arise to me. However it always gives us claims.

An event has just now arose here which has occasioned my presence here and I trust, with proper firmness on the part of the Austrians, that we shall make the French sufferers although for the moment they appear to have an advantage. All neutral powers demand of all ships of war when they enter their ports that they shall abstain from all acts of hostility whilst they remain in that port, in which of course must be meant as the strongest measure that no expedition shall be fitted out in the port. I have made that remark that you should form some judgement of the action committed. And the Commander of each ship or squadron declares on his honour to observe the strictest neutrality. A few nights ago this frigate and other French agents and privateers put out of the port 300 men, surprised an Austrian post about 9 miles from Genoa and brought away many stores and 10,000 pounds sterling in hard cash and returned to Genoa with the booty. The next day they destroyed a magazine of salt belonging to the King of Sardinia under the guns of the town. The party which surprised the Austrian post have been driven back by a larger party of Austrians and the French intended last night (but my arrival prevented the frigate and privateers from moving) intended to have carried a much larger body and to repossess themselves of the post and were to have had support from the French Grand Army at Alberga who were to have fixed themselves at this place called Voltry. The face of affairs is now totally changed. The frigate and corsairs for fear of getting from me what they know they deserve, have got their vessels from the Outer to the Inner Mole inside the merchant ships. But what I want to have settled with this Government is that they shall cause the frigate to be disarmed and kept in the port till the Emperor tells the republic what satisfaction he demands. If this is not accomplished, the moment I sail she will fit out again and be worse than ever. This blow will most probably be in the end most severely felt by the Genoese and also the French. It is a nice point but I have no doubt of carrying it through to the satisfaction of all parties. *Agamemnon* is as well known through Europe as one of Mr. Harwood's ships is at Overy.[1] You will know Admirals Hotham and Goodall have struck their flags.[2] From the latter I have had a very affectionate letter. Holloway is gone home by land. It is not impossible but you may see him at Bath. The Admirals do not return to England till the spring. I am glad you have taken Bett. Thurlow. Better give her good wages, than many others who will rob and plunder small wages.

The fleet is gone to sea with Sir Hyde Parker but every moment we expect Sir John Jarvis's arrival. I shall I assure you be very glad to see England in the *Agamemnon* and I think *Agamemnon* cannot be much longer out, and unless, which is not very likely to happen that the Admiralty may order me to be continued on this command, where I have already given so much satisfaction.

With kindest remembrance to my father, believe me, your most affectionate husband, HORATIO NELSON.

Josiah is very well and Hoste quite recovered.

To Mrs. Nelson, Bath, Angleterre.

No. 136
[Nicolas, II, p. 110, part]

Agamemnon, at Sea,
December 2, 1795

MY DEAREST FANNY,—I am so in the habit of receiving letters that two posts passing and no letter surprises me. If Lord Hood is at Bath his penetration will discover that from my last letter to him of the loss of the Austrians in the action of the 23rd Nov. that the loss of Vado would consequently follow. You may tell his Lordship, and with truth, that I have no doubt but had he commanded in the Mediterranean the Austrians would not have been defeated. Extraordinary as this may appear, I can account very well for it. The French had collected full 100 sail of vessels, in case of failure, to carry off their troops. They had 10 or 12 gun vessels,

[1] Near Wells, north Norfolk.
[2] On November 1 news of Sir John Jervis's appointment had reached the Mediterranean. In the interim period Sir Hyde Parker was in command.

as many privateers, and a man-of-war brig. I wrote to the Admiral the great service the destruction of these vessels would be (many of whom were laden with corn which the French General laid an embargo on), and, as I had not force enough, begged the Admiral, if he came to sea, to look at this fleet himself, and offering, if he would permit me the honour, to lead the *Culloden* and *Courageux* to the attack and with my then squadron of frigates to take or destroy the whole. Had this been done, and done it might have been, I doubt if the French soldiers could have been led to the attack. But my Admiral, for wise reasons I daresay, did not think it proper to attend to my proposal and lessened my squadron to the *Flora* frigate and *Speedy* brig. A gale of wind blew these vessels off the coast, and the French attack at Voltri and expedition ready to sail from Genoa dragging the *Agamemnon* from Vado to Genoa, left these numerous gun boats etc. to harrass the left flank of the Austrian Army, which certainly, had not my squadron been so reduced, could not have happened. I pretend not to say the Austrians would not have been beat had not the gun boats harassed them, on my conscience I believe they would (but I believe they would not have attacked had we destroyed all their vessels of war, transports etc.). The Austrians did not, by all accounts, stand firm. The French, half naked, were determined to conquer or die. The Austrians do lay the blame on the want of co-operation of the English Admiral. They know perfectly the ships were taken from me and had I not, against I own my inclination, been kept at Genoa from 8 to 10,000 men would have been taken prisoners, and General de Vins himself among the number, for the French plan, *well laid*, was to possess a post in the road these people fled by, retreat it could not be called for, except a part of the Army under General Wallis, about 10,000 men, with the others it was the *Devil take the hindmost*. I had a Lieutenant, 2 Mids. and 16 men taken at Vado.[1] The Purser of the ship was at Vado and ran with the Austrians 18 miles without stopping, men without arms, officers without soldiers, women without assistance. Thus has ended my campaign. As our fleet would not assist the Austrians, I believe after the action the General determined not to hold Vado and that the Austrians were glad of the opportunity of withdrawing their troops. They came by the express stipulation of England to the coast and were to take possession of Vado to co-operate with our fleet which has never been near them. However, let the blame lay where it will, I do not believe any party will seriously lay it at my door, if they do, I am perfectly easy as to the consequences. I sincerely hope an enquiry may take place. The world will then know how hard I have fagged.

[1] The lieutenant and party sent to Savona for water in the jollyboat on November 29.

What a military letter. I am on my way to Leghorn to refit, if the Admiral will let me. Not only ship, but ship's company require rest. I hope sincerely we are ordered home. Sir John Jarvis must have some orders about us. We are in a miserable plight. As to myself I am the strongest and least tired of any in the *Agamemnon*. Josiah is very well. Our weather has been intensely cold. Remember me kindly to my father and all our friends, to Lord Hood and family if they are at Bath. I shall write him when I am a little quiet at Leghorn.

Believe me, my dear Fanny, your most affectionate husband, HORATIO NELSON.

Leghorn, December 7th: We arrived here yesterday when I received your letter of October 31st. Sir John Jarvis arrived at St. Fiorenzo the 29th Nov. to the great joy of some and sorrow of others in the fleet.

To Mrs. Nelson, Bath, Angleterre.

No. 137
[Nicolas, II, p. 119, part]

Agamemnon, Leghorn,
December 18, 1795

MY DEAR FANNY,—I have your letters of Nov. 5th and 15th. I know not why Stanley should be cross with us. We can have done nothing to offend him. However, in another year we shall have a right to call for the legacy and interest and I will if possible have it on the day or I will put into a lawyer's hands to talk to them. I feel we have been cruelly used by all except Mr. Bailey and you have nought but civil words from him. Stanley is not an executor if I recollect right. I pray God Admiral Waldegrave [1] may bring out orders for the return of the *Agamemnon* by the first convoy. I rejoice as do many at Sir Charles Middleton [2] being out. Every one knows that Laforey [3] was unfit for the command. It is active young men who are wanted and not drones. I own I wish Maurice had taken his station again at the Navy Office. If he really was so necessary they would for their own ease have got him forward in the office. However, I am a very imperfect judge and can only hope he has done well in refusing. I assure

[1] Came out with a squadron under Jervis—was third in command. Later Admiral Baron Radstock. Died 1825.

[2] Middleton left the Admiralty Board in November 1795. Created Baron Barham, he was First Lord of the Admiralty 1805–6. Died 1813.

[3] Rear-Admiral Christian was sent out to the West Indies to reinforce Sir John Laforey, who resigned his command and died on the passage home, aged sixty-seven.

you I will endeavour to buy something for Mr. Bolton's girls but, to say the truth, when you begin in a large family you know not where to stop. Much better if you like it some time or other give them £10 and tell them to buy a couple of caps or gowns.

The Austrian army, which has been so completely defeated, has lost but very few men compared to the enemy, one about 4,000 the other full 10,000. I have had letters from my poor Lieutenant and Midshipmen who are prisoners, telling me that few of the French are more than 23 or 24 and very many not more than 14 and all without clothes and says he is sure my barge's crew would have beat 100 of them and that could I but see them I would not believe, if the world was covered by such people, that the Austrian army could have been beat by them. The oldest officers say they never heard of so complete a defeat and certainly without any reason. The King of Sardinia was very near in the panic concluding a hasty peace, which also must have been bad. However, I believe we shall make peace, when must the Emperor, and the successes which I hope will tumble on us from West Indies as also from Germany will enable us to make a good one. I only hope we shall be able to keep St. Domingo. If we can, the expenses of the war are nothing to what we shall gain. The French have sent a squadron towards Constantinople and many think the Turks will join them. We have a squadron under Captain Troubridge gone after them. If he gets hold of them he will not easily quit it. Capt. Knight and six lieutenants of the *Victory* are now at Leghorn on their way to England. Mr. Hinton formerly 1st Lieutenant of *Agamemnon* is now Capt. Hinton, as is late Lieutenant Andrews now Captain Andrews, both got their promotion from the services of *Agamemnon*. Reports say I am to be offered either *St. George* 90, Sir Hyde Parker going in to the *Britannia*, or the *Zealous* 74 as Lord Harvey wants a 90. I do not at present think I shall take one or the other, but much must depend on the prospect of *Agamemnon*'s going to England. If she is to be kept here till a peace, I may as well have a good as a bad ship but if there is a prospect of *Agamemnon* going home nothing shall induce me to change, except which cannot be looked for, that the Austrians are again ordered to take the coast of Genoa and I am established as a Commodore which would have been the case had they remained.

Josiah begins to threaten you with a letter and time may produce it. Sir John seems determined to be active and I hope he will continue so. With kindest remembrances to my father, believe me, your most affectionate husband, HORATIO NELSON.

To Mrs. Nelson, Bath, Angleterre.

No. 138

Leghorn,
December 25, 1795

MY DEAR FANNY,—I have just received your letter of Nov. 25th and most sincerely wish you and my dear father many happy returns of the season. Not having seen Sir John Jervis or Admiral Waldegrave arrived I cannot form an idea what ships are to go home. Many more want to go than the Admiral will part with, but he cannot for any length of time keep out the *Agamemnon*. She is rotten and must go home, I hope the first convoy. My health, which you have from a very long report of Captain Montgomery [1] for I have not seen him since the beginning of July, has not been bad, quite the contrary, but it is no wonder that a man that runs a race should be tired. However, I can truly say none in the *Agamemnon* has stood the fag equal to myself. Andrews, who is a Captain, is very ill, perhaps dangerously so. He is at Pisa, where I should gladly go but it is at a distance from my ship. Active employment I like but the cold at Vado was piercing. This was the only unpleasant part of my command. Wherever the blame of a want of naval co-operation will fall is not for me to say. It is sufficient for me that His Majesty's Minister, with the Austrian Army, fully acquits me of all blame, and my own conscience does the same. Reports say General de Vins is dead. He was very infirm and grief, added to his disease, has probably shortened his days. We are in daily expectation of the Admiral at this place and in ten or twelve days I hope to be ready to leave it. The French Army have behaved very ill to the Genoese, plundered their churches and levied contributions on the inhabitants. In Corsica things are by no means quiet, the people are uncivilized and cannot bear control. Paoli expected to have been Viceroy or at least to have governed the Viceroy, and, neither being the case, he opposed the government and having sowed the seeds of discontent, we all know it is difficult to eradicate.

What a scandalous report of poor Mrs. M. [2] Thus all poor women who are left in the world have their characters taken away but few give credit that a civil thing is done by a man to a woman without a criminality. I do not believe a more amiable woman or a better character exists on earth. I feel quite hurt and I daresay that the reporter, if her character could be traced, is a bad woman. You fancy I know Mrs. F. Kelly by telling me of her misery. That of outliving their income is too common a failing

---

[1] Captain Augustus Montgomery had been one of the squadron sent to England in September with the convoy from the Levant.
[2] Mrs. Moutray.

and so far from people living happier at the time they are spending money [far] from it. I am satisfied the contrary must be the case. Every day must give some moment for reflection. As to Allison's [1] death, I am not surprised at it. His drinking must sooner or later, I knew, carry him off, and for himself and family, considering the derangement of intellect it may be considered a mercy. As to Mrs. M. and Mrs. B. [2] meeting it may be all well but the gentlemen must be unpleasant for no two people have I fancy a greater contempt for each other.

I lament the fate of the West Indian fleet but hope they will soon get out again for till we are paid I shall always have fear and trembling for our legacy. The not paying the interest has been scandalous.

With kindest remembrances to my father, believe me, your most affectionate husband, HORATIO NELSON.

Josiah is very well but as I am on shore he knows not I am writing. He says he will one day write but I write so often he is sure there [is] no occasion for him.

To Mrs. Nelson, Bath, Angleterre.

No. 139
[Nicolas, II, p. 123, part]

Leghorn,
January 6, 1796

MY DEAR FANNY,—I do not yet hear of this promotion of flags and I sincerely hope it will not take place for some time to come, more especially as I hope *Agamemnon* will go home the first convoy. All our talk is of peace but I verily believe without the smallest foundation. The French I am sure this spring will make a great exertion to get into Italy and I think Sir John Jervis must be active to keep them out. 15 sail of the line will be ready at Toulon the 1st of February with 140 sail of transports and 200 flat boats adapted for the coast of Italy. The prevention of the intentions of the enemy requires great foresight for if once landed our fleet is of no use and their fleet will retire into Toulon or some safe port. Had they done so last year what would have been the use of our action, and so it will be again, the French will improve on their last year's folly. I am convinced in my own mind I know the very landing place. The French must, if they mean to carry on the war, penetrate into Italy. Holland and Flanders, with their own country, they have stripped of its wealth. Italy is the gold mine and also a country, if once entered, without resistance.

[1] Lieutenant Allison died soon after reaching England.
[2] Nelson's two married sisters, Mrs. Matcham and Mrs. Bolton.

On the Rhine the enemy have still great force and I do not believe the Austrians will get any farther on that side.

January 8th: Our news of the French retiring from Holland confirms me in their intention to force Italy. Nothing else in appearances can save them in any peace which may be coming forward.

The history of Andrew's promotion shows when a thing is done how many claim the merit but, as he is made in the group of those whose ships behaved well in the action of March last, I feel he was made for the distinguishing services of *Agamemnon.* I know not if gratitude for exertions in his favour will be remembered, perhaps not. Suckling seems again discontented. He is gone to the hospital by way of being, I fancy, clear of the ship but I shall never allow the follies of others to make me uneasy again.

Poor Aunt Mary. I am sorry for, but at her time of life she cannot expect to have good health. I only hope she does not want for any of to her luxuries of life. Pray send her a little something which you think may be acceptable.

My officers and people who are prisoners in France are exceedingly well treated and particularly so by the sea officers and, as they say, because they belong to the *Agamemnon* whose character is well known throughout France.

Roger Martin may have an appointment in India but £4,000 a year I do not credit. Such places are very scarce and are the reward of long services. By your not mentioning I suppose you never hear of Stanley, but I believe he is not one of the executors. I wish to God our legacy was safe in England. I am sure in a Court of Justice the interest would be ordered each year for such was certainly the meaning of Mr. Herbert and it is mean in the executors to withhold it. Another year will soon pass away and then I will not stop one day.

We are ready for sea but no orders from the Admiral. With kindest remembrances to my father, believe me, your most affectionate husband, HORATIO NELSON.

To Mrs. Nelson, Bath, Angleterre.

No. 140

Leghorn,
January 14, 1796

MY DEAR FANNY,—I have received your letter of Dec. 16th and although my letters may be long in coming yet rest assured I never miss an opportunity of writing when I am absent from a place of the post. The time between Oct. 19th and Nov. 6th was the time I was from Leghorn to my arrival in Vado Bay. Tomorrow I sail for Corsica, therefore you must expect some distance of time before another letter comes to Bath. Our fleet has been one month at sea and the Admiral has not sent a ship of any kind for letters, therefore neither those in the fleet or their friends in England have had any communication. I expect the Admiral will send *Agamemnon* to sea so soon as he arrives in St. Fiorenzo. I hope so for I detest laying idle when my ship is ready for sea.

We are all much surprised at a truce between the Austrians and French for two months. All these things of mutual convenience clearly indicate that peace is at no very great distance, although from many circumstances I shall not be surprised at one more campaign, for from the King's message I do not flatter myself that it is so near as was thought.

I rejoice Maurice goes once more to the Navy Office. I hope he has saved a little and as his abilities, it would appear, are wanted there, we may reasonably hope he will rise in the office. I never heard any expressions of the Rector, nor do I believe he could or would have the inclination to express his sorrow at our brother's appearance of gaining a little. I should, I own, have been much flattered had such an appointment as was told you have taken place but I do not at present give entire credit to the history.

Our winter here is nothing, for this month past we have not had a winter's day. I hope it is as favourable in England.

I cannot think there is a prospect of our fleet coming home or one more ship than is necessary for the convoy, for the French fleet and transports will be at sea before February finishes, and I doubt not but they will improve from the lesson they learnt last March. Had they fought and brought out their transports Italy would have been lost. 140 sail of transports are collected at Marseilles and Toulon and 200 small flat bottomed boats for the passage of rivers and moving a great body of troops from one place to the other along the coast. I may be mistaken but I cannot yet believe it.

January 15th: The Admiral is just arrived at St. Fiorenzo and as by the death of Lord Hervey[1] the *Zealous* is vacant, as also the *St. George*, the Admiral has offered me the choice of either, but I shall refuse both on many accounts. I have but a moment to finish this letter as my ship is getting under sail. Believe me, my dear Fanny, your most affectionate husband, HORATIO NELSON.

Kindest remembrances to my father.

Josiah is perfectly well.

To Mrs. Nelson, Bath, Angleterre.

---

[1] Captain Viscount Hervey, eldest son of the Earl of Bristol, died in January 1796.

APPENDIX

Admiral Hotham to Nelson [1]

Britannia, Leghorn Road,
September 4, 1795

DEAR SIR,—Although I am hardly able to hold a pen,[2] yet I cannot refrain congratulating you upon your late success; and notwithstanding your last enterprise did not in its consequences end so well, yet the attempt was not the less meritorious, nor does it reflect less honour upon those who were engaged in it than if it had been attended with a more favourable termination to their spirited exertions.

I am truly sorry. With every good wish for your success, my dear Sir, most faithfully yours, W. HOTHAM.

Nelson to the Duke of Clarence [3]

Agamemnon, Vado Bay,
October 1st, 1795

SIR,—I was honoured by your Royal Highness' letter of 24th August last night, and am truly flattered by your kind expressions of remembrances of our very long acquaintance. Many opportunities have been afforded me this war and I have the consolation to think that I have let none slip to do my utmost and to this day all my actions have been approved by my commander-in-chief. In different situations not all of them very dangerous I have been 112 times in action since my arrival in the Mediterranean and twice wounded although thank God not dangerously. And I am full of gratitude to the King for my appointment to the Marines, which I have every reason to believe was given me by His Majesty's command and I hope one day to receive some honour from His Majesty's hand. Your Royal Highness I hope will before a very long time be placed in that situation which both your birth, abilities and rank in our service entitle you too.

I shall now tell you our news. On the 13th September six sail of the line left Toulon supposed for the West Indies. Admiral Man with the same number is going after them, but Hotham is slow in his movements.

---

[1] N.M.M. MS. 9960, Croker collection in the Phillipps papers.
[2] The writing is very shaky and weak.
[3] N.M.M. M. 17, Autograph collection—from a series of twenty-seven letters written by Nelson to the Duke of Clarence.

If he has a failing, and we are none of us without them, it is taking too much time to deliberate whereby opportunities are lost. We have felt this on more than one occasion. Holloway will be flattered by your remembrance of him. He is an honest good man and I wish he had what he wishes for himself, a commissionership of the Navy in London.

Our situation here is drawing fast to a crisis. If the Austrians will not attack the French I have no doubt but the French will attack them. God knows the politics of the Court of Vienna but our endeavour during the war has been to get an army into Italy. Now it is come, they made a very handsome attack, took possession of Vado struck such a panic into the French that every boat and vessel was pressed to carry off the troops and cannon and baggage expecting the Austrians to follow up their blow. This not being done, the French took post on a ridge of mountains called St. Esprit, which has every day increased both in strength of posts and number of men. General de Vins on my first coming here said it was then too strong for him to attack as he would probably lose so many men as to disable him from any further operations. He wished much for a conference with Admiral Hotham to concert a plan for landing a large body of troops to the westward of their works, but Admiral Hotham not thinking it right to come here, and my squadron being reinforced I proceeded to examine the coast to the westward as far as Nice, and found a place where I could have disembarked an army. My plan and my reasons for that plan I stated at large to General de Vins, and it has since had the fullest approbation of his Majesty's ministers both at Turin and Genoa. General de Vins in answer to my plan proposed another much more extensive but in so vague a way that I was obliged to call for particulars which I at last got, and I was obliged, it requiring so many transports, to make my application to Admiral Hotham for more ships. Thus has time the whole summer been worn away and almost induced me to believe that the Austrians never intended to go farther than their first position taken June 24th.

The Admiral has just answered my requisition for transports and 2 74s by telling me that at present he is equipping the squadron for the West Indies, and that the General must wait a little. I must not tell this answer to the General, who I am almost confident has been forced into this plan by my propositions and would desire nothing more than to put his troops into winter quarters. But when I recollect the Austrian army in the year 46 crossing the Var on the 14th December I shall not nor will Mr. Drake who is appointed to reside at head quarters, let the General rest. But I really believe if the interior does not call forth the French army from the frontiers but that they will use every effort to recover Vado. They already begin to push at the Austrians. But whenever any event takes place here worthy your Royal Highness' notice I will instantly write you.

My worthy friend Capt. Locker the other day wrote me that you wished to know the particulars of a court martial held on a land officer. An officer serving on board the *Diadem*, Capt. Tyler, behaved in the most insolent manner to his captain, for which Tyler wrote to the Admiral for a court martial, which was granted. The charge being proved the court passed sentence on him. The officer refused to plead before the court and delivered in a paper stating that it was the opinion of his brother officers that he was not amenable to a naval court martial and that his conduct to Captain Tyler was proper. After this it went on to say that although a naval court martial might be proper in cases of mutiny or crimes of equal magnitude, yet for such an offence as this it ought not to try him more especially as a land court martial could so easily be held. Such was the substance of his paper and the most insolent conduct ever held before such a respectable court not one member of which had been less than 15 years a post captain.

Permit me to reason a little on the conduct of the army officers generally speaking embarked on board the fleet. They say when they take their commissions or a soldier is enlisted he only swears to obey the land articles of war. Chance puts them on board ship but cannot make them subject to naval laws, as to be amenable to the others they entered and none others are mentioned. Yet when they are on board ship for any crime of their soldiers if to them they apply to the captain for punishment an acknowledgement of the power of naval laws, and which must bind equally the officer as the soldier. When a marine is enlisted he is sworn to the same test as a soldier in a regiment, the same reasoning will hold good when he finds on coming on board ship he is subject to other laws he never before heard of, and in my opinion a much harder case than either is a poor man torn from his wife and family and made subject to laws he never consented to or enlisted to serve under. The foundation of naval and military laws are the same, to enforce obedience, discipline and respect.

Can it be thought proper that one sixth part of every ship's company, may be guilty of mutiny etc. and are not to be subject to the naval laws, for if it is acknowledged they can in any case whatever be tried their reasoning falls to the ground. When our articles of war passed into a law all, where marching regiments who were embarked on board our ships of war and the word soldier mentioned in every article, can mean only soldiers belonging to the regiment embarked. A marine might with more propriety say there is no mention of a marine and therefore I am not subject to these laws. But there is many of the articles of war which say if any person in or belonging to the fleet are guilty of such crimes they shall be punished by the sentence of a court martial. In every country are people residing in that country subject to its laws. Our sea laws are known and acknowledged and every person who is on board the fleet even as a passenger I have no doubt is in many cases which are clearly pointed out by the articles of war, subject to those laws. And as on shore the pleading ignorance to the laws of any state may mitigate but certainly will not free the person from punishment, the last part of the act says nothing in this act shall extend to the trial of any officer or soldier embarked on board a transport a sufficient proof that the legislators of that day had no doubts or intention not to submit soldiers embarked on board the fleet to punishments inflicted by the act.

I do not think that Parliament will alter the established laws of the Navy and by which the glory of England has been supported for so many years.[1] All must be who serve in the Navy obedient to its laws if it is altered for any consideration we are lost for a sailor will not be bound by one law and a soldier laughing at him. Believe me ever your Royal Highness' most faithful servant, HORATIO NELSON.

To His Royal Highness Duke of Clarence, St. James's, London.

Nelson to the Duke of Clarence
(Draft) [1]

Agamemnon, off Marseilles,
October 27, 1795

The Admiral who I left at Leghorn on the 20th instant having desired me to send some of my squadron to look into Toulon and to endeavour to get information what the enemy's fleet are about, having looked into Vado Bay and found General de Vins and the French army as I left them very neighbourly, the Neopolitan cavalry gone into winter quarters 100 miles from Vado, and all in appearance very quiet, I thought I could not possibly employ my time more beneficially than by taking a frigate with me and going to the western coasts of France myself.

[1] This matter was the subject of much discussion in England, and the possibility of introducing a Bill was debated following the issue of an additional Article of War by the War Office, which was later withdrawn.
[2] N.M.M. MS. 9960, Croker collection in the Phillipps papers—copy retained by Nelson.

We have been here 48 hours and not yet seen a single vessel although directly off the greatest mercantile sea port in France, but before this letter is closed I hope to be able to tell your Royal Highness the news and politics of Marseilles as also the situation of the Toulon fleet, as the first proper wind I shall examine that port. I have not been with the Austrian army the whole campaign since their taking of Vado and consequently I must have had my opinion of what might and what could not be done, perhaps I might say from my situation of what ought to have been done and what I have no doubt could have been done, after the taking of Vado with an army three times the number of the French. Why was not that flying, disheartened enemy pursued? It was not through an enemy's country the pursuit must be made, it was through a country which sincerely wished both parties at the devil and through part of the dominions of the King of Sardinia. Thus I see no reason why the pursuit was not made. Not a hill was fortified to stop the progress of a victorious army, on the contrary so far from preparing for resistance that every back nay every foot was arrested to carry off the French bag and baggage. The panic had reached even Nice itself which perhaps might have fallen without a blow. However a large army would have been there to have undertaken the siege three months of summer before then, from what cause must I suppose this step was made, from either the inactivity of the General, or orders from Vienna. I own myself rather of opinion it proceeds from the latter, one excuse of General de Vins to me was that about 40 miles at the back of Alberga was a part of the French army encamped at a place called Omea which if he proceeded along the sea coast westerly would be on his right flank and as he proceeded in his rear. This appeared specious but when I knew that 5 times the number of Piedmontese troops were watching this army, and the moment they quitted their stronghold, would have followed them, all this pretext fails.

As I am of opinion that the total failure of the Italian campaign except that of halting the French from advancing which on my conscience I believe never was their intention proceeds from the conduct of the Court of Vienna, I must consequently think it is useless giving them such a large sum of money, from my observation and knowledge all their conduct in Italy has been trick and finesse. Certainly they will never undertake another campaign unless more money is given them. It pays their army which they wish to keep up, but as to their wishing that army to be risked in the common cause I cannot bring myself to believe it. I have seen the Austrians determined not to fight, I have seen the Piedmontese the same, with the highest contempt for each other, the ministry of the Court of Turin I cannot have an high opinion as you will believe from an answer I was

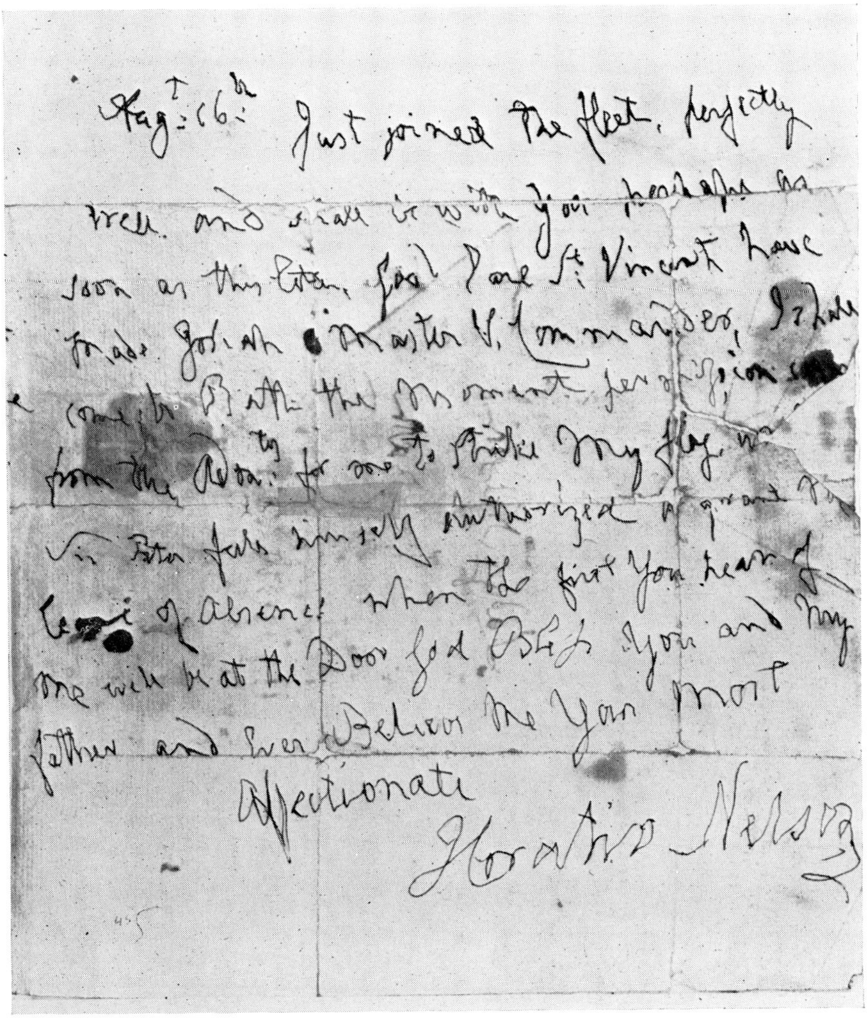

PLATE VIII. Postscript to Nelson's first letter to his wife, written with his left hand (see p. 333).

obliged to give them to a most extraordinary request or rather desire. I give it you verbatim, viz.

'Whilst I have the honour to Command his Britannic Majesty's squadron in the gulf of Genoa, I will allow no intercourse whatever to be held with France which it is in my power to prevent. This is the firm resolution of a British Officer determined to do his duty to his King and Country.'

My answer to his Majesty's minister at Genoa will give a pretty good idea of my feelings. I own I think it the most impudent proposal which could have been made but my answer cannot be misunderstood.

A very brief account of the Vado Campaign for the perusal of Sir John Jervis [1] *[sent to him by Nelson, December, 1795]*

[Nicolas, VII, p. 19]

On the 3rd of July 1795 Admiral Hotham received letters from Mr. Brame, His Majesty's consul at Genoa, enclosing one from General de Vins telling him that the Austrian Army had taken possession of Vado and requesting a co-operation and that the French fleet were returned into Toulon.

On the 4th I sailed with a small squadron from St. Fiorenzo.

On the 6th I fell in with the French fleet and it was not till after the action of July 13th that I sailed again for the coast of Genoa. My orders were to confer with Mr. Drake His Majesty's minister at Genoa on such points as might be essential towards co-operating with General De Vins.

I anchored in Genoa Mole on July 18th and sailed with Mr. Drake on the 20th.

On the 21st I anchored in Vado Bay where we met Mr. Trevor His Majesty's minister to the court of Turin and had an immediate conference with General De Vins. Extract of my letter to Admiral Hotham.

'General De Vins seems glad of our arrival but I do not at present see any immediate prospect of the army's getting to the westward. It appears to me the General wishes famine to do more than the sword. The Austrian general has fitted out some privateers and taken several vessels loaded with corn for France.'

[1] N.M.M. MS. 9578, St. Vincent papers. A summary account written for Sir John Jervis (an incomplete draft is in the Croker collection). The enclosures and the account were published separately by Nicolas, the latter only coming to his knowledge in time for inclusion in the appendix to the last volume.

R

The 25th the cutter carried the General to look at the enemy's advanced posts at Borgetta. From my arrival to the first week in August the General never seemed to doubt his ability to drive the French out of the whole riviera of Genoa and even of taking Nice itself, but he always expressed his wish to have a conference with Admiral Hotham whom I had always reason to assure him would on his arrival from off Toulon anchor in Vado Bay.

On the 14th August our fleet was in sight to the westward and on the 15th I received letters from the Admiral telling me he could not at present anchor in Vado Bay as the fleet was in want of wood, but that he should return from Leghorn in a very few days to water in Vado. In the evening I went on board the admiral to endeavour to induce the Admiral to stop for a few hours as General De Vins was very anxious to see him and would come on board to concert a plan of operation with him. But the Admiral did not think it right to stop and proceeded to Leghorn.

The General seemed much hurt and requested of me to get clear answers from the Admiral to the following questions.

viz. Will the Admiral return to Vado from Leghorn?

Ansr. Uncertain, but I rather think I shall not have an opportunity of returning there owing to the intelligence I have received from the Admiralty which renders my presence immediately necessary at another place.

Ques. Will the Admiral assist and cover the landing of from six to ten thousand men on the coast of Provence?

Answ. It will not be in my power to do so, on account of the fleet being required for another service as stated in the preceding answer.

Ques. Will the Admiral undertake to prevent the Toulon fleet from molesting my operations?

From this time August 19th to the end of the month the General was taken up in examining the enemy's posts and as I thought preparing for an attack.

August 21st: Extract of a letter from Mr. Jackson His Majesty's Charge des affaires at Turin in the absence of Mr. Trevor. Viz 'I was truly sorry to see that Admiral Hotham could not go into Vado Bay, for though I am persuaded that the reasons alleged are perfectly proper, yet I very much fear it will not be seen with due candour by General De Vins who besides may make it a reason for continuing in his present inactivity or affect to do so.

August 22nd: Mr. Drake arrived to talk with the General but we could make nothing of his intentions.

September 4th: Extract of a letter from Mr. Jackson. 'I shall be very glad to see that General De Vins will have stopped your intended cruise off dell Mell and have employed your squadron in some co-operation with his forces whose inactivity is as unaccountable as it is prejudicial.'

September 8th: From Mr. Drake. 'I am fully persuaded from your and my own opinion respecting the future inactivity of the Austrian army.'

September 4th: Not finding the General likely to move I proceeded down the coast as far as Nice and sounded most part of it.

On the 7th saw our fleet standing to westward. On the 12th returned to Vado and delivered the paper marked 1 [1] to General De Vins to which I received the answer No. 2 which occasioned the letters 3 [2], 4 and 5 to pass between us. Extract from my letter Sept. 17th to Admiral Hotham: 'It has sometime appeared to me that the General intends to go no father than his present position and to lay the blame of the miscarriage of the enterprise against Nice (which I had always been led to believe was the object of his army) to the non co-operation of the British fleet and the Sardinian army, to leave the General no room to insinuate such a want on our part has been the object of my paper of the 12th and my letter of the 17th. If the General's answer should be the desire of transports I think we have them, a passage of 24 hours is the outside. But I own I believe he will now find other excuses, and was you to grant the whole fleet for transports I verily believe some excuse would be found. This Sir is my public opinion and which I wish not to conceal.'

September 19th: Received 5 from General de Vins wrote Admiral Hotham by express 6.[3] Mr. Drake has the Admiral's answer but the purport of it was that on consultation with the flag officers of the fleet he had refused the co-operation as a wild scheme. This answer on consultation with Mr. Drake was never communicated to General de Vins nor did he ever ask for it.

September 23rd: From Mr. Drake. 'General De Vins' excuse about the court of Turin having made peace is a mere pretext. To leave him no loophole I have written to him today to assure him formally and ministerially that it is not true and you are fully at liberty to repeat to the General in the strongest manner these assurances from me.'

From Mr. Trevor September 25th: 'Every day since I first had the honour of seeing you has been marked by some fresh proof of your zeal and ability had it been equally seconded by land much might have been and still may be done. Though I cannot help seeing the proposition made to you on the 14th exactly in the same light that you do. We must all of us act as if we thought differently, and take care to leave no pretext which

[1] See below, p. 245, Nelson to De Vins, September 12.
[2] See below, p. 246, Nelson to De Vins, September 14.
[3] See below, p. 246, Nelson to Hotham, September 20.

can be laid at our door. If the troubles in the interior do not cut out work for the troops at home I am of opinion that the most rigorous efforts will be made to recover Vado.'

From Mr. Trevor October 8th: 'I am glad you kept the Admiral's answer secret. It was however on the whole I think favourable since it appears that but for the messenger from the Admiralty your application would have been complied with, but before any actual execution be given to it, we should be assured that the General was in earnest when he made the proposition. Till then I conceive all we have to do is to tell him (that is as soon as the Admiral authorizes you and Mr. Drake to do so) that we are ready to execute our naval share of the business whenever he pleases, and I trust Mr. Drake will succeed in making the Admiral feel the necessity of his really co-operating with zeal in whatever can be attempted and of taking away every pretext which the Austrians are so ready to seize to cover their own abominable inaction. With respect to their being driven from Vado I think the enemy will make every effort to do so. I think the present army must be drilled in order to force General De Vins. I still think however that the French will attempt it if possible and that if they do no very vigorous resistance will be made.'

From Mr. Drake October 26th: 'I returned hither from my military excursion on Friday. I intended to have gone from Turin to Savona but I was so fully persuaded from everything I heard and saw during my tour that there is no hope of stimulating the Austrian General to any active operations during the campaign that I thought it better to return to Genoa. I shall be very anxious to hear the result of your visit to the Admiral and I hope he will have adopted your proposition.'

The object of my visit was to ask the Admiral to give me two 74 gun ships and as many transports as he had in Leghorn with the *Camel* and *Dolphin* to have carried the 10,000 men as desired, but the Admiral did not think it right to send a ship. But reduced my force and ordered me in addition always to undertake the reconnoitering the port of Toulon.

On the 1st I chased a very large convoy into Allassio and by the 8th they were increased to full 100 sail including gun boats and other vessels of war, but they were too well protected for me to make any attempt with my small squadron.

On the 10th the French took the Austrian post at Voltri. On the 11th it was retaken. On the 12th the French were making every attempt for a most vigorous and bold attempt to establish themselves between Voltri and Savona in a strong post, and were in hopes of carrying an insurrection of the Genoese peasantry. My presence was required at Genoa to prevent this expedition by Mr. Drake the Austrian minister and by the Austrian General commanding at Vado.

On the 13th I went to Genoa and was kept there contrary to my inclination till after the defeat of the Austrian Army. November 23rd. However I have this consolation that to the *Agamemnon*'s staying at Genoa do many thousands of Austrians owe their safety by the pass of the Borgetta being kept open, and amongst others do General De Vins himself owe his safety to the *Agamemnon*.

Enclosure No. 1: Nelson to General De Vins [1]

Agamemnon, Vado Bay,
September 12, 1795

Having been down the coast to the westward as far as Nice the following is the result of my observations, and the services which I can undertake to perform with His Majesty's Squadron should General De Vins be inclined or think it right to get to the westward of his present situation. I can embark four or five thousand men with their arms and a few days' provisions on board the ships of the squadron and will engage to land them within two miles of San Remo with their field pieces.

It is now necessary for me to point out the necessity of possessing San Remo and its situation with respect to the sea as it is the only place between Vado and Ville Franche where the squadron can anchor in safety. The town is situated in the middle of a small bay, where the squadron can anchor in almost all winds; in some respects it is as good as Vado Bay, in others for security of large ships it certainly is not. It has a mole where all small vessels can lay and load and unload their cargoes, an advantage which Vado has not.

2ndly. Respecting provisions for the Austrian army, I will undertake to provide sufficient convoys that they shall arrive in safety.

and 3rdly. There can be no doubt but the embarkation of the troops, should such a measure be necessary, can always be covered by the squadron.

Respecting the defence of St. Remo by land should the enemy bring a very large army against it, I cannot take upon me to be a judge but from the little I have seen, I believe it to be easier defended than Vado Bay. The possession of St. Remo as head quarters for the magazines of stores and provisions would enable General De Vins to turn himself to the eastward or westward. The enemy at Oneglia would be cut off from provisions and a body of men can be landed to attack it when ever it might be

[1] Printed by Nicolas, Vol. II, p. 80, with date 'about 9th of September'.

judged necessary. The enemy to the eastward at St. Espirit etc. would be cut off from all supplies as the corsairs etc. from Vado would as at present stop all supplies from Genoa.

What obstacles there may be inland, I cannot be a judge of, but I think it my duty to lay before General De Vins the support by sea which I can give him should his Excellency think it right to proceed to the westward. The army at Oneglia and to the eastward is very much supplied by land, which I have not only learnt from information but from my own observation the road being full of mules with bags of flour, tents, etc.

Nice from the vicinity of St. Remo would be completely blockaded by sea and the British fleet twenty-three sail of the line are now off Toulon.

Enclosure No. 3: Nelson to General De Vins
[Nicolas, II, p. 82]

Agamemnon, Vado Bay,
September 14, 1795

SIR,—I am honoured with your Excellency's letters of this day's date. My reason for the necessity of possessing St. Remo was not that it was a better anchorage than Vado as I say the contrary, in my observations, but that it is the best between Vado and Nice and perfectly safe for all small vessels.

I cannot or do not pretend to judge of the movements your Excellency may think proper to make, but I wished to inform you of the support and assistance it is in my power to give you and on which you may depend in every arrangement making for getting to the westward.

I beg leave to transmit you a copy of Admiral Hotham's letter to me of August 19th which I believe is a full answer to one part of your letter.

I beg leave to assure your Excellency that I am ever ready to give you every assistance in my power and that I am with the greatest truth, your Excellency's most faithful obedient servant.

To His Excellency Baron De Vins.

Enclosure No. 6: Nelson to Admiral Hotham

Vado Bay,
September 20, 1795

SIR,—I have had a meeting with General De Vins this morning, who informs me that yesterday his troops carried a post of the enemy's in the centre of the mountain St. Espirito and that his troops are now within half musket shot of some other which if possible he means to attack. He is going to the advanced post himself.

The General also tells me that the moment he knows the time the transports will be ready he will have the troops ready and that he will head them himself and has no doubt of being successful. 4 or 5,000 peasantry are ready to take a battery of eight guns where the landing is to be effected. For such a short voyage a few ships will carry the men. If the *Dolphin* is at hand, or the *Camel* cleared they would take a great number. I hope the General will be left without an excuse.

I am with the greatest respect your most faithful servant, HORATIO NELSON

Admiral Hotham.

Enclosure (not numbered): Nelson to the Commander of the Neapolitan Flotilla

[Nicolas, II, p. 90]

Agamemnon, Vado Bay,
October 1, 1795

SIR,—The enemy's gun boats having very much annoyed the Austrian camp near Loano I must desire that you will till further orders consider the preventing the enemy's gun boats from annoying the Austrian camp as the greatest and only service which I, at present, wish you to perform. And I hope from the zeal which the officers of the King of Naples have always shewn that you will soon find an opportunity of attacking and destroying these gun boats of the enemy's.

If you can spare any of the feluccas from this service, I shall be glad to have two of them stationed between Vado and Genoa to prevent the enemy's row boats from Genoa from molesting the vessels with provisions for the army at Vado.

I am sir your most obedient servant, HORATIO NELSON.

To the Commandante of the Neapolitan flotilla.

Enclosure (not numbered) Nelson to General De Vins

Agamemnon, Vado Bay,
October 12

SIR,—I am honoured with your Excellency's letter of yesterday's date and beg you to be assured that the security of your army from any attacks by sea is never neglected by us. The news from Genoa is too romantic to give a serious consideration too. His Excellency Mr. Drake from whose situation at the head quarters of your Excellency's army, I am obliged to communicate all my movements, will inform you of the disposition I have made of my sovereign's squadron entrusted to my directions.

Believe me to be with the highest respect your Excellency's most obedient servant, HORATIO NELSON.

His Excellency Baron De Vins (a copy)

[*Endorsed by Nelson:* 'Letter to General De Vins October 12th 1795 in answer to his expecting the French to land in his rear.']

Enclosure (not numbered): Nelson to General Wallis
[Nicolas, II, p. 95]

Agamemnon, Vado Bay,
November 7, 1795

SIR,—I was honoured last night with your letter of yesterday's date. I hope every general officer in the army will give me credit for my desire of doing everything in my power to render them assistance and I will order a frigate and brig to cruise off Cape Noli in order to keep those gun boats in some check. The captains of the ships who have anchored off Pietra declare to me that it is impossible to lay there in the least swell, as it is a quick sand, and both frigate and brig were with difficulty saved when there a few days ago. Indeed Sir, though I shall order the ships off Noli as you seem to wish it, yet I must apprize you that the first strong wind off the land may drive them to sea, and that the same wind is favourable to the enemy's gun boats, and I am sorry to observe that Languebia and Alassio are good places to ride at anchor in, when the same wind would drive any vessel on shore who may be at Pietra, but the moment I hear of any attack you may be sure I shall come down in the *Agamemnon* and render you every assistance in my power.

I have the honour to be Sir your most obedient servant, HORATIO NELSON.

General Comte Wallis.

Enclosure (not numbered): Nelson to General De Vins
[Nicolas, II, p. 96]

Agamemnon, Vado Bay,
November 8, 1795

SIR,—As you are in expectation of a general attack by the French and that the enemy's gun boats may be very troublesome by coming on your flank, as I hold my ships in momentary readiness to come to your assistance, I beg leave to suggest as the quickest means of my knowing of the attack that signals by guns (if possible) may be established from Pietra to the fort in Vado.

You may rest assured that the moment I know of the attack that a very short time shall carry the *Agamemnon* and every vessel I can collect to Pietra for believe me I have the most sincere disposition to co-operate with your Excellency in the destruction of our enemies and that I am with the highest respect and esteem your Excellency's most obedient servant, HORATIO NELSON.

His Excellency Baron De Vins (a copy).

Enclosure (not numbered): General de Vins to Nelson

MONSIEUR,—J'ai l'honneur de recevoir vos lettres du 4 et de 8 de ce mois., elles font honneur à votre zelle. Monsieur, je suis fachée de n'y pouvoir repondre comme je le desire, mais je suis si rempli des douleurs, qu'il me faut dire en moins de mots ce que je puis.

Il paroit que l'ennemi voyant notre position quoi inattaquable a abandonné le projet d'attaque, il a même retirée le plus grande partie des batiments qui etoient entre Borghetto, et Albango, ainsi il serait tres mal fait d'exposer un batiment qu'elconque à faire naufrage contre ces mauvaises côtes. Je vous pris donc seulement, d'avoir la bonté d'ordonner, quand la mer ce permette, qu'une fregate fasse la croisiere, pour en imposer a l'ennemi.

J'espere dans peu d'être à Vado moi-même, dés que ma santé me le permette et ce sera la que j'aurois l'honneur de combiner les signeaux et de vous assurer de vive voix d'être tout l'estime imaginable, monsieur, votre très humble et très obeissant serviteur, B. DE VINS.

La Pietra, 9 novembre 1795.

Nelson to Sir Hyde Parker [1]

A

[Nicolas, VII, p. 27]

Agamemnon, Genoa Road,
November 20, 1795

SIR,—Upon consultation with his Excellency Mr. Drake I have determined on sending a vessel to you with the enclosed reports of the state of the

---

[1] N.M.M. MS. 9578, St. Vincent papers—being a copy sent to Sir John Jervis for information.

ships in Toulon. It is needless for me to make any further observation on their contents, than that if the enemy's squadron come on this coast and land 3 or 4,000 men between Genoa and Savona I am assured that either the whole Austrian army will be defeated or they must instantly retreat into Piedmont and abandon their artillery and stores.

We are well acquainted with the French plan and of the well founded expectation they have of raising an insurrection of the Genoese peasantry in a particular valley between this and Vado.

I have not (which probably you know) been on former occasions backward in representing to Admiral Hotham my thoughts that at one time or other the French would make a push on this coast and my wishes for a reinforcement of two 74 gun ships and that the frigates should not be diminished. The latter I am sorry to say is done.

The extraordinary events which have taken place here, the expedition which would now sail from this port was I to withdraw the *Agamemnon*, will render it a measure of necessity always to keep a superior force to the French at this place with orders to attack if they presume to sail. They have broke the neutrality and the Genoese have not called on me for my word to respect it, they are fully aware (I think) what my answer must be.

Should the French squadron come into Genoa the debarkation can take place round the lanthorn at St. Pierre d'Arena. The Genoese have not the means of preventing it. And the safety of the *Agamemnon* becomes very precarious.

The government two nights ago ordered a guard of 40 men for Mr. Drake's house about 5 miles from Genoa as they were fearful for his personal safety. I believe they intend to recommend his residing in the town, but which Mr. Drake is determined not to do.

I have taken the liberty of breaking open the rendezvous which you sent for Captain Freemantle and I am sir with great respect your most obedient servant, HORATIO NELSON.

November 21st: I am sorry to add that I have received two letters from Leghorn telling me that the *Mozelle* is not arrived there and as she left Vado 13 days ago for Leghorn I am from her very bad state under some apprehensions for her safety. The *Speedy* brig is also missing 17 days. But our weather is so extremely bad in this gulf that sails nor ships or people can remain at sea for a long time. This morning at daylight the Austrians took possession of the French empty magazines at St. Pierre d'Arena and their sentinels are now close to the gates of Genoa. Mr. Drake thinks General de Vins has done wrong in doing it, he demanded satisfaction and payment of the Genoese government and without waiting for their answer has taken satisfaction himself, had the General done so at first he would have found full magazines instead of empty ones. By his conduct he has liberated the Genoese from their difficulties. Things here are so changeable that I cannot guess what may happen tomorrow. You may be assured I shall pursue a steady moderate line of conduct. H. N.

Peace is the universal cry as the King went to Parliament. This comes through France.

B

[Nicolas, VII, p. 29]

Agamemnon, at Sea,
December 2, 1795

SIR,—Although from circumstances I have reason to believe that you are acquainted that Vado is in possession of the French yet I think it my duty to acquaint you of as much of the matter as I know. Reports say the *Speedy* brig went into Vado as also a frigate and three merchant ships therefore as I have seen none of them which I own I am a little surprised at, I take for granted they are returned to St. Fiorenzo. Mr. Drake and myself hired a vessel at Genoa to carry despatches to you and I took the liberty to break open Capt. Freemantle's letter to find out where the fleet was.

The purport of my letter was to send you a report of the state of the ships in Toulon, the certainty of the intended debarkation between Genoa and Savona and a letter from Mr. Drake. I directed the master of the vessel if he fell in with any ships of ours to deliver the dispatches to him, if not to deliver them to the Consul at Mahon.

Not having any ships with me I had it not in my power to prevent the enemy's gun boats from annoying the flank of the Austrians army which I am given to understand the Generals mean to make the most of. However I am satisfied as is I believe the whole army that I have done every thing in my power to render them assistance. My being at Genoa by the requisition of the General at Vado, the Imperial minister, the Colonel commanding the troops at St. Pierre d'Arena and of Mr. Drake, although contrary to my wishes has fortunately been the means of saving about 8 or 10,000 Austrians and most probably De Vins himself, who came the road which but for my prevention would have been in possession of the French. I assure you, Sir, I never more regretted not being able to divide the *Agamemnon*.

General Wallis is retreated to Ormea with about 10,000 men. This is all we know that are collected, for the troops from Vado, Savona and on the coast between Savona and Genoa run away I am told in the utmost confusion, and are gone towards Milan.

I am sorry to say I have a lieutenant, 2 midshipmen and 16 men taken in the town of Savona, which the French before did not take possession of, nor did the Austrians. The guns in the batteries at Vado were spiked, but I suppose they will soon be cleared again. I was in Vado Bay on the 29th November and saw the French in full possession. *Meleager* joined me on the 30th at night and I have directed Captain Cockburn to cruise off Vado to prevent any of our ships from going in and to perform such other services as on consultation with Mr. Drake may be most for his Majesty's service.

I am, sir, your very obedient servant, HORATIO NELSON.

Sir Hyde Parker.

Mrs. Nelson to Nelson [1]

I

Kentish Town,
September 30, 1794

MY DEAREST HUSBAND,—Yesterday was your birthday. Mr. Suckling drank it with no small pleasure, gave some of his best wines and a Norfolk man deserved two geese. We were cheerful. Mr. Rumsey and family were of the party. Mr. Mentz as usual intreated his best respects to you and said many handsome things which I received with pleasure knowing how deserving you were of them. A happy birthday for me, the next I hope we shall be together.

Your letter and my son's of the 5th September I have received and look every day for one telling me you are coming. Everybody that Mr. S. and Maurice has asked if they know who are the captains that are coming home seems to say, you of course, that the ship must want much rest. Maurice came here last Sunday. He is much wanted at the Navy Office, but I do not know that they have offered him what would make it worth his while to quit his present station, for his half pay is £130 yearly and profitable one now. He is grown stout.

Your assurances of health and I hope the prospect of soon seeing my dear husband and child has made me happy beyond expression. It has given health for before you wrote me you were well and Calvi was taken,

[1] B.M. Add. MSS. 34,988. As only a few of the letters Nelson received from his wife have been preserved, they have not been numbered consecutively but in four series according to their dates.

I was fallen into the same way I was last year, now I am quite well. Mr. Suckling behaves in kindest manner. Miss Suckling I shall always have a sincere regard for. Mrs. S. is equally kind. My dear son's letter did contain news. I thank him for it and hope he is quite right in what he says.

Lord Southampton is gone to demand the Princess of Brunswick for a wife for the Prince of Wales, everybody congratulates themselves on the change he is going to make; Mrs. Fitzherbert has been long dismissed. Her violence of temper and some improprieties gave disgust. Everybody are full of the wicked design that a French watchmaker had to take away the life of our king. They were three concerned, the French man, who had made a tube, which upon blowing with his mouth a poisoned arrow was to have struck our King, a saddler and a chemist in Fleet Street. The saddler's conscience tormented him. He went and disclosed it. They are all taken up. The Playhouse was to have been the scene of wickedness, the signal for the watchmaker a call of 'riot'. I wish these French away I never liked them.

The West Indies is now a scene of mortality. Never was such a fever there before. An officer who was tried for not knowing his own things has seen most of the Court Martial dead before the trial was over. The hurricane they have had I hope will be of service to them. Guadeloupe is not yet retaken. Capt. Roberts is a prisoner, recovered his wound. [I am] glad Maurice Suckling is well. Pray [take] care of yourself. How I shall rejoice to see you. You must save yourself as much as you possibly can.

Sir Andrew Hammond [1] has a house at Hampstead. I shall call on Lady H. and the first time I can on Lady Hood. Lord H. has had leave to come by land or in his ship. The French have ships cruising.

Mrs. Matcham I have not heard from since I came to town, but Maurice tells me they went to Tunbridge. Surely there never was such an unsettled man. The journey I hope will be of service to her. You may depend upon it, it is a violent cold she has caught. Capt. Suckling embarks again for the continent. They are all well. Suckling Nelson and the two clergymen of Aylsham are very good friends. Mr. S. says he liked to have my letters sent to him for then he knew you were well. He is very much interested about you. Our father is well. Mr. and Mrs. and Miss Suckling send their love to you. If any little thing falls in your way bring it for Miss S. as a keepsake. I feel for her. An attachment between her and Captain Whigley: he is on the continent, her father knows it. He is to sell out. Don't take notice of it, it is not known. How is Frank? [2] I have seen his beautiful china.

---

[1] Sir Andrew Hamond was Comptroller of the Navy 1794–1806.
[2] Nelson's servant and coxswain, Frank Lepee.

Bless you my dearest husband, your affectionate wife, FRANCES NELSON.

To Captain Nelson, *Agamemnon*. To the care of J. Udney Esq., His Britannic Majesty's Consul, Leghorn. Post paid 1.5.

II

Kentish Town,
October 6, 1794

MY DEAREST HUSBAND,—From your letter of September 12th I flatter myself you will soon be at Portsmouth, therefore I am anxious you should know where to find me. From your sister's indisposition it was necessary for her to come to town for advice. She is better, change of air has been of great service. She is to move about till it is known whether she is bleeding or not. I feel myself particularly obliged to Mr. S. for his invitation which came so fortunate, for our father could not conveniently go to Bath till the first week in November. How anxious I am to see my dear husband and child, what happiness. Let me beg you to be particularly careful of sleeping at the inns.

It is dreadful to hear of the fevers and disorders that rages in the West Indies, indeed it has not been very healthy at Portsmouth and many other places. Are we to be blessed with peace? It is said that the ships coming from the W.I. ought to perform quarantine. The fever is so very infectious. I wrote you how handsome your uncle had been to me. Nothing less than £100 present.

My love to my son. My heart is full: may I see you in good health. God bless my dearest husband, your affectionate wife, FRANCES NELSON.

Mr. S. and family send their love to you and to Mr. J.[1]
This letter I have sent to Lady Parker.[2]

Captain Nelson, *Agamemnon*.

III

Kentish Town,
October 16, 1794

MY DEAREST HUSBAND,—Your letter off Genoa September 28th I received

---

[1] Josiah Nisbet.
[2] Wife of Sir Peter Parker, commander-in-chief at Portsmouth and a friend of Nelsons. By this means the letter would go through naval channels.

yesterday. It made me happy. The prospect of soon seeing everything that is dear to me, what a blessing. Can I ever be thankful enough? If you have heard from me lately, the reason of my leaving your sister Matcham you are no stranger to. She is better although not much. The surgeon whom they employ insists upon it, she breeding very contrary to his opinion. However they recommend a constant change of air and is still in London. I went to see her last week.

Great talk of the Princess of Wales elect.[1] Capt. Payne is to be commodore of the ships which are going for her. You will be concerned to hear poor Mrs. Scrivener is no more. She has by all accounts ended her miserable life. Mr. S. is stranger than ever. Has given both his houses and land to Mr. Revd. Mr. Howman which he had at Exmouth and is now living at Clifton.

Mr. Suckling tells me Charles Mills[2] is come to England. He made enquiries where I was so I suppose I shall see him. Still terrible accounts of the sickness in the West Indies. A reinforcement of ships and troops are gone out. It is said the merchant ships are to perform quarantine. It is sickly at Portsmouth. I have wrote to Lady Parker and sent her a letter which I begged she would deliver to you. Mr. Suckling and family are very kind and attentive and I felt myself obliged to them in giving me an invitation just at the time they did, for it was truly convenient.

Our father proposes going to Bath the first or second week in November. Suckling will have then finished with Cambridge. William Nelson through our father has made proposals for the purchase of Hilborough living. Mr. Suckling has consented provided you like it. Nothing decided is to be done till you come home. I told Mr. S. that Mr. Nelson had spoken to you about it. Mr. Matcham I believe begins to be tired of his purchase, but that is between you and I. Mr. S. will tell it you.

I could not bring myself to tell you of the misfortune Price has met with but fearing you might ask for Sam, poor fellow he was drowned some time at Hampstead, a heavy affliction has been to the father.

Captain Suckling returned from the continent and is going again. Melancholy account from that quarter. The French victorious. They have squadrons out in hopes of intercepting the fleets that are expected home. The Mediterranean fleet is expected every day so that *Victory* and *Agamemnon* will come together. I am happy at the thought of soon seeing my dearest husband and child. Anxious I shall be till I see you. I humbly pray God to bless and protect you and my Josiah.

[1] The Prince of Wales married Princess Caroline of Brunswick in April 1795.
[2] A nephew of Mr. Andrew Hamilton, who had married Mrs. Nelson's cousin, Martha Herbert.

Mr. S. was exceeding pleased to hear from you. All the family unite in love, best wishes to you. A thousand compliments from Hampstead. Milman and Price make many enquiries after you. I hope Frank Lepee is well. His china is beautiful. Your affectionate FRANCES H. NELSON.

I thank my dear son for his line. I am truly happy to hear he is good and well. The pleasing prospect of our soon meeting.

To Capt. Nelson, *Agamemnon.*
To the care of the Principal Officer of His Majesty's Navy, Gibraltar.

IV

Kentish Town,
November 2, 1794

MY DEAREST HUSBAND,—My disappointment at not seeing you and my child as soon as you gave me some hope that I should is very great. The thoughts of soon seeing my affectionate husband had made me quite well, but still I flatter myself it will not be very long before you will come home. This winter will be another anxious one. What did I not suffer in my mind last? I trust in that good providence who has shown great mercies to us.

My letters are dispersed, some to Gibraltar. You will get them I fear when my little news will be quite old. A promotion of Admiral down to Captain Bligh now Admiral Bligh (Charles Holmes E. Calmody, J. Bourmaster, Sir G. Young, J. Henry, Richard Rodney Bligh), Sir Alexander Schomberg, and Hon. P. T. Perceval still at the top of the list.[1] Admiral Elphinstone is not sailed or is the fleet of trade arrived. Horn Tooke, Hardy, Bonny etc. are now on their trial for high treason. A wickeder set surely never lived. Many fear they have acted with so much caution that they will not be hanged. Things had got to too great a height in the Scotch conventions, the terms these creatures had given to their meetings. The Dragoon Guards who in England with their line of new raised fencibles are quartered in and near London. The information that the ministry has is beyond description good. A party had met, inimical to our country, chance threw a gentleman in their way, tickets were dispersed, he put his hand out, one was given, with the name of one of the members, in he went and after he had heard all that was going forward,

---

[1] Sir Alexander Schomberg, promoted captain in 1757, and the Hon. P. Perceval, promoted captain in 1766, were the most senior captains in the Navy. Neither reached flag-rank.

how was he to get out again? He told the doorkeeper a gentleman was waiting without and that it was time for him to come in so he made the best of his way and told it to the minister. This same person married a sister of Mrs. S.

I have seen Mrs. Mills just the same as ever, talks of her brother's fortune. Young Morton and Mrs. Hamilton [1] don't speak. Bad crops. Not a word of even the *interest* of the legacies. Charles Mills is come home to be a W.I. merchant, his own concerns, those of Mr. Hamilton and Mr. Nisbet will instil him to make proposals to any house. The fever that rages in the W.I. is truly terrible. Not a line from Mr. Stanley. I thought of your writing when I was happy enough to see you, most likely I should get no answer was I again to write: Mrs. Stanley is with Mrs. Finch who I am sorry to tell you has been in great trouble and is now left with four little children. Admiral F. [2] died at Dr. W. where he had been some little time. From what Mrs. M. told me Mrs. F. had not been kindly treated by his mother. Adm. F. was subject to violent fits of passion.

Captain Payne is to bring home the Princess of Brunswick, the Prince it is said is quite happy at the thought of his being domesticated. Pringle [3] is sorry that he has his flag. Mrs. M. says he calls it empty honour. I was surprised to see Capt. A. Sutherland Commissioner at Gibraltar. Our good father next Wednesday sets off for Bath, arrives in London on Friday, rests at Mrs. Matcham's a few days and then I go to Bath with him to stay for the winter. I hope you will not stay long out and that we may have peace but the sound of such word I never hear.

Mr. Suckling always kind and sincerely interested in everything which concerns you. Laughs now and then at me, he can tell by my countenance what my good man writes me. Your letter of 27th September to be sure did give me pain. I had hoped to have soon seen my dear friend and my dear young man. If he is good I shall rejoice and be happy, so many turn out ill that truly parent anxiety is not to be wondered at. I feel comforted he is with [you]. Adml. Bourmaster is going to the W.I. with a fleet. Capt. Kelly is very well and is expected home. [4] Mrs. Matcham writes me she is better. Mrs. Bolton, Mr. Bolton and the children are all well excepting George who has a low fever. I wrote you the Rector had made proposals for the living. They are accepted but Mr. S. would not do anything but

---

[1] Mrs. Hamilton had inherited her father's fortune; but if she had no heirs, it was to go to her cousin, Magnus Morton. This happened in 1819 and he added Herbert to his surname.

[2] The Hon. William Clement Finch, rear-admiral 1753–94.

[3] Thomas Pringle, Nelson's friend from his time in the West Indies. Promoted rear-admiral in 1794; died, a vice-admiral, in 1803.

[4] Captain William Kelly had commanded the *Solebay* in Sir John Jervis's fleet in the West Indies expedition.

S

give his consent as you were expected soon. Mrs. S. tells him he is very lazy. Miss S. and I are very good friends. Bring her some little thing.

I pray God to bless you and my child, your affectionate wife, FRANCES H. NELSON.

All here send love to you. Mr. S. is much pleased to hear from you. They complain tell Frank of his never writing.

Capt. Nelson, *Agamemnon.*
To the care of J. Udney Esq., His Britannic Majesty's Consul, Leghorn. Post Paid.

V

Bath,
November 17, 1794

MY DEAREST HUSBAND,—By your letter of October 3rd I fear very much you do not receive the many which I have written you. No opportunity did I ever neglect, it has been my greatest pleasure excepting receiving one from you. No end of my anxiety. When shall I be blessed with seeing you and my child. I hope the French will not get out so as to give you an opportunity of engaging them, could I hope for this, I should endeavour to make myself easy. My mind and poor heart are always on the rack.

Sir A. Hammond and Lady I was fortunate in finding at home. She gave me great hopes that Lord Hood would bring you home, and I cannot think he will let you stay long out there. It may be a fortunate circumstance that you did not come with the fleet from Gibraltar as the French have a large squadron out to intercept the fleet which are not all arrived, and Lord Hood, who they wish much to take. It is said Admiral Bligh is taken in the *Alexander*,[1] who was one of the ships from Gibraltar.

Had you received my letters you would have known our father's plan of going to Bath, and that I was to have been with him. I was two months with Mr. Suckling after Mrs. Matcham was obliged to go to London for advice. She is better. Mr. M. is well. Our father is pretty well; complains very much of a general weakness and walks very little, says his feet hurt him. Bath did a great deal for him last winter, and as the journey is got over, I hope he will soon feel better.

To see my dearest husband and child and to have peace, my joy and thankfulness will be great indeed. I pray God to protect you, take care of your health, I flatter myself it is as good as you tell me it is. It is a very old

[1] The *Alexander* (Captain Richard Bligh) was obliged to retire after a prolonged engagement.

date 3rd October hope tells me I shall soon hear from you. A letter gives me more comfort than I can express. New King St. No. 17 is to be the resting place for the present. Change of air has been of service but when the mind is always harping upon the only friend and that the dearest we can be blessed with, any place after a time we get tired of. So we are together I am happy.

Capt. Kelly is expected home. Mr. Weatherhead who went out to Sir J. Jarvise is dead. More ships are gone out with troops. Guadeloupe [1] is not retaken. Poor Mrs. Robertson is left with four little children. Captain Robertson [2] headed the seamen and they say the English unfortunately fired upon each other. She has £100 a year and her children £25 a year, that is what has been done. I wrote you all the little news I heard. Our father desires his best and affectionate love to you, will write you soon. We came here yesterday and I have been busy in looking for lodgings. A large French out. Will write my dear child my love to him.

My dearest husband I pray God to guard and protect you and my son. Do write. Your affectionate wife, FRANCES H. NELSON.

VI

New King Street, Bath,
November 27, 1794

MY DEAREST HUSBAND,—Your not receiving any letters lately from me truly gives me concern. Many are at Gibraltar, I never missed but one packet and that was owing to Mr. Suckling's expecting you I may say daily. By this time I hope you have heard from me. Take notice of the dates and mark them at the bottom of your letter. The first I wrote from here was on the 20th and as I hear the mail for Leghorn is made up once a week I will take my chance. No kindness or attention from my dear husband but what I feel most sensibly. Lord Hood's arrival gave me hopes of a letter: suppose he did not make Gourgon in his way. From what Sir A. Hammond told me, I did think Lord Hood would have brought you home.

The French illuminated at Brest when they carried in the *Alexander*, Admiral Bligh. They have constantly fresh squadrons at sea between Bay of Biscay and the Channel. They have been too successful in taking trading ships. Will Lord H. send for you? It is much in his power to do so.

---

[1] Jervis had captured Guadeloupe, but was unable to hold it against a French attack, his forces being reduced through yellow fever and no reinforcements being available.
[2] Captain Lewis Robertson was shot while leading a party of seamen in support of the army at Grozior.

The comfort we have in your assurances that your health is good it is the greatest of blessings. Do take care of yourself. I shall be anxious for your coming home and I truly hope the French will not think of any more engagements.

Nothing of the payment of the interest of the legacy. I met Patterson who tells me Mr. Pinney is just arrived. They will call upon us and I may hear of some rogue's trick to keep the interest from you. Our father seems to think if Mr. Bailey was inclined to pay the interest you have not given me sufficient power to receive it as my discharge is not valid.

Since I left town Miss Suckling writes me her father was seized with one of his fits of coughing which they thought would have strangled him. Dr. Broklesby attended him and he is much better. He is attached to you, but so many are his demands. Miss Hawkings met me and the old lady soon paid me a visit. Great alterations in the Andrews family. 2 of the girls and a younger brother gone to the East Indies with the polite Nabob (who never called on our good father) 2 younger brothers in the 81st regiment gone to the West Indies.

Our father sends his blessing to you and will write the first week in December. He tells me he is glad he has got me again and let you live where you will, he must be with you. M. N.[1] is doing well, getting a little money. Mrs. Bolton and her husband are well. The heir [2] growing a great man. Sir Richard Bickerton has General Vaughan on board his ship gone to the West Indies. I write my child. How is Frank? Kelly is very well. Mrs. Morton [3] has lost a son and heir to Monpelier.

God bless you and grant you a safe return home. Your affectionate wife, FRANCES H. NELSON.

Captain Nelson, *Agamemnon*, Leghorn. To the care of J. Udney Esq., His Britannic Majesty's Consul.   Post paid 2/10.

VII

[Bath]
December 4, 1794

MY DEAREST HUSBAND,—This instant left Lord and Lady Hood, who received me with every mark of affection and said all that would gratify an affectionate wife, begged that I would frequently call and consider myself at home.

[1] Nelson's brother, Maurice.
[2] Thomas Bolton, born 1786, later second Earl Nelson, died 1835.
[3] Magnus Morton had married Christina Forbes of Nevis.

Lord Hood assured me you are well, expects you will be at home in less than three months. God grant it. My child is well so he says and that he saw you on the 12th of October.

Our good father is well, sends his love to you. This is to go thro' his lordship. Have only time to tell you I am your affectionate wife, FRANCES H. NELSON.

Dec. 4th. I have not heard from you this age.

Capt. Nelson, *Agamemnon.*

VIII

New King Street, Bath,
December 10, 1794

MY DEAREST HUSBAND,—I have now before me letters of October down to the 31st. Thank you very much my dear for them. Lord Hood enclosed you a letter from me last week. Was as affectionate as if I had been his child assures me I shall soon see you and one of the finest colts he ever saw in his life. Lady Hood speaks much of you. Will never forget the letter you wrote her, showed it to the Lord. I dined with them was cheerful and well dressed. Lord Hood declared he would write to you the next day and tell you I was well. He made me happy by telling me he never saw you look better in his life and thought you were stouter. He has spoke of your services and the situation you had been constantly in particularly one at Bastia to the Speaker of the House of Commons, the Lady said if justice was not done you it would not be Lord H's fault. I assure you many are dissatisfied at G. S.[1] behaviour, they think he should have said more. Some say that as your situation and his were the same it was his modesty. However he is coming home. Col. Trigg is to have the command. Guadeloupe is retaken. You never heard of any poor creatures so oppressed as they were by, *they say,* those who had the command. Col. Gordon is now on his passage home to be tried. It is shocking what is related but I don't believe half.

All that we know in Nevis are still well. Mrs. H. more amiable than ever. Mrs. Morton has miscarried and lost a son and heir to Mountpelier. Stanley has never answered my letter. I have only had 50 pounds from Mr. Baily therefore there is a small sum, if I can get it I will take great care of it for you. I wrote you from Kentish Town how much I had spent, 50 pounds from Marsh and Creed, enough by me to pay for a small pianoforte 25 guineas and what will amply supply all my expenses till I am

----
[1] General Stuart.

blessed with a sight of you. No stage coach I give you my honour do I travel in, do anything in your absence that I thought would give you an opportunity to say that you wished it had been otherwise. No, not for the world.

Our good father has recovered his fatigue, begun the waters, desires me to thank you for your letter and your donation will be distributed in the best manner he can think of. That the 2 guineas I had long paid. Your horse that has been taken the greatest care of, is they are afraid growing quite blind therefore our father after he had my consent has decided to sell her. The expense has been a good deal in keeping her. Nobbs is discharged, grew worse than ever. Has left the village. Maurice is at Netley Camp very well. No prospect of peace although everybody is constantly wishing for it. Wherever Lord H. is this war you are to be with him.

Mrs. Holwell and Miss Somes are here. I have been to one concert since I came here with some pleasant young women whose mothers are our father's acquaintance. We are to stay here till you come home. Mr. Matcham is well. Mrs. Matcham is better. Mr. & Mrs. Bolton are well. I never hear the wind but my dear husband and child are fully in my thoughts indeed they are never never absent from my mind. As long as my letters come regularly once a fortnight I am very well. Poor Frank I own I was afraid some thing was the matter, that he was not so good as formerly. I am very sorry that he is in so deplorable a way. I hope he never is with you. You may be able to get him in G.H.[1] you are sure of Capt. Locker. My love to my dear child, God bless you. Your affectionate wife, FRANCES H. NELSON.

If you can get a little cambric for ruffles and pocket handkerchiefs well and good but pray don't load yourself with presents thank you. Our father's love to you and Josiah.

Capt. Nelson, *Agamemnon*.   To the care of the Consul at Leghorn.

IX

Bath,
December 16, 1794

MY DEAREST HUSBAND,—On Sunday last coming from church I fortunately met Capt. Shield who had left you after the date of your letter. Dr. Harness took pleasure in introducing him to me as he could and would give such good accounts of you. Capt. Shield is gone to London by the desire of Lord Hood. A change in the Admiralty, Lord Spencer first lord,

---

[1] Greenwich Hospital, where Captain Locker was the Lieutenant-Governor.

it is hoped the Admiralty business will now go on properly. Lord Hood I
think has been neglected. One of the newspapers has abused him shamefully. His stay will not be long here. They have been kind and attentive. I
was last night at the ball with them. Dr. Harness [1] I am very much pleased
with, he spoke so handsomely of you and did tell me many little things
which to bystanders might be thought trifling, but to me highly gratifying.
I have heard of your breakfast on the fig tree. My son they all say I shall
not know him. I wish you were in England and that we were blessed with
peace. I am glad you have got a French master, you will be able to give
me instruction and I shall be happy to receive it.

24th. This day I have received your letter of November 15th and hope
you will soon be home. It seems Admiral Elphingstone was to have gone
out; the death of his brother Lord Elphingstone has made him wish to
stay in order to settle some family affairs. His brother must have been
dead some time as his sister Mrs. Drummond has been out of mourning
ever since we came to Bath. Mrs. D. and I were coming from the Octagon
this morning and she told me that her brother was not going to the
Mediterranean this winter.

Four sail of the line has sailed for the Mediterranean and others
ordered immediately to be got ready. Lord Hood I am assured by the Lady
has said everything of you to those in town. I tell you what is told me.
Admiral Cosby was at the ball, he came to Lady H. he spoke of you on
high terms, seemed of a communicative temper but had not an opportunity of saying much, however he did say no man in the Mediterranean
had done what you had, such a conspicuous figure and supposed they
would not let you stay out much longer. I told him what Lady Hood had
told me, that you would be in England in three months.

Miss Walpole writes me Earl Fitz-William is Lord Lieutenant of
Ireland and has appointed Mr. Hussey usher of the Black Rod. Mr. H. is
going over immediately. Mrs. Hussey remains in England. I wished very
much you had sat for your picture. I am told Italy is the place to have it
done. Is it possible? I mean a small one. 5 of the mutineers of the *Culloden* [2]
are ordered for execution. Sir Thomas Shirley has been very particular in
his enquires after you, has paid me a visit and brought his sister and
family to see me.

Our father is better. It is a good thing he is here. The cold has set in
very severe. The secret expedition is put off for some time. Maurice talks
of coming here. All the family are well. Mrs. Hoste thanks me very much

[1] Physician to the Mediterranean Fleet.
[2] Captain Troubridge handled the mutiny in the *Culloden* very firmly—ten men were
brought to trial, eight were condemned, though three subsequently were pardoned.

for my letters as she so seldom gets any from her son but of very old date. She received one a few days dated 7 May. It is said Mr. Pitt is going out and that Mr. Windham [1] is to be prime minister. Capt. Inglefield is to be at Bath today. Mrs. Kelly writes me Capt. Kelly is watching ships that are very valuable Point Peter and he is determined to have them. All Lord H.'s commissions are confirmed. H.'s expected another Eustatia business, these great fortunes will vanish. Our father sends his love to you and Josiah and number of very fine things from the Hoods to you. I dine there today. The Scotch people [2] send their best compliments and good wishes to you and love to my child. Remember me to him. I pray God to bless you. Your affectionate wife, FRANCES H. NELSON.

Captain Nelson, *Agamemnon*, Leghorn.   Care of Consul.

X

Bath,
December 17, 1794

MY DEAREST HUSBAND,—I have been particularly fortunate in receiving your letters of October 31st and November 21st the latter came last Sunday. I am thankful to hear your health is good. Lord Hood says you never looked better. They pay me particular attention. Nothing *now* is like you. Lord Hood once asked me if I knew who had bought Petersham, answer no. I know nothing of his Royal Highness. I went to the play with them, dined and taken a long ride but as to a word of news that is never to be heard there, of all the silent men surely he is the most so, not a word of the contents of your letter. I was determined to make him smile. He had hold of both my hands, and said he hoped I heard from you. I told him yes and as his lordship's letter was dated two days after mine I had an inclination to be jealous and that I should write you so.

Mrs. Holwell is here but not very well. She is a good woman. The Court of Enquiry sits on Capt. Molloy [3] the 31st of this month, parties run high. The contributions that has been raised on the inhabitants are all to be refunded, therefore I suppose estates and carriages must be done without and what is worse than all, it is said that the young men who have been made there are not to be confirmed. The love of wealth ruins many. Mr. John has been to see us. Many enquiries after you. He begged our good father to go and see him.

[1] M.P. for Norwich, Secretary for War; died 1810.
[2] The Lockarts and Miss Nisbet.
[3] Captain Molloy, of the *Glory*, was dismissed his ship for not taking up proper station in the battle of June 1.

Charles Mills called yesterday says the West Indies is worse than ever. Mrs. Hamilton never stirs out, has thirty *cats*. His uncle a good man but he must say deserves all he meets with. Stanley a great man, but is lost to all sense of kindness. The Forbes are going to the West Indies in a very great hurry, how could it be otherwise they lived quite in style.

You will be surprised to find most articles of life much increased. Our father desires me to say your bill he had given orders how it should be disposed of to the best of his judgement. I must tell you he won't let me pay a part of the housekeeping, only of the house rent. He says he will spend his money first and if that won't hold out, he shall attack your purse whether you have the bag or himself it matters not. I shall make Mr. Pinny who is coming here tell me how I am to draw upon Baily for the money.

I read the Norfolk news to our father. A pretty estate of 300 acres to be sold near Cromer. Suppose said Mr. N. you buy it that will just do. The Rector we seldom hear from. Maurice is very busy preparing for a secret expedition so he writes us. My child I figure to myself good obedient to you and I hope tells you all the secrets of his heart. If he does you will keep him good. At his time of life much is to be feared, thank you for having a French master. Do make him clean his teeth not cross ways but upwards and downwards. When I expected you I went and had my teeth put in order and wish I had done it some years back they look much better than you ever saw them.

I don't know that you will approve of what I am going to say but it is human nature. The French I wish may keep their fleet in Toulon. My dear I rejoice not to have seen any such wicked report of your being taken nor do I think it has reached England, but thank you a thousand times for every tenderness you show me. Last night was at the concert a very good one. Learning of music that is an expense to you. I practise a great deal but am not satisfied with myself. Have seen Mrs. Southerland seems highly delighted with her husband's situation she hopes he will never go to sea again.[1] Love to my child, your affectionate wife, FRANCES H. NELSON.

[P.T.O.]

Keep all the little things which you tell me you have got, till we meet. I hear of great delays in some departments. Capt. Troubridge has had terrible mutiny on board *Culloden*, 10 will be hanged. Obliged to order a line of battle ship to sink her before they would hear reason.

Captain Nelson, *Agamemnon*, Leghorn. Care of Consul.

[1] Captain Andrew Sutherland, who had served in the West Indies with Nelson, was appointed Commissioner at Gibraltar in 1794.

XI

New King Street, Bath,
December 28, 1794

MY DEAREST HUSBAND,—Since I have heard the mail was twice a week
made up for Leghorn it is impossible to withstand the pleasure I have in
writing you. On Christmas Day I sent you an epistle. The weather was so
extremely cold that our father would not let me carry it to the post office,
therefore Will was trusted with the charge.

Since then little has arrived, excepting the arrival of Lord and Lady
Bridport. Lord Howe has received an express to go to sea. The French
are out. A powerful fleet indeed 30 sail. Lord Howe could not set off
today on account of indisposition, but I heard Lord Hood tell his brother
that he understood Lord Howe was to go tomorrow, if that is not the case
Lord Bridport will have the command. I was introduced to Lord and Lady
B. I think courteous and says pleasant things. I was for going off as I
heard them announced, but they would not let me and Lady H. told the
Admiral that I was for going. Afterwards I had no inclination, he was very
cheerful and much more of a communicative disposition than Lord H.
who is the most silent man I ever knew.

Confusion seems to reign in every department. It is said the Portland
Party will take the lead. The object of the French is to take the Mediterranean fleet and the West India one, both rich. Sir Harry Burrard is coming
with the Mediterranean fleet. Capt. Inglefield's son is on board, he seems
to say the ship is so fast a sailer that little is to be apprehended on her
account. This said Captain has been here a few days, he called on our
father, and in conversation said he was going out to Corsica resident
commissioner. I suppose a good place. He also said nothing prevented
Lord Hood from being called to the House of Peers but the confusion an
election would make in the city of Westminster. Exactly what I had set
down in my mind although I have heard much of his being neglected.
They suppose Mr. Hood will not go again to the West Indies. I cannot
help hoping after what everybody that has come from Corsica says of you
justice will be done. I am hurt and think it very hard you are not ordered
home. The French has constantly large squadrons out and a good sailing
ship is of great consequence now. Capt. Nugent has the command of the
Glory in consequence of Capt. J. Pakenham being ordered to Bath.

I dined at Lord Hood's on Christmas day when I met Mr. Petre one
of the Corsican deputies, he was very pleasant and of a cheerful disposition, would not speak French on any account, said he had had enough of
that. [*Part missing*]. Capt. Inglefield has just called to take leave is going

to London. Mr. Linzey was with him much indisposed, they begged I would give their best compliments. Our father is much better than when he came to Bath. The Hoods pay him proper attentions.

Josiah, Captain Inglefield told me was a name he often heard my dear husband call: he said he is a fine fellow. I am very well but so sadly disappointed at your not coming home. The blessings I have are never out of my mind. I am thankful. God grant you health. My love to my child. Our father sends his blessing to you. Maurice is well and so are all the family. Bless you my dear husband, believe me, your affectionate wife, FRANCES H. NELSON.

Have sent Aunt Mary a hamper carriage paid of good things.

Captain Nelson, *Agamemnon*, Leghorn. To the care of the Consul.

The Rev. Edmund Nelson to Nelson [1]

A

Bath,
August 5, [1795]

MY DEAR HOR,—We yesterday received yours of the 2nd ult. which from the intelligence it brought that you and our young friend were then in health was the most acceptable regale that could be given to a wife, and two affectionate parents. But indeed I did expect that you had then been a partaker with us of the pleasure we feel in your appointment to the Marines, which perhaps we relish in a very high degree as it is the general voice, it is well and properly given. How eminently does such a situation shine above whatever is obtained by interest or bribery, when it falls upon the unworthy man. We begin to be somewhat anxious to know what effect this event may have upon the arrangement of your own public matters, which you are the sole and best judge of, and our wishes to receive you must be subordinate to your opinion, interest and reputation. Mrs. F. H. N. was never in such good health as here and with some cheerful neighbours etc. I hope her time of widowhood passes with as little alloy as can be expected, and we often are fixing the cottage retirement you are looking forward to. As to myself, every month in this place of warmth, ease and quietude adds something to my strength, and if I live to have a conference with you every arrangement that is likely to make us all happy I hope will take place.

---

[1] Monmouth MSS., Nelson papers, Vol. IV. These are selected from the twenty-four letters Nelson received from his father preserved in that collection.

Never have I heard so general a complaint of scarcity as in this season. Corn there certainly is enough yet every eye is watching when the harvest shall be ripe, which is generally thought to be plentiful. The distillery is stopped; hair powder is ordered to be disused by the military. Only one sort of bread is allowed, no pastry used. Every precaution is taken to keep up the spirits of all, and if possible to quiet the murmurs of the many, whose cry is 'Peace and Bread'. The latter there is, bless God, a near prospect of. When or how the former will be enjoyed is not mine to say, yet it looks as if the actions of Spain is or must be a step towards a general pacification. We are every day teased with newspaper accounts of an action in the Mediterranean but no couriers arrived and we are in suspense. The emigrants at Quiberon are entirely defeated. Monsieur D'Artois is just arrived at Plymouth. My Norfolk intelligence is my good sister [1] is in much sorrow at the loss of her son Edmund, a good young man. Our old neighbour Mr. Raven is gathered to his fathers.

Only have I to add that so affectionate a son merits all a kind father can bestow, his fervent prayers that God may long preserve you. Adieu. EDM. NELSON.

Sir J. Jarvis is going to you.

To Captain Nelson, *Agamemnon*. To the care of John Udney Esq., His Britannic Majesty's Consul at Leghorn.   pd. 1s. 5d. Aug. 5.

B

Bath,
September 3, 1795

MY DEAR HOR,—If your promises and assurances could be made good by any prudent act of your own, they would remain as unalterable as a Persian or Median law, and we should as surely expect you home in October as we do the shoals of herrings on the Norfolk coast. But we see this must not be our dependance. Circumstances with you vary with every lunar change, and what some months past seemed a sure consequence of things I fear is now clouded in an impenetrable mist. If you then saw peace coming forward, with all her smiling train, now her progress towards us is very slow, and as a traveller up a steep and slippery ascent, her efforts to visit this country are baffled and lose their footing. Our naval successes hang out happy signals but they are not answered by continental victory.

[1] Alice, who married the Rev. Robert Rolfe.

The unhappy emigrants could gain no footing in their native country; the hearts of some recoiled and could not support the trial of fighting against their own household, laid down their arms or turned against their leaders, others fell captives into the hands of their cruel foes and are destroyed, some returned to British asylums, and are again embarked to join the Royalists. Thus stand things here. But it will be the language of the many that this Pittian Minister will not attend to the loud calls of his countrymen 'Give us Peace'.

It has pleased the great and good God to give us plenty, and weather such as have scarcely ever been left, to get in the abundant crops which still I hope and even now desire and invite you to partake of. And having the treasure of a self approving mind in justice to that self, you may awhile retire from incessant fatigue and let others hear a little of the roaring cannon. I trust the fatigue of life is over with you. In days of peace you will enjoy your cottage, and even in a future war, or the still further protraction of this, you may expect and claim some rest in a home department.

Your good wife is perfectly well and as happy as the state of things will admit. I myself have, agreeable to your very good wishes, taken a small house [1] here for 3 years and shall not visit Burnham till next summer. Suckling is there the sole regent and I find a sovereign remedy in ease of body and a quiet mind yet still much remains for our personal conference in and for the arrangement of private and family concerns.

Give my best love to Josiah. Merit and Poll are both in health. God bless you. Farewell. EDM. NELSON.

A Dutch War is commenced.

To Captain Nelson, *Agamemnon.* To the Care of John Udney Esq., His Britannic Majesty's Consul at Leghorn.   pd. 1s. 5d.

[1] The house, 17, New King Street, Bath, had fallen vacant through the death of the owner, Mrs. Searle.

Chapter 4

FLAG-RANK AND RENOWN
1796–1797

Introduction

It had needed all the courage of Nelson and his invincible *Agamemnons* to keep alive the fighting spirit in the face of Hotham's apathy during the closing stages of the Vado campaign. Fortunately the arrival of a new and active commander-in-chief brought a tardy recognition of Nelson's zeal. The business of the Mediterranean fleet was still to watch Toulon, guard Corsica, protect British trade with the Levant, and aid the Austrian army in its continued effort to clear the French army from the passes into Italy through the foothills of the Maritime Alps. The bay of St. Fiorenzo on the north-west tip of Corsica was the best fleet anchorage, and Leghorn was still used as a repair and victualling base, although it was not so satisfactory since the Grand Duke of Tuscany had made peace with France in February 1795. However, there was still an overland route open for mail and dispatches between Leghorn and Hamburg.

Nelson met Jervis in St. Fiorenzo Bay on January 15, 1796, and was able to put him wise about matters which had probably lain beyond Hotham's ken. On January 27 he was able to write home from the Gulf of Genoa, where he was again preparing to aid an Austrian army, that there was 'some little envy' in the fleet amongst his brother-captains, one of whom had said to him: 'You did just as you pleased in Lord Hood's time, the same in Admiral Hotham's, and now again with Sir John Jervis. It makes no difference to you who is commander-in-chief.' Nelson 'made a pretty strong answer to this speech', which he would not have recorded if, in his own opinion, it had not contained a modicum of truth. As usual his new-found appreciation and a promise of active service made him feel astonishingly fit and well, so that he remarks, 'you will find me grown very stout'. For as he writes home later, 'If I ever feel unwell, it is when I have no active employment.' That Jervis had declared against copying Hotham's pleasure in the flesh-pots ashore was commented upon by Nelson on February 12 when he reports, 'the new admiral will not land at Leghorn'. Although in Hotham's time Nelson was longing to get home, he was soon announcing that Jervis wanted him to stay and was prepared to make it worth his while to do so. So Mrs. Nelson was again made aware that her husband was not coming home yet awhile, and as for Josiah and his letter-writing, 'he waits probably for some great news to tell you'.

After being sent to look into Toulon, by March 25 Nelson was back off Genoa, but now he knew the *Agamemnon* would soon be flying his coveted distinguishing pendant and as a commodore he would be able to call himself a flag-officer. No doubt also as a result of his talks with Jervis, he was seriously considering how he could hurry up the promotion of Josiah to lieutenant, and regretting that he had never placed Josiah's name on the books of the *Boreas* in the old-established manner of building up a fictitious record of sea time. He thought perhaps his brother Maurice at the Navy Office would be prepared to cheat a little amongst his records on Josiah's behalf. Certainly Nelson became quickly one of the established favourites of Jervis, and what made the good opinion of Jervis particularly valuable was the good relations and easy confidence existing between Jervis and Lord Spencer, the First Lord of the Admiralty, which meant that Jervis's recommendations were nearly always quickly implemented. This harmonious understanding between commander-in-chief and the Government was something which not even Nelson's hero the great Lord Hood had ever been able, or probably even dreamed of trying to accomplish.

Although on April 24 Nelson wrote home, 'Sir John was a perfect stranger to me, therefore I feel the more flattered', Harrison, Nelson's first biographer, records an earlier meeting, 'on no less authority than that of the Earl of St. Vincent himself'. It occurred when Jervis was a member of Parliament (between 1784 and 1793) and was returning from the House of Commons, when, in the Treasury passage, 'he perceived Captain Locker at a distance, whom he instantly knew from the singularity of his looking through an eye-glass fitted at the head of his cane. Sir John immediately hailed his old friend: and Captain Locker, coming up, expressed his happiness at seeing Sir John Jervis as he wished he said to introduce his *élève* Captain Nelson.' In this way, by one distinguished captain introducing his favourite pupil to another, the traditions of the Royal Navy were handed down in the safe keeping of its promising young officers. And Jervis probably understood Nelson better than his other admirals had done. Nelson was only one of a number of promising young officers Jervis chose to favour, and Jervis considered favouritism the secret of efficiency. Nelson comments proudly on Jervis's pleasure in his 'firmness of conduct', but whilst Jervis worked hard to get Nelson his flag, he confided to Sir Gilbert Elliot that the Commodore did not always weigh the consequences, and he congratulated Elliot on having 'a little damped the ardour' because 'his zeal does now and then (not often) outrun his discretion'. But Jervis could never enough admire and extol Nelson's 'zeal and activity' and his 'unexampled vigilance'. And Jervis was not niggardly in bestowing praise or blame. Troubridge was perhaps his real favourite, who in the *Culloden* was soon to lead the British line of battle on the St. Valentine's day fight, and whom, alone of all his underlings, Jervis considered 'capable of commanding the fleet of England'. This commander-in-chief was continually pressing onto the First Lord's bounty the claims of his favourites, and such men as Nelson, Troubridge, Alexander Hood, and Hallowell he loved dearly and brought forward as being 'very great characters'. It was from Jervis that Nelson received the training that enabled him two years later to refer proudly to his own 'Band of Brothers', who had in fact been chosen for him by his commander-in-chief.

Meanwhile, in the Gulf of Genoa, Nelson found the French and the Austrians encamped in the vicinity of the town. On April 9, his broad pendant now proudly flying, he met the British minister, and learnt, 'The Austrian general is seventy-four years of age, but I am told has the fire of youth joined to it.' However, he must have had some doubts of such a happy conjunction of qualities, for in his next letter, 'we hope the discipline of the Austrians will in time get the better of the French.' But that same April 1796, the half-starved and half-naked soldiers of France were responding to the burning words of an even greater than Nelson: 'Soldiers of the Army of Italy, will you lack courage?' The brilliant Italian campaign which Bonaparte was to launch could not be halted by the British Mediterranean fleet. On April 19 Nelson found 'the Austrians are beat at all points' and 'the French fight on shore like our seamen, they never stop and know not the word halt.' And the only consolation he could report was a saying of the French, 'We are masters on shore and the English at sea.'

Although the war ashore was so disappointing, Nelson remained happy and busy. He able to send home the good opinions of his superiors with such cautions to his wife as 'Pray do not let this go farther than my father, not even to the Rector or the Matchams. It is all pleasant to me and I know must be so to you.' It is noticeable that he did not like his two brothers-in-law, Matcham and Bolton, and indeed amongst his relations really seemed to care only for his wife and stepson, father, and brother Maurice. He was a little disappointed in his stepson. 'Josiah is well, teeth good, 5 feet 4 ins. in height', is an unusually informative if laconic report. But his progress in polite learning was slow. His mother was sure he must now speak French. 'You seem to think Josiah is a master of languages. I must say he is the same exactly as when an infant and likes apples and port wine but it will be difficult to make him speak French, much more Italian. However, I hope his heart is good and that is the principal.'

On May 20 Nelson was able to write that Berry had joined the ship, and a little later he is writing cheerfully of his wife's recommendation that he should make Berry a captain. His little jokes are addressed equally to his wife and father. He reads their names with surprised pleasure in an old newspaper as having taken up their winter residence together at Bath. And he repeats his father's well-remembered sayings. 'Put a letter in the post and it will go', is one of them. Indeed, the post seems to have been remarkably reliable before the days of trains and aeroplanes. Nelson's own comment applied then as now: 'Half the letters which *miscarry are not wrote*.' And Nelson confided to them his own private reflections and ambitions. 'Had all my actions been gazetted not one fortnight would have passed'; and 'Let those enjoy their brag and one day or other I will have a *large gazette* to myself.' On May 11 he was still in the Gulf of Genoa, recording it was three years since he had sailed from Spithead. He was still hoping to get his flag as a rear-admiral, but Lord Spencer made no promotions, and as an established commodore with a captain under him, as he had after September, and the confidence of his commander-in-chief, there was not so much urgency for this happy event. On June 13 he wrote home to say he had at last left 'poor old *Agamemnon*', and moved into the *Captain*, 74 guns, taking with him certain of his officers and his barge's crew. The *Agamemnon*, frapped together like St. Paul's ship, was sailed home into dockyard hands.

In July 1796 the French captured Leghorn and started a revolution in Corsica against the British rule under the viceroy, Sir Gilbert Elliot. Whilst the British occupation of Corsica denied the French arsenal at Toulon essential naval stores, particularly timber, it was dependent itself on trade with Leghorn or Genoa for foodstuffs. Its use as a naval base became problematical, and Nelson, in the *Captain*, was sent to seize the island of Elba as an alternative. He instituted a very strict blockade of Leghorn. On September 10 he writes of interviewing the Doge of Genoa, with a view to persuading him to resist French demands, but on the 19, as a result of the Genoese batteries opening fire on his ships, Nelson seized the island of Capraia, to the north of Elba, in retaliation for this act of aggression. By September 30 he was able to write that he would now probably be home by Christmas because of important new developments which he could not trust to a letter. Jervis had received orders from home to evacuate the Mediterranean.

T

The retreat from the Mediterranean was decided upon by Pitt and his ministers when the declaration of war by Spain threatened Jervis with a combination of the Spanish and the French fleets at Toulon. The decision to withdraw was taken quickly and later rescinded when it was too late. Nelson was justly indignant after his three years of Mediterranean 'fag', having had from the beginning a poor opinion of the Spanish fleet. 'At home they know not what this fleet is capable of performing', he complained, 'any and every thing.' He considered the British fleet 'equal to meet the world in arms' and 'with a commander-in-chief fit to lead them to glory'. Meanwhile, rumours of peace had added fuel to the fires of rebellion in Corsica, and Nelson forgot his indignation in the dangerous work of carrying out the evacuation. He had not forgotten his disgust of the army's procrastination. 'As for Corsica I have seen the first and last of it. I was the cause of giving many lucrative employments for the army which they were incapable of getting for themselves and I took them off the island when they were equally helpless.' The garrison was taken to Elba, and Nelson rejoined Jervis at Gibraltar and the Viceroy visited those Italian states which the French had not overrun, whilst he awaited the Government's intentions concerning Elba.

Jervis, receiving orders to evacuate Elba, sent Nelson back again in the frigate *La Minerve*, of 38 guns, Captain George Cockburn, with a 32-gun frigate, the *Blanche*, under his orders. On the way there they fought two Spanish frigates and captured the *Sabina*, which was recaptured by a superior Spanish force, with a prize crew on board. At Elba Nelson had to wait for the Viceroy, who was at Naples. Captain Fremantle in the *Inconstant* fetched Sir Gilbert Elliot from Naples and married Betsy Wynne in Lady Hamilton's house. Mrs. Fremantle sailed with her husband back to Elba, and on 11 January wrote in her diary, 'Old Nelson very civil and good-natured, but does not say much.' He was in his fortieth year: she called herself 'an old lady of nineteen'. Leaving a garrison and frigate at Elba, Nelson embarked the Viceroy and his suite and the naval stores in three detachments, on January 29, 1797. Nelson, in *La Minerve*, determined to look into every port of the enemy on his way back to join the admiral. At Gibraltar he exchanged with the Spaniards for his men lost in the *Sabina* as the prize crew, including Lieutenant Hardy. And in the Straights of Gibraltar his frigate was chased by a superior Spanish squadron and, when holding his own with difficulty, a man fell overboard. Hardy had charge of the boat which tried without success to pick up the man. Nelson had the main topsail backed to recover the boat and Hardy, but the leading Spanish ship, scenting danger, delayed too. Nelson that foggy night found himself in the midst of the Spanish fleet, and despite having the Viceroy on board, considered a flying visit to the West Indies to give warning if the Spaniards were bound that way. Next morning it seemed better to rejoin Jervis and warn him, which they were able to do at daybreak on February 13. Nelson transferred his flag back to the *Captain*, and the Viceroy and suite went on board the *Lively*, frigate, having obtained the admiral's permission to watch the promised battle and take the despatches home. Colonel Drinkwater, a member of the Viceroy's suite and historian of the siege of Gibraltar, wrote an account of the battle which contains Nelson's sentiments freely conveyed to him after the battle.

The battle off Cape St. Vincent, fought on St. Valentine's day, February 14, 1797, is of course one of the great occasions in Nelson's career, and his conduct excited the admiration of the fleet. He now became a naval hero in his own right, and earned, too, some criticism for 'bragging', to use one of his own terms, which he undoubtedly called down upon his own head. Fleet actions in those days were fought by a British fleet under a code of rules and signals, the Fighting Instructions, which had grown as the results of experience and genius from the days of the Armada. The old wooden walls, with their tiers of muzzle-loading smooth-bore guns, were ranged for battle in line ahead, so as to be able to fire their broadsides into the enemy and not into each other. The line of battle was the weapon which the admiral first formed and then wielded. The many courts martial after a sea-fight, by which an officer might be branded as a coward and broke, generally sat to decide whether or not a captain had obeyed the admiral's signals, and held his position in the line.

When first discovered on the morning of February 14 the Spanish fleet was separated into two portions, which were trying to join up. Jervis was able to form his line of battle, fifteen sail of the line, and, on the starboard tack, sailed between the two parts of the Spaniards' seventeen and ten sail of the line, both on the port tack, with the individual ships getting into line, but the parts not joined. This was the position as battle was joined, ignoring the preliminaries. Jervis ordered his line to tack in succession when its head, Troubridge in the *Culloden*, had passed through the gap. The English ships would thus have ranged up into a line to windward but astern of the seventeen Spaniards. The ten Spaniards astern had been forced to turn away by the superior British fire. The seventeen Spaniards now took the opportunity of bearing away, intending to pass astern of the rear of the British line and rejoin their comrades. Nelson, his red broad pendant at the main truck of the *Captain*, was thirteenth in the line of battle of fifteen ships. On his own responsibility, seeing the Spanish manoeuvre, he wore round the *Captain* without orders, and placed his ship in the way of the Spaniards. Jervis had intended, by separating a third from the main body, to overpower the larger portion of the Spanish fleet whilst holding off the remainder, and his purpose might have failed if the junction which Nelson prevented had taken place. As a result the *Captain*, 74 guns, was heavily engaged with the *Santissima Trinidada* of 136, a four-decker, said to be the largest in the world. The four-decker escaped, but the commodore boarded and received the submission of two flag-ships, the *San Nicolas*, 84 guns, and *San Josef*, 112 guns. The disabled *Captain* was grappled with the *San Nicolas*, and the decks of the first prize were used as a bridge across which to board and capture the *San Josef*. Thus, at the end of the battle, of the four Spanish prizes taken, two had surrendered to Nelson. The *Santissima Trinidada* had rehoisted her flag and escaped.

His 'brag' was to write out an account of the action in his own words, attested by Miller and Berry, and send it home to Captain Locker a week later to be published in the newspapers. Colonel Drinkwater describes Nelson's visit to the *Lively*, frigate, the morning after the battle, before calling on board the *Victory* to congratulate the admiral, and Drinkwater's own popular narrative was centred on Nelson's achievements. William Parker, the rear-admiral in the *Prince George*, complained to both Jervis and Spencer of a slight to the part played by his own flag-ship, but got no encouragement from either. The 'Patent Bridge' by which Nelson had used one enemy ship as a spring-board for another was widely accepted as Nelson's own patent. It was new and singular and caught the popular imagination of seaman and landlubber alike. Thomas Bolton, Nelson's brother-in-law, told Nelson's biographer, Harrison, that after the battle, Jervis, when Nelson boarded the *Victory*, literally clasped him in his arms, although he was dirty and disfigured, with a great part of his hat shot away. Those were heroic days, when men were not shy of showing their feelings. The Commodore had himself headed the boarders, after Berry had assisted him into the main chains of the *San Josef*, 'vehemently exclaiming "Westminster Abbey! or glorious victory!"' These famous words were recorded by Colonel Drinkwater in the first edition of his 'Narrative', published anonymously immediately after the battle, and received the approval of both the gallant Commodore and his lady. The Colonel prepared a second edition in 1840, when Nelson's vehement battlecry was silently omitted. This significant omission probably represented a change in taste rather than a correction of fact.

Mrs. Nelson must have been a little bewildered by the sudden excitement which greeted the news of this happy victory. Josiah, who had, by his own choice, stayed in the *Captain*, rather then share his step-father's cruise in *La Minerve*, behaved well at St. Vincent and was soon painted by Orme a small figure with a large dirk, standing with Captain Miller on the fo'c'sle head of the disabled *Captain* summoning reinforcements to take possession of the *San Nicolas* so that the boarding party could attack the Spaniards firing from the stern windows of the *San Josef*.

On March 3 Nelson wrote home from the *Irresistible* at Lisbon that 'I shall come one day or other laughing home when we will retire from the busy scenes of life.' But he promised now no date for his homecoming. Josiah was serving with Mrs. Nelson's friend, Berry, already a captain in command of a sloop. Nelson was promoted a rear-admiral in February in the ordinary course of events, and on April 2 he learnt he would get the Order of the Bath. This reward had been chosen by Spencer as a result of a hint dropped to Elliot before the *Lively* had sailed with the dispatches. 'My chains, medals and ribbons with a contented mind are all sufficient', he told his wife, and added that Josiah might now be addressed as Lieutenant Nisbet.

In April Nelson made another voyage up into the Mediterranean to fetch the troops and naval forces left at Elba, now finally to be evacuated. The Austrian government complained so bitterly that they had been deserted by the British fleet that Spencer wrote to St. Vincent suggesting that a squadron of frigates be sent into the Adriatic and that, if St. Vincent could spare any two-deckers, then Admiral Nelson was the proper man to detach in command. St. Vincent could not spare a line-of-battle ship, and proposed sending Captain Hope with frigates, but nothing came of it. Spencer's suggestion is interesting as showing how readily Nelson's name came to his mind.

At the end of May Admiral Nelson's flag was transferred to the *Theseus*, 74 guns, and he commanded the inshore squadron off Cadiz, still having Captain Miller with him. On July 3 the *Seahorse*, frigate, Captain Fremantle, with his wife on board, joined Nelson and anchored with the inshore squadron. On July 3 and 5 Cadiz was bombarded. On the night of the 3rd, Nelson and Fremantle and a barge's crew fought hand to hand with the boat of the commanding officer of the Spanish gunboats, which they captured. St. Vincent gave over the bombardment, which was costly and futile. On July 11 Nelson wrote home of trouble in the fleet: 'Our mutinies are I hope stopped here, the Admiral having made some severe examples, but they were absolutely necessary.'

On July 15, following a proposal put forward by Nelson a couple of months earlier, the admiral was detached with a squadron of three ships of the line, three frigates and the *Fox*, cutter, to capture Teneriffe and a Spanish treasure-ship sheltering there. Captain Troubridge in the *Culloden* was to command the land forces. On July 22, men were landed, and brought off again later, dead with fatigue, having accomplished nothing. Fluky wind and shoal-water had prevented the ships getting in close enough to destroy the batteries. Mrs. Fremantle noted that 'the *Theseus* men the most tiresome noisy mutinous people in the world.' The ship had had a bad reputation, but St. Vincent had considered that Admiral Nelson and Captain Miller would soon put that right, and on June 15 Nelson had written to his wife of a letter from the ship's company promising their devotion and wishing success to their officers.

At two o'clock in the morning of July 25, a second desperate attempt was made, led by Nelson in person. The surf was high and resistance stiff, and the boats lost their way. The casualties were 250 killed, wounded and missing, and only the courage and resource of Troubridge saved the day ashore, when he threatened to burn down the town and made his own terms with the very chivalrous governor. Nelson was shot in the right arm as he stepped ashore, and Josiah, who had insisted on accompanying him, made a tourniquet of his neckerchief and got him back to the ship. The *Fox*, cutter, was sunk by a shot below the water-line and Lieutenant Gibson and ninety-seven men drowned. Nelson, severely wounded, insisted on helping to haul some survivors into the boat. He climbed on board the *Theseus* with little assistance and returned the salute of his officers on the quarter-deck. His arm was amputated immediately. There is no mention in his wife's account, which must have been based on his stepson's, that he was first taken alongside the *Seahorse* and refused to go on board for fear of alarming Mrs. Fremantle. In her diary she ignores this story too, which is therefore probably apocryphal. Captain Bowen of the *Terpsichore* was killed and Fremantle wounded in the arm. John Weatherhead, one of the *Agamemnon*'s midshipmen, now a lieutenant in the *Theseus*, was killed. The admiral decided to ask permission from St. Vincent to sail home in the *Seahorse* with the Fremantles, to recover from his wound, and Mrs. Fremantle helped to nurse the two men on the voyage. Nelson was sometimes 'in great spirits', but she thought it 'looks shocking to be without one arm'. 'Fremantle suffers cruelly', his wife noted, and the admiral was 'a very bad patient'. On August 5 Nelson wrote to his wife, 'Josiah under God's providence was principally instrumental in saving my life.' And he added, 'I beg neither you or my father will think much of this mishap. My mind has long been made up to such an event.'

The letters printed in the Appendix show that at the time Hotham hauled down his flag Nelson was in correspondence with Lord Spencer, the First Lord of the Admiralty, and was trying to obtain his broad pendant and promotion to commodore direct from the Admiralty. He also kept up his promised correspondence with the Duke of Clarence, in which he outlined his deeds and ambitions. His letter of April 23, 1796, describes how his efforts to support General Beaulieu with the guns of the *Agamemnon* were frustrated by the disorganization of the Austrian troop movements. The extracts from Jervis's correspondence with Nelson and Sir Gilbert Elliot illustrate the business carried on by the commander-in-chief and the nature of his responsibilities. Sir Gilbert Elliot remained Nelson's personal friend and both relied on his services and forwarded his interests. In August 1796 they concocted a little military expedition in which Nelson, by virtue of being a Colonel of Marines, wanted to command troops on shore. Elliot tactfully put the matter in General de Burgh's hands and looked round for reinforcements without effect and the scheme came to nothing.

Mrs. Nelson and her father-in-law were settled at Bath throughout 1796 and 1797. A series of fifteen letters between February and June 1797 has survived. They tell Nelson the family gossip—how, for instance, George Matcham was causing his father-in-law anxiety by trying to live beyond his means. She constantly missed her husband, but was cheered by his successes, and his naval friends were quick to congratulate the admiral's wife after his promotion was gazetted just before the news of the battle of Cape St. Vincent, for her husband's part in which she received the most welcome congratulations and attentions. She turned to her anxieties for his safety. 'What can I say to you about boarding? You have been most wonderfully protected. You have done desperate actions enough, now may I, indeed I do beg, that you never board again. *Leave* it for the *Captains*.' Lady Saumarez had quoted her husband as saying his conduct was above praise. Saumarez, in a letter to his brother written from the *Orion* off the Tagus on March 6, had said, 'Be not surprised if, with our *desperate* Commodore, you hear of our taking the whole Spanish fleet, should we fall in with them.' So no doubt Nelson's poor wife heard rather a lot of his fire-eating and worried accordingly. On April 10 she picks up her husband's prophesy in his letter from Lisbon of March 3 that one day he will come 'laughing back'. But when? She bought Colonel Drinkwater's 'Narrative', written anonymously, before May 15 and enjoyed his account of the battle in which her husband was mentioned with such generous praise. In May Captain Berry came home and fascinated her with his descriptions of her husband and son. She showed the Leghorn miniature which she wore and he thought it no good likeness. 'Oh! how happy I felt', she wrote, when for the first time, on May 18, she addressed Rear-Admiral Sir Horatio Nelson, K.B. The loss of many of her letters is explained by the story of her husband's having burnt them in Josiah's presence the night before the attack on Teneriffe.

When the *Seahorse* arrived at Portsmouth the admiral hauled down his flag and proceeded to Bath and joined his wife and father, after an absence of four and a half years. One evening she heard his voice in the street telling the coachman where to set him down. Despite the pain the stump of his arm caused him, he was remarkably active. The medical history of Nelson's wound, taken from official sources, is printed in the Appendix. That Nelson was shaken both in mind and body by his recent reverse is shown in his letter to his friend Sir Andrew Hamond written on September 8: 'My pride suffered, and although I felt the second attack as a forlorn hope, yet the honour of our country called for the attack, and that I should command it, I never expected to return and am thankful.' How he appeared to his old friend Sir Gilbert Elliot is described in a letter to his wife: 'I dine today [October 5] with Lord Hood at Greenwich; Nelson and his lady carry me there. Nelson looks better and much fresher than I ever remember him. His arm is, however, by no means well, owing to some awkwardness in the operation. The ligature has not come away, and they are afraid that it has taken in the artery or even a sinew. They must wait till it rots off, which may be a great while. If they should attempt to cut it (it is two inches up the wound) and they should cut the artery, they would be obliged to amputate again higher up, which is not easy for the stump is very short already. He suffers a great deal of violent pain, and takes opium every night. He is impatient for the healing of the wound that he may go to sea again. He writes very tolerably with his left.' Fortunately for Nelson's peace of mind, his conduct received official approval. On September 27 he attended a levée at St. James's and was presented to the King on the occasion of his arrival from Teneriffe. His brother William, who accompanied him, was presented for the first time. After the levée, a chapter of the Order of the Bath was held in a closet, and Sir Horatio Nelson was invested with the red riband of the late Lord Howard. At the Drawing Room the next day, he was presented as a Knight of the Bath, again with his brother. During the autumn he and his wife realized their dream 'cottage' and bought the house and estate of Round Wood near Ipswich for two thousand pounds.

Thanks to his wife's careful nursing, his health was restored, and on Sunday, December 10, an officer returned thanks to Almighty God for his perfect recovery from a severe wound, and also for the many mercies bestowed upon him, at his parish church, St. George's, Hanover Square. On December 13 he was passed fit for service. Already he had warned Captain Berry, who was about to be married, that he would be soon wanted as a flag-captain. Nelson was promised the *Foudroyant*, newly building, but as she was not yet completed was given the *Vanguard* instead. Berry commissioned her on the December 19, the same day that Nelson attended the service of thanksgiving in St. Paul's when the enemy flags captured in the recent naval victories were ceremoniously laid on the communion table. Among them were the Spanish colours of the *San Nicholas* and *San Josef*, which Nelson had decided should be included in his new heraldic arms. On December 28 he received the Freedom of the City of London and in the New Year the admiral and his wife joined his father at Bath for a series of family reunions.

No. 141

[Nicolas, II, p. 124]

Agamemnon, St. Fiorenzo,
January 20, 1796

MY DEAR FANNY,—We joined Sir John Jervis yesterday and was received not only with the greatest attention but with much apparent friendship. His offer of either the *St. George* 90 or *Zealous* 74 was declined but with that respect and sense of obligation on my part which the handsome conduct demanded of me. I found the Admiral anxious to know many things which, I was not a little surprised, had not been communicated to him from others in the fleet, and it would appear that he was so well satisfied with my opinion of what is likely to happen, of the means of prevention etc., that he had no reserves with me of his information, opinions and thoughts of what is likely to be done, and concluded by asking me if I should have any objection to serve under him with my flag. My answer was, that if I was ordered to hoist my flag, that I should certainly be happy in serving under him, but that if *Agamemnon* was to go home and my flag not arrived, I should on many accounts wish to go to England and still if the war went on should be very proud of the honour of hoisting my flag under his command. Thus, my dear Fanny, although I wish to get home, yet my fair character makes me stand forward to remain abroad, and I rather believe that Sir John writes home this day that if the fleet is kept up here, that my flag on a promotion may be sent out. The credit which I derive from all these compliments must be satisfactory to you, and, should I remain till peace, which cannot be very long, I sincerely hope, make your mind easy.

Notwithstanding all I have said I think most likely my promotion will soon be out and I shall have a land voyage but be it as it may. I shall take it easy. *Agamemnon* is just going to sea and I can assure you that my health was never better than at the moment of writing. I never felt so mild a winter and I hope my father feels its mildness as well as I do. God bless you and, believe me, ever your most affectionate husband, HORATIO NELSON.

I have often heard that a postscript is better than a letter. Sir John has hinted to me that if I am not promoted I shall go home the first convoy. Keep this secret except to my father, as also the other part of the letter.

To Mrs. Nelson, Bath, Angleterre.

No. 142
[Nicolas, II, p. 126, part]

Gulf of Genoa,
January 27, 1796

MY DEAR FANNY,—I wrote you a line just as I was getting under sail from St. Fiorenzo. The fleet was not a little surprised at my leaving them so soon, and there is some little envy, I fancy, attached itself to the surprise, for one captain told me 'you did just as you pleased in Lord Hood's time, the same in Admiral Hotham's, and now again with Sir John Jervis. It makes no difference to you who is commander-in-chief.' I made a pretty strong answer to this speech. My command here is to prevent any small number of men from making a descent in Italy.

Your last letter was Dec. 16th but on the 29th the post arrives at Genoa and I hope to get some letters from Leghorn. I hear no more of this promotion. I sincerely hope they will put it off a little longer unless, which I cannot well expect, they send me out my flag, for this country certainly is the place for not an over strong man. I fancy you will find me grown very stout and my health was never better than at this moment.

I can tell you nothing new, except that I have taken, or rather detained, two ships laden with corn for France. The condemnation of the cargoes depends entirely on the politics of England. I do not expect to reap any other advantage than having it said I did my duty.

I send a frigate to Genoa, therefore must conclude by assuring my dear Fanny that I am your most affectionate husband, HORATIO NELSON.

You will not forget my kind remembrances to my father.

To Mrs. Nelson, Bath, Angleterre.

No. 143

[Nicolas, II, p. 127, part]

Leghorn,
February 12, 1796

MY DEAREST FANNY,—I came in here last night with a convoy from Genoa where I found Sir John Jervis and the whole fleet. I sail again tomorrow for my station. A letter from you, I fancy, went off for Genoa a few hours before my arrival. As to news, we have little more than the great preparations the French are making for opening the campaign in Italy, and if the Austrians and Piedmontese do not exert themselves I think Turin will be lost and of course all Piedmont. Sardinia is in rebellion, therefore Kings will be reduced in Europe. God knows I now see no prospect of peace. Before the King's message [1] to the House I had hopes but from that moment I gave it up. The message was forced and so worded that it was easy to see no peace was intended by it except such a one as the French are not humbled enough to grant. The convoy is not yet ordered for England but I trust *Agamemnon* will be one of the ships. Admiral Linzee goes home certainly and if the *Princess Royal* does not go home he will hoist his flag in the *Agamemnon*, but I believe it will be April before any convoy is ready and from our sailing I think we shall be two months to Spithead—miserable time.

Josiah is very well and is daily threatening to write you a letter. Our new Admiral will not land at Leghorn. The late one [2] was so much here that Sir John is determined to act in the contrary way. Reports say the French will have their fleet at sea again. If they do I think they will now lose the whole of them, for we have a man of business at our head.

With best regards to my father, believe me, your most affectionate HORATIO NELSON.

To Mrs. Nelson, Bath, Angleterre.

No. 144

[Nicolas, II, p. 127, part, under date February 12]

Agamemnon, off Heires Islands,
February 17, 1796

I received your letter of Jan. 18th after mine of Feb. 12th was gone to the Post Office. I hoped Mr. Baillie would from his fair words have at

---

[1] The King's speech on the opening of Parliament on October 29, 1795, referred to prosecuting the war with the utmost vigour until a just peace could be made.
[2] Admiral Hotham.

least done as much for you as for Mrs. Kelly but her brother is to be courted. He may probably be useful to the house. However, the four years will soon wear away and then we shall get it all together and peace will by that time, I hope, be arrived, when a cottage of our own and an income to live, if not in luxury, in comfort, I doubt not but we shall possess in an ample degree. I cannot bring myself to believe that jealousy could have been the cause of lessening my force at so critical a time. I attribute it to ignorance and inattention. My conduct has no mystery. I freely communicate my knowledge and observations and wish my Admiral may make proper use of it. God forbid I should have any other consideration on service than to serve my country. I appear to stand well as yet with Sir John Jervis and it shall not be my fault if I do not continue so. I am now sent by him to examine into the state of the ships in Toulon. Their numbers we know full well but the accounts of their state are so contradictory that it leaves us uncertain. I will tell you their state when I finish this letter.

You observe that Lady H. tells you that but little is known in the fleet since Sir John's arrival. So much the better. Lord Hood knows that it is unsafe to open one's mouth in a fleet.

1st April reports say the convoy will be ready, but no ships are yet named and till reinforcements arrive I do not see Sir John can part with a single ship for he is now inferior to the French at Toulon. They have built 5 sail of the line since we left Toulon.

I rejoice to hear poor Aunt Mary is better. If you think of anything pray send it her, £5 or £10 cannot be laid out more to my satisfaction.

I am glad to hear you have so pleasant a party. You know F. Parsons was always a favourite of mine. Remember me to her, Mrs. Estridge, Aunt Webbe, the Tobins etc. This Dr. Randolph must be a wonderful man by your account but really I do not believe the world is one bit worse than when our great-grandmothers rode double, except perhaps from a freer communication with the world people are less ashamed.

February 28th: I am now on my way to Genoa, having been joined by the Admiral on the 23rd off Toulon. The French have 13 sail of the line and 5 frigates ready for sea and 4 or 5 fitting in the arsenal, two of which are in forwardness. Sir John from his manner I plainly see does not wish me to leave this station. He seems at present to consider me as an assistant more than a subordinate for I am acting without orders. This may have its difficulties at a future day but I make none knowing the uprightness of my intentions. He asked me if I had heard any more of my promotion. I told him no. His answer was 'You must have a larger ship for we cannot spare you either as Admiral or Captain.' However, we keep going on and if *Agamemnon* is ordered home I hope to come in her but if it is right for me to stay, stay I must.

Genoa, March 2nd: Just arrived. Have received here your letter of Jan. 10th. The pride cannot lay in Holloway, it is in his wife, a very great lady.[1] His making are savings for he had no occasion to spend anything and I have heard him, he did lay out more than £100 and mine has been full £2000. As to prize money, he has not received so much as myself, therefore it is all a boast.

Josiah is very well but I almost despair of this letter. He waits probably for some great news to tell you. God bless you. With kind affections to my father and believe me ever your most affectionate husband, HORATIO NELSON.

To Mrs. Nelson, Bath, Angleterre.

No. 145

Leghorn,
March 11, 1796

MY DEAR FANNY,—I have received your letters of Feb. 4th and 10th as also my father's. I rejoice Maurice is going back to the Navy Office and shall be glad to hear he has actually taken his seat there. I wish he may be able to keep 2 horses although I do not wish him to do it for it will prove that as under-commissary it not only much safer but also much more profitable than a captain.

We do not here see any immediate prospect of a peace. On the contrary, everything denotes vigorous and final campaign. I know not the Admiral's mind but as I wrote you before, I scarcely think he will permit me to leave this country, but a very short time must determine for most of the fleet is ready. All is alarm here. The French are expected to make a push to get possession of Leghorn. We must look out sharp and I hope if they come by sea we shall prevent their destination and, if by land, if the Austrians are active they will stop their progress. The Grand Duke has refused the passage of the Neapolitan troops through his dominions. In short, his ministers appear to be the friends of the French and, if so, how can the progress of these fellows be stopped.

I shall be anxious to hear Aunt Mary is better. Captain Andrews I suppose you have seen by this time. He told me he should go directly to

---

[1] Captain Holloway married Miss Waldron of Antigua before he left the West Indies in 1781.

Bath. You must take this short letter for I am writing to Naples and Corsica and am on the wing for sea.

Believe me ever, your affectionate HORATIO NELSON.

Kind remembrances to my father. Josiah very well—so is Hoste.

To Mrs. Nelson, Bath, Angleterre.

No. 146

[Nicolas, II, p. 140, part]

Agamemnon, off Genoa,
March 25, 1796

MY DEAR FANNY,—Here we are moving about and waiting for the event of opening the campaign. The French army are exerting themselves, so are the Austrians and Piedmontese. I cannot bring myself to think that the Toulon fleet who I saw on the 20th in Toulon will venture to fight our fleet on the sea. They may perhaps attempt to cover a convoy of transports into Italy or perhaps Sardinia but should Sir John Jervis have the good fortune to fall in with them I am sure he will give them a finishing stroke. I fear we shall be confined in this Gulf of Genoa and more so now than for some time past, although lately the Admiral has not given me any great hopes of going home with this next convoy. The following is an extract of his public letter—'I have received by the *Blanche* your two letters of the 16th and one of the 19th instant together with the several enclosures and copies of your correspondence at Turin, Genoa and Naples, and I feel the greatest satisfaction in communicating this public testimony of my thorough approbation of your late and recent correspondence and conduct.' His private letter—'No words can express the sense I entertain of every part of your conduct and correspondence with Messrs. Trevor and Drake and I shall be most happy to manifest it in the most substantial manner. A distinguishing pendant you shall most certainly wear and I will write to Lord Spencer about you. In short there is nothing within my grasp that I shall not be proud to confer on you.' All this is certainly flattering and pleasant. These blossoms may one day bring forth fruit but I doubt it. My expenses here are too much and it is not the Marines that compensates. I cannot help wishing for peace and retirement to a cottage. This must, we all know, be the last campaign and we shall make a good or bad peace as we are successful or otherwise. We have just got accounts that Admiral Waldegrave who was sent to Tunis has taken out of that port three frigates belonging to the French, the *Nemesis* one of them. There I lost my fortune by having such a head as Admiral Linzees for our guide. I just see Admiral Christian has a Red Ribbon. It has given me pleasure to see that merit although unfortunate is not always neglected. [1]

Josiah is very well. So soon as I hear Maurice is fixed at the Navy board I shall get his time out. I do not believe he was borne on the *Boreas's* books, how I regret it, but at that time he was not intended for the sea. *Champion* and *Unicorn* may look at *Boreas* and *Agamemnon*. As my changes take place so I shall tell you. A very short time must determine, only recollect all this is *honour* and for this have I fagged. God bless you and give us a happy meeting and soon is the most sincere wish of your affectionate husband, HORATIO NELSON.

To Mrs. Nelson, Bath, Angleterre.

No. 147

Agamemnon, off Genoa,
April 1, 1796.

MY DEAR FANNY,—As far as relates myself or ship not an occurrence has happened since I wrote last week. We are watching and expecting movements of the two armies. The French are advanced with 4000 men to within 9 miles of Genoa and have talked high of possessing themselves of the town but I fancy it has been more to endeavour to awe the Genoese into the loan of money demanded of them than from any real design but at present it has had a very contrary effect to what they imagined. The militia has been embodied and every preparation made to prevent the French from entering the town and as the French have conducted themselves very ill, instead of warm friends which they had when at a distance, made almost enemies of the Genoese. The Austrian Army is only 35 miles from Genoa. Only two of the old Generals are suffered to remain. General Beaulieu commands instead of De Vins who is very much in disgrace.

I have not had any letter from England of a later date than Feb. 10th but we have many mails due and at present my letters must make a long circuit to come to me. The post comes in from Leghorn today. We are now getting very fine weather and the campaign is only pleasure in summer but I shall guard carefully against another winter. You must be content with a short letter for as I have already wrote there is nothing here.

---

[1] Admiral Christian twice had his West India fleet scattered by gales while trying to work out of the Channel in the winter of 1795.

With kindest remembrances to my father, Josiah is very well as is Hoste etc. Believe me, your most affectionate husband, HORATIO NELSON. To Mrs. Nelson, Bath, Angleterre.

No. 148

Agamemnon, Genoa,
April 9

MY DEAREST FANNY,—Although I have been all day writing and meeting ministers yet I should feel ungrateful was I not to write you a line.

I anchored here yesterday and my broad pendant is now flying.[1] It has been done handsomely by Sir John Jervis. Your letter of Feb. 25th and my father's of March 7th I received yesterday.

We are here in expectation every moment of the campaign commencing. Probably the grand attack will be in two or three days, perhaps sooner. The Austrian General[2] is 74 years of age but I am told has the fire of youth joined to it. I trust we shall do better this campaign than the last.

I hope by your account the legacy will be paid soon, at least the interest. The fancy that it could be omitted for want of a word in the will would fall before a jury. The contention of the donor was clear and in respect to Josiah is particularly so, for it says the interest is to go towards his education etc. I am glad Maurice is again in the Navy Office but his situation although explained by himself does not appear so good as he had before. However, I am glad he is there. His sending the wine was kind but why he sent it in my name instead of his own I cannot conceive. You will I am sure send something. I had a letter from Hilborough and rejoice to hear Aunt Mary is better. My brother it seems is going to make a long tour. Perhaps this will find him at Bath. I shall write him very soon. You must take this short letter with my best affections. Every yours most faithfully, HORATIO NELSON.

Kindest regards to my father. Josiah well, full of business.

To Mrs. Nelson, Bath, Angleterre.

No. 149

Genoa,
April 16, 1796

MY DEAR FANNY,—Yours of March 14th I received yesterday. I cannot write much, my hands are so full of letter writing but all is comprised in

[1] See Appendix, p. 338, Sir John Jervis to Sir Gilbert Elliot, April 5, 1796.
[2] General Beaulieu, a Belgian in command of the Austrian forces.

PLATE IX. Engraving of the portrait of Rear Admiral Sir Horatio Nelson, K.B., aged thirty-nine, painted by Lemuel Francis Abbott for Lady Nelson (see p. 441: Lady Nelson's letter to Nelson, July 23, 1798).

saying I never was better. We are seeing actions every moment and hearing the firing in the mountains but neither party seem yet to have made any great advantage, but we hope the discipline of the Austrians will in time get the better of the French. You may remember an expression very common in my mouth—it is better to be the envied man than the pitied one. I have not rose by keeping Kelly down, I should have been sorry if I had and Kelly has made money and I have made none. This will be the last campaign and I shall get to the cottage. You must take a very short letter and often.

With kindest remembrances to my father and such as are with you, believe me ever your most affectionate HORATIO NELSON.

To Mrs. Nelson, Bath, Angleterre.

No. 150

Genoa,
April 19, 1796

MY DEAR FANNY,—The Austrians are beat at all points and God knows what may be the consequences, perhaps an immediate peace. God bless you, believe me, ever your most affectionate HORATIO NELSON.

I find I have time to add a postscript. The success of the French is wonderful. Not less than 11,000 Austrians have been taken since the 13th in the morning and 4 or 5,000 killed. The French have doubtless lost much but scarcely any taken. The Austrians are now got into a plain and if they cannot withstand the French there they can nowhere. I fear for the fate of the King of Sardinia. He refused a peace at the express desire of England and the Emperor. I am in wonderful good health, but feel a little. I only hope we shall meet them at sea. The French fight on shore like our seamen, they never stop and know not the word *halt*.

This Captain Stanhope [1] I never saw but his character is that of a very sensible man but a very odd character. He never cut a respectable figure in our service.

Josiah is well, teeth good, 5 feet 4½ inches in height. Best affections to my father.

To Mrs. Nelson, Bath, Angleterre.

[1] Captain Henry Stanhope, brought to a court martial on charges from his lieutenant while serving abroad, was acquitted, but received a cool reception when he returned to England in 1796.

U

No. 151

[Nicolas II, p. 161]

Agamemnon, Gulf of Genoa,
April 24, 1796

MY DEAR FANNY,—I have just received your letter of March 21st. You did most perfectly right in not trusting to the movements of a sailor, and you will know from my late letters that Sir John Jervis has such an opinion of my conduct that he is using every influence both public and private with Lord Spencer for my continuance on this station. I am sure you will feel how superior is the pleasure of knowing that my integrity and plainness of conduct is the cause of my being kept from you, to receiving me as a person whom no Commander-in-Chief would wish to keep under his command. Sir John was a perfect stranger to me, therefore I feel the more flattered and when I reflect that I have had the unbounded confidence of three Commanders-in-Chief I cannot but feel a conscious pride and that I have abilities. Rest assured, my dearest Fanny, of my unabated and steady affection which if possible is increasing by that propriety of conduct which I know you are pursuing. Whilst the war lasts I must serve somewhere and for health and nearness to England I know of none equal to this. I thank you for telling me of the gown you are working to receive me in but for fear you should not have finished it I have one, lawn I fancy, and worked the most elegantly I ever saw. If Admiral Linzee goes home, which I believe is likely to happen, I have some thoughts of sending a parcel by him, but most probably he has so many things of his own that mine would be seized, perhaps I shall keep them to bring home myself, but this I shall think on.

Sir Hyde Parker has left the fleet for England. It seems Lady Parker has behaved infamously ill and almost ruined his future peace of mind as well as his pocket, but the newspapers will soon tell all.[1]

Admiral Linzee has long had leave of absence which he did not choose to accept. It almost makes me laugh. So soon as he heard of Sir Hyde's misfortune he told Sir John Jervis he would accept of the Admiralty leave and go home in the first convoy. His desires will I am pretty sure be complied with and the Admiral has told me in that case I am to hoist a broad pendant with a captain under me and to command a Division of the fleet for now Sir Hyde is gone he has nobody with any nerves about him and therefore, ill as he can spare me from my present very important service, he must have me near him. Pray do not let this go farther than my father,

---

[1] Sir Hyde Parker was given leave to return to England owing to domestic troubles. He married for the second time in 1800.

not even to the Rector or the Matchams. It is all pleasant to me and I know must be so to you.

As to the French fleet coming to sea, that cannot be sure, but if they do, depend on it we shall thrash them.

What can I say to Huggins? If I write it can only be a civil letter, but I will do it soon as you wish it. Lt. Berry[1] is not arrived, therefore I have not seen the patterns.[2]

April 28th: You will soon hear of our little brush at Loana.[3] We took four vessels, of very little value to us although of great loss to the enemy. I hope tomorrow to get a letter. I am steering for Genoa with that expectation.

Do not tell this news to anyone. If it ever gets into the Gazette it is time enough.

If my brother is with you say I don't write for that reason but shall when I think he returns to Hilborough. Josiah is very well, indeed he is never sick. Extraordinary, I have not had a line from Mr. Hoste since I drew the last bill, although it must be known I advanced the money every day for 14 months before I asked for it, and another is now rising very fast. I am very angry. Poor Mrs. Kelly; if she is angry at every good deed of mine, I hope she will die of the spleen. From my heart I wish Kelly every success and honour.

29th: No letter. All bad news—armistice with the King of Sardinia, in a few days peace, Austrians retreating, all will before long make peace, then I shall certainly come home.

Believe me, my dear Fanny, your most affectionate HORATIO NELSON.

Kind remembrances to my father.

To Mrs. Nelson, Bath, Angleterre.

No. 152

Agamemnon, Gulf of Genoa,
May 11, 1796

MY DEAREST FANNY,—It is three years this day that I sailed from Spithead. I believe no person in England would have supposed any ship could have been kept so long abroad or that the war would have lasted. However, England will soon carry it on alone if she is still determined to go on and

[1] Edward Berry, nephew of a Norwich clergyman, a protégé of Sir John Jervis, was specially recommended to Nelson by his wife. He received rapid promotion, served as Nelson's flag-captain, and died Rear-Admiral Sir Edward Berry in 1831.

[2] Probably the epaulettes Nelson had asked about (see letter No. 125).

[3] By smart boat action, Nelson had taken four ships at Loana, carrying stores and ammunition.

instead of having all Europe in our alliance and pay we shall have them in a certain degree all against us.

Reports are prevalent of a promotion of flags before the King's Birthday.[1] If so, think it very probable that I may not be employed in this country. Maurice can tell you immediately after the promotion by enquiry at the Admiralty. Long ago I have made up my mind not to be captain of any other ship than the *Agamemnon,* and should the Admiral direct me to hoist a broad pendant with a captain under me on board any ship in the fleet and the Admiralty not order me to hoist my flag this will very much facilitate my journey to England. A land voyage in summer is not so dreadful although perhaps as expensive. We must hope for the best. This is certainly in point of climate the most desirable of any station but no more prize money is to be made here than anywhere else, at least I do not hear that the war is profitable to the Navy in general. The Ipswich business is all at an end.[2] I cannot say I am sorry for it. There is nothing I can get in my professional line and more might have been expected than I could possibly obtain, not but I should like to be in Parliament, if I went in properly and in a certain degree independent (I mean of any private individual).

I have received your very short letter of March 31st. The French have a squadron which will certainly sail from Toulon the moment anything calls our fleet from off that port. Some think they are bound to the East Indies but all is uncertain.

Josiah I believe has entirely lost his cough. I know this is the best news I can tell you. God bless you and believe me your most affectionate husband HORATIO NELSON.

Josiah is very fond of reading letters but I cannot say so much for writing them. My kind love to my father.

To Mrs. Nelson, Bath, Angleterre, via London.

No. 153

[Nicolas, II, p. 173, part, and order transposed]

Agamemnon, Leghorn,
May 20, 1796

MY DEAREST FANNY,—I received the day of my arrival your affectionate letter of April 18th. What can be the reason of Mr. Baillie's conduct? It certainly was the intention of Mr. Herbert that the interest should be

[1] June 4.
[2] In November 1795 Nelson received a proposal to enter Parliament as member for Ipswich. He replied that he could only do so in support of the Whigs and Duke of Portland. The scheme was abandoned. Sir Andrew Hamond, the Comptroller of the Navy, represented Ipswich from 1796–1806.

regularly paid and I have no doubt but a Court of Law would order it. I recollect in particular the will says the interest of the £500 for Josiah shall go towards his education but the principal not to be paid till he is 21 I believe. Now how can the will of the donor be complied with if the interest is not regularly paid? It requires no lawyer to give an opinion on this part of the will. I wish you would get from Doctor's Commons a copy of the will and codicils, then you can for 2 or 3 guineas ask a lawyers' opinion whether the interest ought not to be paid by the trustees. If they say yes, it should be regularly demanded of the trustees for us and for Josiah. The paper can be sent to me as a letter. Huggins can do nothing.

Admiral Linzee is sailed this morning for England in the *Egmont* 74, Capt. Sutton, one of the best conditioned ships in this country. It is proof that all still goes by interest. *Egmont* of all ships ought to have been kept in this country. As to myself I can say nothing. If I am not to hoist my flag in this country, most probably I shall be in England before the convoy. If I am ordered to hoist it the compliment is great and therefore we must both rest contented for a little time. The war will not last much longer. The French must be tired and I believe all our *Allies* are the same.

Lieutenant Berry has joined the ship. He seems a gentleman and an officer from appearances. I have no doubt but I shall like him. How vexed I am about Suckling. He will never now I fear become respectable. If he has again taken to drink the more he drinks the better, it will the sooner finish his disgrace and the part we must all bear in it. My poor father, how he must feel when he knows it. This may find you possibly at Mr. Suckling's. If so, I beg you will say every kind thing for me. We are certainly under greater obligations to him than to anyone. He is a good man and respectable character.

The Duke of Parma and the Duke of Modena have both made treaties with the French, paid large sums of money and in the treaty it is specified that certain pictures are to be delivered to be sent to Paris. The palace of the Louvre is to be the finest gallery of pictures in the world. The Pope has sent to offer ten millions of crowns to prevent their coming to Rome. It is said they have refused unless the famous statue of the Apollo of Belvedere is sent to Paris. What a race of people, but they have done wonders, and yet I believe they will not get farther than they are at present. Reinforcements are coming to join General Beaulieu and the inhabitants of the Tirole a hardy and warlike people, are rising to join the General. If all the States of Italy make peace we have nothing to look to but Corsica which, in the present state of its inhabitants, is not, in my opinion, an object to keep us in the Mediterranean. We shall, I hope, quit it and employ our fleet more to our advantage.

I can only say Josiah is well, indeed he is never sick. I am sorry I cannot say so much of Hoste.[1] He is a very delicate boy. I have not heard from his father this long time. Believe me ever, my dear Fanny, your most affectionate husband, HORATIO NELSON.

To Mrs. Nelson, Bath, Angleterre.

No. 154

Agamemnon, Gulf of Genoa,
May 27, 1796

MY DEAREST FANNY,—Since I wrote you last I have received your affectionate letter of the 24th April. I hope your patience will yet hold out. It is a virtue no doubt, although I cannot say I possess it in a great degree. However, the time will come when we shall get to this cottage. I agree with you it must be a little one but that I regard not. You will know long before me whether I come home or not. A few days I suppose will determine it. If they allow me to remain here it will be a great mark of favour for I know very many who are moving all their interest to get out on this station.

I am glad the Rector was pleased with his expedition. You make me laugh at the account of his gaiters. What is become of George Tobin?[2] He is a fine young man and it is a pity he is not got forward. After the war there is no chance. I am sorry poor Dolly[3] is put upon your house. The Matchams must have known it was distressing both my father and you but I believe they do not think much of anyone but themselves. I have never had a line since I sailed. It is true I have not wrote but my sister can have but little to do compared to me.

Admiral Linzee is sailed. I hinted that if I sent things by him it would be very troublesome getting them on shore, which he agreed *most perfectly in*, therefore I did not choose to run the risk. However, they are of little value yet I should not like to lose them by carelessness.

I am quite angry about Suckling. If he now behaves ill, he deserves not pity.

As to news, all is so bad I know not what to say. The Pope has paid largely to save Rome. I suppose Naples must also pay. The Emperor and

[1] About this time Nelson sent Hoste ashore at Leghorn to recover from an attack of fever.

[2] Son of a West India merchant and friend of Nelson's. He was made lieutenant in 1790 and promoted commander in 1798.

[3] Dolly Jaccombe, a former maid servant of Nelson's father. Her own family being unable to nurse her, she went to Bath, where Mrs. Nelson cared for her. She died there after a long illness.

Spain are trying which shall succeed with Naples, one for war, the other for peace. The Emperor must either directly have 100,000 men in Italy or make peace. How that will affect England I know not. If we can make a good peace, I wish it, but hope we shall not be so pusillanimous as to give up all our conquests. From India reports say we are successful in the highest degree,[1] therefore we have a great deal to set off against the French conquests elsewhere.

Josiah is not learned in the French language for, although we have Frenchmen on board, they cannot speak English, therefore not much can be got from them as masters.

I shall write Mr. Suckling very soon and am truly sorry to hear he has been ill. Pray say every kind thing to him from me and to Mrs. S. etc. Roger Martin (but the chance is against such a gay youth living in that country) may make a fortune but I believe they are not to be had so quick as formerly. You will not forget me where proper and believe me ever, my dear Fanny, your most affectionate HORATIO NELSON.

To Mrs. Nelson, Bath, Angleterre.

No. 155

[Nicolas,II, p. 184, part]

Captain, at Sea,
June 13, 1796

You will see, my dear Fanny, by the date of my letter that I have at last left poor old *Agamemnon*.[2] Whether it is right or wrong time must determine. If my flag is ordered to be hoisted in this country it is well, if not I shall probably be at home before *Agamemnon*. Captain Sutton of the *Egmont* was to have gone in the *Egmont* but the Admiralty having ordered the *Princess Royal* and the worst line of battleship, the *Agamemnon* was of course the ship, and Captain Sutton had sent him commissions for himself and officers for *Agamemnon*.[3] This Sutton did not like and requested to remain in the *Egmont* till she was ordered home. In this state things remained for a week and had the cornships momentarily expected from Naples arrived, I should have sailed for England. The Admiral has on every occasion behaved with the greatest attention to me and if I am to serve it is better that I should serve in this country where I am known and respected than to take my chance of being sent home and

[1] The second Mysore war was being successfully prosecuted against Tipoo Sahib.
[2] Nelson moved into the *Captain*, 74 guns, with five lieutenants and other officers on June 11, exchanging with Captain John Smith, who took the *Agamemnon* home.
[3] See Appendix, p. 336, Sir John Jervis to Nelson, May–June 1796.

ordered to another. All the *Agamemnon*'s officers are changed except Suckling and the Master.[1] The latter has a wife and large family and Suckling thinks now his elder brother is dead that his father wishes him to be home for a little while. In some respects he may be an odd man but I do not believe any one person in the world has a better heart or that will do more real good if providence ordains that he should be master of the Wotton estate.

I have sent my small present for you by him, and you will not feel it necessary to give away any of them unless you like it, who gives to you, but in this do as you please, and do not tell anyone the trifling things I send you. I have desired Suckling to land them singly and to send them singly to Mr. Thomas's No. 164 Strand, London, but so soon as you hear of *Agamemnon*'s arrival you will write Mr. Suckling and tell him what you wish, and any alteration in the mode of sending them you think proper. If you are in Norfolk they had better be sent singly from Portsmouth or Chatham to Mr. Thomas's and he can send them in two or three packages. The black silk stockings I mean for my father if he chooses. If he takes only a part, give my brother Suckling two pair.

June 19th: I have just left Sir John Jervis. The French are fitting and if Richerry[2] from Cadiz joins they may come out but we shall certainly beat them if it pleases God to give us the opportunity. Indeed the French say 'We are masters on shore and the English at sea'. God bless and preserve you.

June 21st, Genoa: Come in for water and to write 20 letters. Naples has made peace. The French are certainly fell back. Reports say Beaulieu is getting reinforcements and has given them a check. The peasants it is said have killed great numbers but these fellows multiply like locusts.

Ever your most affectionate husband, HORATIO NELSON.

Best regards to my brother Suckling. Will write him soon.

To Mrs. Nelson, Bath, Angleterre.

No. 156

Captain, off Leghorn,
July 7, 1796.

MY DEAR FANNY,—From the many extraordinary events which have lately taken place and which you will hear of long before you receive this letter all our posts at least for the present are stopped. I shall send this by

---

[1] Lieutenant Maurice Suckling and John Wilson. Suckling's elder brother had died in the West Indies in 1795. Suckling married shortly after his return to England, turned farmer, and inherited his father's estate of Woodton in 1819.
[2] The rear-admiral commanding the French forces at Cadiz.

way of Genoa hoping it will reach you. A packet is to be established by way of Spain but I believe letters will reach us directed to the care of Joseph Brame Esq., English Consul at Genoa.

You will hear I hope soon that Leghorn [1] is liberated from its present tyrannical rulers. I am ordered to blockade it with my squadron and therefore it will not be such a one as that of Genoa. I have sent a declaration to all the Governments that not a vessel will be permitted to enter or to leave the port of Leghorn till it is restored to its legal government.

I have received your letters of May 12th yesterday and of May 22nd 4 days past.

You must take a short letter for I have very many to write although not one to England except this. Josiah is well. Ever, believe me, my dearest Fanny, your most affectionate husband, HORATIO NELSON.

You will readily conceive the distress of hundreds who were obliged to embark, some without a change of linen, and ladies and gentlemen are stuffed on board small vessels and on shore at Fiorenzo in a manner they little expected. Kind love to my father.

To Mrs. Nelson, Bath, Angleterre. [*Redirected to Lyme, Dorsetshire.*]

No. 157

Captain, at Sea,
July 21, 1796

MY DEAREST FANNY,—I am on my way to Genoa and hope my letters will get safe to England. The Admiral has established packets to Barcelona from Corsica and if we have not a Spanish War this will do very well. Your letters I do not expect to receive for some time for which way they will travel is unknown to me.

You will hear we took possession of Porto Ferraio [2] a short time since and I hope the inhabitants will find an increase of happiness instead of that misery which the unfortunate Leghornese are experiencing. The Austrians I believe by this time have advanced and from many causes I yet have hopes that this will be a most glorious campaign. The King of Naples although he has signed an Armistice, is still in the field with 80,000 troops and declares unless the French instantly leave Tuscany he will renew hostilities and attack Leghorn. This would be right for then I should

---

[1] The French took possession of Leghorn on June 27.

[2] In the island of Elba. This was a necessary precaution in the defence of Corsica, now threatened from Leghorn. It surrendered on terms (see Appendix, p. 341, Sir Gilbert Elliot to Nelson).

have an opportunity of acting with the King of Naples. The Pope has also made an armistice and submitted to such terms as the people of Rome will never submit to, viz. the taking away 100 of the statues and busts.

Genoa, July 23rd: I arrived last night and have letters from Venice assuring me of the defeat of the French before Mantua on the 15th at night.[1] The Austrian Army is advancing and the French retreating. I have only time to say Josiah is well. Ever your most affectionate husband, HORATIO NELSON.

To Mrs. Nelson, Bath, Angleterre. *[Redirected to Lyme, Dorsetshire.]*

No. 158

[Nicolas, II, p. 230, part, order transposed]

Captain, North Road of Leghorn,
August 2, 1796

MY DEAREST FANNY,—Yesterday brought me your letter of June 6th, therefore I do not suppose I shall lose a post. The Leghorn letters for the English are stopped in Germany and sent to Porto Ferraiso and so to Corsica. I have often reason to observe a frequent saying of my father's— 'Put a letter in the post and it will go.' Half the letters which miscarry *are not wrote.* I have never been on any secret expeditions except one when I did not command and therefore lost the opportunity of making a fortune. As to my letter of some affairs not being gazetted, had all my actions been gazetted not one fortnight would have passed. Let those enjoy their brag and one day or other I will have a large Gazette to myself. I feel that one day or other such an opportunity will be given me. I cannot, if I am in the field of glory, be kept out of sight. They, if any such there are, can only hurt me by unemployment. Lord Spencer has wrote to Sir John Jervis how desirous he is of giving me my flag but as circumstances are he does not choose to face a promotion, at the same time fully approving of the pendant. I hope you will see that I have done enough since your recommendation has been with me to make Mr. Berry a Captain. Probably my services may be forgot (by the Great) by the time I get home but my own mind will not forget nor fail to feel a degree of consolation and applause superior to undeserved rewards. Wherever there is anything to do, there providence is sure to direct my steps, and ever credit must be given me in spite of envy.

[1] This proved only a rumour; the siege of Mantua was not raised till July 30.

You ask me when I shall come home. I believe, when an honourable peace is made or a Spanish war, which may draw our fleet out of the Mediterranean. God knows I shall come to you not a sixpence richer than when I set out, but I verily believe with a much better constitution. If I ever feel unwell, it is when I have no active employment, that is but seldom.

The Ipswich business is over. I do not feel much regret at not being in England. Who would have paid the money? I could not. I had a letter a few days past from the Duke of Clarence assuring me of his unalterable friendship. Will this ever do good? I will however take care it shall do me no harm.

The blockade is such a one as never took place before and you will see it will soon have its effect to remove the French. The Great Duke has no revenue, his people ripe for revolt against his ministry and for insurrection against the French. I have their confidence and before you receive this letter some event will happen which restores Leghorn to its legal government. But even the French respect me; their Minister at Genoa on occasion of answering a note of mine returning wearing apparel [1] says 'Your nation, Sir, and mine is made to show all the people of the earth examples of generosity as well as valour.' I shall relate another anecdote, all vanity to myself, but you will partake of it. A person wrote me a letter and directed as follows 'Horatio Nelson, Genoa'. On being asked how he could direct in such a manner his answer was, in a large party, 'Sir there is but one H. N. in the world.' The letter certainly came directly. At Genoa, where I have stopped all their trade, I am beloved and respected by both Senate and lower order. If a man is fearful of his vessel being stopped, he comes and asks me; if I give them a paper or say all is right, they are content. I am known in Italy, not a kingdom or state where my name will be forgot. This is *my* Gazette.

I have just had a letter from Mrs. Bolton and Maurice. Mr. M.[2] I suppose does not choose my sister to correspond.

August 9th: Poor little Hoste yesterday had the misfortune to break his other leg but it is set and I hope will do well. How unfortunate. I now hope all our affairs in Italy will take a favourable turn.

With kindest love to my father. Believe me, your most affectionate husband, HORATIO NELSON.

Josiah is very well, never sick.

To Mrs. Nelson, Bath, Angleterre.

[1] Nelson returned some clothes and personal papers belonging to a French officer found on board a ship he had taken, with a note 'Generous nations are above rendering any other damage than such as the known laws of war prescribe.'
[2] George Matcham, Nelson's brother-in-law.

No. 159

Captain, Leghorn Roads,
August 11, 1796

MY DEAREST FANNY,—Yesterday brought me your letter of June 16th. Our public news is to the 7th July. I know not of Admiral Barrington's[1] secret expedition, therefore you can hear of nothing very extraordinary; that I am always expeditious you know and am never so well pleased as when I have active employment. It pleases God always to prosper all my undertakings and I doubt not but he will continue his goodness to me. As to Josiah he has not served his time and it is impossible, as far as I know of the Service, to get him made a Lieutenant and this war will not last till his time is out,[2] when I know it will be difficult to promote him, but I cannot help it, I wish I could.

We are keeping this place blockaded in a manner I flatter myself unexampled. Not a boat gets in or out or an inhabitant gets a dish of fish without coming on board me to get a pass to fish for it. I have not only the approbation of my Admiral, the Viceroy of Corsica, but even from the Foreign Ministers whose ships are necessarily detained in the Port of Leghorn.[3] I know I cannot communicate my vanity to anyone who will partake more sincerely of it than you and my father. Shall I give you the French or translate, perhaps the last, viz. 'by the obliging letter you addressed to me on the 1st of this month I received the confirmation of the public voice, who all accord in pronouncing on the subject of your character and your loyalty. I myself rejoice that I have had experience, and after your manner of acting I am persuaded that I shall have the satisfaction of making known to all Swedes your name as a person who they have great obligation to, and wishing to soften the horrors of war uniting it at the same time with zeal for the service of your master and with the love of justice, the execution of the will of your sovereign could not have been placed in better hands. By the news of today I hope the war will take a better turn. I again thank you, Sir, for your manner of acting, and if the Viceroy of Corsica and Admiral Jervis still think it a political measure to detain Swedes without cargoes in Leghorn, yet I shall feel equally obliged by your kindness. The Swedish vessels which you have prevented from entering Leghorn speak all the same language of your civility and attention. I long for opportunities of proving to you how much I respect you etc.' and from the Neapolitan Minister as follows viz. 'I have received with the

[1] Admiral Samuel Barrington had served in the West Indies with Rodney. He had no employment at this time and died in 1800.
[2] A midshipman had to do six years at sea before he could qualify for lieutenant.
[3] The blockade of Leghorn, a neutral port occupied by the French, involved diplomatic issues. Nelson had suggested that Swedish vessels should be allowed to leave, but only without cargoes. A similar concession was made to the Neapolitans.

greatest satisfaction your esteemed favour of Aug. 3rd. I will not fail to lay before the King my master this proof of the justice you pay to a Monarch whose sentiments have always been conformable to them which animate His Britannic Majesty and his meritorious officers. I avail myself of your generous permission for the departure of the Neapolitan merchant vessels without cargoes from this port etc.' An officer loses nothing but on the contrary gains much for his King and Country in courteous behaviour to foreigners. I do the same strict things but yet the people are contented.

I would recommend you to eat the hams and tongues; although it will not be a very very long time before I see you, yet it may be too long to keep hams.

All this part of the world who have seen republican principles hate and detest the name. God forbid England should be so miserable. She would be poor indeed. The dominion of modern republicanism is so cruel to the very poor as well as to the rich that England never I hope will submit to such slavery. Our liberty is I hope too firmly fixed to be moved but with our lives. Every village thro' which the French retreat takes arms against them and even kill those who are sick, and this is in a country where the will of the monarch constitutes the law. Whoever has travelled through Tuscany and indeed all Italy will tell you no country is equal to it for the real riches of the country people.

August 15th: I have just received an order to be an established Commodore with a Captain[1] under me. We are all well and the French will soon be out of Leghorn. If you hold any communication with the Hostes you may tell them that poor William has broke his other leg but at the same time you may most truly assure them that he is in a fair way of doing well. Poor fellow, how unlucky he has been. Josiah is well, indeed he is never sick. His constitution is robust. With kindest remembrances to my father, believe me, your most affectionate husband, HORATIO NELSON.

To Mrs. Nelson, Bath, Angleterre.

No. 160.

[Nicolas, II, p. 252, part]

Captain, Leghorn Roads,
August 23, 1796.

MY DEAREST FANNY,—Your letters of June 26th and July 11th I have received, and continue to direct by way of Leghorn, in which place I shall

---

[1] This promotion meant ten shillings a day extra pay for Nelson. Captain Charles Stuart, who took command on September 25, was superseded as flag-captain by Captain Ralph Miller on December 8. Miller, who distinguished himself at the battle of Cape St. Vincent and the Nile, was killed accidentally in May 1799.

write you very soon, and, so soon as our affairs are settled with the Great Duke I am to pay a visit to his Holiness the Pope. I do not think he will oppose the thunder of the Vatican against my thunder and you will I dare say hear that I am at Rome in my barge. If I succeed I am determined to row up the Tiber and into Rome. I cannot bring myself to believe we shall have a Spanish war.[1] The Dons must be great fools and will lose much. What should make you fancy Sir John Jervis[2] is going home? He has not the smallest idea. To say the truth, I should not be a candidate for staying out with Sir Hyde.[3] He did not treat me very well the time he had the command before and I should be sorry to put it in his power again, but we cannot always do as we please. I have wrote to Marsh and Creed this day desiring them to settle my account to the 11th June, the day I left *Agamemnon.* I have desired them to send the account to you (you must tell them where you are) and to pay you whenever you think proper to draw for it. You will not find it much but if any place in Norfolk is to be come at which may suit us I wish you would buy it. We can always sell again if it does not answer our expectations, a little land and we can improve a cottage. Do not be afraid, I shall most certainly like your choice. I am glad Kelly is coming home. I hear him very well spoken of by those who served in the West Indies with him. I believe your cousin is not quite of so open a disposition as K. is. They all think I have made a great deal of money and so let them. You seem to think Josiah is a master of languages. I must say he is the same exactly as when an infant and likes apples and port wine but it will be difficult to make him speak French, much more Italian. However, I hope his heart is good and that is the principal. Poor little Hoste is getting better very fast. Why should they not write to you? Do they suppose I have stole their money but if so they are below my notice, but I shall not show it to the younger. His account this year will be larger than the last and it must be when every article is to be bought. Why should I give it them. He has not cost half what his brother has. I will answer for it, but never mind them. Do not take notice that you feel the neglect.

We have just got accounts that the French are surrounded near Verona. Pray God they may be annihilated.

Ever my dear Fanny, believe me, your affectionate husband, HORATIO NELSON.

Best love to my father etc.

To Mrs. Nelson, Bath, Angleterre.

[1] Spain declared war in October 1796.
[2] In spite of much ill health, Jervis remained in the Mediterranean until June 1799.
[3] Sir Hyde Parker did not return to the Mediterranean, but was given command on the Jamaica station. Nelson served under him in the Baltic in 1801.

No. 161

[Nicolas, II. p. 262, part]

Genoa,
September 10, 1796

MY DEAREST FANNY,—Much against my inclination my time has been taken up here in a business Ministerial but, our Minister being at Venice, it has fell on me. The Senate here are puzzled how to act best for their country. We have right and the French have might. I hardly can guess how it will end. I have memorial'd the Senate had an audience of the Doge but still these wise heads are puzzled. The French threaten and we talk not very low. The Doge was very curious about me. He asked my age, said he had heard much of me, that the blockade of Leghorn was strict beyond what he could have thought possible, at the same time publicly thanked me for my goodness on many occasion to Genoese vessels. It has hitherto been my good fortune to have combined the strictest rigor of my duty with gaining the goodwill of the parties interested. My conduct has been open: this has been my secret and it has answered. I sail tomorrow morning for Corsica where all is in almost rebellion and I do not see how it will end. We have French reports of new victories. It is extraordinary, these Austrians do not stand as they used to do.

With kindest regards for my dear father, believe me your most affectionate HORATIO NELSON.

To Mrs. Nelson, Bath, Angleterre.

No. 162

Captain, Harbour of Capraia,
September 19, 1796

MY DEAREST FANNY,—The Government of Genoa having shown an evident partiality for the French, and fired on my ship for several hours together without any just cause to provoke it, and their conduct in this island being equally inimical to the English, and having sequestered the property of the English at Genoa, the Viceroy with myself thought it proper to instantly take satisfaction, and therefore attacked and took this Island yesterday,[1] the garrison having surrendered prisoners of war,

---

[1] The island surrendered without opposition. Jervis, in his dispatch to the Admiralty, praised Nelson's 'skill, judgement and enterprise' and 'the good training of those under his command'.

I sincerely hope this spirited measure will induce the Government of Genoa to recollect herself. This moment I have dispatches from the Viceroy telling me of the determination of Genoa long ago to break with us. I have for the insult offered to me taken what Genoa will think a severe and a just revenge.

I have just your letter by the cutter from England, with one from Lord Hood, Admiral Young, and my dear father. I can assure you not more than one week has ever elapsed without my writing you and sometimes oftener than once a week, therefore never believe I forget you. I suppose they lay at Leghorn till the French came and are lost. Genoa port is uncertain, direct again to Leghorn. You must be content with a short letter for I am in the act of writing several public letters and much arrangement to make for this new conquest. I will write my father very soon. I grieve to hear such a bad account of yourself. Cheer up, I shall return safe and sound. The busy and active scene is my delight. Josiah is perfectly well. Reports are that a Spanish war is certain but I cannot believe it. Ever, believe me, my dear Fanny, your most affectionate husband, HORATIO NELSON.

To Mrs. Nelson, Bath, Angleterre.

No. 163

Bastia,
September 30, 1796

MY DEAREST FANNY,—I received last night your letter of August 12th and do not be surprised when I tell you that it is far from impossible I may eat my Christmas dinner with you and my dear father. Do not think I am coming home in disgrace. My character never stood higher than at this moment but I cannot trust to a letter what is the cause of this sudden change.[1]

Believe me ever, your most affectionate husband, HORATIO NELSON.

Best love to my father. Josiah is well.

To Mrs. Nelson, Bath.

[1] On September 25 Jervis received orders to evacuate Corsica and leave the Mediterranean.

PLATE X. Oil painting of Rear-Admiral Lord Nelson, aged forty, by Leonardo Guzzardi, signed and dated 1799; from the Trafalgar House Collection.

No. 164

[Nicolas, II p. 290, part, dated 'about October 17th']

Diadem,[1] Porto Ferraio,
October 13, 1796

MY DEAR FANNY,—We are all preparing for an evacuation of the Mediterranean, a measure which I cannot approve. At home they know not what this fleet is capable of performing, *any and everything*. Much as I shall rejoice to see England in a private view, I lament in sackcloth and ashes our present orders, so dishonourable to the dignity of England, whose fleets are equal to meet the world in arms, and of all fleets I ever saw I never saw one equal in point of officers and men to our present one, and with a Commander-in-Chief fit to lead them to glory. God knows what detachments may be made, I hope not one to the West Indies, if it is, I fear the lot will fall on me, and I am for staying here, or coming to you, my dearest Fanny. By Christmas we shall be home. I cannot write much for my hands are full, as you will believe, all the arrangements for the evacuation have been left to me.[2]

With love to my father, believe me your most affectionate husband, HORATIO NELSON.

To Mrs. Nelson, Bath, Angleterre.

No. 165

Bastia[3]
October 19, 1796

MY DEAR FANNY,—I do not feel at this moment myself at liberty to say more than that I am in perfect health and rich in the good opinion of my Admiral and the Viceroy. This truly is all my riches, I fear I spend more than I get.

With kindest regard to my father, believe me, my dear Fanny, your most affectionate husband, HORATIO NELSON.

Josiah is most perfectly well.

To Mrs. Nelson, Bath.

[1] Nelson transferred his flag to the *Diadem*, Captain Towry, on September 27, when the *Captain* was sent to Ajaccio. He took a flag-lieutenant and a signal-lieutenant with him.
[2] See Appendix, p. 340, Sir John Jervis to Sir Gilbert Elliot.
[3] Nelson had returned to the *Captain* on October 16.

x

No. 166

San Fiorenzo,
October 24, 1796

MY DEAREST FANNY,—I yesterday with no small degree of pleasure received your 3 letters of Aug. 8, Aug. 24th and September 4th. Assure yourself, my dear Fanny, that my sincere love and affection is by no means weakened. As to coming home, who can say what tomorrow may bring forth. A few days past I wrote you it was probable we should all dine in England. Now that prospect is thrown a little forwarder. It is said we are offering to make peace. I hope not. It will put it with those insolent people farther off.

I arrived here this day from Porto Ferraio where I have safely lodged the garrison and émigrés from Bastia. The evacuation took place in a manner pleasant to my feelings. Not a creature was left who wished to come off although the French had been 5 hours in possession of the town, and brought off with me the two field pieces, although the Army said it could not be done, and was absolutely the last man who quitted. It appeared to others to be a fag to me but I assure you I am never so well pleased to be in active employment, more especially when my services are well received by my Commander-in-Chief. God knows if in England they will do anything for me. I can't help it. The Dons are coming up but in such a plight that they cannot stand against our fine fleet, when we are all united, which I expect will very soon be. There is nothing our tars look for so earnestly as an opportunity of giving the Dons a total defeat. In England they are ignorant of the capability of this fleet, the finest without exception that ever graced the ocean, and commanded by a first rate naval character.

I rejoice to hear you are so well. Take care of yourself and do not be uneasy about me. I hope to come to you covered with laurels. As to my health I am grown stout and never was so well. If we quit this country the West Indies is my lot. Not that it matters much where an officer serves, so but he does well. I have never heard from Mrs. Matcham since I left England and in good truth I have not time to write, seldom being in the way of these vessels which come from England. Josiah is most perfectly well, as is Hoste.

Believe me, as ever, my dear Fanny, your most affectionate HORATIO NELSON.

Do not forget me to my father.

To Mrs. Nelson, Bath, Angleterre.

No. 167

[Nicolas, II, p. 300, part]

Captain, at Sea,
November 7, 1796

MY DEAR FANNY,—I wrote you a line by the *Camelion* a few days before our sailing from San Fiorenzo, as I had done a short time before from Bastia. The first was a short letter for I dare not trust to paper the plan which was to be pursued. However, by this time you will learn the determination for this fleet to remain in the Mediterranean. As for Corsica I have seen the first and last of it. I was the cause of giving many lucrative employments for the army which they were incapable of getting for themselves and I took them off the island when they were equally helpless. It will appear extraordinary but they allowed the Corsicans at Bastia to sequester and seize all the English property, to lay a privateer across the Mole and in short by every way to insult them, and had I not arrived, I am sure they would have taken the Viceroy from them and have submitted to any terms the townspeople demanded and this with a force of 1800 men in possession of the citadel, but all were panic struck. In one quarter of an hour I settled the whole matter for I sent to the Council of 30 who acted for the Corsicans or French, and told them if the sequester was not taken off in that time, the armed Corsicans retired and that I was molested in taking off what I thought proper, I would blow the town down. The Corsicans down muskets and run. From this moment all was quiet and I saved £200,000 sterling worth of stores and property. In short it is impossible to say what I did not do. The scrap of paper sent from the General to the captain of the fleet will say more for me than I can say for myself, except that I did bring them off and the two field pieces, which the army brought from the citadel to protect their rear, I brought off as a point of honour, and I landed them all safe at Porto Ferraio, a secure place which I had taken for them. Not a sixpence worth of property belonging to the merchants was left behind. The pleasure of my own mind will be my reward, except having the honour to maintain the Viceroy, Secretary of State and about 40 other persons at an enormous expense, but such things are. So soon as we have defeated the Spanish fleet, which I doubt not with God's help but we shall do, I have two or three little matters to settle in Italy and then I care not how soon I return to you. Do not flatter yourself I shall be rewarded. I expect nothing, therefore shall not be disappointed.

November 11th, off Minorca: We are so far with our convoy. Perhaps we shall [see] Gibraltar. If we do I shall write you from thence but this goes on board the Admiral to take its chance for a passage. Josiah is most perfectly well. With kindest regards to my father, believe me, your most affectionate husband, HORATIO NELSON.

I shall not forget George Jolliffe. He is on board the *Inconstant*.[1]

N.B. We took Bastia with 1250 men.

I send the General's[2] note to you as I [am] more interested and feel a greater satisfaction in getting your and my father's applause than that of all the world beside.

To Mrs. Nelson, Bath.

No. 168

Captain, off the Island of Ivica,
November 22, at night

MY DEAREST FANNY,—Although I see no prospect of sending this letter yet I like to have one ready to send off. My last was by the *Cygnet* cutter which I hope will arrive safe.

You will know from Admiral Man's[3] arrival what a state we must be in. I am surprised that any officer, especially as he thought our force united was too weak to meet the enemy, could desert his brethren and how he could get English captains to support his measure I am astonished at, yet Man is as good a man and with as upright intentions as ever lived. However we are in for the plate and must endeavour to win it. We are pursuing our route towards Gibraltar with each a merchant ship in tow, and determined our Admiral is to face the storm, hoping the government in England will not leave us long without assistance. Sir John Jervis honours me with his confidence and you know me well enough to be assured that in no way will I desert him. We have had exceeding bad weather and foul winds but perseverance is the Admiral's as well as my motto. All will end well. It cannot be otherwise in a good cause conducted with good sense. It will give you pleasure to find I have gained no small degree of credit by the evacuation of Bastia. The Admiral has to Lord Spencer attributed the bringing off the troops, and saving them and the Viceroy, together with the cannon and stores, to the *firmness* of conduct in Commodore Nelson. The task was arduous but I have so much been in the habit of good fortune that nothing is despaired of by me and it even in the execution exceeds my expectations.

This day I saw in reading a newspaper your name and my good father's

[1] Commanded by Captain Fremantle. George Jolliffe was promoted lieutenant in March 1797.

[2] General de Burgh.

[3] Admiral Man, sent to Gibraltar with a squadron for provisions, instead of rejoining Jervis took the advice of his captains and returned to England. No court martial was held, but Man had no further employment at sea. He was one of the Lords Commissioners of the Admiralty 1798-1801.

as arrived at Bath. It is impossible to express what I felt at only seeing it and I trust the time will come when I shall see you there myself. Not that I expect a peace till the Dons try what they can do. Had Admiral Man come up we should have done them by this time, and I trust Don Langara would once more have been a prisoner to us. Our chief is equal to conduct us to honour, and we are equal to obey his wise directions, but he feels Man's retreat severely, says nothing, not even complains of Man, but laments his rash step. I do not believe any officer ever was left in so delicate a situation and few, very few, would have firmness to bear up against it. Our great support and able counsellor the Viceroy of Corsica will now probably soon proceed to England. In him we lose a treasure never to be regained. He loves the Navy and we, at least all the good of us, I hope, love him.

I see by the papers Kelly is arrived. When you write to Plymouth remember me kindly to him and her. I hope he has something handsome. We have a report that Captain Holloway was blown up in the *Amphion* at Plymouth.[1] I most sincerely hope it is not so. He has a young family, totally unprovided for. Besides it is so unfashionable mode of leaving the world, but I hope it is only report. I can say nothing how to send letters, to Porto Ferraio I think is still the best mode, that is Leghorn, if the post office says no other way, and also by the conveyance of the Admiralty. Every fortnight or oftener a vessel comes to us. Your last was Sept. 6th but by the first vessel from Ferraio I expect later. We have papers to Oct. 22nd a fortnight since.

December 1st: All well, close to Gibraltar. Write no more by Italy. Send to the Admiralty, Admiral Young[2] or Mr. Nepean.[3] Captain Berry[4] desires his compliments. He is thankful for your interest. Believe me ever, your most affectionate husband, HORATIO NELSON.

To Mrs. Nelson, Bath.

No. 169

[Nicolas, II, p. 311, part, dated 'about 10th December']

Captain, Gibraltar Bay,
December 9, 1796

MY DEAREST FANNY,—The fleet is on the wing from Gibraltar and you will hear where it is gone without my writing it. As to myself, I hoist my

---

[1] The *Amphion* was blown up accidentally, but her captain, Israel Pellew, escaped with little injury.
[2] Admiral William Young was one of the Lords Commissioners of the Admiralty 1795–1801.
[3] Evan Nepean was secretary to the Admiralty 1795–1804.
[4] Berry, although promoted captain, did not get a command of his own until the spring.

pendant in *La Minerve*[1] frigate tomorrow norming and am going on an arduous and most important mission which, with God's blessing, I have little doubt of accomplishing. It is not a fighting mission,[2] therefore be not uneasy. I feel honoured in being trusted by Sir John Jervis in the manner I am. Josiah has not made his mind to stay or go with me. I leave it to himself. You will soon hear from me again.

God bless you and my dear father and believe me your most affectionate husband, HORATIO NELSON.

To Mrs. Nelson, Bath.

December 10th: Received yours Oct. 3rd.

No. 170

[Nicolas, II, p. 311, part, dated 'about 10th December.']

La Minerve,
December 12, 1796

MY DEAREST FANNY,—I have wrote you by this vessel but I know a last letter is the best, therefore I write another line. If I have money enough in Marsh and Creed's hands I wish you would buy the cottage in Norfolk, and be assured that I believe it to be impossible I shall not follow the plough with much greater satisfaction than viewing all the magnificent scenes of Italy.

Josiah stays by choice in the *Captain*. He is most perfectly well and his knowledge of the world is as forward as I wish it.

Believe me ever, my dear Fanny, your most affectionate husband, HORATIO NELSON.

Love to my father.

To Mrs. Nelson, Bath.

No. 171

La Minerve, Gibraltar Bay,
December 14, 1796[3]

Yesterday brought me your letter of October 13th and I rejoice to hear my father is so well. I have no idea that it will be very long before we all are

---

[1] *La Minerve* was commanded by Captain George Cockburn, the first lieutenant being Thomas Hardy. Jervis could not spare a 74-gun ship for this task, his forces being much reduced by Man's return to England.

[2] Nelson received orders to withdraw the naval establishments and transport the troops from Porto Ferraio to Gibraltar and Lisbon. As the general had no such orders, the troops were not embarked.

[3] This letter is worn and torn at the folds (see p. 350, Mrs. Nelson's remarks, February 26, 1797).

in England and the war finished. Respecting Tofts[1], I certainly should like it very much, but I fear it is beyond my powers, *far very far*. You know them as well as I do. When the war is finished and our money matters made up, you will see what can be done. I should have been much distressed had Captain Andrews been appointed to my ship. He has taken to hard drinking, which would not have suited me. I have a much better man with me. Poor Suckling will drink, he is too late to reform in that respect and we must make the best of it. I wish he could get a living of £100 a year but that I own I see no prospect of. As to his expenses, my father cannot nor ought not to go too far. As to wine he nor those of much larger incomes can afford to drink it, and a man can live very happy without the sight of it. You will know by my account from Marsh and Creed how money stands and you may safely dispose of all in their hands. The prizes taken will continue to give me enough for expenses. The legacy is too distant in its payment to be reckoned but whatever you do, depend on it I shall be satisfied with. Hoste has wrote to his father and so have I. He is most perfectly well and a good young man as ever lived. I am just getting under sail.

Believe me ever your most affectionate HORATIO NELSON.

Make my respects to Admiral Barrington.

To Mrs. Nelson, Bath.

No. 172

Porto Ferraio,
December 29, 1796

MY DEAREST FANNY,—I have only time to tell you that I am most perfectly well and doubt not but with God's blessing I shall execute my present mission with credit to myself and consequently with advantage for my country.[2] I shall write again in a few days. With kindest love to my father, believe me your most affectionate husband, HORATIO NELSON.

Dr. Harness[3] desired his compliments.

To Mrs. Nelson, Bath.

[1] Tofts, a house in Norfolk, which Nelson's brother William had suggested he might buy.

[2] Nelson anchored at Porto Ferraio on December 26, having captured the Spanish frigate *Sabina* on his way. The prize was lost the next day when Nelson was counterattacked by a larger force.

[3] Dr. John Harness returned as physician to the fleet with Sir John Jervis.

No. 173

[Nicolas, II, p. 235, part, order transposed]

La Minerve, Port Ferraio,
January 13, 1797

MY DEAR FANNY,—I have not had a letter since I wrote last by way of Florence but that never stops my pen.

We have nothing new stirring here. The armies seem tired of fighting, and each I believe wish for an armistice which in Italy I hope will not take place. As to peace now Mr. Pitt has got money I do not expect it, and the Directory have no inclination. Lord Malmesbury[1] will come back as he went, but the people of England will I trust be more rigorous for the prosecution of the war which now only can insure an honourable peace.

Lady Elliot is at Bath. I hope you know her, she ought to make herself acquainted with you. I expect Sir Gilbert Elliot here every hour. He goes down to Gibraltar with me. He is a good man and I love him.

Naples is alarmed at her peace. The French minister is travelling towards Naples with a train of 300 persons a printing etc., company of comedians etc. The Pope has not made his peace and is now most seriously alarmed, but as we have good news from Mantua I hope the French will not be able to make farther progress this winter. As this line goes to Florence to take its chance of reaching you I shall not say much indeed it is dangerous to write anything like news.

With kindest love to my father, believe me, my dearest Fanny, your most affectionate husband, HORATIO NELSON.

To Mrs. Nelson, Bath, Angleterre.

No. 174

[Nicolas, II, p. 330, part]

La Minerve, Port Ferraio,
January 27, 1797

MY DEAREST FANNY,—The *Minerve* is completely refitted and I am only waiting for the weather moderating to proceed to sea with a small convoy to proceed down the Mediterranean therefore the next letter I shall probably write you will be dated from Lisbon where I hope to arrive safe with my charge, but in war much is left to Providence. However, as I have

---

[1] Lord Malmesbury went on an embassy to Paris to negotiate a peace, but was unsuccessful.

hitherto been most successful, confidence tells me I shall not fail, but as nothing will be left undone by me should I not always succeed my mind will not suffer, nor will the world I trust be willing to attach a blame where my heart tells me none will be due.

Sir Gilbert Elliot and his suite[1] go down in *La Minerve* therefore I shall be sure of a pleasant party let what will happen.

There are four mails now at Florence from England. I long to hear from you, but as I have wrote you in future your letters had better come through the Admiralty till I can tell you what route by post to send them. As for news beyond my immediate concerns the public prints must tell you more than I can therefore the whole I can say which I feel you will prize more than any other news is that I am in most perfect good health. Our winter here has been very disagreeable and on the continent vast falls of snow. I am anxious to know how my father bears it. I do not believe it can be very long before I shall have the happiness of seeing my dear Fanny. Believe me ever your most affectionate husband, HORATIO NELSON.

To Mrs. Nelson, Bath, Angleterre.

No. 175

Off Cape St. Vincent,
February 13, 1797

MY DEAREST FANNY,—This moment joined the fleet and Sir Gilbert Elliot goes on to England in the *Lively*. Yours of the 18th December I have received. I can only say God bless you. Fame says I am near £3000 richer by the Spanish war. For your sake I hope it is so.

Do as you like about the house near Norwich or anywhere else. I shall like it if you do. We want a real fixed home. I will write you an account of my wealth as soon as I know it.

Sir Gilbert Elliott will know you if it is possible for him to come to Bath. You will love him as we all do.

With love to my father, believe me, your most affectionate husband, HORATIO NELSON.

To Mrs. Nelson, Bath.

[1] Clarke, in the extract he quoted in his *Life of Lord Nelson*, added the phrase 'amongst whom is Colonel Drinkwater', which has been repeated by Nicolas, but there is no mention of his name in Nelson's letter.

No. 176

Irresistible,[1]
February 16, 1797

MY DEAREST FANNY,—I am most perfectly well and rich in honour as is Josiah and Hoste. It would not be right to attempt detailing the action as it will come from a much better pen than mine.[2]

God bless you and my dear father and believe me ever, your most affectionate husband, HORATIO NELSON.

Mrs. Nelson, Bath.

No. 177

Irresistible, Lagos Bay,
February 22, 1797

MY DEAR FANNY,—Our prizes being now refitted and the *Captain* put in a tolerable state we are to put to sea the first favourable moment for Lisbon. I do not believe we shall have the good fortune to meet the Spanish fleet or depend on it we shall have some more of them. Berry I have no doubt will be a post captain and two of my lieutenants made masters and commanders.[3] I send you a detail of the transactions of the *Captain* they are so extraordinary that I have had them authenticated by the officers of my ship.[4]

I have some thoughts of sending the Spanish admiral's sword to be hung up in the Guild Hall at Norwich if it will be acceptable. I have barely time to write this line. The *Hope* lugger just arriving from Gibraltar does not anchor but proceeds direct for England.

With kind love to my father, believe me, your most affectionate husband, HORATIO NELSON.

To Mrs. Nelson, Bath.

[1] Nelson rejoined the fleet on February 13 and returned to the *Captain*. During the action off Cape St. Vincent, fought on February 14, the *Captain* was much damaged and he transferred to the *Irresistible*, Captain George Martin.

[2] The official despatch from Sir John Jervis was taken to England by his flag-captain, Captain Calder, who arrived on March 3. No mention was made in it of Nelson's individual achievements, but in a private letter to the Admiralty, Jervis singled him out for special praise.

[3] Berry was promoted post-captain on March 6, 1797; Lieutenants Peter Spicer and James Noble were also promoted.

[4] Nelson's account of the action was published and reprinted in the *Naval Chronicle* in 1799. He sent copies to his wife, Captain Locker, the Duke of Clarence and Admiral Waldegrave. The original MSS., authenticated by Captain Miller and Captain Berry, was retained by Nelson.

A few remarks relative to myself in the Captain *in which my pendant was flying on the most glorious Valentine's Day 1797*[1] *[Nicolas, II, pp. 340–347]*:

At 1 a.m. the *Captain* having passed the sternmost of the enemy ships which formed their van and part of their centre consisting of 17 sail of the line they on the larboard we on the starboard tack, the Admiral made the signal to tack in succession. But I perceiving the Spanish ships all to bear up before the wind or nearly so, evidently with an intention of forming their line going large, joining their separated division at that time engaged with some of our centre ships, or flying from us. To prevent either of their schemes from taking effect I ordered the ship to be wore and passing between the *Diadem* and *Excellent* at ¼ past one oclock was engaged with the headmost and of course leewardmost of the Spanish division, the ships which I know, were the *Santissima Trinidada* 126, *San Josef*, 112, *Salvador Dell Mundo*, 112, *San Nicholas*, 80, another first rate, 112, and 74, names not known. I was immediately joined and most nobly supported by the *Culloden* Capt. Troubridge. The Spanish fleet from not wishing (I suppose) to have a decisive battle hauled to the wind on the larboard tack, which brought the ships afore mentioned to be the leewardmost and sternmost ships in their fleet, for near an hour I believe (but do not pretend to be correct as to time) did the *Culloden* and *Captain* support this apparently but not really unequal contest, when the *Blenheim* passing between us and the enemy gave us a respite and sickened the Dons. At this time the *Salvador Dell Mundo* and *San Isidro* dropped astern, and were fired into in a masterly style by the *Excellent* Capt. Collingwood, who compelled the *San Isidro* to hoist English colours, and I thought the large ship *S.D.M.* had also struck, but Capt. Collingwood disdaining the parade of taking possession of beaten enemies most gallantly pushed up with every sail set to save his old friend and messmate who was to appearance in a critical state, the *Blenheim* being ahead and the *Culloden* crippled and astern. The *Excellent* ranged up within 10 feet of the *San Nicholas* gave a most tremendous fire. The *San Nicholas* luffing up the *San Josef* fell on board her and the *Excellent* passing on for the *Santissima Trinidada* the *Captain* resumed her situation abreast of them and close alongside. At this time the *Captain* having lost her fore topmast, not a sail, shroud or rope left, her wheel shot away and incapable of farther service in the line or in the chase, I directed Capt. Miller to put the helm a starboard and calling for the boarders ordered them to board.

The soldiers of the 69th regiment with an alacrity which will ever do them credit and Lieut. Pierson of the same regiment were amongst the foremost on this service. The first man who jumped into the enemy's

[1] Monmouth MSS., Nelson papers, Vol. IV.

mizen chains was Capt. Berry late my first lieutenant (Capt. Miller was in the very act of going also but I directed him to remain) he was supported from our spritsail yard which hooked in the mizen rigging, a soldier of the 69th regiment having broke the upper quarter gallery window jumped in followed by myself and others as fast as possible, I found the cabin doors fastened, and some Spanish officers fired their pistols, but having broke open the doors the soldiers fired and the Spanish brigadier (Commodore with a distinguishing pendant) fell as retreating to the quarter deck on the larboard side near the wheel. Having pushed on the quarter deck I found Capt. Berry in possession of the poop and the Spanish ensign hauling down. I passed with my people and Lt. Pierson on the larboard gangway to the forecastle where I met two or three Spanish officers prisoners to my seamen and they delivered me their swords. At this moment a fire of pistols or muskets opened from the Admiral's stern gallery of the *San Joseph* I directed the soldiers to fire into her stern and calling to Capt. Miller ordered him to send more men into the *San Nicholas*, and directed my people to board the first rate which was done in an instant Capt. Berry assisting me into the main chains. At this moment a Spanish officer looked over the quarter deck rail and said they surrendered. From this most welcome intelligence it was not long before I was on the quarter deck when the Spanish captain with a bow presented me his sword and said the Admiral was dying of his wounds below. I asked him on his honour if the ship was surrendered. He declared she was, on which I gave him my hand and desired him to call to his officers and ship's company and tell them of it which he did, and on the quarter deck of a Spanish first rate extravagant as the story may seem did I receive the swords of vanquished Spaniards which as I received I gave to William Fearney one of my barge men who put them with the greatest sang froid under his arm. I was surrounded by Capt. Berry, Lieut. Pierson 69th Regiment, John Sykes, John Thompson, Francis Cook all old *Agamemnon*'s and several other brave men, seamen and soldiers. Thus fell these ships.

N.B. In boarding the *San Nicholas* I believe we lost about 7 killed and 10 wounded, and about 20 Spaniards lost their lives by a foolish resistance none were I believe lost in boarding the *San Josef*.

Anecdote

Francis Cook took me by the hand on the quarter deck of the *San Joseph* saying he might not soon have such another place to do it in, and assured me he was heartily glad to see me.

H. N.

There is a saying in the fleet too flattering for me to omit telling.—viz. 'Nelson's Patent Bridge for boarding first rates.'

Don Francisco Wyntheyson Rear Admiral killed on board the *San Joseph*. Commodore Enrique Macdonald killed when the *Captain* boarded the *San Nicholas*. Original authenticated by Captain Miller and Captain Berry with myself.

Commodore Nelson's receipt for making an Olla Podrida

Take a Spanish first rate and an 80 gunship and after well *battering* and *basting* them for an hour keep throwing in your *force balls*, and be sure to let these be well *seasoned*. Your *fire* must never *slacken* for a moment, but must be kept up as brisk as possible during the whole time so soon as you perceive your Spaniards to be well stewed and blended together you must then throw your own ship on board the two decker back your spritsail yard to her mizen mast then skip in to her quarter gallery window sword in hand and let the rest of your boarders follow as they can. The moment that you appear on the 80 gun ship quarter deck the Spaniards will all throw down their arms and fly, you will then only have to take a hop skip and jump from your stepping stone and you will find yourself in the middle of the first rate quarter deck with all the Dons at your feet.

Your Olla Podrida may now be considered as completely *dished* and fit to set before his Majesty.

Nelson his art of cooking Spaniards.

From another part of the Fleet:
The conduct of the *Captain* was sober from beginning to end—He never was equalled and I dare say never will.

From another:
What has happened could only happen to you.

[*Note in Lady Nelson's hand, c. 1806:* This [*the Olla Podrida receipt*] was inclosed to me soon after the 14th Feb.

Copies of letters which Lord Nelson received and sent me. FRANCES NELSON AND BRONTE.]

No. 178
[Nicolas, II, p. 358, part]

Irresistible, Lisbon,
February 28, 1797

MY DEAREST FANNY,—We got up here with our prizes this afternoon. The more I think of our late action the more I am astonished. It absolutely appears a dream. The *Santissima Trinidada* of four decks lost 500 killed and wounded. Had not *Captain* been so cut up I would have had her but it is well. Thank God for it. As to myself I assure you I never was better and rich in the praise of every man from the highest to the lowest in this fleet. I have some reason to believe I shall be in England sooner than I expected. If certain events take place I will not stay here but more of this as the plot thickens.

I this day received your letter of January 16th, that of the 9th not come to hand. Lisbon is the place at present. A packet is come in and I hope to have later letters tomorrow. I go to sea the day after tomorrow in this ship with a squadron and shall return by the time the fleet is ready for sea. Don't think I am forced to go out as Sir John is all kindness to me, but I cannot bear an idle life and it may be every way beneficial to me. I am afraid I over reckoned my balance in my agents' hands, but I believe this Spanish war will give us a cottage and piece of ground which is all I want.

1st March: The packet goes at daylight in the morning therefore I must conclude. Assure yourself as ever being your most affectionate HORATIO NELSON.

To Mrs. Nelson, Bath.

No. 179

[Nicolas, II, p. 358, part, under date February 28]

Irresistible, Lisbon,
March 3, 1797

MY DEAREST FANNY,—I have received your three letters of December 27th, January 9th and another without date, I suppose the latter end of January. I admit they are full which I should regret were they not, for they are invaluable to me. I grieve when I hear you are unwell. I shall come one day or other *laughing back* when we will retire from the busy scenes of life. I do not mean to be a hermit. The Dons will give us a little money but I dare not guess, others say at least £5000 since the Spanish war but as yet I have not touched a farthing.

I have sent Josiah with Captain Berry[1] who wished to have him and he will learn more with him than he could with me and he must be broke of being at my elbow. I assure you I love him and I am confident it's reciprocal. His understanding is manly and his heart is as good as we can wish, but the same shyness is still visible it is his nature and cannot be altered but how much better than if he was forward. Hoste is with me here, in the action

---

[1] Berry was given command of a sloop.

he made me promise never to leave him again. All from the *Captain* are promoted and I regret Josiah has not served his time. I have wrote to Maurice to see if he cannot get a little cheating[1] for him it might be done and would be invaluable. I am getting from Captain Stirling a certificate and I wish one could be got from Captain Sotheby[2] for if they will cheat, I shall do the same for *Boreas*, for if the war lasts another year he must be made at least a Lieutenant and I hope farther. His abilities are superior to many who command ships.

You complain of my short letters but had not the wind been contrary I should this morning have been at sea therefore you must be content with short letters. I hear the Spanish convoy is out of Cadiz bound for the West Indies I regret our destination but cannot help myself. I still hope there is something left at sea for me. I have 19 sail of ships under my command.

I have received my dear father's letters and one from Mrs. Matcham without date which I shall answer if possible with every good wish. Believe me, your most affectionate husband, HORATIO NELSON.

Secret:

I have authorized Sir Gilbert Elliot if he hears of any honours likely to be conferred to decline for me all such; they are, with a small fortune, great incumbrances. I have sent the Spanish Admiral's sword to Mr. Windham[3] for the city of Norwich.

To Mrs. Nelson, Bath.

No. 180

Irresistible, at Sea off Cadiz,
March 14, 1797

MY DEAREST FANNY,—I have been hunting anxiously for the Viceroy of Mexico but as yet without success, but as I am sending a ship in to Lisbon I write you a line in particular as I did not answer part of your letter respecting my brother Suckling. You will credit me when I say that I know not who I have a right to ask to speak to the Chancellor to do a thing which I own would not require much interest. As to Sir Gilbert Elliot, had he the power with the Chancellor, I well know he has much to ask for himself, and when I tell you that as *Viceroy* having displaced two nephews of the Chancellor's it is not likely he could ask anything from that quarter.

---

[1] By having his name entered on the books of a ship fictitiously.
[2] Two captains who had commanded ships in the West Indies when Nelson was in the *Boreas*.
[3] William Windham, M.P. for Norwich.

As to Lord Chatham he has formerly treated me so ill that it's not probable he would step forward to oblige me, and I cannot think it right I should try him. Upon reflection I am sure you and my father will agree with me. When we see how the 14th February turns men's minds towards me as a public officer, having nothing to ask for myself, with proper apologies, the Chancellor might forgive me my stating the situation of my father and brother to him, but I by no means would build any prospect of success from such a measure. I would probably depend on the humour it found the *great man in*. So much for *that*.

I have been examining my agent's accounts and I find that when all my accounts for *Agamemnon* are closed and that till August 11th when I became an established Commodore, my agents will have about £1472 sterling in their hands. I shall send a bill for my flag pay to February 11th will be £432, my marine pay to February 11th about £400 more making according to my calculations as follows

	£	s.	d.
In Marsh and Creed's hands as Captain when accounts are settled	1472	0	0
Flag pay to Feb. 11th.	432		
Marine pay to Feb. 11th	400		
	£2304		

I hope instead of drawing to considerably increase my fortune. It is said and I believe it cannot be much less or anything that £5000 will be my share of prize money to March 1st. This you will keep to yourself but from you I can have no wish to keep any secret, therefore you will now know how far you can go and that £2000 can be spared for a home. We must not be vagabonds any longer.

There is one thing I have made my mind to that is in any common event to ask leave to strike my flag next October till the spring of the year. This I am as much determined on as an officer ought to be. The Admiralty cannot I conceive either refuse or take ill my request. So ends money. If my father wishes for any part of it I beg he will take it that would give me more real pleasure than buying house or land.

Josiah is with Captain Berry in a very fine sloop and Berry shall have such a cruise as I hope will make Captain B's fortune. I expect the Admiralty will make him post and two of my lieutenants captains, with kind love to my father, believe me ever, your most affectionate husband, HORATIO NELSON.

Sir James Saumarez[1] is one of my squadron and is very well dines here this day.

To Mrs. Nelson, Bath.

No. 181

Irresistible, off Cape St. Vincent,
March 22, 1797

MY DEAREST FANNY,—A vessel we have just spoke bound to Lisbon enables me to say we are all well expecting the Viceroy of Mexico and that the Spanish fleet are safe in Cadiz. They acknowledge the *Santissima Trinidada* struck which is satisfactory to me who had my share in her attack. The Commander-in-Chief is sent to Madrid as a prisoner under an escort of horse, and the officers cannot come on shore for fear of the populace.

With love to my father, believe me ever, your most affectionate husband HORATIO NELSON.

Josiah is very well. Captain Berry gives me very good accounts of him.

To Mrs. Nelson, Bath.

No. 182

[Nicolas, II, p. 369, part, no date, only month—April]

Captain,[2] off Cadiz,
April 2, 1797

MY DEAREST FANNY,—You will believe whether my letters are long or *short* which last they generally are, still my heart is entirely with you. Your letter of March 11th, my father's of the 14th with 40 others came to me yesterday afternoon. It is well when we seem to satisfy all the world for the Spaniards are not less lavish of their praises of me than are the people of England. Lord Spencer (this keep to yourself except my father) has by the King's command signified to me His Majesty's intention to confer on me the most honourable order of the Bath, as a mark of His Royal approbation of my conduct on many occasions during the present war.[3] As to fortune we must be content with a little and the *cottage*. Near Norwich, or any other place you like better, will I assure you content me. I do not say if the

---

[1] Saumarez, who had served under Sir Peter Parker with Nelson, had joined Jervis's fleet just before the battle of February 14; he was one of Nelson's senior captains at the battle of the Nile. Died 1836, Admiral Lord Saumarez.

[2] Nelson rejoined the *Captain*, Captain Miller, on April 2.

[3] A baronetcy was the usual honour for a junior flag-officer in an important action, but Nelson had indicated his views on the subject to Sir Gilbert Elliot and explained he could not afford any hereditary honours.

Y

government offered me £300 or £500 per annum I would refuse on the contrary I should be obliged to them, but it is a thing I cannot ask, but then we could afford no more than a cottage. My chains medals and ribbons with a contented mind are all sufficient. When you write to Josiah you may address yourself to Lieutenant Nisbet and I hope he will be a Captain if the war lasts till October next. William Bolton, and Hoste with Weatherhead will also be promoted by Lord Jervis but I fear about their time. I have sent to Maurice to take out so much of a Capt. William Bolton's time, that is all fair. Weatherhead, Mr. Coke has interested himself about and I hope will get over his want of time, but I fear he has not interest for such a thing.

I have handsome letters from the Duke of Clarence and Lord Hood. I have very many letters to write therefore I must finish for the present. We have just chased two Spanish ships of the line into Cadiz where we are blockading them up. I do not expect to see them this summer out again. With love to my father, believe me, your most affectionate husband, HORATIO NELSON.

April 3rd: I forgot to answer one part of your former letter about a young lad. You must explain to the lad and his mother and if he comes out I will certainly do my best for him.

To Mrs. Nelson, Bath. [*Re-addressed by the Rev. E. Nelson:* James Tobin's Esq., Berkeley Square, Bristol.]

No. 183

Captain, off Cape St. Vincent,
April 9, 1797

MY DEAR FANNY,—As Captain Berry is just going away I send a line merely to say I never was better in health. As Captain Berry[1] will tell you all the news about us I shall write no more, only to assure you that I am ever your most affectionate husband, HORATIO NELSON.

To Mrs. Nelson, Bath.

No. 184

Captain, off Cadiz,
April 12, at night

MY DEAREST FANNY,—I have just received your affectionate letter of March 17th and have barely time to write you a line as I am going on a detached service. The Dons are all in port and I believe it will be a very

---

[1] Berry arrived in England in May and visited Mrs. Nelson in Bath (see Appendix, p. 367, Lady Nelson's letter of May 28).

difficult matter to get them out again for what a fleet we have 22 sail of the line 8 three decked ships three of whom are first rates. What can the Dons do against such a fleet? Nothing, the greater their numbers the greater their confusion.

Josiah is a lieutenant, Sir John Jervis gave him a commission April 8th which is gone home for confirmation. He is now officer of the watch. I want Hoste, Bolton and Weatherhead to be made when I shall be easy but as yet I cannot cheat for their time.

Remember me in the most affectionate manner to my father and believe me to be your most affectionate husband, HORATIO NELSON.

Send me Mr. Scrivener's direction I wish you would write him a line and say nothing would have given me more pleasure than to have told him of my movements had he told me where to direct to him. Remember me kindly to him. Sir James Saumarez has just left me perfectly well.

To Mrs. Nelson, Bath.

No. 185

Captain, 20 leagues from Corsica,
April 21, 1797

MY DEAREST FANNY,—Fortune still continues to favour me in the service of my country. I was sent to protect our convoy from Elba down the Mediterranean. The same wind which carried me in 6 days close to Corsica drove from their station off the south end of Minorca 4 sail of the line a frigate and a brig French which were cruising there to intercept our convoy. This morning I had the happiness to join them and they are now I hope safe under my wing, and we are steering for Gibraltar. The French are masters of all Italy and within 150 miles of Vienna but I hope yet the Archduke may give them a total overthrow, either that or an ignominious peace must soon be seen.

You must take short letters. Remember me most kindly to my father and believe me ever your most affectionate husband, HORATIO NELSON.

To Mrs. Nelson, Bath.

No. 186

Captain, 20 leagues east of Gibraltar with all the convoy,
May 5, 1796[1]

MY DEAREST FANNY,—As a cutter goes to the fleet the moment I see the Rock to announce our happy arrival, I send you a line merely to say we are

---

[1] An error for 1797. The convoy had the troops from Porto Ferraio on board.

all well. Our passage down has been as fortunate as could be hoped, and our troops are as healthy as our ships. As for news you will not expect it, for I have heard not a syllable since I wrote you last April 21st. I cannot believe the Spanish ministry will ever suffer their fleet to come out again. They must know it would be giving them to us. I expect to be two days at Gibraltar to water and victual where I hope to find letters from you, by the *Lively* which must be arrived before this time. With best and kindest remembrances to my father, believe me your most affectionate husband, HORATIO NELSON.

To Mrs. Nelson, Bath.

No. 187

[Nicolas, II, p. 388, short extract]

Theseus, off Cadiz,[1]
May 27, 1797

MY DEAREST FANNY,—I have been so taken up with the exchange that has happened as you will see by the top of my letter that I have hardly had time to read your several letters which I found at Gibraltar and on board the *Ville de Paris* up to April 30th, believe my dear Fanny nothing gives me equal pleasure.

My health is good and all pleasant about me and rich in the opinion of my Commander-in-Chief. As to other riches we find to our mortification that Lord Hugh Seymour is cruising on our station to intercept the galleons which are momently expected at Cadiz. This we cannot but think a most cruel thing, leaving us here with so great an inferiority in numbers to the enemy and sending 4 sail of the line to reap the fruit of our toil which has been obtained by sweat of blood. This act of cruelty committed by one of our task masters. The whole [squadron] feels and are louder than myself 'share our dangers, share our riches' but to obtain the latter at our expense is hitherto unprecedented. We cannot come to our families rich in ought but honour. How government can answer for this act I cannot guess but I have done.

We are at anchor off Cadiz in sight of the whole Spanish fleet but I do not believe they will venture out again, if they do we shall all be soon in England with a fleet of prizes.

I recollect enough of your letter which I cannot get at to say a word about a house. Wherever in Norfolk you approve town or country, I shall be satisfied. You may build upon £5000 in addition to my half pay, it may

---

[1] On May 24 Nelson transferred to the *Theseus*, 74 guns, taking Captain Miller and some officers with him. He was given command of the in-shore squadron off Cadiz.

be more but this you are sure of besides your money from Mr. Herbert and if Lord Hugh does not waylay us it will I doubt not be much more. I recollect the house in the upper close Norwich. Do I desire as you like, as to pension I expect none, I will write my father very soon.

Josiah is well as are all of us, with love to my father, believe me your most affectionate HORATIO NELSON.

Charles Dillon drowned November 1796.[1]

I have some Naples sashes to send you and a gown also 5 elegant drawings of the action when opportunity offers, but when the convoy comes I may not be able to have an intercourse with them for all our movements are quick. I am glad Culverhouse[2] called on you, he is a good man, Mr. Windham nor the Mayor of Norwich have not answered my letter which is very odd. I care not about the entail of Mr. Herbert's estate but it [is] unhandsome. As to Mrs. Kelly she is all self. We have got our medals but no chains. It is not to be equal to the 1st of June. We are not pleased at the difference.

To Mrs. Nelson, Bath.

No. 188

[Nicolas, II, p. 397, part]

Theseus,
June 15, 1797

MY DEAREST FANNY,—I have received your affectionate letters of May 8th, 15th and 29th and from the complexion of the times I most fervently hope we shall have a tolerable peace. The vessel which brought these letters being to return within an hour of my getting them must make me write a short letter to say we are well and Josiah very much improved. I hope he will make a good man.

Although the fleet has taken some prizes, yet I think you must not reckon on more than £5000 besides the £2000 from my agents. Where ever you buy the house, depend on it I shall be content. I am tired of the war and long for nothing but to get to you. On the 1st of October, peace or war I hope to sail for England. Nothing but a conviction in my own mind of enemy's fleet coming out of port in a week afterwards should tempt me to stay one day after that time.

The *Theseus* was one of the ships concerned in the business at home for which scare her late Captain Aylmer left her fancying her crew intended to

---

[1] This in reply to an query from his wife (see Appendix, p. 361, Mrs. Nelson's letter of April 10).

[2] John Culverhouse, lieutenant of the *Minerve*; promoted captain in 1802.

carry her into Cadiz and had always a party of marines under arms. I have found a more orderly set of men. A few nights ago a paper was dropped on the quarter deck. I send you a copy.

> 'Success attend Admiral Nelson
> God bless Captain Miller we thank
> them for the officers they have placed over us.
> We are happy and comfortable and will shed every drop
> of blood in our veins to support them, and the
> name of the *Theseus* shall be immortalised as high as
> *Captain*'s ship's company.'

I must not get too far or you will not get your letter. I command the advanced squadron and have to hope the Dons will have the goodness to come out very soon. Then I stay not one hour after it. I have my dear father's letter of May 22nd God bless him and you and believe me your most affectionate husband, HORATIO NELSON.

Joliffe[1] is acting lieutenant of the *Bellerophon*. I never have had an opportunity of knowing him personally, but have had the opportunity of being in a small degree useful to him. Lt. Thompson I know very well a most excellent officer is 1st lieutenant of the *Irresistible* and if the Spanish fleet comes out will assuredly be a captain is in my squadron. Three last verses of a poem, I know not the author.

> 'True British valour has appalled
> The proud insulting foe
> What late was Nelson's Olio called
> Has laid the Dons full low.
>
> This hero brave old England's boast
> Grappled two ships along
> Forced them to strike on their own coast
> And lasting laurels won.
>
> Long will this fact in history shine
> Give me the fair sex say
> A Nelson for my valentine
> On this auspicious day.'

AN OLD SAILOR.

To Lady Nelson,[2] Bath.

[1] See letter No. 167, p. 308. Joliffe and Thompson were recommended to Nelson by his wife (see Appendix, p. 364, May 8, 1797).
[2] The first letter bearing this form of address. Nelson's knighthood was gazetted on May 27.

No. 189

[Nicolas, II, p. 399, part]

Theseus, off Cadiz,
June 29, 1797

MY DEAREST FANNY,—Your letter of May 29th I received 7 or 8 days ago and yesterday yours of June 5th. I wrote April 20 or 21st and sent it to the *Ville de Paris*[1] by a cutter, and also another in the beginning of May, but I did not join the fleet till 25th May since which time I have wrote frequently. Rest assured my dear Fanny, of my most perfect love affection and esteem for your person and character, which the more I see of the world the more I must admire. The imperious call of honour to serve my country is the only thing which keeps me a moment from you, and a hope that by staying a little longer it may enable you to enjoy those little luxuries beyond necessaries which you so highly merit. I pray God it may soon be peace and that we may get into the cottage. Nothing but a thorough conviction that I should do wrong (which you would not I am sure wish me to do) shall induce me to stay here beyond October 1st.

I have to thank many friends for their kind congratulations and have had a long letter and genealogy from the York genealogist[2] however I have referred him to Maurice telling him to enquire who is to pay the fees for I shall not. The Admiralty have paid Sir J. J. and will I suppose pay mine but this I have desired him to ascertain.[3] I have sent Maurice my supporters, crest and motto, on the one side a sailor properly habited holding in his hand the broad pendant on a staff, trampling on a Spanish flag, on the other the British lion tearing the Spanish flag the remnants hanging down and flag in tatters. Crest the *San Josef*. Motto: The Rector's turned into English 'Faith and Works'. I hope you will like them.

I have not a moment to spare. The Admiral tells me I shall be too late which I fear. Josiah is well. God bless you and believe me, your most affectionate HORATIO NELSON.

To Lady Nelson, Bath.

[1] Flagship of Sir John Jervis, now Earl of St. Vincent.
[2] Sir George Naylor, York Herald in the College of Arms, and genealogist of the Order of the Bath.
[3] The fees for registering Nelson's arms and supporters, and for his nomination and installation as a Knight of the Bath, came to £428 7s. 5d., which was paid by the Treasury.

No. 190

[Nicolas, II, p. 399, part, under date 29 June]

Theseus,
June 30, 1797

MY DEAREST FANNY,—I was yesterday obliged to cut my letter short, and it was all that Weatherhead could do by exertion to get it aboard the *Raven*.

Flags of truce which come frequently to us tell us that Pitt has resigned and that peace is almost certain. I pray God it may be true and that I may very soon return to a cottage which I hope you will have been able to purchase before this time. I do not see the necessity of your taking the trouble of seeing it. We must rely on some person's judgement.

Our hopes are again revived of seeing the Viceroy of Mexico. One of his convoy has fallen into our *mouths* but he had not sailed when this vessel left Havannah May 9th but he was daily in expectation of a 74 with money from Mexico and on her appearance off the harbour the fleet was to immediately put to sea. But I would not recommend that we should purchase a very *large* estate on the expectation it would be too good luck, and the Dons have numbers of small vessels at sea to give them notice of our position.

I fancy you may rely that I shall bring my head back for I am confident the Dons will not come out till they are more afraid of the consequences of staying in port than coming out to meet us. Our fleet as yet is most perfectly quiet and orderly and will remain so if government act with proper spirit at the Nore[1] and execute some of the principals. It would be great humanity, for some unfortunate fellows will mutiny too late and will suffer from mistaken humanity. If government gives in, what can we expect of this fleet? I shall believe we shall all be at Spithead. Mankind are all alike and if these people find their brethren in England get their ignorant wishes complied with by being troublesome, it is human nature for others to take the same methods.

Bolton is a lieutenant of a 74 and will be removed into the first good frigate which may be vacant. Hoste would have been the same but I cannot get his time out. Poor Weatherhead cannot be managed. When peace comes I shall change him into a frigate which will remain out.

With your approbation I intend my next winter's gift at Burnham to be fifty good large blankets with the letter N wove in the centre that they may not be sold. I believe they may be made for about 15 shillings of the very

---

[1] The mutiny at the Nore had followed that at Spithead, and there were further outbreaks in the North Sea, Mediterranean and Jamaican fleets during the summer.

best quality and they will last some person or other for seven years at least, and it will not take off from anything the parish might give. I wish enquiry to be made and the blankets ordered of some worthy man, I believe they are made at Frone. They are to be at my father's disposal in November.

Josiah is very well and threatens to write you a letter but I would not have you expect one. My situation with Sir John Jervis is as usual he will not be very fond, should unfortunately the war continue, to let me go home but it must be something very good to induce me to stay after September 30th. Give my kind remembrance to my father etc. etc. when you write and believe me your most affectionate husband, HORATIO NELSON.

P.S. None of us have got our proper notification of our honours, we expect a ship from England every day.

To Lady Nelson, Bath.

No. 191

Theseus,
July 4, 1797

MY DEAREST FANNY,—The *Kangaroo* is in sight and is to hold no connection with, at present, our uncontaminated fleet, therefore you must have this line or nothing. I am most perfectly well and ever believe me my dearest love, your most affectionate HORATIO NELSON.

Josiah is perfectly well. Kind remembrances to my father, no letters from the vessel are yet delivered to the fleet.

To Lady Nelson, Bath.

No. 192

Theseus,
July 11, 1797

MY DEAREST FANNY,—Boyle of the *Kangaroo* is in sight who proceeds directly for England and the convoy is also in view from Lisbon by whom I hope for letters from you.

We have nothing new here. Our bombardment of Cadiz[1] and the Spanish fleet have forced the latter into a nook of the harbour. What a despicable set of wretches they must be. They will not come out this war,

---

[1] Cadiz was bombarded on the night of July 3, and again on July 5, much damage being done to the town.

at least whilst we are off the port. Reports are that the Havannah convoy is stopped but I do not believe it on the contrary I believe they are near Europe.

Our mutinies are I hope stopped here, the Admiral having made some severe examples, but they were absolutely necessary.[1]

We are all well and I adhere to my resolution of leaving this fleet on October 1st. With most affectionate regards believe me your most affectionate husband, HORATIO NELSON.

To Lady Nelson, Bath.

No. 193

[Nicolas, II, p. 412, part]

Theseus,
July 12, 1797

MY DEAREST FANNY,—I am always sorry when you are disappointed, but if you recollect that I was absent on service it must be very uncertain when I should return to the fleet. From April 12th to May 23rd was my absence for although a cutter left me when I joined the Port Ferraio convoy to announce my junction and although I wrote one on May 1st yet only the former got to the fleet, the latter I found at Gibraltar and brought it myself to the fleet. Never fancy for a moment you are absent from my thoughts or that I neglect writing. Yesterday after Boyle left me I received yours of June 19th and my father's of June 12th. You will receive my letters wrote since my return in due time but when you know I am sent from the fleet you never ought to calculate on a letter till you know from myself of my return. But you believed the convoy would arrive with the cutter but the fact is the cutter was 7 days in doing what took the convoy 32 days to Gibraltar and there I left them and they did not join the fleet till the 7 or 8 of June, but I have done.

I never saw Sheppards Spring[2] nor do I fancy if it was within our purse it would suit us. A cottage is absolutely all that we can look to, and £2000 is the fullest extent which we can afford for it, and if you do not object I should like Norfolk in preference to any other part of the kingdom but do as you please and I have no doubt but I shall be satisfied. I should be glad if the house was bought.

I am sure the time is past for doing anything for George Tobin, had

---

[1] Four mutineers of the *St. George* were tried by court martial. They were hanged the next day, July 8, although it was a Sunday.
[2] The house near Ringwood built by the Matchams.

he been with me which was offered he would have long since have been a captain, and I should have liked it as being most exceedingly pleased with him. You surprise me about Lieutenant Pierson[1] I never heard a syllable about it. However they know their own concerns best but I should not have approved of him for a son-in-law, although I believe him to be a very good young man, but I don't think he will make a pleasant husband. He is too *nice* in his dress and fidgetty and has not the knack of being contented with his situation.

Respecting Hoste I have desired his father to send out his time and he may of course apply where he pleases for interest with Sir John Jervis and if you write him pray say so. I still adhere to my determination of going home on October 1st or immediately as we have an account of peace. Sir John has promised me a frigate to take my body and my rags may travel in due time by the *Theseus*.

It was not Captain Wilsford but a Colonel Drinkwater, who wrote the last siege of Gibraltar, who wrote the history of the action. Capt. W. has not abilities for such a thing. His compliments to me are great but I am confident not a word beyond the truth. My late affair here will not I believe lower me in the opinion of the world and I hope it will be my last exertion this year.

Your former direction was right and this not so, but any direction will find H. N. you will recollect the Italian compliment I told you of. 'There is but one H. N. in the world.'[2] I have had flattery enough to make me vain and success enough to make me confident. Josiah is very well he reads all your letters. He does not believe Mr. P.[3] will marry any one who has not a great deal of money and he believes Mr. P. will turn merchant. I have wrote this long letter to be ready for I never know half an hour. The happy termination of the mutiny at the Nore gives us all great pleasure.

Ever believe me your most affectionate husband, HORATIO NELSON.

July 14th: As I may be absent for a short time do not be anxious about letters for you cannot hear from me.

To Lady Nelson, Bath.

No. 194

Theseus,
July 14, 1797

MY DEAREST FANNY,—I have ordered the undermentioned agents to pay to you or your order such proportions of prize money as may be due to me as a flag officer in Sir John Jervis's fleet for prizes placed in their hands.

---

[1] Lieutenant Charles Pierson, who married Lieutenant William Bolton's sister, Mary Ann Bolton, had been with Nelson during the Corsican campaign and on February 14.
[2] See letter No. 158, p. 299.
[3] Lieutenant Charles Pierson.

Santa Natalia (*Lively*).   Maude, Downing Street—about £600 sterling supposed.

El Mem Amigo
Monseratta   } Messrs. Atkins, Walbrook, London— sup-
Santa Teresa   posed upwards of £100

Jean Baptista by the *Lively* { James Sykes, No. 22 Arundel
Andromache and N*iger*   Street, Strand—not known,
                                                     believed about £60.

I fancy you will not find it amount to much, £7 or 800 but it is better in your hands than that I should pay my agents for receiving it. You must not expect to hear very soon from me as I am going a little cruise.[1] You had better write an order for the above agents to pay you or your order.

     Ever your most affectionate HORATIO NELSON.

To Lady Nelson, Bath.

No. 195
[Nicolas, II, p. 436, under date 3 August]

Theseus, at Sea,
August 5, 1797

MY DEAREST FANNY,—I am so confident of your affection that I feel the pleasure you will receive will be equal whether my letter is wrote by my right hand or left, it was the chance of war and I have great reason to be thankful, and I know it will add much to your pleasure in finding that Josiah under God's providence was principally instrumental in saving my life.[2] As to my health it never was better and now I hope soon to return to you, and my country I trust will not allow me any longer to linger in want of that pecuniary assistance which I have been fighting the whole war to preserve to her. But I shall not be surprised to be neglected and forgot as probably I shall no longer be considered as useful. However I shall feel rich if I continue to enjoy your affection. The cottage is now more necessary than ever.[3]

[1] In April Nelson had proposed that an attack should be made on Teneriffe, in the hopes of capturing the Spanish treasure-ships. The plan was put into effect when news was received that *El Principe d'Asturias* was at Santa Cruz.

[2] The attack on Santa Cruz was made on July 24 (see Appendix, p. 371, for Nelson's narrative). It was unsuccessful. Nelson was badly wounded in the right arm, which was amputated by the surgeon, Thomas Eshelby. This is the first letter written to his wife with his left hand. A copy of it, in Lady Nelson's hand, is among the Bridport papers at the N.M.M. Josiah, by his promptness, stopped the bleeding of Nelson's wound (see Appendix for Lady Nelson's account, p. 374).

[3] A property near Ipswich was put up for sale by auction on September 26 which Nelson bought for £2,000 (see Appendix, p. 379).

You will see by the papers J. Weatherhead[1] is gone. Poor fellow he lived 4 days after he was shot. I shall not close this letter till I join the fleet which seems distant for it's been calm these 3 days past. I am fortunate in having a good surgeon on board, in short I am much more recovered than any could have expected.

I beg neither you or my father will think much of this mishap. My mind has long been made up to such an event. God bless you and believe me your most affectionate husband, HORATIO NELSON.

August 16th: Just joined the fleet, perfectly well and shall be with you perhaps as soon as this letter.[2]

Good Earl St. Vincent has made Josiah master and commander.[3] I shall come to Bath the moment permission comes from the Admiralty for me to strike my flag, unless Sir Peter[4] feels himself authorised to grant me leave of absence, when the first you hear of me will be at the door.

God bless you and my father and ever believe me your most affectionate HORATIO NELSON.

To Lady Nelson, Bath.

APPENDIX

Lord Spencer to Nelson[5]

Admiralty,
January 15, 1796

SIR,—I have to acknowledge the receipt (on the 11th instant) of your letter from Genoa dated the 14th November last inclosing a public one to the Board which I laid before them.

I hope you will give me credit when I assure you that I should feel considerable satisfaction in having it in my power to gratify your wishes respecting a distinguishing pendant, as I know of no one whose zeal and activity in the service is more deserving of any distinction which can with propriety be conferred, but as the service on which you have been employed in Vado Bay is of so very temporary a nature and as there are already so many flags employed on the Mediterranean station, I am afraid

---

[1] Lieutenant John Weatherhead.

[2] Nelson returned to England in the *Seahorse*, arrived at Spithead on September 1 and was granted leave to strike his flag and go on shore for the recovery of his wounds.

[3] Josiah Nisbet was given command of the *Dolphin*, hospital ship.

[4] Sir Peter Parker, Nelson's admiral when he was in the *Albemarle*, was commander-in-chief at Portsmouth.

[5] N.M.M. MS. 9960, Croker collection in the Phillipps papers.

it will be impossible for me at present to recommend the adoption of the measure.

I am sir with great respect your very obedient humble servant, SPENCER.

Captain Horatio Nelson, H.M.S. *Agamemnon*, Leghorn.

Nelson to the Duke of Clarence[1]

Agamemnon, off Genoa,
April 23, 1796

SIR,—I wish it had been in my power to give your Royal Highness a good account of the opening of the campaign, but as the news good or bad must be known I think it is proper for me to give you an exact account of what has passed.

I shall first call to your recollection a letter of mine during the winter wherein I tell you that I am informed from the French themselves that they would open the campaign with 80,000 men and by the first of May would lay siege to Turin or Milan. My information I have never known much to fail at least in the attempt, and it is I grieve to say most likely to be accomplished. I shall give your Royal Highness a brief account of the campaign as far as report goes for we have no official information from the General.

On Monday April 11th the Austrians took possession of Voltri with 10,000 men. About 300 of the enemy were killed, wounded or made prisoners, about 4,000 men effected their retreat from the attack being given 12 hours before the time fixed by General Beaulieu and before the General's arrival or I am satisfied not a French man could have escaped and by what has followed the disasters commenced from the escape of these troops. Our ships so entirely command the road that had the General's concerted time and plan been attended to, I again assert none of the enemy could have escaped. These troops retired during the day and night of the 11th to Monte Nota about 8 or 9 miles back of Savona where the enemy had about 2000 men posted. At daybreak General Argenteau attacked this post with about 4000 men not knowing of the reinforcement. He was repulsed and pursued with great loss, 900 Piedmontese troops 500 Austrians, field pieces etc. fell into the enemy's hands. The killed we know not but it was hard fought. On the 13th and 14th the French forced Dego and Speigno which were well defended but they were carried by superior numbers. On the morning of the 15th the Austrian troops posted at Sassello on the right flank and rather in the rear of the enemy (as we should say on the starboard quarter) attacked the enemy at Speigno and

---

[1] N.M.M. M. 22, Autograph collection—from the same series as the letter of October 1, 1795.

totally routed them, retook the 20 pieces of cannon which the Austrians had lost but also all that of the enemy, but unfortunately pursuing his advantage too far he fell in with the main body of the enemy who after an obstinate resistance of 4 hours totally defeated him, to add to this misfortune General Beaulieu had sent 5 battalions from Aqui to support this brave officer Colonel Waskanovick, but alas they arrived too late and added to the triumph of the enemy. By the best accounts I can learn the Austrians have not lost less than 10,000 men, killed, wounded and prisoners. The French loss has also been great but they can better spare their men than the Austrians. General Beaulieu has now withdrawn all his troops from the mountains and is encamped at a place called Bosco on a plain between Novi and Alexandria. I am yet in hopes if the French attack him on the plain he may yet get on by giving them a total defeat. The Austrians seem to have been ruined by loss of posts. I dare say it was necessary to possess them but they were lost by superior numbers coming against them. One column of 20,000 French is on the side of Ceva one of the passes into the plain of Piedmont. If they carry this post the road to Turin is open.

Genoa, 2 oclock: The mails are just arrived from Milan and I rejoice that affairs are not so bad as was reported. General Arginteau is arrested and sent prisoner to Pavia on strong suspicion of treason. Reports say the French are repulsed at Ceva with great loss but the Turin post is not yet arrived.

Believe me ever your Royal Highness's most faithful servant, HORATIO NELSON.

Lord Spencer to Nelson[1]

Admiralty,
May 26, 1796

SIR,—I have to acknowledge the receipt of your letter of the 29th of April, and beg you will not make any apologies for writing, as it is very satisfactory to hear from you when we can in any way. On this occasion we have not received any letters from Sir J. Jervis therefore your intelligence respecting the vessels cut from under the batteries of Loano is the only one we have of it. I very sincerely hope that the six sail you mention may come out, as I have no doubt they will be well accounted for if they do and we much want to hear of some good news by sea to make amends for all the disasters we have lately had to lament on shore.

I am sir, with great truth your very obedient humble servant, SPENCER.

Captain Horatio Nelson, *Agamemnon.*

[1] N.M.M. MS. 9960, Croker collection in the Phillipps papers.

Sir John Jervis to Nelson[1]

A

Victory, off Toulon,
May 11, 1796

DEAR SIR,—Your coup at Loana will have a good effect. I have only to lament the severe wound Lt. Noble has received, which I flatter myself will not deprive you, and his country of such a character. . . .

So much has passed between Lord Spencer, Baron Hotham, and me on the subject of Capt. Sutton going home in the *Egmont*, and the *Goliath* coming out indents so exactly with it, that I shall order Admiral Linzee to hoist his flag on board her, and give him charge of the convoy, and as I cannot possibly do without you in the Gulf of Genoa, I am arranging the fleet in two divisions, for I will not have a third commander under the rank of Admiral unless you are the man. I probably shall receive Lord Spencer's answer to my letter about your flag and learn what the Board says of your present situation and broad pendant soon, which will point out the rest. . . .

Most truly yours, J. JERVIS.

B

Victory, off Toulon,
May 22, 1796

DEAR SIR,—The messenger having brought orders respecting the strength of the convoy which requires my sending the *Princess Royal* and *Agamemnon* instead of the *Egmont*. I send commission for exchange between Captain Sutton and you, trusting that you will serve with me to the end of this war. I shall not think it right to remove the squadron from the Gulf of Genoa while there is a ray of hope that the Austrians will rally, but you may take your twenty days at Pisa baths, leaving the *Egmont* in Leghorn Road for the protection of the factory, and you will be at hand to attend anything which may require your personal interposition.

You mentioned an officer of the army that was useful to you, I therefore have desired Admiral Linzee to remove him, and the same number of men we took from the *Egmont* into her with you, your officers and boat's crew.

When the service you are now upon is over, and you join me, I shall

---

[1] Extracts from the letters received by Nelson: N.M.M. MS. 9960, Croker collection in the Phillipps papers.

continue your broad pendant until your flag or some other arrives. Mrs. Calder writes that the promotion is to take place soon. I therefore hope I shall see your flag hoisted e'er long. Most truly yours, J. JERVIS.

C

Victory, off Toulon,
June 1, 1796

DEAR SIR,—Capt. Sutton declining the exchange I suggested for his accommodation, I cannot consistent with my instructions keep the *Agamemnon* crippled as she is any longer, in these seas. I deplore the loss of your services and if Sir Charles Knowles continues in the sentiments he expressed to a brother officer at San Fiorenzo a few days ago I will make another effort to keep you with me, by settling an exchange with him, on a presumption that your health will enable you to serve, of this you alone are competent to decide. What ever may be the event, you will hold a lasting place in the esteem and regard of, dear sir, your very sincere and obedient servant, J. JERVIS.

D

July 13, 1796

DEAR SIR,—Mr. Gregory who made great haste to England and back brought me a letter from Lord Spencer expressing a great desire to promote you to the flag, but confessed he could not face another promotion. He however has approved of the distinguishing pendant. I forwarded a letter from his Lordship to you via St. Fiorenzo two days ago. . . .

E

July 14, 1796

DEAR SIR,—I congratulate you most heartily upon the event of your enterprise at Porto Ferraio. The Pope having made his peace, I have counter-ordered *Petterell*, *L'Eclair*, *La Sardine* and *Comet*. The three first named will be at yours and the Viceroy's orders, the last must return to me. I very much approve all the steps you have taken about Leghorn and will give you an official to say so by the *Excellent*. . . .

F

Secret   September 5, 1796

DEAR SIR,—Lady Jervis wants an elegant light plain velvet for a birthday suit on the Queen's anniversary, the colour to be a rich blue, will you have

z

the goodness to employ one of your friends at Genoa to get it for her? The velvet must be of the finest kind, otherwise the weight of it will be too much for her to carry. I am totally ignorant of the quantity, but it is only for a robe, the petticoats now worn, being always of white crape or gauze which the ladies embroider or ornament for themselves. I dare say Madame Coffurene knows all about it. . . .

G

Victory, off Toulon,
September 25, 1796

Secret

DEAR SIR,—All our operations are at an end by the arrival of orders to evacuate Corsica and retreat down the Mediterranean. Thus circumstanced I fear nothing can be done in favour of the merchants at Genoa. I however inclose a letter with a flying seal to the Consul which you will avail yourself of or not as you shall judge best. You must go over to Bastia immediately and co-operate with the Viceroy in retiring the troops from the outposts, keeping Leghorn in blockade to prevent a descent pending this difficult operation. Yours most truly, J. JERVIS.

H

Victory, San Fiorenzo Bay,
13 October, [1796]

DEAR SIR,—The moment I was assured of your arrival at Bastia I felt perfectly at ease with respect to the embarkation etc. My letter of this morning informed you of my wishes touching Leghorn, which in truth you have anticipated. Capt. Calder is endeavouring to send you two transports under the care of the *Excellent*. I wish you to keep up the water of the line of battle ships, as to the rest you will do it better than I can direct. Yours most truly, J. JERVIS.

Sir John Jervis to Sir Gilbert Elliott[1]

A

Victory, San Fiorenzo Bay,
April 5, 1796

. . . I enclose Capt. Nelson's intelligence from Genoa, he is very sanguine in his expectations of a vigorous campaign on the part of the Austrians,

[1] Extracts from the letters received by Sir Gilbert Elliott: N.M.M. MS. 9217, Minto papers.

and I have added to his squadron and dubbed him a Commodore with view to an effectual co-operation. He sailed at the same time with the *Speedy* and transports to resume his station. . . .

B

Victory, off Toulon,
July 14, 1796

. . . I refer you to Commodore Nelson for everything relative to co-operation with Corsican privateers, which appears a very good plan, he is a reasonable and disinterested man in money matters and will come into every proposition you make. . . .

C

Victory, off Toulon,
July 25, 1796

. . . I am very glad you have a little damped the ardour of Commodore Nelson respecting the republic of Genoa, he is an excellent partisan but does not sufficiently weigh consequences. . . .

D

Victory, off Toulon,
August 12, 1796

It being by no means improbable that Langara and Richery may attempt to cut me up, I think it right to concentrate my force and have dispatched orders by the *Lively* to Commodore Nelson to send the *Captain* and *Diadem* to me immediately, he will hoist his broad pendant on board a frigate as an established Commodore and I will give him all I have.

E

Victory, off Toulon,
August 15, 1796

I do not lose a moment in sending back the *Comet* to authorize Commodore Nelson to keep the *Captain* and *Diadem* for some time longer in order to facilitate the coup you propose, heavy artillery and every other implement will be furnished from his squadron. When Leghorn is evacuated the Commodore has directions to proceed to Civita Vecchia with your manifesto, which I subscribe to most willingly. . . .

F

Victory, off Toulon,
August 22, 1796

. . . I agree with you in every part of your reasoning respecting Leghorn, the Commodore is the best and fittest fellow in the world to conduct the naval part yet his zeal does now and then (not often) outrun his discretion. If Marshall Wurmset has fairly beat the enemy in the field, prison and the stiletto will do the rest and the attempt on Leghorn ought to be made. . .

G

Victory, off Toulon,
September 25, 1796

Secret

In my judgement the best mode of evacuating Corsica is to contract the posts with as much secrecy as possible, and I have directed Commodore Nelson to come over to you immediately to concert the means. . . .

H

Victory, off Toulon,
September 26, 1796

. . . I wish very much to be at your elbow, but critically circumstanced as I am I dare not leave this position at present. The moment I know of Admiral Man being en route to join me, I will make the best of my way to you, in the mean while Commodore Nelson, whose zeal and activity cannot be exceeded, will carry into execution all your plans. . . .

I

Victory, in San Fiorenzo Bay,
October 17, 1796

. . . In any event the evacuation of the island of Corsica if it had not been at this moment begun is absolutely necessary—in the first place because my instructions have not varied upon this head, in the second that should the fleet be compelled to go to Naples or Sicily you would be at the mercy of those devils at Leghorn, who malgre the unexampled vigilance of Commodore Nelson and his squadron would get over and carry Bastia weakly garrisoned as it is. . . . .

Sir Gilbert Elliot to Nelson[1]

A

Bastia,
July 6, 1796

Secret

MY DEAR SIR,—I have this moment sent a letter to San Fiorenzo to acquaint you that it is resolved to attempt possessing ourselves of Porto Ferraio and that the troops may embark this very evening. I am therefore to request such naval aid as you are able to afford. Whatever you can spare should come instantly to Bastia. If the expedition should have sailed before the arrival of what you send, I will endeavour to have the intelligence meet you at sea, in which case the ships had better make directly for Elba. We have transports here, but the *Vanneau* and *Rose* are our only men of war. I have already hinted to the Admiral the possibility of my calling on the Navy for aid on this service and there can be no doubt of his approving it. I should hope the operation would not be tedious.

Understanding that you have sailed from San Fiorenzo I send this to meet you at sea.

Believe me your obedient and faithful humble servant, GILBERT ELLIOT.

To Commodore Nelson, H.M.S. *Captain.*

B

Bastia,
July 17, 1796

MY DEAR SIR,—This is I fear the first opportunity I have had of thanking you for your zealous and successful services and those of your squadron at Porto Ferraio, but I have not omitted the mention of them elsewhere, and I shall not be suspected by you of being insensible to them. The fact is that a point of delicacy towards the Governor of Porto Ferraio forced me to be mysterious to the last moment, and I was on this account so long in soliciting your aid that I was very nearly deprived of it. All proved fortunate at last however and I congratulate you once more with all my heart on this fresh sprig of laurel added to your former crown.

Capt. Cockburn has delivered to me your letters and all the good intelligence you have been so good as to send. He has also brought me back the bills which I had drawn payable to your order, not having been able to negotiate them at Genoa. Understanding however, that if they were

[1] N.M.M. MS. 9960, Croker collection in the Phillipps papers.

made out in smaller sums, they might be negotiated, I have furnished them with other bills, payable also to your order, which I hope you will be so good as to dispatch without delay to Genoa, for we are *entirely exhausted* and nothing that I know of is more *urgent* in Corsica, than to obtain a very *speedy* supply of cash. I reserve myself on the subject of the Genoese memorials concerning the capture of their vessels, for a separate letter and I beg you to believe me ever my dear Sir, yours most faithfully and affectionately, GILBERT ELLIOT.

Nelson to Sir Gilbert Elliot[1]

Captain, Leghorn Roads,
August 5, 1796

Private

MY DEAR SIR,—Leghorn is from all accounts last night in such a state that a respectable force landed would, I have every reason to suppose, insure the immediate possession of the town. I know many things must be considered, not less than 1000 troops should be sent to which I will add every soldier in my squadron and a party of seamen to make a show. In every way pray consider this as private and excuse my opinions. I well know the difficulty of getting a proper person to command this party. Firmness and that the people of Leghorn should know the person commanding will most assuredly have a great effect. A cordial co-operation with me (for vanity apart no one is so much feared or respected in Leghorn as myself) is absolutely necessary. A declaration from your Excellency would I am sure have the happiest effect. I am going farther. We know the jealousy of the Army against the Navy, but I am by the King's commission a Colonel in the Army from June 1st. 1795. I should like such a man as Duncan, he receiving your directions to consult no one but myself, but I have most unfortunately a Major, now I fancy Lieutenant Colonel, Saunderson on board who could not serve under Major Duncan. If I landed as Colonel of course I should command the whole, and I most certainly should not call Mr. Saunderson to my councils. But I feel almost the impossibility of your settling this business although I am sure it would be for His Majesty's service and if my character is known the internal regulations of the troops should rest by order under the Major Duncan, and I should only interfere in the great scale.

I will however it may hurt the feelings of Major Saunderson keep him on board with six soldiers. He shall never command in co-operation with me, therefore do not let this be an objection.

[1] N.M.M. MS. 9217, Minto papers (Nicolas, Vol. II, p. 233, without all the names).

You will consider, Sir, all these points and form a much better judgement than I can, only give me credit that the nearest wish of my heart is to serve my King and Country at every personal risk and consideration.

Believe me ever your Excellency's most faithful, HORATIO NELSON.

It has ever pleased God to prosper all my undertakings and I feel confident of his blessing on this occasion. I ever consider my motto 'Fides et opera'.

N.B. 24 hours will do the business. Send an active officer.

To His Excellency the Viceroy.

Sir Gilbert Elliot to Nelson[1]

A

Bastia,
August 6, 1796

Secret

MY DEAR SIR,—I am much pleased at your concurring so heartily in the idea I mentioned in my last letter, and at your thinking it so practicable. To say the truth I have already written to the Admiral on that subject, and expect his answer daily.

You know my dear sir, my entire and unlimited confidence in you, and the high opinion I have acquired, not by report but by the testimony of my own eyes and experience of your zealous, and as you say, hitherto successful services. You will therefore attribute it to anything but want of confidence or friendship if I find it absolutely impossible to fall in with the idea you have suggested concerning the command on shore. You may have heard in part, but you never can know or even imagine, what I have had to do and to endure from professional feelings, and jealousies in the military. I do not mean as between Army and Navy but with my own situation, and with each other. What you mention would blow us all up at once. However the truth is that if the expedition takes place I have reason to think the General[2] himself would command the troops, as it is of sufficient importance and magnitude to justify that step and to give him an inclination to be present in person. If I were writing to most other men I should fear personal feelings in you on this explanation, but I know enough of you to be quite certain that the King's service is the sole object that can either interest your feelings or animate your exertions, and I am therefore afraid of no devilry.

[1] N.M.M. MS. 9960, Croker collection in the Phillipps papers.
[2] General de Burgh, commander of the forces in Corsica.

Now for the business itself. I am not prepared to say positively *yes*, because the General to whom I communicated fully my wishes on this subject this morning, has not yet entirely formed his opinion on the practicability. You shall hear from me *very soon*. In the meanwhile I may say that on canvassing the matter pretty fully with the General this morning, I was confirmed in my opinion that we can spare 1500 regulars and add 1000 Corsican volunteers if not more. The General seems to think it possible we might be ready to embark in ten days and I am sure it could not be sooner. I reckon our force about 3000 including marines and seamen. Surely the Tuscans would join us. You will find General de Burgh one of the most gentlemanlike in the world. He is cool and well skilled in his profession; and his reputation for spirit and courage is established on sure testimony of his former conduct and actions, which have been very distinguished in this war.

For artillery, especially heavy, if wanted we must be obliged to you. If the thing is determined on, the preparation will be set about tomorrow, and you shall have the earliest possible notice. In the meanwhile the most perfect secrecy will be observed by us.

Believe me ever my dear Sir, your most faithful and affectionate GILBERT ELLIOT.

To Commodore Nelson.

B

Bastia,
August 30, 1796

MY DEAR SIR,—You know ere now, the final relinquishment of our expedition. I am much mortified at the necessity I was under to abandon it from a variety of reasons which seemed to conspire against this very important enterprise. The matter is now completely settled by the departure of the 100th Regiment, which is ordered immediately to Gibraltar. Mr. Wyndham went to Naples to solicit co-operation from thence. I wrote to Sir William Hamilton to the same effect, but they will not stir while the affairs of Lombardy are doubtful. I must ever be grateful to you however for your zeal on this and all other occasions of public service.

We have completely defeated two republican attempts to create fresh sedition in Corsica, within this month. All is quiet for the present. But looking out for Gentili and his ragamuffins from Leghorn. The Admiral has determined to give us effectual aid in guarding the coast on both sides of the island. I cannot sufficiently admire the resources he finds where other men would only grumble and despair.

Pray send us better news than of late. The Spanish war seems to blow over. I hope the Austrian peace will do so also.

I am writing in more than usual haste and can only beg you believe me ever my dear sir, most faithfully and affectionately yours, GILBERT ELLIOT.

To Commodore Nelson.

Mrs. Nelson to Nelson

I

Bath,
February 8, 1797

MY DEAREST HUSBAND,—I hope you will receive many of my letters through the hands of Admiral Young. He has been very kind in promising to forward them for me.

My anxiety to hear from you was very great. I waited patiently as long as I could, at last I wrote to Lord Hood, who made all the enquiries he could for me and sent me Admiral Young's letter when I had the great happiness of learning you were quite well after the action with the Spanish frigates, thank my God for it. Admiral Y. says I must not expect to hear from you, therefore am endeavouring to make myself as easy as my great anxiety for you will let me. There is a report that Sir. J. J. has received the reinforcements I hope it is true that will be some comfort to me, as I *know where you are* (I am told it) or wrote it in confidence.

I pray God to protect and grant you a continuance of your great successes. I long for to be with you. He thought it was good to make holiday and to feast a little. Our good father I am sorry has not been quite so stout lately, he is better again I assure you, it was a fever and cold. I had never seen him so much indisposed. He has taken his walk again and I flatter myself he will be well soon, these colds have been general. Will was much alarmed although dead drunk. I was quite well again, but fright I believe has given me a cold. Bett Thurlow who has long thought Bath did not agree with her left me in the midst of it and without my having a servant. I am better without her, she was dissatisfied and never contented and a most wretched temper. The characters of servants in this town is I am sorry to say very bad and of the two evils I preferred her, knowing her temper and only wished her to stay till we returned into Norfolk or my dear husband was in England.

Our father's stay here I sometimes think uncertain. However the Matchams have just wrote they shall be with him in May to look for a house. They are determined upon disposing of Shepherd Spring, and have written to London to a friend upon the subject. This determination has given our father uneasiness, he thinks Mr. M. will soon be tired of a situation near Bath. However they are fixed upon it. Maurice I hope will write to you himself. He wrote me a long letter. I wrote to him to make enquiries of you for me, he did it but he could not tell me as much as Lord H. Maurice has received orders to be in readiness but what they intend doing with him, he could not tell me. Sir A. Hammond says he cannot be spared, £300 a year and his old situation are his terms. It is to be finally settled when Lord Spencer returns to London, he is here.

A gentleman belong to the Pay Office accosted our father the other day in the Pump Room: told him he was an acquaintance of Mr. Nelson and to his knowledge the business stood still in the absence of Mr. M. Nelson and that they all knew they could not do without him at the office. Mr. Nelson says this person who had a long chat in the Pump Room was not a young man and looked like a gentleman. I hope his wishes may be complied with. I am sadly afraid S. Nelson is still going on in his old way, so Maurice writes me, that I keep to myself. No occasion to make so good a man as our father more uneasy about him than I know he is already. Mrs. Bolton I heard from, all well. If what I hear is *true* about Sir J. Jervis, the fleet etc. I begin to think you will all be drawing homewards by and by. Sir G. K. Elphingstone, Sir J. J. and Adm. Hotham are to be peers very soon for certain. Don't say I never told you *news*.

Oh my dear husband God bless and protect you, your affectionate wife, FRANCES H. NELSON.

I wrote to Josiah.

Capt. Sotheby I hear is at Clifton. The Achills are at Bath. Lady B.[1] is on board with her husband.

II

Bath,
February 15, 1797

MY DEAREST HUSBAND,—No letter from you since you left Gibraltar. I have written to you generally once a week and sent my letter to Admiral Young. Now I will try the patience of a friend General Trigge, who it seems has written his wife a very cheerful witty letter, upon your telling him 'He looked too old to have a mother living', he says you are a most excellent commander but no courtier. 'Now indeed' said Captain Trigge to me 'My brother is really a good looking man.'

I supped last night at Admiral Dickson's[2] the first time of my doing

---

[1] Lady Bickerton.

[2] Admiral Dickson, promoted rear-admiral in 1794, continued in active service, but without distinction.

such a thing since we came to Bath. Our good father promised to go to bed. I was at home earlier than I expected, it was curiosity, for I heard much of the style etc. of the night entertainments. However this was truly a few acquaintances. Two card tables and all stayed to supper. Admiral Mason is very ill, a stroke of the palsy. Admiral D. seems to think we shall never see him again, it has affected Adm. D. spirits very much. I asked Capt. Trigge for some news of you. He assured me there was not any stirring worthy of telling you.

Everybody are full of the talk of an invasion, that the French are desperate enough to attempt it, but all hands agree in being assured that they will be unsuccessful. While the French were off Ireland, the bank in that country would not discount. The Irish I hear are very much dissatisfied with the conduct of the Fleet. The disposition of the defenders and White Boys were strongly marked in favour of the English government, they showed a determined resolution that they should not land, that they were oppressed and wanted to be relieved but not by French masters.

Norfolk and Suffolk have taken the alarm, a camp is to be formed early in the spring in that part of the Kingdom, such a commotion in this country is attended with great and serious consequences. The miseries it has brought on private families can never be done away. Estates are every day offering for sale. Where this general calamity will end the wisest are quite at a loss. The surrender of Mantua some think may bring forward a general peace. 'They say if the Emperor deserts us we are gone.'

I pray most sincerely Sir J. Jervis has joined you long before this time. Not a syllable do we hear from or of him, only that he was to be made an Irish Lord; that has not taken place. We see Lord Keith Elphingstone and Lord Hotham have kissed hands. I hope Maurice writes you all the news. The accounts from all parts of the West Indies are truly afflicting. The deaths of the unfortunate men who are sent out there are not noticed. Government supresses the accounts reaching the public as much as possible.

I think the contractors for medicines have much to answer. Mr. Searle called on our father and said he was intimately acquainted with one of the Directors of Apothecaries Hall, and that day the directors had received an order to pack up fourteen thousand pounds worth of medicine for the West Indies. The bark which had been sent out had grown in this country, and even the James' powders were so adulterated that no quantity remained I think their act is truly wicked. I am sure the contractors were French people for they do not allow there is a Supreme Being.

I have now on a pair of bracelets made of the chain you sent me. They are beautiful. The Italian flowers I have worn, they have been much noticed. I had occasion to enquire the character of a woman servant of

Mrs. Dillon. She speaks very little English however she told me the Col. [her husband] had charged her to tell Mrs. Nelson the truth for he had heard of Com. Nelson. It was fortunate the Col. had charged her to tell the truth which was three gentlemen were trying to get her and that she had not character enough for *you*. I have a very nice young woman, she comes from Torbay and does not care where she lives.

Our father is better than when I last wrote to you. He seems to have quite unloaded his mind to me about the Matchams. He has again written to them, begging they would consider what they were about, as to his part he did not think they had income enough to live in the neighbourhood of Bath. He says he is sure Mr. M. will never be a settled man. Mrs. Suckling has written me. The sunshine I want must come from the Mediterranean. A feeling temper was certainly a great inconvenience but what will be the pleasure when I see my dear husband. We were speaking of the chance of your coming home which people think very probable. And then your good father says you must not go to the West Indies. The idea of it I verily believe would end his days. He certainly gets very infirm and this fever and cold have shook him very much, but I assure you he is better than when I wrote to you.

He desires me to give you his blessing. I pray God to bless and protect my dearest continuing his great successes. Believe me your affectionate wife, FRANCES N. NELSON.

I long to hear Josiah is with you. Mrs. Napier is very well. Compliments to General Trigge.

Commodore Nelson, *La Minerve*. To the care of General Trigge, Gibraltar.

III

[Nicolas, II, p. 354, extract]

Bath,
February 23, 1797

MY DEAREST HUSBAND,—Yesterday's Gazette authorises our good father and myself to congratulate you on being a flag officer, may it please God your fame and successes increase and continue under this promotion.[1] I never saw anything elevate our father equal to this. He repeated with pleasure the last words 'His good uncle told him that he would live to see you an Admiral.' I was taking my walk. Capt. Frane who is wonderfully polite, made *all* the haste he could from the coffee house to tell the news.

---

[1] There was a promotion of nine post-captains, all of eighteen years' seniority. Nelson's name stood sixth in the list.

All the world were trying to go to the Catch Club on the Ladies' night, tickets were not to be bought. My chance of getting one I thought none, however I asked Sir Thomas Shirley who exerted himself very much and to our great surprise he succeeded and near ten o' clock he sent me a ticket. Our father begged me to go. I dressed and away I went observing to our father 'The Admiral's wife had got a ticket.' Twenty guineas Mrs. Stanhope told me were offered for a lady ticket. There is but one lady night in the season. Everybody of title or fashion were there. Capt. Sotherby has made a second visit, this was a complimentary one.

Now to our own affairs. Mr Baily has behaved very handsomely I wrote to him since my letter to you last week, which I sent to Admiral Young requesting him to give me a satisfactory answer about the interest of the legacy and the annuity which was due in '93. He answered me by bringing £450 in less than a week. He had received orders from Stanley to pay the interest from the legacy, but that I must state an account of the annuity and that he would send it to the West Indies for Mr. Norton and Mr. Hamilton to sanction payment, and that he had strongly recommended their doing it. By my uncle's will they may not pay it unless they like it. Had the times been what they are not, I would have sent part of the money to your agents. When I hear much wiser and experienced people than I can possibly be speak of the necessity of having cash by you I shall keep it, but I may not have it in the same house. I made an offer on any part of it to our father who declined it for the present. All I could say it was your money, and I was sure it was much at his service. He said he was sure of that. Baillie still assures me he will advance the money, the legacies, at the shortest notice for you, and wished it had been double. Kelly drew a bill for the interest which Mr. B. wrote Mrs. K. rather than she should be put to any inconvenience he would advance the money for her, but that he did not or would not allow any gentleman to write to him in the stile Capt. K. had, and that Capt. Kelly might get the money in future from Mr. Stanley, for that he would not advance him any. The estates were very considerably in his debt. Stanley I am told is in debt. How that happened I cannot conceive.

The Bristol men have formed themselves into a body of a thousand men to be a sufficient force to keep the French prisoners while the regular troops march forward to the sea coast. The merchants pay all expense. Mr. E. Baillie government have requested to take the command as Colonel. They say it will be a fine body. Tobin's age exempts him, but two of his sons serve, and says if there is an absolute necessity he will fall into the ranks. Everybody have their alarms. The wooden walls of old England are in the mouth of every one. They pay their commanders little attention but in the time of need.

Admiral Nelson will now be soon home, so they tell me. However I will direct this letter to General Trigge and on Monday the Admiral[1] shall have a letter for you through Lord Hood. Make my compliments to General Trigge, assure him Mrs. Napier desires me to send letters or anything else. She is without exception one of the most charming women I ever had the pleasure of knowing. The Dicksons have left Bath. They talk much of the increase of expenses. It is said money lightly got generally goes fast. He has built a most elegant house, hot houses, etc. His waggon came here for chimney pieces etc. 9 in number.

I long to hear from you. Josiah has not wrote to me since. Our father sends his blessing to you, he is better and I am quite well. I hope you are the same. God bless and protect my dearest husband and child and grant us a happy meeting. Your affectionate wife, FRANCES H. NELSON.

To Rear-Admiral Nelson, *La Minerve*, Gibraltar. To the care of General Trigge, Gibraltar.   Post paid.

IV

Bath,
February 26, 1797

MY DEAREST HUSBAND,—I have this moment returned from calling on Lady Saumarez who tells me she can send you a letter for me. I therefore can only say our good father and myself are well. I have looked for a letter from you this age. The one from Gibraltar December 14th is almost worn out. I have it in my pocket. I have had a letter of congratulations from the Rector and his wife.

Aunt Mary and all send you many good wishes, the Rector thinks of taking his doctor's degree and are determined upon making you a visit as soon as you are landed. I forgot to mention your agents not sending me the account as you desired. I shall write again tomorrow.

Our father's best wishes to you. God bless my dearest husband and believe me your affectionate wife, FRANCES NELSON.

To Rear-Admiral Nelson, *La Minerve*.

V

[Nicolas, II, p. 358]

Bath,
March 11, 1797

MY DEAREST HUSBAND,—Yesterday I received your letter of February 16th, thank God you are well and Josiah. My anxiety was far beyond my powers

[1] Admiral Young.

of expression, M. Nelson and Capt. Locker behaved humanely and attentive to me. They wrote immediate. Capt. Locker assuring me you were perfectly well, Maurice begging me not to believe idle reports, the Gazette saying you were slightly wounded. Altogether my dearest husband, my sufferings were great.

Lady Saumarez came running to tell me she had letters from her husband all this was on this day week. He speaks generously and manly about you and concluded by saying 'Com. Nelson's conduct was above praise.' You were universally the subject of conversation. Lord, Lady and Lady Mary Howe amongst others sent to know how you were, and if I had heard from you. The letters that I have had from common acquaintances will take me at least a week to answer them. But not one from my cousin Kelly. Mr. Sutherland's letter was very handsome. 'I have this instant heard of Sir J. Jervis's battle in which Adm. Nelson bore a most conspicuous part, as he has in every service he was engaged in. The naval officers I heard speak on the subject in the course of yesterday and today all declare that 'he has displayed more professional skill more zeal and more intrepidity than any officer who served this war', and I think it impossible that he can escape being made a lord or at least a K.B. for such honours are sometimes bestowed on men who really deserve them. Be this as it may happen, yet it is the general *wish*!'

Lord Hood wrote that he was astonished to hear that you were there, that he congratulated us on the glorious share Adm. Nelson had in the late action with the Spanish fleet. Lady is very ill and from what his Lordship says, I don't think she will rally again, and begs I will write him all you say about the action. Yesterday after I received your letter I went to Colonel Glover's morning concert, you had I think his regiment on board *Agamemnon*. The colonel or his wife told me something about it. I thought Baron Dillon would have kissed me he said 'Madam, I have seen you at Mr. Glass's therefore I will speak and sincerely do I wish you joy.' In short he announced who I was, they all made their bow, enquired if I had heard from you, hoped you were well. 'What does Adm. Nelson say about the battle, does he not give you the particulars?' The Baron who is very much respected, indeed beloved by everybody, said you had something else to do. I was very glad when they had taken their seats and the misses taken their seats at the pianoforte. This concert consists entirely of gentlemen and lady performers. All the Glovers are musical.

I had a letter from poor Mrs. Bolton expressing her joy in your being well and their concern at not hearing from Wm. Bolton. I have received (yesterday) your letter off Cape St. Vincent Febry. 13th. Mile End House is not yet disposed of, 38 acres of land may be had with it. I will make further enquiries about it. The distance is a great one from London. Our father thinks it too small, the eating room may be, but if it answers in all respects but that a window may be thrown out. I wish you would say something more positive about it.

Our good father has bore his great joy of your being well and the many congratulations very well: but he attempted to walk out, but was obliged to return, however he is pretty well. I shall not be myself till I hear from you again. What can I attempt to say to you about boarding. You have been most wonderfully protected. You have done desperate actions enough. Now may I, indeed I do beg, that you never board again. *Leave* it for *Captains*.

How rejoiced Jo. must have been to have seen you, although it was but an absence of two months.[1]

Tomorrow is our wedding day, when it gave me a dear husband, and my child the best of fathers. I hope he will deserve all the blessings Providence has bestowed on him. Maurice Suckling has written me his very best production, they are the sentiments of an affectionate heart. He would like to be employed with you but won't stir till he hears what command you are to have, in the Channel or North Seas. Now I shall tell M. S. your flag is sent you 3 days back. Do come home this summer or in the autumn. It is said a change in the administration would certainly have taken place had not this wonderful and fortunate victory taken place. Admiral Parker it seems had written the *Captain* and *Culloden* bore the brunt of action. This instant have I received a letter from Lord Hood telling me Sir Robert Calder was gone to Portsmouth.

Thank you my dearest husband a thousand times for your letter of February 22nd. God bless and protect you and my Jos. crown all your endeavours with success and grant us a happy meeting. I can bear all my extreme good fortune. Your affectionate wife, FRANCES H. NELSON.

Our father sends his blessing to you and offers up his prayers for your protection. God bless you.

To Rear-Admiral Nelson, *Captain*. By favour of Sir Robert Calder.[2]

VI

Bath,
March 20, 1797

MY DEAREST HUSBAND,—In Friday the 17th I received your letter which came by Capt. Pierson.[3] His cousin Miss Aspinal brought it to me, dated

---

[1] While Nelson was in the *La Minerve*.

[2] Calder, who had brought the dispatches back from Sir John Jervis, was knighted. He rejoined the Mediterranean fleet at the end of March.

[3] Captain Charles Pierson of the 69th Regiment.

1 of March. I hope you received my letters by the packet. Several I had sent to Admiral Young and directed to General Trigge and one by the packet to take its chance.

Lord Hood requested me to give him all the account I could of this battle. When I received your letter Lagos Bay 22nd February with the action of the *Captain*[1] I consulted our father whether I should send it to him, he consented and I did send it to his Lordship, who when he returned it said a number of handsome things. 'The glorious share Adm. Nelson had in the action will immortalize his name in the pages of the history of England.' That he had an opportunity of shewing where he knew it would be of service—that it was a most excellent clear account of the battle. He said a great deal more I assure you. I hope I have not done wrong. I have lived long enough to dread envy.

Our father grows quite important, he says he is sure nothing will be done. He had yesterday a letter from Lord Walpole (Lady W. had been ill and our father made enquiries after her) who assured him nothing was yet talked of in London but *Nelson*. Everybody was loud in his praises, sends an extract of Capt. Collingwood's letter to his cousin Sir Edward Blackett who after saying everything that a generous mind could say, that brave honest Nelson with his little crew did wonders, but tells all that you did. General Tarleton's brother Mr. Tarleton and his wife called on me yesterday, she is a relative of Collingwood. He spoke very handsomely of you and 'besides Admiral Nelson's conduct has been very great in the Mediterranean' asked me if I had heard what was to be done for you.

Mr. Scrivener has written a very affectionate letter to our father, regrets he has never heard from you since he left Exmouth, gives an account of a very large breed of fowls which is his amusement. I had a letter from Mrs. Suckling, very polite, and of the Rumsey school mentioning the prize money. Capt. Nailor expected to get £100. Mr. Suckling has given up writing and Maurice wrote us he was grown a very old man. I sincerely hope my dear husband that all these wonderful and desperate actions such as boarding ships you will leave to others. With the protection of a Supreme Being you have acquired a character or name which all hands agree cannot be greater, therefore rest satisfied. What does Josiah say to all this? He is seasoned.

I don't hear a word of any changes taking place amongst your fleet. I mean in regard to the commander. I fancy I understand what you mean, I will keep it to myself. I feel a happiness which I cannot describe at the very idea of your being so much nearer to me. It seems as if I could almost

---

[1] Nelson's account of the proceedings (see letter No. 177, p. 314).

2 A

shake hands with you. As to Josiah, I shall not know him—so I am told. Mr. Ewin of Norwich promised to keep a good lookout for a cottage and land for you. We never heard from him. I expect a description of Mile End House, then I shall be a better judge but buying a house without either of us seeing it I don't like, indeed I am sure our father will never think any large enough that I shall. I am not disappointed in what you say about the balance in your agent's hands. I have never believed what people have said about your prize money.

Adm. Dickson made loud complaint about Lord Hood's secretary who still had his money in his hands for corn vessels. Never woman felt herself more thankful than I do at the very great mercies which have been shown me. God grant his protection to you and Josiah. I am happy.

I have had Govr. Bruce to see me. He sent me *The Times* which had 'Nelson art of cooking' the same your kind and affectionate disposition led you to send me. The Govr. declared 'it was the Man'. Mr. Daniel the attorney general from Dominique called. They had the honour of knowing you very well. Govr. Bruce spoke of Prince William, who recollected him the other day at the levee, of course loud in his praises—spoke of his sense.

The weather has and is very trying to old people, it is piercingly cold, so much so that I dare not go out but to the post office with this letter when I will try and know when the bag is made up for Lisbon. I will write once a week regularly. I have answered M. Suckling's letter, told him, 'that Lord Hood wrote me the *Gibraltar* was fitting up for you', and begged him to write to your brother if he wanted to know anything about you. No letter from one of the Burnhamites. The woman servant that I have, lived with a rich Portugal merchant, therefore I am willing that you should partake of the good things, I hear that place abounds with. There is a talk of a change in administration.

Miss Athill my great favourite tells me everybody talks of peace. We expect to hear from Mrs. Bolton. We have had a sincere (I do think) congratulatory letter from Mr. Hoste. The account of battle Maurice begged he might have it, when he has read it, etc., etc. it is to be sent to William, who assures our father he don't *mind* postage if it is to hear of *you*. My spirits were agitated most wonderfully, but they are calm again.

God protect you our good father send his blessing and love to you believe me your affectionate wife FRANCES H. NELSON.

Mrs. Shenstone tell us Lady S.[1] speaks of the Admirals and Captains

---

[1] Lady Spencer, wife of the First Lord of the Admiralty.

as a chosen band, they all can do the same great actions. Mile End House won't do. It is very much out of repair and no wash house.[1]

To Rear-Admiral Nelson, *Irresistible*, Lisbon.   Post-paid.

VII

Bath,
March 26, 1797

MY DEAREST HUSBAND,—I have had no letter from you since the one dated March 1st. therefore I have very little to say, excepting I hope in God you are well and Josiah. The newspapers have told the world that Admiral Nelson has sailed with a squadron on purpose to take the Spanish flotilla. I sincerely hope to hear Sir. R. Calder has joined Sir J. Jervis with the reinforcements. Lady Northesk[2] called on me on Saturday. Her mother has been confined to the house or would have called on me. This day I shall return the visit. She told me Lady J. had received letters of a very late date from Lisbon.

I had a letter from Maurice yesterday he tells me 'The Navy Board yesterday informed me that they had replaced me in my former rank in the office and had ordered me a salary of three hundred a year. I am perfectly satisfied.' I rejoice at it most sincerely, he tells me he has many letters to send you by Capt. Hollowell, one from Sir R. Hughes who is going on in the same old way. Our father has at last received a letter from old Crow[3] I thought he was afraid of saying too much. 'Although he was desired by a numerous set of respectable people to express their admiration of your extraordinary gallant conduct and hoped it would not be long before he was blessed with the sight of such a son that few had to boast.'

The Rector wrote us a very affectionate letter: he is determined to make you a visit, he will set off as soon as you arrive, he is *determined* on it. They have invited me to spend the summer with them. Our father has talked of going into Norfolk. He sometimes expresses his anxiety about Suckling, but any movements of his must be regulated by Mrs. Bolton, as he has offered to accommodate her and girls for 6 months. Mrs. Bolton's girls go to the Matchams in May, therefore everything will soon be determined upon. I shall send you a barren letter but indeed one hears of nothing but banks stopping. The Bury bank has stopped payment. Lord Cornwallis has

---

[1] A recipe has been written as a postscript: 'Love apple catch up in necked narrow bottomed jars. Semolina a root of a tree grounded very good for puddings, orange flower water—citron port wine.'

[2] Lady Northesk, the niece of Sir John Jervis, married William Carnegie, later Admiral Lord Northesk.

[3] A Norfolk friend and neighbour.

lost thousands, Sir Charles Davis is a very great sufferer. Mr. Maynard who is here from Suffolk has lost five hundred, which he says is a serious inconvenience. The Cambridge bank is broke. Bridport bank totters, Bristol bank is not thought to stand very firm. Mr. Baillie gave me two bank notes of Bristol, each twenty pounds, I got rid of one as soon as I received it, the other stuck fast, I sent it to Mr. Tobin last week and requested him to get a Bank of England note for me. I hope he will succeed, scarcity of money is very great. The times are very unpleasant. Our father tells me the old women get hold of me and make me quite melancholy. It is not the old women that make me look grave. I leave you to guess where my thoughts are. They will fly across the sea and settle on board ship. Mr. Tarleton and his wife are here. Mr. T. tells me the Duke of Clarence begins to be a favourite of his Majesty's. Many who thought him wanting in common sense find they are deceived. We have been blessed with fine rain. It was seriously wanted. Bread began to be raised.

One of the handsomest letters I have received was from Scotland. Miss Nisbet hopes government intends the Admiral a title and something better, sends her love to Josiah, 'and desires me to tell him I hope he will tread in such steps of honour and glory and one day equally be the pride and boast of his country.' If you go to Gibraltar do notice G. Tobin. Mr. Tobin is sure you will like him, 'for he would take a *lion* by the beard, as to Harry he likes a good dinner and minds the counting house.' Our good father has answered old Crow's letter very charmingly, says envy itself dare not show its head. He will write to you next Monday. He is grown young. These blessings in his declining days cheer him. He desires his love to you and prays God to bless you. My love to Josiah, God bless you both and continue your great success. Believe me your affectionate wife, FRANCES H. NELSON.

Compliments to Capt. Collingwood. I hope the Portuguese make much of you. I long to hear from you.

To Rear-Admiral Nelson, *Irresistible*, Lisbon.   Post paid 1/8d.

VIII

Bath,
April 3, 1797

MY DEAREST HUSBAND,—As I wrote you I made my visit to — and my Bristol friends and returned yesterday. My absence was one week. Our good father was very glad to see me telling me I had made a long visit. I was in hopes of writing you yesterday but hope my letter will be in time for the mail. I have now to thank you for your letter of April 3rd off Cadiz. We are generally open to flattery and your telling me 'my heart is entirely with you' is too pleasing not to notice it, particularly as I feel every affectionate and sincere attachment for my dear husband.

Lord Keith told me the Red Ribbon was to be sent out to you in the ball room in the hearing of several persons. I rejoice you have at last begun to be noticed in a proper manner. The Ribbon won't satisfy me. I expect they will give you a handsome pension, if they do not you must ask for it. They cannot refuse. Everybody expects you will have one. The merchants of Bristol are loud in their praises. Mrs. Pinney declares Mr. P. talked in his sleep of you. Mr. Pinney's heart was so full when he saw me, that he could not speak, his congratulations were pleasant they were from his heart.

The first Bristol news was that Mrs. Kelly had written Miss Tobin, her brother and Mrs. Hamilton had consulted the first lawyers in England, whether they could cut off the entail of Mr. Herbert's estate. They had received a satisfactory answer. Mrs. Hamilton had offered Morton thirty thousand pounds, which he had accepted and that Mr. and Mrs. Morton were coming to England. Mr. M. was to spend a short time with his wife and then return to the West Indies. Mrs. Morton's income would be five thousand a year. I had certainly heard some vague reports of this kind but as experience had taught me not to believe one half of what I heard I gave little credit. However on Sunday noon at Mr. Pinney's I had a visit from Mr. E. Baillie. A packet had just arrived from the West Indies. Mrs. Hamilton had written to Mr. B. telling him what she and Morton were going to do. Mr. B. began to tell me that Hamilton had wrote him that from my uncle's estates he should ship four hundred hogsheads at least, which will pay off, Mr. B. says, all the debts and legacies. I then mentioned what I had heard about young Morton and Mrs. Hamilton. Mr. B. said it was true in some measure for that Mr. S. and himself had for some time been consulted. Mr. H. offered Morton Dasent's estate and I think Mr. B. said ten thousand sterling. As Mr. B. is trustee he says not only for the estate but the legacy which may hereafter become due, he shall be very careful how he acts and assures me that he would not lose sight of your interests. They are all loud against Mrs. Hamilton as she has no children. Why not let her father's female heirs have a chance? You sent me so good an example of not caring for great riches that I should be unworthy of you were I to repine at what they are now doing, only for your sake, as they say the chance was not so very great, I hope they will live to enjoy what they now think will make each party happy. Hamilton they say is a slave to his unhappy temper, however he will gain much.

We had a line from Mrs. Matcham, all well. Mrs. Bolton will be soon

with them. I have seen lodgings at Clifton. Our father I don't fancy will like to move. I will not urge it unless the summer is very hot. Admiral Barrington called on us this day, sat one hour. He says Pringle will soon be in England, they have left him in an unpleasant situation, have taken too many hands from the men of war to put on board the prizes and does not feel himself pleased. I thank you for my dear Josiah's promotion, my love to him, he shall soon hear from me. I hope you are right in regard to his further promotion. I trust he will do you credit. Mr. Hoste is here called twice on our father last week flying gut. Mrs. Hoste is laying in. Mr. Hoste is gone to London to see if he can get his son's time made out, as he was upon some books. Our father's blessing and love to you God bless and protect you and Jo, and grant us a happy meeting, your affectionate wife, FRANCES H. NELSON.

A thousand compliments from Bristol.

To Rear-Admiral Nelson, *Captain*, Lisbon.   Post paid 1/8.

IX

Bath,
April 3, 1797 [1]

MY DEAREST HUSBAND,—I have wrote to you by the *Lively*, at least I directed a letter from our father. Lord Hood writes me he can send another letter, therefore it gives me an opportunity of enquiring after you and Josiah, not but I think the packet is as good a conveyance as any. As to news we have none not even a little chat, excepting meeting last night Mr. Lucas from Norfolk he says Admiral Duncan speaking of your engagement nothing could ever be done to equal it, therefore he hoped never to meet an enemy, everything must fall short of such an action. The Norfolk man wanted to know what title they were to give you for they must give you what you please. They don't like their present member for Yarmouth Mr. Joddrill, he has never been near the place since his election. A navy man was absolutely necessary for them. I said Sir J. Jervis had offered his services, it was very true but they wanted a man that the ministers would recommend else they would not get anything done. Mr. Lucas mentioned a house and twenty acres of land that would soon be offered for sale eight miles from Norwich either in the Bury or Bungay road, which I am not certain. The house is not large, two very good parlours and a study, the house was Sir Barney Bargraves; he mentioned several large overgrown houses. No bidders for Lyndford. I wrote you about the house near Nor-

------
[1] The second letter of this date.

wich, the roof was fallen in and otherwise very much out of repair. Land is increasing in value. Sir Frank Laforey called on us yesterday, he is going to London, has asked for a frigate, is to have one. His accounts from the West Indies are very alarming. The French have seized all the American vessels going to the islands and sent them to St. Martins. The want of corn and flour is very great, they are fearful of being in extreme distress. The West Indian seas swarm with privateers from Guadeloupe.

Captain Stanhope's business is accommodated: Lord Keith had nothing to say against him, excepting that he thought him not quite so respectful as he might have been and the Admiralty lawyers could not find that a court martial could be granted, upon which Capt. Stanhope asked for the *Neptune* and he has her. He came down on Saturday. Mrs. Stanhope tells me all this, she says she and her children were to return with him to Woolwich as it would be some time before the ship would be ready for sea.

Our father's cough is better, he is writing to Mrs. Bolton to enquire how she intends disposing of herself and her children after her visit to the Matchams, therefore I shall tell you in my next how matters are going on. I would fain go into Norfolk but our father seems to say a great many inconveniences would attend it, plenty of time yet to talk about it for much depends upon Mrs. B. I long to hear from you, some say you are gone to the Western Islands, other off Cadiz. God grant you are well and that I may soon hear from you.

Did I write you I had Lady Northesk's visit. I like Mrs. Rickets,[1] she is a pleasant well bred woman. The ladies of quality have fashion in their mode of speaking, laughing, or smiling, at every word they say which I don't like. Such revolutions in our dress since you left me. Now our waists are lengthened, heads dressed *flat* at the *sides*, very high in front and low upon the forehead, short sleeves, some ladies showing their elbows, short petticoats, nay above the ankle with the fashionable, and little or no heels to the shoes. Gloves almost beyond the pocket of anyone, none but the long ones are of use. None less than 3/-, a pair. Coloured and white the same price. I have just heard that Admiral Kingsmill's secretary has absconded and joined the French fleet, the same of Lord Corhampton's secretary changing all the signals. I think more of this on account of you not hearing it. When shall we meet and have rest? I hope before long. God Almighty bless and protect you and Josiah continuing to you your great success. Believe me my dearest husband your affectionate wife, FRANCES H. NELSON.

To Rear-Admiral Nelson.

---

[1] Sister of Sir John Jervis and mother of Lady Northesk.

X

Bath,
April 10, 1797

MY DEAREST HUSBAND,—Your letter of March 3rd I received last week and am glad you have had my letters, that you were kind enough to say gave you pleasure: they are full, but truly of nothing. Your affectionate concern for my want of health, has its healing balm. The heartfelt satisfaction at your expression of returning to me 'laughing—back', gives me a pleasure, a something which I am certain none can feel but those who are sincerely attached to a husband. They are fine feelings but exquisitely painful. I have never shed a tear on Josiah's account but when I have known he was not with you. You are the best judge. Capt. Berry is a gentlemanly man his character is quite established, and he has taken a mode to convince the naval world how very high he stands in your estimation. I think you have paid him a very handsome compliment.

The newspapers have added to my apprehension by saying there are three line-of-battle ships with the Spanish convoy. I shall rejoice to hear from you. God protect you. Lord Hood wrote me that he had received an answer from Capt. Hollowell saying he had received my letter for you. Lord Hood hopes you may be successful. You can't think what attention he pays me and the very handsome letters I receive from him. Some I save for you to read. I hear the medals are gone out. Are they very handsome? If you have received our father's letter which was sent to Lord Hood, there you will find what Mr. Norris wrote the Rector about titles. I have at last got a letter from Mrs. Kelly but not a word that she rejoiced at your safety or any kind expression excepting she hoped that I had lately heard from you and dear Josiah. After the many engagements he had been in she hoped by this time he had been a ——. Kelly was gone on a cruise with Sir R. C.[1] They were to see the India fleet to a given latitude and then were to come home. Many ships are gone to look for this Spanish flotilla.

We have heard from Mrs. Matcham, they talk of coming here before our father visits Norfolk but his idea of going into Norfolk seems to be given up and that he will remain at Clifton with me. His cough is very troublesome. I would not wish to go to Clifton this summer but indeed a little country air will do me good. Bath is so hot in the summer and so stinking that very few remain in it. I have been often told this situation was too low. It is very near the river, but when I considered, after making enquiries as to the rent of houses in good situations and found the rent differed so materially I was determined to remain for our father has several

[1] Sir Roger Curtis.

times requested that I would consent to his taking a house elsewhere. This house £90 a year: Gay St. £160, the higher you go the dearer. However I hope you will be home before long and then we will be snug. I am sure I shall be quite well then.

Maurice Suckling is appointed 5th Lieutenant of the *Neptune*, I have taken it into my head that he will not like to remain there. I fancy the Captain of her is anxious to have everything in greater order than before, however I told him Suckling was your relation and had been many years at sea with you, so that if he can be civil I hope that he may. Mrs. S. and I are very good friends. Mrs. Bolton and the girls are to be with Maurice Nelson this day, where they stay a month and then go on to Ringwood. I expect after their visit is over at Ringwood, they will come here, for the Boltons, at least William Bolton's family are going in the winter to Ipswich.

I have this instant received a kind letter from Mrs. Pinney who had forgot to ask me before to the Sheriff's ball. A Pinney is one of them. I have no desire of being in a great crowd therefore shall not go. You cannot conceive how very quiet I am grown. Our father declares he has more spirit than I have. I believe it, but I mean to grow quite gay when I see my dearest husband and Josiah. Give my love to him. After Easter I have some thoughts of going to Bristol for a few days. It is very cold today but I have been to church and am now going to the Post Office. Our father's love and blessing to you God bless and protect you and Josiah and grant us a happy meeting soon. Believe me my dear husband, your affectionate wife, FRANCES H. NELSON.

Mr. Nelson begs you will enquire if Charles Dillon[1] is on board the *Captain* by trade a painter a native of Bath. We have no Navy here but Admiral Stanhope and his wife who is sister to Sir Digby Dent. I believe I wrote you Sir D. D. had apartments in Holy Rood House. Poor Dent[2] a lieutenant in a cutter.

To Rear-Admiral Nelson, *Irresistible*, Lisbon.

XI

Bath,
April 17, 1797

MY DEAREST HUSBAND,—I have had the pleasure of receiving your letter of March 14th the contents were highly gratifying, and be assured the confidence you kindly repose in me shall not be abused. The sum you

---

[1] Nelson's answer was brief: 'Charles Dillon drowned—November 1796' (Letter No. 187, p. 325).

[2] Nelson's lieutenant in the *Boreas*; had no further promotion.

mentioned for house and land I think quite sufficient, we must have nothing to do with more spare bedrooms than one or two. Mr. Sanby's house which he built some time back it is thought will be for sale, if so I will certainly have inquiries made about it, it is quite modern and was intended for the use of Mrs. Sanby who is dead. The very great advance of everything and the additional taxes since you left the country is beyond any idea you can form. As to Suckling our father saw the truth in everything you said, you have been explicit which is the only way. Time may produce something to his advantage. At present the minister amuses us with the journey of Mr. Hammond to Vienna. A general peace is the alluring prospect which is held out, therefore I am in hopes by the time you mention, October, I may have the happiness of seeing you.

We had a letter yesterday from Mrs. Bolton, the girls and herself are arrived at Maurice's. She promises to write as soon as she arrives at the Matchams'. The proprietors of the estate wished to make additions to the house which is the reason of her quitting it so soon. She says she will not visit our father this summer which makes our father think she will spend next summer with him. He desired me not to say anything to you about his going into Norfolk as he might change his mind. Truly this plan has been altered some few times. I wish him to keep to his present idea: the journey is very long and this violent cough and cold which he has had for some time has shook him.

On Saturday I am going to Bristol for a few days, I am to look if we can get a very small house or lodgings where no other lodgers are taken. He seems to be fixed upon drinking the water there. They have found a spring on the top of the hill which is thought to be equally good with the old one. Capt. Culverhouse called on me. He came on purpose to Bath. He assures me your bruise is of no consequence and that you were quite well. He begged I would not scruple to ask him questions, and he would answer them. Angry with the Gazette, so is everybody.

The Ansteys have told the very handsome compliment which Sir J. J. paid Captain Sotherby in a letter to the Admiralty. That he requested Captain Sotherby might be sent out to him, as he could not dispense with the services of so gallant and able an officer. I give you word for word. It was first told me by his cousin Westerns and this day my hairdresser told it me. I am going to the ball. Mrs. Glass and daughter called this morning. She sings wonderfully well. Mrs. Admiral Stanhope was a Miss Dent, she tells me Dent's friends have tried everything to get him made a Captain, he has five beautiful children and his wife is near her time. The Admiral is confined with the gout. Maurice Suckling and his wife are in London on their way to Woolwich.

In the first part of my letter I forgot to mention £500 it would take for furniture and very plain too. Ben Suckling's cost £800. Lady Saumarez told me that I could get a letter from you. Sir J.[1] letters are so long that I verily believe he mentions what you give them to *eat*. I asked her the news, she said nothing but shewed a large sheet of paper full. They leave Bath soon. I hope Josiah is well. My love to him. We have not heard from the Rector lately. I think I shall soon hear from my dear husband. God bless and protect and continue your great success. Our father sends his love and blessing to you. Believe me my dearest husband, your affectionate wife, FRANCES H. NELSON.

Our father takes my letter to the post. Hurry—Polly is very well talks.

To Rear-Admiral Nelson, *Irresistible*, Lisbon.

XII

Bath,
May 8, 1797

MY DEAREST HUSBAND,—Your letter of April 12th I had yesterday the pleasure of receiving, and thank you for the good accounts you give of our lieutenant. I hope he is everything, excepting his retired disposition, you can wish. A happy medium is desirable but it cannot always be obtained, and his reservedness may keep him out of scrapes.

The Norwich paper tells us Prince Henry of Gloster and Rear-Admiral Nelson have been presented with the freedom of the city. I am pleased with the Norwich people as they did it the same day with the Prince. Our father's heart often overflows at the mention of you. He asked me if that compliment would satisfy me. I told him yes. He anxiously looks forward to the time you mention of returning home. The truce with the Emperor and France has again revived the idea of peace. Mr. Burke is still here. He tells Mr. Tarleton that Mr. Windham's abilities are great that he had for some time back disapproved of measures and that Mr. W. knew it, and that Mr. W. had for some time back been in the minority in the Council, that if other measures are not pursued our finances are ruined,—that he was going past fast and should not see it. He looks miserably ill. You will see by the papers our additional taxes, the turnpike tax for government is called the 'Public Robber'.

Mr. Hoste drank tea here last night, made many handsome speeches. I fancied he felt a little. I was very polite and took care not to be a bit stiff. He has mentioned Mr. Vane's house. Our father is determined he will

---

[1] Sir James Saumarez.

have an opportunity of saying 'You found that neighbourhood too thin [to think] of returning to it again.' I will certainly write to Mr. Scrivener and say all you have desired me. Lord Peter and Mr. Wilson have bought two of Mr. Nelthorp's farms. As to Mr. Hoste, he could not tell us any news, spoke much of Mr. Coke's and his friends' petition which everybody says was one of the most ridiculous things that ever was penned, in short Mr. Coke has lost himself very much in the county.

Prince Henry of Gloster has made himself very popular at Norwich by his very moderate mode of living. One course for dinner, no removes, shilling whist. A gentleman asked him if he wished to bet, he said half crowns he had no objection. Everybody who asked him, he accepted their invitation and the last accounts we had from little Young he was then going to Holkam. Mr. Moss of Norwich sent very handsome message to our father saying that as he heard Adm. Nelson wished and was looking out for a house in Norfolk, he would make enquiries and let him know.

Mr. Ewin it seems is but a poor hand. I have had a letter from your agents offering £2000 to me to purchase a house for Admiral Nelson but at the same time says the *Agamemnon*'s books are not settled. Mr. E. Baillie's son, the eldest I mean, will in a few days be married to Betsey Pinney, she is a good looking young woman. They say he has been wild and expensive however he has been living with his father for some time and has conducted himself with great propriety. Major Baillie is married to a clergyman's daughter who went out to India in the same ship. She was going to her relation Lady Shaw. It is said Lady Parker intended to follow him, some say she is on her passage.

I have had a request from Mr. Lockhart to make you. 'There is on board the *Irresistible*, Captain Martin, Lt. Andrew Thompson, for whom Sir J. Stuart interests himself very much and will take it as a particular favour if you will recommend him to Adm. Nelson's protection, if he could do him any service in the way of promotion.' I shall write them that I have mentioned Lt. T. to you, but at the same time shall tell them of Josiah and 3 young men that you wish to get forward. Do notice this young man; have you noticed Joliffe? Mr. Lockhart cannot resist the opportunity of congratulating Mrs. Nelson with his own hand on the glorious conduct of her husband. His gallantry is above praise and will renew the old gentleman's age to hear so many just encomiums on his illustrious son. Mr. L. hopes the ladies do not forget, requesting you to remember him to the good old doctor. Mr. L. always called our father 'Dr. Nelson'. Our father desired me to send you Mr. L.'s letter. We have not yet had a letter from Mrs. Bolton. I sometimes think our father won't stir. He says he feels he gets whimsical and wants a great deal of room and is afraid of being disturbed. I shall not urge his stirring. He sends his love and blessing to you. My love to our Lt. Josiah. Do you think I shall know him?

God bless my dearest husband and protect him and Josiah. Crown you with success and grant us all a happy meeting. Your affectionate wife, FRANCES H. NELSON.

Captain Shank desires his best compliments to you. Lady Saumarez is here and very well.

To Rear-Admiral Nelson, *Captain*, Lisbon.

XIII

Bath,
May 15, 1797

MY DEAREST HUSBAND,—Although you did not mention where you were going in your letter of April 12th, I heard it from Admiral Barrington who first asked me if you had told me. My answer No, then said the Admiral *I will tell* and so he did, had it from good authority, General Rainsford.

Captain Shank thinks you will proceed to Elba. I hope soon to hear of your return to the fleet, indeed you fag too much. October is always uppermost in my mind. I pray God we may meet not to part again. I had a kind letter from Maurice, telling me all he had heard, which was the same as the Admiral's. He had seen Captain Woodhouse, Spicer and Noble who all assured him you were well, congratulates me on Josiah's promotion and seems very sanguine in his further rise. I suppose you will hear from Mrs. Bolton who writes me Mr. B. has hired Mr. R.'s farm, for 15 years and of her kind reception at Shepherd's Spring. Our father talks of inviting her and the girls in September to spend a few weeks before she returns into Norfolk.

We have had a letter from the Rector of Hilborough telling of one hundred acres of land to be purchased near Pickenham. It has a very poor farm house and old out buildings, thinks that you may like to build and that you could let the land that you did not want. However I have said nay: that will never do these times. Building is so very expensive and besides our father says the situation is a very bad one. Mr. Hoste was here on Thursday he thinks Mr. Hogge's house at Aylsham will soon be to dispose of, as Mr. H's female attachment lives in London, and has promised that he will request a friend of his who lives in that neighbourhood and is acquainted with Mr. H. to let him know whenever it is to be offered for sale, but he thinks it has not much land. He describes the house as being very good, few rooms but those are large and well fitted up.

You will see by the papers the unhappy situation this country has been from the seamen, wishing for an increase of pay and their dislike for some particular officers. Sir Bickerton, Mrs. Shaw tells me she hears from her husband, although the sailors have suffered him to return to his ship, still threaten his life. After they had once driven him on shore and allowed him to return he addressed them on the impropriety of their conduct, the great lenity of his Majesty etc. (it would have been well had he stopped there) but he said he knew he had a set of rascals to deal with, that expression has made them more inveterate than ever. However he is still on board his ship. Mrs. Athill who has been very kind to me I feel most sincerely for. Lady B.[1] is at Portsmouth her sister is gone there to her. What a lesson it is to those entering life to use the power which certain situations give them with moderation and great evenness of temper.

I have bought the narrative of the action of the 14th of February.[2] I like it because it has done my dear husband justice. It was written by a land officer on board the *Lively*. The late Viceroy's wife of Corsica[3] I hear was not liked. She would not mix with the inhabitants. I readily believe her to be very proud. The day I returned her visit I thought she received me as if I was honoured. I told our father on my return that Lady E. had forgot she was not the person she was at Corsica, however she is mistaken, it is not in her power by her acquaintance to honour your wife, and so little do I covet the acquaintance of the fashionable that I would rather shun it. Not that I think the air of London particularly infectious. The late poor Lady Derby. No one would perform the charitable office of burying her. Lord D. refused, and the D. of H.[4] likewise did the same, there she lay for a considerable time. At last the D. of H. feelings were roused, a spark of natural feeling being left, and he buried his sister. She was still his sister, let her conduct been ever so bad. Her unfortunate daughter whom Lord D. disputed, but the laws of his country not, has married a subaltern in the Dragoons, and is in great distress.

I have taken up much of my paper relating this history so that I can only make short enquiries after the Lieutenant who I do hope is well. Give my love to him and tell me if he adds a little gravity to the change.

God bless you my dear husband, your affectionate wife, FRANCES H. NELSON.

Lady Saumarez and her party has left Bath. Mr. W. Hoste leaves Bath

---

[1] Lady Bickerton was Miss Ann Athill.
[2] The account by Colonel John Drinkwater, who had been deputy judge-advocate in Corsica. In his *Narrative of the Battle of St. Vincent*, Drinkwater praised Nelson's services, which he considered had been underestimated.
[3] Lady Elliot.
[4] The Duke of Hamilton, brother of Lady Derby.

next week. Mr. Coke it is said has some thoughts of living at Worham as he cannot afford to live at Holkham.

To Rear-Admiral Nelson, *Captain*, Lisbon.

Our father's blessing and love to you. Will write on Thursday or Monday next.

XIV

May 28, 1797

MY DEAREST HUSBAND,—Our father wrote to you last Monday the very great pleasure Captain Berry gave us. He assured us you were quite well. Oh! how happy I felt. He dined with us and was not out of my sight but when he went to dress for dinner, still I had more questions to ask, was sorry when he took his leave. He is one of the most grateful creatures I ever met, with the pleasing message of your coming home in short he ingratiated himself very much in our good opinion. I think I shall know the lieutenant, although I am told his eyes are dark. I was highly gratified in hearing he loved you, and that he is good. I hope it is all truth for therein consists much of my happiness. Captain Berry begged to see your picture which he had seen me wear. I showed it, but he will not allow it's like you. I wish I had one good picture of you. You must give me one when you come home.

Last night's Gazette[1] authorises me to add something more to my usual address, which you have so long toiled and worked for, that it sits as easy upon me as if I had been born to it, that and much more do you deserve from your country. As I wrote you before, that the ribbon won't satisfy me. How I am looking forward to our meeting. God grant it may be soon not to part again.

There is much talk of Lady B. returning from Portsmouth. The account she gave is very bad however she and her sister lived on board for days. Most extraordinary doings, the papers will tell you of the licentious conduct of drunken men. The Royal Marriage has amused a little. When the P.R.[2] was introduced to the Duke of Wurtemburg she started back and was in tears. The Duke appeared distressed and hurt. His Majesty begged His Highness to consider when the Princess saw him it brought to her mind she was to quit her native country and everything that was dear to her, upon which the Duke embraced her saying he hoped they were the first and last tears she would shed on his account. I assure there are more gallant and kind things said. We have everything Wurtemburg.

---

[1] Announcing Nelson's knighthood.
[2] Charlotte, the Princess Royal, was married on May 18, 1797.

I thank my dear husband for the two sea pieces Captain Berry brought me. I have them both up in the room where I always sit. The bunch of Roman pearls and silk handkerchief which Mrs. Fremantle[1] gave you, and a very pretty work bag which he brought me. I was not for taking it, but he assured me it cost him 4/6 therefore I took it. I thought the pearls had been real and I took them to a jeweller to have them dressed, they were composed of rice, therefore they were not to be touched. They look well in bandeaux round the head which is now the fashion.

Miss Cholomondeley gave a letter of introduction to Mr. Hardman. He was very polite and attentive and brought me one of the narratives of Lord St. Vincent's victory (I think of my husband's) neatly bound. I took it and the one I bought I sent to Suckling Nelson, who will be highly gratified. He writes us some of the Burnhamites show what they most likely wish to conceal, jealousy. It rains very much, however Captain Frane is come, I was obliged to wish the Captain a good day as I was writing to you. He begged his most respectful compliments.

The Rector writes us Mr. Partridge's house is to be sold at Calton with 30 acres of land. The house is too large 3 parlours and a drawing room. Mr. Moss and Ewin are both to let us hear when they hear of anything. They will ask much more than I would venture to give. Stocks 3 per cent on 47.

A letter this day from Mrs. Matcham, she says Mr. Matcham will be at Bath in three weeks to look for a house. He has advertised Shepherd's Spring, if they sell it, they move directly. Mr. M. is very well and Mrs. M. and the children.

Mrs. Bolton and the girls are to come to Bath before they go to Norfolk. All the family are glad our father has given up the thoughts of going into Norfolk and say honestly they don't think him able, however he has just said he is very able to do it. I am sure if he has a wish to go I shall again beg he will not stay thinking to accommodate me. I certainly can spend 6 weeks at Kentish Town. Captain Locker always invites me. He has not been very well lately. I had a long letter from Miss Locker and a very long one from Mrs. Wigley,[2] they are in town. She presses me very much to make them a visit, but that I shall not do, they have taken a house at Worster.

Mr. Hoste when he took his leave thanked us very much for the great civilties we had shown him. A Mr. Brown called on me on Saturday. His son George Brown had received great kindness from you. I was assured

---

[1] Captain Fremantle married Betsy Wynne in Naples in February 1797. He was with Nelson in the attack on Santa Cruz and brought him home in the *Seahorse*. His wife, who was on board, helped to nurse Nelson.
[2] Miss Suckling married Captain Wigley.

PLATE XI. Stipple engraving of Lady Hamilton, drawn, engraved and published by Thomas Cheesman, London, February 10, 1797.

with Mr. Brown's humble duty and humble thanks to you and hopes for an opportunity of doing it personally to you, but as you were not in England, he heard I was at Bath therefore he came from Bristol to offer his thanks, that he could not express the obligations he and his son and all his family were under to you, all he could say he was truly sensible of them. Our father's blessing to you. God bless you my dear husband and protect you and Josiah. Your affectionate wife, FRANCES H. NELSON.

To Rear-Admiral Sir Horatio Nelson, K.B., *Captain*, Lisbon.

XV

June 19, 1797

MY DEAREST HUSBAND,—Our father wrote to you last Monday, little has occurred since worth mentioning particularly as I have not had the great pleasure of hearing from you. Mr. Matcham came here on Friday, house hunting. He has seen many, objections are started. Rent far beyond what he expected. Everything has been said to him of the expenses which are almost unavoidable in this place, and indeed in most places in the kingdom (excepting Shepherd's Spring) if you attempt to live like a gentleman.

When you come home this house is to be offered, provided we have peace. He seems to say he will accept it for your sister to lay in which she expects will be in September. Mrs. Nelson told Mrs. M. to accommodate him, we would remove higher up the town if you were not in England. In short our good father sees they are heartily tired of Shepherd's Spring and does not want them to engage in any house, thinking six months in *this* would heartily tire them and then they might form some idea of the expenses. So now I leave them, excepting telling you Mr. and Mrs. Matcham are well. He says your sister's health was never better. His children all but George, have a scorbutic humour, but they have independent of that good health. Mrs. Bolton and her girls he speaks kindly of. How long they stay with him will depend upon their movements. The girls he says are sensible and affectionate to their mother. Lieut. Pierson has been staying some time with Mr. W. Bolton, he has not it seems been idle, as he has made an offer to Miss Mary Ann Bolton. All parties are agreed and they are soon to be married. This may be old news to you, but it was new to us and from Mr. Matcham. Mr. Bolton writes Mrs. Bolton his crops promise abundance, everything looks well around him. I heartily rejoice at it and I am sure you will.

The newspapers will tell you all the public news. It is better than it has been for some time. The private accounts of the cheapness of provisions at Paris is beyond all belief 2d. ½lb. for meat, 1½d. for bread, if it is so England

2 B

will have no inhabitants whenever we are blessed with my dear husband, our lieutenant and peace. Our good father says 'if letters are as long getting to you as they are long coming to us you can hear but seldom.' Captain Welsford begged I would present his compliments to you. We all had a great deal of talk of you. I think he wrote the narrative. His mode of speaking of you was couched in the handsomest manner, he is gone to Cheltenham. Poor Andrews is rather better. Mrs. Hamil his sister and her children are gone to see him. Miss Andrews I don't think seems to have any affection for him.

I hope I shall soon hear from you and Josiah indeed I am very anxious. God Almighty protect you and my Josiah. The time draws near when you thought of returning, it seems just at hand, which most probably increases my feelings and anxiety. The time Susannah was with Maurice, he had taught her music. They speak French. I had almost forgot Mr. Hoste begged that I would mention to you, a letter which you had received *from him* saying whether you would wish him to apply to Mr. Cooke or any other friend about letters of recommendation for his son to Lord St. Vincent. Mr. Schutz from Brancaster called upon us last week. Suckling is well. He is a lively sensible man. Talked of our 'Norfolk hero'. He was quite delighted. Weatherhead's letters to his father Mr. S. seems to know by heart.

George Tobin still a lieutenant. All Mr. Tobin's expensive presents to some lords and ladies and captains cannot get him made. After my son I will then beg you to remember my cousin. I can't write you a cheerful letter because I have not had a letter from you. Our father's love and blessing to you. God bless and believe me my dear husband, your affectionate wife, FRANCES H. NELSON.

Our father smiles at my direction to you, so this time I have directed in the same manner he did.

To Rear-Admiral Horatio Nelson, K.B., *Captain*, Lisbon.   Post paid 1/8.

Maurice Nelson to Mrs. Nelson[1]

Navy Office,
May 10, 1797

MY DEAR MADAM,—My not writing you before was entirely owing to my not having anything particular to relate. My sister and the girls went to Ringwood on the 2nd of the present month so that I should suppose you will hear of them very soon. Report has for some time past given my

---
[1] Monmouth MSS., Nelson papers, Vol. IV.

brother the Red Ribbon and that he is also to have a baronetage. I sincerely wish it may be so. I am certain his services merit all the country can bestow. The last letter I had from him is dated the 28th of March, fearful he should not fall in with the Viceroy of Mexico. Capt. Woodhouse who arrived on Friday from Lisbon I saw on Saturday who said he left my brother perfectly well on the 13th April on which day the *Captain* and 3 other ships of the line separated from Sir J. Jervis to cruise off Carthegena. I hope in God it will be a successful one. I am very glad to hear Josiah has got the first step. I hope it will not be long before the other follows. Captains Spicer and Noble late lieutenants of the *Captain* I have lately seen. They both speak in raptures and look upon my brother as their father.

I am glad Norwich have given the freedom of the city to him. I understand Lynn will follow the example (thro' Mr. Lane) and that they wish the sword had been presented to them. News I know of none: the report is that the unhappy differences in the Fleet are settled. I wish it may be so.

Give my duty to our father and believe me yours affectionately, MAURICE NELSON.

To Mrs. Nelson, New King Street, Bath.

Sir John Jervis to Lady Nelson[1]

Ville de Paris, at anchor, before Cadiz
August 16, 1797

MADAM,—Sir Horatio Nelson has added very considerably to the laurels he had won before the assault upon the town of Santa Cruz in the Island of Teneriffe. He is wounded but not dangerously and I hope your Ladyship will be soon made happy by his presence in England, whither he will proceed the moment the *Theseus* joins.

I have the honour to be with very great respect. Your Ladyship's very faithful and obedient servant, J. JERVIS.

To Lady Nelson, Bath.

A Detail of the Proceedings of the Expedition against the Town of Santa Cruz in the Island of Teneriffe[2]

On Friday the 21st of July ten leagues to windward of Teneriffe I directed to be embarked on board the *Seahorse*, *Terpischore*, and *Emerald* frigates

[1] Monmouth MSS., Nelson papers, Vol. V.
[2] N.M.M. MS. 9217, Minto papers. Minuted by Sir Gilbert Elliot: 'Sir Horatio Nelson's narrative of his attack on Teneriffe. Given by him October 1797.' St. Vincent's dispatch with the news of this attack arrived in England on September 1, the same day as Nelson. The official dispatch included a short report from Nelson with a list of killed and wounded.

one thousand men (including two hundred and fifty marines under the command of Captain Thomas Oldfield) the whole commanded by Capt. Troubridge attended by all the boats of the squadron, scaling ladders and every implement which I thought necessary for the success of the enterprise. I directed that the boats should land in the night between the fort on the north east side of the Bay of Santa Cruz and the town, and endeavour to make themselves masters of that fort, which when done to send in my summons (marked No. 1), the liberal terms of which I am confident you will approve.

Although the frigates approached within three miles of the place of debarkation by 12 o'clock, yet by the unforeseen circumstance of a strong gale of wind in the offing, and a strong current against them in shore, they did not approach within a mile of the landing place when the day dawned, which discovered to the Spaniards our force and intentions. On my approach with the line of battle ships, Captains Troubridge and Bowen with Captain Oldfield of the Marines came on board to consult with me what was best to be done and were of opinion if they could possess themselves of the heights over the fort aforementioned that it could be stormed, to which I gave my assent, and directed the line of battle ships to batter the fort in order to create a diversion but this was found impracticable, not being able to get nearer the shore than three miles, from a calm and contrary currents, nor could our men possess themselves of the heights as the enemy had taken possession of them and seemed as anxious to retain as we were to get them.

Thus foiled in my original plan I considered it for the honour of our King and country not to give over the attempt to possess ourselves of the town, that our enemies might be convinced that there is nothing that Englishmen are not equal to, and confident in the bravery of those who would be employed on the service, I embarked every person from the shore on the 22nd at night.

On the 24th I got the ships to an anchor about two miles to the northward of the town and made every show for a disposition of attacking the heights, which appeared to answer the end from the great number of people they had placed in them. The *Leander*, Captain Thompson, joined this afternoon and her marines were added to the force before appointed and Captain Thompson also volunteered his services. At 11 o'clock at night the boats of the squadron containing between 6 and 700 men, 180 men on board the *Fox* cutter and about 70 or 80 men in a boat we had taken the day before proceeded towards the town. The divisions of boats conducted by all the captains except Fremantle and Bowen who attended with me to regulate and lead the way to the attack. Every Captain being acquainted that the landing was to be made on the mole and from whence they were to proceed as fast as possible into the great square where they were to form and proceed on such services as might be found necessary. We were not discovered till within half gun shot of the landing place, when I directed the boats to cast off from each other give an hurra and push for the shore.

A fire of 30 or 40 pieces of cannon with musketry from one end of the town to the other opened on us but nothing could stop the intrepidity of the Captains leading the divisions. Unfortunately the greater part of the boats did not see the mole but went on shore thro' a raging surf which stove all the boats to the left of it. For the detail of their proceedings, I send you a copy of Captain Troubridge's account to me and I cannot but express my admiration of the firmness with which he and his brave associates supported the honour of the British flag. Captains Fremantle and Bowen, myself with 3 or 4 boats, stormed the mole altho' opposed seemingly by 4 or 500 men took possession of it, and spiked the guns, but such a heavy fire of musketry and grape shot was kept up from the citadel and houses at the head of the mole, that we could not advance and were nearly all killed or wounded.

The *Fox* cutter in rowing towards the town received a shot under water from one of the enemy's distant batteries immediately sunk and Lieut. Gibson her commander with 97 men were drowned.

I must not omit to acquaint you of the satisfaction I received from the conduct of Lieut. Baynes of the Royal Artillery, not only from the ardour with which he undertook every service but also from his professional skill.

Captains Troubridge, Hood, Miller and Waller landed with part of the boats just to the southward of the citadel passing thro' a raging surf which stove all the boats and wet all the ammunition. Notwithstanding all these difficulties they pushed over the enemy's line wall and batteries and formed in the great square of the town about 80 marines, 80 pike men and 180 small armed seamen, where they took possession of a convent from whence they marched against the citadel, but they found it far beyond all their power to take.

At daylight (from prisoners taken) Capt. Troubridge found there were 8000 Spaniards in arms, 100 French with 5 field pieces assembled at the entrance of the town, and seeing the impossibility of getting any assistance from the ships, at 7 o'clock he sent Captain Hood with a message to the Governor, that if he was allowed freely and without molestation to embark his people at the mole head, taking off such of our boats as were not stove and that the Governor should find others to carry off the people, the squadron now before the town would not molest it. The Governor told

Captain Hood that he thought they ought to surrender prisoners of war, to which he replied that Captain Troubridge had directed him to say that if the terms he had offered were not accepted in five minutes he would set the town on fire, and attack the Spaniards at the point of the bayonet, on which the Governor instantly closed with the terms, when Captain Troubridge with his party marched with the British colours flying to the mole where they embarked in such of our boats as were not stove, the Spaniards finding others to carry them off to our ships.

And here it is right I should notice the noble and generous conduct of Don Juan Antonio Gutierrez the Spanish Governor. The moment the terms were agreed to he directed our wounded to be received into the hospitals and all our people to be supplied with the best provisions that could be procured and sent offers that the ships were at liberty to send on shore and purchase whatever refreshments they were in want of, during the time we might lay off the island.[1]

Lady Nelson's Memorandum of the Events of July 1797[2]

The night Sir Horatio Nelson lost his arm he called Lieut. Nisbet into his cabin whose watch it was to assist him in sorting Lady N. letters in order to burn them saying they would not fall into the hands of anyone. After this business was done he said ' what are you equipped for? the care of the ship falls to you.' 'The ship, Sir, must take care of herself.' 'You must not go, supposing your poor mother was to lose us both, what will she do?' 'I will go this night if I never go again.' In the act of Sir H. putting his foot over the boat he was shot thro' the elbow. Lieut. N. who was close to him saw him turn his head from the flash of the guns, say to him 'I am shot thro' the elbow.' Upon which he seated him in the boat. The sight of the blood pouring from the arm affected him. Lieut. N. took off his hat in order to catch the blood and feeling where the bones were broken he grasped the arm with one hand which stopped the bleeding, the revolting of the blood was so great that Sir H. said he never could forget it and he tied up his arm and placed him as comfortably as he could with his two silk neckerchiefs from his throat, and then found one Lovel a seaman and 5 other sailors to assist in rowing him off. The tide had receded which caused great difficulty in getting the boat into the water. After 5 men had with difficulty got the boat into the water, Lieut. N. taking an oar, the first

---

[1] This account is a copy of the original dispatch sent by Nelson to St. Vincent, which was one of the first documents signed with his left hand.

[2] Monmouth MSS., Nelson papers, Vol. V. This account was written about 1806 for the life of Nelson being prepared by the Rev. J. Clarke.

thing which aroused Sir H. N. was the voice of Lieut. N. desiring the steersman to row under the batteries, upon which the sailor said 'Sir, we will never get the Admiral on board.' Sir H. called 'Josiah lift me up', which he did by placing his back against one of the benches and from the very heavy fire of the battery he saw his perilous situation and said 'Strike out to sea', upon which Lieut. N. said 'No Sir, if we do that we never get you on board', he then said 'Take you the tiller', and to the sailors 'Obey Lieut. N.' upon which they steered close under the batteries, thro' a heavy fire and tempestuous sea the spray from the shot coming and not long before they come to the ship pick up 2 or 3 of the *Fox* cutter's men. When the boat reached the side of the ship Nisbet called out 'Tell the surgeon the Admiral is wounded and he must prepare for amputation', upon which they offered to let down the chair, Sir H. Nelson said 'No I have yet my legs and one arm', and he walked up the side of the ship, Lieut. N. keeping so close that in case he had slipped he could have caught him.

On getting on the quarter deck the officers as usual saluted him by taking off their hats, which compliment Nelson returned with his left hand as if nothing had happened.

Lovel took off his shirt and gave him slips to tie the poor arm round his neck.

Lord Nelson said in ten minutes more he was no more.

The Rev. William Nelson to Nelson[1]

Hilborough,
October 7, 1797

Private.

MY DEAR BROTHER,—I think I never left *even you* with an heavier heart than I did last Friday, more particularly as it was your birthday. Could I have been certain of my churches I certainly would have stayed three or four days longer, and as ill luck would have it when I got home everyone was calling out why I did not write? Mr. Yonge is home and his curate is at liberty and we could have gone on without any difficulty.

As Lady Nelson has not put any private mark in the cover of the newspaper I conclude and hope you are doing well even tho' it is but slowly. I this day met Bayly a Swaffham surgeon and esteemed a very good one. I mentioned particularly the apparent pain in your *right hand*, he said it was a sure sign of a nerve being taken up with the artery, indeed he says it is hardly possible to avoid it, as there are so many and such small ones:

[1] Monmouth MSS., Nelson papers, Vol. IV.

that you must now have patience and all will do well, but he thinks the ligature had better not be forced too much; he thinks you are very safe with Mr. Cruikshanks,[1] who certainly is very eminent.

I mentioned the circumstances of your Norwich freedon to old Mr. Day, who left Norwich yesterday, he had heard you had not yet received the freedom, which was sent out to you written on parchment and the seal of the city affixed thereto, and therefore he thinks you had better defer your *public* letter, till you get it, which he has no doubt you will do in time. He tells me the report last week at Norwich was, that Dr. Prettyman was to have the residentiary of St. Paul's and vacate Norwich, and a person a good deal connected with the church assured him he knew it as a *fixed* and *certain* thing that you had secured the *vacant stall for me*, and that the Lord Chancellor had promised it to me and all was settled; I thought *your bows* to the *Great Seal* would produce something. Now they think Prettyman does not vacate, and I am to have the first vacant preferment in any Cathedral wherever ministers may have it to dispose of. I smile, and nobody will believe the contrary. I heartily wish they would prove their words, I am fully convinced could you do it, it would not be left undone a single day. Pray continue your bows to the Great Seal. Who knows what may happen now the iron is hot.

Nothing was done at Lynn at the feast, and I rather believe the Corporation is divided, and they say they have their reasons. Mr. Tharpe and Mr. Wilbraham sent you game last Thursday, other people will send at different times.

I hear Mr. Coke means to move for a public letter to be written to you from the magistrates of this county, it was to have been done at the sessions last Thursday but I have not yet heard, if it was you have received it.

I beg nobody but Lady Nelson may see my letter, not even the Boltons or Matchams on any account but keep it quite secret what I have written. Only remember when you think you want me let me, know and I will come to you. Our love and best regards attend you and Lady Nelson and believe me your truly affectionate brother, WILLIAM NELSON.

I have not yet been able to make much out about the pedigree, I have put it in a train but am afraid little can be done. When I know, you or Mr. Nayler shall hear. I congratulate you on the safe arrival of the Spanish prizes. All the doctors say that you must drink port wine; and I have sent you by the coach this evening six pigeons, carriage paid.

To Sir Horatio Nelson, K.B., No. 141, New Bond Street, London.

---

[1] William Cruikshank, the London surgeon; died 1800.

Commissioners for Taking Care of Sick and Wounded Seamen to the Admiralty[1]

Office for Sick and Wounded Seamen,
March 26, 1798

SIR,—Rear Admiral Sir Horatio Nelson K.B. having by his letter of the 21st instant requested us to give directions for his being allowed such a sum for Sick Quarters between 3rd September 1797 and the 13th December following as we may think proper for an officer of his rank, we send you enclosed a copy of the Rear Admiral's said letter and of the two papers which accompanied it, and request you will be pleased to lay them before the right honourable the Lords Commissioners of the Admiralty and we beg to be favoured with their Lordships' direction thereon.

We are Sir, your most humble servants,

R. BLAIR,
W. GIBBONS,
JA. JOHNSTON,
GIL. BLANE.

To the Honble. Evan Nepean Esq.

Enclosures

No. 1: The Surgeons' Company to the Honourable Commissioners of His Majesty's Navy[2]

Lincoln's Inn Fields,
March 1, 1798

GENTLEMEN,—In pursuance of your letter of the 13th December we have examined into the claim made by Rear Admiral Sir Horatio Nelson, for the expenses attending the cure of his arm, and we are of opinion that the sum of £135. 1. 0 the amount of such claim being for chirurgical and medical expenses is reasonable and proper to be allowed.

We are gentleman, your most obedient humble servants,

J. EARLE	C. HAWKINS
WM. LONG	JOS. WARNER
W. LUCAS	S. HOWARD
WM. COOPER	G. CHANDLER

[1] N.M.M. Admiralty records Adm/F/28.
[2] Letter from the Surgeons' Hall, where Nelson had attended, when his wound had healed, to claim his expenses.

An account of Admiral Nelson's expenses attending the cure of his wound from the 25th July 1797 to the 13th December following:

	£	s.	d.
Paid Lewis Remonier for assisting in amputating my arm and for attendance from 25th July 1797 to the 17th August following during which time he sat up 14 nights.	25	4	0
Paid Thomas Eshelby for amputating my arm, quitting the *Theseus* and attending me to England in the *Seahorse* frigate from the 25th July to 3rd September	36	0	0
Paid Mr. Nicholls at Bath for dressing my arm and attendance from the 3rd to 18th September	12	0	0
Paid Mr. Spry for medicines at Bath	2	0	0
Dr. Faulkner[1] for advice	1	1	0
Paid Mr. Cruikshanks[2] for 30 days' attendance	31	10	0
Paid Mr. Rush[4] ⎫ Earle ⎬ per advice Keate ⎭	3	3	0
Paid Michael Jefferson[4] for attendance from 19th October to the 13th December 1797[5]	24	3	0
Paid for sick quarters from 3rd September to the 13th December 1797 being 102 days	—	—	—

No. 2: Sir Horatio Nelson to the Commissioners for Sick and Wounded Seaman

No. 96, New Bond Street,
March 21, 1798

GENTLEMEN,—The Surgeon's Company not having filled up the blank opposite the Sick Quarters but told me that as they could not be judges of

---

[1] Nelson's physician in Bath.

[2] Nelson was attended daily by Mr. Cruikshank for the first month he was in London, September 19 to October 19.

[3] A consultation was held on October 19. John Rush, a senior army surgeon and inspector-general of hospitals; James Earle, Master of the Surgeons Company, surgeon at St. Bartholomew's Hospital, and Thomas Keate, surgeon to St. George's Hospital, advised against a further operation, although the wound was not healing satisfactorily.

[4] Michael Jefferson had been surgeon in the *Agamemnon* and *Captain*.

[5] On December 13 the wound began to heal, the poison having worked its way out.

what was proper to be allowed to an officer of my rank they left it open for the decision of the proper board, and as I apprehend this expense comes more immediately within the cognizance of your department I request you will give directions for my being allowed such a sum for Sick Quarters as you may think proper for an officer of my rank.

Enclosed I send you a copy of the account allowed by the Navy Board, also a copy of the report of the Surgeons' Company thereupon. I am etc., HORATIO NELSON.

To the Commissioners for Sick and Wounded Seamen.[1]

Description of Round Wood, near Ipswich

Particulars and conditions of sale of the following estates to be sold in auction in nine lots by Roper and Doughty at the sign of the White Horse, situate in Ipswich in Suffolk on Tuesday the 26th day of September 1797 at eleven o'clock in the forenoon:[2]

Lot 3. 'A modern built messuage: consisting of a small hall, 2 genteel parlours, a dressing room, kitchen, back kitchen, dairy, cellar, 3 wine vaults, 4 good bed chambers, 2 dressings rooms, and 2 servants' chambers; also a large barn, stables, cow-house and other offices; a well planted garden together with 50 A. 1 R. 35 P. by survey of exceeding rich arable land in high cultivation situate in the parishes of St. Margaret in Ipswich and Rushmere and in the hamlet of Wix Ufford in Ipswich. The house is now occupied by Capt. Edge under an agreement determinable on 6 months' notice; the land was late in the occupation of the said John Kirby.

The buildings and 31 A. 3 R. 16 P. of the land comprised in this lot are copyhold of inheritance of the Manor of Christchurch otherwise Withepole House, in Ipswich subject to a fine arbitrary on death or alienation, and to an annual rent of 17s. 1d.; the residue of the land is freehold.

The lot is assessed to the land tax £7 2s a year.'

[1] The letter has been minuted by the Secretary to the Admiralty: 'Own receipt and acquaint them [the Commissioners] that their Lordships do not think it right to allow him to make any charge for Sick Quarters and refer him to the Navy Board who will grant him such allowances as are proper to be made to him agreeably to H.M. order in Council.'

[2] B.M. Add. MS. 30,170. Sale catalogue. Round Wood was bought by Nelson for £2,000. The articles of agreement were signed on November 13 with John Kirby, Captain Berry being the witness.

Nelson to Lord St. Vincent[1]

London,
October 6, 1797

MY DEAR LORD,—Waller is gone but I shall send this letter after him and as reinforcements do not get from Portsmouth very actively I have no doubt of catching him. My pension will Lord Spencer says be the same as those of 1st June £712 with the deductions. Lord Howe made many of not only handsome but kind enquiries after you. The King asked how your general health was. I told H.M. that considering the great fatigue you was undergoing that your health was tolerable.

My poor arm is the same as Dr. Weir left it. The ligature still fast to the nerve, and very painful at times. The moment I am cured I shall offer myself for service and if you continue to hold your opinion of me, shall press to return with all the zeal although not with all the personal ability I had formerly. Sir Gilbert Elliot is a warm admirer of yours. His affairs were so uncomfortable respecting Corsica that he had not the heart to write to anybody. I told him of your goodness to his son. As to politics I am not likely to know anything. Couriers are said to be daily passing to France but peace does not seem expected. I had the pleasure of being introduced to Sir Charles Grey. He is not the least like Capt. Grey except in the eyes. Frederick is in town but cannot get employed much to his regret.

Lady Nelson desires to present her best respects and with me most anxiously hopes Nisbet continues to merit your kind protection. Command me here in any way which can be useful and believe with the greatest affection your most obliged HORATIO NELSON.

I beg my compliments to Grey and all my friends about you. I have seen your sword. It is very handsome.

To Earl St. Vincent.

---

[1] N.M.M. MS. 58/040, Autograph collection. Part of this letter was printed by Clarke and McArthur, from whom Nicolas took his copy (*Despatches*, Vol. II, p. 448). The original letter has just been deposited in the N.M.M.

Chapter 5

THE HERO OF THE NILE
1798

Introduction

Despite his ill success off Santa Cruz, Nelson had not lost the confidence of his commander-in-chief, now the Earl of St. Vincent. Already on September 14 he was writing to Lord Spencer: 'I beg that Admiral Nelson may be sent to me.' At the end of February 1798 Nelson and his wife returned to lodgings in Bond Street, and on February 28 Nelson took Captain Fremantle to a levee. On March 14 he took leave of George III. Lady Spencer used to speak of Nelson's appearance, when he was suffering from his wound gained at Teneriffe and visiting the First Lord to talk of the needs of St. Vincent's fleet: 'A most uncouth creature', she thought him, sickly, and his general appearance 'that of an idiot', but when he spoke 'his wonderful mind broke forth' and he riveted her whole attention. He continued to visit her daily during his stay in London. He told her that his wife was beautiful and accomplished, that her tenderness to him was angelic, and that she had dressed his wounds and saved his life. Lady Spencer made it a rule never to receive officers' wives, but relaxed this rule for Nelson and entertained them both to dinner on his last night in town. 'His attentions to her were those of a lover. He handed her to dinner and sat by her; apologizing to me, by saying he was so little with her, that he would not, voluntarily, lose an instant of her society.' All the accounts of Nelson remark on his good spirits and anxiety to get back to sea. Berry had carried the *Vanguard* round to Portsmouth and Nelson's flag was hoisted on March 29. Probably the packing of his baggage had presented difficulties, particularly as he had new servants, including the famous Tom Allen, from Burnham Thorpe. Many things he could not find when he unpacked, and his first letters are short and rather irritable, understandable when an admiral first goes to sea with one arm, and cannot find his possessions.

There were other tiresome delays; there was money owing to him from the fathers of the little boys he took with him; and he did not much care for his new secretary, Mr. Campbell. The list of missing articles grows, and unwanted articles, such as the weights for the kitchen scales, turn up. It would appear they must have packed in a hurry from their London lodgings. There is wine to send to Ipswich, including a present from the Governor of Teneriffe, Nelson's late victorious enemy.

The *Vanguard* sailed with a convoy on April 9 and arrived at the Tagus, St. Vincent's base, on April 23. Here Nelson found Josiah in command of the *Dolphin* and wishing to get to sea. His stepfather was not overpleased to see him. The fond tolerance had given place to petty fault-finding. Lisbon was the necessary base for the fleet blockading Cadiz. Lord Spencer and St. Vincent had corresponded about the possibility of Portugal making peace with Spain and excluding British ships. Nelson refers to this fear, which he had probably discussed with Lord Spencer. St. Vincent, was at sea off Cadiz on the look-out for some Spanish ships which were expected, and Nelson joined him, evidently prepared once again to take command of the inshore squadron and harry the defences every night. He writes as much to the Duke of Clarence and regrets to his wife that he has not brought out bomb-vessels for the proper destruction of Cadiz and the unfortunate Dons. He was soon to realize that greater deeds were within his grasp.

Since the evacuation of the Mediterranean, brilliantly carried out by the British fleet, and especially by the rearguard commanded by Admiral Nelson, St. Vincent had been hankering to get back there and he had not spared the First Lord his hankerings. Without the British fleet British trade in the Mediterranean was dead. And now, faced by the imminent loss of the Tagus and a base at Lisbon, St. Vincent failed to see how he could maintain a watch on Cadiz with a base at Gibraltar which sailing ships could only leave with the aid of the levanter, and Gibraltar was also too vulnerable, for the stores could be destroyed by bombs. But if the fleet was driven from its watch on Cadiz it could reoccupy the Mediterranean and harass the French lines of communications, and stir up Austria, Sardinia, the Two Sicilies and Turkey to resist the French. He thought a range round the Mediterranean was quite feasible and might do considerable damage to the enemy. Meanwhile his information from Leghorn reported great activity at Toulon, with troops and transports and a fleet preparing for an expedition; probably against Ireland, thought St. Vincent. And on May 1 St. Vincent wrote to Spencer that the arrival of Lord Nelson had given him new life, and he was putting the *Orion* and *Alexander* and some frigates under his command and sending this squadron to endeavour to ascertain the real objects of the preparations making by the French. Nelson carried his convoy on to Gibraltar and there watered his squadron.

St. Vincent had unwittingly forestalled the Cabinet: such was the responsibility of a commander-in-chief on a foreign station in 1798. The

Austrians had made peace with France by the Treaty of Campo Formio (October 17, 1797), but the occupation of Rome and Switzerland in 1798 alarmed the Court of Vienna, who also saw in this a threat to the court of Naples, and the Empress of Austria was naturally interested in supporting her mother, the Queen of Naples. An Austro-Neapolitan alliance was being discussed, and although the British ministers were unaware of this, they could see that the two countries might be willing to set up a new coalition against France. The Austrians had complained about a war loan and also thought the retreat of the British fleet from the Mediterranean was the direct cause of their defeat by the French as well as being a breach of the last alliance. The British ministers would not consider a further loan but they decided on April 28 to send a strong fleet into the Mediterranean, to back a new coalition against France.

At first there was no particular fear for Egypt from the French preparations, but rather for Naples. As far back as January 10 St. Vincent had written: 'In respect to an active squadron taking a range round the Mediterranean, I do not perceive any great obstacle. It must have occurred to your Lordship that the smallest infraction of treaty by Sardinia, Tuscany, or Naples would be immediately followed by the French army in Italy.' It had occurred to his lordship. On April 6 Spencer, at Pitt's request, sent Grenville his ideas on the possibility of St. Vincent's fleet re-entering the Mediterranean when his fleet, which Spencer considered 'the best formed to act together that perhaps ever existed', should be excluded from the Tagus. Then he thought it might be expedient 'to send Lord St. Vincent with the fleet he now has to sweep round the Mediterranean and do all the mischief he can to the French navy there.'

On April 29 St. Vincent was warned of the arduous nature of the measures the ministers now had in contemplation and was given the choice of taking his whole fleet up into the Mediterranean, warning the Admiralty, so that new steps could be taken to deal with the ships in Cadiz, or else to detach a squadron: 'I think it almost unnecessary to suggest to you the propriety of putting it under the command of Sir H. Nelson whose acquaintance with that part of the world, as well as his activity and disposition, seem to qualify him in a peculiar manner for that service.' On May 1 Spencer promised St. Vincent reinforcements, consisting of eight ships from the coast of Ireland under Sir Roger Curtis, so that St. Vincent could remain off Cadiz and send a strong force up the Straits. St. Vincent's agent from Leghorn, now in London, thought the armament designed for the Levant, but Spencer did not believe it. On May 19 St. Vincent was able to write home that the ships were ready to intercept Nelson in the Mediterranean.

The reinforcements changed places with the inshore squadron at night so as not to alarm the Dons. After which Lord Spencer was kept starved of news until St. Vincent's letter of July 15, which enclosed copies of five letters from Nelson to St. Vincent and the remark: 'Not fit for the eye of a gossiping board, it is proper your Lordship should see the inmost recesses of such a soul as Nelson's.'

Meanwhile Nelson had entered the Mediterranean with three seventy-fours, the *Vanguard*, *Orion* (Captain Sir James Saumarez) and *Alexander* (Captain Alexander Ball), and all the frigates that could be spared. And St. Vincent had sent to join his flag under Troubridge, in the *Culloden*, a chosen band of ships and men, the men those 'choice fellows of the inshore squadron', 'the élite of the navy of England'. Thirteen seventy-fours, a fifty and an eighteen-gun brig made up the fleet, for when they joined forces they found the *Vanguard* had been dismasted in a gale and was now repaired but that the frigates had parted company and not rejoined. This was a heavy blow because Nelson was unable to extend his look-out without frigates and this lessened the chance of intercepting the French armament at sea, the warships being encumbered by the transports and storeships.

Back in England, by June 11, Nelson's friend Elliot, now Lord Minto, knew that he had actually gone up into the Mediterranean with only three sail of the line and that St. Vincent would send nine more to join him when he had received reinforcements. The news was not out because the ministers were waiting until the reinforcements had joined Nelson. Minto got the information from Lord Gambier, a 'gossiping' Lord of the Admiralty. Lord Minto had in fact actually seen Lord Spencer on April 24, putting forward Nelson's name very strongly for the Mediterranean adventure which he already suspected would be planned, and he wrote to Nelson the very next day apologizing for having done it without his sanction. There is no doubt but that Nelson's name came very readily to the lips of all knowing men concerned in those days to find a very energetic naval officer. Minto's personal approach to the Board explains Gambier's apparent indiscretion.

The story of Nelson's search for the French fleet should surely rank in popular fame with his pursuit of Villeneuve across the Atlantic. On June 10 Troubridge joined Nelson. On the 14th they learnt the enemy had been seen at sea off Sicily. Captain Troubridge was sent into Naples in Hardy's brig, the *Mutine*. On June 20 they were passing through the Straits of Messina. On the 22nd they learnt Malta had fallen to the French. In the Appendix is given the intelligence Nelson obtained that day, and submitted to his five senior captains for their advice, which was to press on for Egypt. They pushed on to Alexandria, but the British consul was away and the Turks were surprised and ignorant of any threat. The British fleet had, as it

PLATE XII. Oil painting of the Reverend Edmund Nelson, aged seventy-eight, by Sir William Beechey, R.A. (see p. 552: Lady Nelson's letter to Nelson, March 4, 1800).

turned out, by taking the shorter route, got ahead of the French armament, which arrived the next day. This could scarcely have happened if Nelson had not lost his frigates, which indeed were sighting and scaring the French as they in their turn tried to rejoin Nelson. So back towards Naples, first watering at Syracuse, which took five days. Whether or not Lady Hamilton obtained secret orders from the Queen of Naples to open Neapolitan ports to the English will remain a matter of opinion or a mystery. It did not much matter, as Nelson's orders were to force Neapolitan ports or else quit the Mediterranean, and by forcing them he also forced Naples into conflict with the French and into the arms of the new coalition.

From Syracuse, with a happy intuition, the British fleet steered back to Alexandria, and the battle of the Nile fought on August 1 was the result. The excitement in the squadron must have been intense when first the masts of the transports anchored in Alexandria's two harbours and then the warships came into view, carefully anchored in Aboukir Bay. Nelson's immediate attack, at sunset, with orders to be ready to anchor by the stern an obvious though new manœuvre, found the French unprepared. The attack was led by Captain Foley in the *Goliath*, the fastest ship. Nelson hailed Hood in the *Zealous* to ask whether he could pass ahead of the French line. Hood did not know and would try, but Foley sailed past him and seems to have made his own decision to envelop the two sides of the French line. Lord Minto's son, George Elliot, serving as a midshipman in the *Goliath*, records that Captain Foley had a French atlas which suggested, fortunately correctly, that there was sufficient depth of water for the line of battle to round the head of the anchored French line of battle. The French were short of men and did not expect an attack that night and their ships were not cleared for action on the shore side. In the morning the batteries would have opened from what was later named Nelson's Island, and could perhaps have done some harm. Villeneuve, the French admiral who escaped in the *Guillaume Tell* to fight again, and lose to Nelson again, was blamed for not warping his ship to windward; not that it would have been an easy manœuvre, but he could have hauled his ship out of line or have slipped and got under way and engaged the enemy somehow. As it was, the Frenchman engaged fought very well, and were chewed up, ship by ship. If Nelson had not been wounded, no French line-of-battle ships would have escaped. This is no reflection on his captains, his gallant Band of Brothers, but once the battle was over, then the squadron required the leadership of Nelson to secure the total annihilation of the enemy, by taking steps to overpower the two French ships of the line which had not been engaged.

2 c

After the victory the dispatches carried by Captain Berry were sent to St. Vincent in the *Leander*, unfortunately made a prize by a Nile fugitive *Le Genereux*. Thus the news sent direct to the Admiralty and taken over land by Captain Capel did not reach England until October 2 by which time Dundas was asking Spencer whether or not he realized the danger to India, because Bonaparte's exploits in Egypt were well known.

Three short letters from Nelson to his wife before and after the battle suggest that some are missing. Then a longer letter describing the *Vanguard's* arrival at Naples introduces us once more, suddenly and dramatically, to Lady Hamilton, as 'the very best woman in the world' thumps to the deck in a faint and bruises herself. According to his lady, Lord Spencer also 'fell on the floor insensible' when told incautiously by his secretary of this same famous victory. Josiah adds a short note to his stepfather's letter, and a surprisingly long poem is copied out by him. For once his mother got good measure. Josiah, who had joined Nelson after the battle, was now captain of *La Bonne Citoyenne*. According to a prejudiced source, James Harrison, who wrote a biography of Nelson at Merton in 1806, Josiah was drunk and abusive at Nelson's birthday party given at Naples on September 29, and was later forgiven through the Hamilton's intercession. Nelson stigmatized many young and some old officers for drunkenness, commoner in 1798 than today, and one had to be at least a prince, like William, to escape his censure. The Duke of Clarence told Nelson's biographer, the Rev. J. S. Clarke, that Nelson was a remarkably sober man. 'During an intimacy of twenty four years,' Clarke noted, 'H.R.H. never saw Nelson intoxicated. The Duke thinks that during three years in the West Indies Nelson never tasted wine. His custom was to drink only one glass of champagne after dinner. Except Commissioner Coffin the Duke never saw so sober a man.' So perhaps this was Josiah's failing which Nelson could not cure. There is no doubt that Nelson's complaints of Josiah's conduct, real or imagined, must from now on have pained his wife, who was also a fond mother.

The twenty letters from his wife to Nelson show her distress at his accounts of the missing chattels, for she too sees a one-armed admiral at sea. 'But another time I shall take more care and hope we shall have proper servants.' Then there is her pleasure at moving into Round Wood, and her pleasure at his father's pleasure, which was as near as she could get to his own. She keeps the surrounding county families at a distance, and indeed her anxiety not to offend Nelson by making improper friends is agonizing. The company of Mrs. Berry pleases her, and she is gracious to her husband's naval friends. Much time was spent in looking after two nieces, the Bolton twins, now seventeen years of age. Like all Boltons,

Nelson was told, they had bad tempers, and were outspoken, but she adds
'I would do anything for them as your nieces.' Her neighbours do not
please her, and she still delights in the small scandals that they used to
discuss as young lovers in the West Indian days. She longs for news, and
when it comes she wakes up to find herself famous. Lady Hamilton sends
her a poem by Miss Knight and writes friendly letters which were also
sincere. They would surely have welcomed her out there. Unfortunately
the series of her letters stops short before the official despatches of the Nile
had reached England, but a selection of family letters has been added to
show how the news was received.

The Times first mentioned 'Admiral Nelson's Victory' in its issue of
October 2. Captain Sutton of the *Prince of Wales*, packet, had arrived
with despatches from Vienna. The Mediterranean was now reported under
the British flag, and this would act as a general good influence throughout
Europe. 'We can only hope', the leading article went on to say, 'that
Bonaparte is on the point of terminating his brilliant but short career on
the sands of Egypt.' The official announcement of the happy event was
described in the next issue. 'The Park and Tower guns and the merry peals
of the bells from the steeples of several churches soon announced this
happy news to the public.' The Admiralty messenger, Mr. Winchester, had
been sent express to the King at Weymouth, 'in order that his Majesty
might learn the glad tidings before he went to rest.' 'The illuminations at
night were general throughout the metropolis and its neighbourhood. The
Admiralty and the Navy and Victualling offices of course took the lead in
point of splendour, and such was the zeal shown by the public at large that
to particularize any house would only appear invidious. It is sufficient to
say that all ranks of people seemed to participate in the glorious news.'
'Rule Britannia' was sung at Drury Lane Theatre, with a new verse linking
Nelson and Britannia as Mistress of the Seas, and also 'Britons strike
home'. On October 4 *The Times* described the illuminations as being even
better and much more brilliant than the night before. On October 5, still
under the heading 'Admiral Nelson's Victory', the news from Weymouth
was that the Royal Family had attended the theatre the day before, the
manager had addressed the company, and a song was sung, one line of
which recorded: 'Even Arabs shout Britannia rules the waves.'

The *San Fiorenzo*, frigate, had taken the Royal Family for a sail, and
after dark she was outlined in 'variegated lamps' and rockets were fired.
On Saturday, October 6, *The Times* thought, 'Mr. Fladong's hotel in
Oxford Street stood one of the premier in point of splendour. It was parti-
cularly tasteful and elegant. It consisted of festoons of variegated lamps.
The initials of the admiral suspended from a knot, a beautiful star and large

anchor. The whole had a pleasing effect.' On October 8 *The Times* notes
that 'Mr. Nelson, the father of the gallant admiral, has long resided at
Round Wood Farm, near Ipswich, beloved and respected by his neighbours.
Lady Nelson, since the absence of her husband, has lived with him.' At
Plymouth, the celebrations had included church bells, dressed ships, a
feu de joie round the citadel ramparts, and illuminations. On October 9 *The
Times* hoped on another occasion of public rejoicings steps would be taken
to prevent excesses. Carrying loaded fire-arms in the streets should be
declared 'a nuisance'. Throwing squibs into carriages endangered lives,
and a worthy magistrate had been hurt and blinded. On October 10 *The
Times* advertised a performance at the Westminster Bridge Theatre of a
grand performance of 'Nelson's Triumph or Bonaparte in the Dumps'.
This showed the fleets in action, the Mansion House and London illuminated, Wapping in an uproar, Admiral Nelson's ships with variegated
lamps, ending up with a beautiful firework display.

Lady Nelson missed all these excitements, but instead of going to
Bath for the winter, she took lodgings in London and, now a Baroness,
attended the Queen's Drawing Room with the 'principal female nobility
and gentry'. Sometime in the middle of November she met Lord Minto
and showed him Nelson's letter of May 24 in which he described the
dismasting of the *Vanguard*. Minto thought the letter so fine he obtained
leave to copy it for his wife. Brother William, forseeing further social
activities in London, decided his daughter, now aged eleven, should go to
school there, under Lady Nelson's kindly eye. He sent his brother good
advice on points of heraldry and genealogy and then turned his attention
to designing a suitable full-dress livery for Lady Nelson's menservants.
Meanwhile the ministers were busy appraising the new political situation
and wondering how best to take advantage of a French army in Egypt
and an English fleet with indisputable command of the waters over which
that army must be supplied.

No. 196[1]

March 29, 1798
Wind—N.E.

MY DEAR FANNY,[2]—At half past five I arrived here,[3] and what you will be
surprised to hear, with great difficulty found *one* pair of raw silk stockings.

[1] This and the next six letters (Nos. 196–202) have been separated from the others
and are now only known through being printed by Nicolas and by Pettigrew, both of
whom had access to the originals which they quote.
[2] Pettigrew, *Memoirs of Lord Nelson*, Vol. I, p. 114.
[3] Portsmouth, where he hoisted his flag in the *Vanguard*, Captain Berry, the *Foudroyant* not being ready for him.

I suppose in some place or other I shall find my linen, for there is scarcely any in this trunk. The wind is fair, and on Saturday morning I go on board, and with the lark on Sunday I am off.

All here are full of inquiries about you. No letter from Mr. Cooper[1]— it is shameful.

Kind love to my father and Kitty,[2] and ever believe me your most affectionate HORATIO NELSON.

No. 197[3]

March 31, 1798

MY DEAREST FANNY—I go on board at two o'clock and if possible I shall sail early tomorrow morning. I have not the scrap of a pen from Mr. Cooper. More than £45 I have laid out for his son.

Mr. Marsh has given Allen[4] no account of his money which you gave him to buy into the funds. Get it.

God bless you all, and ever believe me, your most affectionate HORATIO NELSON.

I have opened my letter to say thanks for your letter. In due time send me Marsh and Creed's account. I have no wishes but for a speedy peace.

I have wrote Mr. Cooper to send you an order for £45.

No. 198[5]

April 1, 1798

MY DEAREST FANNY,—We put to sea this morning with the convoy, but the wind at noon came to the westward which obliged us to return to St. Helen's: thus have I lost the finest East wind that has blown this year, and there can be no guess when we may have another; so much for Admiralty delays: however, I shall not go out of the ship unless upon duty, and get off as soon as possible.

My place is tolerably comfortable, but do not shine in servants. A Captain Peyton, a fellow-traveller of yours, is a passenger with me, as are two land officers for Gibraltar. Captain P. is going to the *Defence* in the room of Captain Wells.

---

[1] Mr. Cooper had a son under Nelson's care.
[2] His niece, Catherine, Mrs. Matcham's eldest daughter, married Lieutenant John Bendyshe, R.N., in 1820.
[3] Pettigrew, *Memoirs of Lord Nelson*, Vol. I, p. 114.
[4] Tom Allen, Nelson's servant, who came from Burnham Thorpe.
[5] Nicolas, *The dispatches and letters of Vice-Admiral Lord Viscount Nelson*, Vol. VII, p. cxlix—from autograph.

The Matchams, I think, are getting to Bath sooner than they first intended; but whatever may be other people's opinions, I am clear it is right you should be in your own cottage.[1]

May God Almighty bless you, will ever be the fervent prayer of your most affectionate husband HORATIO NELSON.

To Lady Nelson, Bath.

No. 199[2]

St. Helen's,
April 3, 1798

MY DEAREST FANNY,—The wind still continues as foul as it can blow, but as I am now fixed on board, it is my intention not to move out of the ship, to which I begin to be reconciled. As to news, I cannot tell you a word beyond my own ship. If you look at Queen Square Chapel, it will tell you to write or not, but on the sealed side of the letter write, 'If the *Vanguard* is sailed to be returned to Lady Nelson, Bath.'

I can only, my dear Fanny, repeat, what I hope you know, that you are uppermost in my thoughts.

With my kindest love to my father, believe me your most affectionate HORATIO NELSON.

I cannot find my black stock and buckle. I find the weights for your scales are on board this ship. Love to Kitty, my sister, Mr. Matcham etc.

No. 200[2]

St. Helen's,
April 5, 1798

Pray, my dear Fanny, did you put up the three Portugal pieces—joes? For if you did, they cannot be found. If they are not sent, so much the better. My black stock and buckle has not yet appeared, nor are the keys of my dressing-stand sent. If they were left with the stand in London, the man has neglected to pack them up. I can do very well without these things, but it is a satisfaction to mention them.

All my passengers are gone on shore, till the wind comes fair; but I shall, if possible, remain fast on board. We have had very blowing weather, and there seems no prospect of a change of wind. My baro-

---

[1] As a tenant, Captain Edge, was living in Round Wood when Nelson bought it, he had to wait for six months, till May, before he could take possession of it.

[2] Nicolas, Vol. VII, p. cxlix.—original MS. in his possession in 1846.

meter[1] told me the weather would be bad. So far it answers, and I find an amusement in attending to it.

A gentleman is just going on shore, who takes this letter; therefore I can only say, God bless you, my father etc. Your ever affectionate HORATIO NELSON.

No. 201[2]

St. Helen's,
April 7, 1798
Wind S.W.

MY DEAREST FANNY,—I have looked over my linen, and find it very different to your list in the articles as follows: thirteen silk pocket handkerchiefs: only six new, five old. Thirteen cambric ditto: I have sixteen. Twelve cravats: I have only eleven. Six Genoa velvet stocks: I have only three. You have put down thirty huckaback towels: I have from 1 to 10. Eleven is missing from 11 to 22, that is Nos. 12 and 21; therefore there is missing No. 11–22, and to 30: ten in all. I only hope and believe they have not been sent. I do not want them.

Have you the two old pieces of gold which my father gave me, for I have them not? and yet I am pretty positive I brought them home: if you have them not, they are lost.

When my print comes out,[3] you must send one to Captain James Macnamara.[4] If directed at Sir Peter Parker's, he will be sure to get it, and he is very anxious about it.

My health never was better, and only wishing for a fair wind. God bless you. HORATIO NELSON.

Have received only one letter: love to all.

No. 202[5]

St. Helen's,
April 7, 8 p.m.
April 8, noon:Wind S.W.

Many thanks, my dearest Fanny, for your two letters. From my heart, I

---

[1] When he was in the *Victory*, Nelson kept a daily weather log of the barometer readings. A barometer given by Nelson to Captain Cockburn of the *Le Minerve* is now in the National Maritime Museum.
[2] Nicolas, Vol. VII, p. cl—autograph.
[3] From the portrait by Lemuel Abbott (see Appendix, p. 436, Lady Nelson's letter of June 25).
[4] Captain Macnamara, who had served with Nelson during the Vado campaign and commanded the *Southampton* at the Battle of Cape St. Vincent, had been Nelson's companion in 1783 when they spent a few months in France together.
[5] Pettigrew, *Memoirs of Lord Nelson*, Vol. I, p. 115.

wish it was peace, then not a moment would I lose in getting to my cottage. I wrote you this morning about my things. I have bought a *new* stock buckle at double the price of the old one, which, eighteen years past, cost 1*s.* 6*s.*, just a penny per year, and it was certainly now worth 1*s.*

Cooke and Holford, No. 7, Beaufort Buildings, Strand, wrote me they have £108 0*s.* 8*d.* for me, which I have desired them to send you, but I believe it is not payable before May; but if you do not get it sooner, inquire when you go to London.

Governor Phillip is a good man, remember me kindly to him and her.

As to those people swearing off, if they are *any one* indicated, they will at least stand in the pillory. Mr. Pitt will get money whilst it is to be had, and for this world I would not take a false oath. You will take care and secure a few hundred pounds, for if England to herself is not true, our funded debt must fall, and with it who can tell *what*.

May God Almighty protect you is the most sincere prayer of your affectionate husband, HORATIO NELSON.

Kind love to my father, Kitty, my sister, and Mr. Matcham. Compliments to Mr. and Mrs. Sherston.[1]

No. 203[2]

St. Helen's,
April 7, 1798:Wind E.S.E.

MY DEAREST FANNY,—The wind is fair and we are getting under sail and I pray God to bless you and soon to send us peace when believe me nothing in this world can exceed the pleasure I shall have in returning to you. I hope to find Josiah as good as he ought to be, when I shall be happy.

I have paid the duties for my wines and Mr. Cambell[3] is gone on shore to enquire what the land carriage will be to Ipswich. If your cellar will not take the pipe, I am sure you may put it in the back pantry. On the other side I send you a perfect list. Mr. Bolton or Admiral Reeve will give house room, if Captain Edge[4] cannot receive it. The collector of the Customs here (Portsmouth) thinks it very dangerous sending it by water from its being necessary to change vessels so often. I shall determine when Mr. C. comes on board and write it at the bottom of my letter.

---

[1] Mrs. Sherston was a distant cousin of Nelson's.
[2] Monmouth MSS., Nelson Papers, Vol. III, continuing after No. 195.
[3] John Campbell, Nelson's secretary, who was recommended for other employment by Nelson after the battle of the Nile: 'He has not activity enough for me.' Campbell, then purser of the *Canopus*, died at Plymouth 2nd September, 1799.
[4] The Round Wood tenant.

I have packed up a box with the spare papers and your weights.

1 o'clock: just received your letter of the 7th. The large Portugal pieces not to be found. The paper marked small Portugal pieces I have and its contents. The value is less than the suspicion. As to the times we must hope the best. God bless you and believe me with the sincerest affection ever your HORATIO NELSON.

I wish you would write to Mr. Cooper and say that I have put myself to great inconvenience in advancing money for his son and desire him to repay you according to my desire. And also that he will write me to Lisbon who is to pay his son's bills in London for no one will take a bill in Norfolk. Captain Edge ought to have given more notice, you will. There is something about the taxes is the cause. Do not sign any papers for Captain Edge without sending them to Mr. Notcutt[1] or Mr. Bolton to look at. Mr. Cambell not being come off I cannot tell you about the way the wine is to travel, but write to Mr. Bolton to receive and to see it safe lodged. I am at this moment in a great wrath at Mr. C. keeping a whole fleet and was it not for the loss of 10 men I would assuredly leave him. You must write to Mr. Bolton to pay the money.

God bless you. At sea 6 p.m.

I have wrote a line to Mr. Cooper and if you do not hear in a week write to him. Clerk engages to deliver the wine at Ipswich for £17 14. 0d. and one pipe to be left at London.

Wine for Ipswich:—

1 Pipe of port
1 Hogshead of Busellis
1 Quarter cask of Ponte
1 Quarter cask of old Malaga
4 cases of Pachoretta Tent and
2 dozen of Teneriffe sent me by the Governor in the whole about 19 dozen.

To Lady Nelson, Bath.

No. 204

[Nicolas, III, p. 9]

Vanguard, Tagus,
April 24, 1798

MY DEAREST FANNY,—We arrived here yesterday in 14 days from St. Helen's. Lord St. Vincent is at sea off Cadiz, having wished to prevent some

---

[1] His lawyer.

Spanish ships from getting out of Cadiz but without effect, for one ship of the line the *Monarca* and 2 frigates got out on the 12th. The *Neptuna* a 84 and 2 more frigates are also on the wing, but I hope they will not escape the vigilance of the Earl.

The *Dolphin* is here and Josiah is very well.[1] I hope he will make a good man when we shall be happy. I have just seen Mr. Hunter[2] who appears a very gentlemanlike man. Josiah has not cultivated this acquaintance so much as he ought. He is tired of being confined in the Tagus and wishes to be at sea. Captain Berry is not so well as I wish him and has got the jaundice, but he is better than he was.

If possible I shall sail tomorrow to join the fleet. I can hardly describe to you the miserable appearance of this place after seeing England, and, whenever the French choose to say: 'Turn out the English and we will make peace', that moment we shall be turned off and the port shut against us. So we are treated by this power which we are keeping an army to protect. I pray fervently for peace.

With kind remembrances to my father and friends believe me, ever your most affectionate husband, HORATIO NELSON.

To Lady Nelson, Bath. [*Readdressed:* Wm. Suckling, Esq., Kentish Town, Middlesex.]

No. 205

[Nicolas, III, p. 11, part]

Vanguard, off Cadiz,
May 1, 1798

MY DEAREST FANNY,—I joined the fleet yesterday and found Lord St. Vincent everything I wished him, and his friends in England have done me justice to him for my zeal and affection. I am sure his Lordship will omit no proper opportunity of giving Josiah the other great step but I have my fears that he will not be much longer in this command for I believe he has wrote to be superseded which I am sincerely sorry for, it will considerably take from my pleasure in serving here, especially if the command is for a month only left with Sir William Parker,[3] but I will hope the best.

The Dons have I find long expected my return with bomb vessels, gunboats and every proper implement for the destruction of Cadiz and their fleet. They have prepared 3 floating batteries to lay outside their walls

---

[1] Josiah had commanded the *Dolphin*, hospital ship, since August 24, 1797. He had spent most of the winter in the Tagus.

[2] Consul at Madrid.

[3] Nelson had had some difference with Parker, who was senior to him in rank, over the Spanish prize money after the battle of Cape St. Vincent.

to prevent the fancied attack, and lo the mountain has brought forth a mouse. I am arrived a single ship and without the means of annoying them. The Admiral will probably (*secret* is going) detach me with a small squadron not on any fighting expedition,[1] therefore do not be surprised if it is some little time before you hear again from me.

The Portuguese money nor stock and buckle cannot be found. I direct this to our cottage where I hope you will fix yourself in comfort, and I pray that it will very soon please God to give us peace. England will not be invaded this summer. Bonaparte is gone back to Italy where 80 thousand are embarking for some expedition probably Sicily, Malta and Sardinia and to finish the King of Naples at a blow. There are others who think this mighty army is for Portugal, to be landed at Malaga and march thro' Spain. If they do I think they will just stop at Cadiz and take care of the Spanish navy. In short Spain is sick of the war, they have everything to lose and nothing to gain.

With every affectionate wish which a fond heart can frame believe me as ever your most affectionate husband, HORATIO NELSON.

Love regards and compliments where proper.

To Lady Nelson, Round Wood, Ipswich, Suffolk.

No. 206
[Nicolas, III, p. 12, part]

Vanguard, Gibraltar,
May 4, 1798

MY DEAREST FANNY,—I have received your letter of the 15th and 19th April. They would console me had I any misfortunes, which thank God I never had but be assured your letters add much to my comfort. As to the missing things they will never be found here, therefore must be forgot. Ward's is a curious letter, I am not surprised at the money being stolen and, as I shall have to pay the £175 the commissioners of customs will not trouble themselves about my money. Do you object to pay the bill if presented, requesting the commissioners of the customs to order my money to be paid. I shall write Ward however a civil letter.

I came here with the convoy which came out with me and may be a month before I join the Commander-in-chief. Sir John Orde is here giving fêtes etc., but I have no turn for such things when we had better be

---

[1] Before he received special orders from England, St. Vincent had proposed that Nelson should carry out a reconnaissance in the Mediterranean.

alongside a Spaniard. A propos my frigate the *Sabina*[1] is at Algeçiras about 5 miles from this place she looks well and if I catch her at sea shall certainly make free to take my property. The folks here are certainly very civil but merry and wise we had better be filling water and getting quickly to our excellent commander-in-chief than playing here. I dine today with Commissioner Ingelfield[2] he enquired after you as did Mrs. Trigg. I saw Kelly he is as fat and merry as ever and is a favourite of the Earl's. Collingwood is well and as good as ever. I am glad to see that Lady Spencer is safe. She wrote me a very civil letter about my taking her recommendation and assured me Josiah should not be forget.

I have scarcely time to say more than that you are perfectly right to get into the cottage as soon as possible. I do not believe government will by force take your house and if they did by a proper letter, I am sure it would instantly be resigned again for if they kept you in the street I would instantly strike my flag and come home to protect you, but I do not believe the story.[3]

With love and compliments where proper, believe me, your most affectionate HORATIO NELSON.

To Lady Nelson, Round Wood, Ipswich, Suffolk.

No. 207

[Nicolas, III, p. 17]

Vanguard, Island of St. Peter's in Sardinia
May 24, 1798

MY DEAREST FANNY,—I ought not to call what has happened to the *Vanguard* by the cold name of accident, I believe firmly that it was the Almighty's goodness to check my consumate vanity. I hope it has made me a better officer, as I feel confident it has made me a better man. I kiss with all humility the rod. Figure to yourself a vain man on Sunday evening at sunset walking in his cabin with a squadron about him who looked up to their chief to lead them to glory and in whom this chief placed the firmest reliance that the proudest ships in equal numbers belonging to France would have bowed their flags, and with a very rich prize laying by him. Figure to yourself this proud conceited man, when the sun rose on

---

[1] The Spanish frigate which Nelson captured on December 19, 1796, but lost the next day.
[2] Captain Inglefield had succeeded Captain Sutherland as commissioner at Gibraltar in 1796.
[3] Lady Nelson has added an explanatory note: 'There was a talk of the houses for barracks' (see Appendix, p. 426, her letter of April 17).

Monday morning his ship dismasted his fleet dispersed and himself in such distress that the meanest frigate out of France would have been a very unwelcome guest. But it has pleased Almighty God to bring us into a safe port, where altho' we are refused the rights of humanity, yet the *Vanguard* will in two days get to sea again as an Englishman of war. The exertions of Sir James Saumarez and Captain Ball[1] have been wonderful and if the ship had been in England months would have been taken to send her to sea. Here my operations will not be delayed four days, and I shall join the rest of my fleet on the rendezvous. If this letter gets to you be so good as to write a line to Lord Spencer telling him that the *Vanguard* is fitted tolerably for sea, and that what has happened will not retard my operations.

We are all health and good humour. Tell Lady Saumarez Sir James never was in better health.

With kind love to my father believe me ever your most affectionate husband, Horatio Nelson.

I have wrote to Lord Spencer by another but I still wish you to write a line to say we are all well for yours may arrive and his Lordship's miscarry.[2]

Vanguard's damages:

Foremast
Foretopmast
Foretopgallant mast and all the } gone overboard.
  yards forward
Bowsprit sprung in three places.
Maintopmast and topgallantmast with all the yards
  except topgallant yard and rigging—gone overboard.
Mizentopmast topgallantmast and all the yards
  belonging to topgallant yard—gone overboard.
A topsail yard washed out.
The mainchains, starboard
  quarters gallery washed away
  with one boat and a bower anchor.

Mr. Thomas Meek (who was recommended by Mr. Hussey, my brother Suckling etc.) killed and several seamen hurt.

To Lady Nelson, Round Wood, Ipswich.

[1] Captain Alexander Ball, of the *Alexander*, one of Nelson's senior captains, distinguished himself at the battle of the Nile. He was chiefly responsible for the long siege of Malta, which surrendered in the autumn of 1800.

[2] This letter was shown by Lady Nelson to many of her friends; some of them made copies of it. She sent it to Lord Spencer (see Appendix, p. 447, Lady Nelson's letter of September 11).

No. 208

Vanguard, off Naples,
June 15, 1798

MY DEAREST FANNY,—I wrote you a line from St. Peter's in Sardinia. My situation since then is much altered for the better having now a respectable fleet to support me.[1]

My health never was better and you may rest assured that it will always be my pride to do those things which may not be unpleasant to you to hear me named. You must be content with short letters.

With kind love to my father and all about you, believe me your most affectionate HORATIO NELSON.

To Lady Nelson, Round Wood, Ipswich.

No. 209

[Nicolas, III, p. 44]

Vanguard, in Sicily,
July 20, 1798

MY DEAREST FANNY,—Except that my health is perfect I have not a word of news to tell you. I have been sent after the French fleet but have not been able to find them to my great mortification or the event I can scarcely doubt.

Since I wrote you a line from off Naples we have been off Malta, to Alexandria in Egypt, Syria into Asia and are returned here without success. However no person will say that it's been for want of activity. I yet live in hopes of meeting these scoundrels but it would have been my delight to have tried Buonaparte on a wind; for he commands the fleet as well as army.

I hope my dear Fanny that you find everything comfortable where you are. Recollect that I am at no personal expense therefore I hope you will not be sparing of money. Glory is my object and that alone.

God Almighty bless you. Ever your most affectionate HORATIO NELSON.

Love to all with you.

To Lady Nelson, Round Wood, Ipswich, Suffolk.

[1] On June 5 Nelson received despatches from St. Vincent ordering him to seek out and destroy the French armament, known to be assembling at Toulon, and informing him that Captain Troubridge, in the *Culloden*, was joining him with a squadron of eleven ships.

No. 210

August 11, 1798

MY DEAREST FANNY,—I am thank God as much better as could be expected,[1] and what I hope will make Europe happy is the certain destruction of the French army. The people of the country are rising against them every hour. Such are the blessed fruits of our conquest.[2] Victory is certainly not a name strong enough for such a scene as I have passed.

I shall most probably be in England in November but more of this hereafter.

With kindest love to my father and all our friends. Believe me ever your most affectionate husband, HORATIO NELSON.[3]

To Lady Nelson, Round Wood, Ipswich, Suffolk.

No. 211

[Nicolas, III, p. 125, part]

Began at Sea,
September 16, 1798

MY DEAREST FANNY,—It is hardly possible for me to know where to begin. My head is almost turned by letters already and what am I not to expect when I get on shore. Noise enough to distract me. My head is healed and I am better.

The Kingdom of the two Sicilies are mad with joy from the throne to the peasant all are alike. From Lady Hamilton's letter the situation of the Queen was truly pitiable. I only hope I shall not have to be witness to a renewal of it. I give you Lady Hamilton's words: 'How shall I describe the transports of the Queen? 'Tis not possible. She fainted, cried, kissed her husband, her children, walked frantic about the room, cried, kissed and embraced every person near her exclaiming: "Oh, brave Nelson; Oh God bless and protect our brave deliverer. Oh Nelson, Nelson, what do we not owe you. Oh victor, saviour of Italy. Oh that my swollen heart could now tell him personally what we owe to him."' You may judge of the rest, but my head will not allow to tell you half. So much for that.

[1] During the battle of the Nile fought on August 1, Nelson received a wound on his forehead which he feared was fatal, but his surgeon, Michael Jefferson, pronounced it to be little more than superficial.

[2] See Appendix, p. 417, Sir William Hamilton to St. Vincent on the effects of the victory.

[3] This letter shows signs of being much handled and is torn.

My fag without success would have had no effect. But blessed be God for his goodness to me. I have your letters of May 22nd, June 11th and July 16th. The box you were so good as to send me with plates, seal etc., if sent by *L'Aigle*[1] is *lost* but never mind that, I feel equally your kindness. Do not send any more. What is likely to go on here time only can shew. I am sure I cannot guess, but as the French have only one regular ship of the line 'tis not likely I shall see any more fighting. As to Round Wood if the place or neighbourhood is not to your satisfaction, I hope the country will put me in a situation of choosing another, but my dear Fanny unless you can *game*, and talk scandal, that is *lies*, most probably your company will never be coveted by country town tabbies. Young people have more goodness than old cats. I put Hoste into a sloop of war. I hope Lord St. Vincent will allow him to remain in her. His father is under no obligation to me. If he writes *stuff* tell him so. All must go to Earl St. Vincent I have not power to make a cook. The Queen of Naples has given Hoste a very elegant diamond ring value at least £500 sterling. So much for being a messenger of good news.[2] Sir James Saumarez[3] is on his passage home, so that Lady Saumarez will have the pleasure of his company this winter. Had his wound been very little deeper it would have done his business but as it is, he is not the worse. Josiah is in the *Bonne Citoyenne*.[4] I see no prospect of his being made post. I wish he was as great a favourite of Lord St. Vincent's as I wish him, but that is not my fault. However, I hope he will do well in time. He is young and will not endeavour to make him agreeable for his interest or comfort.

September 25th: The poor wretched *Vanguard* arrived here[5] on the 22nd. I must endeavour to convey to you something of what passed, but if it was so affecting to those only who are united in bonds of friendship what must it be to my dearest wife. My friends say everything which is most dear to me in this world. Sir William and Lady Hamilton came out to sea attended by numerous boats with emblems etc. My most respectable friends had really been laid up and seriously ill, first from anxiety and then from joy. It was imprudently told Lady Hamilton in a moment. The effect was a shot. She fell apparently dead and is not yet perfectly recovered from severe bruises. Alongside my honoured friends came, the scene in the boat

[1] *L'Aigle* was wrecked near Tunis in July 1798. Josiah Nisbet had been a passenger in her (see Appendix, p. 454, Maurice Nelson to Lady Nelson, October 19, 1798).

[2] Hoste had been entrusted with Nelson's dispatches for Naples after the battle of the Nile. He commanded the *Mutine* when Captain Capel proceeded overland with the dispatches for the Admiralty.

[3] Saumarez sailed for Gibraltar with six of the French prizes (see Appendix, p. 419, St. Vincent to Sir William Hamilton).

[4] Josiah was superseded in the *Dolphin* on July 6, 1798. He took command of the *Bonne Citoyenne* on September 13.

[5] Naples.

appeared terribly affecting. Up flew her ladyship and exclaiming: '*Oh God is it possible*' fell into my arms more dead than alive. Tears however soon set matters to rights, when alongside came the King. The scene was in its way affecting. He took me by the hand, calling me his deliverer and preserver, with every other expression of kindness. In short all Naples calls me '*Nostra Liberatore*' for the scene with the lower classes was truly affecting. I hope one day to have the pleasure of introducing you to Lady Hamilton. She is one of the very best women in this world. How few could have made the turn she has. She is an honour to her sex and a proof that even reputation may be regained, but I own it requires a great soul. Her kindness with Sir William to me is more than I can express. I am in their house, and I may now tell you it required all the kindness of my friends to set me up. Her ladyship if Josiah was to stay would make something of him and with all his bluntness I am sure he likes Lady Hamilton more than any female. She would fashion him in 6 months in spite of himself. I believe Lady Hamilton intends writing you.

May God Almighty bless you my dearest Fanny and give us in due time a happy meeting. Should the King give me a peerage I believe I scarcely need state the propriety of your going to court. Don't mind the expense. Money is thrash. Again God Almighty bless you.

Ever your most affectionate HORATIO NELSON.

You cannot write to Naples by common post. The Admiralty or Secretary of State is the only way.

To Lady Nelson, Round Wood, Ipswich, Suffolk.

No. 212

[Nicolas, III, p. 134]

September 28, 1798

MY DEAREST FANNY,—I only this moment have heard that a courier is going off in a very few hours for Vienna therefore I can say in that moment with truth that I am much recovered. The goodness of Sir William and Lady Hamilton is beyond everything I could have expected or desired. The preparations of Lady Hamilton for celebrating my birthday tomorrow are enough to fill me with vanity. Every ribbon every button has 'Nelson' etc., the whole service are 'H. N. Glorious 1st August'. Songs, sonnets are numerous beyond what I ever could deserve. I send the additional verse to 'God save the King' as I know you will sing it with pleasure. I cannot move on foot or in a carriage for the kindness of the populace but good Lady

2 D

Hamilton preserves all the papers as the highest treat for you. The Queen yesterday being still ill sent her favourite son to visit and bring me a letter from her of gratitude and thanks.

Josiah is well and could he be here six months Lady Hamilton would much fashion him which indeed he wants.

> Join we great Nelson's name
> First on the roll of fame
>   Him let us sing
> Spread we his praise around
> Honour of British ground
> Who made Nile's shores resound
>   God Save the King.

Write Lady Saumarez that I have this moment a letter from Sir James dated September 17th perfectly well with the squadron. Miserable accounts of the *Guillaume Tell*.[1] I trust God Almighty will yet put her into the hands of our King. His almighty hand has gone with us to the battle, protected us and still continues destroying the unbeliever. All glory be to God, the more I think, the more I hear, the more I am astonished at the extent and good consequence of our victory. I leave Josiah to insert a paper.

To Lady Nelson, Round Wood, Ipswich, via London.

[In Josiah's Autograph:]

DEAR MOTHER,—I am now Captain of *La Bonne Citoyenne* and expect to go off Malta very soon with the Admiral. Malta is expected will be given up to the English directly they appear off there.

Believe me your affectionate J. NESBIT.

On the Arrival of Admiral Nelson[2]

> He's come the British hero see advance,
> His country's glory and the dread of France
> Each patriot's bosom glows with warm desire
> To view the hero they unknown admire.
> Each in idea would a portrait frame
> A portrait such as suits with Nelson's fame
> By most (as judging by the actions wrought)
> Of age advanced he's painted in their thought
> While Nelson yet but in the prime of life,
> With aged veterans vies with noblest strife.

---

[1] One of the two French ships of the line which escaped from the battle of the Nile.
[2] A poem printed in Naples at this time. Author unknown—possibly Josiah.

Their warlike virtues in his bosom dwell
Not rash, but brave, 'tis prudence guides his helm,
With generous zeal inflamed to serve the state
Brave Nelson fought and scorned the frowns of fate.
His tranquil bosom fearless of surprise
From innate virtue felt its courage rise.
In combat terrible but victory won
He shewed the Christian and the hero one
Humanity again resumed its place
And Nelson's bent before the throne of grace
No vain presumption filled the hero's breast
He felt that heaven the enterprise had blest
And deaf awhile to every vain applause
With bended knee adored the Great first cause
In whose blest aid depends all human force
Who crowns at will, or stops the victor's course.

No. 213
[Nicolas, III, p. 138, part]

Naples,
October 1, 1798. October 6.

MY DEAREST FANNY,—I have your letters of June 18th, 25th July and although I have them of a later date yet they are additional proofs of your kindness. Our time here is busily employed and between business and what is called pleasure I am not my own master for 5 minutes. The continued kind attention of Sir William and Lady Hamilton must ever make you and I love them and they are deserving of the love and admiration of all the world.

You would know before this of the capture of the *Leander*[1] I hope poor Berry is safe. It has been a great misfortune I dare say he feels but I hope the King will consider his situation. We have just got news of my letter getting to Constantinople. The Grand Signior has ordered me a rich jewel[2] if it was worth a million my pleasure will be to see it in your possession. My pride is being your husband, the son of my dear father and in having Sir William and Lady Hamilton for my friends. While those approve of my conduct I shall not feel or regard the envy of thousands. The King

[1] Captain Berry was sent with duplicate dispatches in the *Leander*, Captain Thompson, which was captured off Candia on August 18 by *Le Genereux*. He was wounded and taken prisoner, but released on parole and arrived in England in December.
[2] The *chelangk* or plume of triumph.

yesterday gave us a great dinner on board ship and his whole fleet fired a royal salute when my health was drunk. Part of the band of brothers[1] go to sea tomorrow, Josiah with them and more of us will be soon after them. God almighty bless and protect you from all harm is the constant prayer of your affectionate husband, HORATIO NELSON.

Kind love to my father.

Could I my dear Fanny tell you half the honours which are done me here not a ream of paper would hold the heads. On my birthday night 80 people dined at Sir William's, 1,740 came to a ball, 800 supped conducted in such a style of elegance as I never saw or shall again probably. A rostral column is erected under a magnificent canopy never Lady Hamilton says to come down while they remain in Naples. My father will tell you all about it, in the front Nelson, on the pedestal 'veni vidi vici', anchors inscriptions having [*part missing*] were numerous.

> The British Nelson rivals Caesar's fame
> Like him he came, he saw, he overcame,
> In conquest modest as in action brave
> To God the glory pious Nelson gave.
>
> From Gallia Bonaparte sailed
> Nelson from Albion's sea
> Chains were our lot if one prevail
> The other sets us free.
>
>   C. K.[2]

A little circumstance happened yesterday which does honour to the King and is not unpleasant to me. I went to view the manufactory of china, magnificent. After admiring all the fine things sufficient to seduce my money from my pocket, I came to busts in china of all the royal family; this I immediately ordered and when I wanted to pay I was informed that the King had directed whatever I chose to be sent and free of all costs. It was handsome in the King and my taking nothing but the busts of the royal family must please them. God bless you. Mr. Fuller[3] will never be unkindly treated in the final debt.

To Lady Lady Nelson, Round Wood, Ipswich, Suffolk. [*Readdressed:* No. 141, Bond Street.]

---

[1] Nelson's term for his fellow-officers; also used by Sir William Hamilton.
[2] Lines by Miss Cornelia Knight, authoress, daughter of Sir Joseph Knight. She lived in Naples with her mother and after the latter's death was in the Hamilton's household. She returned to England with them in 1800.
[3] Tenant of the farm at Round Wood.

Memorandum[1]

Constantinople, October 3, 1798
Lord Grenville's Office,
November 3, 1798

A superb *aigrette* (of which the marginal sketch gives but an imperfect idea) called a chelengk, or plume of triumph, such as has been upon very famous and memorable successes of the Ottoman Arms conferred upon victorious (Musselmen) Seraskers (I believe never before upon a disbeliever) as the 'ne plus ultra' of personal honour as separate from official dignity. The one in question is indeed rich of its kind; being a blaze of brilliants crowned with a vibrating plumage; and a radiant star in the middle, turning upon its centre by means of watch work which winds up behind. This badge was absolutely taken from one of the imperial turbans and can hardly, according to the ideas annexed to such insignia here, be considered as less than equivocal to the first order of Chivalry in Christendom—such at least was my aim in the indication.

> [*Sketch of the aigrette is given with the note:* N.B. The top should have 13 fingers or sprigs in allusion to the 13 ships taken]

[*Endorsed:* 'This was sent me by Lord Nelson. FRANCES H. NELSON AND BRONTE.']

APPENDIX

Will of Sir Horatio Nelson
March 21, 1798[2]

This is the last will and testament of me Sir Horatio Nelson, knight of the most honourable order of the Bath, Rear-Admiral in his Majesty's Navy. In the first place I charge all my real and personal estates with the payment of my debts and legacies item I give to my brother Mr. Maurice Nelson two-hundred pounds to my son-in-law Josiah Nesbit five hundred pounds and to Francis Lepe fifty pounds and I give and devise unto my dear wife Dame Frances Herbert Nelson all my freehold and copyhold lands tenements and hereditaments to hold to her heirs and assigns for ever and I also give

---

[1] Monmouth MSS., Nelson papers, Vol. V. This information on the significance of the *chelengk* was provided by Mr. Spencer Smith, the British plenipotentiary at Constantinople. Lord Grenville was at that time Secretary of State.

[2] Monmouth MSS., Nelson papers, Vol. III.

to my said wife all the rest of and residue my personal estate and effects but in case my dear wife shall happen to depart this life in my lifetime or in case she shall survive me and shall die without having made any will or disposition of the estates and property hereby by me devised to her then and in either of the said cases I do give to my said son-in-law Josiah Nesbit the legacy or sum of ten thousand pounds instead of the said sum of five-hundred pounds hereinbefore by me given to him and I appoint my said wife sole executrix of this my will but in either of the before mentioned events I do appoint the said Josiah Nesbit executor of this my will.

In witness whereof I have to this my last will and testament set my hand and seal this twenty-first day of March one thousand seven hundred and ninety eight.

HORATIO NELSON. [seal]

Signed sealed published and declared by the said Sir
Horatio Nelson the testator as and for his last will
and testament in the presence of us who in his
presence at his request and in the presence of each
other have subscribed our names as witnesses hereto

THOMAS COMBE of Bishops Court, Chancery Lane
THOMAS SMITH
WILLIAM RYDER

St. Vincent to Nelson[1]

Ville de Paris, before Cadiz,
May 21, 1798

MY DEAR ADMIRAL,—I look for the reinforcement every hour the *Valiant* lugger having joined on the 19th with advices that Sir Roger Curtis with his whole squadron was ordered to proceed to join me from Cape Clear where he was cruising he was not to touch at Lisbon it is therefore reasonable to expect he will appear in a day or two: in the meanwhile the ships named in the inclosed list are completed to 6 month's provisions of all species except bread and wine of which they have as much as they can stow and their water kept up from day to day and the instant Sir Roger Curtis appears, they will proceed to endeavour to intercept you in your way down. Should they be so fortunate as to accomplish this object you will take everything out of the *Orion* she can spare, consistently with her passage to Gibraltar, where you will direct her to proceed to complete her water and provisions to four months of all species and join me at this anchorage. And you may inform Sir James Saumarez that I have assurances from the

[1] N.M.M. MS. 9848, Hamilton papers, copy of letter made by Sir William Hamilton.

Admiralty the *Orion* and *Colossus* shall be soon ordered to England, where he expressed so very anxious and importunate desire to go in a conversation I had with him on the poop of the *Ville de Paris* that I feel myself bound not to place him in a situation likely to defeat the object of his desires.

Very sincerely yours, St. VINCENT.

Troubridge . . .	Culloden	Vanguard . . .	Ad. Nelson
Foley . . .	Goliath	Alexander . . .	Ball
(Louis) . . .	Minotaur	Hector . . .	Aplin
Peyton . . .	Defence	Leander 50 . .	Thompson
Darby . . .	Bellerophon	Flora . . .	Middleton
(Westcott) . . .	Majestic	Alcmene . . .	Hope
Gold . . .	Audacious	Terpsichore . . .	Gage
Hood . . .	Zealous	Espoir . . .	Bland
Holowell . . .	Swiftsure	Bon Citoyen . . .	Precalet
Miller . . .	Theseus		(Retalick)

Nelson's Questionnaire[1]

June 22, 1798

The vessel spoke with this morning is from Malta one day, he says the two frigates in sight are French, that the French colours and garrison are in Malta, that the Fleet and transports left it six days today, but they did not know where they were going, some said to Sicily.

With this information what is your opinion? Do you believe under all circumstances which we know that Sicily is their destination? Do you think we had better stand for Malta, or steer for Sicily?

Should the armament be gone to Alexandria and get safe there our possessions in India are probably lost. Do you think we had better push for that place?

Replies of the Captains:

June 22, 1798

From the intelligence received respecting the French fleet I am of the opinion that they are gone toward Alexandria, and that it is best for his Majesty's Service that we should steer in that direction. Had the French fleet any intention of attacking Sicily immediately and made for that island when they left Malta, we were off Saragossa yesterday and should certainly have had information of it. ALEXANDER M. BALL (H.M.Ship *Alexander*).

[1] N.M.M. MS. 9960, Croker collection in the Phillipps papers. The questionnaire is holograph (unsigned) by Nelson; the replies by the senior captains are signed.

I am clearly of opinion that the French armament are steering for Alexandria, and that it would be most advisable to pursue them, immediately. E. Berry (H.M.Ship *Vanguard*)

Vanguard, at Sea,
   June 22, 1798.

Admitting the account of the French fleet's having passed Sicily, and left Malta, on last Saturday to be true, it is most probable they are gone to the eastward, and as the wind now is, it would be losing much time endeavouring to regain Sicily, which by the account from Naples does not appear to be their object. H. D. Darby (H.M.Ship *Bellerophon*).

Vanguard,
   June 22, 1798.

The French fleet having left Malta six days ago, had their destination been the island of Sicily, there is reason to presume we should have obtained information of it yesterday off Syracuse or the day before in passing through the Pharo of Messina—under all circumstances I think it is most conducive to the good of His Majesty's service to make the best of our way for Alexandria as the only means of saving our possessions in India should the French armament be destined for that country. James Saumarez (H.M.Ship *Orion*).

Vanguard, at Sea,
   June 22, 1798.

I am of the opinion that Sicily is not the object at present of the French armaments, or the Governor of Saragosa would certainly have sent off information when we passed so close yesterday; from the length of time the enemy has left Malta if they were going to Sicily they must have landed at least 4 days since, and of course it would have been known all over the island.

Considering all circumstances I am led to think Egypt is their present destination, and that it will be best for His Majesty's service to endeavour to overtake and destroy them as their getting possession of Alexandria or

any port in Egypt will put our possessions in India in a very perilous situation. T. TROUBRIDGE (H.M.Ship *Culloden*).
Vanguard,
   June 22, 1798.

Nelson to St. Vincent[1]
(Copy)

Vanguard, at Sea,
June 29, 1798

MY LORD,—Although I rest confident my intentions will always with you have the most favourable interpretations yet when success does not crown an officer's plan, it is absolutely necessary that he should explain the motives which actuate his conduct and therefore I shall state them as briefly as possible.

Captain Troubridge joined me on the 7th June. From calms it was the 12th before I got round Cape Corse (I must here state that I had nothing in the shape of a frigate but the *Mutine* Brig),[2] I then sent the *Mutine* to look into Telamon Bay which as all the French troops had not left Genoa on the 6th I thought a probable place for the rendezvous of a large fleet, for completely ignorant as I was of the destination of the enemy I felt it my duty to take every precaution not to pass them. On the 13th the *Mutine* looked into Telamon Bay but found nothing there, I ran the fleet between Plenosa and Elba and Monte Christi and on the 14th at noon, was off Civita Vechia when we spoke a Tunisian cruiser, who reported that he had spoke a Greek on the 10th who told him that on the 4th he had passed through the French fleet off the N.W. end of Sicily steering to the eastward. From this moment I was in anxious expectations of meeting with dispatch boats, Neapolitan cruisers etc., with letters for me from Naples giving me every information I could desire (but my hopes were vain). On the 15th I made the Pensa Islands when not finding a cruiser I sent Captain Troubridge in the *Mutine* to talk with Sir William Hamilton and General Acton and to state my distress for frigates.

On the 17th in the bay of Naples I received my first letter from Sir William Hamilton and in two hours Captain Troubridge returned with information that the French were off Malta on the 8th going to attack it, that Naples was at peace with the French republic therefore could afford us no assistance in ships, but that under the rose, they would give us the use of their ports and sincerely wished us success, but did not give me the

---

[1] N.M.M. MS. 9578, St. Vincent's papers—printed by Nicolas, Vol. III, p. 38.
[2] Commanded by Captain Hardy, who was promoted flag-captain in the *Vanguard* when Berry went home with dispatches.

smallest information of what was, or likely to be the future destination of the French armament. With this comfortable account I pushed for the Faro of Messina. On my way I heard of the French landing in Malta, and that on Tuesday the 12th they had taken the old city, that the fleet was anchored between Goza and Malta.

On the 20th off Messina the English consul came on board to tell me that Malta had surrendered on the 15th, the Russian minister having arrived the day before from Malta when the intelligence came over, but I received not the smallest information or notice from the Sicilian government. Keeping the Sicilian shore on board on the 21st I was close off Syracuse and hoisted our colours. A boat in the evening towed out a mile but although I brought too and sent the *Mutine* in shore, she rowed back again. On the 22nd in the morning being off Cape Passaro the *Mutine* spoke a brig which sailed from Malta the day before. The master reported that Malta surrendered on Friday the 15th June and that on Saturday the 16th the whole French fleet left it, as was supposed for Sicily, that a French garrison was left in the town and French colours flying. The wind at this time was blowing strong from the W.N.W. The vessel had been spoke three hours before and was gone out of my reach. I could not get to Malta till it moderated and then might get no better information.

Thus situated I had to make use of my judgement with information from Naples that they were at peace with the French Republic, that General Bonaparte had sent on shore to Sicily that the King of Naples need not be alarmed at the French armament for it had not Sicily for its object. It was also certain the Sicilian government were not alarmed or they would have sent off to me. I recalled all the circumstances of this armament before me, 40,000 troops in 280 transports, many hundred pieces of artillery, waggons, draft horses, cavalry, artificers, naturalists, astronomers, mathematicians etc. The firstr endezvous inc ase of separation was Bastia, the second Malta. This armament could not be necessary for taking possession of Malta. The Neapolitan ministers considered Naples and Sicily as safe. Spain after Malta, or indeed any place to the westward I could not think their destination, for at this season the westerly winds so strongly prevail between Sicily and the coast of Barbary that I conceived it almost impossible to get a fleet of transports to the westward. It then became the serious question where are they gone. (Here I had deeply to regret my want of frigates and I desire it may be understood that if one half of the frigates your Lordship had ordered under my command had been with me, that I could not have wanted information of the French fleet.) If to Corfu in consequence of my approach (which they knew from Naples on the 12th or 13th) they were arrived by this time, the 22nd.

Upon their whole proceedings together with such information as I have been able to collect it appeared clear to me that they were either destined to assist the rebel Pacha and to overthrow the present government of Turkey or to settle a colony in Egypt and to open a trade to India by way of the Red Sea, for strange as it may appear at first sight, an enterprising enemy if they have the force or consent of the Pacha of Egypt may with great ease get an army to the Red Sea and if they have concerted a plan with Tippo Saib to have vessels at Suez, three weeks at this season is a common passage to the Malabar coast, when our India possessions would be in great danger. I therefore determined with the opinion of those captains in whom I can place great confidence to go to Alexandria, and if that place or any other part of Italy was their destination I hope to arrive time enough to frustrate their plans. The only objection I can fancy to be started is you should not have gone sail a long voyage without more certain information of the enemy's destination. My answer is ready, who was I to get it from? The government of Naples or Sicily either knew not or chose to keep me in ignorance. Was I to wait patiently till I heard certain accounts if Egypt was their object, before I could hear of them they would have been in India. To do nothing was I felt disgraceful, therefore I made use of my understanding and by it I ought to stand or fall.

I am before your Lordship's judgement (which in the present case I feel is the tribunal of my country) and if, under all circumstances, it is decided that I am wrong[1] I ought for the sake of our country to be superseded, for at this moment when I know the French are not in Alexandria I hold the same opinion as off Cape Passaro, viz., that under all circumstances I was right in steering for Alexandria and by that opinion I must stand or fall. However erroneous my judgement may be I feel conscious of my honest intentions which I hope will bear me up under the greatest misfortune that could happen to me as an officer, that of your Lordship's thinking me wrong.

I have the honour to be with the highest respect your Lordship's most obedient servant, HORATIO NELSON.

To Earl St. Vincent.

Nelson to Mr. George Baldwin[2]

Merton,
January 23, 1802

SIR,—I have been honoured with your letter of the 19th desiring to know whether I considered you as our Consul in Egypt in 1798 and what

---

[1] Captain Ball, to whom Nelson showed this letter, thought it was too derogatory and 'may induce a suspicion that you are not perfectly satisfied with your own conduct'.
[2] N.M.M. MS. 55/080, De Coppet collection.

consequences I thought ensued from your not being at Alexandria when I arrived off that place in June 1798. I own I was much disappointed at not finding you at your post for I certainly thought you was consul at Alexandria by my writing you two letters of which I send you copies (but I must inform you that we sea officers are never told who are our consuls at different places or whether they are removed or changed). With respect to my opinion of what would have been the consequences had I found you at Alexandria there can be no doubt but that I should have been off Alexandria when the French fleet arrived, and most assuredly the army could not have landed in the complete order it did had an action taken place on the first day of July which assuredly it would have done had the Turks received me as a friend instead of an enemy, as the answer I received was that neither English nor French should enter the port of Alexandria. And I believe if you had been there to explain between me and the Turkish governor that I should have remained a few days to get some water and refreshments.

I am sir with great respect, your most obedient servant, NELSON AND BRONTE.

To George Baldwin, Esq.

Private

Nelson to St. Vincent[1]

Vanguard, Syracuse,
July 22, 1798

MY DEAR LORD,—I have very many letters and papers to send you, but as I have no frigate to send and at this moment cannot think it right to send *Orion* you will feel for my situation—I am as completely ignorant of the French fleet as the day I left Cape Passaro, this I am clear in that on Monday the 18th June the French began to come out of the harbour of Malta, by Tuesday night they were all out and on Wednesday morning they were seen with a strong wind at W.N.W. steering before it; this has been proved to me by 14 persons: beyond this all is conjecture, had they gone to the westward I rest confident every port and point of Sicily would have had information for me, I dare not say more, for I am sure we are betrayed, and it is far from impossible but this letter may never get to Naples. At least I expect the French minister will copy it, therefore I here assure him, that if it is possible, I will get at the French fleet. Ours is without a sick man. I have detailed every circumstance even to my thoughts.
God bless you, ever your faithful HORATIO NELSON.

[1] N.M.M. MS. 9578, St. Vincent papers—printed by Nicolas, Vol. VII, p. cliii.

Our treatment in the Sicilian ports is shameful. If they had the force this Government say they are bound by their orders to prevent our entry. Acton promised to send orders, *None has been sent*—what think of this?

[*Endorsed:* Sir Horatio Nelson, 22nd. July 1798. Recd. 25th Augt.]

Sir William Hamilton to St. Vincent[1]

Naples,
August 12, 1798

MY LORD,—I profit at the opportunity of the Spanish prize, the *Dorothea*, being sent to your Lordship by Capt. Dixon of the *Lion*, to inform your Lordship of the many disappointments we have had since I wrote last on the 18th of June by Capt. Bowen of the *Transfer* sloop. The shameful surrender of Malta to the French republic was the first and great disappointment for in all probability the business would have been completed by the brave squadron under the command of Sir Horatio Nelson in sight of Malta. The last ships of Bonaparte's fleet left Malta only the 19th of June, and Sir Horatio Nelson was in sight of the place on the 21st. I have the honour of inclosing copies of the 3 letters that I received from Sir Horatio Nelson from Syracuse, when he returned with the squadron to that port the 20th of July after having been 600 leagues in 27 days and as far as Alexandria, without getting any intelligence of the enemy or having met with any one of his frigates, which is most extraordinary, as we knew of seven frigates and cutter being gone towards the Levant to look out for the Rear-Admiral for more than three weeks passed. I received yesterday from Messina the letter inclosed and directed to your Lordship from Capt. Hope with the letter for Sir Rober Calder likewise inclosed. Capt. Hope will have informed your Lordship of the intelligence he got of the French fleet from Candia. Surely there never was such a chain of disappointments and yet we must hope for the best at last. Wherever the French fleet shall have taken refuge they will certainly be found, (having had sufficient time) well fortified.

I say nothing of the *Lion* and its prize the *Dorothea* as certainly Capt. Dixon will have made his regular report to your Lordship.

Your Lordship will observe in Sir Horatio Nelson's letter to me of the 22nd of July, heavy complaints of the Governor of Syracuse for having made the smallest difficulty in admitting the whole of His Majesty's squadron into that port. But really this government could not throw off the mask until the treaty they have made with the Emperor of Germany

[1] N.M.M. MS. 9848, Hamilton papers—draft in Sir William's autograph.

was returned, ratified, from Vienna. That treaty was only signed at Vienna the 16th July and I had the official notice from the Marquis de Gallo here of his Sicilian's Majesty ports being now open to the King's ships without any limitation, only the 31st of July.

I thought this news would be of such importance to Admiral Nelson that I sent off Capt. Bowen in the *Transfer* sloop on the 1st August to Syracuse to inform him of it and to deliver to him your Lordship's dispatches to Naples brought by the *Lion* Capt. Dixon.

I flatter myself your Lordship will not disapprove of this measure altho' I find that Admiral Nelson left Syracuse the 26th of July and I fear that Capt. Bowen is following him.

I need not say anything of the Portuguese squadron as the Marquis Niza who sailed yesterday for Syracuse has written to your Lordship by the *Dorothea*. Good God! but thank God also what a difference there is in the discipline, manœuvres etc., of all foreign ships more or less and those of Great Britain. The loss of the fine Portuguese brig will surely be a very unpleasing news to your Lordship and lost so foolishly.

His Sicilian Majesty who was well acquainted with and very fond of the Marquis Niza when he was at Naples some years ago went on board of his ship before he came to an anchor in this port and I know has done all in his power to persuade the Marquis not to be in a hurry to join Admiral Nelson. This government has been also underhand, tampering with me to persuade him that it would be of more use to the King's service for him to remain cruising in these seas than to go and join Admiral Nelson, as a second small squadron was ready and expected to sail soon from Toulon to join Bonaparte. I have constantly given my opinion as an old soldier having served 12 years in the Army, that unless the orders from our superiors were discretionary, they must be obeyed, let what may be the consequences. I went on board the *Principe Realle* the day before yesterday and told my mind freely to the Marquis Niza, and we agreed that I should go to General Acton and if the Neapolitan government had nothing material to propose and that could alter that resolution, the Marquis had determined to sail the next day to look out for and join Admiral Nelson. In my conversation with the Marquis I discovered however that he is much embarrassed about going into the Archipelago, as he said the Portuguese were not in Peace with the Porte and until he should have joined Admiral Nelson might be under many difficulties among those islands! In short, altho' he is sailed for Syracuse I doubt much of his being in haste to join the Rear-Admiral and having reflected that the *Incendiary* fireship might at this moment be very necessary to Admiral Nelson's operations I wrote a billet yesterday morning to the Marquis, a copy of which and of the Marquis' answer are here inclosed and I flatter myself that your Lordship will see that I have done as much as I could in this business for the King's service. It is well however that the Marquis Niza has left Naples for he would have been without a man on board his ship. No less than 170 men of his ship's crew having deserted it since he came into this port. The Marquis appears to be perplexed and unhappy and I verily believe he is sensible that the command he has is much above his ability.

The agent of the Ragusa Republic resident at Naples came to me three days ago by order of that Government desiring me to inform our Government, your Lordship, and Sir Horatio Nelson, that a French ship of the line and a brig with a commissary on board had come to the port of Ragusa the 6th of July and demanded in the name of the French government a loan of one million livres tournois for two years and that unless it was paid in twenty-four hours they would take possession of their port and overturn their government. It ended in the Ragusans paying all the money they could possibly raise at Ragusa, which was six hundred thousand livres, which the French carried off to Corfu the 26th of July, as your Lordship will see detailed in the inclosed copy of a paper left with me by Sigr. Connecilo the Ragusan agent.

Sir Horatio Nelson sent me the particulars of what would be wanting for the repairs of the *Vanguard* and I have given them to General Acton who has promised to get them ready here as soon as possible but his Excellency complains that your Lordship has detained at Gibraltar a vessel with masts belonging to His Sicilian Majesty.

We know nothing here of Mr. Littledale; but as I think it prudent to be prepared with bread at least should the King's squadron return here Mr. Gibb a principal British merchant here at my desire ordered a considerable quantity of biscuit to be baked without any view of profit to himself but to be made over to Mr. Littledale should he arrive at Naples.

I am happy at having remained at Naples altho' I have had the King's leave to return home for more than a year passed my presence being necessary. Your Lordship'l see that, as we have not a consul at Naples, the load of business falls upon my shoulders, and if I had gone to England the King's service would have suffered greatly. It is highly probable that this court must break witb the French republic in a few days, as on the confines of this kingdom the Roman peasants have murdered the French who were robbing them of their harvest and some peasants pursued by the French have come to the Neapolitan out-posts for protection and it is said that the French have killed some Neapolitans, if so I know it is determined that the Neapolitan army shall march on to Rome. For my part I hope so as we shall be in a much worse position here remaining in what is called peace and giving leave for more French troops to come into Italy. W. H.

P.S. I have the honour of inclosing likewise a private letter from Sir Horatio Nelson directed to your Lordship.

Nelson to St. Vincent[1]

Off Candia,
September 1, 1798

MY DEAR LORD,—You will think me quite mad to pester you with so many letters; I now only do it to send you a copy of my letter to Mr. Jackson at Constantinople, and if the Grand Signior will but *trot* an army into Syria, Bonaparte's career is finished, as for Naples she is saved in spite of herself, they have evidently broke their treaty with France, and yet are afraid to assist in finishing the vast armament of the French, four hours with 4 bomb vessels would get all in a blaze, and we know, what is an army without stores. I shall try the Marquis de Niza if he will go to Egypt but I hardly expect his compliance, I have just sent Sir James an order to send me *Minotaur* and *Audacious* with all the salt provisions he can spare but I have my doubts if the ships victualled to six months of that article. *Culloden* sails dreadfully, but we have not a sick man in the three ships with me. As to myself I know I ought to give up for a little while. My head is splitting at this moment, but of this hereafter. You will give me credit for serving as long as I can. My friend Ball is the polite man he entertains the captive Admiral,[2] and the 1st Captain of the fleet who was saved out of *L'Orient*. The Admiral being wounded I shall let go on his parole at Naples and all the rest in our ships.

God bless you. Ever yours most affectionately, HORATIO NELSON.

I am glad to think you are a little mistaken in Nisbet. He is young but I find a great knowledge of the service in him and none that I see as to seamanship in any. He may have laid too long in Lisbon, I hope the best. Captain Bowen is gone hunting for me I have heard of him at Cyprus. Captain Foote fortunately took the dispatches away from him, and told Captain Bowen that he should come to where he had seen the F. fleet but Captain Bowen has *wisely* gone the round. I left word at Syracuse I should go to find the French.

[1] N.M.M. MS. 9848, St. Vincent papers—printed by Nicolas, Vol. VII, p. clxii.
[2] Rear-Admiral Blanquet.

Sir William Hamilton to St. Vincent[1]

Private.

Naples,
September 29, 1798

MY LORD,—Your Lordship may well imagine the extreme joy that Lady Hamilton and I felt on the arrival of the *Mutine* Capt. Capel at Naples with the glorious news of the complete victory gained over the French fleet by our dear friend Sir Horatio Nelson and the brave band so well chosen by your Lordship at the ever memorable battle of the Nile on the first of August last, a victory unparalleled in the annals of either ancient or modern history. After having felt so much our selves one of our first thoughts was the consolation your Lordship must have received in hearing of so complete a success obtained by a chief and a band of heroes chosen by yourself and all trained in your own school. In short no words can express half what is felt here, and the consequences of this most important and well timed action are incalculable.

Sir Horatio Nelson who has given us the greatest satisfaction by accepting an apartment in our house will tell your Lordship how sensible their Sicilian Majesties, their ministry and this nation in general are of having been snatched from the jaws of destruction by the timely aid of the powerful squadron detached by your Lordship to their assistance. The King of Naples went out to meet our brave Admiral and instantly went on board the *Vanguard* and taking his deliverer by the hand expressed in the warmest terms of gratitude the high sense His Majesty had of the essential service the Admiral had rendered to him, his family and kingdom.

There would be no end if I was to tell your Lordship the proper honours and distinctions that are shewn to Sir Horatio Nelson and his illustrious associates every moment here, but what pleases Sir Horatio, Capt. Troubridge and Capt. Ball most, is the friendly and unreserved assistance they get in the refitting of their ships: nothing that His Sicilian Majesty's dockyards and magazines can possibly furnish has been denied them, and they will all be ready for sea in a very few days.

The glorious victory of the first of August is like the church of St. Peter's at Rome, it strikes you at first sight from its magnitude but the more you examine into its dimensions and details the more wonderful it appears. God be praised—if the first of August does not humble the pride of our perfidious enemy I know not what will.

The first good effects of this signal victory is the insurrection at Malta which will probably fall soon altho' this government does not yet at least

---

[1] N.M.M. MS. 9848, Hamilton Papers—draft in Sir William's autograph.

2 E

openly assist the insurgents in that island. I am convinced that Capt. Capel's arrival at Vienna with the glorious news of the Battle of the Nile will have determined the Emperor to march forward. Sir Horatio Nelson's arrival at Naples appears to have determined this government to do so and drive the French out of Rome without waiting any longer for the Emperor's determination.

As I take it for granted that Lady Hamilton will not fail of profiting of the present opportunity to give your Lordship joy on this most happy occasion and that Sir Horatio Nelson will have given you an account of the present state of His Majesty's ships here under his command, I have nothing further to add but my best wishes for a continuance of every success to the glorious fleet your Lordship has the honour to have under your command and that has already rendered itself immortal—and seems to be in a fair way of giving the long wished for peace to Europe.

I have the honour etc. . . . .

Sir William Hamilton to St. Vincent[1]

Naples,
October 5, 1798

My Lord,—I cannot let my friend Capt. Bowen depart without writing to your Lordship another line of congratulation on the glorious victory of the first of August which will be an eternal honour to your Lordship, the Admiral and the chosen band that have so handsomely and completely executed your Lordship's orders and by which in all probability peace and order will soon be restored to three parts of our globe that were already greatly distressed and disturbed by the rascally French republic calling itself the queen nation.

Letters received yesterday by this Government from Constantinople dated the 7th of September say that the Grand Signior on receiving Sir Horatio Nelson's letters with the account of his having either taken burnt or destroyed almost the whole of the French fleet, at the mouth of the Nile, near Alexandria, had instantly declared war against the French republic, deposed the first Vizier and Mufti on suspicion of their having favoured the French party, and sent the ambassador of the French republic and his whole legation prisoners to the Seven Towers having found concealed in his house seven thousand stand of arms and some small cannon.

The same official letters say that the Grand Signior had ordered a valuable jewel to be sent as a present from him to our brave friend Sir Horatio

---

[1] N.M.M. MS. 9848, Hamilton papers—draft in Sir William's autograph.

Nelson and that the Russian fleet already joined to the Ottoman were ordered to sail directly for Alexandria and an army of 60 thousand men to march immediately against Bonaparte. This is the first great consequence of the glorious 1st of August and I hope it will determine the Court of Vienna and this court to do what they could and ought to have done long ago—drive the French out of Italy and crushed the little rising republics. The Admiral and I do not mince the matter in giving this our opinion on every occasion to His Sicilian Majesty and his Ministers. It is a curious moment for the arrival of the new French ambassador Monsr. La Combe St. Michel to this court. He presented his credential letter only the day before yesterday.

Sir Horatio Nelson will have certainly informed your Lordship that his reception at Naples from the highest to the lowest has been such as it ought to be. All confess him to be their saviour and deliverer. We have no other quarrel with this government but for their losing these precious moments, and doing nothing for themselves. They have either at Malta or elsewhere given every possible assistance in their power to His Majesty's ships under your Lordship's command that were in some little want of their assistance of which the Admiral will have informed your Lordship officially.

I have the great satisfaction of assuring your Lordship that Sir Horatio Nelson's health is much improved since he came to Naples, but his activity is such that I believe no self consideration can keep him much longer here.

When my conscience will permit me to leave Naples and profit of the King's leave to return home on my private affairs there and I can with propriety get a passage to Gibraltar in one of the store ships, Lady Hamilton and I hope for the great satisfaction of being able to pay our respects to your Lordship on our way home either at Gibraltar or Lisbon.

I have the honour etc. . . .

St. Vincent to Sir William Hamilton[1]

SIR,—I have the honour to acquaint your excellency that Sir James Saumarez approaches this promontory fast with his glorious trophies the hulls of which are seen from the Signal House.

I congratulate you most heartily upon this greatest of all events, and assure your excellency of the perfect esteem and regard with which I have the honour to be your very faithful and obedient servant, ST. VINCENT.

Gibraltar,
    October 18, 1798.

[1] N.M.M. MS. 9848, Hamilton papers.

Lady Hamilton to Nelson[1]

October 26, 1798

MY DEAR FRIEND,—I must say one word more to you. We have just had another letter. The good Signor has written to the King of England to beg his permission that you may wear the order or feather that he took out of his own turban to decorate you, and which is a sign of sovereignty. I do not know exactly how many piastres its worth, but unprecendented the present. 'Vivo il Turco' says Emma.

If I was King of England I would make you the most noble puissant *DUKE NELSON, MARQUIS NILE, EARL ALEXANDRIA, VISCOUNT PYRAMID, BARON CROCODILE*, and *PRINCE VICTORY*, that posterity might have you in all forms.

Pray if the Turkish frigate comes to you I beg you to bring it here, that I may have the pleasure of entertaining the good turban'd soul and sending him home satisfied and convinced than an English woman has a soul for I fancy they don't believe we have one, and showing him our gratitude for the justice his master has done to the friend of our hearts, for so Sir William and I call you.

Once more God bless you and believe me ever your grateful EMMA HAMILTON.

If you see dear Captain Bell pray remember me most kindly to him, and to all brothers, Gold, Troubridge, Louis.[2]

To Rear-Admiral Sir Horatio Nelson, K.B., at sea.

Lady Nelson to Nelson

I

Bath,
March 30, 1798

MY DEAREST HUSBAND,—Unless I write before I have the pleasure of hearing how you are after your journey you will not in all probability hear from me before you sail as the Portsmouth post comes in at 8 o'clock. I arrived yesterday quite in time for dinner. Our father looks well; his spirits as good as I could expect them and I will try and exert mine.

God bless and protect you. My love to my child how truly fortunate he will be to have you near him. I hope he will profit. Our father talks of going the beginning of May. The Matchams are to be at Bath, bag and

---

[1] B.M. Add. MSS. 34989, Bridport papers.
[2] The captains of the squadron formed an Egyptian Club in commemoration of the battle and presented Nelson with a sword.

baggage next Wednesday. My little blue pillow is sent with your things. If you think it will be of use to you keep it, if not send it to me. In the hurry the old watch was brought away, that with other things shall be sent to you. I find I have Marsh and Creed's accounts to March 23, 1798. Shall I send you the account or a copy? The papers belonging to you both public and private were all tied up together. I hope you will have everything you can wish to be comfortable. Do tell me if anything is wanting and I will take care and get it myself and send it. I beg you will give my compliments to Lady Parker. I sincerely hope you will be a true prophet: 'That you will be in England this year and peace, all before Christmas.'

I can't fill my paper this day believe me my dear husband, your affectionate wife, FRANCES H. NELSON.

Our good father's love and blessing to you. Mr. Ewin thinks the times are so bad that he never mentioned them. The assessed taxes have surprised the generality here they not expecting they would have amounted to half the sum. How differently are the opinions. Bath is full with country families supposing it a safe place. Be assured I will implicitly follow your advice, in doing which I shall feel an inward satisfaction. I have examined all my drawings, they look bright and well. I will soon see to the packing of them and shall be anxious to see them safely hung up in our cottage, not castle. Pray take care how the box is unpacked that was sent by coach, the one marked china.

To Rear-Admiral Nelson, K.B., *Vanguard*, Portsmouth.

II

Bath,
April 4, 1798

MY DEAREST HUSBAND,—Many thanks for your letter. I was very much afraid the wind was contrary altho' our good father would have it was not so. However I would not hope or flatter myself I should hear from you. Now we are separated I sincerely wish that the wind will soon change but at this moment it blows a severe storm. I wish you had better servants. No possibility of getting any now. I forgot to mention a circumstance to you relative to a manservant which did live with Mr. Gordon and is now on board the *Vanguard*. The man lived seven years with the gentleman that Mr. Gordon had him from, brought a good character, lived with Mr. G., I think nearly two years, when there were several things missing, such as tumblers, a few tablecloths and things of that sort, suspicion falling on this man, he confessed he had been the thief, but it clearly was the first offence therefore Mr. G., promised if he would enter on board a man of war, he would not prosecute him. I tell you this that if you are very much distressed you may be upon your guard. I will write to Marsh and get Allen's money.

I am sure you would smile to see the sevants I found on my return. An old Catholic cook near 60 years of age, a girl of fourteen and Will who he intended to have sent immediately to Suckling (who I found was ready to receive Will upon condition he never was to work in the garden) but upon my appearance Will remains. I have been very steady in your plan of my going to the cottage and the first or second week in May I go to town and as soon as Graham can send the furniture I follow and will remain and take charge of my dear husband's picture which I will only allow to remain a short time in the exhibition. Suckling writes Dixon Hoste has sworn his income to be £60. I am determined to write to him soon, saying that as we left town before his arrival he would not know where to direct to me. Mr. Cooper's behaviour has been shameful and if I do not hear from him I will soon write to him. I have been requested to take Mary Cooper as my servant, that will be refused. The servant I have will do very well.

Captain and Mrs. Phillips came immediately to see me, pressed me to dine would take no refusal and yesterday we dined there, where we met Mr. Eyre, one of the Illuminati,[1] he filled me with the horrors. Capt. P. begged he would tell me something cheerful, however that was not his disposition. At tea our party was made more cheerful by the arrival of young ladies and a Capt. Orm, who is well acquainted with Capt. Troubridge and made many enquiries after you, he knew you as a lieutenant, said a great many pleasing and handsome things. Mrs. Godfrey and Miss Fanny Berry are now in the room. I feel that I have a great deal to say. My mind feels composed and quiet when I consider how very lately I have seen you. God grant that we may not be very long before we meet and then I shall hope we may live for some years together without being so very often separated. God bless you and believe me, your affectionate wife, FRANCES H. NELSON.

Kitty says she put in your box of sundries, 3 black stocks and Ryson is certain you will see the buckle and stocks in the trunk in paper. Wrote to the Duke of Portland and it is expected will be ordered away. Too late to notice your affec. letter of April 3. Write tomorrow.

To Rear-Admiral Nelson, K.B., *Vanguard*, Portsmouth.

If the *Vanguard* is sailed to be returned to Lady Nelson, Bath.

---

[1] The name given to a secret society in Germany, holding deist and republican opinions, was adopted by some young Englishmen.

III

Thursday [5 April] 1798

MY DEAREST HUSBAND,—I had written to you yesterday before I had received your kind and affectionate letter. Indeed I have always felt your sincere attachment and at no one period could I feel it more strongly than I do at this moment and I hope as some few years are past, time enough to know our dispositions, we may flatter ourselves it will last. You will I hope find all your things I am much mortified at their being displaced. Have the small paper parcels opened. I yesterday wrote you what Kitty said, that she had put into the box of sundries 3 velvet stocks and Ryson is quite sure the stock buckle and velvet stocks are in the trunk. Do say if they are found. Have you stockings enough? I wish very much you would examine the parcels and box yourself. The great bundle of papers which was tied up in a common coloured handkerchief in that I put several things myself. I have nothing here which would be of the smallest service. The Matchams arrived yesterday. They are gone to unpack and put their house to rights. Kitty went to them after breakfast. Your sister is delighted at leaving the Heath.

Mr. Matcham last week fell from his horse at 3 o'clock in the morning in liquor, however she knew nothing of it, and he was not hurt. The horse went home, and Tom seeing it sent it back by a careful person and Mr. M. rode home.

The news is melancholy today from Ireland so Capt. Welsford says, who is ordered upon a recruiting party. How cruel it is for men of great wealth to be swearing off the taxes. Conceive of Mr. Braithwaite keeping 16 horses and says he uses but four, 9 men servants and enters four. Mr. Sherston it seems told him it was a shame that everybody was throwing the load off their shoulders. His opinion of the times are the same as my dear husband's and he means to do exactly what you have desired me to the cottage.

The wind is very contrary how it blew all last night. God grant you his protection and that we may meet again. As to peace I most ardently wish for it particularly as you will then be satisfied to live quietly at home. I can't help feeling quite unsettled and a little hurried for when my spirits are not quiet you know I am but a poor creature.

Our good father's love and blessing to you. He will take a little money I have offered him just what he pleases. God bless you my dearest husband, your affectionate wife, FRANCES H. NELSON.

To Rear-Admiral Nelson, K.B., *Vanguard*, Portsmouth.

If the *Vanguard* is sailed to be returned.

IV

April 7, 1798

MY DEAREST HUSBAND,—I wrote to you on Thursday the wind still continuing contrary gives me an opportunity of asking how you are. I can feel your disappointment in being contrary to your wishes detained at St. Helens. I comfort myself in thinking you are safe and hope the ship runs no risk in losing any part of her masts etc. I see no daily paper and the Bath newspapers tell little Portsmouth ship news.

Yesterday I received a letter from Mr. W. Bolton telling me Capt. Edge had called to give him notice that he should quit the house this week. Had Capt. Edge wrote us a line three weeks back, it might have made some difference in our plans. I will write immediately to Mr. B. requesting him to get a proper person to take charge of the house coals to be found and board wages. I shall be very anxious to get down. Our father has tried to let the house, however he has now given up all thoughts of success. He took the £100 which I offered him this day hoping that would serve him till Christmas. He did not like to take so much from you. The expense of his going to see Suckling could not be avoided.

The post has knocked and brings me your letter of April 5th and am as positive as I can be that the small silver pieces and ditto gold pieces with three large gold pieces were put in the trunk, or the three large joes were put in your black letter case. All I can say I have them not, and have and will make the most diligent search. Ryson is positive a small parcel written upon [some description of money] was put in the trunk and I think the superscription was 'Portugal Pieces'. It is a sad thing to lose money and I think you will find it yet. As to the black stock and buckle I think it will come to hand. I wish very much it had been in my power to have sent your things more comfortably, but they going at different times and a change of servant in the midst of the few last days we were in town has made all this confusion. I charged Allen[1] to take care when he opened the trunk at the inn to lock the door of the chamber as the trunk was mostly filled with small parcels. I have a few old looking keys, but don't think they belong to your dressing stand and cannot say a word about them. I have a cravat of yours, Ryson says she sent more cambric pocket hands. than were put on the list. Another time I will take more care and hope we shall have proper servants. Can't Allen find the keys in his trunk? I will leave this mortifying subject although I would give something if you would take the trouble to say you have again searched. I am so glad you find amusement from your barometer. Kate has been out this morning I have just been

---

[1] Tom Allen, Nelson's servant.

asking her whose memory is better than mine and she says the money was sent in the trunk. I think we can't all be mistaken. Don't say much to Allen and I will give the search I have promised and I assure you I rejoice to see you so exact. Times will make us all very careful.

Mr. Matcham brings melancholy news from his Irish friends who are resident here, and have properties there. Clubs have been found out here that bode no good. God bless you. Believe me your affectionate wife, FRANCES H. NELSON.

Mr. Coke's assessed taxes £800.

To Rear-Admiral Nelson, K.B., *Vanguard*, Portsmouth.

If the *Vanguard* has sailed, to be returned to Lady Nelson, Bath.

No letter from Mr. Cooper.

V

Bath,
April 17, 1798

MY DEAREST HUSBAND,—I had the pleasure of receiving your letter of the 9th and am very glad you were not detained longer at Portsmouth. God grant you his protection and continuance of the great successes which have attended you, and a happy meeting to us in old England and that soon.

My letter to you of the 9th April was returned to me yesterday, with one from Capt. Lloyd who wishes you and your chief well, assures you he shall never forget you. At the time of his writing he was in bed and supported by pillows, two hours after you saw him, he took to his bed and had never been out since. A letter from Mr. Ward of Nevis the copy of which you shall have on the other side, likewise one from Mr. Noble of Bristol, Mr. Cooke and Halford acknowledging your letter and will do as you desired etc. Mrs Gray's packet was put into Mr. Purvis's box. Mrs. Baillie has a son and the mother writes me that it was the most joyful event of Mr. P. and her life. My old aunt Mrs. P. writes me is in a dangerous way. No prospect of Charles Tobin ever getting well. All these things will most likely prevent my staying more than a day at Bristol. However I must go for a day.

Our good father seems determined upon going immediately into Suffolk with me, he does not see any great necessity for his going to Burnham etc., he would have liked if I had not engaged myself to the Sucklings. I offered to put off my engagement but that at present he does not consent to. The Matchams are very pleased with their new abode. Miss K. M. is going to boarding school. Kitty Bolton[1] has had a letter from Lieut.

---

[1] Nelson's neice, Catherine Bolton, married her cousin, William Bolton, who had been one of Nelson's midshipmen in the *Agamemnon*, in 1803.

Bolton, I think her affections are engaged, but she tells me she loves him the same as if he were her brother, a dangerous kind of love. I think I have now told you all the family occurrences.

I wrote to Mr. Hoste and will write to Mr. Cooper as the week has lapsed without scrape of pen. Mrs. Falconer[1] made me a visit, a thousand kind enquiries of you. Her doctor declares had he been a single man he would have embarked with you. I called on Mrs. Rickets this morning, her spirits are much mended. She delights in talking of her brother,[2] leaves Bath on Saturday. I had written you a very long letter April 9th.

Kate and I are certain the huckaback towels were packed up, for I made her put the numbers which were at the washerwoman's down in her pocket book 7 in all and I myself put the greater part of them in the box of sundries which went by the coach. Mr. Baddley put me under some alarm telling me all the empty houses in Suffolk were by the orders of government to be taken and converted into barracks so I wrote immediately to Graham to send the furniture down and requested Mr. B. to have the bedstead put up and to say I was coming, therefore my visit will only be three or four days at K.T.[3] I will send your cravat seal etc., in May.

Be assured my dear husband my study and the wish of my heart is to add to your happiness I am not insensible of your affection to me and I sincerely hope my Josiah you will find deserving of your fatherly care and protection. My love to him, I shall long to hear of your arrival at Lisbon. God bless you is the prayer of your affectionate wife, FRANCES H. NELSON.

Mr. and Mrs. Tarleton are arrived they met the ringleaders, who were taken up at Manchester going to London. He is much alarmed and wishes he was safe again in his house. I shall send Mr. Ward's letter to Marsh and Creed.

Rear Admiral Nelson, K.B., *Vanguard*, Lisbon.

VI

Bath,
April 23, 1798

MY DEAREST HUSBAND,—I wrote to you last Monday and hope you received my letter for it contained Mr. Ward's letter of Nevis giving you an account of money which was missing out of your chest at Nevis. I shall answer his letter and show Marsh and Creed Mr. W.'s letter that if any

[1] Wife of Dr. Falconer, who had attended to Nelson's wound while he was in Bath in September 1797.
[2] Lord St. Vincent.
[3] Kentish Town.

steps are necessary to be taken on behalf of you it may be done. I have wrote to Mr. Cooper and enclosed to Mr. Ives of Cottishall requesting him to forward my letter to Mr. C. saying Mr. C. son said he was an acquaintance of his father's and my not knowing the proper direction to Obry Hall had made me take that liberty. No answers yet. Mr. Hammond of West Acre had heard of an attorney of that name and it was the same. No good was attached to it. However he wrote to a friend of his, the report of Mr. C. is truly unfavourable. Duns, bailiffs, are nine tenths of the year his constant attendants. Mr. H. thinks he will pay you, but if I do not get the money I will write to some person at Norwich and I hope you will send the young attorney home for if so much difficulty attends this first payment what will it be by and by.

Mr. Hoste is very sorry he did not see you but hopes you will take his son and that it will not be inconvenient to me to wait 10 days longer for the money. What can I say to such shabby people. I will wait ten days and then I will write again, by that time I leave Bath, it will bring it to the 3rd or 4th of May which was the time I had fixed in my mind to go,—contrary to the opinion of many who have kindly offered their advice gratis. My promise to my husband is binding I cannot break it even in what the world calls trifles.

The Rector has written a long letter only stating facts: 'The general indecorum besides pillage the constant attendant of large encampments with many other inconveniences.' If I knew our father's sentiments in regard to himself I would not wish him to run any risk on my account by living so near the sea. The pictures and pianoforte are packed and going out of the house and I shall not be very comfortable till I follow. I shall pass a week at K.T. Our father has just told me he shall be soon after me, for what can he do by himself? Will on Thursday begins his journey into Norfolk, his behaviour is so exceedingly bad that it is not to be borne with: in short we run no little risk either to be robbed or to have the house burned.

A thousand reports are in circulation, all I hope we shall be true to ourselves. I wish I could be with you. I should be better satisfied. I hope they will send you the newspapers regularly that will tell you know on a large scale but now and then a little anecdote such as the D. of Northumberland having one hundred thousand pounds in the American funds and taking advantage of the lenity of the assessed taxes such as his having eight children, not a drop of the Percy blood remaining.

I have had a handsome letter from Capt. Cockburn of *La Minerve* telling me about your M.[1] wine. I have told him what you did with your wine

[1] Madeira.

at Portsmouth. I begged him to pay the duties and if the wine could be safely sent by the waggon from Plymouth, I begged him to see the cask properly secured and fit to undertake so long a journey, and when he had determined upon which way it was to be sent, to let me know and to say the amount of expenses and I would remit him the money immediately with thanks. I hope all this business is to your mind. Adml. Sawyer has been very polite. I long to hear your opinion of Josiah. You must tell me the truth. God bless you and believe me, your affectionate wife, FRANCES H. NELSON.

Our father will write the first of the month. Love attend you. My best affection to Josiah.   P.P.1/8d.

Rear-Admiral Sir Horatio Nelson, His Majesty's Ship *Vanguard*, Lisbon.

VII

Kentish Town,
May 6, 1798

MY DEAREST HUSBAND,—I hope it will not be long before I hear from you, of your good health, safe arrival and my Josiah's conduct such as you approve. Various were the reports at Bath a few days before we left it, of engagements which Lord St. Vincent had had with the Spanish fleets. One day he was beat, the next day he had taken twelve sail of the line, in short I was almost done up, seized with violent perspirations from which I took cold, but I daresay I shall be soon well. Poor Mrs. Godfrey burning with heat, quite in a fever; but in the midst of her own anxiety she said she felt most sincerely for me, for that she had never seen any poor creature so affected. My mind was relieved when I found no dates were to be had when these actions had taken place, and Admiral Barrington giving his opinion that it was all a fabrication.

I had, my dear husband, all my treasures in your absence well packed by Champness and safely lodged at Wiltshire's Warehouse before I left Bath, with a proper direction to be forwarded to Round Wood etc.

I left Bath the 3rd. Arrived on 4th. The next day Mr. Suckling took me to town. Called at the carpet warehouse and Graham's was going on with my orders to Graham when I received a summons from coachman that he must go for his master at the Custom House, so that my business is but half finished, and I have a great deal to do in a very few days, as our father fixed to leave Bath tomorrow week, intends staying one day in town to see Mr. Suckling, which I think only what is right. I received a letter yesterday from Capt. Cockburn—it came from Bath. His ship is at Portsmouth and he writes me he has paid the duties and sent it by Clark's waggon who has engaged to deliver it safe at Ipswich and begs not to trouble me with the expenses as you and him will settle it when he returns to Lord Vincent which will be very shortly. I shall write to him again and beg to pay the money. No letter yet from Mr. Cooper. I mean for Mr. Nottcut to write to him. Tomorrow we go a strong party to the Exhibition.[1] Mrs. Wigley has been there and she says she did not see a picture of yours. The bust is there, but she thought it too old for you. If my picture of you is not there, I shall desire Abbot to have it properly packed and sent to Round Wood. Orm[2] must have made a great deal of money. The little picture he published of you has sold beyond description. Mrs. Tarleton as soon as she heard you were to be bought, she was determined to have you, but was told by the bookseller, he had a load of Admiral Nelson's but had sold every one of them, that he had written for another load and one should be saved for her. Dr. Falconer has got the Admiral but he will have one of Abbot's and which ever he thinks the most like shall be framed.

Mr. Suckling as usual is very kind, always speaks of you with the greatest affection. Mrs. Wigley regrets she did not see you. I tell her she must come and see us. My next letter will be very long. This I take myself to London, therefore have only time to assure you my dear husband of my most sincere and affectionate attachment.

Believe me your faithful wife, FRANCES H. NELSON.

Monday 7th: Love to my dear Josiah. Post paid 1/8d.

Rear-Admiral Nelson, K.B., *Vanguard*, Lisbon.

VIII

London,
May 15, 1798

MY DEAREST HUSBAND,—I have just had the pleasure of hearing from Maurice Nelson that he has seen a letter dated Lisbon April 28th which mentions you are well, thank God for it, and may the Almighty continue his goodness to me in the preservation of your life. I long to hear of my Josiah, I hope you will find him a good man. Our father will be in town this afternoon. He stays with old Mrs. Matcham, dines at Kentish Town on

---

[1] The Royal Academy exhibition. Lemuel Abbot's portrait of Nelson was not exhibited this year; it had been painted while Nelson was in London during the winter 1797–8.
[2] Daniel Orme, portrait painter and engraver.

Thursday, and on Friday or Saturday we set off for Round Wood. Had our father stayed a few days longer at Bath, it would have suited me better. I called on Lady St. Vincent, she has had no letters from her Lord lately. She seems a good woman, spoke very humanely and tenderly of the unfortunate Lady Elizabeth Rickets. She is generally pitied. If Lord St. Vincent should ever say anything on the subject do lean on the poor woman's side; Lady E. has written to him begging that he would intercede with her husband to grant her one interview. I could write a great deal.

Captain Peard is determined to be divorced. Mrs. Thomas tells me poor Mrs. Peard won't live long. He won't see her. Mrs. Thomas will go on another message not to prevent my writing, therefore my letter in spite of my inclination will be short. Cooke and Holford has paid me, promised to send me £40 soon. I have had £100 from Marsh. When I have paid every bill I send you exactly the expenses of the furniture. I have collected a few little things for you. Two very good silver plates, bought them second hand, had them cleaned and your crest engraved upon them. Find it very inconvenient to be at Kentish Town. Shopping takes much time.

Mrs. Wigley makes kind enquiries after you. Mr. W. seems a very softly man was quite offended that he should be thought like you. The little woman will chat—

My love to my child. God bless you my dear husband and believe me, your affectionate wife, FRANCES H. NELSON.

Mr. and Mrs. Suckling, Mr and Mrs. Wigley beg to send kind love. M. Nelson will send this letter for me. Gave him one last week—Monday.

Rear-Admiral Sir Horatio Nelson, K.B., *Vanguard*, Lisbon. 1/8d.

IX

Round Wood,
May 28, 1798

MY DEAREST HUSBAND,—On Sunday the 20th of May we arrived at Round Wood, the satisfaction I felt was very great in being under your own roof. No thanks to any earthly being. Our father was for staying, although the house had little or no accommodation. He viewed everything attentively and I never saw him so thoroughly satisfied as he was and says the more he examines everything the better he is pleased. The house is quite large enough and the walls are of a good thickness. The trees thriven well, they have been planted five years, and your tenant Mr. Fuller thinks from their present height in five years more the house will be quite sheltered. A little more ground planted in trees will still add to its beauty.

We were obliged to take up our quarters at Ipswich that day. However on the Monday, our father's patience could not hold out, till I called on Mrs. Bolton to thank her for her civilities and a chaise to be ordered, but he set off with the footman I hired at Bath and walked up a high Suffolk hill and we are very comfortably settled. But before I proceed with my narrative I must tell you how very much he has been distressed by the servant he hired at Bath leaving him, in a fit of insanity as he supposes. Your father and Miss Martin had just walked into Mrs. Martin's parlour, Kensington, Mr. N. says to deliver his fellow traveller, to her mother, safe when the servant set off running in the most extraordinary manner ever seen, and has never to our knowledge been heard of. Since we arrived here Mr. N. had his clothes examined that they might be packed up, when they were found in so disgraceful a state that he gave orders to the footman to burn them, and he thinks violent medicines has been improperly taken. He was the completest servant I had ever seen: so that we have but one footman, quite enough.

The pump upon examination and some money laid upon it, will do, the water is particularly good, it has been dug several feet deeper, it must have new works, the wise ones of this part of the country agreeing that Round Wood stood so exceedingly high that the uncertainty of finding water was great therefore it was worth the great expense of cleaning the old well, which has turned out well. A closet taken down in the eating parlour to admit a sideboard and a window in the damp dressing room, thrown out to the east (the little one which is in it now to be stopped up to the north) are the only expenses which are necessary besides the fixtures until I have the happiness of seeing you. Our father thinks you must throw out a good dining room next to the present eating room and a bedroom over it, then you will have a good room to yourself and a very good house good enough for anybody. Our father's dislike to Mr. W. B.[1] is great, I begged him not to show it. Mr. B. was looking at the pump he did not exactly approve of what one of the workmen said, but concluded his speech with saying: 'There must be a court martial held and I will sit upon it,'— besides he is an officious man. He nearly made a mischief between the workmen, however I will make use of him when it suits my convenience. He is to pay me next week the balance of your account. Mr. Hoste has taken no further notice. Mr. Cooper is an infamous character, you will never get your money. You had better send that knowing young lawyer home. The papers relative to the Round Wood farm Mr. Ryder gave me. Tomorrow I take them to Mr. Norcutt with a written desire of Mr. Ryder for a paper which Mr. N. has omitted sending. Mr. Norcutt is an old infirm man with

[1] Mr. William Bolton.

a good character. Mr. Ryder's charges five guineas which I paid and he gave me a receipt. I have received my dear husband your letter No. 3 *Vanguard* Gibraltar May the 4th. I thank you for it and rejoice you have seen my Josiah and that the lady of the Admiralty[1] promises not to forget him. Captain Berry mentions him in a flattering manner to his wife. I sincrely hope he will deserve every thing you have done for him and indeed I think he will.

On Friday 25th Mr. Bolton and Susanna[2] came to dinner (Mrs. Bolton is well) they dined Mr. Bolton left Susanna and the next day she went to Ipswich. Mrs. Bolton is to come as soon as I have got a bed fitted up. Mr. Nelson said: 'I don't make use of a dressing room, therefore I think you had better have a bed put in it at once for one of the girls,' so I did it. The boys have dined here they are fine boys, but from their age quite children. I shall exactly follow your directions about the £175 had I not been so exceedingly hurried down I should have seen Capt. Cockburn for he was in London. Capt. C. will not allow me to pay him the expenses of the wine, he writes me you and him will settle it. The little trunk I was obliged to send to Mrs. Godfrey, who writes me she will take it to your brother Maurice, who I shall write to and beg he will deliver it to Capt. C.

Mr. Norcutt has sent me word that he will call on Wednesday on his way to Woodbridge. Then I shall be able to give you a full acount of your affairs here. I gave Mr. Marsh your account up to the 23rd March to copy that it might be sent to you by Capt. C. I can't tell you yet the expense of furniture. God bless you my dearest husband believe me your faithful and affectionate wife, FRANCES H. NELSON.

My love to Josiah. Our father's blessing to you, 'tis an excellent way to number letters. This is I think my sixth letter, No. 1 and 3 received from you. 2 silver plated plates, knife, seal, prayer book, and a hussey, 2 pr. of buckles, tape and bobbins. Italian paste.

Rear-Admiral Nelson, K.B., *Vanguard*, Lisbon.

X

Round Wood
June 11, 1798
(No. 9)

MY DEAREST HUSBAND,—Last week I received your letter No. 2 where it had been laying I cannot think. The Boltons received one the same time

---

[1] Lady Spencer.
[2] Nelson's niece, twin sister to Catherine Bolton.

dated Tagus May 17th. The newspapers say you are with Lord St. Vincent, they all mention the great force the French have at Toulon. From the professions of friendship you have had from your chief I hope he will never send you upon any service without a sufficient force and I pray God to continue his protection to my dear husband and child and to crown them with success. Bolton does not mention Josiah therefore I conclude he is with the fleet. Since I have requested W. B. to pay the balance of your accounts of monies advanced for his son I see very little of him. However I am determined you shall not lose it, for my want of asking for it. I have not yet heard from Mr. Norcutt, which makes me fear the money you advanced for the young lawyer is gone.

I think I wrote to you last Monday week (No. 8) there was to be a court held this month when all the business relative to this estate would be settled but I hear nothing of it as yet. Mr. T. Bolton dined here yesterday, with his 2 sons, Miss. S. Bolton and your sister, who with the boys and Miss Kitty are going home. Your father sends them in a post chaise. Mr. B. talks of going to Cranwick in October—he looks well. Your good father told me Mr. B. never once said he thanked him or myself for the expense we had been at for his daughter Kitty, he thinks they expect too much of you and he says enough to put me upon my guard. I must say they are cunning people, and often times little things show the disposition. Last Sunday Susannah came from Ipswich early in the morning to spend the day with Kitty. When I was ready for church I called for the girls, Kitty answered: 'Susannah can't go to church.' Upon which I said: 'Why?' 'She has no gloves.' 'And did she come from Ipswich without gloves?' 'No, but they are not good enough.'

Capt. and Mrs. Boucher and Adml. Reeve[1] have been very attentive. I dined last Monday with Capt. Boucher, they give no dinners, but invited the Miss Lloyds, their particular friends to meet me, they are nice women. We are very gracious when we meet but they say their little ponies will just take them to Ipswich and if they unfortunately knock them up, they must stay at home. We all went to the ball which was thinness itself, I was sorry for it was the King's birthday. However we did our best. On Friday Adml. Reeve gave me a handsome dinner, two courses everything in season. He requested I would do him the honour of going to the promenade, which I consented too, provided it was not in the fields it was a weekly meeting at 9 o'clock in the Assembly room, which gave the military, the neighbourhood and the townspeople an opportunity of meeting for 2 hours. I stayed till 10 o'clock having had quite enough for my shilling. One of the girls were with me. I left her with Mrs. W. B. I have had a visit

[1] Vice-Admiral Samuel Reeve; died 1803.

2 F

from Major and Mrs. Heron, they live in the town, have laid down their carriage. I shall return everybody's visits.

Postchaise hire comes to too much money I find everything very dear. The military does not incommode us. We often see them exercising their horses on the Woodbridge road, and that is all we can say of them: excepting General Balfour who desired Admiral Reeve to introduce him to me. The General made very handsome enquiries of you, offered his services to me in an equal handsome manner.

I went to a gardener's to see for a few flowers to ornament Round Wood. The show of carnations (of which I am particularly fond) was very great. I enquired the beauties of two, I next observed the green of one was particularly fine. 'And what are the colours of that?' The gardener's answer: 'Admiral Nelson a curious plant named last year.' Upon which we all looked at the man (he was deaf) he concluded we were cheapening of this rare plant and he assured us he had but that one it was worth to him one guinea and would not take two for it. Adml. Reeve then told him who I was and asked if him he had not seen me before, upon which he said: 'No.' You never saw a creature so pleased. We were a large party, your sister, one of the girls, Adm. Reeve, Major Heron etc., he left his flowers to take care of themselves and to talk this affair over to each of the company. I am to have two layers from it, and I am to give 10/6, a little extravagance but the name is excuse sufficient.

Adm. R. brought home some hardy flowers from Italy. Josiah was fond of gardening. I wish he would select a few carnations and geraniums. Round Wood wants a little money to be laid out on it. The first are the necessary repairs. The walls in general (I mean garden) must be immediately done. It has been much neglected. The fixtures are all finished putting up and in my next letter I will tell you what I have paid.

I find by a letter from your brother Maurice, Capt. Cockburn is not certain of going to Lord St. Vincent, but that it will be soon determined. Maurice has got the trunk. The stock buckle, and stocks are found. Our father sends his blessing to you. Believe me my dear husband, your affectionate wife, FRANCES H. NELSON.

My love to Josiah. I hope Lord St. Vincent won't come home—if he does very likely you will. I wish for peace, pray to God to grant you a return. My J. I think will be a good man. We have a room for each and one to spare.

Rear-Admiral Nelson, K.B., *Vanguard*, Lisbon.

XI

Round Wood,
June 18, 1798
(No. 10)

MY DEAREST HUSBAND,—Since I wrote to you last Monday little has ocurred in our private affairs till today, and now it is over it seems little. A boy who was painting the troughs round the house slipped—he has escaped unhurt but truly the fright has upset me for the day.

You will see by the papers the alarm we were under last Thursday and remained so for some hours. A fleet of merchantmen were becalmed off Hollesley, expresses were immediately sent to the General. The troops they say behaved remarkably well, in getting themselves in readiness. The officers speak handsomely of them. Our good father seemed very uneasy, talked of Bath he still had the house, there is no saying how I should feel were an enemy actually landed but in the fright I said I must stay in the cottage. I have had a visit from one of the great of Ipswich, Mrs. Trotman, who is half in love with Sir A. Hammond. She pronounced him a charming man and Mr. Cricket was very much liked, offered her open carriage and would call for me. The offer I declined in the handsomest manner I could, alleging my fears etc.

Mrs. Butcher was telling me of the motley crew that graced this London, then I told her how I had escaped. Mr. W. Bolton keeps himself quite away since I applied for the money. Mr. Pearson[1] called on Saturday and on Sunday he was going to Hollesley, his intended being there on a visit to your sister. I think P. is fairly taken in. Mr. W. B. must be very poor indeed, or a very sad character that the money is not forthcoming. My maid tells me they say at Ipswich his family is supported from the gaming table. True it is that he is always there so his family says, but they call it the coffee house. I shall receive greater civilities from Capt. Boucher than anyone else, not but Adm. Reeve is all attention, but he is fid fad.

I assure you it takes a great deal of furniture for this small house, and Graham has not sent all that was ordered. Our father desires me to ask you whether Mr. Fuller is to have the farm another year, and that when you wish him to quit it, you will give him notice. Mr. F. is very desirous to be your tenant. We have had a fine rain it was much wanted. I have shut up two windows and opened one, which add much to the house. At least it makes the walls dry, and no dampness is now seen. There will be nothing done to the outside, papering and painting is much wanted but it cannot

---

[1] Lieutenant Pierson's engagement to Miss Mary Anne Bolton was now recognized.

be done while we are in the house. Kitty is gone home and Susanna is here. Mrs. B. said she should like Kate to go home therefore I said if she liked Susanna to stay with me a few weeks I should be glad to see her. Kate was so positive that your father has said more than once: 'I see you will have the last word, so you shall for me.' I wished I could make them cleaner and nicer in their persons. I would do anything for them as your nieces. Mrs. Berry is coming to see me. She says to spend a short time.

I have had no letter from you since the one dated May 4th—I long to hear. My love to my dear Josiah. God bless and protect you, my dear husband. Believe me ever your affectionate wife, FRANCES H. NELSON.

XII

Round Wood,
June 25, 1798

MY DEAREST HUSBAND,—I write, not that I can tell you a word of chat, the time seems particularly long since I have heard from you, I wrote to Maurice last week begging him to tell me all he knew, which was very little 'that Lord St. Vincent was gone upon this expedition and that everybody as well as myself were anxious to hear from the Lord and yourself.' This intelligence does not in the least quiet my anxiety, I trust in God you are well, and that he has granted you success. I enclosed my letter No. 10 to M. which contained a copy of a letter from Mr. Ward relative to the *JANE and ELIZABETH*. I deviated from my general mode, but I was a little indisposed which prevented my writing on the Monday. M. promises that it shall be sent by the first government dispatches.

The prints of you are out from the picture of Abbot's. I am to have my picture your brother writes in ten days. He does not say a word of the likeness. You told me I think you had subscribed for ten, Abbot says twenty. I shall take ten and desire him to keep some back till I hear from you. Pearson has called again and he looks very grave. We were talking of the increased expenses of everything he said he could just manage to keep himself out of debt, and that was all he could do.

Since I wrote last Tuesday I have had a visit from Lady Harland. She and Mrs. Boucher are gentlewomen. I have had visits from a few others what are called ladies, but I don't like them. Lady H. told me she had heard you had bought this place as a breathing place just for the summer. I have now taken seriously into consideration your wine and I hope with the assistance of Capt. Boucher it will be properly drawn off. Capt. B. told our father it was necessary to have a place parted and properly built up for the bottles. Our father seems thoroughly satisfied he understands what he is about. Tomorrow Admiral Reeve, Capt. B. and his wife dine with us. They come early in the day, that he may set seriously to work. He has got all the bottles, and he intends examining to see if the wine wants fineing. He says it does not, he would recommend that it should not be touched, as it will only impoverish it.

The crops look delightful. Oats they cut in ten days. A plentiful harvest, at least the prospects are such. Seems the only thing which brightens the countenance. Everybody is gloomy. Mrs. Berry came here last Friday, she seems a very mild good young woman. Tell Capt. B. I set her to work upon the sofa cover and the numberless cushions you had in the *Captain*, and by the time we have completely finished what we have taken in hand, she will be fully qualified to make furniture for the bedstead. It serves to amuse just now. It requires a great deal of contriving. How very fortunate your time is so much taken up, that it must prevent you from thinking. We have little else to do.

Your brother Suckling is to be here the first week in July. He says they have had very fine rains, but not a word of news does he tell us. Admiral Colpoys I hear is so very low spirited that his friends seem quite concerned, they say he has never enjoyed himself since he left his ship. He has a sister in Ireland and nieces, I think that alone would awaken the feelings of any man.

No money from Messrs. Bolton, Hoste and Cooper. I shall write to my dear child next week and give him a commission to procure a few hardy shrubs and seeds for us. We have a great many larks and plenty of black birds. One very fine morella cherry tree which I intend to have netted that I may have the pleasure of preserving them for you in brandy. The pump does very well therefore I now begin to think we have been very successful. Our good father will write to you next week. I hope and long to hear from you. God bless you my dear husband and believe me your faithful and affectionate wife, FRANCES H. NELSON.

Capt. and Mrs. Boucher, Mrs. Berry and I dined yesterday with Adml. Reeve. Drank tea with a great rich man Mr. Trotman.

Rear-Admiral Sir Horatio Nelson, K.B., *Vanguard*, Lisbon.

XIII

Round Wood,
July 9, 1798
(No. 11 or 12 I think)

MY DEAREST HUSBAND,—We write although we think opportunities will seldom offer to you. The newspapers gives a fresh account of your movements almost every day. Yesterday the report was you had appeared off Malta the island was in possession of the French, the Maltese rose and killed the French troops: our anxiety and wish to hear from you is very great. I trust in God you are well and I do flatter myself you will be successful. We only take the Ipswich paper, but the news we hear from Capt. Boucher who takes a walk now and then to tell us, and Capt. Hatley was here yesterday.

Our good father wrote to you last Monday, therefore I must give you some account of the race week, the jubilee of Ipswich. Mrs. Berry and Miss S. Bolton and myself went to two balls and one breakfast. The balls were well attended by the county families. Lord and Lady Broom, Lord and Lady Rouse, the Rowleys, Sir Harry and Lady Parker. Admiral Reeve introduced them to me. I found Lady P. a very proud woman and Sir H. a very great man. He asked me where you were. My answer was ready: 'I did not know.' The newspapers said you were gone up the Mediterranean. He was just come from London and he did not believe it. You might be sent up the gutt of Gibraltar. I mention a report of Lord St. Vincent being on his passage home, he said no such thing. There was at one time an idea of Lord Bridport's health being so bad, that he would be obliged to give up his command, if that had been the case, Lord St. Vincent would have the Channel fleet and his brother Sir Hyde would then have taken Lord St. Vincent's command. These great people stayed at Admiral Reeve's. I was asked to dine there but truly neither inclination nor strength would hold out, particularly as we were not to go to the ball till 9 o'clock. Lady L. Broom stood by me some time. She looked as if she wished to speak to me.

The Middletons are the only country family who have been attentive. Admiral Reeve told me country families always wished to know how long new comers intended staying, before they made any advances to be acquainted. 'Shall I give them a hint you would wish to be acquainted?' I said: 'No, upon no account.' 'Do you think Admiral Nelson will live here?' I told him you bought it with that intention and if you found it pleasant you would spend some months in the year. The families I have mentioned drive four horses and still live in great style.

Mrs. Berry and I dined the day we went to the breakfast with Capt. Boucher. There we met Mr. Harry Bunbury, he made kind enquiries of you. We found him a useful man in the ballroom, he told us who all the famous characters were. Our old beaux (the Admiral) being very deaf we could not at times make him hear us. Pearson looks very so so. There was a supper. I had almost forgot I was asked if I would not join the party of country families, I declined it and took tea with a cheerful party, Bouchers etc. I feel your consequence. Never to force myself in any titled company that does not seek my acquaintance. Suckling Nelson is with us, the first night he was very ill but he is better. Closer than ever, seldom goes to Hilborough, he tells us Lady Spencer is at the doctors, whose health declines fast. The Cooks have laid down their set of horses and drive one pair. Allin's estate to be sold. Wm. Hoste [1] and his wife are going to live in a very small house at Lynn, the estate let, in short he says all that part of Norfolk is deserted. Mount Idea still to be sold. Mr. Dixon Hoste [2] met Suckling at Deerham and desired him to tell me he was going to London and that I should hear from him.

The cases of wine has been opened rum, claret and other liquors they contained bottles leaking for want of good corks, some half emptied and in such state that Capt. Boucher advised us the corks in the bottles must be drawn. The wine had best be put into pint bottles as it is rare wine (the sweet) and not to be had but very few tables now. If I have an opportunity I shall certainly send you corks. Our good father complains much of his sight. He wants more to be amused. I do all I can and he seems sensible of it. Mrs. Berry's manners are very gentle and she is very good. I like her very much.

I wish I could hear from my Josiah. I hope he is with you. Abbot has promised your brother Maurice to send me your picture, which I grow impatient to have. My spirits are a little fagged, every day I hope to hear from you. God bless and protect you my dear husband. Believe me your affectionate wife FRANCES H. NELSON.

Love and blessing to you—Love to Josiah. Mr. Bolton called here in his way to Cranwick. He is very —— and so are all the family.

Rear-Admiral Sir Horatio Nelson, K.B., *Vanguard*, Lisbon.

Post Paid 1/8.

XIV

Round Wood,
July 16, 1798
(No. 13)

MY DEAREST HUSBAND,—I only write to tell you of my extreme anxiety to hear from you, no one period of the war have I felt more than I do at this moment. I really am so affected that it has enervated me beyond description still I think all will turn out to your most sanguine wishes. I hope

[1] Uncle of Midshipman Hoste. Mr. William Hoste had married a Norfolk heiress.
[2] Father of William Hoste, Nelson's midshipman.
[3] Thomas Bolton, Nelson's brother-in-law.

in God it will. The papers tell us you have been to Naples, but was not satisfied and immediately sailed for Malta. I wish I knew that Josiah was with you. A line from him would do me good. I can only hope his duty to his profession and his love for you employ his time. I am one of the old fashion mothers and think there is a something called natural affection. I am sure I feel it for him. Mrs. Berry is still with me. I find her a very pleasant young woman. Not in the least gay. We go to Capt. Boucher's just when we like.

Yesterday we called upon them after church and brought them up to dinner which cheered us all, for I assure you we all have talked of the situation you are placed in till we are almost stupefied. Our father was glad to have somebody to talk to. How any creature could possibly tell us this was a good neighbourhood. We talked of it to Capt. Boucher, he said by no means. The Berners never mixed with anybody. Sir W. Rowley was full 17 miles from us. Sir R. Harland was a very gay young man and no gentlewoman ever went to his house, once a year at the races he either gave a breakfast or a dinner. General Dalrimple, Sir Robert Harland's brother-in-law lives with him. The world thinks Sir R. H. is fond of gaming and has lost very much at play that he will soon be fleeced by his relation. We have been to see his beautiful seat Wherstead, the house not finished. A want of money they say is the cause. A well behaved man shewed us the house and when he came to the bedrooms he threw the doors open for us, he remaining outside, Mrs. B. Mrs. Berry and myself were not at all gratified by the indecent ornaments of a gay young man, fine, naked figures and very handsome looking glasses at the bottoms of the bedstead, so we left this handsome house and on one of the most beautiful prospects I ever beheld, not much impressed with favourable sentiments of the owner.

The Queen of a certain town that you called upon who made handsome promises about introduction and such civilities, I find as arrant a courtier as ever lived, a tongue well dipped in oil and fashioned early in life by a gay disposition and I am happy to say I am not at all of her clan therefore the communication there will be very little. She is likewise reckoned to play a steady game. Her house is opened to all card players even her old acquaintance, who have from prudence given up card playing, she never invites saying: 'Capt. you and your wife seldom play which is the reason I never send you a card, but any time you like to come I shall be glad to see you.' Even the Admiral does not escape her.

The window shutters are not all made, but this week I think will nearly finish the carpenter's work. Our father thinks it best only to patch up the rails and fences which to be sure are very bad. It will cost you a good deal to put the house in good repair but everything that can be done shall, excepting the two parlour window shutters, if it is possible the shutters shall remain as they are while we are in the house, altho' they admit wind enough when they are done up to make it a matter of some moment, where to place the candlesticks.

John Thompson[1] called here this morning. He has been a prisoner in France made his escape with five others that were confined in a church, they took everything from him. Mrs. Berry recollected his face, we had a long dish of chat. He wished himself often enough with you. Can't stoop nor go aloft poor fellow. He looked very thin could hardly eat. He took care that he had money enough to carry him to London. He told us the common people in France they were told wished for peace, they heard little. I asked him how he knew where you had a house. He said he was asked if he knew you. He said monstrous well for he sailed with you five years, all this at an ale house in the neighbourhood. Give Mrs. Berry's love to her husband and she will write to him on Thursday.

I have had a letter saying he is in hopes of having all your business settled at the Custom House to your satisfaction. Thomas Allen's money is quite safe. Our father's blessing attend you. God bless and preserve my dearest husband. Believe me your affectionate wife, FRANCES H. NELSON.

Rear-Admiral Nelson, K.B., *Vanguard*, Lisbon.

Post Paid 1/8.

XV

[Nicolas, III, p. 125, extract]

Round Wood,
July 23, 1798
(No. 13 or 14)

MY DEAREST HUSBAND,—I am now writing opposite to your portrait, the likeness is great. I am well satisfied with Abbot. I really began to think he had no intention of letting me have my own property which I am not a little attached too, indeed it is more than attachment, it is real affection. It is my companion, my sincere friend in your absence. Our good father was delighted with the likeness. The room is very near 11 feet, therefore it stands very well opposite the east window. Abbot's bill with the few proofs and prints I have ordered amounts to £18 for when Mr. Nelson

---

[1] A sailor from the *Agamemnon* whose conduct was specially mentioned by Nelson on February 14, 1797.

wrote me they were not like. I only ordered for those we named, and the names you wrote down, I will pay Abbott immediately. Crook and Halford have just wrote me they have the sum of £385.12.8d. for you, which I shall desire them to send me, specifying what vessels the money is for (putting it down in the same manner you did, that I will do myself). My eyes are very weak, my hearing at times is very indifferent, which makes me think it is at times a little nervous, and I shall be better when I hear from you.

The communication you can have from this country I suppose is more frequent than any we can hope for from you. I have had no letter since the one dated May 18th. Every day the papers says something of your movements.

Mr. W. Bolton has paid me £60 and has promised to settle the remainder soon. His house in Ipswich is advertised to be sold, but I think it is with a view to purchase one in a better part of the town. If it is true what a good friend of ours hears, it is too good to quit the town. Mrs. Berry leaves me soon which I am sorry for, her father expects some of Capt. Berry's family to be with him at the Assize week therefore she goes to receive them. I have had one of the girls with me till the week before the last. Our good father frets so much at their awkwardness and high temper, besides giving so decided opinion in politics that I am almost afraid of having them any length of time with me.

Capt. Auffee has been here. I asked him for the news. He says none. I should tell you he is the man who prevented his father from striking his mother for which he was turned out of the house and from his conversation this morning I don't believe has ever been in it since. Mr. Suckling now writes they will be here the 3rd week in August. They may afford us a little chat for we see very few people. I wrote you there was no neighbourhood.

Trees are to be planted next to those already forming what is called a belt which in a few years will make a plantation. I assure you the sweep to the front door admits of a carriage and four horses with ease, having once seen such a sight—the Middletons. Your father asked me whether I would not ask the rector and his wife soon, I have promised to do it, but as they take two beds we must give timely notice. I am obliged to keep three women servants, could not get on with two altho' I tried very much for I assure you the expense of housekeeping is very great, altho' we dine off cold roast beef not being able to procure fish or fowl. I wish I knew some cheerful story to tell you. My mind and ideas will brighten up when I can get a letter from my dear husband.

I wrote you I hoped my Josiah was with you and as Bolton has not mentioned him lately we begin to think he is. My love to him. Our father sends his blessing and love to you. God bless and protect you and believe me my dear husband, your affectionate wife, FRANCES H. NELSON.

Rear-Admiral Nelson, K.B., *Vanguard*, Lisbon.

Post paid 1/8.

XVI

Round Wood,
July 30, 1798

MY DEAREST HUSBAND,—I have to thank Mr. Nepean for your letter of June 15th off Naples which he sent me on Thursday, the one you mentioned writing at St. Peter's I have not received unless it was dated May 18th both of which I thank you for and need not tell you how truly welcome they were. Sincerely do I rejoice in your good health and spirits, thank God for that and the many blessings we enjoy, and I humbly hope He will guide, protect and crown your endeavours to serve your country with success. Our good father and myself have little to do but to talk of you excepting having last week a pipe of Madeira drawn off which Capt. Boucher super intended. 41 doz. has been its produce. I don't mean to touch any of these good things till you come to the cottage, for I understand Madeira is excellent and the port old and very fine, and a great deal more wine than you have, can be put in the cellar. You will smile at my resolutions, which is of sending you good corks if I have the opportunity.

I long to hear if you have received the box containing various good things which was to be sent by Capt. Cockburn. One of the blades to your knife the case would not hold, I put it in my purse with intent of sending it in one of the small parcels or in the Squire's box of spices.

Dr. Foster came for Mrs. Berry. She was sorry to leave me, but Mrs. Berry and Mr. and Mrs. Carpenter were going there for the Assize week. But upon recollection I wrote you all that news. Dr. Foster told me J. Berry, a young merchant was going to take a house in Albemarle St. He knew his income was not sufficient to pay the house rent. Money matters in that family will, I think, make a grand blow up. Fortunately for Capt. Berry he is absent and Dr. Foster is determined to make J. Berry pay Capt. Berry's share, as to the sister they are frighted she can't bring their brother John to say what they are to expect. That's the news I heard from that quarter. I wish exceedingly to write you a cheerful letter. We see nobody—indeed there are no families to visit.

The cottage is well built and when a few trees are added to those already planted will make it very warm but at present it is rather exposed being reckoned the highest spot within ten miles. I wrote you I had got your portrait. It is indeed my friend. Sir R. Calder and Capt. Gray's coming home has made a grand bustle in my mind. Capt. Boucher can tell us nothing and the Admiral is absent from Ipswich, in quest of health which he hopes to find in hot sea bathing.

I wrote to Maurice last week (indeed I have had lately two letters from him telling me all he heard) requesting he would enquire if the *Dolphin* was with you, which I flatter myself she is, therefore I will send my love to my Josiah. Our father sends his blessing and will write next Monday. God bless you my dear husband and believe me your affectionate wife, FRANCES H. NELSON.

XVII

Round Wood,
August 13, 1798
(No. 14)

MY DEAREST HUSBAND,—Last Monday I did not write as it was our good father's day, but he complained much of his sight in the course of the week. He says he has made shift to fill his paper. One of his great amusements my reading the London packet which affords us a little chat, as the Admiral has been absent who is one of our newsmongers. However, he is returned from his hot sea bathing which seems to have given him strength and spirits to encounter a visit to some friend which probably will give him a little gout. His news from Chatham, Admiral Lutwidge was well. Turned out of his lodging. Madam obliged to go from thence for want of accommodation. Dined with the Hartwells. Everything going in style, a ball etc. Capt. Holloway and his wife were at Chatham. They were invited but did not attend this gay house.

I see by the paper Sir R. Calder is a baronet, I suppose the lady is satisfied. Admiral Reeve is surprised at his coming home, for his love of money is great. However I am told the Earl and him did not agree. I begged of Lord Hood to accept of a proof print of your portrait by Abbott. His lordship who you know is an elegant writer, wrote me one of the handsomest letters I ever received assuring me he considered it a very high compliment, speaks of you as my gallant and beloved husband wishing he could have received one line from you requesting that I would write him as soon as I heard from you. Lord Hood says he has been seriously ill with the shingles which were great blotches round his body four nights he could not rest in bed, he had once been on horseback, and thought he should again get about. His eldest grandson had a commission in the Guards.

I had a letter from Miss Nisbet the other day, she enquires kindly of you, regrets exceedingly she cannot hear of or from her dear young captain. She drank his health on his birthday. I wrote her immediately and told her the news which Mr. Bolton told me that Josiah had gone to join you and to be made Post in *La Bonne Citoyenne*. Sincerely do I hope its true and long before this he is under the eye of his mentor. Admiral Cornwallis has adopted Captain Whitby as his son, so Mrs. Sherston writes me. Mr. Pearson has just left me and from what he has been telling I think he finds he has been doing an imprudent thing in making an offer before he had an income. In my humble opinion he has given all parties an opportunity of getting quit of him if they please. He tells me he has this visit told Mr. Bolton he never would have made the offer if he had not at the time thought himself sure of promotion and that he has likewise told Miss Mary Anne if there is anything in his conduct that she thinks anyway reprehensible it is not too late to speak. He is determined to solicit the Duke of York for employment in any part of the world.

Harvest this year has been particularly fine and early got in. The weather is very fine, nice clear sky which helps to cheer us. I was determined to see if I could write without tormenting you with my anxieties, every day produces hopes of hearing from you. Maurice has promised to write me. I hope in God you are well. My love to my Josiah. The Matchams have been to Ringwood for ten days. They are all well.

I feel a great deal of load off my mind since I heard of Josiah going to you. Mr. Pearson has seen somebody lately from Lord St. Vincent's fleet, he says they all speak well of Josiah. I hope its true. God bless and preserve my dear husband and child and give us a happy meeting. My letter this day fortnight, I sent to Mr. Nepean.

Believe me your affectionate FRANCES H. NELSON.

XVIII

Round Wood,
August 26, 1798
(No. 15)

MY DEAREST HUSBAND,—The newspapers will give you an account of the various reports which they have every day tantalized me with. My hopes were all alive my heart has beat many a time of late with the hope of seeing your own handwriting with the welcome news of your good health. 15th June the latest date, therefore you will not wonder at my anxiety. Since I wrote to you I have had a long letter from Mrs. Sherston. Her brother has again turned his thoughts to nautical life, he is on board the *Nonsuch*. Mrs. Sherston wrote to Capt. Wolley recommending her brother to him, and requested the favour to make him a lieutenant. Capt. Wolley assured her his recommendation alone to Lord Spencer could have little effect but a letter from Sir Horatio Nelson to Lord Spencer he was certain would ensure him success, therefore Mrs. Sherston will be obliged to you to exert your interest for a relative who has been at different times within these 25 years in the King's service. She says she will never give you any further trouble about B. Nelson as the height of her ambition is to see her brother a lieutenant. She does not attempt to say a word in vindication of his conduct which it seems has been very improper on various occasions. This letter I answered. Your father very much approved of what I said on the subject which was shortly: 'That Capt. Wolley could be little acquainted with Lord Spencer's situation, to suppose lieutenants were so easily made, that had Mr. B. Nelson been on board your ship, after your 6 lieutenants were made and some other young men you were particularly attached too, he might then have stood some chance.' Our good father supposes this Mr. B. Nelson must be bordering on fifty, it seems he married some very bad woman which Mrs. Sherston says he has got quit off. The laws of his country had liberated him from a jade of a wife. I will leave this subject and tell you how closely Mr. Swanston has attacked me to recommend his son to you, if first, to be your agent.

I wrote him it was impossible for me to say anything on the subject you were engaged with Messrs. Marsh and Creed. I have now had another letter which shows how some people confer favours. I will send you an extract: 'Mr. Drake wishing to assist men in bringing up my son to the business of agent has suggested the idea, viz., that as frequent opportunities would occur to the Admiral of appointing officers who Mr. Drake conceives would pay the greatest deference to his recommendation of an agent, he thought application on that ground would not be improper, which he proposed to my consideration and has himself accordingly spoke to Capt. Holloway and will speak to other gentlemen of his acquaintance, as opportunity offers.' After saying in a polite way that I was in hopes my first letter I thought fully explained my sentiments on the subject I would repeat a conversation which has passed in regard to my son. 'Who have you desired Josiah to make his agent?' 'I never recommend, he must choose himself. Therefore I leave you to judge whether I could say anything on the subject, besides Adml. Nelson would not I am certain tie down any young man by asking him a favour, who he had just conferred one upon. I leave Mr. Drake to do what he pleases in this business.' How can I ask you to do things for people that it is impossible for me to be interested for? Only wishing every body to do well and that of recommending agents a particularly delicate thing, particularly when there can be no good security.

Tuesday last the Squire and Price arrived safe from Kentish Town Mr. Romsey was extremely ill, he begged his daughter not to leave him. Mr. S. had been very ill with what Mrs. S. terms thorough scouring, after a stoppage of 2 days and a night, but she wrote me it had been of service to him, however the medical people recommended change of air, and he had set his mind upon going to Barsham. Stayed two days with us and was so exceedingly well pleased with his reception that he not only drank your health success and your speedy return to me, but thanked me for his very handsome entertainment. The few people I knew I would not invite till they came, which were the Bouchers, Will Bolton and Pearson. The next day two from Mr. Berners, Major McKensy a Devonshire man, and Major Anfrene, Mr. and Mrs. Heron, Mrs. Bolton who has been here the whole week. I take her home tomorrow. One of the girls returns with me. Your father wished her to spend a cheerful week and I am sure I was glad to see her. They talk of going into Norfolk in October. Mr. Bolton looks well he was very kind in sending me fine lobsters and a hare. It is very hard to get victuals, no fish and poultry very bad. I am told when we have peace there will be plenty.

I wrote you Mr. W. Bolton paid me the beginning of the month. He wishes very much his son was only in one of the ships under your command. Our father I think likes him better. General Balfour called this morning, had no news. Have had a kind letter from Miss Walpole begging to know if I had heard from you. The Brooks of Nacton wished to be acquainted with me, but did not know whether I wished to be visited. She gives them a great character. Very intimate friends of theirs.

Give my love to my Josiah. I know he loves me dearly though he has quarrelled with a pen. Our good father sends his blessing to you.

God bless you my dearest husband, believe me your affectionate wife, FRANCES H. NELSON.

P.S. *[from Mrs. Bolton]:* God bless and preserve you my dear brother and accept my best love and wishes. Miss B. desires to join me. S. BOLTON.

XIX

Round Wood,
September 11, 1798

MY DEAREST HUSBAND,—We were happily relieved on Sunday from a load of anxiety by your letter of May 24th off Sardinia, which had on the wafer

side: 'Sir Horatio was well on the 22nd July your h.s. Maud and Son.'
It is impossible to say what I have suffered, I thank God you were saved.
What a storm. On that very Sunday May the 20th it blew a storm at
Ipswich. Mr. Harrison at the Admiralty wrote to me on last Saturday
saying 'there was a letter in town from Sir Horatio to your ladyship but
Lord Spencer would not delay telling you Sir Horatio Nelson was well on
the 19th of July. His lordship was fearful your letter was of an old date.
Should it not be so his Lordship will thank you for any information you
will be pleased to give him, as no letters have been received immediately
from Sir. H. Nelson.'

I felt myself so truly thankful to Lord Spencer that I sent your letter
to him, writing his Lordship as civil a note as I could and requesting to
have my letter by return of post which I have had this morning, with a
handsome note from his Lordship, who I think had not received your
letter of May off Sardinia.

The newspapers have tormented and almost killed me in regard to the
desperate action you have fought with the French fleet.[1] How human
faculties can be brought to make others intentionally miserable I cannot
conceive. In my opinion a news paper writer, or a fabricator for them, is
a despicable creature bearing a human shape. I trust in God for a continuance of his protection over you and to grant my dear husband a happy
return to me and our good father, who has exerted his spirits pretty well.

The Rector was here last week, he was obliged to leave us on the
Friday. We sent him a copy of your letter on Sunday. I am very anxious
to hear Josiah has joined you. He left Lord St. Vincent's fleet in June.
Mr. Suckling left us yesterday in his way to town he looks but poorly. I
shall send this letter to Mr. Nepean and request the favour of him to
forward it to you. Mr. Palmer has been very kind in making enquiries if
government had any intelligence from you, this he did 10 days back. I feel
most sensibly how much you have to do and must beg you will let your
mind and body rest as much as possible. I don't suppose you have
received any of the almost weekly letters I have written to you. Except to
church I have been out nowhere lately.

I took Mrs. Bolton home and brought Kitty and George [2] with me,
George for advice, he has what is called a scalt head, they are now giving
him mercury, he cannot be sent to sea for two or three years at least not
being able to read three lines in any book. They are both gone to see the
soldiers exercise. Everybody are soldiers. W. Bolton sports a red coat and

---

[1] The dispatches of the battle of the Nile did not reach England till October 2, but
rumours had been circulating for some time.
[2] George Bolton, then aged eleven.

PLATE XIII. Caricature by J. Cruikshank, published October 1798, of Admiral Nelson 'bringing home two uncommon fierce French crocodiles' from the Nile.

helmet cap (and indeed many other clergymen) Suckling had in inclination to mount a red coat, however our father and the Rector said No. Cook and Halford wrote to me they had £114 of your money which I will [draw] by and by. I will write next Monday. God bless you my dear husband and believe me your affectionate wife, FRANCES H. NELSON.

Our good father sends his blessing to you. We offer our daily prayers for you. My love to my dear child.

I wrote to Lady Saumarez and will to Mrs. B.

Rear-Admiral Nelson, K.B., *Vanguard*, Mediterranean.

XX

Round Wood,
October 1, 1798

MY DEAREST HUSBAND,—The 20th July is the date of your letter which I received the middle of last month. The newspapers let me rest a week, then began again with their conjectures and this last week have positively asserted you have gained some advantages over the French fleet assuring the public you arrived safe with your prizes at Naples. Government has sent some part of the above to Lloyds. I long to hear from you. A letter of one line will rejoice my heart, and I think I shall soon be gratified, God grant I may.

The cottage is in good repair. The window shutters are all finished, which makes it very comfortable. Our good father finds the air particularly clear and sharp. He told me it was the keenest air I had breathed he was sure for years. It is all true but I have taken less colds here than anywhere for years. However I have promised to go to Bath with him whenever he wishes. My own plan was to have left Round Wood in January but from all that has passed I think it will be the middle of November, provided Mrs. Bolton and her two children leave us. I expect her in ten days.

Every bill will be paid, the expense of drawing off the wine, bottles etc., came to £30 all very carefully put away against your coming home, in all 150 doz. I believe I mentioned to you the house was to be painted, and a part papered, I am almost afraid of papering all, the expense will be very great. Mention what you wish me to do. I feel very much your kindness in desiring I would indulge my self in everything you can afford. I go on in the same careful way I began. Six constantly in family, besides one of the Boltons and for six weeks back George, I assure you makes my weekly bills high.

Miss Patty Berry is spending a few days with me. Her brother John and

2 G

NELSON'S LETTERS TO HIS WIFE

his wife are gone to Trosendon to shoot for a week, from thence to
Norwich to show himself after his voyage. Miss P. Berry is going to
Norwich to Mrs. Berry in hopes of persuading her to go to the gay town.
What will Capt. Berry say to all this? Capt. Charles Rowley has been
obliged to give up his ship and is ordered to Cheltenham. Capt. B. Rowley
is stationed in Ireland. Lady Harland told me yesterday that his friends
were rather uneasy about him. Those who were in the same ship were not
perfectly in good humour. I think that is all the news I picked up there.
I met the Admiral just as I was going out of the house, who very politely
begged I would dine with him, the Bouchers were to be there. So we all
(three in number) went and spent a cheerful day. Very little variety here
and when you make your appearance in the town you see plenty of soldiers
and that is all. No kind of trade, or the least bustle.

Capt. Cockburn[1] writes me he expects to leave England and will
take charge of anything for you. I have by this day's waggon sent a box
containing 9 small stone jars of cherries in brandy, five of currant jelly
and five of apricot. The season was particularly unfavourable for preserving. The torrents of rain bruised the fruit very much. Sugar has raised in
price beyond belief. We now drink sugar at 1/6 per pound.

We lately heard from Mrs. Matcham who is all anxiety to see her
father. Miss Martin is returned from India. She and old Mr. M. are there.
Tell Capt. Berry his old flirt that he often escorted to Kensington is fashion
mad, exhibits without powder which makes her look particularly amiable.
Miss Patty begs you will tell her brother that her mother is going to Dover
St. Their house is to be painted. I trust I may say all the family are well.

Our good father will write next. I shall send my letter to Admiral
Young. You can't think how very good Lord Hood has been to me.
Writes very often tells me what he hears, and what he believes. I wish I
could hear of my dear child. God bless and protect you my dearest husband
and believe me to be your affectionate wife, FRANCES H. NELSON.

Rear-Admiral Nelson, K.B., *Vanguard*, Mediterranean.

Horatio Nelson to Nelson[2]

Hilborough, Near Brandon,
October 17, 1798

MY DEAR UNCLE,—When the news of your victory arrived at Bury I was
carried to the Angel Hill to see the soldiers fire a feu de joie. I am now

---

[1] Captain Cockburn sailed from Portsmouth in the *La Minerve* on November 21.
[2] N.M.M. MS. 9292, Bridport papers. Horatio Nelson, the only son of the Rev.
William Nelson, was then ten years old.

home for the fair holidays and am employed all day in writing songs and verses about you. I hope I shall see you home in the Christmas holidays. Charlotte sends her love to you and Captain Nisbet.

I am my lord your dutiful and affectionate nephew, HORATIO NELSON.

> 'But the best piece of prose I have heard a long while,
> Is what gallant Nelson has sent from the Nile,
> And had he but told us the story in rhyme,
> What a thing it would be; but perhaps he hadn't time,
> Then I'll do it myself; oh! what glorious news,
> "Nine ships of the line, that's a ship for each muse."'

Note by Horatio's father, the Rev. William Nelson: The above is the conclusion of an epilogue written by Mr. Palmer of the Temple, son to your friend Mr. Palmer. After a humorous defence of rhyme, the poet says as above. It was received with the most rapturous bursts of applause.

Rev. William Nelson continues:

MY DEAR BROTHER,—As I wrote to you so lately as last week from Ipswich and Lady Nelson was kind enough to inclose it with hers, I don't know that I should have written to you again so soon if Horatio had not in a manner insisted on writing to you himself, and my father likewise rather wished it and desired me to remind you that if you was not satisfied with the title ministers had conferred upon you and any addition was to be made that I would remind you that the title of *Orford* [1] was now extinct; not that I ever wish to see the name of Nelson forgotten. I have no doubt but Parliament will settle the same pension upon yourself and the two next possessors of your title which they have done upon Earl St. Vincent and Viscount Duncan. The Irish Parliament have already mentioned it, and Lord Altamont son-in-law to Lord Howe has spoken very strongly upon the subject. [2]

The newspapers are giving preferment both to our father and myself, and the following paragraph has appeared in several. 'His Majesty has intimated to his ministers that he expects some dignitary should be given to the father and brother of the gallant Lord Nelson, who are both in the Church.' We are much obliged to these writers and heartily wish we could hear it from better authority, but are afraid we shall not.

Mrs. Nelson sends her love and hopes you will now come home and enjoy the honours you have so dearly earned, with your good lady and

[1] A title which would show Nelson's connection with the Walpole family.
[2] The Irish Parliament did not vote Nelson a pension and he got a smaller one from the Parliament at Westminster than St. Vincent or Duncan.

your friends. You have now done enough, let others take their turn, your country cannot require more at present. We are to have a grand ball in honour of you at Swaffham next Tuesday and Mrs. Nelson has sent for a dress for the occasion.

I send this by the Lisbon mail in hopes it may meet you there or at Cadiz on your passage to England, where you may speedily arrive safe and in perfect health is the fervent prayer of your most affectionate brother, WILLIAM NELSON.

Aunt Mary is tolerable and sends her love to you.

Right Honble. Lord Nelson, at Lisbon, or with Earl St. Vincent's fleet off Cadiz.

Maurice Nelson to Lady Nelson[1]

A

Navy Office,
July 26, 1798

MY DEAR MADAM,—Sir Robert Calder is just arrived (on the score of ill-health) from Lord St. Vincent's whose dispatches are dated on the 11th instant. He brings an account of the capture of the *Sensible* French frigate on the 27th June by the *Seahorse*, who was going with stores to my brother. The French frigate had on board Bonaparte's second in command who was carrying dispatches from Malta to the Directory as also all the trophies taken there. She left it on the 18th of June on which day Bonaparte also sailed thence up the Mediterranean, and as it is generally supposed my brother sailed from Naples on the 17th June, there is every reason to think he will fall in with him in a few days after.

I trust in God he will and that we shall soon hear of him.

Adieu—God bless you, and believe me yours affectionately, MAURICE NELSON.

To Lady Nelson, Ipswich, Suffolk.

B

Navy Office,
October 4, 1798

MY DEAR MADAM,—You of course received this morning my brother's letter by Captain Capel,[2] as I did one yesterday of 3 lines merely to tell me

---

[1] Monmouth MSS., Nelson papers, Vol. IV.
[2] Captain Capel arrived in London on October 2.

that Mr. Davison was appointed sole agent to the prizes. I have seen a letter from Mr. Campbell the secretary who says my brother was wounded over the right eye and that he was in perfect health and spirits and there was not the least danger in the wound and that it would be quite well in the course of a week or ten days. These were his very words, therefore you may make yourself perfectly easy. Letters were yesterday received from him at the Admiralty dated the 27th August. He was then cruising near the Island of Rhodes.

Lord Spencer sent for me this morning and after congratulating me upon the victory obtained over the French fleet said His Majesty had been pleased to create my brother a peer but as he had never heard my brother say what title he would wish to take he had sent for me to ask my opinion. As we had never had any conversation on this subject I told his Lordship I was at a loss to say, but that I rather wished the name might be retained. His Lordship said he was perfectly of my mind and that it should be so fixed. His Lordship did not tell me and I did not think proper to ask what degree of peerage was to be conferred. If you have ever heard my brother say what title he should like, tell me and I will see his Lordship again. He likewise desired I would not at present make this public.

Give my duty to our good father and believe me your truly affectionate brother, MAURICE NELSON.

To Lady Nelson, Ipswich, Suffolk.

C.

Navy Office,
October 6, 1798

MY DEAR MADAM,—I am sorry you have been so unwell and the fatigue you must experience just now I fear will not expedite your recovery. I can say nothing more on the subject of my brother's peerage than what you will receive in my letter this morning.[1] I again repeat I am dissatisfied. As to any remainder of the title, nothing certainly can be done in that until my brother arrives.[2] However I now declare to you that William may have all the honours to himself. It will be my wish and request to my

[1] B.M. Add. MSS. 34988. In the letter written on October 5, Maurice Nelson expressed his dissatisfaction at his brother's honour: 'I am by no means satisfied with it, and if I had been authorized I should have rejected it with contempt, but as I was not, I held my tongue. I only hope he may be better pleased with it than I am.' St. Vincent had received an earldom and Duncan a viscountcy for their victories, which were not popularly considered so eminent. Nelson was created Baron Nelson of the Nile.
[2] Maurice, who had no children, died in 1801. The succession to Nelson's title was finally settled after the battle of Copenhagen, for which he received a viscountcy.

brother not to put my name in the patent. However at present no other person than my brother and his heirs will be named in the patent. I move in too humble a sphere to think of such a thing.

Give my duty and believe me yours most affectionately, MAURICE NELSON.

I shall write a few lines to William.

To Lady Nelson, Ipswich, Suffolk.

D

Navy Office,
October 19, 1798

MY DEAR MADAM,—I have been fearful you were not well as I had not heard from you for some time. As I know unpleasant news flies fast enough, I forbore saying any thing respecting Captain Nisbet, however I will tell you all I know of the matter, which is contained in a letter from the Consul at Tunis to the Navy Board, I don't recollect the date, some time the latter end of June I think. After mentioning the loss of *L'Aigle*, he says ' I have hired a vessel for the use of Captain Nisbet who is going in search of Admiral Nelson's fleet, with one hundred men.' From which circumstance we conjecture Captain Nisbet and his men were passengers in *L'Aigle*.

Captain Berry I am much afraid has been taken by one of the ships that escaped or that the ship has been lost (*Leander*) from her having been so much crippled in the action. The former is the opinion of the Admiralty, the latter of Lord St. Vincent, from whom letters were received yesterday dated 1st October.

You have been at a grand ball and received great attention. I have been at a grand dinner on the invitation of Mr. Pitt who made a point of my being there. He was not well enough to attend, but I was carried by Sir Andrew Hamond, and introduced by him to Mr. Rose, Lord Spencer and many other great men. Among the rest was Lord Hood who was particularly civil, enquired much after you, and said he expected to hear from you. He asked about the remainder of my brother's title. I said I knew nothing about it and that I apprehended nothing could be determined respecting it until his arrival. His answer was—I wish he was here.

Mr. Rumsey called upon me yesterday to say that he thought my uncle in such a way that it was impossible he could survive long, and said both himself and Mrs. Suckling thought it right I should be made acquainted with the state he was in, and that he (Mr. Rumsey) considered me as the heir to his estate. However I endeavoured to convince him that, that could not be the case as I had often heard how the young men had disposed of his property. What I said did not convince him, he said it was impossible and took his leave. I went to Kentish Town this morning and saw him very feeble indeed and I think in exactly the same way as the late Comptroller[1] was, he seems perfectly easy and sleeps a great deal (by far too much) I confess I saw no appearance of his dissolution being soon but that he might continue in his present state for some months; his voice is strong, he said he should never get well again, and that he attributed his present complaint to his journey into Suffolk. He has certainly a confirmed dropsy but Mrs. Suckling says the water has not increased for some days past, neither has it diminished, and she was also fearful that he would not be able to bear the medicines that was given him. She desired to be kindly remembered to you and said she hoped you would excuse her writing. Mrs. Wigley was expected there today.

The box for my brother I sent by the *Barfleur* (I think I told you so before) and is I hope arrived at Lisbon before this time. Admiral Young told me that two of my brother's ships had arrived at Naples and that he was expected there every day, but I have some idea he got his information from the French papers. I am glad to find I am not the only person who is dissatisfied with what has been done for my brother, but the Admiralty say they could not do more. However I cannot help thinking that when he arrives the King will confer upon him some other degree of peerage.

Thank you for desiring Mr. Hoste to send me some game. I think with you that Mr. B.[2] farm is a large one, but if he can stock it I don't see why he should not do as well as his neighbours. Do you remember the prints of Lord St. Vincent's action are at Marsh and Creeds for you? Say what you would have done with them. Give my duty to our good father and love to my sister and the girls and believe me your truly affectionate brother, MAURICE NELSON.

I suspect my letter have offended William as I have not heard from him but I wrote my mind.

Captain Locker to Lady Nelson [3]

Barking Essex,
at W. Smith's Esq.,
October 1798

MY DEAR LADY NELSON,—I am just arrived from Malvern Wells and am invited here to stay till my apartments are ready to receive me being

---

[1] Captain Maurice Suckling.   [2] Mr. Bolton, his brother-in-law.
[3] Monmouth MSS., Nelson papers, Vol. V.

newly painted and repaired or I should have paid my respects to you long ago by letter. I now most sincerely wish your Ladyship joy of the late happy event and am glad to find my worthy and gallant friend has providentially escaped with so little harm and I trust from what I have heard he will be soon perfectly well and that your Ladyship may soon see him in the highest health and the happiest meeting is my most hearty wish. I have this moment received a letter from Lady St. Vincent which I have copied and enclosed for your Ladyship's reading—and shall write to her Ladyship by this post to say I have done so.

I think the Malvern waters has been of great service to me, but I am still lame, as it is an old wound. If my sons and daughter were here they would join me in our best congratulations and our most sincere wishes for your Ladyship's happy meeting with his Lordship to whom I beg my most kind and sincere regards, and to those I know of his fleet with every good wish I am your Ladyship's most sincere and faithful servant, W. LOCKER.

P.S. I have wrote this in a room full of people and therefore hope your Ladyship will be able to make it out and excuse the writing. My daughter is with Mr. and Mrs. Law at Tunbridge Wells. When you write to my worthy friend Lord Nelson remember me and mine most kindly.

Enclosure:

DEAR SIR,—I beg you will accept my sincere congratulations on the important victory obtained by our friend Nelson over the French fleet. The becoming sense of piety he shews on the occasion crowns all. I wish much to write to Lady Nelson but am totally ignorant of her address, and should esteem it a favour if you would send me a line informing me where I should direct to her Ladyship. I do not mean to trouble you to write yourself, but Miss Locker or one of your sons would have the goodness to inform me. I wish to hear Lord Nelson's wound is recovering fast. By the last dispatches from Lord St. Vincent he was well, but he will be in infinitely better spirits when I hear again. The happiness he will derive from the high credit done to his judgement on this occasion will almost exceed description. I hope to hear yourself and family are well and remain dear sir your faithful etc., etc., M. ST. VINCENT.

Rochetts: October 8th 1798.

[*Cover addressed:* To Right Honourable Lady Nelson, Near Ipswich, Suffolk. *Post mark:* 11th October 1798.]

Mrs. Lockhart to Lady Nelson [1]

Camalthan House,
October 8, 1798

MY DEAR SISTER,—I was happy once more to receive a letter from you in which I was happy to find you was well. Amidst the universal congratulations of the whole nation, permit me to add mine, but my anxiety is great to be indulged with a few lines from you saying how Sir Horatio Nelson does, in whose health and happiness I must ever feel deeply interested. How do you feel yourself? For withal your joy there is a damper, and I must again intreat you to make your maid write me if you cannot. And what is become of our dearest Josiah? You was always steady and not apt to be led away with the vanities of this world, but you really will now require more than common principles to withstand all that I hope in God await you.

The town of Glasgow illuminated for your hero's victory, which was more than they did for Lord Duncan's, tho' a Scotsman. Even a village, the property of my husband had a bonfire and got drunk upon the occasion, which he sent them word he would pay with great pleasure, as he never had his health drank with such a hero's before. I was so anxious to learn of Admiral Nelson that I was once going to write . . . *[part missing]*.

Whenever I meet with a private opportunity going to London I will send you two embroidered screens done upon white satin worked by Mary and Isabella which I beg your acceptance of to allow them a place in Sir Horatio Nelson's house. I was in hopes of sending them some time ago, but the opportunity failed me. I will direct them to the care of Mrs. Thomas.

Mr. Lockhart speaks for himself below, the rest of my family unite in every kind and heartfelt congratulation to you and anxious wishes for Sir Horatio Nelson's speedy recovery, with your affectionate sister, MARY EMILIA LOCKHART.

Best respects are offered to good Mr. Nelson. I have a very good English governess and knows none in want of one.

[By Mr. Lockhart:]

Amidst the public rejoicings with which Sir Horatio Nelson's splendid and unexampled victory has filled the whole kingdom, Mr. Lockhart begs leave to add his private congratulations, to the wife and the father of this illustrious hero. Happy old man to live to see his son the glory and the pride of his country.

To Lady Nelson, Round Wood, Ipswich, Suffolk.
Franked by Alex Trotter.

[1] Monmouth MSS., Nelson papers, Vol. V.

Lady Nelson to Lord Hood [1]

A.

Round Wood,
Thursday, October 4, 1798

MY DEAR LORD,—Altho' I am exceedingly indisposed, I have sent you my dear husband's letter and will answer your question. Any request of your Lordship's will readily be complied with. And I will remember it knowing that there are very few my husband feels a stronger attachment for. I must beg you will not notice to any one, what he says about coming home.

The first title certainly *Alexandria.*

His father and myself thinks he will like Baron Nelson. His unbounded affection for his father would make him wish to have it Baron Nelson. I will write again tomorrow.

Have sent by coach this night brace of pheasants and a hare directed for your Lordship in Wimpole Street. My best respects to Lady Hood.

Your Lordship's affectionate, FRANCES H. NELSON.

B

Round Wood,
October 18, 1798

MY DEAR LORD,—My cough is still very troublesome, but that has not been the cause of my silence, the constant expectation of Capt. Berry who will give me full accounts from my husband, and the anxiety I have been under for my son, which was relieved yesterday by Mr. Pearson, who told me Capt. Nisbet was at Tunis procuring men for Lord Nelson; that Mr. M. Nelson had desired him to tell me.

The honours which have been conferred on Lord Nelson is I am told the subject of conversation everywhere. It does not meet the approbation of the public, as to my own feelings, they were mortified in the extreme, so much so that I was going to direct my letter to my husband, as I usually did; but Mr. Nelson requested I would give him all every mark of distinction which his own title would allow.

When Mr. Nepean sent for Mr. M. Nelson and told him that his brother was to be created a baron!—he was so much hurt, and surprised, that he never made any reply, but bowed and took his leave.[2]

---

[1] N.M.M. 50 MS. 0096, Hood papers.
[2] See Maurice Nelson's letter, p. 453.

Since my dear Lord, my husband, has gained this victory I have been honoured with the notice of the great in this neighbourhood—truly I don't thank them: they ought to have found their way to the cottage before,—that is my way of thinking. Mrs. Berners and Mrs. Middleton paid me great attention when I first came here; this is the second day I have been writing thus far to your Lordship. Since writing the above Miss Berry, who is staying with me, has received a very distressing letter from her mother, who is under great fears for the safety of Capt. Berry. The newspapers seems to think the *Leander* is taken—if your Lordship can give us any information on the subject I will thank you. I have enclosed Lord Spencer's letter for your Lordship's perusal. I have been noticed in a handsome manner by Lord Chatham who requested General Manners and General Belfour to introduce him at Round Wood. I afterwards met all these great generals with the addition of Sir W. How on Westerfield green. The window of the chaise being frequently down, gave me rather more fresh air than was necessary. A little ass's milk will I hope set all to rights again.

The neighbourhood gave a very handsome ball and supper on Tuesday. I was there and great attention was paid me. I cannot conclude without telling your Lordship of the very extraordinary applications I have had made me: 'If I would only ask Lord Spencer, it would be complied with, immediately.'

I beg my kindest regards to my good Lady Hood, Mrs. Holwell and family.

Your Lordship will believe me your affectionate FRANCES H. NELSON.

C

Round Wood,
November 11, 1798

MY DEAR LORD,—Mr. Nepean sent me the enclosed letter this morning; when your Lordship has read my dear husband's letter, pray sent it me. We leave Round Wood on Friday for London. I have written to Jones if his lodgings are vacant I would prefer them. If Lady Hood goes to St. James's I hope she will allow me to be her attendant.[1] I would not wish her to go out of civility to me. The fatigue is great. You will see I do not go to please myself.

My best and kindest love etc., to Lady Hood, your Lordship and family. Yours very sincerely, FRANCES H. NELSON.

To Viscount Hood, Royal Hospital, Greenwich.

[1] Lady Nelson attended the Drawing Room on November 22, when she was presented to the Queen by the Countess of Chatham. Her name was included by *The Times* 'among the principal female nobility and gentry'.

Lady Hamilton to Lady Nelson [1]
'For Lady Nelson with Lady Hamilton's Compliments'
THE BATTLE OF THE NILE
1ST OF AUGUST 1798
A PINDARICK ODE
Naples 1798

Dedication:

To His Excellency the right honourable Sir William Hamilton, K.B.,
minister plenipotentiary of His Britannic Majesty
at the Court of the two Sicilies, etc., etc., etc.

SIR,—It was your wish that I should consecrate a few lines to the celebration of one of the noblest actions that ever graced the splendid annals of our naval history. No other motive could have induced me to undertake so arduous a task; though, had I found my abilities equal to my feelings, the subject itself would have inspired me with the most ardent desire of recording the praises so justly due to the Hero of the Nile and his brave associates.

However the following ode may be deemed inadequate to the glorious theme, I take the liberty of offering it to your Excellency, as to the friend of Sir Horatio Nelson, as to a minister whose zeal and talents have ever stood foremost in promoting the happiness and real interest of his own country and of that in which he resides; and, may I be allowed to add? as a tribute of gratitude from a daughter of the waves for the distinguished attentions conferred on the British Navy by Sir William Hamilton and his amiable lady.

I have the honour to be sir, your Excellency's obliged humble servant,
ELLIS CORNELIA KNIGHT.

Naples: September the 16th, 1798.

[Ode of 17 stanzas of 8 lines each follows: the last four are given.]

XIV

More had he said; but from his humble tomb
The shade of laurel'd Pompey rose;
He views the Britons victors of their foes;
The Nile with wrecks overspread, the curling smoke,
The captive banners seal the doom
Of haughty France, and break her galling yoke:
'See, proud oppression falls,' the Chief exclaims,
'Perish her empire 'midst these sanguine flames!

[1] This copy of the Ode printed in Naples has been signed by Lady Hamilton: Monmouth MSS., Nelson papers, Vol. V.

XV

'Blest leader, whom thy country's voice approves,
Whom rescued nations must adore;
Whom I, though lost on treacherous Egypt's shore,
Exulting greet, and in the Paeans join.
Each son of fame the Hero loves;
Nor will I envious at thy deeds repine,
Though once my name stood foremost in renown
Of all whose brows adorn'd the rostral crown.

XVI

'O may that Crown long grace thy honour'd head
With ever blooming laurels twined
And oaken wreaths by sapient Heaven assigned
The growth of Britain, and to Britons due,
Who kingdoms free from servile dread!
And thou benign with these illustrious few
Who share thy toils and emulate thy worth,
Hear the prophetic words to which thy deeds give birth

XVII

'Though vice and guilt their numerous conquests boast,
Yet virtue has her sails unfurl'd
To save a sinking, a deluded world;
Her sons assert her empire o'er the main,
Spread terror round each hostile coast
And teach mankind to bless her generous reign:
Britannia's palms shall break the guilty charm
Rouse latent valour, and bid Europe arm.'

Lady Hamilton to Lady Nelson [1]

December 2, 1798

I hope your ladyship received my former letter with an account of
Lord Nelson's arrival and his reception from their Sicilian Majesties and
also the congratulations and compliments from this amiable and adorable
Queen to your ladyship, which I was charged with and wrote a month
back, but as the posts are very uncertain you may not have received that
letter.

[1] B.M. Add. MS. 34989, Bridport papers.

Lord Nelson is gone to Leghorn with the troops of the King of Naples and we expect him soon back. As the King is gone to Rome with his army he urged of my Lord Nelson to be as much at or about Naples as he could, not only to advise and consult with her Majesty (who is regent) for the good of the common cause, but in case of accident to take care of her and her family.

Lord Nelson is adored here and looked on as the deliverer of this country. He was not well when first he arrived, but by nursing and asses' milk he went from Naples quite recovered. The King and Queen adore him and if he had been their brother they could not have shewn him more respect and attentions. I need not tell your Ladyship how happy Sir William and myself are at having an opportunity of seeing our dear, respectable, brave friend return here with so much honour to himself and glory for his country. We only wanted you to be completely happy. Lord Nelson's wound is quite well.

Josiah is so much improved in every respect. We are all delighted with him. He is an excellent officer and very steady and one of the best hearts in the world. I love him much and although we quarrel sometimes, he loves me and does as I would have him. He is in the way of being rich, for he has taken many prizes. He is indefatigable in his line, never sleeps out of his ship and I am sure will make a very great officer.

Lady Knight and her aimiable daughter desire to be remembered to your Ladyship. I hope you received the ode I sent. It is very well written, but Miss K. is very clever in everything she undertakes.

Sir William desires his kind compliments to your Ladyship, and to Lord Nelson's dear respected father. The King is having his picture set with diamonds for his Lordship, and the Queen has ordered a fine set of china with all the battles he has been engaged in and his picture painted on china.

Josiah desired his duty to your Ladyship and says he will write as soon as he has time but he has been very busy for some time past.

May God bless you and yours my dear Madam, and believe me your Ladyship's ever sincere friend and humble servant, EMMA HAMILTON.

Sir William is in a rage with ministry for not having made Lord Nelson a viscount, for sure this great and glorious action, greater than any other, ought to have been recompensed more. Hang them I say.

To Lady Nelson, Round Wood, Near Ipswich, Suffolk.

[Endorsed by Lady Nelson: 'Lady Hamilton's letter to Lady Nelson Naples 2 October 1798.'[1]]

---

[1] Lady Nelson has read the date incorrectly—it is December, not October.

The Queen of Naples to the Marquis Circello [1]

(Translation)

[1798]

I write to you with the greatest joy. The brave and gallant Admiral Nelson has gained a most complete victory. I wish I could give wings to the bearer of this news, and at the same time of our most sincere thanks.

Italy is saved on the part of the sea, and that is only due to the gallant English. This action or better named total defeat of the regicide fleet is owing to the valour and courage of this brave Admiral seconded by a marine which is the terror of its enemies. The victory is so complete, that I can still scarcely believe it and if it was not the English nation which is accustomed to perform prodigies by sea, I could not persuade myself of it. This has produced a general enthusiasm.

You would have been moved at seeing all my children boys and girls, hanging on my neck, crying for joy at the happy news, which has been doubled by the critical moment in which it is arrived. Fear, avarice, and the malicious intrigues of the Republicans have made all the cash disappear, and there is no one who has courage to propose a plan to put it in circulation. And this want of cash produces much discontent. We are distressed by the Republicans with all these troubles which afflict this charming country Italy. Many who thought things coming to a crisis began to take off the mask, but this joyful news the defeat of Bonaparte's fleet, who I hope will perish with his army in Egypt, makes them more timid, and does us great good. If the Emperor at present will move with activity, it is to be hoped that Italy may be saved. We are ready and eager to render ourselves worthy of being the friends and allies of the brave defenders of the seas. Present my respects to the King, and Queen of England, make my compliments to Lord Grenville, to Pitt and to Lord Spencer who has the honour to be at the head of this heroic navy, give them my thanks for sending the fleet, and tell them that I rejoice in this event, as much for our own advantage which is very great, as for their honour and glory. Assure them of my eternal gratitude. I hope that by the orders which you have received by the last couriers, we shall be more secure, and that by a good understanding we shall be able to save Italy and to afford to our defenders advantages that will bind them to us for ever.

The brave Nelson is wounded: he has the modesty never to speak of it. Recommend the hero to his master. He has made every Italian an enthusiast

[1] Monmouth MSS., Nelson papers, Vol. V. The Marquis Circello was the Neapolitan ambassador in London. This letter had been marked in pencil: 'Sent by Lady N. to J. McA.' It was printed in full in Clarke and M'Arthur's life of Nelson. The original letter was written in French.

for the English nation, great hopes were entertained of some advantages from his bravery, but no one could flatter themselves of so complete destruction. All the world is mad with joy.

Extracts from 'The Times'

Wednesday, November 21, 1798

PARLIAMENTARY INTELLIGENCE

House of Lords—Tuesday, November 20

The King entered the house about three o'clock and being seated on the throne the Commons attending the bar, his Majesty opened the session with the following most gracious speech:—

'MY LORDS and GENTLEMEN,

The events which have taken place in the course of the present year, and the signal success which by the blessing of Providence has attended my arms, have been productive of the happiest consequences, and have essentially promoted the prosperity and glory of our country.

The unexampled series of our naval triumphs has received fresh splendour from the memorable and decisive action, in which a detachment of my fleet under the command of Rear-Admiral Lord Nelson attacked and almost totally destroyed a superior force of the enemy, strengthened by every advantage of situation. By this great and brilliant victory, an enterprise, of which the injustice, perfidy, and extravagance had fixed the attention of the world, and which was peculiarly directed against some of the most valuable interests of the British Empire, has in the first instance been turned to the confusion of its authors; and the blow thus given to the power and influence of France has afforded an opening, which, if improved by suitable exertions on the part of other Powers, may lead to the general deliverance of Europe. . . . '

Thursday, November 22, 1798

PARLIAMENTARY INTELLIGENCE

House of Lords—Wednesday, November 21

The House having met at two o'clock, the Address of Thanks, which had been agreed to yesterday, in consequence of his Majesty's gracious speech, passed through the usual stages, and was ordered to be presented to his Majesty.

PLATE XIV. Caricature by J. Gillray, published December 1798, of the Hero of the Nile, wearing in his hat the chelengk given him by the Sultan of Turkey.

Earl Spencer after a few observations, in which he extolled the skill and bravery of Admiral Lord Nelson, moved the Thanks of the House to his Lordship, and the officers and seamen serving under him, for their able and gallant exertions in defeating and almost totally destroying the French fleet off the mouth of the Nile on the 1st of August.

The Duke of Clarence delivered a very warm encomium on the brilliant achievements of the gallant Admiral, and in a strain of the most heartfelt praise described the late glorious action as the most unparalleled event, in point of splendour and extensive advantages, that had ever occurred in the naval history of this or any other country.

Lord Minto having made a few remarks in commendation of the gallant Admiral, the Thanks of the house were unanimously voted. . . .

Extract from Lord Minto's speech in the House of Lords made on the motion to return thanks to Lord Nelson and his officers, November 21, 1798

Were I to indulge myself on the details of this memorable day, and in tracing all its beneficial consequences, I should quickly be drawn out of my own depth, and beyond the limits of your Lordships' time. I refrain therefore, content with having used the opportunity of rendering to this great man, and signal event, the homage at least, of an ardent and humble affection. I will indeed, trust that the sentiments I profess towards my extraordinary friend will not be deemed entirely of a private nature, and may be admitted into somewhat of a higher class; since they were excited by a daily and hourly contemplation, for a considerable period of time, of the most unremitting exertions of zeal, ability, application and courage in the service of his country; not on one occasion, but on all; not in one branch of service, but in all; in a long course of naval vigilance and perseverance, in battles at sea, in sieges on shore.

That friendship, I say, is somewhat more than private, which was not indeed created, for it had an earlier date, but which was raised in my breast to the highest pitch of admiration and devotion by those exploits, which it is the singular felicity of my life to have witnessed with my own eyes on the ever memorable St. Valentine's day; I mean on the 14th of February, when the Spanish fleet was defeated off Cadiz by the great and immortal St. Vincent. It was on that day my illustrious friend performed those prodigies of valour and conduct never equalled, I believe, before in the history of the war, nor ever to be surpassed, if it be not, indeed, by this very battle of Aboukir; for it is the peculiar privilege of my friend, that from the beginning of his life, there have been few of his actions which could be surpassed, unless it were by some other action of his own.

There is one other point of excellence to which I must say a single

2 H

word, because I am, perhaps, the man in the world who has had the best opportunity of being acquainted with it. The world knows that Lord Nelson can fight the battles of his country; but a constant and confidential correspondence with this great man, for a considerable portion of time, has taught me, that he is not less capable of providing for its political interests and honour, on occasions of great delicacy and embarrassment. In that new capacity I have witnessed a degree of ability, judgment, temper and conciliation, not always allied to the sort of spirit which without an instant's hesitation can attack on one day the whole Spanish line with his single ship, and on another, a superior French fleet, moored and fortified within the islands and shoals of an unknown bay; what can I add to these two short facts? They are themselves a volume of praise and must leave behind them all the common and vulgar forms of panegyric. It is enough for me to declare my hearty concurrence with this Vote.[1]

Charlotte Nelson to Nelson[2]

[Hilborough,]
February 5, 1799

MY DEAR UNCLE,—I hope you are well and that I shall soon see you in England, for I am afraid I have quite forgot you, but as I see your picture every day and hear so much about you it is impossible not to long to be acquainted with one who is so nearly related to me.

My aunt Nelson has recommended a school to Mama in London called Camden House, which I reckon very much of, and shall reckon of it much more if you and my aunt Nelson are in London as I hope you will be.

There are new songs come out every day on the Battle of the Nile, which I learn to play and hope I shall have the pleasure of playing them to you. I am now learning a grand march on your victory and another called Lady Nelson's Fancy, which I hope you will like. My aunt Bolton is come to live at Cranwich about five miles from hence, and is pretty well.

I remain your Lordship's dutiful niece, CHARLOTTE MARY NELSON.

The Rev. William Nelson to Lady Nelson

Hilborough,
April 1, 1799

MY DEAR MADAM,—When I was at Brecon last week, I saw Mrs. Thomas Berney who enquired particularly after my children and upon my saying

[1] Nicolas, Vol. III, pp. 77–8. Taken from a copy in the Nelson papers. This is the speech to which Lady Hamilton refers in her letter to Lord Minto dated March 6, 1800, an extract from which is printed in the Appendix to Chapter 6, p. 522.
[2] N.M.M. MS. 9292, Bridport papers. Charlotte was the only daughter of the Rev. William Nelson; she was born in 1787.

that we had thoughts of sending Charlotte to some school in or near London, immediately mentioned a school at Chelsea, called White-lands House, the conduct and management of which she said she knew to be unexceptionable and the attention paid to the health and morals of the young ladies unequalled by any other school in or near London. I told her that at present the business was in your Ladyship's hands, but I would write to you upon the subject, and if you were not fixed, we should be happy to pay attention to her recommendation; Mrs. Berney further added that Mrs. Clarke and Thomas the governesses of the school were well behaved good tempered accommmplished people, and that she looked upon them more as sisters, than anything else; we must all allow Mrs. Berney is a good judge, being so very accomplished herself. As you seem to have some objections to Camden House, if you approve of this Mrs. Nelson will write to the governess to know when the school opens again after the Whitsun holidays, but she will first wait for your answer, because we shall take no further steps unless you fully approve of it.

With regard to the full dress livery, I cannot say that I am a competent judge, I should think a London tailor who is used to make them for the nobility who frequent St. James's will immediately know from seeing the undress.

However my idea is this. The coat lined with yellow and yellow button holes, the collar and cuffs black velvet the same as at present, only it should have a standing collar, the waistcoat yellow, and I think there should be shag breeches the colour of the waistcoat, the coat, and coat and waistcoat pockets and collar should be embroidered with a worsted lace composed of the colours of the livery with the cross which composes part of [the crest] worked upon it, one or two gold epaulets as [you] please on the coat and a gold laced hat [that is] my general idea, I have only seen Lord Walpole's full dress which is something in this manner; the buttons should have either the aigrette or *San Josef* crests upon them.

Mrs. Bolton is here. I shall write to my father on church matters either by tomorrow's or the next day's post. Hilborough is not vacant yet.

I am your ladyship's most obliged friend, WM. NELSON.

I have not heard from Mr. H. Tobin. When you go to Bristol I will thank you to receive it, and when I have the pleasure of seeing your ladyship you can give it to me. I believe it is near twenty pounds.

To the Right Honourable Lady Nelson, Bath.

Chapter 6

NEAPOLITAN CHAINS
1798–1800

Introduction

The festivities at the Bourbon court after the victory of the Nile would have turned the head of a successful general and saviour of the state far less susceptible to honours and flattery than Nelson. Besides, he had been wounded and was still sick and overwrought. At the Hamiltons' he obtained luxuries, care and comforts, such as asses' milk, unknown on board of a man-of-war. He had always been inclined to consider his services inadequately rewarded and was again unhappy on this account. Therefore he was very open to receiving fulsome flattery and high-sounding rewards from the Neapolitans. He had had his orders to defend the territories of the King of Naples, and he was prepared to exercise, even to overstrain his authority as a British admiral to enable him further to gratify the whims of his new-found friends, the Hamiltons and the interesting and illustrious daughter of Maria Theresa, the sister of Marie Antionette, the mother of the Empress of Austria and the virtual ruler of the Kingdom of the Two Sicilies. Meanwhile Captain Ball blockaded Malta and Nelson remained based on Naples. There was an uneasy treaty between Naples and France, and with the encouragement of Nelson's victory and the comforting presence of his warships, the Queen and Acton planned to recover Rome in French hands. The Austrians lent their General Mack to lead the Neapolitan army, and Nelson, despite his former experiences with Austrian generals, was very enthusiastic on the chances of a victorious campaign.

The ministers in England, surprised by the very completeness of Nelson's victory and their new control of the Mediterranean, naturally began to consider afresh how best to take advantage of the turn of Fortune's wheel. Meanwhile the ambassador at Naples was told to discourage warlike moves against the French for the time being until new plans had been formed. Unlike Nelson although he was on the spot, Pitt and Grenville and Spencer no longer held any illusions that it was possible to catch armed Frenchmen napping. Nelson's and the Hamiltons' admiration for the Bourbon rulers of Naples was not shared by all their subjects. Ferdinand had rough, simple tastes, including a great love of hunting and fishing, which endeared him to the lower classes, including the fishermen of Naples. He had advanced ideas on patronizing special factories on his estates. But the upper and middle classes, in Bourbon fashion, were denied any part in the government and encouraged to grace the court and enjoy themselves but otherwise lead idle lives except under royal command. Thus the poorer classes of Naples, known as the *lazzaroni*, supported the royal family, and the nobility and landowners, often well educated and enlightened, turned to the study of the arts, and also of politics which they were denied in practice. As a result the French Revolution and the principles it propagated appealed, in the case of the people of Naples, more to the upper than to the lower classes.

King Ferdinand, devoted to his amusements, his hunting and fishing and palace industries, was the despair of his Queen and Acton the Englishman and former naval officer who for many years was either the Prime Minister or else acting as such whilst some other favourite held the office. The Queen looked to her daughter, the Empress, to send her Austrian troops. And Gallo, the Neapolitan minister at the Austrian court, produced General Mack. No move was made without Nelson's approval and attendance. He was their saviour and his warships moved like inviolate castles, able to threaten the coast roads at any point and to carry stores and snap up any enemy ships. Nelson, who had always preached boldness and was later to assert that 'no captain can do very wrong if he places his ship alongside that of an enemy', reviewed the Neapolitan army the command of which Mack had assumed, and counselled an immediate advance on Rome and a surprise landing in the rear of the French at Leghorn by troops which he would transport in his ships. The latter expedition he was well able to carry out. Austria would promise no help unless the French attacked first, and Nelson upbraided the timid Neapolitans with cowardice so as to get the army on the move.

Nelson sailed to Leghorn, which surrendered unconditionally to a summons, and leaving infantry there under General Naselli, he returned to Naples on December 5. Meanwhile Mack's advance on Rome took the French by surprise, but as France and Naples were at peace the scattered French forces obligingly withdrew and were re-organized in the rear. Ferdinand entered Rome in triumph on November 29. He left hurriedly on December 7 to avoid capture, and two days later the French were back in Rome. The King's sudden return spread alarm at Naples. His fears were indeed well founded. Everything went wrong. The Neapolitan Jacobins took courage. The Queen panicked, as did the Hamiltons. The attachment of the lower classes, the *lazzaroni*, to the Monarchy hardened and crowds prevented the open flight which they had sensed. Therefore the notorious withdrawal of the court to Palermo was carried out in secrecy, with subterfuge balls and an underground passage and Lady Hamilton arranging all, and the wooden walls and Nelson's tars giving complete security, despite a gale of wind. The pitiful lession of Marie Antionette possibly explains her brave sister's panic. It ruined her dominance over the King and she never recovered whatever popularity she lost. A strange feature was that the Neapolitan army was totally defeated without war with France being declared. And as a result of this disastrous campaign both Nelson and Hamilton were in disgrace at home for advising it, when Hamilton's clear orders had been to keep the Neapolitans quiet and not to send their armies out to certain defeat at this time. The sudden change of fortune which had resulted in the flight to Palermo and the loss of many of the Hamiltons' private effects, (Nelson saved much in his ships) left the Hamiltons worried about the future, although fairly comfortable in their new house, the Queen inconsolable, and very much in Emma Hamilton's confidence, and the King as happy as ever, busy hunting over fresh grounds and declaring he did not want to return to Naples.

At home the policy regarding the war in the Mediterranean had changed and Naples loomed less large in the minds of the planners. It was decided to seize Minorca as a naval base and to blockade Egypt more thoroughly so as to destroy the French army. Sir Sidney Smith, a brave and flamboyant character, a naval captain who had burnt some of the French ships at the evacuation of Toulon and whom Nelson thought little of, was sent out, independently to carry out this blockade. Nelson was very angry and talked of getting permission to sail home immediately in the *Vanguard* with his friends, the Hamiltons. At the end of October 1798 Lord Spencer had detailed the objects of the naval campaign in the Mediterranean as being firstly the protection of the coasts of Sicily, Naples and the Adriatic and active co-operation with the Austrian and Neapolitan armed forces; secondly, the cutting off of communications between the French army in Egypt and supplies from France; thirdly, the blockade of Malta, and fourthly, co-operation with Turkish and Russian squadrons in the archipelago. St. Vincent thought it would be practicable to blockade Toulon again if supplies could be obtained from Leghorn. On October 6 he sent Commodore Duckworth, whom he considered had 'a fair share of forbearance', and General Stuart, who was 'niggard in his praise of the navy', to capture Minorca, which fell on November 19. On December 23 Spencer was writing to St. Vincent expressing the hope that Austria would back Naples. It will be noted that Nelson's acts became wrong when they were unsuccessful, and although Mack had moved against the French when denied further Austrian support, the French were surprised and were only able to capture Naples as a result of the inefficient leadership of quite a respectable Neapolitan army. Meanwhile the British fleets in the Atlantic were covering and attacking whenever possible the French and Spanish fleets, sheltering at Brest, Rochfort, Ferrol and Cadiz. The bright radiance cast over the gloomy scene by the glorious victory of the Nile had made British naval policy very aggressive, which made the dalliance at Naples and Palermo of the victor of the Nile particularly noticeable.

Attention was rudely called to Nelson's new-found lethargy when the French Minister of Marine, Admiral Bruix, escaped from Brest in April 1799 with a strong force, which due to Keith's firm tactics, failed to enter Cadiz, but swept into the Mediterranean. Admiral Bruix had a force sufficient to do untold harm, and he also managed to keep friend and foe guessing. St. Vincent was determined to prevent a junction between Admiral Bruix and another enemy force, and also to defend Minorca, which was lightly held. Bruix's threat lasted from April to October 1799, and he considered taking supplies to Egypt as well as crushing the British squadrons off Malta, Corfu and Naples. Nothing came of his brilliant evasion of the main British forces, but his was a very serious threat to Britain's newly realized dominance on the inland sea. In the meantime the French had captured Naples, in the face of stern popular resistance savagely suppressed, and set up the Parthenopean Republic, run by the Neapolitan middle and upper classes, who were in opposition to the monarchy. This republic can be described as brilliantly futile, but its members were many of them brave and cultured, and it has left a reputation as an experiment in ideal government, probably beyond its worth. The French forces were few and interested in sending money and valuables home to France. This plundering made discontented many who had had Jacobin sympathies and welcomed the arrival of the French. The King's viceroy, Cardinal Ruffo, raised a revolt on the mainland and from small beginnings was soon able to promise the recovery of Naples. A British squadron under Troubridge in Naples Bay aided the cardinal's growing army.

In May 1799 Captain Sir Sidney Smith had relieved Troubridge off Alexandria and with two ships of the line was helping the Turks to defend Acre against Napoleon's intended march into Syria. Ball was blockading Malta with three ships; Troubridge, with four, was attacking Naples, and Commodore Duckworth had four defending Minorca. On May 12 a report reached Nelson at Palermo that Admiral Bruix had entered the Mediterranean. He sent the vessel on to tell Troubridge to bring three line-of-battle ships to Palermo and also notified Ball to send two ships. Troubridge joined Nelson off Palermo in a gale on May 17, and between May 21 and 28 Nelson looked out for the French fleet, stationing his ships off the north-west of Sicily. On May 29 Nelson returned to Palermo and on June 8 shifted his flag into the *Foudroyant*, 80 guns, Captain Hardy. On June 13 Nelson sailed for Naples with Neapolitan troops under the Hereditary Prince, but returned and disembarked the troops when he received intelligence from Lord Keith concerning the French fleet. In view of Keith's orders he again took up a position to protect Sicily, between June 16 and 20. Then he returned to Palermo, and taking the Hamiltons on board, sailed with a powerful squadron for Naples. On June 24, when off Ischia, he learnt of the capitulation of the forts which were holding out at Naples against the forces of Cardinal Ruffo with his allies.

Nelson's conduct at Naples between June 25 and August 4, 1799, has been seized on by his detractors and apologists, who, it might seem, have been so busy abusing each other that it is difficult to piece together Nelson's part in the affair from out of the shambles. It is safe to say that Nelson behaved quite correctly according to his own code and the code of his age. His contemporary detractors were also his personal enemies, by reason of politics and moral beliefs, and it was not usual to spare accusations. At the time, the truth was hard to come by. Most of the unforgivable sins Nelson is said to have committed at Naples never took place, at least in the manner which turned them into crimes against humanity for which Nelson was directly responsible.

When Nelson sailed with the Hamiltons to recover Naples for its lawful rulers he carried with him the full authority to act as a viceroy on Ferdinand's behalf, superior to Cardinal Ruffo, whose absolute loyalty was suspect, both because of his successes, which had bred jealousy, and his leniency to certain known rebels who wished to change sides. The court represented the party jealous of Ruffo and they dared not act until Nelson's powerful squadron had anchored in Naples Bay in battle order. Nelson immediately declared that the terms of the capitulation which stipulated that the rebels were to reside in Naples or be transported to France, as they chose, were annulled. It is fair to Ruffo to remember that he expected the arrival of the French fleet rather than Nelson's, and therefore wished to gain possession of Naples quickly, and was on this account ready to grant easy terms. Nelson claimed that if indeed he had been the French fleet, Ruffo's easy terms would have meant nothing to a French admiral, who would have repossessed himself of Naples and thrown out the Cardinal's forces in double-quick time.

The cardinal protested, with reason, at Nelson's assumption of over-riding powers. The King wrote to him demanding his submission or return to Palermo to be disgraced. The Neapolitan Jacobins, their plans disordered, and deserted by the French, and certain that resistance was now useless, gave themselves up, possibly still expecting clemency, though certainly well aware of the new state of affairs which Nelson's arrival had brought about.

Nelson's temper was shown when the rebel Neapolitan admiral, Caracciolo, was arrested and brought on board the *Foudroyant*, bound and weary. Captain Hardy, who had known him as the captain of a Neapolitan warship, recognized him and had him unbound and offered refreshment. Nelson had him tried by a court martial of Neapolitan officers and hanged the same evening from the yard-arm of a Neapolitan frigate. Caracciolo had no defence according to martial law because he had opened fire on ships of the Neapolitan Navy. He had visited Naples, by permission, to try to save his possessions, but the French marshal, Macdonald, who had commanded the garrison at Naples before the French withdrawal, records: 'He afterwards fell a victim to the English Admiral Nelson, who cruelly and ignominiously caused him to be hanged from the yard-arm of his own ship, a death with which I have always deeply reproached myself, as it was I who overcame his reluctance, and gained him to our side.' Perhaps the most ridiculous calumny of Nelson is that he was pleased to be rid of Caracciolo because he was jealous of his fame as a naval officer superior in talents to himself.

There were three forts held by enemies at Naples, two in the hands of the rebel Neapolitans and one held by the French. The Neapolitans surrendered and were held as prisoners under the guns of Nelson's ships, on board the transports which they had hoped would take them to Toulon. Lists of prisoners were compiled and the chosen victims extracted for trial and punishment by Neapolitan courts. The remainder were forced to sign confessions promising they would not return to Naples. Unfortunately revised lists were made and some rebels spared at first were later added to the accused. The Hamiltons, far from encouraging the excesses, seem to have counselled moderation after an example had been set. Unfortunately the trials and executions continued far too long, even after the King of Naples arrived and took up his quarters with Nelson on board the *Foudroyant* on July 10.

On July 13 Nelson received orders from Lord Keith, who was his senior officer in the Mediterranean, to take all the ships he could possibly spare to the defence of Minorca. Kieth, with thirty-one sail of the line, had learnt that the enemy were approaching with forty-three sail. Nelson considered he was bound by his word not to desert the King and Queen of Naples until they were restored and secure. He also considered that the defence of Naples and Sicily was of paramount importance. 'It is better to save the Kingdom of Naples and risk Minorca than to risk the Kingdom of Naples to save Minorca.' Therefore he defied Keith's orders and remained at Naples. For this disobedience he was rightly condemned by Keith, St. Vincent, the Board of Admiralty and its First Lord. Lord Spencer softened the Board's censure, but already it was becoming common knowledge that Nelson was tied to the Neapolitan cause by chains that grappled his affections as well as his reason and strong sense of duty.

On August 5 he took the King back to Palermo and landed him on the 8th, and remained there until October 5. On September 1 Nelson became the commander-in-chief in the Mediterranean, when Lord Keith had chased the enemy out of the Mediterranean, being off Ushant on August 14. Nelson was perhaps obsessed by the importance of preserving Sicily, but Keith had little sympathy with Nelson's independent ideas and a keen eye for the ridiculous. He was writing on April 19 to his sister of 'the Queen, Lady Hamilton, General Acton and Lord N———n cutting the most absurd figure possible for folly and vanity.' But Nelson and his friends the Hamiltons seem to have sensed none of the ridicule their capers were encouraging. On September 11 Nelson wrote home from Palermo, 'my time is so fully occupied that I never set foot out of the writing room, except now and then in an evening with Sir William and Lady Hamilton to the palace.' This must have caused Lady Nelson to think. And on September 23 he replied to her enquiry about Berry's return as his flag captain that he would be 'wore to death by being obliged to fag and think of those things which my present excellent Captain Hardy takes entirely from me.' Lady Nelson, whose best friend Lady Berry had become, would again feel unhappy at this retort to a polite enquiry. But perhaps his letter of January 9, 1800, when Nelson declared petulantly that Lisbon, to which her doctors wished to send his wife, was 'the most dirty place in Europe", must have told her plainly that he did not miss her presence as much as she missed him. And he added Josiah had been 'too much spoilt by me in his younger days.' And in answer to another polite enquiry as to whether Lady Hamilton had received some prints sent her by Lady Nelson some months back: 'Lady Hamilton has never received from you the scrap of a pen or any prints.'

In his dealings with Neapolitan affairs, Nelson had acquired a personal ascendancy, which satisfied his vanity, and which also depended on the daily intercourse with the Hamiltons, especially because Nelson knew little French and no Italian. As Nelson became aware that his conduct was suspect, and his high-minded pursuit of the business of his profession was now linked with a supposed infatuation, he naturally became more stubborn. Sir William handled the Neapolitans cleverly with the aid of a famous British admiral. With the aid of his coolness and 'phlegm' he had kept the peace between Nelson and Cardinal Ruffo. He knew that the King's warrant to arrest the cardinal was held locked in Nelson's writing-box and never used. He would have dealt more circumspectly with Caracciolo's case, only here Nelson dealt with a service matter. He knew and appreciated St. Vincent and admired and liked the chosen officers of Nelson's squadron, Troubridge, Ball, Hood, Hallowell, Darby and Miller, who returned and valued his friendship and hospitality. Nelson was forced by circumstances into his obstinate defence of his conduct at Naples which was commented upon adversely by his best friends.

By 1800 St. Vincent and Lord Spencer hoped Nelson would come home. Lord Minto wrote to his wife from Vienna on March 23: 'I have letters from Nelson and Lady Hamilton. It does not seem clear that he will go home. I hope he will not for his own sake, and he will at least I hope take Malta first. He does not seem at all conscious of the sort of discredit he has fallen into, or the cause of it, for he writes still not wisely about Lady Hamilton and all that. But it is hard to condemn and use ill a hero, as he is in his own element, for being foolish about a woman who has art enough to make fools of many wiser than an admiral.' On January 20 he joined Keith at Leghorn and they visited Malta together. On February 18 the squadron captured the *Le Genereux*, which had escaped from the battle of the Nile. And on March 24, Berry, again commanding the *Foudroyant*, but with Nelson's flag at Palermo, was able to announce the capture of the *Guillaume Tell*, 80-guns, the last French line-of-battle ship which had escaped from the Nile. Berry had missed Nelson's presence, animation and decision in a confused night's action. 'How often I went into your cabin, last night, to ask you if we were doing right', he wrote, and added he was 'praying earnestly for you to fly on board.'

Nelson wished to sail home with the Hamiltons in his flag-ship the *Foudroyant*, having seen the Queen of Naples safely on her way to visit her daughter at Vienna. But Lord Keith, now the commander-in-chief in the Mediterranean, rightly refused to detach an 80-gun ship for this purpose. So the party made the journey overland. Nelson clearly tells his wife to meet him in London at the lodgings Davison will obtain for her. Yet he writes from Yarmouth to say he will bring the Hamiltons to dine with her at Round Wood. Nelson was received with honour by his countrymen, but it was a confused homecoming in the eyes of his puzzled wife.

The letters from home start again in June 1799 and continue through the winter. The family circle has adapted itself to the position Nelson's fame has given it. Round Wood now seems dull. A visit to Bronte or even Lisbon would, Lady Nelson thinks, help her to recover her spirits, fading for want of news from her husband, whose return is so constantly promised by her naval friends. For the winter 'a small ready furnished house at 7 guineas a week' in St. James's Street, London, is the temporary house of Nelson's wife and father, now an inseparable pair. The relations are a little troublesome, particularly William, who hankers after preferment in the Church for himself, and hopes for a more stylish mode of living when his brother comes home. His grand ideas perplex his father, and Lady Nelson cannot bring herself to ask favours on his behalf. The worry and strain contribute to the father's illness which so alarmed Lady Nelson and stopped all her social engagements for part of the winter. But the old man recovered and was able to sit for his portrait to Sir William Beechey. The offer of a passage to the Mediterranean tantalizes Lady Nelson, but she does as her husband wishes and waits at home for him, her spirits drooping. The time between his letters is so long, and when they come they are so short and not very cheerful. The news of Josiah is not good either. He is rough, he has almost broken his stepfather's heart. Then some improvement is noted, only to be followed by further criticism. She wrote the last letter printed here in April 1800 and waited another seven months before she saw Nelson once again.

No. 214

[Nicolas, III, p. 151, part, under date October 24]

Off Sicily,
October 22, 1798

MY DEAREST FANNY,—Whilst I lay in port my business real and formal was so much that I had scarcely time to read, much less to write letters except upon business. Respecting the agency you answered perfectly right I never have nor ever will desire any person to appoint an agent. I have never done it for my own brother when it might have been useful. As to Mr. Shentone's brother how can I recommend a person of whose merits I can know nothing. Is he fit to be entrusted on his watch with the lives of a ship's crew? If Captain Woolley will send me a letter that he is fit for a lieutenant, in that case I will ask Lord Spencer but what reason have I to suppose I have any interest in that quarter. *Is not the 'Foudroyant' given to another cruising at home and not sent to me although I was promised it.*[1] However thank God I have done without her.

Lady Hamilton promised she would write you a line of what passed on the day of my sailing and I dare say has done it, for it is impossible for me to express the affectionate kindness both Sir William and her ladyship has shown me. I had not a wish which was not anticipated and all their study was how to please me best. Never, never shall I forget them. Except from you my dearest Fanny, did I ever before experience friendship? Here could have been no interested views. May God bless and reward them tenfold.

Off Malta, October 24: Josiah is not made post, all are put over his head. I am just off here. The French are not yet turned out but I shall do my best in negotiating. There is no fighting I assure you, if there was it should be settled before night. Our hearts are in the trim and God is with us, of whom then shall we be afraid?

God bless you, ever your affectionate HORATIO NELSON.

To Lady Nelson, Round Wood, Ipswich, Suffolk.

No. 215

Caserta,
November 1, 1798

MY DEAR FANNY,—I arrived in the bay of Naples last evening, from off Malta where I have left a squadron to blockade it.[2] The island of Gozo (a little island near Malta containing 16,000 persons) surrendered to me on the 28th ult. and I have brought the French garrison prisoners (217) to Naples. I am pretty tolerable, Josiah is well and improving.

I have barely time to say this much as a courier goes off in 10 minutes for Vienna and London. Pray write to Berry tell him how much I feel for his delay, as to ill luck, where so much honour was gained I will not call [it] and desire him to say everything handsome to Captain Thompson, whose letter is at sea in search of me.

Kind remembrances to my dear father etc. and believe me ever your most affectionate HORATIO NELSON.

Naples just going to war.

[1] The *Foudroyant* was cruising off Plymouth commanded by Captain J. Elphinstone. Lord Keith arrived in the Mediterranean with his flag in the *Foudroyant* in January 1799.
[2] A squadron of three sail of the line, a frigate and a fireship was put under the command of Captain Alexander Ball.

No. 216

Naples,
November 19, 1798

MY DEAREST FANNY,—I have received your letter of October 1st thro'
Admiral Younge. It is very good of him.

I am perfectly well and keep to my resolution of going home next
spring. We are embarking troops for —— and I sail tomorrow at daylight.[1]
I suppose this will find you and my dear father at Bath but I shall direct
it to Round Wood. Josiah is with me and well.

May God bless you and my dear father is the constant prayer of your
affectionate husband, NELSON.[2]

To Lady Nelson, Round Wood, Ipswich, Suffolk.

No. 217

Leghorn,
November 29, 1798

MY DEAREST FANNY,—I brought here a cargo of Neapolitan troops and
yesterday night took possession of the town and fortress of Leghorn. I am
tolerable,[3] and shall sail tomorrow for Naples. As mine is a truly active
scene you cannot hope for long letters, but believe me ever with the truest
affection, your NELSON.

Kind love to my father and my sister and Mr. Matcham. October 1st
your last letter.

To Lady Nelson, Bath.

No. 218

[Nicolas, III, p. 194, order transposed]

Naples,
December 11, 1798

MY DEAREST FANNY,—You will of course get my letter from Leghorn. I
arrived here on the 5th and the poor Queen has again made me promise
not to quit her and her family till brighter prospects appear than do at
present. The King is with the army and she is sole regent. She is in fact a
Great King.

---

[1] Five thousand troops were embarked for an attack on Leghorn.

[2] News of his elevation to the peerage as a baron reached Nelson about November
18. After that date his usual signature was 'Nelson'.

[3] Writing to Lord Spencer on the same day, Nelson ended his letter, 'I will be active
as long as I can, but my strength fails daily.'

My correspondence has now the additional increase of a Turkish and Russian admiral which with what I had before takes all my time, but Lady Hamilton's goodness forces me out at noon for an hour. What can I say of her and Sir William's goodness to me. They are in fact with the exception of you and my dear father the dearest friends I have in this world. I live as Sir William's son in the house and my glory is as dear to them as their own. In short I am under such obligations that I can never repay but with my etermal gratitude.

The improvement made in Josiah by Lady Hamilton is wonderful. She seems the only person he minds, and his faults are not omitted to be told him but in such a way as pleases him, and his, your and my obligation are infinite on that score. Not but dear Josiah's heart is as good and as humane as ever was covered by human breast, but his manners are so rough, but God bless him I love him dearly with all his roughness.[1]

I have not received the scrap of a pen from England since the 11th October. Lord St. Vincent is in no hurry to oblige me *now*.[2] I am got her fancies too near him in reputation. In short I am the envied man, but better that than the pitied one. Never mind, it is my present intention if matters are in a good train to leave the country in March and to be in England in the latter end of May or beginning of June and to rest the four months.

May God bless you my dear Fanny and my father is the constant prayer of your most affectionate NELSON.

To Lady Nelson, Bath.

No. 219

Palermo,
January 2, 1799

MY DEAR FANNY,—Since yours of October 8th I have not had the scrap of a pen from England as nothing has come from Lord St. Vincent except Sir Sidney Smith who passed on to Constantinople. My time and mind has been fully occupied. I wrote you a line from Naples a few days before the embarkation of the Royal family who thank God (except Prince Albert of 6 years) were safely landed on December 26th.[3]

[1] There is a pencilled note by Lady Nelson at the end of this letter: My son did not like the Hamiltons and would not dance—No reflections on any people are proper.'
[2] The first criticism Nelson made of St. Vincent, but his later letters show that it was only a peevish outburst.
[3] Owing to the advance of the French forces, preparation for the evacuation of the Sicilian royal family from Naples to Palermo in Sicily were started on December 20. They embarked on board the *Vanguard* the next day. Prince Albert, aged six, died during the passage.

The first week in March it is my intention if I get leave to quit this situation for, as a piece of my command is lopped off by the great S.S.S.[1] there can be no occasion for a Nelson. However my mind is satisfied with myself, and although I shall return much poorer than when I set out, yet my heart is at ease. I must have a house in London if possible. I should like the one that was Captain Suckling's [2] or one like it. The rooms must be light and airy, but this is supposing my pension is handsome. I wish you to think if Round Wood pleases you if not, look out for another, in either case, we must have a good dining room and bed chambers, a kitchen must be thought of and room for servants with coach house and stables. Now I wish you to decide whether it's better to build on a place we may not like, or buy a place ready built to our hands, but if we have money a neat house in London near Hyde Park, but on no account on the other side of Portman Square. I detest Baker Street. In short do as you please you know my wishes and income. A neat carriage I desire you will order and if possible get good servants. You will take care I am not let down. The King has elevated me and I must support my station in short whether I am at home a month sooner or later a house in London must be had furnished and ready for us.

I suppose this will find you at Bath. If Lord Hood is there remember me most kindly to him, and any other of our friends. To my dear father say everything which is kind. I love, honour, and respect him as a father and as a man and as the very best man that ever I saw.

Sir William and Lady Hamilton desire to be kindly remembered to you both, and hope to be your sincere friends as they are mine. May God bless you and believe me ever your affectionate husband, NELSON.

You will not forget me to my sister and Mr. Matcham.

To Lady Nelson, Bath.

No. 220

Palermo,
January 17, 1799

MY DEAREST FANNY,—I have just received your letter of November 19th, the last was October 8th. I am glad you are going to Bath as that place will not only agree better with our dear father than Round Wood but be more pleasant and cheerful for you. Indeed my command here has no occasion to be envied and if I can with propriety get away I shall do it. Indeed I have wrote to request permission.

---

[1] Sir Sidney Smith was given an independent command of Constantinople and in the Levant seas. Both Nelson and St. Vincent resented this appointment.
[2] His uncle, Captain Maurice Suckling.

We have had a dreadful winter and if it has been in proportion in the north it must be cold indeed. I wish I could say much to your and my satisfaction about Josiah but I am sorry to say and with real grief, that he has nothing good about him, he must sooner or later be broke, but I am sure neither you or I can help it, I have done with the subject it is an ungrateful one.[1]

May God bless you and my dear father and ever believe me your affectionate husband, NELSON.

To Lady Nelson, Bath.

No. 221

Palermo,
February 2, 1799

MY DEAREST FANNY,—I have received your several letters to the 26th November for which I sincerely thank you. With more writing than two hands could get through you must take a line for a page and a page for a sheet of paper.

Josiah has got a commission for *Thalia* [2] I wish he may deserve it. However he has had more done for him than any young man in the service and made I fear the worst use of his advantages.

We are here as badly situated as heart can wish but I have no permission to quit my post and of course I must remain.

Tell my dear Kate I have just received her and Mr. Matcham's kind letter, but it will be a week before I can answer it but they are sure of my most affectionate regards. Maurice seems hurt with me but without reason. I shall never do an unkind thing by anyone or omit a favourable opportunity of serving my family.

May God bless you, my dear father and all my relations about you is the sincere prayer of your affectionate NELSON.

To Lady Nelson, Bath.

No. 222

Palermo,
March 21, 1799

MY DEAR FANNY,—Nothing worth relating has occurred since I wrote you last. We go dragging an existence from day to day. How matters will end

[1] The chief causes of complaint against Josiah seems to have been his roughness and quick temper. On January 7 Nelson sent him to Constantinople with the Turkish ambassador.

[2] Josiah remained in the *Bonne Citoyenne* until March 2 and took command of the *Thalia* on April 2.

21

God only knows. If the Emperor of Germany marches into Italy, the King of Naples may again mount his throne and the French be driven out of Italy, where they are plundering in a manner that would disgrace a house breaker in our own country.[1]

The Turks and Russians have taken Corfu.[2] They tell us a squadron of their ships are coming to this country, but it is troops not ships which we want.

Josiah is off Malta and I wish he may act as he ought. It would be a comfort to me. You must excuse short letters for neither my head or hand can get thro' my business.

Remember me affectionately to my father and sister and believe me your affectionate NELSON.

To Lady Nelson, Bath.

No. 223[3]

Palermo,
April 10, 1799

MY DEAR FANNY,—Yesterday brought me your letters of December; they had been stopped in Italy, and now came by way of Venice. I had three days ago received two of February 5th and 11th. You must not think it possible for me to write even to you as much as I used to do. In truth, I have such quantities of writing public letters, that my private correspondence has been, and must continue to be, greatly neglected.

You would by February have seen how unpleasant it would have been had you followed *any* advice, which carried you from England to a wandering sailor. I could, if you had come, *only* have struck my flag, and carried you back again, for it would have been impossible to have set up an establishment at either Naples or Palermo. Nothing but the situation of affairs in this country has kept me from England; and if I have the happiness of seeing their Sicilian Majesties safe on their throne again, it is probable I shall yet be home in the summer. Good Sir William, Lady Hamilton, and myself, are the mainsprings of the machine, which manage what is going on in this country. We are all bound to England when we can quit our posts with propriety.[4]

---

[1] Naples had been declared a republic by the French on January 13, 1799.
[2] Corfu surrendered to the blockading Russian and Turkish squadron on March 1.
[3] This letter escaped from Lady Nelson's hands and passed into the possession of Dr. T. Pettigrew, who printed it in his *Memoirs of Lord Nelson*, Vol. I, p. 220. The present whereabouts of the letter is not known.
[4] Sir William had leave to return to England on his private affairs.

As to my entering into the situation of affairs with Mr. Suckling [1] and his numerous family: in the first place, I never knew of his death till I read it in a magazine, and as yet the other executors have never wrote me a line. However, if I can be useful by acting to his family, I feel myself bound by every tie of gratitude, to do it, and on that account I am not sorry that he has disappointed the expectations of many that he would have left me something considerable. I always loved and respected my dear uncle while living, and shall do the same now he is dead.

Josiah is now in full possession of a noble frigate. [2] He has sent to say that he is sensible of his youthful follies, and that he shall alter his whole conduct. I sincerely wish he may, both for his and your sake. You will not, I am sure, forget me to Mr. Hamilton when you write, nor to our friends at Bristol. As to our dear father, say everything which is kind, and also to my sister, and Mr. Matcham, and believe me your most affectionate NELSON.

No. 224

[Palermo,]
May 5, 1799

MY DEAR FANNY,—I have barely time to write a line to say I am as well as my busy station will allow. Their Majesties are now holding themselves in readiness to again embark in the *Vanguard* and I sincerely hope I shall have the happiness of soon landing them again in their capital.

I can only say God bless you and my dear father and believe me your affectionate husband, NELSON.

I have left off all private correspondence I have not hand enough to write public letters therefore pray tell my friends so who may with reason complain of my apparent neglect. The enclosed has been a voyage to Tuscany.

To Lady Nelson, Bath.

No. 225 [3]

Palermo,
May 10, 1799

MY DEAR FANNY,—If I do not write to you so often, nor such long letters as I have formerly done, pray attribute it to the true cause—viz., that in truth my poor hand cannot execute what my head tells me I ought to do. As to writing a line to anyone else, they may take it ill or well, as they please.

[1] Nelson's uncle, Mr. William Suckling, who had died on December 15, 1798, had made Nelson one of his executors and left him £100.

[2] *Thalia*, 36 guns.

[3] This letter was in the possession of Sir Harris Nicolas in 1846; its present whereabouts in not known. This text is taken from Nicolas, Vol. VII, p. clxxxi.

We now live in some hopes that the French will be drove entirely out of Italy. If so, I shall seriously think of going home. Both Lord Spencer, Earl St. Vincent, and their Sicilian Majesties at present prevent me, by their opinion that I am of some use here.

How does our father? It is very odd, that I have not received a scrap of a pen from him since he knew of the battle of the Nile. You must remember me kindly to all our family, and my father, who I love dearly; and believe me ever your most affectionate NELSON.

No. 226[1]

Vanguard, at Sea,
May 24, 1799

MY DEAR FANNY, We are all well cannot be better and anxiously looking out for the French fleet. I send you a letter from Josiah which I hope will comfort you, with kindest regards to our father, believe me ever your affectionate husband, NELSON.

To Lady Nelson, Round Wood, Ipswich, Suffolk.

Thalia, off Malta,
May 4, [1799]

DEAR FATHER,[2]—I am sorry to find from Mr. Tyson's[3] letter that you thought I was very imprudent in messing in the gunroom, which I had not the least idea of doing only until I got to Palermo where I could fit myself out.

I have now determined to do everything in my power to deserve the unmerited promotion which you have given me and hope my endeavours for the future will always meet with your approbation as you are the only person on earth who has my interest truly at heart and I trust and hope my future conduct will effectually do away with my former folly.

I have been off Linosa and have taken two vessels by one of which I shall send this letter tomorrow. Captain Ball has given me another cruise off Linoso and I hope we shall take something more.[4]

And believe dear Father your affectionate son, J. NISBET.

To Horatio Lord Nelson, etc. etc. etc., Palermo.

[1] The original of this letter has disappeared. This text is taken from a copy which has been bound up with the letters in the Monmouth collection. It is in the same hand as the copy of Nelson's letter of August 11, 1794 (No. 83, p. 118).
[2] N.M.M. MS. 9594, Nelson Ward collection.
[3] John Tyson, Nelson's secretary at this time.
[4] The *Thalia* was under Ball's command, blockading Malta.

No. 227

Palermo,
June 5, 1799

MY DEAR FANNY,—We are waiting events with more anxiety than you can conceive. 11 sail of the line are now anchored in a line ready to resist an attack if the combined fleets should escape Lord St. Vincent.[1] But I fear both French and Spaniards will get into port and that we shall have the torment of blockading.

Except being anxious I am in perfect health but had I two hands I cannot get thro my pen and ink work although I find I can write a letter sooner than direct another person to do it. But as I have told you before all my private correspondence must drop and my friends must forgive me or not as they please.

Josiah is here and promises to do every thing in his power to make us happy I hope to God he will.[2] Your last letters are in March. Josiah has them all.

May God bless you and my dear father with all our friends and relations is the fervent prayer of your affectionate NELSON.

To Lady Nelson, Round Wood, Ipswich, Suffolk.

No. 228

Foudroyant,[3] at Sea,
June 17, 1799

MY DEAR FANNY,—I catch a moment to say God be with you. Our friend Lord Keith has placed me with 18 sail of the line in the most cruel of all situations [4] but I must submit and will not more complain, but my country will feel for my treatment as do those who are with me on shore or afloat.[5]

My health is tolerable, but my mind full of sorrow, not for myself for I care not, but for my country and the world. Remember me kindly to my dear father and believe me ever your affectionate NELSON.

[1] St. Vincent had left Gibraltar with twenty sail of the line to try to prevent a junction between the French and Spanish fleets.
[2] Josiah was with Nelson, the *Thalia* being employed as a look-out.
[3] Nelson transferred to the *Foudroyant* on June 8, taking Captain Hardy and several officers with him.
[4] As he was about to sail for Naples and help to reinstate the King, Nelson received orders from Keith to proceed to Maritimo, wait for reinforcements and search out the French fleet.
[5] St. Vincent resigned the command to Keith, owing to his ill health, on June 10.

I have just received a report that a body of 500 Russians marched into Naples on the 14th.

To Lady Nelson, Round Wood, Ipswich, Suffolk.

[*Readdressed:* 92, Sloane Street, London.]

No. 229

[Nicolas, III, p. 411]

Naples,
July 14, 1799

MY DEAR FANNY,—I have to thank you sincerely for your 4 letters to April 15th. The *William Pitt* cutter being taken with 5 mails on board has deprived us of much news.

I rejoice that you sent Mr. Bolton the money and I wish it to be made up £500. I never regarded money or wanted it for my own use, therefore as the East India Company have made me so magnificent a present, I beg that £2000 pounds of it may be disposed of in the following manner.[1] £500 to my father, £500 to be made up to Mr. Bolton and let it be a God send without any restriction, £500 to Maurice and £500 to William, and if you think my sister Matcham desires it do the same for her. If I was rich I would do more but it will very soon be known how poor I am except my yearly income.

I am not surprised at my brother's death.[2] Three are now dead younger than myself having grown to man's age.[3]

The *Thalia* is just gone to sea. I hope Josiah is in some respects altered for the better. My situation here is not to be described but suffice it to say I am endeavouring to work for good.[4]

May Almighty God bless you, my dear father and all my brothers and sisters is the fervant prayer of your affectionate NELSON.

Pray my apologies to Mr. Tobin, I have not strength to write him a letter.

---

[1] At a Court of Directors held in April 1799, the East India Company gave Nelson £10,000 for his victory of August 1.

[2] Suckling Nelson died on April 30, 1799.

[3] Nelson was mistaken: two of his younger brothers had died young men, the third, George, in infancy.

[4] Nelson had returned to Palermo on June 21, embarkéd Sir William and Lady Hamilton and proceeded to Naples, where the republican forces were collapsing (see Appendix, p. 503, for Sir William's letters).

No. 230

[Nicolas, III, p. 434]

Naples,
August 4, 1799

MY DEAR FANNY,—A few days ago brought me your letter of May 6th from Clifton, but since then I see by the papers you have been in London. I am glad you went to court on the King's birthday. By the next I have no doubt but the world will be at peace and if Lord Keith had fallen in with the French fleet we should have had it by this time. Thank God all goes well in Italy and the kingdom of Naples is liberated from thieves and murderers, but still it has so overthrown the fabric of a regular government that much time and great care is necessary to keep the country quiet. Their Majesties have confidence in my councils which they know to be disinterested and are fixed in the belief that whatever I undertake is sure of success and indeed this is general to the Kingdom. However flattering this may be, it has its alloys for if anything was to go wrong my popularity would be over.

The first of August[1] was celebrated here with as much respect as our situation would admit. The King[2] dined with me and when his Majesty drank my health a royal salute of 21 guns was fired from all H.S.M's. ships of war and from all the castles. In the evening there was a general illumination. Amongst others a large vessel was fitted out like a Roman galley. On the oars were fixed lamps and in the centre was erected a rostral column with my name, at the stern elevated were two angels supporting my picture. In short the beauty of the thing was beyond my powers of description. More than 2000 variegated lamps were fixed round the vessel, an orchestra was fitted up and filled with the very best musicians and singers. The piece of music was in a great measure my praises, describing their distress, but Nelson comes, the invincible Nelson and we are safe and happy again. Thus you must not make you think me vain so far very far from it and I relate it more from gratitude than vanity.

I return to Palermo with the King tomorrow and what may then be my movements it is impossible for me to say. As to the co-operation of Turks and Russian fleets I see none of them.

May God bless you all. Pray say what is true that I really *steal* time to write this letter, and my hand is ready to drop, and as to my eyes I cannot

---

[1] The terms for the capitulation of the last republican-held castles were agreed on July 31, which made possible the celebrations of August 1 in commemoration of the battle of the Nile.

[2] The King of Naples had been on board the *Foudroyant* since July 10.

see half what I write. My dear father must forgive my not writing so often as I ought and so must my brothers and friends but ever believe me your affectionate NELSON.

To Lady Nelson, Round Wood, Ipswich, Suffolk.

No. 231
[Nicolas, III, p. 460, part]

Palermo,
August 23, 1799

MY DEAR FANNY,—I have received your letters of May and to June 27th. You must not expect a long letter, indeed you tell me you do not. The last letter of the King's minister here Sir John Acton, is as follows

'My formal demand is however to beg of your Lordship to protect the Two Sicilies with your name and presence till at last all Italy is perfectly quiet.'

Therefore whatever my state of health is I cannot move. My flag is in Transport, for I will not let the *Foudroyant* lay idle.[1]

I have wrote fully to my father about Bronte [2] and send you a little history of it. The present is magnificent and worthy of a king. As this goes by a cutter for Mahon it may be some time before you get it but a courier goes tomorrow for Vienna and England by whom all my public and private letters are sent.

God bless you and believe me ever your affectionate NELSON.

No. 232

Palermo,
August 24, 1799

MY DEAR FANNY,—I have received all your letters of May and to June 27th. We are now in a state of the greatest anxiety respecting Lord Keith and the combined fleet.[3] If he gets up with them, they will be, I am sure, annihilated. As to myself he has so pushed me with orders that had I obeyed them literally the Kingdom of Naples would certainly at this moment have been

[1] The *Foudroyant*, Captain Hardy, sailed for Malta on August 14 and Nelson shifted his flag to the *Samuel and Jane* transport.
[2] The dukedom of Bronte in Sicily was conferred on Nelson by the King of Naples in appreciation of his services on August 13.
[3] Keith had left the Mediterranean in pursuit of the French fleet at the end of July. His orders to Nelson had been to concentrate on the security of Minorca, rather than Sicily.

in the hands of the French and this country in a state of confusion. The Turkish and Russian squadrons are just arrived but they inspire no confidence, it is England alone that is looked to. Therefore I see no prospect of my leaving this station at present.

I had a letter some time ago from Mr. Tobin requesting me to interest myself for his son being made post by Lord Spencer. This request after what you know passed to get G.T.[1] made a captain cannot be pressed. Was he on the same station as myself I assure you I should have great pleasure in using my influence with the commander in chief.

I have wrote to my father about Bronte, and also to my brothers about the descent of the title.

God bless you my dear Fanny and believe me your affectionate NELSON.

What am I to do about George Bolton?[2] Do as you like about sending him to school or to sea.

No. 233

Palermo,
September 11, 1799

MY DEAR FANNY,—I will not omit this opportunity of sending a line as they say the post is now open from Leghorn to England, merely to say I am tolerable and when the intense heats are over I hope to rub through the winter, by which time the war will be concluded. I have wrote to you lately in all ways by sea and land, but short letters, for my time is fully occupied that I never set my foot out of the writing room, except now and then in an evening with Sir William and Lady Hamilton to the palace.

I never expect to see even Bronte although I am told its situation is beautiful. In various ways I have wrote to my father, Maurice and William. If the print of Orme and the other of boarding the *San Nicolas* are out I wish for 2 or 3 for the young Prince Leopold[3] and for this house. Also if any are out of the Nile I beg to have some. Davison[4] or Maurice will do me that favour and a few of the late caricatures. A good laced hat and a plain one will be very acceptable.

With my most affectionate regards to my father and all friends believe me ever your affectionate NELSON.

To Lady Nelson, Round Wood, Ipswich, Suffolk.

[1] George Tobin.
[2] His nephew, aged twelve.
[3] The son of the King of Naples, who was being trained as a midshipman.
[4] Alexander Davison, Nelson's agent and friend.

No. 234

Palermo,
September 23, 1799

MY DEAR FANNY,—Yesterday brought me your letters of July 28th and August 3rd and I thank you for the indulgence you give me of writing short letters. I wish from my heart Josiah may answer your expectations. He is placed in an enviable situation.

Respecting the purchase of the land for £8000, do as you please about it. To me it is perfectly indifferent. My income is certainly now very handsome but even the settlement of the Bronte estate will cost me £1000 before any income comes to me. You will know what is in my Bankers' hands and whether it is eligible. Do as you like best.

I have not heard whether Sir Edward Berry comes out or not. I have doubtless many obligations to him, but his health is such that I shall be worn to death by being obliged to fag and think of those things which my present excellent Captain Hardy takes entirely from me.[1]

If the enemy should again get a fleet into the Mediterranean, Lord Spencer will I hope send me out the *San Joseph* which would gratify me, but I am vexed to think the ministers have done nothing for either my good father or brothers. I feel it very much and at present I believe they cut me off £1000 a year less than either St. Vincent or Duncan.[2]

Remember me most kindly to our dear father I am confident he has wrote often but it is true that only one letter has ever reached me. I have not wrote to Mr. Tobin about George for I can in truth do nothing unless he was here and I had the command.

May God bless you and believe me ever your affectionate NELSON.

No. 235

Port Mahon,
October 15, 1799

MY DEAR FANNY,—On my way to Gibraltar I fell in with Sir Edward Berry[3] and he gave me your and our father's letter (a very few days before

---

[1] Captain Hardy had been Nelson's flag-captain since the battle of the Nile when Berry was sent home with dispatches.

[2] Nelson was voted a pension of £2,000 a year by Parliament. St. Vincent and Duncan had received pensions of £3,000 for their victories. Nelson tried to obtain promotion for his brother Maurice in the Navy Office and for his father and William in the Church.

[3] Berry superseded Hardy as flag-captain on October 13, and Hardy was sent home with dispatches.

I received two from my father one in May one in June and several from you and Maurice that had been laid aside at the Admiralty.)

The accounts brought by the ship from Gibraltar and Lisbon forced my return here. I should have been truly glad to have seen the Old Parsonage and if it pleases God to give us peace, see it I will. I am in truth most heartily tired of war. Sir Edward Berry will tell you of the death of George Bolton.[1] I am glad not to have seen the child for Berry speaks very highly.

I am here and endeavouring to arrange matters for the reducing of Malta. I am fagged out. I shall not write to my father by this opportunity. I have only to say may God bless you both and believe me ever your affectionate NELSON.

To Lady Nelson, Bath.

No. 236

Palermo,
November 7, 1799

MY DEAR FANNY,—Since my arrival from Minorca I received your letters of June 7th and 13th which came by way of Vienna, which shews the uncertainty of the movement of letters. I have now all my newspapers to September 29th but not the scrap of a pen from any one.

My task here is still arduous for I cannot get the General at Minorca to give me some troops for the service of Malta and I have not force enough to attack it. This and other things have half broke my heart but I trust that one day or other, I shall rest from all my labours. I still find it good to serve near home. There a man's fag and services are easily seen. Next to that is writing a famous account of your own actions. I could not do justice to those of my friends who rescued the Kingdom of Naples from the French and therefore Parliament does not think of them.

I have just received from the Grand Signor a diamond star with a crescent in the centre[2] which I wear above that of the Bath. But these jewels give not money meat or drink and from the various circumstances of my having much more expenses than any commander in chief without any one profit it has been a heavy money campaign to me. I shall mention the circumstance to Lord Spencer but I doubt if he will do anything for me. I trust that the war will very soon be over.

---

[1] Sir Edward Berry had brought Bolton out from England with him in the *Bulldog*, but he died before reaching the Mediterranean.
[2] The Order of the Crescent, created specially for award to non-Mohammedans.

May God bless you and my dear father and believe me ever your affectionate BRONTE NELSON.[1]

To Lady Nelson, Bath.
[*Readdressed:* 54 St. James' Street.]

No. 237

Palermo,
December 15, 1799

MY DEAR FANNY,—Although I have been writing till I am almost totally blind yet I will not let this opportunity slip of sending a line not to say I am contented and happy for neither one or the other is near me but enough of that.

It was only a few days past that I received your letter of August 20th with one from Sir Edward Berry. I hope so soon as the East India money is paid that my present for my brothers and sisters will be paid, and it is my intention if my *right* is allowed for the rich Spanish frigates to do something for Mr. Bolton and my dear sister.[2] If I do not write to her she must not think that she is out of my thoughts and whoever knows me knows that I despise money except as it may be useful to my friends. I have in my own mind given up for the improvement of Bronte two years' rents, for it is my intention to fulfil a prophecy that one day it should be called Bronte the happy.

The *Foudroyant* and every ship up there is off Malta endeavouring to bring that tedious blockade to a close but from every quarter I find such difficulties thrown in the way that often makes me very uneasy, but I trust in my usual good fortune to see its surrender. You will rejoice when I tell you that I have most favourable accounts of Captain Nisbet's conduct.[3] I trust for his sake that he has seen his follies. Remember me most kindly to my father and the Matchams, and believe me as ever your affectionate husband, BRONTE NELSON.

To Lady Nelson, Bath.
[*Readdressed:* St. James' Street, London.]

[1] Nelson's signature at this time varied. Usually he followed this form, sometimes more fully 'Bronte Nelson of the Nile'. His foreign title was not formally recognized until 1801, when he adopted the signature 'Nelson and Bronte' which he used until his death.
[2] See Appendix, p. 536, Lady Nelson's letter of October 27. Nelson later gave his sister £100 for educating her family.
[3] Josiah was now under Rear-Admiral Duckworth, who told Nelson he hoped to keep him under his command 'as I augur much better of him than your lordship and would try to bring him round.'

No. 238

Palermo,
January 9, 1799[1]

MY DEAR FANNY,—I have received by Lord Keith your letter of November 13th and two in October. Whatever any physicians may say about Lisbon I can have no idea that the most dirty place in Europe covered with fog can be even wholesome; to old débauchés who must lead a more regular life from the want of any decent society, it may be of benefit on that account, but I will answer on no other. My abhorrence of it is such from two days' acquaintance that I would rather take a house in the worst part of Portsmouth, and what a sea voyage. Having said this it is for you to judge. I shall never go to Lisbon for if I can get that far, Portsmouth will be the place to find me.[2]

We must have peace for our allies seem only to think of themselves and then England will see the necessity of taking care of herself. The arrival of Lord Keith has not surprised, for I never yet have received any particular mark of favour, and have been kept here with all the expenses of a commander in chief and not one farthing of profit. From the day I left England I have never received one farthing of prize money, except £500 in dollars for what was taken when I was last in this country and I am forced to an expense of many thousands a year. From Bronte it is not my intention to take any money for several years. It shall be improved and made the happiest place in Europe. The King has just given me the honour of naming all public officers and my friends, judges etc. etc. in short I am absolute in church and state except acknowledging the King as head of the church for the Pope is no longer the head of it, although we are tolerably bigoted.

I have taken a farm of 700 acres the finest corn land in Europe and have directed the building an *English* farm house and I hope to make all Sicily bless the day I was placed amongst them. I am glad my brothers and sisters are paid the money as the East India Company have long paid theirs I thought it would come from that fund. You will not I am sure fail to make my very best regards acceptable to Mr. & Mrs. Hamilton and I sincerely thank them for their good wishes towards me. To my dear father say everything which is kind. I long to see him when it can be done with propriety.

I expect Josiah here every day, I hope he will yet make a good man,

[1] A mistake for 1800.
[2] Lady Nelson's doctor had suggested she should spend the winter in Lisbon (see Appendix, p. 538, Lady Nelson's letter of November 13, 1799).

His abilities are equal to any thing, he was too much spoilt by me in his younger days. Lord Keith is coming to pay us a visit at Palermo and he may if he pleases remove me, but as I have been particularly placed here for the service of the King of Naples I think he will not. He will however always find me ready to obey. The *Foudroyant* has been some time off Malta, her Captain[1] is very well and, as he writes me, very happy. I expect him here every moment. Say every thing which is kind for me to all persons and believe me your affectionate BRONTE NELSON.

Lady Hamilton has never received from you the scrap of a pen or any prints.

No. 239

Foudroyant, off Leghorn,
January 20, 1800

MY DEAR FANNY,—As Lord Keith writes me that he is coming this road I am come here to pay homage to him. Now I have only to obey and God only knows on what service he will order me. In truth I have no great reason to be pleased but I do not think it right to shrink from my duty. Josiah is with me and is much improved. I yet hope he will be a comfort to you. I am glad to hear you are got to London with my father. The scene will divert you and I would have not you consider the expense but use all I have. Except to support my public situation, I want not money. It has been very hard how I have been kept here since May 1798.

I am just going on board Lord Keith. Allen has overset the ink. God bless you and believe me ever your affectionate BRONTE NELSON.

To Lady Nelson, No. 54 St. James' Street, London.

No. 240

Leghorn,
January 25, 1800

MY DEAR FANNY,—We are just weighing with Lord Keith for Palermo and Malta. Yesterday I received your and my father's letters of December. I am so so.

May God Almighty bless you both is the fervent wish of your ever affectionate [BRONTE NELSON][2]

To Lady Nelson, 54 St. James' Street, London.

[1] Sir Edward Berry.
[2] The signature has been cut away.

No. 241

Off Malta,
March 10, 1800

MY DEAR FANNY,—Having wrote you by the *Queen Charlotte*[1] who is gone to Leghorn I have now only to say that I have been left here, very unwell and am this day going to Palermo for the benefit of my health.[2]

I have just received your kind letter of December 10th. It blows a gale of wind and the vessel cannot wait.

With my most affectionate regards to my father, believe me ever your affectionate BRONTE NELSON.

To Lady Nelson, 54 St. James' Street, London.

No. 242[3]

Leghorn,
June 20, 1800

MY DEAR FANNY,—Your letter of May 10th found me at this place where I came with the Queen of Naples and 4 of her children, Sir William and Lady Hamilton etc. etc. We are detained by the situation of the armies but a few days will I hope enable Her Majesty to prosecute her intended journey to Vienna, when Lord Keith I think must allow the *Foudroyant* to carry me and my party to England for she cannot be refitted in the Mediterranean.

My health at times îs better but a quiet mind and to give content is necessary for me. A very difficult thing for me to enjoy I could say much but it would only distress me and be useless. I trust I shall find my dear father in as perfect health as his age will allow. I shall come to London or where ever he may be the moment I get out of quarantine therefore I would not have you come to Portsmouth on any account.

Remember me most kindly to all our friends and believe me ever your most affectionate BRONTE NELSON OF THE NILE.

[1] Lord Keith's flag-ship which was destroyed accidentally by fire at Leghorn on March 17.
[2] Nelson's health did not improve and he requested permission to go home on that account.
[3] Several letters are missing for this period.

No. 243

Vienna,
September 20, 1800[1]

MY DEAR FANNY, —Since I wrote you from Trieste we have been so continually prepared to set out that I have not wrote a line till this day. Sir William Hamilton being recovered we set out tomorrow, and shall be in England the 2nd week in October.[2] I have wrote to Davison to take a house or good lodgings for the very short time I shall be in London, to which I shall instantly proceed and hope to meet you in the house.

You must expect to find me a worn out old man. Make my kindest love to my father who I shall see the moment I have been with the King.

May God bless you and believe me your affectionate BRONTE NELSON OF THE NILE.

To Lady Nelson, Round Wood, Suffolk.

No. 244

[Yarmouth,]
November 6, 1800

MY DEAR FANNY,—We are this moment arrived[3] and the post only allows me to say that we shall set off tomorrow noon and be with you on Saturday to dinner. I have only had time to open one of your letters, my visits are so numerous.

May God bless you and my dear father and believe me ever your affectionate BRONTE NELSON OF THE NILE.

Sir and Lady Hamilton beg their best regards and will accept your offer of a bed. Mrs. Cadogan[4] and Miss Knight[5] with all the servants will proceed to Colchester.

I beg my dear father to be assured of my duty and every tender feeling of a son.

To Lady Nelson, Round Wood, Ipswich, Suffolk.
[*Readdressed:* Nerotts Hotel, Kings Street, London.][6]

   [1] As the *Foudroyant* could not be spared to take Nelson home, he struck his flag on July 13 and proceeded overland.
   [2] See Appendix, p. 526, for the details of this journey. They stayed in Vienna for a month, and arrived at Hamburgh at the end of October.
   [3] Nelson crossed from Hamburg in the *King George*, packet, and spent the night of November 6 at Yarmouth. He proceeded to London via Colchester.
   [4] Lady Hamilton's mother, who had travelled from Naples with the party.
   [5] Miss Ellis Cornelia Knight, authoress.
   [6] This is the last letter in the Monmouth MSS. The two letters printed in chapter 7 have been taken from other sources. As it is known that some letters for this period, January–March 1801, are now lost, the numeration has not been continued.

APPENDIX

St. Vincent to Sir William Hamilton[1]

A

Rosia House, Gibraltar,
December 7, 1798

SIR,—I am much obliged by your interesting letter of the 7th November, the occurrences related in which I hope are a happy presage of the downfall of this devouring republic. I have not the honour to be personally acquainted with General Mack, but some of my intimate friends are, and from their description of him he is certainly formed for the situation he is placed in.

The possession of Minorca[2] will stimulate all the discontented in Italy to action, and I shall do everything in my power to feed the stimulus. While you have such men about you as Nelson, Troubridge, Ball, Hood, Hallowell and co. everything is to be looked for, and nothing dreaded on our element. Captain Miller who will have the honour to present you with this, is justly entitled to be classed as one of your heroes, and I shall soon present you with another in Captain Darby of the *Bellerophon.*

Pray remember me in the most friendly manner to Sir John Acton and believe me to be with the most sincere regard and esteem, your Excellency's very faithful and obedient servant, ST. VINCENT.

Right Honble Sir William Hamilton.

B

Rosia House, Gibraltar,[3]
January 17, 1799

SIR,—I am truly sensible of your most obliging and friendly attention in leaving your despatch to Lord Grenville open for my perusal. The Queen's letters are a grand display of magnanimity, penetration and decision, and represent Her Majesty and her faithful friend Lady Hamilton in the most exalted point of view. The fate of Prince Albert is a sad tragic scene in recital, what must have been its effect on the royal mother and Lady Hamilton, who alone was capable of administering comfort to either.

[1] N.M.M. MS 9848, Hamilton papers.
[2] Port Mahon and the Island of Minorca surrendered on November 15 to Commodore Duckworth, later Admiral Sir John Duckworth (died 1817).
[3] Owing to ill health, St. Vincent spent much of his last year as commander-in-chief ashore at Gibraltar.

2 K

I shall make no reflections on the base conduct of the Neapolitan officers and troops under the orders of General Mack. I have too much reason to believe the same thing will happen, both in Spain and Portugal, whenever it pleases the Directory to take possession of those Kingdoms, for the minds of the generality of all orders of men are corrupted and prepared to act upon French principles whenever a force enters either country to put the match to the train.

May I request of your Excellency to lay me at the feet of their Majesties and convey my most unfeigned congratulations on their timely retreat from Naples and to assure them that I shall continue to exert every means in my power for the preservation of their royal persons and the rest of their dominions.

I have the honour to be with great regard and esteem your excellency's most obedient humble servant, ST. VINCENT.

His Excellency the Right Honourable Sir William Hamilton, K.B.

Captain Ball to Sir William Hamilton[1]

Alexander, off Malta,
February 9, 1799

MY DEAR SIR,—I cannot find language to express to you my grateful feelings for your friendly letter of the 31st of last month, written at a time when your mind could not be recovered from the sensation it must have received at witnessing the great political convulsion and transition in the Neapolitan government. Although you have been obliged to make so sudden a retreat, to avoid the consequences of such unparalleled treachery, you have this consoling reflection, that your thirty years' labour in a public capacity has enabled you to render essential services to your country, and to enlighten mankind by your philosophical researches. You have most strictly kept up the character of the English for probity and honour, and your polished and conciliatory manners have procured our countrymen respect and esteem throughout his Sicilian Majesty's dominions.

I beg leave to express that I feel very proud of the kind attention you and Lady Hamilton have been pleased to honour me, but it would be presumption in me not to ascribe a part of it to my very kind and sincere friend, Lord Nelson. His prompt decision and admirable conduct in the battle of the Nile gained me a medal,[2] but the public testimony he is

[1] N.M.M. MS. 9848, Hamilton papers.
[2] A gold medal was given to all captains who took part in the Battle of the Nile. The medals were sent out by Lord Spencer in January 1799 with directions for wearing them.

giving me of his friendship is more estimable and of more intrinsic consequence than all the medals in the world.

Your Excellency will hear of the hard task we have had to support and
animate the Maltese to persevere in their struggle against the French. We
derive this advantage from it, that we have impressed strongly upon their
minds a great love and esteem for the British nation; and they are now
sensible of what they would not believe before, that a British squadron in
the winter months can block them up and starve them. The lower class
of Maltese who are all attached to us have evinced more patience and
cheerfulness under their great hardships than I ever expected from any
nation. They have done the duty of soldiers in the severe weather almost
naked, without pay and their only nourishment bread and a small allowance of pork. They have not shewn much constitutional courage but I
think I have given a physical cause for it. They and their chiefs have lost
all confidence in each other. Their general Carnana within these few
days has lost his senses. I doubt very much his recovering. I have been
obliged to call a meeting of the chief inhabitants to consult upon the means
of extricating them from their difficulties, and we are now obliged to meet
twice a week. Three days ago we met on business, and it was necessary to
assemble the next day for an hour to finish it. As I thought it could be
accomplished without my presence, I expressed my intention of remaining
on board the *Alexander*, upon which they all declared they could not
finish without I presided. I must refer you to Capt. Hardy, Col. Rooke and
the gentlemen who came from Palermo who can give you many particulars
of the strong attachment which the Maltese profess for the English.
But I am extremely anxious to impress upon your mind and that of
Lord Nelson that this has not been effected by any intrigue or insinuation
on the part of the English. I have studiously avoided all overturns and
have constantly held out to them the necessity of being under the protection
of his Sicilian Majesty.

Your Excellency and my Lord Nelson will soon be convinced that I
have most zealously obeyed that part of his Lordship's instructions
directing me to use my influence to strengthen the allegiance of the
Maltese to his Sicilian Majesty and to prevent their pursuing any measures
derogatory to his dignity and right as their legitimate sovereign. They
have appointed three deputies to wait upon his Sicilian Majesty and Lord
Nelson to represent their situation. I believe they are men of integrity.
I beg leave to introduce them to your Excellency's notice. The Baron ——
and the Abbé Savoye I have met very frequently. The latter is a man of
business. He professes good abilities and appears the fittest person. I
hope his Sicilian Majesty will allow them to put themselves under the

protection of His Britannic Majesty during the war. I will answer to keep it without a British garrison if the Government will only allow me the expense of two British regiments and a small military staff. This will be paid them four fold, besides the consequence and advantage of such a port. After the first year Great Britain will not have occasion to remit money. The island will be a great depot for the British manufacturers which will find their way to Tripoli, Tunis, Sicily and the Levant all that I shall have to do will be to draw every quarter for a specified sum. Four thousand a year would pay a Master Attendant, a builders and boats' crews to attend ships coming in and out of port and a number of gun boats. The deputies can inform you of their exports in cotton which is considerable. Most of it was sent to Spain which they will now be enabled to do under the Tunisian flag. But if England and Spain were at peace, the English merchant would take cotton in return for British manufacture which he would carry to Spain and exchange a Spanish cargo for the English market.

If my Lord Nelson should approve of the proposals and the King of Naples would send over five or ten thousand pounds on account of Great Britain it would effectually secure this island to us. If Great Britain will not take them under her protection they will fall into the hands of Russia. You may depend on it Sir, that I have investigated very fully the intrigues carried on by a few individuals with Russia, and the Grand Master which would never have taken place if they had thought the English would have accepted their island. I am of opinion that it would be a good speculation for the merchants to pay the expenses if Mr. Pitt does not see the great advantage which may be derived by keeping possession of it. I will not trespass any farther on your time, than by requesting you to present my respects to Lady Hamilton with every good wish I have the honour to remain with sincere respect and esteem your excellency's most obliged ALEXANDER JOHN BALL.

The Right Honourable Sir William Hamilton, K.B.

P.S. Since closing my letter to the Admiral it has occurred to me, if I should be appointed to the government here by Lord Nelson and the King of Naples it would have a good effect if his Majesty were to give me a public mark of his approbation by investing me with an order suitable to my rank to wear while here only.[1] Be so good to mention this to his Lordship if you approve the idea.

[1] Ball was given the title 'Chief of the Island of Malta' in September 1799, but Valetta still held out and he was not officially appointed governor until the end of the blockade in the autumn of 1800. He remained in that position until his death in 1809.

Lady Hamilton to Nelson[1]

Thursday evening, June 12, [1799]

I have been with the Queen this evening: she is very miserable and says that although the people of Naples are for them in general, *yet* things will not be brought to that state of quietness and subordination till the fleet of Lord Nelson appears off Naples. She therefore begs, entreats you, and conjures you my dear Lord, if it is possible, to arrange matters so as to be able to go to Naples. Sir William is waiting for General Acton's answer. For God sake consider it and do. We will go with you, if you will come to fetch us. Sir W. is ill, I am ill, it will do us good. God bless you, ever ever your sincerely, E. HAMILTON.

Right Honourable Lord Nelson, *Foudroyant.*

The King of Naples to Nelson.[3]

Palermo,
June 25, 1799

MY DEAR AND MOST WORTHY LORD,—I cannot express to you the pain I have felt from Sir William Hamilton's billet to Acton.[4] You would greatly wrong my sentiments if you could believe them capable of changing in so short a space of time.

I write to the Cardinal[5] in the manner that is proper and that he may in all and everything, act in concert with you for the manner of treating with the French, who are at St. Elmo and in the other places, and the rebels. Not to tire you I refer to what Acton has written more fully to Sir William, whilst I conjure you to believe me, full of gratitude and thankfulness, ever the same your affectionate friend, FERDINAND B.

[1] N.M.M. MS. 9960, Croker collection in the Phillipps papers—quoted by Nicolas, Vol. III, p. 491.
[2] Nelson had already received an appeal from the King to proceed to Naples with his squadron. He embarked the Hereditary Prince and sailed the next day, but news of the French fleet forced him to return to Palermo.
[3] N.M.M. MS. 9960, Croker collection in the Phillipps Papers. The original letters and the contemporary English translations have been preserved in this collection.
[4] Nelson sailed for Naples on June 21, taking with him Sir William and Lady Hamilton.
[5] Cardinal Ruffo, who with Captain Foote had arranged terms of capitulation with the last Republican strongholds before Nelson's arrival.

Sir William Hamilton to Sir John Acton[1]

Foudroyant, Bay of Naples,
June 25, 1799

MY DEAR SIR,—Last night all Naples was illuminated and illuminations are beginning tonight. The whole squadron did not get to their anchors until 2 o'clock today in line of battle extending from opposite the Arsenal of Naples towards Portici. The *Foudroyant* is in 43 fathom water. We have had boats with music and crowds of people with revelry the whole day. Capts. Troubridge and Ball were sent early this morning to Cardinal Ruffo with a letter which I wrote to his Eminency by Lord Nelson's desire telling him how much he disapproved of the armistice. The Cardinal always said that he made the armistice as the best he could do in his weak state to save the city of Naples from destruction, that from what he had signed he could not depart but that Lord Nelson was under no engagement and might do what he thought best for the King's service but that he still thought what he had done was the best that could be done for His Majesty's service. As both Lord Nelson and I differ so much from the sentiments of His Eminency, your Excellency may well imagine that in a visit the Cardinal made this evening to Lord Nelson on board the *Foudroyant* nothing more could be concluded but by Lord Nelson's giving his opinion in writing which was no more than that having arrived in the Bay of Naples yesterday the 24th he had found that his Eminency had made a treaty with the rebels that in his Lordship's opinion could not be carried into effect without the consent of His Sicilian Majesty and there it rests.

I hear from those that have been in Naples that in general most are discontented with the armistice and I find that the Royalist and Jacobin parties keep possession of the parts of the city they possessed at the moment of the signing the armistice so that the tree of infamy is opposite the Castel Nuovo and I saw with my glass that the giant opposite the Palace wears still a red cap of liberty.[2] The Cardinal I believe intends to let them know at the Castles of St. Elmo Nuovo and del Ovo that he can not answer for Lord Nelson's allowing of the armistice to continue.

I have written just what has passed since we came here, but I can have no judge how the business will end. Lord Nelson offered to send 12 hundred marines on shore but difficulties were made by the Cardinal as to providing them with quarters. Now Lord Nelson seems to have laid aside all thought of venturing his marines on shore. As Lord Nelson is now telling Lady

[1] N.M.M. MS. 9849, Hamilton papers.
[2] The tree of liberty and the red cap were Republican emblems.

Hamilton what he wishes to say to the Queen you will probably know from the Queen more than I do of Lord Nelson's intentions. I have no more to add this night than that I remain ever desirous of serving their Sicilian Majesties to the utmost of my power and have the honour to be my dear Sir, your Excellency's obedient humble servant, WILLIAM HAMILTON.

The King of Naples to Nelson[1]

Palermo,
June 27, 1799

MY DEAR AND EVER MORE WORTHY LORD,—I could not read without the greatest satisfaction the paper of declaration which you addressed to Cardinal Ruffo, and to which I flatter myself he immediately conformed, as was his duty, and acted in consequence.

I wait with the greatest impatience for accounts from you, that I may take my farther resolutions and ever more recommending to you my honour, and decorum, I beg you always to believe me your same grateful friend, FERDINAND B.

My salutes to Sir William Hamilton and Milady.

Sir William Hamilton to Sir John Acton[2]

A

Foudroyant, Bay of Naples,
June 27, 1799

MY DEAR SIR,—Your Excellency will have perceived by my last that the opinions of the Cardinal and Lord Nelson by no means coincided. However upon cool reflexion Lord Nelson authorized me to write to His Eminency early yesterday morning and assure him that he would not do anything that could break the armistice which his Eminency had thought proper to make with the rebels in the Castle of Ovo and Nuovo, and that his Lordship was ready to give him any assistance that the fleet under his command could afford and that his Eminency thought for the good of his Sicilian Majesty's service. This produced the best effect possible. Naples had been in confusion expecting Lord Nelson to break the armistice, now

---

[1] N.M.M. MS. 9960, Croker collection in the Phillipps papers.
[2] N.M.M. MS. 9849, Hamilton papers.

all was calm and the Cardinal settled with Capts. Ball and Troubridge[1] that the rebels should embark from the Castles of Ovo and Nuovo in the evening and that 500 marines should be put on shore from the fleet to garrison the two castles where now thank God his Sicilian Majesty's flags are flying and the short lived Republican flags are now in the cabin of the *Foudroyant* and so will I hope very soon be the French flag still flying at St. Elmo.

We were with Lord Nelson in his boat seeing the Marines land at the health office. The joy of the people was excessive. The British and Neapolitan colours displayed from many windows and when we took possession of the castles a feu de joye went all over Naples and at night great illuminations as the former nights. In short I am now in the greatest hopes that Lord Nelson's coming here will be of infinite service to their Sicilian Majesties. A little of my phlegm was necessary between the Cardinal and Lord Nelson or all would have blown up the very first day and the Cardinal has written to thank me and Lady Hamilton. The tree of abomination is now cutting down opposite the King's palace and the red cap will be taken off the giant's head. Capt. Troubridge is gone to execute this business and the rebels on board of the polaccas from the castles can not stir without a passport from Lord Nelson.

Caracciolo and 12 of the most infamous rebels are this day to be sent to Lord Nelson. If my opinion is relished they should be sent directly to be tried by the judge at Procita and such as are condemned be brought back and executed here. Caraccioli will probably be seen hanging at the yard arm of the *Minerva* Neapolitan frigate from daybreak to sunset for such an example is necessary for the future marine service of H.S. Majesty and particularly as Jacobinism had prevailed so much in the Neapolitan marine.

St. Elmo has fired every night 7 or 8 shot. We are told it was at some Calabrese that were taking up rebels under the walls of the castle. I believe the honour of reducing St. Elmo will fall to the lot of the British and Russian troops. However we now shall act perfectly in concert with the Cardinal tho' we think the same as we did at first as to the treaty his Eminency made before our arrival. If one cannot do exactly as one could wish, one must make the best of a bad bargain and that Lord Nelson is doing and I hope the result will be approved by their Sicilian Majesties. Salandra's conduct is such that I am convinced that he himself is an honest man and loyal whatever his connections may be. Adieu, ever your Excellency's obedient servant, WM. HAMILTON.

---

[1] The command of all marine forces who were landed was given to Captain Troubridge, with Ball as his second-in-command.

B

On board the *Foudroyant*,
June 28, 1799

MY DEAR SIR,—This morning I received your Excellency's packet of the 25th instant with a letter from His Sicilian Majesty to Lord Nelson which I instantly delivered to his Lordship. We all are of opinion that without the presence of His Majesty the confusion will increase and no regular government be established. We could wish that both the King, Queen and your Excellency could come directly when in a very few days the material points of government might be settled. Lord Nelson sends off the *St. Vincent* cutter to acquaint their Majesties that the *Seahorse* will sail this night for Palermo to be at their Majesties' disposition and Lord Nelson thinks that the *Seahorse* will bring you here very safely and expeditiously. We trust no one with the secret of any probability of their Majesties coming but should they so determine we are firmly of opinion that they will by so doing place themselves on their throne of Naples with dignity and expedition whereas leaving things in their present mysterious state God knows how or when it may end. Lord Nelson's finding that his Sicilian Majesty totally disapproved of what the Cardinal Ruffo has done contrary to his instructions with respect to the rebels in the castles and those rebels being still on board of 12 or 14 polaccas and it being in time to remedy that evil, thought himself sufficiently authorized to seize all these polaccas and anchor them amidst of the squadron and there they will remain at his Majesty's disposition and I wrote at the same time the following letter to the Cardinal by Lord Nelson's desire.

a bord du *Foudroyant* 25 juin 1799

EMINENCE,—Milord Nelson me prie d'informer V.E. qu'en consequence d'une ordre qu'il vient de recevoir de S.M. Sicilienne qui disapprouve entierement la capitulation faite avec ses sujets rebelles dan les Chateaux Neuf and de l'Oeuf il va saisir et s'assurer de ceux qui sont sortis et se trouvent a bord des batiments dans ce Port en se soumettant a l'opinion de V.E. s'il ne servit pas a prospos de publicer dabord a Naples la raison de cette operation de Milord Nelson, et en meme tems de donner avis a ceux des rebelles qui sont echappes des dits chateaux dans la Ville de Naples doivent se soumettre a la clemance de S.M. Sicilienne dans l'espace de 24 heures sous peine de mort. J'ai l'honneur etc., W.H.

How the Cardinal will relish this letter I can not tell, but I know that affairs could not be going on worse for their Majesties' honour than they did before we came to this resolution—in our minds necessary for their Majesties' honour. I have reason to believe Cirillo and all the most guilty were on board these polaccas and the stroke was quiteu nexpected and so will be the arrival of their Majesties and your Excellency should you determine as we sincerely wish. At this season it will be a party of pleasure and their Majesties might do their business and return to Palermo before the world was informed of their departure. Excuse the confusion in this letter we are all hurried to death.

Ever my dear Sir your Excellency's most obedient and attached humble servant, WILLIAM HAMILTON.

C

Foudroyant, Bay of Naples,
June 30, 1799, 11 o'clock morning

MY DEAR SIR,—We have just received the last packets from the Palace of Palermo and am to return your Excellency many thanks for your two letters one dated 27th June 10 o'clock and the other 12 o'clock at night of the 27th. Lord Nelson is highly honoured by the King's letter and much flattered with the entire confidence that their Majesties and your Excellency place in him—but we are all of opinion that at this moment there is by no means occasion to make any use of the full powers you have given to Lord Nelson and come to extremities with the Cardinal, therefore we have thought it prudent to lock the whole of the packet sent to Lord Nelson and not even give the Cardinal the King's letter No. 1 although (as far as we can learn) the Cardinal is surrounded by bad people and has employed many that have served under the infamous republic and gives protections as we are told to some of the most conspicuous of notre Jacobin families. Yet we do not believe his Eminence to have any direct treacherous design. Therefore we think it best for their Majesties' interest to keep smooth with him, and where he will not take upon himself to act, and the King's service require decision, Lord Nelson will act. As your Excellency will see by the printed papers published yesterday and this day at Naples, some of which are inclosed, the Cardinal has joined his forces to assist Capt. Troubridge, gone with the British marines, Portuguese artillery, and Russians upon the attack of St. Elmo. They marched at 4 this morning and as all seems quiet at St. Elmo I rather hope for a capitulation without coming to blows. However your Excellency knows that if Troubridge is once irritated he will spare no pains to carry his point.

In consequence of Lord Nelson's notification numbers are coming to the castles but as he can not know how far they have been engaged with the republic he has allowed them to return to their house promising not to stir out of them until his Sicilian Majesty's pleasure is known. Should any very notorious rebels appear Lord Nelson would confine him on board of one of his ships as he has done by Manthonet, Cirillo and many more from the polaccas that have been the principals. The Cardinal dines with Lord Nelson today, but we keep it a profound secret that we have any letter from his Eminency—so that your Excellency understands all those packets lay dormant in Lord Nelson's writing box and will do so unless there should be a necessity of making use of them, of which I see no probability. I still see the necessity of the King's appearance in this bay. His Majesty would soon see how truly attached the people are to his Majesty and his Majesty would also soon distinguish and separate his true from his false friends. Caracciolo[1] submitted to his fate with courage, but Count Thurn can best describe his exit. Certainly this quick justice has had a great effect and gives the people the greater pleasure. I can not get time to write more. But I think every thing is going on towards a happy conclusion. Still I return to the necessity of the King's appearance at least on board the *Foudroyant* and I hope that his Majesty's flag will be flying at St. Elmo whilst his royal standard is hoisted on board this ship.

Adieu my dear sir, believe me with sincere attachment your Excellency's most obedient humble servant, WILLIAM HAMILTON.

Nelson to Sir John Acton[2]

Foudroyant,
June 29, 1799

MY DEAR SIR,—I long for the arrival of the King and Queen and your Excellency. I send you a proclamation I have requested the Cardinal to get published, his Eminence having declined printing any paper. Capt. Troubridge will have 1300 men from the fleet in the town of Naples this evening, and I shall endeavour to keep terms with the Cardinal till their Majesties' arrival. The last paper of the Cardinal was that no person should be arrested without his order, this is saving the rebels. In short it was a toss up yesterday whether the Cardinal would not have been arrested. His brother is grievously complained of. It is in vain to tease your Excellency farther, I will endeavour to keep matters tolerable. I will

---

[1] Executed on board his Sicilian Majesty's ship *Minerva*, commanded by Count Thurn, on June 29.

[2] N.M.M. MS. 55/080, De Coppet collection. This letter is not given by Nicolas, but is in *Nelson and the Neapolitan Jacobins*, edited by Gutteridge, N.R.S., p. 278. The Italian proclamation is given by Nicolas, Vol. III, p. 396, but from a corrupt text.

answer with my head for the security of their Majesties. May God soon send us a finish to these disastrous events, ever believe me your Excellency's faithful servant, NELSON.[1]

His Excellency Sir John Acton, Bt.

Enclosures: Italian translation of the letter.
Printed notification (in Italian).
English translation of the notification.

'Horatio Lord Nelson Admiral of the British Fleet in the Bay of Naples gives notice to all those who have served as officers civil or military in the infamous Neapolitan republic, that if in the space of 24 hours for those who are in the city of Naples and 48 hours for those who are within five miles of it, they do not give themselves up to the clemency of the King, to the officers commanding in the Castles of Nuovo and Ovo that Lord Nelson will consider them as still in rebellion and enemies of his Sicilian Majesty.

'*Foudroyant*, Naples Bay, 29 June 1799.'

The King of Naples to Nelson[2]

Palermo,
July 2, 1799

MY DEAR AND MOST WORTHY LORD,—Your letter of the 30th of last month, received this evening, has given me the greatest pleasure, seeing that through your activity and firmness affairs have taken a better turn. For the sake of systemizing every thing as it is right, and terminating the business according to our common just intentions, I accept with all my heart the invitation you give me,[2] and please God, shall depart tomorrow evening with the convoy with the troops for Procida, whence with the greatest conveniency we can make all the arrangements, and give all the orders that shall be thought convenient for securing the future quiet and felicity of my faithful subjects.

I chose immediately to let you know this for your regulation at the same time that I beg you to be assured of my eternal gratitude, as well as of my constant esteem and friendship. FERDINAND B.

---

[1] Nelson's letter, which is holograph, has been addressed to Sir John Acton as follows in Lady Hamilton's hand: 'His Excellency Sir John Acton Bt. etc. etc., Palermo.'
[2] N.M.M. MS. 9960, Croker collection in the Phillipps papers.
[3] Nelson had for some time urged the King to come to Naples, and on June 28 had sent the *Seahorse*, Captain Foote, for him. The King embarked in a Sicilian frigate and arrived on July 10. He was accompanied by his ministers and lived on board the *Foudroyant*.

Captain Josiah Nisbet to Lord Nelson[1]

H.M.S. *Thalia,* off Civita Vecchia,
July 27, 1799

MY LORD,—Having in pursuance of your Lordship's orders sailed from Naples Bay on the 11th inst. I was unfortunate enough on the 18th to find my mainmast badly sprung and was obliged to go into St. Stephen's bay to fish it, with orders from Capt. Foote to proceed from thence to join him at Longona, Leghorn or Genoa. I remained in the bay part of the 18th, 19th 20th, 21st and part of the 22nd during which period I had frequent communications with the governor of Orbitello who daily received good news from Tuscany and the Roman states. He informed me he had certain information that the French were preparing to evacuate Civita Vecchia and that they had embarked all their property on board armed vessels then ready to sail for Corsica. That 2000 Tuscan troops were on their march to attack Civita Vecchia and that it was his opinion they were in that desperate state that they would surrender the town upon its being summoned.

I therefore (as I supposed Capt. Foote would have been on his return ere I could have joined him) thought it for the good of His Majesty's service to proceed to this place which I appeared before and summoned on the 23rd. A copy of which summons and the answer of the commandant I herewith transmit to you.

I have since had frequent intercourse with the people from the shore who seems so eager to shake off the tyranny of the French that I have no doubt but that they will act with vigour whenever opportunity occurs. It is my intention to remain here waiting your further orders and with hopes that the measures I have adopted will meet your approbation,[2] I am my Lord, your Lordship's most obedient and most humble servant, (signed) J. NISBET.

To the Right Hon. Lord Nelson, Rear Admiral of the Red, etc. etc.

Sir John Acton to Lord Nelson[3]

On board the *Foudroyant* in the road of Naples,
August 1, 1799

MY LORD,—By the two enclosed papers relative to the Government of Naples and this Kingdom while his Sicilian Majesty continues to reside in

[1] B.M. Add. MSS. 34912, Bridport papers.
[2] Nelson, in answering this letter, expressed his regret that Josiah had not been on the north coast of Italy: 'however I am persuaded it was done for the best.'
[3] N.M.M. MS. 9960, Croker collection in the Phillipps papers.

Palermo your Lordship will see that your example of a prudent moderation in regard to Cardinal Ruffo has been followed by his Majesty. The conduct of his Eminence was highly to be commended in Calabria, his approaches to Naples, his behaviour in the first days when entered in this capital, his unaccountable and I may say shameful capitulation intended for the castles of Ovo and Nuovo did with reason promote a prevention against his way of thinking and principles at the moment. Your Lordship's and Sir William Hamilton's observations on these events at your arrival in Naples Bay rose his Majesty's suspicions, which since have been, I must say, rather confirmed than abated with the reports received in this road. It was in your Lordship's power to arrest the Cardinal and send him to Palermo, as the orders to him and the principal persons in Naples charged with that execution, when you had thought proper, directed, by delivering those letters to their destination. As the Cardinal yielded to your wise and steady declarations, your Lordship and Sir William's advice caused a suspension of his Majesty's determinations. You will see by the enclosed instructions an order for a council to direct the Cardinal, and in a manner to overlook and with a proper vigilancy over his actions that he is tied up, in a manner and secured from doing mischief in the beginnings. If he entertains any further concern, I would say intelligence with the conspirators of his own order, it shall be discovered in a moment and immediately as well as efficaciously remedied.

His Majesty's reasons for running in appearance a kind of hazard are however founded: in the eyes of the nation in general the Cardinal deserves praise for his courage in the first setting out and promoting a royal insurrection in the Calabrias under the religious and the King's banner, which has raised and inflamed the rest of the five southern provinces. This service is real. The meanings of this man in advancing to Naples, the corrupted people that flocked around him, his brother especially known for bad and dubious dispositions, gave room to entertain an equivocal opinion, but single doubts and no facts properly were ascertained. His ambition on one side known to the court, his weakness in principle on the other and connections in part abated by the arrest and judgment of most of the traitors amongst the nobles, seemed to encourage his Majesty in the determination of forming a government in the form explained with the aforesaid instructions. The first sign afterwards of a doubtful management shall cause the Cardinal's removal instantly, the dispositions being taken for this necessary operation, when ever the case shall indicate the moment to put it in execution. The Cardinal's brother has been sent already to Sicily, many persons have been dismissed from his confidence by the King's direction. In short if a more proper person to keep up the insurgent army which the Cardinal himself has raised, could have been found in this instant, he should have been placed in his room. The organisation of a new army will I hope in a short time cause the dismission of the Calabrese corps, and tie up again by this disposition any further disagreeable and dangerous thought of a sedition. This *and no revolution* is to be apprehended. The Russian Corps is near to arrive, and we do not see that the party of the nobility which has so much worked in the conspiration against his Majesty may in Naples produce a serious disturbance when the people in the capital as your Lordship is a witness, is so much devoted to his Majesty, the same is likewise in all the provinces.

The King in ordering my communication to your Lordship of these determinations, commands that I should repeat his Majesty's acknowledgement to so many conspicuous and essential services rendered to his Majesty and royal family. I am with regard and respect your Lordship's most obedient and most humble servant. J. ACTON.

His Excellency Lord Nelson.

Lord Spencer to Nelson[1]

Private.   Admiralty,
                                                         August 18, 1799

MY DEAR LORD,—I received with great satisfaction on the 10th instant your letter of the 15th July. The account it conveyed of the repossession of Naples and of your having returned the King to his dominions was calculated to give the most sincere pleasure to everyone here, and it has given to no one of your friends more joy than to myself that this restoration should have been effected so entirely by your means with the assistance of the gallant companions of your service.

I am very glad to see that you do me the justice to believe that Captain Troubridge needed no amplification of his merits to induce me to feel them as I ought. I did not fail to represent them to His Majesty as deserving some mark of his approbation and His Majesty has been pleased to signify his intention of conferring the honour of a baronetage on him, as a proof of his Royal favour for the many services he has performed since he has been employed in the Mediterranean. I trust that we shall soon hear of the final completion of the good work you are about by the surrender of Capua and Gaeta, not only as it will secure the tranquillity of the Kingdom of Naples, but as it will set you at liberty to attend to some other points where the assistance of the fleet will probably be very essential to the cause of His Majesty and his allies.

[1] N.M.M. MS. 9960, Croker collection in the Phillipps papers.

I hope I am not too sanguine in expecting to hear a good account of Malta soon, I should suppose that the garrison of that place must have by this time so little hope of being relieved that they will not be disposed to hold out much longer; and though I have full confidence in you and in Captain Ball for co-operating as cordially with the Russians in that part of the world as we are fortunately doing in every other where we have to act together, it would I confess give me peculiar satisfaction to see that island reduced by our naval force without the interference of any other maritime power.

I am willing to hope from your not mentioning your health that you were well when you wrote. I know you must be a good deal hurried and fatigued from the constant exertion and anxiety you have been exposed to, but the complete success with which it has been attended will I doubt not have much alleviated the pressure of such a crisis.

I had great pleasure in giving the rank of commander to Mr. Parkinson[1] as a compliment to the news he brought. I desired the Marquis de Circello[2] to consider his appointment as a testimony of my respect for his Sicilian Majesty who was graciously pleased to charge that minister with a message to me in which he did no more than justice to your most satisfactory exertions for his restoration.

Believe me my dear Lord your very faithful humble servant, SPENCER.

Lord Nelson.

Sir William Hamilton to Sir Morton Eden[3]

Palermo,
September 5, 1799

. . . It will be the fault of their Sicilian Majesties if they do not profit of what Lord Nelson has done for them, but entre nous I fear they will not follow our advice which is to return immediately to Naples and not trust their affairs to any other hand but their own, to make proper examples in the highest and lowest class and then for a general and real indulto. Lord Keith's incomprehensible conduct obliges Lord Nelson to send most of his squadron to Gibraltar and Minorca and I fear that in the protection of this country the Russian and Turkish fleets will do little at least in the winter, as they allow they cannot keep the sea in that season. . . .

---

[1] Lieutenant William Parkinson, sent to England with dispatches.
[2] The Sicilian ambassador in London.
[3] N.M.M. MS. 9217, Minto papers. Sir Morton Eden had been ambassador at Vienna since 1794.

Sir William Hamilton to Lord Minto[1]

A

Palermo,
September 5, 1799

It is only from newspaper intelligence that I conjecture that your Lordship may be at Vienna. With the King's leave in my pocket to return home since two years last June, my conscience would never allow me to profit of it, as I clearly saw that the King's affairs and still more those of their Sicilian Majesties would suffer by my absence, and altho' my health bad and worn out with constant application, I have remained at my post but am amply rewarded in having contributed to reinstate their Sicilian Majesties on their throne of Naples. Lord Nelson has done all in his power to serve their Sicilian Majesties and has been nobly rewarded having been created Duke of Bronte with an estate of 18 thousand ducats per annum at the foot of Mount Etna. We have all indeed received the most flattering marks of the approbation of their Sicilian Majesties and of the nation.

Their Majesties have still much to do before the Government of Naples can recover from its late severe shock and they must seriously think of a total reform in that country to ensure a just and lasting one. I refer your Lordship to Sir Morton Eden to inform you of the particulars of what has happened here as he has read my dispatches to Lord Grenville.

The season is so far advanced that I dare not profit of the *Goliath* that was appointed by Lord St. Vincent to carry us home, as we should arrive in London probably in the midst of winter and as there is a prospect of this being the last campaign I have determined to defer my return to England until next spring particularly as Lord Nelson is so desirous of a continuance of the assistance he gets from Emma and me, his Lordship as you know not possessing any other language than his own. We have lived together either on shore or on board his ship ever since he returned from Egypt and I do assure your Lordship that the greatest pleasure I have ever had is in the having gained the friendship of this great man and been acquainted particularly with the officers of his squadron. I never met with such a set of valuable brave men. I am really now proud of my country. It is the only one that has conducted itself with dignity, firmness and courage at a period that required universal exertion. Mr. Pitt has rendered himself immortal. . . . Emma who desires to be most kindly remembered to your Lordship has made a very conspicuous figure of late and was so useful at Naples in the service of their Sicilian Majesties during our late

---

[1] Sir Gilbert Elliot, created Baron Minto in 1798, was appointed minister at Vienna in 1799 in succession to Sir Morton Eden. N.M.M. MS. 9217 Minto Papers.

2 L

expedition to that capital that she has received magnificent presents from
both with their Majesties' pictures diamonds etc. etc. Every officer immediately employed in their Majesties' service has had a token and a
handsome one their remembrance. Adieu, my dear Lord, your Lordship's obedient WILLIAM HAMILTON.

B

Palermo,
September 22, 1799

. . . You will have seen official accounts of our late successes in the Bay
of Naples, and as your friends Lord Nelson, Emma and I have been the
principal actors you will certainly have been much interested in our proceedings particularly as it has relieved these amiable sovereigns from such
a weight of calamity as they were scarcely able to support. The gratitude
they express for the support they have had from Great Britain, is unbounded. The King of Naples has given his father's diamond sword left
him to protect his kingdoms, to Lord Nelson, created his Lordship Duke
of Bronte, with an estate on the borders of Mount Etna of 18 thousand
ducats per annum. I have got a large diamond in a ring. Emma the King
and Queen's pictures set with diamonds and also ear rings bracelets etc.
from the Queen. The King was 5 weeks with us on board the *Foudroyant*
and saw himself how hard we laboured for him. Every captain employed
on the different services at Naples, Gaeta and Capua have had from the
King handsome presents of snuff boxes set with diamonds and either His
Majesty's picture or cyphers. Although I have had the King's leave to
return home these two years and a half, my conscience would never allow
me to make use of it, and I am amply rewarded by having had a small share
in replacing their Sicilian Majesties on their throne of Naples. Without
Emma and me Lord Nelson would never have stayed long here, but his
Lordship's activity and my phlegm and knowledge of this court and
country kept all together and has enabled us to bring matters to so happy
a conclusion. . . .

There are still eight thousand in the prisons of Naples, Capua and
Gaeta as rebels or Jacobins. Many executions have taken place. . . . It is
to be hoped when a sufficient number of examples shall have been made
that a general and sincere pardon will be granted, and that the court will
return to Naples. Lord Nelson and I are of opinion that they should
return there as soon as possible, but I see that until the promised Russians
arrive at Naples there is no chance of our quitting Palermo, the hot damp
air of which does not agree with any of our constitutions. . . .

The sesaon being so advanced and Lord Nelson living with us and having occasion for us every moment obliges me to defer my journey home until next spring, but I am really so worn out that I should not be surprised if my career should finish at Palermo. The Queen of Naples is also ill and worn out, talking of dying, and what is more extraordinary Emma who looks as well and as blooming as ever talks of death every day. I believe it is the heat and scirocco winds that depress us all for Lord Nelson complains too.

What a pity that Lord Keith did not fight the French fleet when he could near Genoa, but still I hope the business will be happily concluded before next spring. . . .

C

Palermo,
November 8, 1799

. . . Appearances are favourable and that this abominable war may finish with the century, be that as it may, I am grown so old and worn out that I am determined to go home next spring to get a little repose. If by land we shall certainly not think it out of our way to pay you a visit at Vienna, but my ambition is, if the war ends, to go home with our good friend Lord Nelson in the *Foudroyant*. . . .

Horatio Nelson to Nelson[1]

January 18, 1800

DEAR UNCLE,—I hope this will find your Lordship well. I have been at Eton 6 months and like it very much. I hope to have the pleasure soon of seeing you in England. I went to my uncle Maurice's at Laleham which is about six miles from Eton. I spent your birthday there and at another time I went with my uncle to Deptford and saw an East Indiaman called the *Lord Nelson* launched.[2] My uncle named it and threw a bottle of wine at it. We dined with 200 people and stayed to a ball afterwards, and returned with my uncle to his house in London to sleep. He is very good to me and often sends for me.

I hope you will find time to write me a line to Eton. Direct it Mr. Horatio Nelson at Mrs. Middleton's, Eton, Windsor. I hope Captain Nisbet is well. Give my love to him.

I am your Lordship's affectionate nephew, HORATIO NELSON.

Charlotte sends her love.

[1] B.M. Add. MSS. 34988, Bridport papers.
[2] The East India ship the *Lord Nelson*, 819 tons, made her first voyage in 1800; she was lost in 1808.

The Master of the 'Thalia' to John Tyson[1]

Thalia, at sea,
February 19, 1800

DEAR SIR,—I am under the necessity of troubling you to declare whether in my letter to you when at Palermo last concerning Capt. Nisbet's conduct towards me I mentioned Mr. Colquit [2] having treated him, Capt. Nisbet, ill, or had been Mr. Bulkeley's lawyer in the business which took place at Mahon, or in short whether his name was mentioned and whether Lord Nelson received a letter from me wherein Mr. Colquit was mentioned or any allusion made to him in any respect.

The reason I request it is that in consequence of the inclosed No. 1 a copy of which I sent Capt. Nisbet for his perusal that he might not say I had acted underhand with him in the business it referred to, he five days afterwards framed a story the most infamous and false that ever disgraced the mouth of men. He sent for the 1st Lieutenant and told him the story which No. 2 inclosure refers to and confutes. He said he saw a letter on Lord Nelson's table which he did not know but it might have referred to some of the foregoing assertions. Capt. Nisbet himself told me the reason Lord Nelson behaved cool to Mr. Colquit was in consequence of what he, Capt. N., told my Lord Nelson.

Waiting your answer I remain dear Sir your very humble and obedient servant, A. BRIARLY.

To John Tyson.

Enclosure 1: The Master of the 'Thalia' to the Navy Board

Thalia,
February 10, 1800

GENTLEMEN,—I am sorry to be under the necessity of addressing you on so disagreeable a subject as the following but considering it my indispensable duty from the situation in which I am placed as master of this ship not to suffer any false or undue expense of warrant officers' stores (for which I am to sign) to pass unmentioned, I have made it a rule since my first appointment on joining a ship to inform the boatswain and carpenter that they were upon no account to expend any stores committed to their care without letting me know prior to the conversion and to give me copies of

---

[1] B.M. Add. MSS. 34916, Bridport papers. Alexander Briarly had been master of the *Audacious* at the Battle of the Nile and was in the *Bellona* at the Battle of Copenhagen. He remained in the *Thalia* until she returned to England in October 1800. Tyson was Nelson's secretary.

[2] Samuel Colquit, lieutenant of the *Thalia*. He brought several charges against Captain Nisbet, but no public action was taken. Colquit was promoted rear-admiral in 1846.

their working abstracts, that I might be able to check what was expended and know what remained. Notwithstanding which I have not been able to get a clear or just expense from either boatswain or carpenter since my joining this ship in June last, and they upon my remonstrating told me such things were expended so by the Captain's order, or rather direction to them. Particularly the boatswain once told me (in observing a new St. George's ensign blown away in his expense which was not the case) the Capt. had desired it to be expended so, upon which I told him I should try him by court martial if ever it happened again or anything of the sort.

Yesterday morning the carpenter came and told me the Capt. ordered him to convert spare steering sail booms into fidding royal masts and wished to know from me if I would sign to their being carried away and expended as steering sail booms. I answered no certainly I would not sign to their being expended in any other way than that in which they really were. That I told him repeatedly I never would sign any improper expenditure of stores.

At 4 p.m. the Capt accosted me in the following manner, it being then my watch on deck. 'So, Sir, you would not sign the expense of these spars.' I told him I could not unless mentioned for the use for which they were converted. 'Then, Sir, you have behaved like a damned rascal, and I would recommend you to jump overboard, for if you don't I shall soon make you.' I told him this was not language I was accustomed to, neither was he authorised to make use of such to an officer. He answered 'You an *officer*. Damn your eyes, you are no more an officer than the boatswain or carpenter and will recommend them if ever you refuse to sign their expense to knock you down.' I told him to recollect what he was saying and whether I was to be treated in that manner for doing my duty. He still persisted and said 'If you don't leave the ship I shall make her a hell to you. I want no master but a broom stick who I can make do as I think proper.' Thus he continued for half an hour making use of the like language and without any other provocation than what I have stated.[1]

Which I submit to your consideration that you may take such steps as you think necessary to prevent the service suffering by such conduct.

I have the honour to be gentlemen your very humble and obedient servant, A. BRIARLY.

To the Principal Officers and Commissioners of His Majesty's Navy, London. (a copy)

---

[1] In June, Nelson learned from Duckworth that Josiah was at daggers drawn with his officers, but that he had managed to stave off a general inquiry. He recommended that when the ship was paid off 'a few months with Lady Nelson would *now* correct his foibles'.

Enclosure 2: the Master of the 'Thalia' to Captain Nisbet

Thalia,
February 18, 1800

SIR,—With infinite astonishment I hear you asserted I told you Mr. Colquit was your enemy and had volunteered to be Mr. Bulkeley's counsel against you which was the cause of everything that has happened between you and him. In answer to which I take the Almighty God to witness an expression or anything of the sort never escaped my lips. On the contrary when you told me upon deck Mr. Colquit had thought proper to quarrel with you as you supposed we all did, I answered, 'I was certain there was not a member in the mess wished it or that did not wish you well.' As to my speaking to you at Leghorn on our going there from Mahon you well know Sir could not be the case, as the only time we had any conversation was when you beat the man at the theatre and called me to assist you. I begged you would let him alone as it would bring a mob around you which you know was the case. The last time we were at Leghorn I was never alone with you for one moment. Mr. Pughe[1] and you were together several times but I never was. When you told me I had treated you ill, and been your enemy I answered my messmates could declare I had always acknowledged your goodness to me when I was unwell. It is not likely I could have referred to any person if I had told you before they had been your enemies. What you now accuse me of my existence and everything dear to me in this life is and always shall be pledged upon its not being so. My God is it possible a man be injured so for no reason. I should as soon have thought of being accused of murder. Sir, *you* accused me after the court martial of speaking to Mr. Bulkeley and said Mr. Colquit did and was with him while on shore and farther that Mr. Colquit was his lawyer. I told you no, he was not for he had asked him to assist in his defence but he refused. This is all that ever passed between you and I relative to that business which I will make oath to if necessary.

Captain Nisbet. Copy. Sent him the original, no answer.

Enclosure 3: the Master of the 'Thalia' to Captain Nisbet

Thalia,
February 19, 1800

SIR,—I have just heard you asserted I did not deny that part of your story relative to Mr. Colquit being obliged to quit the mess. I declare

[1] Purser of the *Thalia*.

upon my honour that I never heard directly or indirectly from any one member of the mess a hint or idea of anything like it, nor never asserted it myself. Recollect yourself Sir, and you will find that the only thing could possibly have any affinity to that part of the business came from yourself, when you said to me 'Mr. Colquit should be the last man to quarrel with me, for when he had that row with all his messmates I settled the business with Whidby, otherwise he could not stay below, as no one there would speak to him.'

Was it not enough for you Sir to insult my feelings in the manner you did on the 10th of this month, knowing I had it not in my power to retaliate at that time and when you mentioned you would make the ship hell to me? Could I think it possible that an assertion of this nature could be made use of with an intent to make her so? There is one thing I have to observe, it is utterly impossible I could injure Mr. Colquit's character did I know anything bad of it, which I do not.

Capt. Nisbet—a copy. Sent him the original, no answer.

Lady Nelson to Captain Nisbet, her son[1]

April 15, 1799[2]

MY DEAR JOSIAH,—I have written of late very frequently to you and as I generally take my letters to the foreign post office, I hope you may have received them.

I received a letter from my Lord Nelson dated January 25th where he mentions your improvements with tenderness and kindness. His love for you is very great. He flatters himself he shall see you a good and great man. It is in your power to be both. Therefore God bless you, disappoint us not. You are very young and cannot know the world, be satisfied of this truth, and implicitly follow the directions of my husband, who is truly a good man and his military achievements has stamped his character great all over the world.

You are more conspicuous than you imagine. Be assured you are much envied from having such a father to bring you forward, who has every desire to do it. To convince you I have very good reason to write to you on this subject, I will in confidence repeat to you a conversation a captain of the Navy had with an intimate acquaintance of mine, not knowing I was in the least acquainted. 'I am trying all I can to remove Mr. —— first lieutenant of the *Thalia*, for her captain is no great things.' Then vented his ill-natured disposition, never once allowing

[1] B.M. Add. MSS. 34988, Bridport papers.
[2] Wrongly dated for 1800.

himself to think he had been young. This acquaintance of mine is rather what is called passionate. He immediately said 'Do you know you are speaking of the son of a friend of my wife's, and the son-in-law of Lord Nelson's?' 'Yes' was the answer, and immediately this captain turned and left this gentleman, but in a minute returned saying 'For God sake don't mention what I have said.' And the *very next morning* he returned and intreated as a particular favour that the conversation might not be repeated. All this happened a year and a half back.

My dear Josiah take yourself to account every day. Don't excuse any foibles. I do assure you your first lieutenant has always wrote of you in a handsome manner, I have seen his letters to his mother. Silence on this subject.

There is an admiral who has got himself much laughed at in wishing to defame my Lord's understanding. He wishes to be acquainted with me of all things. I suppose to speak well of my husband.

God bless you and believe me your affectionate mother, FRANCES H. NELSON.

Capt. Hardy's compliments to you and my Lord Nelson. He has written several times.

Have you received the medal I sent you? I will enclose this letter to my Lord fearing it might fall into other hands. I never had a secret from him. Berry writes his wife 'you are much improved in manners and person.'

To Captain Nisbet, *Thalia.*

Nelson's Sea Journal,[1] *February 19–20, 1800*

February 19th: Having detached the *Northumberland* and *Alexander* with the *Genereux* to Syracuse I made sail to the westward carrying all which was possible. In the night joined company with the *Audacious* and *Bonne Citoyenne.* At daylight seeing nothing of the enemy's ships and the *Audacious* being filled with French prisoners, and we not having landed our Neapolitan ones, I directed the *Bonne Citoyenne* to proceed to Lampedusa to see after them and then to cruise 7 leagues west of the Island of Goza till further orders.

I bore up with the *Audacious* for Malta in expectation of finding our Commander-in-chief. ½ past 2 passing between Goza and Malta the Island

---

[1] N.M.M. MS. 9960, Croker collection in the Phillipps papers: an extract from Nelson's journal, written the day after the capture of the French line-of-battle ship, the *Genereux*, and a frigate.

of Comino which is fortified lays in the middle a good passage on each side about 1½ over. At 4 joined the Commander-in-Chief who was too great to appear pleased at the captures of yesterday although he said if they had got in, Graham would have been in great danger of being taken.

February 20th: Very unwell. Lord Keith sends me word the Brest fleet 22 sail of the line is said to be coming here, which I do not believe.

The Queen of Naples to Nelson[1]

February 27, 1800

MON BRAVE RESPECTABLE ET CHER AMIRAL,—J'ai ete bien touche de votre attention et lettre pour mon fils Leopold, qui en a ete dans l'ivresse et hors de lui de joie.[2] La nouvelle victoire n'est qu'un lauriers de plus a la gloire imortelle que vous vous etes acquise, et un recompense a vos vertus. J'en ai eue une joie infinie come je l'aurois toujours a tout ce qui vous concerne. J'espere que cet evenement rendra la prise de Malthe plus facile. Que d'obligations je vous ai, et tous les deux Royaumes ont ces memes sentimens. Ayez soin de votre precieuse sante, et contez sur l'eternells reconnoissance de votre sincere amie, CHARLOTTE.

Le 27 fevrier. 1800.

Je vous envois une reponse de mon fils.[3] Puisse-t-il un jour vous imiter, il fera alors ma gloire come il est actuellement ma tendresse.

Sir William Hamilton to Lord Minto[4]

Palermo,
March 3, 1800

[Tells of the capture of the 'Genereux']. . . . We have reason to hope that the whole of the squadron is in our possession and that the enemy's plan of relieving Malta is completely defeated, and the consequence will be the surrender of the Valetta before which are our two admirals Lord Keith and Lord Nelson.

Entre nous it was an ill judged plan to send out Lord Keith to take the command from Lord Nelson whose delicacy you may be sure felt it sensibly, but he had wisdom enough to swallow the bitter pill for the good

---

[1] N.M.M. MS. 9292, Bridport papers.

[2] Nelson captured the *Genereux* on February 18. He sent the French admiral's flag as a present to Prince Leopold.

[3] The Prince's letter written for him, in Italian, is also among the Bridport papers in the N.M.M.

[4] N.M.M. MS. 9217, Minto papers.

NELSON'S LETTERS TO HIS WIFE

of the service of his King and Country and he has been rewarded by having had the good fortune to take the *Genereux*. Nothing now remains to make the glorious battle of the Nile complete but the capture of the *Guillaume Tell* which (as you know) is in the harbour of Malta. I have now lived two years in the house or on board of ship with Lord Nelson and I protest take him all in all I never met with his equal, but your Lordship knows him well. . . .

Lady Hamilton to Lord Minto

March 6, 1800

I have only a moment my dear Lord to send you Lord Nelson's letters from Malta. He has taken *le Genereux* and a frigate with men and stores for the relief of Malta, so that we expect every moment the capitulation of La Valetta. God grant it, but how happy we are that our dear Nelson took them. Now only the *William Tell* remains and he will have her. Glorious Nelson oh how he loves you. He keeps by him your friendly and eloquent speech in the House of Lords after the battle of the Nile and we often read it together and tears of friendship and gratitude run down his honoured face in speaking of you and to me that loves you and remembers with such satisfaction our happy days at Naples. . . . God bless you, my dear lord. Give my love to Lady Minto and kiss the children for your sincere and attached EMMA HAMILTON.

Sir Thomas Troubridge to Lord Keith[1]

A

Culloden, Malta,
May 7, 1800

I am duly honoured with your Lordship's letters of the 20th and 22nd April and beg to assure your Lordship nothing could give me more pleasure than to find by them that my conduct meets your Lordship's approbation. Lord Nelson was here I shewed him your Lordship's letter, but I believe some arrangements with the Court of Naples to carry her Majesty to Leghorn has induced Lord Nelson to keep the *Foudroyant* and to take the *Alexander* with him. . . .

I trust and hope by this your Lordship is in Genoa, it will relieve you much. The *Culloden* is ready to start the moment your Lordship directs. Lord Nelson has given me a discretionary power to go, if the service will admit of it as some ship must be in this bay it would lessen the force.

---

[1] N.M.M. MS. 9281, Keith papers. Copies of Troubridge's letters to Nelson are included among the Keith papers, from which these extracts are taken.

As the business draws to a conclusion we must prevent supplies getting in; I mean to stay until I hear from your Lordship, as it does not appear to me your intention I should go without Lord Nelson was to hoist his flag in *Culloden*. If fortune puts us in possession of La Villette I shall push for Mahon and wait your Lordship's further orders. . . .

B

Culloden, Malta,
May 24, 1800

I am truly honoured with your Lordship's letter of 10th inst. and the one from Lord Spencer. My health has suffered so much from the last stroke of sickness I had, that I really feel myself wholly unequal to the journey by land, if your Lordship will indulge me to carry home the *Culloden* which I should be ashamed to ask if I did not know to a certainty she has been reported this last two years as irreparable and this last accident has made her worse of course. And as it appears to me by all the orders and letters that it is your Lordship's intention she should go immediately to Mahon and thence to England if reported safe. I have no doubts about her going safe, I represented this to Lord Nelson and offered to accommodate both him and Sir William Hamilton long since, conceiving it my duty to make the most of the *Culloden* by that means and probably be the cause of leaving your Lordship an effective ship in the station which you might be induced to spare for that purpose but I see neither will venture in her,[1] I therefore for the good of the service and conceiving I meet fully your Lordship's wishes mean to proceed to Mahon and wait your farther orders for England. I am so shook in my constitution that I foresee the journey overland would leave me on the road an invalid, and most likely return to England an object for an hospital rather than active service. As my mind will have little to disturb it in a single ship and a very few days' difference with respect to getting to England, I trust your Lordship's indulgence in sending me orders to proceed direct in the *Culloden*. . . .

Sir Thomas Troubridge to Lord Nelson

A

Culloden,
May 24, 1800

I received your several orders this morning by Captain Stephenson and shall put them in force as fast as possible. . . . I shall have arranged

---

[1] Nelson thought the *Culloden* too unsafe to sail alone. She returned to England in July 1800.

everything here and leave Army and Navy and inhabitants well supplied and be able to sail Tuesday or Wednesday for Mahon where I hope to find Lord Keith's orders to proceed to England. I feel myself so very unwell as to be wholly unequal to the journey by land, I therefore send *Princess Charlotte* agreeable to your wish for your orders. I feel a strong desire to see you before I go, but I fear I shall be deprived of that pleasure until we meet in England. I had promised myself when I first wrote to your Lordship at Palermo that I should have had the honour to carry you home, my whole study should have been to please and I flatter myself you would have found yourself easy and comfortable on board as would good Sir William and Lady Hamilton. I will venture to say more so than in *Foudroyant*. Be assured my Lord no one loves and respects you more than I do, and I flatter myself I shall soon see your flag flying in the Channel.

I mean to leave the *Strombolo* in this bay as all will be done. The General will not miss *Culloden* and it appears to me by all the orders that I meet the Commander-in-Chief's wishes by carrying *Culloden* to Mahon and there wait for his, Lord Keith's orders, if he dispatches me from thence quick I shall be equally soon as if I went by land and most likely arrive in good health in the other case an invalid, for I assure you I am more shook in constitution than you have any idea of. My mind with only my own ship will be at ease and quiet and restore me, for I am fully persuaded I should be left in Germany if I tried the expedition by land, I hope your Lordship will approve of what I am doing I beg my best respects to Sir William and Lady H. who I fear I shall not have time to write to. . . .

B

Culloden,
May 26, 1800

. . . I shall have finished all here tomorrow and will thank your Lordship to press Lord Keith to send me order for to proceed from Mahon to England; my breast is very indifferent and I spit much blood; I mean when I sail to try a blister on my breast. I beg my best respects to Sir Wm. and Lady Hamilton. . . .

Mr. Murdoch, Madeira, to Lord Keith

Madeira,
May 24, 1800

MY LORD,—I have already had the honour of writing your Lordship by the *Thalia* Captain Nisbet, who after a three weeks' cruise has returned here for some necessary articles he found himself deficient in. Meantime we stand indebted to him for the having kept us so free of enemy's cruisers, that a variety of arrivals have brought us most seasonable supplies and relieved a threatened scarcity. He now farther obliges the trade by seeing clear of the island all the vessels in readiness to sail and they are forward in expressing their wishes that your Lordship may allow of Capt. Nisbet's return to take care of us.[1]

You will probably my Lord, have the pleasure of seeing with this an old acquaintance. Mr. Heron with Lady Elizabeth and their only surviving daughter, to whom Captain Nisbet is good enough to give a passage. They came hither on account of the health of their other amiable daughter but who died just as they arrived. There accompanies them Col. Lumsden who has been with me for some time past on the score of his wounded condition, whom I beg leave to make known to your Lordship. Believe me my Lord, on all occasions with the warmest esteem, your Lordship's faithful and most obedient servant, JAMES MURDOCH.

Lord Spencer to Lord Keith[2]

A

Admiralty,
April 25, 1800

I am sorry to find that Lord Nelson was on the 10th of March thinking of returning to Palermo. I shall be afraid, if he does, that his health will grow worse and he will be obliged to come home. . . .

B

Admiralty,
May 9, 1800

Private and confidential.

The very indifferent state of health in which Lord Nelson has for some time past appeared to be makes me very apprehensive that he may look sincerely to returning home before long; we have therefore left a discretionary power to your Lordship to permit him so to do, if he should for that cause think it necessary. . . .

C

Admiralty,
July 4, 1800

Private.

We continue to look with great anxiety for the return of Sir Thomas Troubridge and I should also like much to know what is become of Lord Nelson. . . .

---

[1] Captain Nisbet returned to England in October 1800.
[2] N.M.M. MS. 9281, Keith papers.

D

Admiralty,
August 18, 1800

Private.

I hope it will not be long before Lord Nelson arrives in this part of the world. His further stay in the Mediterranean cannot I am sure contribute either to the public advantage or his own. . . .

Lord Minto to Lord Keith

Vienna,
August 30, 1800

Lord Nelson arrived here with Sir W. and Lady Hamilton a few days after the Queen of Naples having been detained at Trieste some time by Sir William's illness. Sir W. has had a relapse here; and altho' he has recovered a little yet he is so feeble and so much reduced that I cannot see how it is possible for him to reach England alive. Lord Nelson has been received here by all ranks with the admiration which his great actions deserve, and notwithstanding the disadvantage under which he presents himself at present to the public eye. They talk of proceeding in a few days towards England; and I who am a lover of naval merit and indeed a sincere friend of the man, hope we shall again hear of him on his proper element. . . .

Lord Nelson and Sir William Hamilton

Joint Expence of Journey from Palermo to Trieste, Vienna, Prague, Dresden. Hamburgh, etc., to Yarmouth. 1800[1]

Money drawn for by Lord Nelson:

	£	s.	d.
Mr. Tyson, Leghorn, brought away	258		
Ancona by bill	100		
Trieste by bill	150		
Myself	6		
Vienna August 19th	100		
21st	100		
22nd	300		
Sept. 13th	200		
21st	300		
23rd	100		

[1] N.M.M. MS. 9499, Walter collection—written by Nelson: unsigned and undated.

	£	s.	d.
Prague Sept. 29th	100		
Dresden October 6th	100		
Hamburgh October 28th	400		
29th	150		
30th	656		
Yarmouth November	287		
Colchester	50		
Money borrowed	40		
	3397	6	
Mr. Oliver	34	10	

Drawn for and laid out by Lord Nelson between
July 13th and November 18th   3431 16

Spent by Lord Nelson:

	£	s.	d.
To September 13th	111	10	
21st	100		
Wine for Mr. Greffer	12		
Hamburg October 28th	100		
30th	506	13	3
Yarmouth November	58	10	
	988	13	3

Sir William Hamilton:

	£	s.	d.
To September 13th	205		
Hamburg October 28th	50		
Spent total by Sir William H.	255		
To be deducted from the bills drawn	1243	13	3
	3431	16	
To be divided	2188	4	8
Sir William Hamilton's proportion	1094	2	4
	255		
Due Lord Nelson[1]	1349	2	4

[1] There are some errors in Nelson's calculations here.

Lady Nelson to Nelson

I

June 7, 1799
[London]

MY DEAREST HUSBAND,—I have written a very long letter to you this day and took it to the Admiralty. Mr. Davison has just left us, he says an inland messenger leaves town tomorrow and altho' I have nothing to say but God bless you and grant us a happy meeting, I would write.

Mr. Walpole has sent me a letter to forward to you, his son has called but I was out. I am told he is a charming youth. Our father is going to Windsor tomorrow to meet the Bishop of Norwich, some business relative to the Bishop giving him the living of Burnham St. Albans. I have insisted upon his having your carriage and horses and he will return the following day. There he will meet the Rector and his children. I cannot say his manners are better. The roughest mortal surely that ever lived. He frightened Mr. Buckley the other day in desiring me to take Mrs. Nelson and the children in the carriage. However I assured Mrs. B. it was only an odd method he had acquired in speaking. The Walpoles as usual very attentive to me. I had their chairman to go to the drawing room where I was most graciously received.[1]

God bless my dear husband and believe me your affectionate wife, FRANCES H. NELSON.

My love to my Josiah our father's blessing attend you. I hope to see you in the summer.

Right Hon. Lord Nelson, *Vanguard*, Mediterranean.

II

London,
June 18, 1799

MY DEAREST HUSBAND,—I suppose messengers must be frequently going therefore altho' I have nothing to say, my letter shall be sent to Mr. Davison. The anxiety of my mind has been very great since the French fleet passed Gibraltar. Our friends all give me comfort in saying the Commander will never seek you, and before you can hear of the fleet,

[1] The Drawing Room was held in honour of the King's birthday on June 4. Lady Nelson, according to the *Morning Herald*, was 'most magnificently attired in a superb embroidery of silver, in drapery of stripes, with a robe of silver, ornamented to correspond—a beautiful head-dress, with an elegant plumage of ostrich feathers.'

Lord St. Vincent will be after them. I comfort myself it will be so. My prayers are daily offered for you. God bless you. My Josiah is not absent from my thoughts, I think we shall all have a happy meeting before long.

The various passions that torment the Rector discomposes our good father who has been describing them to me. First of all ambition, pride and a selfish disposition. His pride is wounded at the situation of the Boltons. Mr. B.'s[1] glaring impropriety in taking so large a farm, makes everybody talk. Aunt Mary had heard from her neighbours that Mr. B. has a brother-in-law a great lord, that is to pay all his debts, therefore he will be trusted. The Rector last night advanced before our father, Kitty Bolton and myself that both the boys must be brought up gentlemen, and he did not see anything better than their going to sea. The expense of keeping two boys was mentioned, he said, that I know nothing of. Our good father and myself put an end to this extraordinary conversation by holding our tongues, but this morning he came to talk it over with me, and he says Rector does not know what to do with himself. We were very much pressed to make them a visit at Hilboro' (in our way to Burnham) which we promised to do. Our father was speaking of the accommodation, I said 'They have three good bed rooms, Horatio can sleep in his sister's for she will be at school.' That's no matter, Hor. is never to be turned out of his bed again for anyone, so his father says. I never saw a child stand a fairer chance of being spoiled than he does, his ideas will be great indeed.

I have seen Lord Minto, his spirits were not good. His eldest son has been deaf for a twelvemonth. Our good father has had of me £100 since we came to London, he tells me he fears he shall find many heavy bills at Burnham. One he knows of already of £50. My expenses are very great, entirely owing to the dearness of every article of life, for I have never asked any creature to dine with us excepting the 14th February but the family. The Rector says 'When my lord comes home, things will be in better style.' My answer we are keeping two houses, and this is a very expensive one. They leave town on Thursday or Friday. I have just had the pleasure of receiving your letter of April 17th, thank you very much for it. Believe me, God bless you my dear husband your affectionate wife, FRANCES H. NELSON.

Right Honorable Lord Nelson, *Vanguard*, Mediterranean.

[1] Thomas Bolton, who had settled at Cranwich in Norfolk.

III

[Round Wood],
June 30th, 1799

MY DEAREST HUSBAND,—I am sorry I mentioned my indisposition to you a few days back without saying it is a slow fever, altho' not reckoned dangerous is tiresome, and I fret a good deal. The cottage is pleasant now. This winter has shook numbers. We are anxious to hear from the Mediterranean. God grant you are well. My Josiah I hope makes you comfortable. My affectionate love to him.

I mentioned in my former letter our father's receiving your letter of March 16th, he writes this week George Bolton is soon to go to his uncle Maurice who is to fit him out for his sea faring life. They talk of his going with Sir E. Berry who is quite recovered. He is anxious to hear of your determination, whether you stay in that country or make a visit to this. Mr. Davison says he will take you a house. I leave it to him having told your wishes in regard to situation. Our father intends his curate to live in the house at Burnham Thorpe this summer he will be there a few weeks. The Curate's name (Mr.) Wise, he did duty for Dr. Poyntz by the request of Lady Spencer, but finding some things he said not quite to his mind, he thought himself particularly fortunate in being the successful candidate in doing duty for your father.

You will be truly concerned to hear Mr. Barnard is dead, he drank himself mad and died raving. Mrs. Barnard with five sons in great distress. Sir Mordant has for some time spoke his mind of his son-in-law's conduct. Our father thinks all the great connections will raise something comfortable for Mrs. Barnard, I wish it may be so. God protect her. The Rector said Mr. B. was a disappointed man. He expected her great relations would have got him a living.

Mrs. Suckling called yesterday she says Mr. Hume[1] has allowed Colonel Suckling to receive the £60 which Mr. Suckling left his grandson yearly till you come home. The child is with his father and mother near Windsor. I hope they will send him to school. Horace has got the youngest boy. Tom Bolton is to be educated for the East Indies. Report says my rich cousin is coming home. I wonder how we shall stand in her good graces. I hope well. They make fine crops. I beg my best respects to Sir William and Lady Hamilton.

God bless you believe me your affectionate wife, FRANCES H. NELSON.

Mr. Outram the old purser of the *Enterprize* off the Tower has named his 9th child Frances Herbert Nelson, has written two long letters on the

---

[1] Co-executor of Mr. William Suckling's will with Nelson.

subject—the honour—your goodness. I won't forget joking, but Miss Frances must not be at your honours service. I will send her something. The enclosed is from Allens. Love so our father says.

Right Honourable Lord Nelson, *Vanguard*, Mediterranean.

IV

[Round Wood,]
August 18, 1799

MY DEAREST HUSBAND,—I had the pleasure of receiving your letter of the 14th of July. I rejoice in hearing you are well. The disposal of £2500 to your brothers and sisters I should certainly have complied with. No doubt Mr. Marsh would have advanced the money, but as you mentioned the fund it was to come from [East India Company] who I understand does not intend paying the money into any hand but yours, has made me silent on the subject, particularly as our father gave me that advice. However if you wish it to be paid before you come home I daresay Mr. Davison will advance the money, he offered me the money for the purchase of the land at Round Wood, but that seems at a distance. Mr. Sam Bolton says you must pay £500 more than it is worth in order to make your little farm complete, but it is only 50 acres that is at all desirable for you. Here we are at the Parsonage at Burnham. The Rector and Mrs. Bolton are with us.

Our father intended staying only two Sundays, which made me decline going to Wolterton, but he finds more business than he expected therefore our stay is uncertain. The Rector and myself dined at Holkham last Thursday, a full public dinner. The Walpoles were there, as usual kind and very attentive to me, indeed I feel myself particularly obliged to them. It is unnecessary for me to say the Cokes were very attentive. Mr. Hoste and family were there, he says a great deal of your goodness to his son. Mr. Cook desires his best compliments to you and desires that I would assure you how sensible he feels himself obliged to you for your goodness to Hoste.

The coachman I have been obliged to dismiss, appearances were so much against him that our father said it was impossible to keep him. The stable window was opened and all his great coats, besides other articles were taken out. Mr. Ripshaw the Ipswich jailor was sent for, who examined the bricklayers that were repairing the stables and then our servants and I am sorry to say Mr. Ripshaw whose judgement is thought very good, pronounced the coachman the guilty man. Appearances were very much against indeed and since he left your service the servants of the Walpoles give him a very bad character, his treatment of his wife was shocking. She is at service. Our father spoke to him and begged him to give up the company of bad women which it seems he is particularly attached to and our father told him the gallows was the fate of all that was so given. What effect his kind admonition will have, time will discover.

My love to my dear Josiah. Believe me my dear husband, your affectionate wife, FRANCES H. NELSON.

God bless you.

Received Tuesday afternoon 4 o'clock August 1799 Alexander Davison.

Right Honourable Lord Nelson, *Foudroyant*, Mediterranean.

V

Burnham,
September 8, 1799

MY DEAREST HUSBAND,—I received last night your letter of August the 11th. It had been to Round Wood which deprived me of great pleasure for two days. I am obliged to you for it and sincerely hope you are well. Lord H. assures me you are quite well. God grant it is so.

We leave Burnham on Monday we have been here one month. Our good father seems quite tired of the place. Mr. Howard has a son on board the *Alexander*, a second mate, which our father begs you will notice, if the young man is not in that ship he says he is on board some other in the Mediterranean fleet, these are his words. I think you must be almost tired of the situation you hold in the Mediterranean for it seems to be as responsible on shore as on board ship. God bless you and believe me my dear husband to be your affectionate wife, FRANCES H. NELSON.

I am afraid to miss this post. Sir E. B. writes 'you must send me a line immediately'. God be with you. My love to my dear Josiah. Our father's blessing attends you. I hope the King of Naples will remember your services. I should like very much to spend a few months in a warm climate. I sometimes think you will be home before long.

Right Honourable Lord Nelson, *Foudroyant*, Mediterranean.

VI

Round Wood,
September 23, 1799

MY DEAREST HUSBAND,—Mr. Walpole called on Saturday he tells me his son is afloat and hopes you will see him before long. He embarked in the same ship with Lord Elgin. Sir E. Berry I hope you have seen and George Bolton, how does he like the sea? We have very little chat worth your reading.

The papers give an account of the public news, and indeed when we see an acquaintance all our conversation is on the melancholy weather. You can form no idea of the vast quantity of rain that falls daily. Harvest very backward. I have one piece of news to tell you which causes a few 'is it possible?' Admiral Dickson is going to marry a girl of 18 years, surely he has lost his senses. All true, the Admiral saw Miss Willings (a daughter of one of the minor canons at Norwich) not quite three weeks at Yarmouth. He fell desperately in love, gave balls on board ship, then on shore, in short was quite desperate. The friend of Miss W. saw how matters were going on took the young damsel home which caused the Admiral to send an express that arrived at General and Mrs. White's at 12 o'clock at night. The terms were very liberal and handsome. 'The young lady was to do as she pleased.' Mrs. White says she acted with great prudence and the Admiral will soon be married to Miss W. I have seen her, she looks a gentlewoman, and is very much liked.

I hear Admiral and Mrs. Nugent have separated, a difference of temper she says is the cause. I think it will hurt Lady Parker particularly as Mrs. Nugent had a daughter not long ago which I heard had given much happiness to the Admiral. These affairs make little noise for a day. Mrs. Pearson and her daughter are doing very well. She was brought to bed last Friday.

Miss Susanna I took to the concert last Thursday. We were entertained by seeing an old nabob make love to a very rich porter brewer's daughter. The world says her father can give her £20,000 and still she must marry one of the most unpleasant looking men in the world for the sake of driving four horses. I gratified your good father very much in bringing Miss Susanna home with me. I did it I own with some little fear, her temper they say is not very good, she will meet with no contradiction from me, therefore I hope she will be able to conceal it.

We have just heard from Mr. Matcham, Mrs. Matcham is well and she has a daughter. God bless my dear husband.

Believe me your affectionate wife, FRANCES H. NELSON.

Miss Su[sanna] love to you.

Our good father sends his blessing to you. Love to Captain Nisbet.

Right Honourable Lord Nelson, *Foudroyant*, Mediterranean.

VII

Round Wood,
October 14, 1799

MY DEAREST HUSBAND,—The public news you have by the papers, and truly my chit chat is hardly worth your reading, but such as it is you must accept.

Major Dundas Saunders is quartered at Ipswich. Mrs. Godfrey requested me to visit his wife. which I did and conclude it was acceptable from Mrs. D's returning the visit the next day. Our good father is pretty well, the garden affords him great amusement and now and then some of our acquaintance gives him a nosegay.

Lady St. Vincent writes me her Lord recovers very fast. Sir J. Orde has again made himself the subject of conversation.[1] Matters are very properly set to rights by binding him over 'to keep the peace'. Every man who refuses a challenge exalts himself in my opinion. From all this you may suppose the Earl is a first rate favourite. I long to hear from you. My latest date was August 4th. I wonder Lady Hamilton never acknowledged all the prints I requested Mr. Davison to send her. I packed them up myself and Mr. D told me he would send them by the first good opportunity. This is 10 or 11 months back. Make my best regards to her and ask if they are received.

Mr. W. Bolton come bowing to congratulate me on your being created Duke de Bronte and was surprised I had not heard it. It seems all the papers have mentioned it, excepting the *Sun* and *Star*. I hope this news is true if you have money given to support the rank. I assure you I am frightened at the money I spend, every article of life is so dear. Beef 9/4 a stone. Coals very dear. Since Sir E. Berry and his wife dined with us, I have never had any dinner company.

My love to my Josiah God bless you both believe me my dearest husband your affectionate wife, FRANCES H. NELSON.

Our father's love and blessing attend you.

Right Honourable Lord Nelson, *Foudroyant*, Mediterranean.

VIII

[Nicolas, IV, p. 36]

Round Wood,
October 21

MY DEAREST HUSBAND,—Lieutenant Parker[2] called last night at ten o'clock just to tell me you were well on the 8th September. Thank God for it and may you enjoy health and every other blessing this world affords. The young man's extreme gratitude and modesty will never be obliterated

---

[1] Sir John Orde challenged Lord St. Vincent to a duel, which was refused.

[2] Lieutenant Edward Parker, one of Nelson's protégés, had been sent to Vienna with dispatches from the King of Naples and thence to England. He was promoted captain, and died of wounds after the attack on the French flotilla at Boulogne in September 1801.

from your good father's and my memory. He stayed a very few minutes as the express from Vienna was in the chaise at the door. I was so glad to see anyone who could give me such late accounts of my dear husband and my son, that it had such an effect on me that I could not hear or see and was obliged to call in our good father, who made many enquiries and amongst the rest, if you were Duke of Bronte, not but we were well satisfied you were from a letter I received from my Josiah who gave us a very good account where the place was situated and from whence you took your title. Sicily may be a desirable island to have property in probably better than near Naples.

Captain Oswald[1] called last week, he came from Yarmouth and returned immediately as he was going to the Texel. I long to hear of the arrival of Sir William and Lady Hamilton. The carriage the coachmaker let me have during the building of yours is just worn out, at least the coachman says the wheels will not last long, therefore I intend to deliver the old carriage and take the new one down, and any little alterations can be made immediately. Besides all this I should have such a good opportunity of acknowledging and thanking Sir W. and Lady Hamilton for their attention and kindness to you and my son.

Our good father stays at home and Miss S. Bolton is to accompany me. What a sad thing it is those girls cannot or will not conceal these unpleasant tempers. They are, I tell our good father, very young, he says 'True Boltons, I pity the men that marry them but no man will venture.' You will find George Bolton a very affectionate temper. He speaks of Lady Nelson as a very superior creature only six weeks attention to him. The dampness occasioned by the constant rain is beyond description— However we stand high, therefore under no fear of suffering from it, which is no bad thing I assure you.

Mr. and Mrs. Hamilton are arrived in England. I congratulated her on the occasion and received a letter of thanks and full handsome expressions of you and speaks highly of your goodness to my Josiah. She concludes by saying with economy and good crops she hopes to remain in England.

I shall send this letter to Admiral Young. Our good father sends his love and blessing to you. Believe me my dear husband your affectionate wife, FRANCES H. NELSON.

George Tobin and his little dasher are home. Mr. T. wishes as well as G. T. he could be sent to you, if I could give him any information of your movements which I could not.

Right Honourable Lord Nelson, *Foudroyant*, Mediterranean.

---

[1] Captain James Oswald, sent to England with Nelson's dispatches after the liberation of Naples; died 1822.

IX

Round Wood,
October 27

MY DEAREST HUSBAND,—Our good father and myself were highly gratified at the perusal of the King of Naples' letter and grant of the territory attached to the Dukedom of Bronte. God bless you and grant you health and long life to enjoy all this well earned honour.

Mr. Marsh has been successful in getting the East India Company to pay the £10000. He writes me [he] has bought £2000 in the India stock and wishes I would say what was to be done with the £8000 or should he purchase more in the East India stock. Upon the receipt of this intelligence from Mr. Marsh our father the following day asked me what I intended doing in regard to the sum you had desired me to give to your family out of the donation from E.I.C. I said I would write to Marsh to distribute the money you had mentioned if he pleased, but candidly I did not intend noticing your letter 14th of July which contained your desire till I had wrote to you upon this subject. However our father gave me his opinion in these words 'If his brothers and sisters ever hear that you have a letter desiring a portion of the E.I.C. gift to be given to them and you withhold it, I think it will make an irreparable breach between you and them and Horace may say I knew very well what I was about.' Therefore after this conversation I wrote to Mr. Marsh that you had desired me to give £2500 to your father, brothers and sisters and the remainder I was certain he would take care of. I was no judge nor did I wish to interfere in money matters. Our father intends giving the family notice of your donation but wishes me to shew Mr. Marsh your letter of the 14th of July and not send it, particularly as I am partly obliged to go to London. The carriage Mr. Lukin lent me while he was building yours is so very old and crazy that your father thinks I had better take it up myself. The charges of the waggon is pretty high and the coachman wants to change his horses. All these considerations makes it necessary for me to go. He remains at home and Miss S. Bolton is to go with me.

I hope Sir E. Berry has seen you long before this time, as Lady Berry had a letter a week back dated Gibraltar 2nd of October.

I had a letter from my dear Josiah, he was the first that told us of Bronte. He has had a fever. I have since heard that he was better. I hope it is true. My anxiety for my dear son is great. He thinks you will soon be in England.

Our father will write to you very soon. Believe me my dear husband,
FRANCES H. NELSON.

Mr. Berners has been at Bronte. He gives so delightful an account of it, that with great difficulty I refrain from making you a visit, therefore I hope you will consent to my going out, particularly as my health is really very indifferent. I think our father would go with me. Patty Berry says she would go out with me as femme de chambre.

Right Honourable Lord Nelson, *Foudroyant*, Mediterranean.

Post paid 1/8

The Rev. E. Nelson to Mrs. Bolton[1]

Ipswich,
October 29, 1799

MY DEAR,—I think it probable that you may have received a letter dated from Palermo about the same date with ours, wherein your brother has acquainted you with his intentions respecting the succession to the Dukedom of Bronte, first to his elder brother and his sons, in the same manner to William, next to your sons and next to his sister Matcham's sons and so on to his nearest relations.

But I have farther to inform you of a most benevolent act of this good man which is that immediately after he heard of the handsome present made him by the East India Company he wrote to Lady Nelson saying he desired as soon as the money was paid that £500 might be given to each of his brothers and sisters, that is three hundred pounds to be added to the £200 already received by Mr. Bolton from Lady Nelson. That security will be given up as a part of the above donation, the residue viz. £300 is in the hands of your brother's bankers and in about a fortnight he will be ready to receive orders about it. Mr. Bolton will no doubt appropriate this money to such purposes as may be permanently of benefit to you.

God bless and prosper you and yours, EDMUND NELSON.

To Mrs. Bolton, Cranwich, Near Brandon, Norfolk.

Lady Nelson to Nelson

X

London,
November 13, 1799

MY DEAR HUSBAND,—I called yesterday on Lady Spencer who did me the honour of being at home, therefore I delivered your letter which she did

---

[1] N.M.M. MS. 9590, Girdlestone papers.

not open as Admiral Payne was there. She talked much of you and let me into a little bit of a secret which was 'that you were expected at Minorca'. Her ladyship told me you were quite well. I writ you sometime back of my intended journey to London.

I have seen Mr. Marsh, shewed him your letter wherein you desired the money to be paid your brothers and sisters. He said as Mr. Davison had likewise received a letter on the same subject he would certainly pay the money although he had not received the order from you, which was the way it should have come to him. The money will be paid in a few days.

I was ordered to Lisbon by the physician who attends me, he fears the winter will be too severe for me. Not knowing whether you would like my going out of the kingdom I have declined doing it till I have received your positive consent and approbation. Devonshire I mentioned as a warm place. Too much rain and damp weather makes me suffer very much. Round Wood being very cold for our father and myself. I am ordered to spend some months in London and, as early in the year as I can, bathe in the sea. I am to go and brace my nerves. I have had a very bad cough for some time. I leave London in a day or two. Our good father is not so stout as he was last year, he suffered so much from the severity of the winter.

Mr. Reynolds has this instant left me, he requested I would enclose this letter to you stating the merits of a young friend of his who wishes to serve under your command. This friend of his is Mr. Wm. Layman who has served 5 years and 7 months in the Navy. Mr. & Mrs. Hamilton are in London. I understand they will keep an excellent table when they remove into their new house, No. 1 Harley Street. Poor Hamilton much good may do him the prospect of my cousin's great fortune. She was truly glad to see me, made kind enquiries after you and Josiah, declares Mr. H. has never been in his sober senses since he heard of the Battle of the Nile. Mr. H. absolutely cries with joy when he mentions it. Everybody in the West Indies claimed you as their acquaintance who (Mr. H. says) had seen the hem of your garment.

Your carriage is finished, it is really elegantly neat. In the hope of your coming home as Lord Keith leaves London tomorrow for Gibraltar, I will not use the chariot, that I may have the pleasure of seeing you get into it. Lord Hood left London yesterday for Bath. He wishes very much you were in England. Everybody seems to say you will not remain out there now. Indeed I am rejoiced this said Lord is gone. As they would not give you the command in Lord St. Vincent's absence, I think you are more likely to return, than if there had been the least chance of the Earl's going out. From what Lady St. Vincent told me I should suppose it was impossible for him to return to Gibraltar.

I called at Rochetts in my way to town, he wished to see me, but his nerves were so violently affected that even after taking cordial drops he was obliged to send his excuses saying he could not muster courage to see the wife of the man he so tenderly loves, as he does my dear and gallant lord.

Admiral Pole is a father. I sincerely hope the little girl will live. I take for granted the mother is well. I dine today with Mr. and Mrs. Marsh and tomorrow I leave town in order to bring our father comfortably up as soon as a house can be procured for us. Mr. Davison is looking out for one. I am teased with a sad cough. Change of air I hope will remove it. Maurice looks well, he is in high favour just now with the Hilbro' family. The Rector talked of taking lodgings this Christmas in town; if he thinks it is likely for you to be in London, I am sure he will. I long to hear of my dear Josiah. He was very good in writing to me of your creation to the Dukedom of Bronte. I hope he is quite well. Lady Spencer told me *Thalia* was in a shocking state. Give my love to my son, and believe me my dear husband your affectionate wife, FRANCES H. NELSON.

Miss Susanna sends her love to you and George[1].

Right Honourable Lord Nelson, *Foudroyant*, Gibraltar.

XI

Round Wood,
November 25, 1799

MY DEAREST HUSBAND,—I hear from all quarters that you are expected home, indeed Lord Hood seems to speak from authority. The *Sun* etc. positively say that Lord Keith is to have the chief command in the Mediterranean. From all these things I really begin to flatter myself I shall see my dear husband and son before long, as Lady Spencer told me the *Thalia* was in a very bad state. Our good father is not quite so stout as he was last year. His cough is particularly troublesome, however I hope going to a warmer air will be of service, at least the variety of St. James' Street No. 54[2] will amuse him, particularly as he will hear the political news and the chat of the day.

Mrs. Bolton and Kitty came here yesterday in their way to Hollesley. They stay till Tuesday. All our plans for going to London were arranged for Wednesday. Mrs. B and K are to spend a month out when they return to

---

[1] George Bolton. News of his death at sea had not yet reached his family.
[2] The house Mr. Davison had rented for them for the winter.

Cranwich. Mr. Bolton goes to Norwich. Your sister assures me you have made them quite happy. I have had a long letter from the Rector saying everything that was handsome of you and your generosity towards the family and wishes I would give Mr. Windham[1] a gentle hint that nothing has been done for the Nelson family. I read the letter to our father, he was hurt that William was so pressing and dissatisfied, and agreed with me, not to say a word to Mr. Windham. Some women can say or do anything. I cannot and feel happy it is my disposition by which I never get myself into any scrapes.

The weather has been so very bad and of course the roads impassable, therefore we have had very little intercourse. The troops pass the cottage daily from Yarmouth. I hear Lord St. Vincent still continues indisposed. His lady seemed much attached to me therefore I flatter myself we shall often meet. The Admiral is this moment come, he cannot tell me a word of news, only desires his best regards to you.

Bonaparte is the subject now. Round Wood is in good repair even the shrubs are trimmed up and looks smiling all ready to receive my lord. Mrs. Bolton, our father and all the party desire their love. God bless my dearest husband and grant us a happy meeting and soon, believe me your affectionate wife, FRANCES H. NELSON.

XII

St. James Street 54,
December 3, 1799

MY DEAREST HUSBAND,—You see by the date of my letter we are safely arrived in town a small ready furnished house at 7 guineas per week, consisting of two rooms and a light closet on a floor. Quite large enough for you and my Josiah should you think it right for him to come home. Report says you are at Gibraltar. Time will discover, however I sincerely hope what everybody says in this instance may be true. I wish I could give you good accounts of our good father. He is much altered of late, grown feeble and eats very very little indeed.

Mr. Younge has given him some medicine which has been of service his stomach is very weak. Fish and game are the only things he eats. The cheerful situation we are in amuses him and as he sleeps in the back drawing room he is perfectly quiet at night. He assures me he wants for no attention on my part and I feel a consciousness of doing everything that can add one moment to his comfort.

---

[1] William Windham, M.P. for Norwich and Secretary of State for War.

Sir Peter and Miss Parker called upon us. Good Lady Parker was ill. I called to see her on Sunday. She was better her spirits was so agitated when she talked of you, that I found it necessary to make my visit short. She tells me she has written two long letters to you endeavouring to point out the necessity of your coming home. I hope she will succeed.

I am fully persuaded many are jealous of your character and your countrymen in general will allow you are deserving of all that has been done, but for all the world to acknowledge your great abilities is another thing. I hear Lord St. Vincent was at the levee last Wednesday, the following day he was confined to his bed. The command of the Channel fleet it is said he is to have.

Mr. George Mills, his wife and one child leave England very soon for the West Indies, it seems he had outrun everything he had. Lady Hammond called yesterday. She looks well. Sir A. she says is complaining.

Mr. Davison desires me to say he has written to you so fully by the last packet that he will not tease you by this, being fully convinced he shall soon see you. Mr. Davison says your godson is the finest boy in the world. He can almost speak.

I would not conclude my letter before I made my visit to Earl St. Vincent. He speaks of you in the most affectionate manner. I am quite pleased with him. I have just seen Captain Hood.[1] He tells me he hears you are at Minorca half way home. Mr. Nepean has given me an opportunity of sending my letter.

Believe me my dear husband, your affectionate wife, FRANCES H. NELSON.

God bless you.

Right Honourable Lord Nelson, *Foudroyant*, Mediterranean.

XIII[2]

St. James's Street,
December 10, 1799

MY DEAR HUSBAND, I have seen a letter from Lady Berry to Mr. Davison. She tells him of Sir Edward's letter dated *Foudroyant*, Minorca October 18th and mentions you were quite well which I hope is true. I dined a few

---

[1] Captain Samuel Hood, who had assisted in the operations for the recovery of the Kingdom of Naples; died 1814, Vice-Admiral Sir Samuel Hood.
[2] This letter was sold at Sotheby's on July 8, 1905; Lot 130, the property of Mrs L. F. Holding. The text is quoted by Mrs. Gamelin in *Nelson's Friendships*, and by A. M. Broadley in *Chats on Autographs*. The present whereabouts of this letter is not now known.

days back at Mr. Nepean's. He told me you were at Gibraltar. I thanked him for his intelligence. Would have given something to have asked a question, but that could not be done. Therefore I still flatter myself as you are half way we may stand some chance of seeing you. Captain Foley has this instant left me. From what Captain Hood said I was in great hopes Captain F. had very lately seen you. He is full of the Earl's commanding the Channel fleet. Lord Bridport has sailed again.

Our good father received yesterday from your brother William, teazing him about no dignitaries for the Nelson family. I must write to the Rector and beg him not to be so tiresome, for truly I am nursing and doing everything I can to make your father comfortable and then he is quite upset by one of these epistles, for Mr. W. N. requested me to give Mr. Windham a gentle hint.

Sir Peter and Lady Parker called yesterday. We have agreed to go and see the famous French milliner. Lady P. declares they will put me in a sack and send me to Bonaparte. Her spirits are good indeed. She sends Sir Peter to the Admiralty to hear when you are expected home. I don't know what she is *not* to do Dance and grow young. We dined yesterday (Susanna I mean) with the Hamiltons. I wish I could say Mrs. Hamilton is the least modernized of all the antique figures. She is certainly the most. Mr. Morton pays great attention. Bob Jones tells me Forbes has got Mr. M. to sign some papers for him. I long to hear what you have done for Captain Hardy. His character is excellent indeed. Our father has received direction how to proceed in sending to the stage coach for Horace. Susanna Bolton is to go to buy maps in St. Paul's Churchyard to amuse his children. Our good father's love to you and blessing.

God bless and protect my dearest husband, believe me your affectionate wife, FRANCES H. NELSON.

XIV

St. James's,
December 13, 1799

MY DEAREST HUSBAND,—Admiral Young has this instant left me, and has offered to send a letter for me by a very good conveyance, therefore I have just time to tell you we are pretty well. Cold seasonable weather has set in, a cold dry air, which I am told will do us all much good.

I have seen good Captain Locker who delights in talking of you. He dined yesterday with Lord St. Vincent and promised to let me know the news from that house. Admiral Pringle is in town. I have not seen him. Admiral Barrington tells me he is quite well, looking very funny in his new wig which does not cover his ears in the smallest degree. Powder is quite out of fashion. You can't think how very much Lady Martin admires my black locks, but they won't allow that they are black, but a fine dark brown! A great happiness, we are not of the same opinion even in trifles.

Captain Trigg made very kind enquiries after you and I could fill my letter with handsome speeches if I was not afraid of this messenger going away without my letter. Mrs. Hamilton I hear is ill, I called but was not let in. She has sent for a physician but positively refuses to do any one thing he advises. I never beheld a creature with so much patience as Mr. Hamilton. He will get all her money which I think he deserves. God bless you and believe me my dear husband to be your faithful and affectionate wife, FRANCES H. NELSON.

Our good father's love and blessing attend you, had it not been candle light he would have sent you a line. My love to my dear Josiah if he is with you.

Right Honourable Lord Nelson, *Foudroyant*, Mediterranean.

XV[1]

54 St. James' Street,
December 26, [1799]

. . . Captain Hardy[2] has made us all happy by the flattering accounts he give us of your health. I mentioned your letters were written quite out of spirits. He assures me that is owing to the tiresome people you have to deal with. It is impossible to tell you how much pleasure the arrival of Capt. Hardy has given to all our acquaintance. When I enquired after poor George Bolton, Capt. Hardy did not seem to know anything of him. Susanna was surprised, the conversation dropped and Maurice informed me the next morning that the little boy died on his passage from Gibraltar to Minorca. I own at first I was afraid he had fell overboard. Mrs. Bolton and Kitty have been absent from home some weeks, which frets our good father. Your sister assured us Mr. Bolton was quite easy and happy in his circumstances. I repeat all these things as I find one half of my letters never reach you.

Everything you desired to be sent you will receive by the first frigate. Capt. Hardy told me you would be gratified if I sent Lady Hamilton anything, therefore I shall send her ladyship a cap and kerchief such as are

[1] The text of this letter is taken from A. Morrison, *The Nelson and Hamilton Papers*, Vol. II, No. 439. The whereabouts of the original of this and the other four letters taken from Morrison is not now known.

[2] Captain Hardy had returned to England in the *Princess Charlotte* when Sir Edward Berry replaced him as Nelson's flag-captain.

worn this cold weather. I have ordered a suit of cloths for Her Majesty's birthday.[1] I am frightened to tell you the expense of your new chariot, nothing fine about it, only fashionable, £352 harness etc. for one pair of horses.

Colonel Suckling has called several times, and seems highly gratified by my civility. Good Capt. Locker desires I would give his love to you, in short I was to say everything that was kind and affectionate for him, and at the same time I was to tell you he is grown quite old; one of his hands are stiff which prevents him from writing.

Lord Hood is still at Bath. I must write to him. I have seen Capt. Hardy for he is wonderfully anxious for your coming home. The Parkers are in town. Lady P. was kind and attentive to me. Unfortunately Sir Peter in going upstairs with a candlestick in his hand fell backwards, very much bruised and one of his legs cut in several places. No danger is apprehended from the fall, but although this accident happened upwards of a fortnight he is not out of his room. Admiral Pole looks well, desires to be kindly remembered to you.

I am clothed in two suits of flannel and I hope I shall be the better for it. My health is much mended within this month. And Admiral Pringle desires me to tell you he longs to see you. He has been very ill with a complaint in his head. He is better and they give him hopes of getting quite well. He has bought a house and land on the borders of England, 7 miles from a town, which he finds very inconvenient. I am now going to take this letter to Mr. A. Stanhope who sends all your letters, for I cannot bear the idea of your not receiving them when truly I write once a week.

God bless my dearest husband. Our father's blessing attend you. . . .

XVI[2]

St. James',
January 13, 1800

. . . I have had the happiness of seeing Lieut. Leahey he assures me you are well, which I hope is true. Seeing Capt. Hardy and the lieutenant has put me in spirits and makes me well in spite of rheumatism. Maurice has just left us. He tells Capt. Boyle has received all your boxes. I hope Lady Hamilton will like her cap, all I can say it's the whim of the moment. Sir William I find has determined to leave Sicily in the spring. The honourable Mr. Paget[3] I hear is going to Naples by land. He told Mrs. Coleman his

---

[1] January 19. The Drawing Room in her honour was held on January 18, when Lady Nelson attended.

[2] Morrison, Vol. II, No. 442. The text given there is incomplete.

[3] Arthur Paget, ambassador at Naples in succession to Sir William Hamilton 1800–1, died 1840.

stay abroad was very uncertain, 6 months or 6 years. His plate is handsome. Rundall shewed me a few things, and was given to understand the order might be larger.

Admiral Waldegrave called to hear if you are expected home. I told him what the young men told me 'that you were anxious to return home'. He thought you ought, rest would be of service. Our good father came up in hopes of hearing the chat of the day, however the Admiral had an answer to his question and took his leave. He wishes to be continued on the Newfoundland Station, but Maurice thinks he won't have it. Lord St. Vincent keeps himself very snug indeed, for no one sees him. Some say he is ill. (Lord Bridport I hear from his family has no thought of giving up his command.) He promised to give a dinner on the 14th of February I hope he will. Good Capt. Locker wishes his hand would let him write to you. He looks well, but his memory is very so-so, which makes our good father rather impatient, for he cannot bear to hear the same thing twice. I wish I could say his body was as strong as his intellectual powers. I have almost made him promise to consult some physician about that weakness he has had some years which rather increases. I have had a letter from Mrs. Nelson to say she had rather for her daughter to be with me than anybody, therefore she requested I would receive her, and when school opened I would take her there. The rector she thought would go to London with his children therefore they will all be in London in a few days.

I have paid for your new carriage £342. You will be astonished to find how very expensive everything is grown since you left England, and I sometimes flatter myself it will not be many months before you are convinced of it in person. Our father sometimes seems to have an inclination to go to Bath late in the spring. Mr. Matcham is recovered from his late alarming indisposition. He had lost the use of all his limbs, owing to a cold which was attended by a bilious fever. Mrs. M. wrote to her father they had an offer to sell Shepherd Spring, but they would not do it if they thought you would wish to purchase it. £5000 was the sum offered. Mr. Nelson desired I would answer the letter for him, which I did saying it was impossible for me to say much on the subject, but that from your letters I had no idea of your wishing to make any new purchases, and that Mr. Nelson thought that if they could sell it to advantage it would save them a great deal of trouble hereafter. Mr. Matcham is determined whenever we have peace to go to France, and if there is anything like an established government numbers will do the same. Lord Keith is gone to Minorca. We are anxious to hear if he intends going to Sicily. Some say he will. . . .

2 N

Charlotte Nelson to Mrs. William Nelson[1]

[London,
January 1800]

MY DEAR MAMA,—I thank you for your kind letter and I hope you will find me very much improved in my music when I come home. Papa and my aunt and myself went to Whitelands[2] yesterday and saw Miss Vetch. My aunt went in some of the rooms and thinks it is a very nice house and garden. I think I shall like Miss Vetch very well. I go to school on Monday next. I believe the Miss Tollemaches come next Tuesday. I thank you for your kind offer of giving me a guinea when I get six guineas for my pearl ear-rings.

You will be much surprised to hear I and my aunt and Papa and Captain Hardy went to a grand ball and supper on Tuesday. Captain Hardy danced with me several dances. It was an accident that I went too, my aunt found out I was invited. I enjoyed it very much. Papa went in Susanna's[3] place, as she was not well enough to go. We came home at two o'clock. My aunt was so kind as to lend me a pair of pearl ear-rings and a wreath of flowers to wear on my head and a pair of white kid gloves. So I did very well. My aunt and Papa dined out yesterday.

Papa took my stool to have it done and it is not half big enough. I must take it to school to finish it. My aunt will send by Papa some lamb's wool to do her a handkerchief. Papa has seen Mrs. Stable, and she is to get me some more of it to match my pelisse.

Papa will tell you all the news. I cannot think of any thing more to say. Give my love to my aunt and Mrs. Micklethwaite. I think I shall not write to you any more before I go to school. My aunt is so good as to order me a cake to take with me to school. Susanna still continues very poorly. I remain your dutiful daughter, C. M. NELSON.

To Mrs. Nelson.

Lady Nelson to Nelson

XVII

St. James's Street 54,
February 4

MY DEAREST HUSBAND,—My day of writing to you is come and although I have no one thing to amuse you, still I feel uncomfortable if I do not send you a sheet of paper, therefore accept my best.

[1] N.M.M. MS. 9292, Bridport papers.
[2] The school in Chelsea.
[3] Her cousin, Susanna Bolton, who was nineteen.

Sir William and Lady Calder have made me two visits before I took it into my head to call upon them once. It certainly shows her extreme anxiety for the honour of my acquaintance. Whether I am flattered to be so noticed is another thing. Some I hear thinks she can be very ill natured if she pleases, and a little envy sometimes will intrude on her ladyship's mind.

I called yesterday on Lady Minto, her carriage was at the door therefore I did not gain admittance. I must send the footman to enquire where Colonel Drinkwater is to be found. I like him very much.

We have a sad sick house, every servant one after the other, Susanna very ill with a bilious complaint in her bowels and fever. This day is the sixth she has had a physician. She is better and will be quite well in a few days. Our good father was very ill yesterday, the weakness in his body was so much increased that he could not assist himself, therefore he sent for Mr. Younge who took a surgeon into his room (Mr. Hawkins) who replaced his body up, immediately he had relief and is much better this morning.

I am now going into the city to send this letter by the foreign post. Therefore I flatter myself you will get a few of my epistles. Lord St. Vincent is still ill. Mr. Nepean told me yesterday it was the stone and not the cruel thing they had said of the Earl—poor Earl I had not heard the fashionable report. They are going to Rochetts immediately. I have seen Mr. Palmer who made many kind enquiries of you. I have written to my son and directed his letters to Palermo. I hear the weather is delightful there. The sun does shine upon us today, it's quite a treat.

Maurice was out of town all last week. He promised to see our father today. Mr. Davison often calls and tells him the chat of the day. I don't see much of the Hoods, but they are all well and very much with the Princess of Wales. Mr. Walpole calls frequently. Our good father's love and blessing attend you. God bless you and believe me my dear husband, your affectionate wife, FRANCES H. NELSON.

Right Honourable Lord Nelson, *Foudroyant*, Palermo, Mediterranean.

XVIII

February 11, 1800

MY DEAREST HUSBAND,—I wrote to you last Monday and thought it was right to mention that our good father was very indifferent and I am sorry to say he is not better. Surgical assistance has been very necessary, from extreme weakness his body comes down too frequently, even turning in his bed quickly. Mr. Hawkins has taught our father's servant (who is a good man) to put it up, which he has done these last 48 hours. The least difficulty arising Mr. Hawkins is sent for, day or night. A supression of urine alarmed us all and he has been obliged once to have it drawn off. Mr. H. said he never relieved any person with so little difficulty. But he was the day following sent for for the same purpose, but nature relieved him and he has had no difficulty since. I was not satisfied with the advice of one physician, therefore I desired Dr. Baillie to attend which he did. He approved of everything which had been done or given, rich cordials with some few drops of bitters are the only thing taken as medicine. The laudanum is given in ejections. Be assured my dear no one thing that can can be done for our good father shall be omitted. I flatter myself no one of his children can pay him more attention than he has. His affection for me is great his opinion of me will gratify you. I cannot tell you what he says of me. The two physicians and the surgeon and Mr. Young will remember it. This best of men often talks of you. He told me when he thought and talked of you he shed tears but now he could not relieve himself in that way. When every one was loud about your coming home, he did not expect you because you had not written to me on that subject. Mr. Davison desires me to tell you he has given in your claim as commander for your share of prize money for the Spanish ships that were taken some months back and that he will answer your letter of the 9th December this day.

We were very glad to see your letter to Mr. Davison as I have not received any letter from you since Captain Hardy. If my Josiah is with you give my love to him. God bless you our father sends his blessing to you. Believe me my dear husband your affectionate wife, FRANCES H. NELSON.

The physicians and surgeon say they see no immediate danger in any of our good father's complaints.

The Right Honourable Lord Nelson, *Foudroyant*, Palermo, Mediterranean.

XIX[1]

St. James's Street,
February 17, [1800]

... My two letters to you last week was written very much out of spirits. Our dear father was extremely ill, I never thought of seeing him again

[1] Morrison, Vol. II, No. 454.

sitting by the fireside. That pleasure I have really had. He is very, very weak. He tells me he thinks he may go on for some time longer. The fabric has had such a shake that it can never recover its former strength. I rejoice to see him free from pain and I hope he will remain so. He would not allow any of his children to make him a visit. I think the Matchams will be here in the spring. They are gone into Hampshire to conclude the business of the sale of Shepherd's Spring. These are the chief articles of family news.

A sad account of Captain Pearson's health.[1] He has had a relapse of the yellow fever. I am truly sorry for it. His leave of absence went out some time back. I have seen Admiral Bligh. His account of that terrible fever is truly frightful. He made many enquiries of you.

Colonel and Mrs. Suckling have left town. It was not in my power to show them any civilities. Maurice Suckling has taken a farm within a mile of Horace Suckling. Mr Maurice Nelson told him sailors seldom make good farmers. He said he would do his best. In consequence of our father's illness, I declined going to Mr. Walpole's last night. By way of persuading me, she mentioned that the Prince of Wales, two of his brothers, and the Stadholder, the Duke of Gloucester if he could and a great many fine people. I believe she will give me up for being too humdrum. Sir Peter and his family are all gone into their new house in Wimpole Street. It seems a large handsome house. Lady Berry is expected at Kensington next week. John Berry and his wife are on the eve of embarking for America. The Walpoles are still in the country. Mr. W. Bolton has been staying at Bath for three weeks. He called yesterday. I was not at home. Our father had him up to ask how the four kings went on. Very high play, higher than ever.

Mr. Higgins has written to me on the subject of one of his sons going to sea, a lad 15 years of age. I do not know what to do. Capt. Hardy and everybody was very uncertain of your coming home, therefore I asked Capt. Foley to take him, and he joins the *Elephant* this week. As to public news, the papers give you a full and perfect account. Mrs. Hamilton is a perfect recluse in Harley Street, neither stirs out nor admits any inside her house. Susanna has recovered from her illness, we think she must go home, she requires a great deal of exercise, which she cannot have with me. Our dear father intends writing to you.

God bless you and believe me . . .

My love to my dear son.

[1] Captain Pierson died on his way home from Honduras in 1801.

XX

February 23, 1800

MY DEAR HUSBAND,—Sir Andrew Hammond called this morning not only to give me notice of his son's [1] going to the Mediterranean but to offer me every accommodation the *Champion* could afford if I had a wish to go out to you. I told Sir A. I had the desire, but without your leave I could not think of undertaking the voyage. You may be assured I felt much obliged to them for thinking of me.

I hope our good father is generally free from pain, he is grown much thinner, at times cheerful. He has tried twice to take an airing but thinks it irritates his bowels and causes him much pain. In a day or two I shall persuade him to try a sedan chair. He rises when he can, about 9 o'clock, dines by himself at 4 and sits up till 7 if he can. I think I have given you an exact diary of his movements, with all his years and infirmities he thinks he shall last some time unless a sudden change takes place. He told me yesterday he did not think he could ever leave London. The country surgeons were not to be compared to the London ones and he should be afraid of being butchered like poor Mr. Rolfe, therefore I cannot say anything of my returning to the cottage at present. I have never left him since this severe illness, but once, that was at his own desire to dine at Mr. Davison's who had a cheerful dinner company.

I have been sadly tormented with coughs and by no means very stout yet. However a little hot sea bathing I am told is to make me quite well. The Matchams are anxious to see our father, who seems at times to consent to their coming in my absence. I shall leave him quite easy if I think he is well enough to be left provided one of his daughters are staying in the house.

How sadly tormenting the Rector has been in consequence of the Bishop of Bangor's death, such a long letter he had written our dear father, telling him of your letters to him, extracts of my letters in '97, which only tend to shew your anxiety to get him some dignitary in the church. He now wishes your good father or myself would make some stir, by reminding Mr. Windham or the Chancellor of his promise to you. He wants to tie down the Chancellor to provide for him, so soon as Mr. Methold has a stall. Our good father wrote him a very handsome letter 'telling him if a stall at Norwich was the ultimatum of his ambition he had better at once say so to you, when you had an opportunity of saying so you would and as to my taking any steps to accomplish his wishes it was impossible', therefore he hoped he would rest quiet.

[1] Captain Graham Hamond. Died, Admiral Sir Graham Hamond, 1862.

I have got the flower seeds you sent me, a gardener who works for Round Wood will raise a few for us. Lady Berry is at Kensington. They tell me she is six months gone with child. She is not in the least increased in size. She is to spend a few days with me and to take half Susanna's bed. It will be coming to London, that is the only variety I can offer her. Now it is quite out of the question any person dining with me but Maurice, and I have not been to one public place since I came to London, altho' the Parkers have once kindly offered me two tickets for the opera.

I had some difficulty to prevail on myself to go to the Queen's birthday, I am glad I did it. Admiral Christopher Parker[1] has been dangerously ill. Lady P. tells me he is better. Our good father made me promise to dine with them next Tuesday. God bless and protect my dear husband, believe me your affectionate wife, FRANCES H. NELSON.

I beg my love to my dear Josiah who I hope is with you. Capt. Locker desired me to send a copy of a note.

'Mr. Evined's compliments to the Lieut. Governor and thanks him very kindly for his attention, his wishes are that the Lieut. Governor will be so good as to intercede with Lord Nelson to appoint Mr. James Browne Boyd now a mid. in the *Northumberland* to be a lieutenant.' 3 February 1800.

Have you ever seen the lad Miss Nisbet asked you to notice on board Captain Ball?

Right Honourable Lord Nelson, *Foudroyant*, Mediterranean. By favour of Capt. Hammond.

XXI

St. James's Street,
March 4, 1800

MY DEAREST HUSBAND,—I wrote to you last Monday by Captain Hammond who was to have sailed immediately but now I hear he is waiting for the merchant ships that are going to the Mediterranean. I have not had the pleasure of hearing from you since Capt. Hardy which you will allow is a great while, at least I think it an age.

Mr. Falonnetté sent me one of the silver medals that have been struck at Birmingham (for the King of Naples) in honour of the Battle of the Nile, highly gratifying to me and truly honourable to you. The description would fill my sheet of paper, therefore shall only say it represents

[1] Son of Sir Peter Parker; died 1804.

the *Foudroyant* on the 10th of July 1799 going into Naples. I hope his Majesty will very soon take it seriously into his mind to return to his beautiful capital. Surely men's minds must be quiet now or they never will be.

I think you will be surprised when I tell you our good father is sitting for his picture. Sir W. Beechey is the fortunate man.[1] You must know it is a profound secret. I was to [go to] Sir W. B. ask his price, look at his pictures and then enquire whether he would go to an invalid. The answer 'No' puzzled me, however I said sometimes general rules were broken thro'. Sir W. finding I was rather anxious about this picture said, that really he never went to any person excepting the King and Royal family, the Duke and Duchess of York had that instant left the house. I knew that. 'But Madam may I ask who is the gentleman?' 'Yes Sir, my Lord Nelson's father.' 'My God, I would go to York to do it, yes Madam directly.' He was as good as his word, and has been here twice. I think the likeness will be an exceeding good one. I don't know whether the picture is for you or me.

Mr. Drake called yesterday he is preparing for his journey to the continent. The picture is for you, so I hear this morning. Mr. Davison called yesterday. He says he has written to you.

Mrs. McArthur has kindly brought me your picture which Abbott has drawn for Mr. McArthur[2] with the chelengk . . . [*part of the letter missing*] cats and dogs. I am told not a creature is asked inside of her house. Mrs. Morton was telling me all this. I therefore said it was fortunate Mrs. K. had her brother's house to go to.

My love to my dear Josiah.

Right Honourable Lord Nelson, *Foudroyant*, Palermo, Mediterranean.

XXII[3]

St. James's Street,
March 15, 1800
No. 11.

MY DEAR HUSBAND,—Admiral Young has called to tell me of this conveyance and have just time to say our good father continues to mend, and

---

[1] The portrait is now in the National Maritime Museum.

[2] John M'Arthur, joint editor of the *Naval Chronicle* 1799–1818 with the Rev. J. S. Clarke, and biographer of Nelson. A biographical memoir of Nelson was published in the *Naval Chronicle* in 1800 with a portrait by Abbott showing the *chelengk* in Nelson's hat.

[3] N.M.M. MS. 9960, Croker collection in the Phillipps papers. This is the only letter of Lady Nelson's in this collection.

he sometimes talks of returning to Round Wood when I return from the hot sea bathing which I sometimes flatter myself will be of service to me.

I shall make you smile at my economy. My birthday suit could not be worn after Easter therefore I took the first tolerable Thursday to pay my respects at St. James's which was last Thursday.[1] Our gracious King thought it was a long time since I heard from you, and told me the wind was changed therefore he hoped I should hear from you very soon. The Queen always speaks to me, with so much condescension that I like her very much. And Lady Harrington endeavoured to persuade me to make you a visit. Spoke of the climate how necessary it was to me who had so bad a cough. She little knew how much virtue I had in not going out.

Is my dear son with you? I hope he is. The neutral vessels that were taken by Captain Foley and himself are to be considered as prizes, therefore tell him how to send his money home. Mr. Marsh tells me private bills are very dangerous. With your affectionate advice he will do all things right. A little independence he will find a great comfort.

Aunt Mary is very ill. Mr. Nelson from the letters from Hilbro' does not think she [can] last long. To give you an idea of the extreme danger our father was in, when he was able to sit up the physician called to see him, and when he found him in the parlour, he told me he had seen a prodigy! Mr. Nelson in the parlour. Our good father wrote to you during his illness. His love and best love attend you.

God bless you is the sincere wish of your affectionate wife, FRANCES H. NELSON.

My love to my dear Josiah. The Berrys, the world says, are grown very great indeed. How could they give out Lady B. was with child?

Right Honourable Lord Nelson, *Foudroyant*, Mediterranean.

XXIII[2]

St. James's Street,
March 24, [1800]

. . . The Admiralty yesterday received letters from Lord Keith dated 21st January. He mentions your joining him in good health. Thank God for it. I hope you have seen my Josiah, that you love him not for my sake but his own. Our good father is wonderfully recovered, but still very feeble. Aunt Mary's death has hurried him. Many letters from the Rector passed on the occasion. The will was in our father's possession, but many memorandums were found in chests of drawers. Mrs. Goulty is left £150. Mrs.

---

[1] March 13. [2] Morrison, Vol. II, p. 472.

Rolfe £20 or £30 for the repairs of the house, Charlotte £20. The Rector writes to his father 'Knowing you were left everything, Mrs. Nelson or myself never made use of undue influence with my aunt in her last illness.' And in the same letter hopes with your father's assistance to purchase the house which is left to Mrs. Rolfe as she intends selling it. Our father observed the necessity of committing the Rector's letter to the flames, which I think he has done. I should not be surprised to see Mr. and Mrs. W. Nelson in town about Easter as our father told W. N. his children should spend the holidays with him. Charlotte can be accommodated, but where Horace will be put I can't tell.

Mrs. Miller called and requested you would have the goodness to notice the young man she recommended to you, and gave me a letter to forward to Mr. Vernon Gambier Yates, midshipman on board *Le Tigre*, which I shall this day take to Lombard Street. Capt. Kelly is in town for a few days. I asked what he intended doing in regard to the legacy. 'They know it's due, and I shall be glad to receive it.' 'I will speak to Morton about it.' But I have seen such terrible quarrels in my own family about money that I dread to say a word. Between you and I they are paying Mrs. Hamilton great court. I spoke to Mrs. Hamilton and requested that it might be paid. It had been due upwards of 12 months. What will be done time will discover. The Parkers are very attentive and kind to me. Admiral Parker is in a very ill state of health. Lord St. Vincent is still confined to the house. It has been said his Lordship neglected his health too much in Italy. Lady St. Vincent told me she now began to hope he would get well.

We see very little of Maurice. I will thank you to notice Capt. Hammond. His father and mother have been very civil to me. I had last night the pleasure of reading your letter to our father dated Palermo February 7th. It made him cheerful and I believe made him sit up one hour later. I hope *Thalia* will be your last stay in the Mediterranean, for my son would not like England without you.

So many new fashions about visiting, that were I to attempt to give you an idea it would fill a sheet.

God bless you and believe me . . .

XXIV[1]

March 29, [1800]

. . . I have this instant received a note from Admiral Young who tells me if I can send him a letter for you in an hour he will send it, therefore I have only time to say I have at last had the pleasure of receiving two

[1] Morrison, Vol. II, No. 473.

letters from you dated January 20th and 25th. I rejoice exceedingly I did not follow the advice of the physician and our good father to change the climate, and I hope my health will be established by hot sea bathing and the warmth of the summer.

I can with safety put my hand on my heart and say it has been my study to please and make you happy, and I still flatter myself we shall meet before very long. I feel most sensibly all your kindnesses to my dear son, and I hope he will add much to our comfort. Our good father has been in good spirits ever since we heard from you. Indeed my spirits were quite worn out, the time had been so long. I thank God for the preservation of my dear husband, and your recent success off Malta. The taking of the *Genereux* seems to give great spirits to all. God bless you my dear husband and grant us a happy meeting, believe me . . .

Our father's love and blessing attend you. I don't seal my letter with black least I should alarm you. My love to my dear Josiah.

XXV[1]

St. James's Street,
15th [April, 1800]

MY DEAR HUSBAND,—Mr. Marsh last Thursday had the goodness to bring me your letter of February 27th and one enclosed without a direction, therefore he desired to open it before me, and we found it was for Maurice. I wished you had been in better spirits. I know your health depends greatly on your mind being at ease. I think when Malta surrenders and the Royal family once more quietly seated in their old capital, you will feel yourself at liberty to think of your health and affairs and to show yourself in England. John Bull's eyes sparkle at the sound of the battle of the Nile, and I think your presence would be of service. However your own wishes and experience must be a better guide than anything I can possibly have to offer.

I write so often that truly I have little to say as I have been confined from going into hot rooms owing to a rash which was very troublesome, but am better. Our good father has been rather indisposed for a day or two, but he is better and talks of going in three weeks to Round Wood. He goes by himself, that is to say he takes his servant with him, he talks of being three days on the road. I have offered to stay in London or the neighbourhood if he wishes it. He says no. I am rather alarmed at his going so far from those who have been of service.

[1] The last letter of the collection now in the British Museum (Add. MS. 34988).

Capt. Hardy is returned to town and was to make his bow to Lord Spencer this day. Susanna desires me to tell you Capt. Parkinson is married to a young woman with little or no money. Capt. Hardy is quite concerned at this rash action. Bad health and poverty he says is too much. I can [only] say he called upon me not long ago when he left his crutch at the drawing room door, and one leg still wrapped up in flannel. Hardy says he hears the young woman in Dorsetshire thinks more of a good —— and good settlements than anything else.

Mr. Davison desires me to tell you he has been shut up several days with lawyers and will not write to you till he can give you an account how matters are going on. Lord St. Vincent's conduct in this affair has not pleased him, however he is sanguine and thinks your claims will be attended with success. I hope he is right. You can form no idea of the sum of money it takes to live in the style of a gentleman's family. Mr. D. says 'he shan't lose one farthing that I can get'.

Your affectionate wife my dear husband, FRANCES H. NELSON.

P.S. [*written by Charlotte Nelson, daughter of the Rev. W. Nelson*]

MY DEAR UNCLE,—Here I am very happy and very well and expect to see you home very soon. I am afraid my aunt is going out of town very soon or I should be much happier. CHARLOTTE MARY NELSON.

Charlotte begged that she might write you a letter. Our father's blessing attend you.

Right Honourable Lord Nelson, *Foudroyant*, Leghorn, Mediterranean.

To the care of Messrs. Littledale and Co. Double letter paid 2/-.

Chapter 7

LOVE LIES BLEEDING
1800–1831

Introduction

Admiral Nelson, the Hamiltons, Mrs. Cadogan, who was Lady Hamilton's mother, Miss Knight and the servants made a triumphal journey across Europe, and on their arrival at Yarmouth on Thursday, November 6, 1800, Nelson was given a hero's welcome by his countrymen. The Hero of the Nile was home again at long last and John Bull forgot his customary English phlegm, and deputations and cheering crowds reminded Nelson of the carnivals at Naples two years before. His inseparable friends the Hamiltons were fêted with him. Nelson had written to his friend and business agent Davison from Vienna asking for a house, 'not too large, yet fitted for my situation', to be rented for him in London for a short period, to be ready for his arrival, adding that he should not want to remain in town longer than a month. On landing at Yarmouth he wrote to the Admiralty announcing that his health was now perfectly re-established and that he wished to serve immediately. Indeed, he later, as soon as he had hoisted his flag again, requested that his journey home might be considered as his official removal from the Mediterranean to the Channel fleet and that he might receive full pay over that period, which was refused. On Friday evening, or Saturday, Nelson and the Hamiltons arrived in London, having been acclaimed along the route.

His wife and father were waiting for him at Nerot's Hotel in King Street, on the site until recently occupied by the St. James's Theatre. It is stated that his wife's reception of him was cold and she has been blamed for not meeting him at Round Wood, where he had called with the Hamiltons on the road to London, although he had recently ordered her, by letter from Vienna, to wait for him in London. Likewise, she has been blamed for remaining in England and not joining her sick husband in the Mediterranean. Again, she had obeyed his orders. And this despite Lady Hamilton's kind invitation to stay with them at Naples. Lady Hamilton had also suggested to Nelson that Lady Nelson, she and the Queen of Naples would together form a female counterpart of the Nelson-Hamilton

'Tria juncta in uno', Lady Hamilton, it will be noticed, having the distinction of belonging to both sets. But Nelson had not wanted his wife's
presence at that time, and since then had fallen entirely, when not on
active service, into dependence on Lady Hamilton's attentions. Lady
Minto wrote home from Vienna describing how Lady Hamilton must sit
by his side to cut his meat whilst he carried her pocket handkerchief.
He seldom smiled, except when she whispered to him.

The Earl of St. Vincent, now commander-in-chief of the Channel
fleet, wrote from Torr Abbey, his headquarters ashore, to Nepean, who
had served as his secretary and was now the secretary of the Admiralty,
on November 9. It is evident from Lord Nelson's letter to you on his
landing, that he is doubtful of the propriety of his conduct. I have no
doubt he is pledged to getting Lady Hamilton received at St. James' and
everywhere, and that he will get into much brouillerie about it.' St. Vincent
was a shrewd man of the world. Sir William Hamilton had come home
in disfavour with the ministry. There was no chance of his wife being
received at court, nor was he likely to press the matter, for he was anxious
to secure a pension or further employment, as well as compensation for
his house and property wrecked at Naples. Malta had fallen to British
forces on September 5 and he even considered being appointed the
governor, as this step would please the King of Naples, who claimed the
island.

When the party reached London, Miss Cornelia Knight, who had
long enjoyed the Hamiltons' friendship and hospitality, was warned by
Troubridge to break loose from their way of life and disreputable set of
friends and she went to live with the Nepeans, the family of the secretary
of the Admiralty. There is no reason to suppose that Lady Nelson, who
had regularly entertained serving officers home from her husband's fleet,
was ignorant of what was now common knowledge amongst Nelson's
service friends, that he was making a fool of himself with Lady Hamilton.
But, though her reception of him may have been cool, all for a time was
outwardly well. On Sunday, November 9, as was reported in the press,
Nelson visited Lord Spencer, First Lord of the Admiralty, and perhaps
the man most responsible for sending him to fight the battle of the Nile.
The Admiral was 'decorated with his stars of the different orders with
which he had been invested for his brilliant achievements in the Nile:
and also the medal descriptive of Earl St. Vincent's action.' That day, his
family dined with the Hamiltons at Nerot's Hotel. On the Monday he
again went to the Admiralty in the morning, this time in undress uniform,
after which on his way to the Navy Office at Somerset House he was
recognized and mobbed in the Strand and had to take refuge in the Navy

Office, where his brother Maurice worked. In future, he was always in danger of being mobbed whenever he was recognized in the streets, and he was easy to recognize, in or out of uniform, with his empty right sleeve. The little admiral had become a national hero. That Monday was the Lord Mayor's day, held over from the Sunday. With Sir William, also asked to the feast, Nelson joined the procession on its return, and the citizens took the horses from his carriage when it had reached the top of Ludgate Hill, and drew him to the Guildhall. There, after a sumptuous repast, he was presented with an elegant sword.

Nelson, with his wife and father, stayed on at Nerot's Hotel until the end of November, when a house was taken at 17 Dover Street. The Hamiltons moved to 22 Grosvenor Square, lent them by William Beckford, until the new year, when their own house was ready at 23 Piccadilly. Newspaper accounts show that they all went to the theatre together several times and Nelson led a very social life. So much so, that St. Vincent, who read about it in his newspapers, wrote and kindly warned him against city feasting 'for there is much risk of illness in going out of smoking hot rooms into the damp putrid air of London streets.'

Tuesday, November 11, Nelson spent at the Duke of Clarence's apartments by invitation. On the 12th he and Sir William attended a levée at St. James's and the admiral was presented to the King in full-dress naval uniform, wearing his aigrette, the diamond-studded *chelengk* or plume of triumph given him by the Sultan of Turkey, in his hat, the medallions of the King and Queen of Naples, his orders, and the sword presented to him by the City of London. He told his friend Collingwood of this levée a few weeks later and Collingwood put in a letter from Cawsand Bay: 'He gave me an account of his reception at court, which was not very flattering, after having been the admiration of that of Naples. His Majesty merely asked him if he had recovered his health; and then, without waiting for an answer, turned to General ——, and talked to him near half an hour in great good humour. It could not be about his successes.'

There was a simple explanation of Nelson's cool reception by the King. He came to court decorated with foreign insignia and orders, for the wearing of which he had not obtained the King's formal permission. For a period Nelson altered his signature from the 'Bronte Nelson' or 'Bronte Nelson of the Nile' he had used abroad to plain 'Nelson'. He got the royal licence in January 1801 to use his title of Duke of Bronte, but it was not immediately gazetted. After this he signed himself 'Nelson and Bronte'. The same day as the levée Lord and Lady Nelson dined with the Spencers at the Admiralty. Lady Spencer was a great gossip and she used to compare this dinner with the other dinner before Nelson had sailed in the *Vanguard* for the Nile campaign. She had insisted that Nelson brought his wife to dinner again. She found his conduct utterly changed. He treated his wife 'with every mark of dislike, and even of contempt.' After dinner, Lady Nelson 'peeled some walnuts, and offered them to him in a glass. As she handed it across the table Nelson pushed it away from him, so roughly that the glass broke against one of the dishes.' Lady Nelson burst into tears. 'When we retired to the drawing-room,' Lady Spencer told Lady Shelley, 'she told me how she was situated.' Nelson was cross after his rebuff at the levée and Lady Nelson had broken down before company which was looking for evidence of the tension of which they knew the cause. The next day Lady Nelson was presented to the Queen at a Drawing Room, and her husband came too, attended by captains who had fought at the Nile, including Hardy, who who were all introduced to her Majesty.

It seems likely that when the *Morning Herald* sketched Lady Hamilton's profile for the benefit of its readers in the issue for November 13, the editor had in mind this Drawing Room to which the ambassador's wife had not been invited. Charles Greville, a member of the King's Household, kept his uncle accurately informed as to how his reputation stood both at court and with the Secretary of State's department. He had patiently waited in London so as not to be absent when Sir William returned and he cautioned him to wait on Lord Grenville immediately and before attending the levée. Sir William had been the foster-brother of George III, but as his mother, Lady Jane Hamilton, was the favourite of Frederick, Prince of Wales, this relationship may not have increased his esteem in the eyes of the Queen, who was determined not to receive his second wife at court. We need not blame her prudence, because Sir William's family were of the same way of thinking, and only called on Lady Hamilton and received her visits occasionally because they did not wish to offend an old man of whom they were genuinely fond. They regretted his idolatry and thought the company he now kept doubtful. There was Prince Augustus, later the Duke of Sussex, foreigners and English friends from Naples, but few ladies except those who had been at Naples. A member of the family reported on their appearance: 'Sir William is very thin, much aged, and stoops; but is very cheerful, and has the same pleasing countenance. I was much disappointed in Lady Hamilton. Expected much elegance of figure and manner; she has neither, is tall, and very large. Has good eyes and teeth and much cheerfulness and expression of countenance, of an open disposition. Was not in the least

PLATE XV. Caricature by J. Gillray, published in 1801, of Lady Hamilton as 'Dido in Despair', as Nelson, her 'Aeneas', sails away.

embarrassed, yet behaved with propriety. Too much dress, more a striking figure for the stage, than the elegance of good taste, but very decent. Her neck much covered, and long sleeves, a kind of Turkish dress. She appears much attached to Sir William and he is in much admiration, and I believe she constitutes his happiness. I cannot but lament this idolatry.'

On November 17 Lord Nelson took his seat for the first time in the House of Lords. On December 4, the newspapers reported a visit lately made by the Nelsons and Hamiltons to the Marquis of Abercorn, a distinguished connection of Sir William's. And on the 16th they were reported as having recently been entertained by Mr. Walpole, a family with which Nelson was proud to claim relationship. But Nelson, leaving his lady behind, spent a long Christmas week enjoying festivities and mock pageantry at Fonthill, William Beckford's remarkable folly near Salisbury. Here Lady Hamilton enchanted a large and distinguished company with a performance of her famous attitudes, in which, with a few properties such as a shawl and a scarf and Sir William holding up a candle, she transformed herself into Agrippina bearing the ashes of Germanicus and then swiftly changed into some other classical pose, to the delight of her charmed spectators. Well had Horace Walpole nicknamed her Sir William Hamilton's 'gallery of statues'. Beckford, immensely rich, hoped his kinsman, Sir William, might use his waning influence to obtain him a peerage, for a consideration, and Nelson added his advice to the schemes which were being hatched, but without effect. Mrs. Cadogan was one of the party, and Lady Nelson's absence must have been remarked upon.

On the last day of the old year his Majesty was 'conducted from the Presence Chamber to the Throne in the House of Lords by the noble Admirals Nelson and Hood.' On January 1, 1801, Nelson was promoted Vice-Admiral of the Blue, and attended a levée and was presented in company with other recently promoted admirals on the 7th. On the 9th he received orders to hoist his flag on board the *San Josef*, his Spanish prize taken off Cape St. Vincent, and now lying fitted out and ready for him at Plymouth.

His early biographer, Harrison, writing under Lady Hamilton's tutelage, describes Nelson's unhappiness at home, caused by his wife's haughty conduct towards his family and their children, whom he wished to ask to stay. Quarrels drove him to take long and exhausting night walks through the streets of London, before sheltering with his friends the Hamiltons in the early hours. Whether these tales are inventions or exaggerations, no doubt Nelson and his wife were both unhappy. Originally the niece of the President of Nevis had been the social superior, but now Nelson, who had hobnobbed with royalty, had little in common with an

2 o

English gentlewoman who found the company in the Pump Room at Bath exciting. Nevertheless, they visited and dined out together, but apparently not again after the visit to Fonthill.

Nelson left London with his brother William on January 13, and wrote his wife a short friendly note that night to announce their safe arrival, 'heartily tired', at Southampton. Years later, Mr. Haslewood, Nelson's solicitor, remembered a breakfast scene where angry words had passed, when Lady Hamilton's name had come into the conversation, and linked it with the date January 13, making the episode the immediate cause of a sudden separation. Nelson's friend Sir Andrew Hamond, the Comptroller of the Navy, who had offered Lady Nelson a passage out to the Mediterranean with his son, was a close friend of both parties who considered 'their tempers not calculated to suit each other'. Farington records this judgment in his diary on the authority of Sir Thomas Lawrence, who had it from Hamond. But Farington also tells of a scene at supper at Lord Nelson's when Lady Hamilton had fainted and Lady Nelson did not leave the room to attend her. According to Farington, Sir William, who understood his Emma's guile, 'very much condemned the conduct of Lady Hamilton on this occasion'.

That the quarrel or quarrels were not regarded as final is shown by Nelson's note from Southampton and an undated letter from Lady Hamilton to Lady Nelson of this time, for it refers to Nelson's return to service: 'I would have done myself the honour of calling on you and Lord Nelson this day, but I am not well nor in spirits. Sir William and self feel the loss of our good friend, the good Lord Nelson. Permit me in the morning to have the pleasure of seeing you and hoping, my dear, Lady Nelson, the continuance of your friendship, which will be in Sir William and myself for everlasting to you and your family. Sir William begs to say, as an old and true friend of Lord Nelson, if he can be of any use to you in his Lordship's absence, he shall be very happy and will call to pay his respects to you and Mr. Nelson, to whom I beg my compliments and to Capt. Nesbit.'

If Lady Hamilton did call, it was the last time they met, because Lady Nelson joined her friend Miss Locker at Brighton on January 24, after her father-in-law had returned to Bath. Captain William Locker had died at the end of December, and on January 3 Nelson had followed the funeral in his carriage from Greenwich Hospital to Addington in Kent, calling on the Hamiltons, 'his true friends', when he returned to London.

On his way to Plymouth, Nelson reported to St. Vincent at Torr Abbey. St. Vincent wrote to Nepean: 'Poor man! he is devoured with vanity, weakness and folly; was strung with ribbons, medals, etc. and yet

pretended that he wished to avoid the honour and ceremonies he everywhere met with upon the road.' On the 17th Nelson hoisted his flag in the
San Josef and the occasion was cheered by the whole fleet. He was pleased
to meet Collingwood at this time, but otherwise avoided engagements as
much as possible. No doubt the loss of his arm made him less anxious to
undertake unessential boat work and climbing in and out of ships. He
was writing constantly to Lady Hamilton. Unfortunately, once again he
considered his wife had packed carelessly, and he evidently did not spare
her. 'I have wrote her a letter of truth about my outfit.' This letter has
been lost. He knew she was at Brighton. 'I go to the watering place,' he
scoffed. 'If I do without your consent may God inflict his punishment. I
cannot serve God and Mammon. I long to get to Bronte, for believe me
this England is a shocking place, a walk under the chestnut trees although
you may be shot by banditti is better than to have our reputations stabbed
in this country.'

In a letter of February 18 he tells Lady Hamilton how much he looks
forward to the inexpressible happiness of coming to London and staying
at the hotel nearest to the Hamiltons. St. Vincent had just replaced Spencer
as First Lord in the new government and he fears 'it may be necessary at
Lord St. Vincent's to hold a candle to the devil', a nice way of referring to
the prospect of a duty dinner-party at Admiralty House. 'However, all
matters shall be properly settled between us. I had a letter from that
person at Brighton saying she had heard from my brother that I was ill and
offered to come and nurse me but I have sent such an answer that will
convince her she would not be received. I am almost afraid you will think
I have gone too far, for she must see there is some strong reason but my
intentions are in everything to give you satisfaction, therefore do not be
angry for the strength of my letter. It is not my intention to go on shore at
Portsmouth but on duty to the Admiral and nothing but a gale of wind
shall keep me half an hour ashore, you know my word is my bond.'

It is not difficult to guess at the 'strong reason' which must be hid from
Lady Nelson, for Horatia, Nelson's adopted child, was born to Lady
Hamilton at the end of January. Nelson obtained three days' leave of
absence on February 23, but his wife remained at Brighton. It is most
probable that the prospect of Lady Hamilton's child was the immediate
cause of the rupture, and Nelson's angry letters to Davison at this time
suggest that his business agent was very much in his confidence in arranging the separation which Nelson now deemed inevitable. Nelson had
transferred from the *San Josef* to the *St. George* and knew he was sailing
to the Baltic, second in command to Sir Hyde Parker. The firmness of
conduct, the trait in his character which St. Vincent had so much admired

when deployed against the enemy, was as potent in deciding his private affairs. For better or worse, Nelson had given himself over to Lady Hamilton. On February 14 he had written to her, 'that person has her separate maintenance, let us be happy, that is in our power.' He wrote his letter of dismissal to his wife from the *St. George* on March 4, 1801. His brother Maurice counselled her to ignore it, 'as his brother seemed to have forgot himself'. But Maurice had died before his brother came home in June. As usual, Nelson was generous in money matters and made his wife a handsome allowance of half his income, paid quarterly in advance. She thanked him kindly for it as more than she would have asked for.

What had started as a drift apart quickly widened into a separation which Nelson intended to be permanent. He had in fact burnt his boats, metaphorically, when early in February he outlined for Lady Hamilton the provision he intended making for their child. He proposed, she having been 'the great cause of my performing those services which have gained me honours and rewards', to leave her the rental of the Bronte estates, and she was to have 'the full power of naming any child she may have in or out of wedlock or any child male or female which she, the said Emma Hamilton wife of the Right Honourable Sir William Hamilton may choose to adopt and call her child', who was to inherit the estate and the sword given by the King of Naples and pictures set in diamonds and other valuables held by Davison. He went on to make particular reference to a female child, whose parentage only Lady Hamilton knew, and who was in addition to be bequeathed all the money he should be worth above the sum of twenty thousand pounds. Nelson, in drawing up this proposed codicil for Lady Hamilton's approval in legal language, wished to ensure that in the event of his decease she and not Sir William would have the handling of his estate and the duty of carrying out his wishes. He was much occupied with forebodings, which he managed to communicate to St. Vincent, who took alarm and besought him by letter not to yield to any sudden impulse. It must have cost him much anguish to act towards his wife, whom he acknowledged had always behaved most correctly, in a manner which he would have quickly condemned if done by anybody else. The anger which both the guilty parties showed towards Lady Nelson is very forced. Josiah, up till now, had been his stepfather's heir, after his mother. She must have resented his displacement. She may not have hoped he would inherit his stepfather's titles, but she may very reasonably have expected some honour for him, such as the knighthood William Bolton received when he stood Nelson's proxy at the installation of the Knights of the Bath. Nelson tried to reward Davison by making him his proxy, but was told he must appoint a naval officer. Lady Nelson may have dropped her claims on Josiah's behalf in a desperate attempt to regain her lord's favour. She had always placed him and his pleasure before Josiah's. Such a turn about would explain Lady Hamilton's sneers, first that she wished to place her son, 'the Cub', above Nelson's own kin, and then that she had befouled her own nest by disowning him. But Lady Hamilton's anger had so savagely overwhelmed her habitual good nature when Lady Nelson's defection disturbed what had become her accustomed way of life, that she was capable of making any false accusation against her which seemed to suit the occasion. Nelson tried to fill the gap and give her a female companion by arranging for his brother William's wife to become her neighbour at his expense, although the Hamiltons found the 'Reverend Sir' rather a bore. Nelson arranged for this too by telling the one William not to inflict his company too often on the other. And Nelson also set to work to change the affections of his family from Lady Nelson to Lady Hamilton. Having made his plans he became more reconciled, and of course was now busily engaged on active service, which always improved his mental and physical health. He tried to persuade St. Vincent to re-appoint Captain Nisbet to the *Thalia*, but although seemingly promised, the new appointment was never made.

Nelson had long set Lady Hamilton on a pedestal of virtue that some-times reads strangely. He had written to her on January 29, 'You are kind and good to an old friend with one arm, a broken head and no teeth.' This unflattering picture of himself is borne out by the less adonized portraits, such as that by the Italian artist Guzzardi. Lord Elgin, in October 1799, thought he looked very old and noticed that he had lost his upper teeth: 'Yet,' he adds, 'on business Nelson shows infinite fire and a decision and dismission of difficulties which enables him to animate councils and direct successful operations so as to keep steady the minds of wavering people.' And Nelson never showed his fire and decision better than at the battle of Copenhagen, which he won after disobeying a senior officer and refusing to break off the engagement. Yet, this dis-obedience brought him a viscountcy. Lady Minto's sister felt sorry for Hyde Parker: 'but no wise man would ever have gone with Nelson or over him, as he was sure to be in the background in every case.'

Sir William's letter to Nelson of April 16 describes the jolly way in which the Hamiltons and their friends received news of Nelson's latest victory, which otherwise in England was received rather gloomily, with unusual emphasis on the casualty lists and the widows and orphans. A reason for public concern may have been that the French were the tradi-tional enemies and not the Danes. Public illuminations were forbidden and the money was to be given to the bereaved. However, brother William felt nothing of this and went on cutting his extraordinary capers, to Sir William's obvious astonishment. Sir Nathaniel William Wraxall, who was present at the party given at 23 Piccadilly on April 15 when the news of the victory arrived, gives us further particulars. Amongst the guests were the Duke of Queensberry, the notorious 'Old Q', and Lord William Gordon, soldier and poetaster, both new friends of Nelson through the Hamiltons. Lady Hamilton undertook to dance a 'Tarentella', which demanded a partner, as the dance represented a satyr chasing a nymph. Sir William began it with her, but his seventy-one years at last began to tell, and a Neapolitan duke took over from Sir William; then Lady Hamilton's maid was summoned to relieve the duke, and the maid in her turn handed over to the perfectly black Copt, the Egyptian girl Nelson had given Lady Hamilton after the Battle of the Nile. The account of this marathon performance accentuates the new way of life Nelson had come to regard as his own if never perhaps quite to understand. His wife, to retain his affections, must not only have accepted Horatia and discussed her husband's goodness endlessly with Lady Hamilton, but also have applauded the 'Tarentella' and even danced the part of nymph or satyr under the ogling gaze of 'Old Q'. But she must have realized once and for all she had lost Nelson's heart when, on his return from the Baltic, he was led off on a series of country jaunts, organized by Lady Hamilton for the benefit of his health. The Hamiltons were joined by Nelson and the young officers in attendance on him, his brother William and family, and smart friends, such as the Duke of Queensberry and Lord William Gordon, were also invited. Lord William Gordon described the party in verse, with pointed references to Anthony and Cleopatra while Mrs. William Nelson was addressed concerning her husband as follows:

'But to return to this same worthy Vicar
Who loves, you say, good eating and good liquor,
Know, Lady, that it is our earnest wish
That we, ere long, may greet him Lord Archbish.
For this no common pains, or I'm mistaken;
Our best of friends, the Duke, hath lately taken;
And if a mitre fall not on his head,
Justice and gratitude are gone to bed.'

Nelson himself was the Duke (of Bronte) who had long striven to procure ecclesiastical preferment for his brother.

Lady Nelson was at Bath when the news of the victory of Copenhagen was brought to her in a short note, in the third person, from kind Lord

Spencer, who had himself just arrived at Bath. She went up to London, saw Mrs. William Nelson and attended a Drawing Room, but returned to Bath to look after her father-in-law, although Mrs. Bolton's advice was that she should remain in London so as to welcome her husband's return. A draft of a letter of congratulations to her husband on his latest victory may not have been sent, but Nelson's father did write to him from Bath and mentioned his hopes that his son might now return to domestic joys, and he referred to his son's wife's sorrow at not receiving a line in her husband's hand. But Nelson did not relent and wrote instruction to Davison on April 23 from the *St. George* to signify to her that his mind was 'fixed as fate', and he wanted to be left alone. Davison did write, after Nelson's return to England, diffidently and late on July 12, saying her husband's health required 'a few days' quiet retreat in the country.

In July 1801 Nelson hoisted his flag in command of a special squadron stationed in the Downs and the Hamiltons and William Nelsons stayed at Deal to be near him. An attack on the Boulogne invasion flotilla was a costly failure. On December 18 Lady Nelson wrote her last letter to her dear husband. 'Let everything be buried in oblivion, it will pass away like a dream.' She could offer him a comfortable, warm house in Somerset Street. But Nelson no longer looked forward to love in a cottage. Her letter was returned by Davison unread, marked 'Opened in error'. For Nelson's mind now turned to the country seat he had commissioned Lady Hamilton to purchase for him, Merton Place in Surrey, 'Paradise Merton'. The Hamiltons retained their Piccadilly residence and shared expenses whenever they were with Nelson. But Nelson insisted that everything at Merton should be his own and nothing of Sir William's was allowed there. He handed the management and improvement of Merton over to Lady Hamilton and encouraged her to various extravagances he could ill afford. Merton was to be a home for their daughter, and a home where he could offer open hospitality to his family, and friends. His family came over to him and not only dropped any social intercourse with his wife, but made many disparaging references to her in their correspondence with Lady Hamilton, calling her Tom Tit, a nickname due to her awkward manner of walking. Josiah was nicknamed the Cub. Only Nelson's father remained faithful to his son's wife. Anonymous letters accusing him of being unjust to his son upset the old man. Lady Nelson generously besought him to consult his own happiness and give her up. The father wrote to Nelson asking if he was likely to visit Burnham Thorpe but warning him that gratitude dictated that he should reside with Lady Nelson if he could give her any comfort. This gentle decision infuriated his high-minded son, who wrote a protest under open cover to be forwarded to him by Lady Hamilton, who sent a copy of the letter to Mrs. William Nelson, with comments. The old man capitulated, and when he died at Bath, he was contemplating an early visit to Merton to end his days there in apartments which were being specially prepared for him. The defection of the old father, her devoted friend of so many years, completed Lady Nelson's abandonment by her husband and her family. But he did not quite forget her. His last letter from Bath, announcing an addition to the Matcham family, was dated April 20, 1802. He died six days later, and his daughter-in-law characteristically hurried from London to ease his death-bed. Mrs. Bolton wrote to her, 'Your going to Bath my dear Lady Nelson was of a piece with all your conduct to my beloved father.' She added, 'I am going to Merton in about a fortnight, but my dear Lady Nelson we cannot meet as I wished for everybody is known who visits you.' So Lady Nelson was forced out of her husband's life.

Nelson liked to think of his family coming and going from Merton, Lady Hamilton fell in with his ideas and became indispensable to all the members of it. He helped generously with money for the children's education and she introduced the girls into polite society. Nelson was at home during the peace which followed the treaty of Amiens. At the same time that the threat of war warned him he would soon be called upon to hoist his flag as commander-in-chief, Mediterranean, Sir William Hamilton, who had suddenly aged, removed himself from Merton up to town and died in the arms of Nelson and Emma on April 6, 1803. Next month Nelson joined the *Victory*. The rest of Nelson's life is history. Lady Hamilton's name is linked with his, giving popular support to his supposed dictum, 'If there were more Emmas there would be more Nelson's,' but his wife's name is almost forgotten, except as some poor, well-meaning, colourless person, unworthy of him. Perhaps more credit will be given to Fanny, who showed quiet courage, dignity and good sense in her continued love of a hero who had forgotten her. Nelson's professional reputation, it is true to say, was very much the concern of Lady Hamilton, who fostered it, in her fashion. If Lady Nelson can be said to have failed her husband in any way it was in being unable to recognize and flatter him as a great man.

The documents quoted in this last chapter have been selected from Nelson family letters now preserved at Monmouth, the British Museum and the National Maritime Museum. Few of them have been used by any of Nelson's biographers, who have neglected Nelson's private life for the glory of his public one. The story has been carried on until May 1831, when Lady Nelson died in London. Her memorial in the church at Littleham near Exmouth has the following inscription:

Sacred to the memory of
Frances Herbert,
Viscountess Nelson—Duchess of Bronte
Widow of the late Admiral—Lord Viscount Nelson
and to her son Josiah Nisbet Esq.
Captain in the Royal Navy,
whom she survived eleven months
and died in London May 6th 1831
aged 73 years.

This humble offering of affection
is erected by Frances Herbert Nisbet
in grateful remembrance of those virtues
which adorned a kind mother in law
and a good husband.'

FAMILY CORRESPONDENCE AND NEWS, 1800–1831

Extracts from the 'Morning Herald'

Tuesday, November 11, 1800: Lord Nelson, the gallant hero of the Nile, on his arrival in town, was met by his venerable father and his amiable lady. The scene which took place was of the most graceful description, and is more easily to be conceived than described. This family party, with Sir William and Lady Hamilton, dined on Sunday at Nerot's Hotel.

The Duke of Queensberry, who admires gallantry of every description, paid a visit to Lord Nelson shortly after his Lordship's arrival in town.

Lord Nelson paid his respects to the Admiralty Board yesterday morning, and afterwards, accompanied by a gentleman, walked between eleven and twelve through the Adelphi buildings, and along the Strand, to the Navy Office at Somerset House. His Lordship was in the full dress uniform of an Admiral, and though in appearance somewhat thinner than when he was last in England, looked in perfect health.

He was not recognized until he came into the Strand, where the curiosity of his grateful countrymen became a little troublesome to the gallant Admiral, the inconvenience of which he avoided by going into Somerset House.

Lord Nelson, in every town through which he passed on his way to London from Yarmouth, was received by the populous with the most ecstatic shouts of applause. The Volunteers of Yarmouth, on his departure, attended his Lordship to a considerable distance from the town.

When his Lordship left Somerset House, a very numerous crowd assembled, and accompanied him to Whitehall. It must be truly gratifying to every mind susceptible of great and generous feelings, that time, which too often dims the lustre of the noblest deeds, has not in the slightest degree obscured the glory of the conquerer of Aboukir.

The arrival of Lord Nelson in London cannot fail of reviving in the breast of British gratitude the recollection of his victories. On this occasion, the Manager of Covent Garden has obligingly got up the 'Mouth of the Nile', in which piece the hero of Aboukir will see with what attention his services are recorded, and with what transport received by his country-men.

Thursday, November 13, 1800: Yesterday His Majesty held a Levée at St. James's Palace, which was attended by the foreign envoys, the cabinet ministers, the Archbishop of Canterbury, the Bishop of Durham, Baron Bouille and a number of the nobility. The presentations were:

The gallant Lord Nelson, who appeared in his full naval uniform, decorated with the diamond aigrette, presented to him by the Grand Seignior, which he wore in his hat, besides the medallions of the King and Queen of Naples, the different orders with which he had been invested, and the elegant sword presented to him by the City of London. . . . Sir William Hamilton on his arrival from the Court of Naples. . . .

Lord and Lady Nelson dined yesterday with the Earl and Countess Spencer, at their house in the Admiralty.

Thursday, November 13, 1800: Lady Hamilton.[1]—The lady of Sir William Hamilton, K.B., who with her husband has lately accompanied Lord Nelson to England being variously spoken of as to her personal charms, a short sketch of her exterior may be acceptable to many of our readers. Her ladyship is in her 49th year: rather taller than the common height; still displaying a superior graceful animation of figure, now a little on the wane from too great a propensity to the *en bon point*. Her attitud-inarian graces, so varying in their style and captivating in their effect, are declining also under this unfortunate personal extension. Her teeth are lovely, and her hair is of the darkest brown, immensely thick and trails to the ground. Her eyes are black and possess the most fascinating attrac-tion, but her nose is rather too short for the Grecian contour of her face, which notwithstanding is singularly expressive and her conversaziones, if not solid and argumentative, are at least sprightly and unceasing. Such after ransacking Herculaneum and Pompeia for thirty-eight years is the

---

[1] Lady Hamilton had not been in England since her marriage to Sir William Hamil-ton in Naples. She was not received by any of the Royal Family except the Prince of Wales and Prince Augustus.

chief curiosity with which that celebrated antiquarian Sir William Hamilton has returned to his native country.

Friday, November 14, 1800: Yesterday the Queen held a Drawing Room at St. James's Palace, at which all the Princesses, the Prince of Wales, Duke of Kent and Prince Augustus, with several of the nobility were present.

The gentlemen introduced to her Majesty, were those who were presented to His Majesty on the preceding day.

The ladies introduced were, the Duchess of Dorset and Somerset, Lady Nelson, Lady Stirling, Lady Peele, Mrs. Robert Moore, and Miss Whitworth. . . .

Lord Nelson was yesterday attended at Court by Captain Hardy, Captain Cuthbert, Captain Cowan, Captain Duval and Captain Parkinson, who were presented to Her Majesty by his Lordship, being all heroes of the glorious Battle of the Nile.

Wednesday, November 19, 1800: Covent Garden.—Lord and Lady Nelson, Sir William and Lady Hamilton and the Reverend Mr. Nelson, the venerable father of the hero of the Nile, were last night present at the last new comedy of 'Life' and the musical entertainment of 'The Mouth of the Nile'.

The noble and gallant Admiral as soon as he presented himself to the audience was received with the most ecstatic and reiterated bursts of applause we ever recollect to have witnessed on any similar occasion. While this generous manifestation of regard on the part of the admiring crowd took place, his Lordship standing up in the front of the box bowed frequently to the applauding company in grateful return; and his venerable father, completely overcome with the interest of the scene, at length gave vent to his paternal feelings by a most plenteous flow of tears. 'Rule Britannia' was then called for and sung amidst the general plaudits of the house, after which the performance of the comedy commenced and the whole went off with infinite éclat. At the conclusion of the play Munden sang the last new song of the junior Dibdin, in honour of the splendid achievements of the noble Admiral, which was encored amidst an unprecedented tumult of enthusiastic exultation and applause: his Lordship by a graceful bow returned the flattering compliment. 'Rule Britannia' was then again called for and the demand was instantly complied with. In the entertainment of 'The Mouth of the Nile' Emery's song recounting the exploits of our several naval heroes was also encored: and the whole of the performance being terminated, his Lordship took his departure amidst the joyous acclamations of a full and splendid audience.

The hero of the Nile was in the front of the second box from the stage on the Prince's side, Lady Hamilton being seated on his right, and Lady

Nelson on his left. Sir William Hamilton sat behind his lady, and the Reverend Mr. Nelson in the front of the adjoining box.

Lady Nelson appeared in white with a violet satin head dress and a small white feather. Her ladyship's person is of a very pleasing description: her features are handsome and exceedingly interesting, and her general appearance is at once prepossessing and elegant. Lady Hamilton is rather *embonpoint* but her person is nevertheless highly graceful and her face extremely pretty. She wore a blue satin gown and head dress with a fine plume of feathers.

Prince Augustus, the Duchess of Leeds, Lords Chesterfield and Shrewsbury formed also a part of the brilliant circle.

Tuesday, November 25, 1800: Drury Lane.—The play of 'Pizarro' attracted last night a most splendid assemblage of beauty and fashion. The house was literally crowded in every part, and the performance went off with universal éclat. Kemble in the Peruvian hero never acted better, nor did his great exertions ever produce a more happy effect.

Lord and Lady Nelson, Sir William and Lady Hamilton, formed a part of the brilliant circle. His Lordship on his entrance was received with the most flattering testimonials of public regard; and 'Rule Britannia' with an additional verse in favour of the gallant hero of the Nile was sung amidst the universal plaudits of the admiring crowd. After the play, Dibdin's favourite song of the Navy and Nelson was sung in character by Dignum and deservedly encored: and every opportunity was eagerly seized by the audience to evince the high estimation in which they held the valiant conqueror of Aboukir. The heat, owing to the crowd, was so great that about the end of the third act Lady Nelson fainted away, and was obliged to be carried out of her box. Her Ladyship however soon became sufficiently recovered to resume her seat, and to the great satisfaction of all present remained in the box during the rest of the performance. We understand she has for some days been in a very indifferent state of health.

Tuesday, December 9, 1800: Lady Hamilton has not yet been at Court. The cause is said to be her not having received any answer from her Majesty to the letter of recommendation of which her Ladyship was the bearer from the Queen of Naples.

Monday, January 5, 1801: Lady Hamilton has received no answer whatever to the recommendatory letter which the Queen of Naples wrote to our Queen in her favour, although a Great Personage received it at the Levée from Sir W. H. and was himself the bearer of this courtly epistle to his Royal Consort.

Nelson to Lady Nelson[1]

Southampton,[2]
January 13, 1801

MY DEAR FANNY,—We are arrived, and heartily tired: and, with kindest regards to my father and all the family, believe me, your affectionate NELSON.[3]

Lady Nelson to Mrs. William Nelson[4]

[London],
January 22, [1801]

MY DEAR MRS. NELSON,—Mr. Davison has just left me. I mentioned my intentions of going to Nerots Hotel, which he thinks I had better not do, particularly as the house is taken for me at Brighton.[5] Therefore let me beg of you to go with me, and I will do everything in my power to make it comfortable, or should you rather wish to stay in London, I will stay on purpose till Mr. Nelson's return to you.[6]

I am sure I need not repeat my constant desire to do anything in my power to serve or accommodate my dear Lord's family. Yours very sincerely, FRANCES H. NELSON.

To Mrs. Nelson.

Alexander Davison to Nelson[7]

St. James's Square,
27 January, 1801

MY DEAR FRIEND,—I cannot express how much I was hurt yesterday on receiving your last letter[8] mentioning the reports you had heard respecting my procuring you a house. Such reports could only have been fabricated for the vilest of purposes, and none would have dared to have said such a

[1] From Pettigrew, Vol. II, p. 643. This letter and five others are in the Huntington Library, San Marino, California. See p. 618.

[2] Nelson, with his brother William, left London on January 13 for Plymouth, where his new flag-ship, the *San Josef*, was being fitted out.

[3] Nelson did not use his foreign title of Bronte in England until he had received royal licence to do so.

[4] B.M. Add. MSS. 34,988, Bridport papers.

[5] The newspapers reported on January 24 that Lady Nelson had gone to Brighton. Nelson heard of it and wrote to Lady Hamilton, 'Let her go to Brighton or where she pleases, I care not: she is a great fool and thank God you are not the least like her.'

[6] The Rev. William Nelson returned at the end of the month.

[7] N.M.M. MSS. 9960, Croker collection in the Phillipps papers.

[8] Written on January 24 when Nelson heard a rumour Davison was buying a house for him in London. The best thing for Lady Nelson, he said, 'was good lodgings or a very small ready furnished house'.

thing but those who are alternately both our enemies. I should have felt still more grieved had you given the slightest credit to them, trusting you have known me long enough to be assured I could have no other motive than your interest and happiness at heart and that I could never be such an egregious fool as to go and do that which I knew would be diametrically opposite to your wish and intention, and which the frequent conversations we have had on the subject must have fully made me acquainted with, and farther I think it but justice to assert that I know it is Lady Nelson's wish by no means to have a large house, and which she has repeatedly begged me not to think of, only to *hire* one in an airy situation, but independent of that I am surprised you could for a moment think it necessary to remind me of what I must be fully assured of, that it was your request to hire a neat comfortable sized house. Depend on it, those people who could insinuate that I was acting contrary to what you approved of, must have motives much beneath us to regard or our time to be taken up with this impertinent interference.

I wrote to you on the 24th to Tor Bay conceiving you would have got round. I presume my letter would be forwarded to Plymouth, it containing a copy of Mr. Tucker's last to me, and of my solicitors to the Earl[1] of the 23rd. to which no reply is yet made. I think it probable he may have transmitted it to his attornies, requesting them to form the proper answer. I am glad to hear that in his letters to you, he never mentions the subject.

Mr. Law gives me some expectations of receiving his opinion tomorrow or next day, which with the Earl's reply to my solicitors (if he condescends to give an answer) shall be sent you. In my last I told you the moment I could with safety to your interest quit town, I would set off to meet you at Torbay. Rundle and Bridge are exerting themselves to finish your plate, but it requires time, and being confined to a few hands to work upon it.

I am happy to hear the borough of Plymouth has conferred the freedom upon you, it being our second sea port town makes it more gratifying.

God bless you and believe me my dear friend your ever sincere and affectionate ALEXANDER DAVISON.

Nelson to Lady Hamilton[2]

Brixham,
February 5, 1801

'And as Emma Hamilton the wife of the right honourable Sir William Hamilton K.B. has been the great cause of my performing those services

---

[1] Lord St. Vincent, with whom Nelson was engaged in a lawsuit about the allocation of prize money.
[2] B.M. Egerton MS. 1614. The first part of this letter is a draft codicil to his will.

which have gained me honours and rewards I give unto her in case of the failure of male heirs as directed by my will, the entire rental of the Bronte estate for her particular use and benefit and in case of her death before she may come into the possession of the estate of Bronte she is to have the full power of naming any child she may have in or out of wedlock or any child male or female which she, the said Emma Hamilton wife of the right honourable Sir William Hamilton may choose to adopt and call her child by her last will and testament or by deed declaring her intent, and the sword given by His Sicilian Majesty is to be delivered on her coming to the estate or to the person she may name as directed by my said will and I likewise give to the said Emma wife of the right honourable Sir William Hamilton K.B. a picture of His Sicilian Majesty set in diamonds with the Queen's cypher on the opposite side, whom God preserve, with all the diamonds which surround it, as it is now lodged in a mahogany box in the care of Alexander Davison Esq., St. James's Square, London, and I give all my other boxes lodged in the aforesaid box at Alexander Davison's Esq. in which diamonds are placed, viz. one with the portrait of the Emperor Paul of Russia, one of the King of Sardinia and the one said to have been sent me by the mother of the Grand Signor, likewise to the said Emma Hamilton wife of Sir William Hamilton K.B. to be sold if she pleases and the income to be for her use during her natural life and at her decease it is to be given to a child called —— in whom I take a very particular interest and as Emma Hamilton is the only person who knows the parents of this female child I rely with the greatest confidence on her unspotted honour and integrity that she will consider the child as mine and be a guardian to it, shielding it from want and disgrace, and bringing it up as the child of her dear friend Nelson and Bronte,[1] and to this female child, of which Lady Hamilton shall only be the declarer that it is the one I mean, I give and bequeath all the money I shall be worth above the sum of twenty thousand pounds, the interest of it to be received by Lady Hamilton for the maintenance and education of this female child, the principal to be paid her at the death of Lady Hamilton if she has attained the age of 21 years or that she may marry, the guardians of my adopted child to be named by Lady Hamilton in her will.'

Such is my ideas if you have no objection, if you have I will endeavour to alter them to your wishes. I shall now begin and save a fortune for the little one. . . . Your faithful and affectionate NELSON AND BRONTE.

To Lady Hamilton, 23 Picadilly, London.

[1] Nelson received royal licence to accept the Sicilian title of Bronte in January 1801. He used this form of signature until his death.

Sir William Hamilton to Nelson[1]

A

Piccadilly,
February 19, 1801

MY DEAR LORD,—Whether Emma will be able to write to you today or not is a question, as she has got one of her terrible sick headaches. Among other things that vex her, is that we have been drawn in to be under the absolute necessity of giving a dinner to the Prince of Wales on Sunday next. He asked it himself having expressed his strong desire of hearing Banti's and Emma's voices together. I am well aware of the danger that would attend the Prince's frequenting our house, not that I fear that Emma could ever be induced to act contrary to the prudent conduct she has hitherto pursued, but the world is so ill natured that the worst construction is put upon the most innocent actions. As this dinner must be, or the Prince would be offended, we shall keep it strictly to the musical part, invite only Banti, her husband, and Taylor and as I wish to shew a civility to Davison I have sent him an invitation. In short we will get rid of it as well as we can and guard against its producing more meetings of the same sort. Emma would really have gone any lengths to have avoided Sunday's dinner, but I thought it would not be prudent to break with the Prince who really has shewn the greatest civility to us when we were last in England and since we returned, and she has at last acquiesced to my opinion. I have been thus explicit as I know well your Lordship's way of thinking and your very kind attachment to us and to every thing that concerns us.

The King caught cold at the chapel the fast day and there was no levée yesterday and today the Queen alone will be at the drawing room—and I believe the new ministry[2] will not be quite fixed until the levée day next week. As to my business I have done all I can to bring it to a point. The pension recommended by Lord Grenville was only like Walpole's a nominal £2000. I have represented the injustice of that after my having had the King's promise of not being removed from Naples but at my own request and having only empowered Lord Grenville to remove me on securing to me a net income of £2000 per annum. Lord Grenville has recommended to the Treasury the taking my extraordinary expenses into consideration. I have fully demonstrated to Lord Grenville and Treasury that £8000 is absolutely necessary for the clearing off my unfunded debt

---

[1] N.M.M. MS. 9960, Croker collection in the Phillipps papers.
[2] Pitt resigned on February 5 but the formation of a new ministry under Addington was held up by the King's illness.

PLATE XVI. Lady Hamilton, as Britannia, crowning the bust of Nelson. Stipple engraving by A. R. Burt from a drawing by Thomas Baxter (probably made at Merton), published December 5, 1805.

without making up for my losses. Upon the whole then I do not expect to get more than the net annuity above mentioned and the £8000 but unless that is granted I shall indeed have been very ill used. I hope in my next to be able to inform your Lordship that all has been finally settled. I am busy in putting in order the remains of my vases and pictures that you so kindly saved for me on board the *Foudroyant* and the sale of them will enable me to go on more at my ease and not leave a debt unpaid,—but unfortunately there have been too many picture sales this year and mine will come late.

Adieu my very dear Lord, may health and success attend you wherever you go and I flatter myself this political jumble may hasten a peace and bring you back soon.

Your Lordship's ever obliged and most sincerely attached friend and humble servant, WILLIAM HAMILTON.

B

Piccadilly,
February 20, 1801

MY DEAR LORD,—You need not be the least alarmed that Emma has commissioned me to send you the newspapers and write you a line to tell you that she is much better, having vomited naturally and is now purposing to take a regular one of tartar emetic. All her convulsive complaints certainly proceed from a foul stomach and I will answer for it, she will be in spirits and write to you herself tomorrow. Adieu my very dear Lord I have not a moment to lose as the bell is going. Your ever attached and obliged humble servant, WILLIAM HAMILTON.

Lady Hamilton to Mrs. William Nelson[1]

A

Friday noon, abed.
[February 20, 1801]

I have been ill abed my dearest Mrs. Nelson since yesterday, I could not take leave of you, my soul was torn in pieces. It is such a pain to part with dear friends, and you and I liked each other from the moment we met. Our souls were congenial. Not so with *Tom tit*[2] for there was an antipathy not to be described.

---

[1] B.M. Add. MS. 34989, Bridport papers.
[2] Lady Nelson.

2 P

I am laying down writing to you, so if it is not legible. But my heart says everything that's kind to you and good honest Mr. Nelson. I received yesterday letters from that great adored being that we all so love, esteem and admire. The more one knows him, the more one wonders at his greatness, his heart, his head both so perfect. He says he is coming round to Spithead soon he hopes. I am sorry you was in such a hurry to go. Troubridge[1] comes to town today as one of the Lords, so he is settled for the present, but depend on it, my dear friend, this poor patched up party can never hold long. A new coat will wear many a day and long as the vulgar phrase is, but an old patched mended one must soon go. 'Tis a remedy for the moment. Oh my dear Mrs. Nelson I wish there was a peace, and all parties settled to their liking. I know where you and I would be. Tom tit might go to the devil for what I care.

I am so ill that I don't think we can have His Royal Highness to dinner on Sunday, which will not vex me. Addio mia cara amica. You know as you are learning Italian I must say a word or so. How dull my bedroom looks without you. I miss our little friendly confidential chat, but in this world nothing is complete. If all went smartly one should regret quitting it, but 'tis the way. Little vexations and crosses separations from one's dear friends that makes one not regret leaving it. Give my love to Mr. Nelson. Mr. Denis, the Duke[2] and Lord William[3] desire theirs and believe me, ever ever your attached EMMA HAMILTON.

Sir William's kind regards.

To Mrs. Nelson.

B

London,
February 24, 1801

MY DEAREST FRIEND,—Your dear brother arrived this morning by seven oclock. He stays only 3 days so by the time you would be here, he will be gone. How unlucky you went so soon.

I am in health so-so, but spirits today excellent at what real pleasure Sir William and I have in seeing this our great good virtuous Nelson. His eye is better.[4]

---

[1] Sir Thomas Troubridge, one of the new Admiralty Board, with St. Vincent as First Lord; he received his commission on February 19.
[2] The Duke of Queensbury, Old 'Q' (1724–1810).
[3] Lord William Gordon, soldier and writer of light verse; died 1823.
[4] Nelson's sound eye had been infected while he was at Plymouth and he had been advised to protect it with an eye-shade.

Tom tit does not come to town. She offered to go down but was refused. She only wanted to go to do mischief to all the great Jove's relations. 'Tis now shown all her ill treatment and bad heart, Jove has found it out. Apropos Lady Nelson is at Brighton yet.

The King, God bless him, is ill and there are many speculations, some say it is his old disorder.[1] I can only say to you God bless you I will write longer tomorrow. Ever ever yours, E. HAMILTON.

[*Addressed by Nelson:* To Mrs. Nelson, Hilborough.]

C[2]

February 26

. . . Tom tit at the same place Brighton. The Cub is to have a frigate, the *Thalia*, the Earl gives it, 'tis settled. So I suppose he will be up in a day or so. I only hope he will not come near me. If he does 'not at home' shall be the answer. Am glad he is going, I hope never to— . . .

D

Monday noon,
March 2, 1801

MY DEAREST FRIEND,—Anxiety and heart bleeding for your brother's departure has made me so ill I have not been able to write. I cannot eat or sleep. Oh, may God prosper and bless him. He has wrote to Lord Eldon[3] for Mr. Nelson.

You will have him at Yarmouth in 2 days. Oh how I envy you. Oh God how happy you are to be with that great good virtuous man. My spirits and health is bad indeed. The King is worse today, yesterday was better.

Tom tit is at B.[4] She did not come nor did he go. *Jove* for such he is, quite a Jove, knows better than that. Maurice means to go to Yarmouth. The Cub dined with us, but I never asked how Tom Tit was.

Love to Mr. Nelson, believe me ever ever yours sincerely, E. HAMILTON.

Oh how I long to see you. Do try and come for God sake do.

To Mrs. Nelson, Hilborough, Near Brandon, Norfolk.

[1] Attacks of insanity.
[2] Lady Hamilton wrote to Mrs. Nelson daily at this time. The extract given above is characteristic of her remarks about Lady Nelson and her son.
[3] The Lord Chancellor, an important source of ecclesiastical patronage.
[4] Brighton.

Nelson to Lady Nelson[1]
(Draft)

St. George,
March 4, 1801

Josiah is to have another ship and to go abroad if the *Thalia* cannot soon be got ready.[2] I have done *all* for him and he may again as he has often done before wish me to break my neck, and be abetted in it by his friends who are likewise my enemies, but I have done my duty as an honest generous man and I neither want or wish for any body to care what become of me, whether I return or am left in the Baltic, seeing I have done all in my power for you.[3] And if dead you will find I have done the same,[4] therefore my only wish is to be left to myself and wishing you every happiness, believe that I am your affectionate NELSON AND BRONTE.

Memorandum[5]

[March 4, 1801]

Lord Nelson's annual income is about £4000 a year including £200 a year the interest of Lady Nelson's £4000. My plan is to allow Lady Nelson £2000 a year subject to the income tax which as I pay the tax with my own will reduce my net yearly income to £3600.

Lady Nelson to be paid every quarter in advance viz. 1st January 1801, 1st April, 1st July, 1st October by Messrs. Marsh, Page and Creed £400 each quarter which with the interest of the £4000 will amount to £1800 neat money.

Lord Nelson has directed Mr. Davison to pay every bill and expense of his and Lady Nelson's to the day of his leaving London. NELSON.

N.B. Lord Nelson gives Lady Nelson the principal of the £4000 mentioned above to be at her disposal by will.

[1] N.M.M. 36 MS. 0552, Autograph collection. The original letter is preserved in a collection of Nelson legal documents at the British Museum (Add. MSS. 28333). It is torn, and part of the text is missing. It has been endorsed by Lady Nelson: 'This is my Lord Nelson's letter of dismissal, which so astonished me that I immediately sent to it Mr. Maurice Nelson who was sincerely attached to me for his advice, he desired me not to take the least notice of it, as his brother seemed to have forgot himself.' It is addressed to Lady Nelson, Brighton, Sussex.

[2] Josiah did not get the *Thalia*, nor was another ship given to him. His lieutenant from the *Thalia*, Samuel Colquitt, had brought various charges against him, which Nelson attributed to spite. But in spite of his intervention, Josiah had no further employment. Colquitt was made a rear-admiral in 1846.

[3] On February 14 Nelson had written to Lady Hamilton, 'that person has her separate maintenance: let us be happy, that is in our power.'

[4] By a codicil to his will, Nelson had left his wife £1,000 a year.

[5] B.M. Add. MSS. 28333, a collection of legal documents relating to Nelson. This memorandum is written by Nelson and signed, but not dated. It may have been sent to his agents in this form.

Sir William Hamilton to Nelson[1]

Piccadilly,
March 7, 1801

MY VERY DEAR LORD,—I wish it was in my power to profit of your kind invitation, you would soon see me and Emma on board the *St. George* but I am now totally occupied in preparing for the sale of my pictures and what I have saved of my vases. To my great satisfaction I have found some of the most capital vases and which I thought surely lost on board the *Colossus*.[2] It has comforted me much.

We remain in the same cruel state with respect to the King's recovery. There can be no doubts but that His Majesty is better, however if my conjectures are true the Regency must soon take place as it may be long before His Majesty could be troubled with business, supposing even his fever to have totally subsided and the times admit of no delay.

We see now the certainty of the French squadron's being in the Mediterranean. God knows how all this will end but I hope it will be your Lordship's lot to bring Paul[3] to his senses. God send you every success and send you home safe and well crowned with additional laurels and then I hope you will repose your shattered frame and make your friends happy by staying with them. Emma is certainly much better but not quite free from bile.

Ever my dear Lord your Lordship's most attached and eternally obliged humble servant, WILLIAM HAMILTON.

Nelson to Mrs. William Nelson[4]

Yarmouth,
March 7, 1801

MY DEAR MADAM,—I wish you would take a post chaise and go to London and be near and as much as possible with our dear friend Lady Hamilton who loves and esteems you very much, I will tell my brother that you are gone, therefore he shall either meet you in London or go round by Hilborough and arrange his church duty.

In doing this favour you shall be at no expense[5] and you will most truly oblige your sincere and affectionate friend, NELSON AND BRONTE.

To Mrs. Nelson, Hilborough, Brandon, Norfolk. Turn Barton mills.

[1] N.M.M. MS. 9960, Croker collection in the Phillipps papers.
[2] Wrecked off Scilly Isles in December 1798.
[3] The Czar of Russia, who had revived the Armed Neutrality of the North against England.
[4] N.M.M. MS. 9292, Bridport papers.
[5] On March 11 Nelson asked Davison to pay Mrs. Nelson £100: 'she is in London by my desire.'

Mrs. Bolton to Lady Nelson[1]

Cranwich,
March 8, 1801

Could you for one moment my dear Lady Nelson attribute my silence to neglect? Believe me I was very anxious to hear from you, and nothing but your telling Mr. Bolton you would write to me as soon as you were *settled* prevented you hearing from me for till this week by a letter from Mrs. Matcham did I know you were absolutely at Brighton. Will you excuse what I am going to say? I wish you had continued in town a little longer, as I *have heard* my brother regretted he had not a house he could call his own when he returned.[2] Do, whenever you hear he is likely to return, have a house to receive him. If you absent yourself entirely from him, there never can be a reconciliation. Such attention must please him and I am sure will do in the end. Your conduct as he *justly* says is *exemplary* in regard to him and he has not an unfeeling heart.

I most sincerely love my brother and *did quite as much before he was Lord Nelson* and I hope my conduct was ever the same towards you as Mrs. Nelson as ever it was as Lady Nelson. I hope in God one day I shall have the pleasure of seeing you together as happy as ever, he certainly as far as I hear is not a happy man.

I was glad to find from Mrs. Matcham you had Miss Locker[3] with you. It would not have been comfortable at this to have been alone. We all beg our kind compliments to her and likewise to Captain Nisbet (if with you) I am rejoiced to think he has got the *Thalia*, I know he was so anxious to have her. I hope he will be successful in her.

The newspapers I will take care shall be paid for. Mr. William Bolton is at Bath with his two daughters. He wishes to get the rest of the party to join them but I doubt poor Mrs. Pierson will not be willing. Capt. Bouchier's house I see is advertised to be sold.

I am glad you find Brighton likely to be of service to you. Keep up your spirits as well as you can and all will do well. Your illness proceeds from uneasiness of mind. The Rector and his lady have been home a fortnight. I have seen him once of a morning. Thank God my father seems comfortable. He says to Mrs. M.[4] 'Tell your sister I am better in all respects than when she saw me. I certainly can walk much better.'

My two little girls are both at Edmonton very happy. Mrs. Pierson has introduced them to a lady (aunt to poor Pierson) who lives at Tottenham,

[1] Monmouth MSS., Nelson papers, Vol. IV.
[2] Nelson was in London for three days, February 24–27.
[3] Daughter of Captain Locker, who had died in December 1800.
[4] Mrs. Matcham.

who is very kind to them. She keeps a carriage, the distance is none for a ride. You see I trouble you with all my family chit chat as usual. Mr. Bolton and the girls join in kindest regards to you. Excuse whatever I have said as I most sincerely wish you happy. And believe me your truly affectionate S. BOLTON.

I hope you will sometimes favour me with a letter as I shall be anxious to hear from you. You may be certain if I hear any intelligence that I think will give you pleasure or information you shall have it. If you should wish in the heat of summer for retirement you know where [to] find it and we shall be happy to show you all the attention in our power.

To the Right Honourable Lady Nelson, Brighton.

The Rev. E. Nelson to Lady Nelson[1]

No. 3 South Parade, Bath,
March 14, 1801

MY GOOD MADAM,—Tho' I verily believe you have no intention of making my mind uneasy in any one instance, yet, your very long omission in not noticing me gives cause for abundance of unpleasant feelings respecting yourself, as well as my own thoughts about what indeed in some measure may affect us both. Excuse therefore my enquiry how your own health advances, whether change of place and scenes promises all or part of what was expected. How long do you think of remaining at Brighton? Can I contribute any thing to the farther increase of your comfort or do your mind feel easy and happy in its present state?

My own health God knows is very weak and very uncertain what a day may bring forth.

I shall endeavour to recruit a little by trying the efficacy of Bath water upon a frame broken almost to pieces by time. My daughter I see for a short time every day, tho' seven infants require much care and demand great and anxious attention.

Have you taken or do you think of taking any house in London? Can I be of any use in these things? Believe me curiosity does [not] excite me to make such enquiries but a sincere wish to prove that I am truly yours most affectionately, EDMUND NELSON.

To the Right Honourable Lady Nelson, Brighthamsted, Sussex.

[1] Monmouth MSS., Nelson papers, Vol. IV.

Lord Spencer to Lady Nelson[1]

April 16, 1801

Lord Spencer presents his compliments to Lady Nelson and sends her the account he has received from the Admiralty of the glorious victory obtained under the Command of Lord Nelson over the Danish fleet.[2]

Every one speaks in the highest terms of his Lordship's conduct on the occasion and in a line he has written to Mr. Addington he says that he thinks this action will put an end to all further contest.

Sir William Hamilton to Nelson[3]

Piccadilly,
April 16, 1801

What can I say my dear Lord that would convey the smallest idea of what we felt yesterday on receiving the authentical letters confirming your late most glorious victory and read in your own hand that God had not only granted you complete success against the enemies of our country but in the midst of such perils prevented your receiving the smallest scratch. We can only repeat what we knew well and often said before that Nelson *was*, *is* and to the *last* will ever be *the first*. However we all agree that when we get you safe home once more that you should never more risk your shattered frame. You have done enough and are well entitled to the motto of Virgil 'Hic victor laestus artemque repono.' The famous Broughton after he had beaten every opponent that dared to measure hard blows with him set up an ale house, the Broughton Head, in London, with the above verse of Virgil under it. Some years after he was persuaded to accept the challenge of a coachman and was beaten. Not that I mean to convey that any such thing could happen to your Lordship but you have done enough. Let others follow your good examples, they will be remembered to the latest posterity.

It appeared to me most extraordinary that the 6th inst. the date of your last letter to Emma that the death of the Emperor Paul[4] (which we have no doubt of here) should not be known at Copenhagen. It appears to us that as soon as that great event is known in Sweden and Denmark with the severe blow you have just given the latter, the formidable giant Northern

---

[1] Monmouth MSS., Nelson papers, Vol. V. Lord Spencer and his wife arrived in Bath at the same time as Lady Nelson.

[2] The battle of Copenhagen, fought on April 2. Sir Hyde Parker's despatch was published in the London Gazette on April 15. There were heavy losses: 254 officers and men killed, 689 wounded. Nelson was very grieved that no medal was given to those who had taken part in this battle.

[3] N.M.M. MS. 9960, Croker collection in the Phillipps papers.

[4] The Czar was assassinated on March 24, 1801.

Coalition will of itself fall to pieces and that we shall have the happiness of embracing you again here in a very short time.

You would have laughed to have seen what I saw yesterday. Emma did not know whether she was on her head or heels—in such a hurry to tell your great news that she could utter nothing but tears of joy and tenderness. I went to Davison yesterday morning and found him still in bed, having had a severe fit of the gout, and with your letter which he had just received, and he cried like a child. But what was very extraordinary, assured me that from the instant he had read your letter all pain had left him and that he felt himself able to get up and walk about. Your brother, Mrs. Nelson and Horace dined with us—your brother was more extraordinary than ever. He would get up suddenly and cut a caper rubbing his hands, every time that the thought of your fresh laurels came into his head. In short, except my self, and your Lordship knows that I have some phlegm, all the company, which was considerable after dinner—the Duke, Lord William, Mrs. Este, etc. were mad with joy—but I am sure that no one really rejoiced more at heart than I did. I have lived too long to have ecstasies but with calm reflection I felt for my friend having got to the very summit of glory—the 'Ne Plus Ultra', that he has had an other opportunity of rendering to his country the most important service and manifesting again his judgment his intrepidity and humanity. God bless you my very dear Lord and send you soon home to your friends. Enemies you have none but those that are bursting with envy and such animals infest all parts of the world. The King be assured is (tho' weak) getting well fast. Lord Loughborough told Livingston, who has just been here, that he was with the King the day before yesterday, before and after the delivery of the seals, and that he was perfectly calm and recollected.[1] Ever your sincerely attached and truly obliged and humble servant, WILLIAM HAMILTON.

Lady Nelson to Nelson[2]
(Draft)

[Bath,
April, 1801]

MY DEAR HUSBAND,—I cannot be silent in the general joy throughout the Kingdom, I must express my thankfulness and happiness it hath pleased God to spare your life. All greet you with every testimony of gratitude and

---

[1] The King recovered his health, but lived in seclusion for a time.
[2] Monmouth MSS., Nelson papers, Vol. III. It is not known whether a letter was sent to Nelson at this time, but the draft, preserved by Lady Nelson, has several corrections.

praise. This victory is said to surpass Aboukir. What my feelings are your own good heart will tell you. Let me beg, nay intreat you, to believe no wife ever felt greater affection for a husband than I do. And to the best of my knowedge I have invariably done everything you desired. If I have omitted any thing I am sorry for it.

On receiving a letter from our father written in a melancholy and distressing manner, I offered to go to him if I could in the least contribute to ease his mind. By return of post he desired to see me immediately but I was to stop a few days in town to see for a house. I will do every thing in my power to alleviate the many infirmities which bear him down.

What more can I do to convince you that I am truly your affectionate wife?

The Rev. Edmund Nelson to Nelson[1]

[Bath,
April, 1801]

MY GOOD, GREAT AND AFFECTIONATE SON,—He who created all things, He to whom all creatures bow, He by whom the very hairs of our heads are numbered, have covered your head in the day of battle. He has bestowed upon you great abilities and has granted you His grace to use them to His glory, the good of your fellow creatures and the salvation of your own soul.

I have sometimes a hope of receiving you once more surrounded not with public honours alone, but what must add pleasures to every other gratification, a return to domestic joys, the most durable and solid of all others. Be it so O God.

Yesterday I received your joyous news, but all things have their alloy, Lady[2] was heavily affected with her personal feelings at not receiving a line from your own hand. In all things may you have a right understanding. Writing is not easy task. [EDMUND NELSON].

To Lord Nelson.

Nelson to Alexander Davison[3]

St. George,
April 23, 1801

MY DEAR DAVISON,—You will, at a proper time, and before my arrival in England signify to Lady Nelson that I expect, and for which I have made

[1] N.M.M. MS. 9960, Croker collection in the Phillipps papers.
[2] Lady Nelson.
[3] Nicolas, Vol. VII, Addenda, p. ccix. The original in 1846 was in the possession of Colonel Davison.

such a very liberal allowance to her, to be left to myself, and without any inquiries from her: for sooner than live the unhappy life I did when I last came to England, I would stay abroad for ever. My mind is fixed as fate: therefore you will send my determination in any way you may judge proper; and believe me ever your obliged and faithful friend, NELSON AND BRONTE.

Mrs. Bolton to Lady Nelson[1]

Cranwich,
May 14, 1801

I suppose by this time, my dear Lady Nelson, you are returned to Bath after your appearance in the Drawing Room which I hope you found as pleasant as you expected. I find by a letter from Mrs. Nelson that you saw her. She thinks of bringing Charlotte to Hilborow to spend her holidays, I believe she is heartily tired of London and my brother will not be sorry to come into the country unless Lord Nelson wishes for his company there. I thought perhaps you would have stayed in town until my brother arrived, but you and my father are better judges than I am what is proper and you are with *his* father. Keep up your spirits my dear Madam and all will come right again, for tho' he is warm, he has a truly affectionate mind.

Mr. William Bolton has paid for the Bury papers I think 17s 6d, he says, Mr. Willett said he had a little bill against you for beer or porter, if you give him orders he will pay it. I would have paid him but he says he hopes to see you himself one day.

I have got my family all at home. The girls much improved, Eliza particularly. Anne is grown quite stout, but her shape is got *right*. Mr. and Mrs. Edwards dined with us last Thursday and next week we go there. Great events for Cranwich. The first company I have had to dinner, and the first visit we have made. Hete[2] has just finished her net gown which she hopes to wear on the first of August at a ball at Swaffham. Mr. Bolton's youngest daughter, Rebecca, is with us.

You talk of making a visit to Wolterton. If it does take place, I hope you will favour us with your company, here. Do not say you will not suffer us to take too much notice of you for fear it should injure us with Lord Nelson. I assure you I have a pride, as well as himself, in doing what is right, and that surely is to be attentive to those who have been *so to us* and I am sure my brother would *despise* us if we acted contrary.

[1] Monmouth MSS., Nelson papers, Vol. IV.
[2] Harriet, one of her daughters.

Ah Lady Nelson, you and I have lost our best friend in my dear brother Maurice.[1] What a shock to us all. Did you see the poor blind widow when you were in town? Mr. Bolton and the girls join in best wishes to all the party in both houses.

God bless you, yours affectionately, S. BOLTON.

Right Honourable Viscountess Nelson,[2] Kensington Place, Bath.

Lady Nelson to Nelson[3]
(Draft)

[July, 1801]

MY DEAREST HUSBAND,—Your generosity and tenderness was never more strongly shewn than your writing to Mr. Marsh yesterday morning for the payment of your very handsome quarterly allowance, which far exceeded my expectation, knowing your income and had you left it to me, I could not in conscience have said so much.

Accept my warmest, my most affectionate and grateful thanks. I could say more but my heart is too full. Be assured every wish, every desire of mine is to please the man whose affection constitutes my happiness.

God bless my dear husband. (unfinished).

Mr. Davison to Lady Nelson[4]

St. James Square,
July 12, 1801

MY DEAR MADAM,—I have long wished to write to you which nothing but the want of something to say to you prevented. I have nothing to relate particular, yet it is with unspeakable pleasure I can assure you, that Lord Nelson is better in health than I had ever reason to expect. He had been extremely ill indeed, and there yet remains a very troublesome disagreeable cough. I hope it will go off, and that we shall see him re-assume his former and natural good state of health.

A few day's quiet retreat in the country I trust may be of use to him.[5] I hardly need to repeat how happy I should have been to have seen him

---

[1] Maurice Nelson died suddenly on April 24, 1801, of brain fever. He left a widow, Mrs. Sarah Nelson, who was blind and in poor circumstances. Nelson gave her a pension of £200 a year.

[2] Nelson was created a viscount for his services in the battle of Copenhagen.

[3] Monmouth MSS., Nelson papers, Vol. III. Nelson returned to England on July 1, 1801, having resigned the command of the Baltic fleet owing to ill health.

[4] Monmouth MSS., Nelson papers, Vol. V.

[5] Nelson went with his brother and family and the Hamiltons to Surrey for 'a rural excursion' to recover his health.

with you, the happiest. His heart is so pure and so extremely good that I flatter myself he never can be divested from his affection. I have the same opinion I ever had of his sincere respect for you. I have no right to doubt it.

I understand the good old father intends coming to town. I should like to see him, ere I set off on the 26th for Northumberland.

Mrs. Davison sets out tomorrow with her young family and servants. She desires me to offer her kind respects to you.

Wishing you every comfort I am my dear Madam, your faithful friend, ALEXANDER DAVISON.

To the Right Honourable Lady Nelson, Bath.[1]

The Rev. Edmund Nelson to Nelson[2]

[Bath]
July 16, 1801

MY DEAR HORATIO,—On Tuesday next I intend (God willing) to leave Bath and tho' not very strong, yet, hope to reach Lothian[3] on Thursday, and as I must remain a few days in London, let me not interrupt any of your engagments.

Recollecting that Sir William and Lady Hamilton seemed to be gratified by the flavour of a cream cheese, I have taken the liberty of sending 2 or 3 cheeses of Bath manufacture.

I am my dear Son your most affectionate EDMUND NELSON.

Sir William Hamilton to Lady Hamilton[4]

Burford, 80 miles from London,
Saturday night. [July 27,] 1801

Here we are my dear Emma after a pleasant day's journey. No extraordinary occurrence. Our chaise is good and would have held the famous 'Tria Iuncta in Uno'[5] very well, but we must submit to the circumstances of the times.

Sir Joseph Banks we found in bed with the gout and last night his hot house was robbed of its choicest fruit peaches and nectarines. Amuse

---

[1] Redirected by the Rev. Edmund Nelson to Lymington, Hampshire.
[2] N.M.M. MS. 9960, Croker collection in the Phillipps papers.
[3] The hotel in Albemarle Street where Nelson was staying.
[4] N.M.M. MS. 9960, Croker collection in the Phillipps papers. After the excursion to Surrey, Sir William and his nephew went to view his estates at Milford Haven.
[5] The motto of the Order of the Bath, used by the Hamiltons and Nelson to describe their friendship.

yourself as well as you can and you may be assured that I shall return as soon as possible and you shall hear from me often.

Ever yours my dear Emma with the truest affection, WILLIAM HAMILTON.

My kindest love to my Lord[1] if he is not gone.
P.S. Corn at this market fell £15 a load today.

To Lady Hamilton, 23, Piccadilly, London.

The Rev. E. Nelson to Lady Nelson[2]

[Burnham Thorpe],
August 21, 1801

MY GOOD FRIEND,—I can only repeat what I have often declared that whenever you have a house likely to be your residence, which is convenient for receiving me, I will be ready. If you think you shall add any comfort to your self from my being with you I will certainly be at your command. Whether London is the spot most eligible, supposing all your wishes cannot be accomplished there you must judge, or whether Bath may not be a place more likely to answer every probable purpose of making you as happy as the present appearance of things will permit you to hope for.

Where you fix when your summer excursions end, and what routes you mean to take in the ensuing months, you will communicate to me and in every instance that comes within my power to accommodate be assured, with every friendly regard your most obliged and humble servant, EDMUND NELSON.

Mrs. Bolton will be with me 2 or 3 weeks longer.
Public news is my only gazette.

To Viscountess Nelson, No. 66 Wimpole Street, London.

Nelson to Lady Hamilton[3]

Amazon,[4]
September 26, 1801, 8 o'clock.

MY DEAREST EMMA,—Your kind letters came on board about 6 o'clock. You may rely upon one thing that I shall like Merton,[5] therefore do not be

---

[1] On July 24 Nelson was appointed to command a special squadron based from Deal to protect the coast against invasion.
[2] Monmouth MSS., Nelson papers, Vol. IV.
[3] N.M.M. MS. 9960, Croker collection in the Phillipps papers.
[4] Nelson's flag-ship after the attack on the Boulogne flotilla.
[5] The house near London chosen for Nelson by Lady Hamilton.

uneasy on that account. I have that opinion of your taste and judgement that I do not believe it can fail in pleasing me. We must only consider our means and for the rest I am sure you will soon make it the prettiest place in the world. I dare say Mr. Haslewood acted like all lawyers whose only consideration was for their client but I am sure you will do for me all the civil things towards Mr. Greaves. If I can afford to buy the Duck Close and the field adjoining it would be pleasant but I fear it is not in my power, but I shall know when my accounts are settled at New Year's year.

To be sure we shall employ the tradespeople of our village in preference to any others in what we want for common use, and give them every encouragement to be kind and attentive to us. From my heart do I wish that I was with you and it cannot be long, for today I am far from well, violent headache and very cold, but it may be agitation. Whatever my dear Emma you do for my little charge[1] I must be pleased with. Probably she will be lodged at Merton at least in the spring when she can have the benefit of our walks. It will make the poor mother happy I am sure. I do not write to her today as this goes through the Admiralty but tell her all I would say, you know my unchangeable thoughts about her. I shall have the child christened when I come up. Have we a nice church at Merton? We will set an example of goodness to the whole parish. Would to God I was with you at Laleham, I shall never forget our happiness at that place.

Mr. Davison will pay Mrs. Nelson £50 October 1st. I dare say Mr. Shakespeare has some orders about it. I had yesterday a letter from my father. He seems to think that he may do something which I shall not like I suppose he means going to Somerset St.[2] Shall I to an old man enter upon the detestable subject? It may shorten his days, but I think I shall tell him that I cannot go to Somerset Street to see him, but I shall not write till I hear your opinion. If I once begin you know it will *all out* about her and her ill treatment to her son,[3] but you shall decide.

Our accounts of dear Parker[4] I fear preclude all hopes of his recovery. It was my intention to have gone ashore this morning to have called on Admiral Lutwidge but the wind is blowing fresh from the S.W. I have declined it, for I doubt if I could get off again. At 10 o'clock with your letters came off Dr. Baird's note to say every hope was gone. I have desired that his death should be sent by telegraph to the Admiralty. They

[1] The child whom Nelson adopted, Horatia Nelson Thompson.
[2] Where Lady Nelson was living.
[3] Nothing is known of Lady Nelson ill-treating Josiah: the rumour may have been fabricated when he failed to get another ship.
[4] Nelson's favourite young captain, who was badly wounded in the attack on the Boulogne flotilla.

will surely honour his memory although they would not promote him. What are our feelings my dear Emma? But we must cheer up, and with best regards to Mrs. Nelson, believe me ever forever your most affectionate NELSON AND BRONTE.

Best regards to Sir William.
I send you the last report who knows.

Lady Hamilton to Mrs. William Nelson[1]

[September, 1801]

MY DEAR MRS. NELSON,—I have had many letters from my dear Nelson. He is desperate to get here and be quiet at Merton but he loves his brother and wishes most *ardently* to *see* him situated as he ought. As the thing is come to a conclusion, he wishes for many reasons that things should terminate with *advantage* to his only brother. Ministers are all *deceitful animals* and when *no longer pipe no longer dance* and the war being over if there is not a little management these double dealers may wish for a loop hole to get out from their *promises* but they shall not. Nelson loves his brother, and he will for 3 weeks or a month sacrifice every thing, that no occasion shall be given to *these false* friends to be off their *promises*— I will also give up the satisfaction of seeing, nursing and comforting my dear, much loved, virtuous Nelson for your sakes. So *we* will hold the candle to the devil for once for perhaps. Whilst preliminaries are talking and peace signed, it may be very necessary to be double diligent not to be outwitted by the *arch* rogue Bonaparte: Nelson *weighs* in the scales of politics very *heavy, counts* much. Therefore I have wrote to him as I *write* to *you* with force and sincere. *My heart says* 'come'; my love of his glory and *your husband's cause* says, 'stay, let him finish with éclat'. I love Nelson's glory, his great and glorious deeds have made on my heart an impression *never never* to be effaced. I love you. *You* and your husband are the only people worthy to be by *him beloved*. His poor father is un-knowing and taken in by a very wicked, bad, artful woman, acting *a bad part by so glorious* a son. The sin be on their heads. Would your father have seen with patience if she had lived with milord, *his own* flesh and blood set a *side* for who? For Nesbit's, the doctor's son, a villain who many times called the glorious Nelson villain and that he would do for him, yet this boy the —— son would, if this designing woman had had her way, have put you all aside. And *your* father, Nelson's father, protects this woman and gives a mortal blow to his son. The old man could never hear

[1] N.M.M. MS. 9292, Bridport papers.

her till now and now he conspires *against the saviour of his country* and his darling, who has risen him to such a height of honour, *and for whom*? *A wicked false malicious* wretch who rendered his days wretched and his nights miserable; *And the father* of Nelson says, 'I will *stab* my son to the heart,' but indeed, he says 'my poor father is led now he does not know what he does.' But oh! how cruel, shocking it is and I am afraid the Boltons are not without their share of *guilt* in *this affair. Jealous of you all* they have, with the Matchams, pushed this poor dear old gentleman to act this bad and horrible *part*, to support a false proud bad *woman*, artful, and with every bad quality to make wretched those she belongs to and yet command over her own cold heart and infamous soul to shew an appearance to the bad part of the *world* of gentleness and struggling with oppression, but let her own wickedness be her punishment. Her sins be on her head she abandons her *son* although a villain! 'Tis a bad bird befowls its own nest. [EMMA HAMILTON]

Lady Nelson to the Rev. E. Nelson
(Drafts)

A[1]

[Wolterton,
September, 1801]

MY DEAR SIR,—The reception of my friends on Saturday last was truly gratifying. It makes me more satisfied with myself than ever I was before. Altho' I spend my time cheerfully, I shall certainly make you a visit for two or three days. Do not incommode yourself in the least to receive me as there is a good inn at Norham or the accommodation will do quite well enough at Burnham Market for two nights and the days I can spend at the Parsonage—I think of being with you on the 25th of this month—but you shall hear again from me—Be assured I shall have great pleasure in paying you every attention in my power—and at the same time you do not deprive Captain Nisbet of any rooms in my house—he will be *very, very* welcome in Town—and a back parlour is all he would ever wish for.

The Rev. E. Nelson, Burnham Thorpe, Norfolk.

B[2]

[October, 1801]

MY DEAR SIR,—My visit to Burnham was one of duty rather than of pleasure I assure you it called forth all my feelings. The impression your

---

[1] Monmouth MSS., Nelson papers, Vol. III. Draft in Lady Nelson's hand: unsigned, but with a note, 'This letter was written from Wolterton Sept. 1801.'
[2] Draft as above, with a note by Lady Nelson: 'This in October 1801. Mr. Nelson makes me a visit in November—towards the end—Somerset Street.'

2 Q

situation has left on my mind is so strong that I cannot delay any longer offering my opinion on the subject of your living with me, which from your conversation makes it impracticable; the deprivation of seeing your children is so cruel, even in thought, it is impossible you can any longer the desire [. . . *paper cut away* . . .]

I am not surprised for I knew Lord Nelson's friends could not like it. Even supposing his Lordship resided in Italy the offence would be just the same and in my opinion greater. I told Mrs. M.[1] at Bath, that Lord Nelson would not like your living with me. 'Oh! my dear Lady Nelson. My brother will thank you in his heart for he knows no one can attend to my father as you do.' I had seen the wonderful change pass belief. She had not.

Do not consider the rent of the house one moment. My visit to Wolterton is a pretty long one and I return in a few days there. Be assured if at any time I can be of the least use to you, command my services and you shall always find me the same.

The Rev. E. Nelson, Burnham Thorpe, Norfolk.

The Rev. E. Nelson to Nelson[2]

Burnham,
October 8, 1801

MY DEAR HORATIO,—Upon the happy return of peace I may, with a little variation, address you in the words of an apostle and say 'You have fought a good fight, you have finished your military career, with glory, and honour, henceforth, there is laid up for you, much happiness, subject indeed in this present time, to uncertainty, but in a future state, immutable and incorruptible.' As a public character I could be acquainted only with what was made public respecting you. Now in a private station possibly you may tell me where it is likely your general place of residence may be, so that sometimes we may have mutual happiness in each other, notwithstanding, the severe reproaches I feel from an anonymous letter for my conduct to you, which is such, it seems, as will totally separate us. This is unexpected indeed.

Most likely the winter may be too cold for me to continue here, and I mean to spend it between Bath and London. If Lady Nelson is in a hired house and by herself, gratitude requires that I should sometimes be with her, if it is likely to be of any comfort to her. Everywhere age and my many infirmities are very troublesome and require every mark of

---

[1] Mrs. Matcham.
[2] N.M.M. MS. 9499, Walter collection.

respect. At present I am in the parsonage, it is warm and comfortable. I am quite by my self, except the gentleman who takes care of the churches. He is a worthy sensible sober man, in all respects and as far as rests with him, makes me very happy.

I cannot do any public duty nor even walk to the next house, but my dearest son, here is still room enough to give to you a warm a joyful and affectionate reception, if you could feel an inclination to look once more at me in Burnham parsonage. I pray God to continue his blessings in all stations, places, and undertakings. EDMUND NELSON.

Rev. E. Nelson to Lady Nelson[1]

Burnham,
October 17, 1801

MY GOOD MADAM,—Be assured I still hold fast my integrity, and am ready to join you, whenever you have your servants in the London house as at first thought of. In respect to this business, the opinion of others must rest with themselves, and not make any alteration with us. I have not offended any man and do rely upon my children's affection that notwithstand all that have been said, they will not in my old age forsake me.

If there are good reasons to alter our general plan, I shall reside at Bath all this winter. Shall be glad to hear again from you on this subject as my movements depend now on your self.

The first week in November shall leave Burnham.

Am most truly ready to subscribe my self your obliged humble servant, EDMUND NELSON.

To Lady Nelson.

Lady Hamilton to Mrs. William Nelson[2]

Merton Place,
Saturday, [October 17, 1801]

MY DEAREST FRIEND,—I had letters yesterday from our dear Lord. He has sent me a letter open for me to read and put in the post which I have done this day but I send you an extract.

MY DEAR FATHER,—I have received your letter and of which you must be sensible I cannot like for as you seem by your conduct to put me in the wrong it is no wonder that they who do not know me and my disposition should. But Nelson soars above them all and time will do

---

[1] Monmouth MSS., Nelson papers, Vol. IV.
[2] N.M.M. MS. 9292, Bridport papers.

that justice to my private character which she has to my public one. I that have given her,[1] with her falsity and his £2000 a year and £4000 in money and which she calls a poor pittance, and with all that to abandon her son bad as he is and going about defaming me. May God's vengeance strike me dead if I would abandon my children. If he wants reformation, who should reclaim him but the mother? I could say much more but will not out of respect to you, my dear Father, but you know her, therefore I finish.

On the 23rd I shall be at Merton with Sir William and Lady Hamilton and them with myself shall be happy, most happy to see you, my dear beloved father, that is your home.[2] My brother and sister, the dear children will soon be with us and happy shall we all be, but more so if you will come. Plenty of room for you and your servant, Abram's brother will live with us. Allen's wife is the dairy maid.

Ever my dear father's dutiful son, N. AND B.

This is an extract what do you think of it? When you and Mr. Nelson has read it, pray burn it. I would have sent you the letter but am obliged to send it to day. God bless you. In a hurry. Sir William is gone to fetch Charlotte. Viganoni comes so she will have 3 lessons. 2 today and perhaps 2 tomorrow. Sir William is quite charmed with her. She will have her Italian lesson and French from Oliver. She shall be early at school on Monday morning and as milord is to arrive on Friday[3] at dinner, she shall be here to receive him and go back to school on Monday early.
[EMMA HAMILTON]

Lady Nelson to Nelson[4]

16 Somerset Street,
December 18, 1801

MY DEAR HUSBAND,—It is some time since I have written to you. The silence you have imposed is more than my affections will allow me and in this instance I hope you will forgive me in not obeying you. One thing I omitted in my letter of July which I now have to offer for your accommodation, a comfortable warm house. Do, my dear husband, let us live together. I can never be happy till such an event takes place. I assure you again I

---

[1] Lady Nelson, and Josiah.
[2] His father went to Merton to stay in November. He told Mrs. Matcham, 'Your good brother is truly in better health and happier in himself than in good truth I have in any passed time observed him to be.' He then went to Bath for the winter.
[3] Nelson arrived as promised on October 23.
[4] Monmouth MSS., Nelson papers, Vol. III. This letter, addressed to Nelson at Davison's house, was returned to Lady Nelson with a note by Davison, 'Opened by mistake by Lord Nelson, but not read. A. Davison.'

have but one wish in the world, to please you. Let every thing be buried in oblivion, it will pass away like a dream. I can now only intreat you to believe I am most sincerely and affectionately your wife, FRANCES H. NELSON.

To Viscount Nelson and Duke of Bronte, St. James's Square, London.

Horatio Nelson to Mrs. William Nelson[1]

[Merton, 1802]

MY DEAR MAMA,—I am as happy as a prince, I am now making a little box. When my cousin comes my uncle says we shall go and see everything worth seeing. I have done my task. I arrived here on Wednesday about 9 o'clock. Charlotte is now playing. My little dog Nilus is lost which I am very sorry for. Pray give my love to Papa.

Accept the same from your affectionate son, HORATIO NELSON.

[Postscript added by Lady Hamilton:]

Sir William did not come with us yesterday as he was obliged to attend the British Museum this morning, but he comes to dinner; so does Captain Louis and tomorrow we have Captains Sutton and Plamkin. We have a dreadful cold wind to day. Charlotte[2] is now translating one of Madame de Sevigni's letters. God bless you ever yours most affectionately, EMMA.

Why did you not let me know you had a great dinner? I would have sent you a fine dish of fish. Out upon you, I am angry. What a blessed thing is gold. It is a 'passa por tout'. The rich can do every thing, except what Nelson does—fight.

The Rev. Edmund Nelson to Nelson[3]

[Bath,]
March 23, 1802

MY DEAR HOR,—Your 2 last kind letters I esteem as fresh marks of your affectionate attention to what must give to me every paternal sensation which I can derive from a confirmation of what can contribute to your happiness as a philanthropist, a love of the country in general and of the individuals which compose it. And amongst many others may your lot be cast where there is not only a goodly heritage but also abundance of internal peace such as you have never yet enjoyed much of, but are now of age to enjoy.

[1] N.M.M. MS. 9292, Bridport papers.
[2] As soon as he got to Merton, Nelson made it the focal point for his family. Horace, his nephew, was at Eton, and Charlotte still at school in London.
[3] N.M.M. MS. 9960, Croker collection in the Phillipps papers.

When the expected stranger is arrived in Kensington Place[1] and I can see your sister in a way of recovering, I shall then begin to think of leaving Bath. When I am deprived of Kitty's daily visits to dine with me, my comforts here will be much curtailed. My strength returns very slow, yet still have hopes I shall with the assistance of the May sunshine get able to travel, and smell a Merton rose in June.[2]

Lady Hamilton's promised gazette is very tardy in its appearance, pleasant news is always acceptable.

God bless you and all who dwell under your roof. EDMUND NELSON.

Rev. E. Nelson to Lady Nelson[3]

[Bath]
April 20, 1802

MY GOOD MADAM,—I am truly glad to have it in my power to acquaint you that my dear daughter was yesterday safely delivered of a girl, both in a prosperous way.

Mr. Tarlton gave me pleasing account of your health and that you spoke of leaving London early in the summer. Of this rest assured that in all places I wish for your happiness and am your most obliged humble servant, EDMUND NELSON.

Next month I mean to leave Bath.

To Viscountess Nelson,[4] No. 16 Somerset Street, Portman Square, London.

Mrs. Bolton to Lady Hamilton[5]

Cranwich,
May 6, 1802

LADY HAMILTON,—Many thanks my dear Lady Hamilton for your obliging letter and that you gave such a favourable account of my dear brother's amendment. The death of my dearest father must be great grief to all his children for never was there a more affectionate father than he has been to us, or one I believe more beloved by children, but thank God his life was spared to us so long, and to the last was cheerful.[6]

---

[1] Where Mrs. Matcham was living.
[2] Rooms were being prepared at Merton for his permanent residence.
[3] Monmouth MSS., Nelson papers, Vol. IV. Lady Nelson has added a note: 'Mr. Nelson died six days after he writ this letter.'
[4] The address has been written in another hand.
[5] N.M.M. MS. 9594, Nelson-Ward collection; Morrison, *The Hamilton and Nelson Papers*, Vol. II, No. 666.
[6] The Rev. Edmund Nelson died at Bath on April 26, 1802.

Mr. Bolton is gone this day to Burnham with the Dr.[1] When he returns, shall have great pleasure in fixing the time for visiting Merton.

I cannot close my letter without thanking you my dear Madam for your kindness and attention to my little girls when at Merton.

I am your ladyship's obliged obedient servant, S. BOLTON.

My kindest love to my brother and beg you will make my compliments to Sir William.

[Addressed under cover to: The Right Hon. Viscount Nelson, Duke of Bronte, etc., Merton Place, Surrey.]

Mrs. Bolton to Lady Nelson[2]

Cranwich,
Friday noon, [May 15, 1802]

Your going to Bath my dear Lady Nelson was of a piece with all your conduct to my beloved father. I did not know he was ill till he was no more. To me his loss is great indeed, even as a friend, but more as a parent. He had lived so long that when not with him we always flattered ourselves with a longer time still. He was a truly good Christian and no doubt has met his reward. This must be our comfort and hope to meet again in a better world.

Poor Mrs. Goulty[3] lost her husband about ten days ago. I find my Lord[4] has promised to provide for Abraham[5] by a place in the India House and till then with an allowance.

Mr. Bolton returned from Burnham yesterday where he had been to attend the funeral (or should have wrote to you sooner). He says the church was crowded, every one lamenting as the loss of a friend. I am sure the poor have lost a kind benefactor. Six clergymen attended as bearers. The Dr. Mr. Rolfe and Mr. B.[6] attended as real mourners I am sure, the farmers in the three parishes followed. Thus closed this mournful procession and with it the greatest comfort of my life.

I am going to Merton in about a fortnight, but my dear Lady N. we cannot meet as I wished for every body is known who visits you. Indeed I do not think I shall be permitted even to go to town.[7]

---

[1] Dr. William Nelson, Mrs. Bolton's brother.
[2] Monmouth MSS., Nelson papers, Vol. IV.
[3] Her aunt Thomazine, wife of Mr. John Goulty.
[4] Lord Nelson, who had been too ill to attend his father's funeral.
[5] Servant to the Rev. E. Nelson.
[6] Dr. William Nelson, son; the Rev. Robert Rolfe, nephew; and Mr. Thomas Bolton, son-in-law of the Rev. E. Nelson.
[7] Mrs. Bolton was the last of the family to drop Lady Nelson.

But be assured I always have and shall always be your sincere friend.
S. BOLTON.

To Viscountess Nelson, Somerset Street, Portman Square, London.

Nelson to Mrs. Bolton[1]

Merton,
June 11, 1802

MY DEAR SISTER,—Here is £100 which I shall pay you on the 11th June for three years towards the education of your children. By that time other things may turn up and there is a trifle in case you may want any little thing going thro' London.

All I desire is that you would not say or write me a syllable on the subject for I am sorry I cannot do more being truly your most affectionate brother, NELSON AND BRONTE.

To Mrs. Bolton.

Thomas Bolton to Nelson[2]

[Cranwich,
December 30, 1802]

I have sent you by Josiah Griggs two cows which I hope you will approve. They will be at the 'Pyed Bull' at Islington on Sunday next at 10 oclock. You'll be so good as to order some body there to take care of them. I shall pay the man for the driving etc. I have received Doctor Nelson's notices for cotton. I set off for Norwich Thursday and I shall send a turkey directed to No. 23 on Saturday. I hope Lady Hamilton will like the cow, it's an extravagant price, I am well assured she is a good one.

		£	s.	d.
December 28th 1802	One cow bought at Hilborow with calf in about 6 weeks	10		
	One cow with a calf 10 days old	16		
	Expenses getting her home		2	6
	Driving to Islington	1	1	0
		27	3	6
	Allow for the calf	1	1	0
		26	2	6

[1] N.M.M. MS. 9590, Girdlestone papers. At this time Nelson was paying £150 a year 'to assisting in educating my nephews'. His half-pay as a vice-admiral was £465 and he had a naval pension of £923 for the loss of one arm and one eye.
[2] N.M.M. MS. 9960, Croker collection in the Phillipps papers.

I bought 20 Scots today to fat, which cost me £320 which is £16 each. If we give these prices for lean stock, meat cannot be cheaper. I think you had better be selling your hay. If the winter continues open hay will be cheaper. I was glad to hear you had got through for the conveying Mr. Axe's estate,[1] it has made you complete.

With best respects to Lady Hamilton, I remain your Lordship's much obliged friend and humble servant, THOMAS BOLTON.

Everything goes on well at Bridgham and Mr. Comyns[2] will soon have his glebes laid together.

George Matcham to Nelson[3]

January 9, 1803

MY DEAR LORD,—I am happy that our opinions coincide in respect to the mortgage. If you will have the goodness to order the interest to be paid to my bankers Lefevre Currie and Co. Cornhill I will thank you and as it is equally agreeable to you to have it paid half yearly, it will be an accommodation to us.

The *Moniteur* has latterly been so violent in its invectives that despairing of a long peace, we had almost relinquished the hope of going abroad. France is I think out of the question, but a Dutch gentleman, our neighbour, has given us so favourable an account of Germany, both for our comfort and finances, that we have turned our thoughts towards a residence there for a few years. It will also be advantageous for the education of our children. Our neighbour recommends Dresden, but Vienna appears to me most eligible. Having been there, I am a little judge of the situation and pleasantness of the environs and Mr. Oliver assured me it was one of the cheapest residences in Europe. As he resided there a long time I have taken the liberty of inclosing a letter to him for his advice and particular information. He once offered to conduct us there. Should he be inclined to go we would frank his journey and make him a recompense if his demands are suitable to our means. This his letter may determine. When we shall be able to proceed we cannot say, as there is a prospect of another addition to our family connections, and we know not whether it would be more convenient to dub the stranger German or English. God bless us all and direct us for the best.

[1] The extra land Nelson bought at Merton.
[2] Nelson's chaplain in the *Vanguard* in 1798, who had been given the living of Bridgham in Norfolk.
[3] N.M.M. MSS. 9960, Croker collection in the Phillipps papers. Nelson's brother-in-law had travelled a good deal in the East before he settled in England as a country gentleman; died 1833.

Lady Nelson we understand has taken a house at Clifton. She called upon us. Mrs. Matcham was at home but she did not come in nor make the least inquiry about us, but left a card and rolled off as she came in Lord Hood's carriage and four. We should have told her, as we have always declared, it is our maxim if possible to be at peace with all the world.

With best wishes to your happy circle, I am my dear Lord yours most sincerely, G. MATCHAM.

Mrs. Bolton to Lady Hamilton[1]

Cranwich,
March 21, 1803

LADY HAMILTON,—Thanks my dear Lady for your letter I am afraid all hopes of keeping my dear brother with us is now over. Bonaparte must be severely punished for his insolence. God preserve and restore him again to us in safety, then what a happy party we shall all meet at Merton. May it be soon is my prayer. I find by a letter from Captain Bolton[2] Sir Wm.[3] has taken a medicine which has made him better. This mild weather must be greatly in his favour. I sincerely hope he will be restored to you.

Will your Ladyship permit me the privilege of friendship to request your interest with my Lord in favour of Captain Bolton? The nearer he is placed to him the better I shall like it. Granting his request will cause an additional obligation on me. The young man himself is anxious to serve with Lord Nelson, which makes me say the more.

Mrs. Pierson and her little girl are with us, the child is the exact image of poor Pierson. She begs her compliments. I am sure had the Dr. or Mrs. Nelson known the present situation of affairs they never would have left you.

Mr. Bolton is gone to Retford assizes as one of a special jury in a cause for defamation, the plaintiff Sir Edward Ashley. Erskine and Garrow are to plead, therefore a seat in the jury box will be no unpleasant thing.

Whenever you have a moment to spare give me a line just to say peace or war and when and where my Lord is going, for the papers are no dependence. Give my kind and affectionate love to my brother. I do not write to him as I know you will express my feelings and anxious wishes for him.

I am my dear Lady Hamilton, your sincere friend, S. BOLTON.

[1] N.M.M. MS. 9594, Nelson-Ward collection; Morrison, Vol. II, No. 706.
[2] William Bolton, midshipman in the *Agamemnon*; promoted captain in 1801.
[3] Sir William Hamilton.

Nelson to Mrs. Bolton[1]

Merton,
March 30, 1803

MY DEAR SISTER,—I have strongly memorandum, Lord St. Vincent for Captain Bolton to be sent to the Mediterranean and if we unfortunately have a war his promotion may be looked upon as sure, and as he is likely to be related,[2] my interest for his welfare must increase. I really believe him to be a most excellent young man.

Dear Sir William is very, very bad, he can't, in my opinion, get over it and I think it will happen very soon. You will imagine Lady Hamilton and my feelings on the occasion. Indeed all London is interested in the fate of such a character.[3]

Kind regards to all at Cranwich and believe me ever your most affectionate brother, NELSON AND BRONTE.

Wrote last Saturday. I forgot.

[P.S. by Lady Hamilton:] I have only to say, dearest Mrs. Bolton, Sir W. was so ill yesterday he could not live we thought. Today he is better. I am worn out but ever your affectionately. E.H.

To Mrs. Bolton, Cranwich, Near Brandon, Norfolk.

Nelson to St. Vincent[4]

May 19, 1803

MY DEAR LORD,—This will be presented to you by my nephew Sir William Bolton[5] and now he stands in so near a situation to me it must be my anxious wish to get him employed and with me and promoted.

If the Devil stands at the door the *Victory* shall sail tomorrow forenoon. Keep your health my dear Lord and ever believe me your most obliged and affectionate NELSON AND BRONTE.

Earl St. Vincent, K.Bth.

[1] N.M.M. MS. 9590, Girdlestone papers.
[2] He was engaged to his cousin, Catherine Bolton, Nelson's neice.
[3] Sir William left Merton and died at his house in Piccadilly on April 6, 1803.
[4] N.M.M. MS. 9292.
[5] Bridport papers. Captain Bolton and Miss Bolton were married on May 18. He was knighted the next day when he stood proxy for Nelson at the ceremony of installation of Knights of the Bath, which Nelson could not attend as he had gone to Portsmouth to join the *Victory*, his new flag-ship.

Mrs. Matcham to Lady Hamilton[1]

A

No. 2 Portland Place, Bath,
December 1, 1804

Many thanks my dear Lady Hamilton for your kindness in writing which is more than I deserve for my seeming neglect but you may suppose I have not much spare time for writing when I tell you that we are always fifteen in family which it has been no little business to settle in our new habitation. . . . The Lady[2] is I believe at Bath, but too great a distance for us ever to see her. We have been at a ball, a concert and a play this week but she was not at either. My only desire is that we shall not be in the same room and circumstances are now so well understood by our friends that I don't think it likely we shall ever meet her. . . .

B

Bath,
January 20, 1805

MY DEAR LADY HAMILTON,— . . . As you have had no letters from our dear friend most likely this Spanish war will detain him for some time longer, but if it pleases God to give him health he may now have an opportunity of adding money to glory. We were in the same room with Lady N. a few nights since, for the first time since she came to Bath. She had then an opportunity of showing her insolence as far as looks could express, so I was told by some friends of mine who said she looked as I passed her in that scornful way, which could not but be noticed by all that saw her. But be assured there is a strong party against my brother whom we know to be all goodness and liberality. Different tales are told in different parties, but I think a time must come when everything will appear in a true light. . . .

Miss S. Bolton[3] *to Lady Hamilton*

Bath,
July 7, 1805

MY DEAR LADY HAMILTON,—We are all anxiety as you may readily conceive for news, you are we know even more anxious than we are. We often talk of you and wish ourselves with you that we might talk it over. . . . We

[1] This and the two following letters are from N.M.M. MS. 9594, Nelson-Ward collection; Morrison, Vol. II, Nos. 798, 806, 819. Extracts only are quoted here.
[2] Lady Nelson.
[3] Susanna Bolton, niece of Nelson, twin sister of Catherine Bolton; died 1864.

hear that Tom Tit has been very ill and been attended by two physicians. She is now however got quite well. She looks shockingly really and very old. Mrs. Matcham often wishes she was in heaven, we join, and make no doubt we have your good wishes on the occasion. She is still in Bath. . . .

Mrs. Bolton to Lady Hamilton[1]

A

[August, 1805]

Thanks my dear Lady for your scrap. It was indeed short and sweet, for sweet was the intelligence that my dearest brother was arrived in England.[2] What a Paradise he must think Merton to say nothing of the Eve it contains. I need not give you joy for I am sure you have it. The Dr. is at Mrs. Berney's but depend upon it, they will soon be with you and fill your house. When you give me a hint I will come. God bless you, you have no time I know to read my thrash. Your affectionate S. BOLTON.

B

Bath,
October 17, 1805

MY DEAR FRIEND,—I shall obey your commands or rather I may say wishes, and be at Merton next Tuesday night. . . . I saw Tom Tit yesterday in her carriage at the next door come to take Lady Charlotte Drummond out with her. She looked then much as usual had I seen only her hands spreading about I should have known her. I hope by the last Lisbon mails you have got letters from my dear brother and that I am sure will drive away all the blue devils in spite of screech owls rooks etc. You must keep up your spirits. What in the world will my Lord think if he comes back and finds you grown thin and looking ill? . . .

Lord Barham to Lady Nelson[3]

Admiralty,
November 6, 1805

MADAM,—It is with the utmost concern that in the midst of victory I have to inform your ladyship of the death of your illustrious partner Lord Viscount Nelson.[4]

---

[1] N.M.M. MS. 9594, Nelson-Ward collection; Morrison, Vol. II, Nos. 825, 846.

[2] Nelson arrived at Spithead, after his long Mediterranean service and chase to the West Indies, on August 18. He proceeded at once to Merton.

[3] B.M. Add. MS. 28,333. Lord Barham was First Lord of the Admiralty 1805–6. As Sir Charles Middleton he had been Comptroller of the Navy and served on the Admiralty Board. He died in 1813.

[4] The news of the Battle of Trafalgar reached London on November 6.

After leading the British fleet into close action with the enemy and seeing their defeat he fell by a musket ball entering his chest.

It is the death he wished for and less to be regretted on his own account. But the public loss is irretrievable. I can only add that events of this kind do not happen by chance. I recommend therefore your ladyship to His protection who is alone able to save or to destroy.

Being with much esteem madam your faithful and most obedient servant, BARHAM.

Lady Walpole to Captain Nisbet[1]

Wolterton,
November 7, 1805

No words my dear Sir can express our feelings at this present moment, you must forgive our anxiety for Lady Nelson, if I trespass upon you. I beg of you to tell me how she supports herself under the shock of Lord Nelson's death.

I well know how sincerely she will feel, notwithstanding all that has passed, as I know how well she loved him. He fell gloriously, but the nation will ever lament their brave defender, and the last act of his life was the gaining a most glorious victory for his country.

When she can bear it, may I beg of you to assure her how anxious we are for her. Lady Berry is here and desires me to to say that she shall be most happy to go to Lady Nelson directly if she can give her any satisfaction or any comfort. She came here yesterday for a few days and this news is just arrived.

Believe me my dear Sir, your ever obliged KATHERINE WALPOLE.

Lady Berry would not at this moment give Lady Nelson the trouble of a letter as I am writing.

Earl Nelson to Lady Nelson[2]
(Draft)

34 Fitz Roy Square,
November 9, 1805

DEAR MADAM,—I have just gone through the painful task of perusing the last will of that great man whose name I have now the honour to bear.

---

[1] Monmouth MSS., Nelson papers, Vol. V.

[2] N.M.M. MS. 9292, Bridport papers. Nelson's brother William was created Earl Nelson on November 9. As his heir he inherited the Dukedom of Bronte.

Being appointed (jointly with Mr. Haslewood) executor it becomes my duty to acquaint your Ladyship with so much of the will [as] more immediately concerns your [ladyship I] shall give direction for your being fu[rnished] as soon as possible with a complete copy. And if I could feel pleasure amidst so many mournful reflections as press upon my mind it would be in the opportunity afforded me of renewing with your Ladyship that intercourse of kind offices which I once hoped would have always marked our lives—which untoward circumstances have occasioned some interruption of, but which I trust will never again be suspended. Believe me to remain with truest regard dear Madam, your most affectionate brother, NELSON.

The right honourable the Viscountess Nelson.

Captain Hardy to Lady Hamilton[1]

Victory, St. Helen's
Wednesday night (December 4, 1805)

MY DEAR LADY HAMILTON,—I lose not a moment to acquaint you with our arrival and inclose you by Chevalier[2] the last letters written by our most dear and ever to be lamented friend. Be assured my dear Lady Hamilton, that I will do everything that lays in my power to serve you and I trust you will believe that I am your sincere friend, T. M. HARDY.

Nelson's last Will and Testament[3]

May 10, 1803

This is the last will and testament of me Horatio Viscount Nelson of the Nile and of Burnham Thorpe in the county of Norfolk and United Kingdom of Great Britain and Ireland and Duke of Bronte in the kingdom of farther Sicily.

First in the event that I shall die in England I direct my executors hereinafter named (unless His Majesty shall signify it to be his pleasure

---

[1] N.M.M. 47 MS. 9421. Trafalgar House collection.
[2] Nelson's servant, recommended by his friend Alexander Davison.
[3] N.M.M. MS. 9641, duplicate copy of Nelson's will. The original is kept at Somerset House. Nicolas, Vol. vii, p. ccxxi.

that my body shall be interred elsewhere) to cause my body to be interred in the parish church of Burnham Thorpe in the county of Norfolk near the remains of my deceased father and mother and in as private a manner as may be and I direct that the sum of one hundred pounds shall be divided amongst the poor of the several parishes of Burnham Thorpe (aforesaid) Sutton and Norton all in the county of Norfolk that is to say one third part to the poor of each of the said parishes the same to be distributed at the discretion of the respective curates or officiating ministers of those parishes and in such manner and proportions and to such objects as they respectively shall think fit.

And I give and bequeath to Emma Lady Hamilton widow of the right honourable Sir William Hamilton Knight of the most Honourable Order of the Bath my diamond star as a token of my friendship and regard I likewise give and bequeath to the said Emma Lady Hamilton the silver cup marked E. H. which she presented to me. I give and bequeath to my brother the reverend William Nelson doctor in divinity the gold box presented to me by the city of London also I give and bequeath to the said William Nelson the gold sword presented to me by the captains who fought with me at the battle of the Nile. Also I give and bequeath to my sister Catherine Matcham the sword presented to me by the City of London. Also I give and bequeath to my sister Susannah Bolton the silver cup presented to me by the Turkey company. Also I give and bequeath to Alexander Davison of St. James's Square in the county of Middlesex Esquire my Turkish gun scymeter and canteen. Also I give and bequeath to my late captain and worthy friend Captain Hardy all my telescopes and sea glasses and one hundred pounds in money to be paid three months after my death. And I give and bequeath the sum of one hundred pounds to each of my executors hereinafter named to be paid or retained at the end of three months from my death.

And I give and bequeath to my before named brother William Nelson and William Haslewood of Craven Street in the Strand in the county of Middlesex esquire all the residue and remainder of my goods chattels and personal estate whatsoever and wheresoever (except the household goods and furniture wines plate china linen pictures and prints which shall be in my house at Merton at my decease and also except my diamond sword and jewels hereinafter bequeathed and also except any other articles which I do or shall or may by this my will or by any codicil or codicils hereto otherwise bequeath and dispose of) to hold to them their executors administrators and assigns upon trusts and for the ends intents and purposes hereinafter limited expressed declared and contained of and concerning the same

vizt upon trust that they the said trustees and the survivor of them and the executors and administrators of such survivors do and shall as soon as may be after my death convert into money such parts of the same personal estate as shall not consist of money and do and shall lay out and invest in the purchase of three pounds per cent consolidated bank annuities so much and such part of the money and also the money which shall belong to me at my death as by the dividends interest and income thereof will produce the clear yearly sum of one thousand pounds and do and shall stand and be possessed of the said bank annuities upon trust that from time to time during the natural life of Frances Herbert Viscountess Nelson my wife they the said trustees and the survivor of them the executors or administrators of such survivor do and shall permit and suffer or authorize and empower the said Viscountess Nelson my wife and her assigns to receive and take the dividends interest and income of the same bank annuities when and as the same shall become due and payable in addition to all other provisions made by me at any time heretofore for her and in addition to the sum of four thousand pounds lately given by me to her and which sum of four thousand pounds it is my will that she shall retain I direct and declare that the provision made for her by this my will and also the said four thousand pounds shall be accepted and taken by her in lieu and full satisfaction of all dower right and title of dower and free bench of her the said Viscountess Nelson my wife of and in all or any of the freehold and copyhold lands and hereditaments of which I am now seized or possessed or of which I have been or shall be seized or possessed at any time during her coverture by me and I also declare and direct that in case the annual income to arise or be produced from the bank annuities to be purchased with the residue of my personal estate shall be insufficient to answer and pay the sum of one thousand pounds a year then the deficiency shall be answered to the said Viscountess Nelson my wife out of the rents, issues and profits of my barony town and feud lands and hereditaments in Farther Sicily hereinafter devised and I charge the rents, issues and profits thereof with the payment of the said yearly sum of one thousand pounds or such part thereof as the bank annuities to be purchased with the residue of my personal estate shall be insufficient to answer and pay so that in all events the said Viscountess Nelson my wife shall be entitled to receive a clear annual income of one thousand pounds during her natural life provided always that nothing contained in this my will shall extend or be construed to subject my real estates in England to the payment of the said annuity of one thousand pounds or any part thereof . . . provided always and in case a pension or pensions to the amount or value of one thousand pounds a year or upwards shall in my life time be granted to the said Viscountess Nelson my wife by His Majesty or by Parliament then and

2 R

in that case the said sum of one thousand pounds a year to be granted to
her as aforesaid shall be in lieu of the provision of one thousand pounds
a year hereby made for her and then and in that case the same provision
shall cease and be void [1] and in that case the whole of my residuary personal
estate shall be divisible and distributable on my death in the same or the
like manner and to the same persons and in the same proportions as if the
death of my said wife had taken place at the instant of my death. . . .
[Other annuities to his family, etc.; provision for the estate in Sicily.]

And I give and bequeath the diamond hilted sword given to me by
his said Sicilian Majesty the diamond aigrette presented to me by the
Grand Signior, my collar of the order of the Bath, medals of the order of
St. Ferdinand and insignia of other orders to the said William Nelson
and William Haslewood in trust that the same may be held as or in the
nature of heir looms as far as the rules of law and equity will permit. . . .
[Disposal of Merton.]

In witness whereof I the said Horatio Viscount Nelson and Duke of
Bronte have to the fourteen first sheets of this my last will and testament
contained in fifteen sheets of paper set my hand and to the fifteenth and
last sheet my hand and seal have also affixed my seal to the top of the
first sheet where the several sheets are fastened together and have executed
a duplicate hereof this tenth day of May in the year of our Lord one
thousand eight hundred and three.

NELSON AND BRONTE.

Witnessed:

HORATIO LEGGATT.

WILLIAM SLAUGHTER junr. clerks to Messrs. Booth and Haslewood.

HENRY FLETCHER.

Mr. Western to Lady Nelson [2]

11 Gray's Inn Square,
February 4, 1806

MY LADY,—I yesterday waited upon Earl Nelson with your Ladyship's
letter, who after telling me it was the intention of the executors to provide

[1] It has been stated that when Lady Nelson was voted a pension of £2,000 a year by
Parliament in February 1806, this clause took effect. The letters which follow show this
was not so and she enjoyed the annuity and the pension.
[2] Monmouth MSS. Nelson papers, Vol. V. This and the following letters have been
selected from the full correspondence preserved by Lady Nelson. Mr. Western was her
solicitor.

for the annuity given to your ladyship as soon as they received sufficient funds for that purpose, referred me to Mr. Haslewood.

From Mr. Haslewood I understand the only funded property of which Lord Nelson died possessed was the sum of £15600 three per cents, and that his Lordship was indebted to Mr. Davison in the sum of £3000 and the executors have since borrowed £2000 more from him.

From the prize money which is expected to be received and the produce of the estate at Merton which is to be sold in the spring, there will be more than sufficient for the payment of all the debts, legacies and other charges and Mr. H. assured me it was the intention of the executors to provide for the payment of your annuity out of the first monies that might be received which they expect will be in the course of three months and that they consider your Ladyship as intitled to half a year's annuity due at Christmas last.

As your Ladyship cannot call upon the executors for the payment of your annuity till the expiration of 12 months from the death of Lord Nelson, I think your Ladyship cannot do better than wait the time Mr. Haslewood has mentioned when I hope every thing will be settled to your Ladyship's satisfaction.

I have the honour to be your Ladyship's most obliged servant, JAMES WESTERN.

To the Right Honourable Viscountess Nelson, Duchess of Bronte.

Sir Robert Burton to Lady Nelson

London,
May 17, 1806

DEAR LADY NELSON,—I have had two or three interviews with Mr. Western, who seems a judicious man and to have your Ladyship's interest at heart. He has shewn me the letter received from Mr. Haslewood which makes it absolutely necessary to serve the executors with a requisition on behalf of your Ladyship to perform the trusts of Lord Nelson's will, as well respecting his immediate payment of the half annuity due, as the investment of the fund to answer the future payments thereof, which either from ignorance or design, they seem desirous to postpone to other payments in direct contradiction to the trusts in the will.

And if this is not immediately complied with I know my friend Sir Samuel Romilly the Solicitor General, will upon my account give us his best advice how to proceed. I have no difficulty about the mode, nor of effecting the *justice* due to you, but I shall wish to have the sanction of such an authority.

I beg the favour of you to give my best respects to Captain Nisbet, and to be assured that I am with all truth and respect your Ladyship's faithful and most obedient servant. ROBERT BURTON.

Mr. Western to Lady Nelson

11 Gray's Inn Square,
October 17, 1806

DEAR MADAM,—I have great pleasure in informing your Ladyship that the executors of Lord Nelson have purchased the sum of £33,333. 6. 8. 3 per cent consols to provide for the growing payments of the annuity left you by his Lordship's will, and that the executors are willing to execute a power of attorney to enable your banker to receive the dividends as they become due.

Inclosed is a receipt for the year's annuity due at Midsummer after deducting the property tax, which I will trouble you to sign and return to me and the amount shall be paid to your account at Messrs. Marsh and Co. as soon as I receive it.

I beg to congratulate you on the speedy termination of the Chancery suit and have the honour to remain, your Ladyship's most obliged servant, JAMES WESTERN.

Lady Nelson to William Marsh [1]

Clifton,
October 20, 1806

MY DEAR SIR,—I have sent you Mr. Western's letter which will tell you my business with the executors is settled. The stamp receipt which he sent me I signed, it was to empower my bankers to receive the amount of my annuity which was due last June. I am glad the business is all settled. Purchase £1,000 (one thousand pounds) money into the same stock for me. I shall then have enough in your hands to answer my expenses till January. As I have no intention of going to town till the spring, I desired Mr. Western to deliver his bill to you. As to the amount, I can form no idea, but I beg you will do what is proper and customary on these occasions.

---

[1] Lady Nelson's agent.

Many thanks for your letter and the inclosed was quite new to me. I deferred answering it till I could get at a box, which contained what I had promised. Your Mr. Purvis is returned from Lymington and I shall soon to Bath. I must own Malvern air possesses qualities far beyond description.

Believe me dear sir, your sincere and obliged, FRANCES H. NELSON AND BRONTE.

Mr. Western to Lady Nelson

A

11 Gray's Inn Square,
October 23, 1806

DEAR MADAM,—On Tuesday I received from the executors of Lord Nelson the sum of £918.15. which I have paid to your account at Messrs. Marsh and Co. At the time I received the money from Mr. Haslewood I of course told him the executors would be expected to pay the costs incurred by filing the bill in Chancery. Mr. Haslewood tho' he admitted the executors were liable to the costs seemed to think it harsh that they should be called upon to pay them and expressed a hope that your Ladyship would not insist upon it.

I do not myself see the least pretence they can have for asking to have the costs given up, particularly as it was their own conduct that made it necessary to apply to the Court of Chancery, neither do I think they are intitled to any particular marks of favour from you, but as the proposal came from Mr. H. I think it right to acquaint your Ladyship with it, and to wait your directions before I apply to them again.

The taxed costs of filing the bill to which the executors are liable will amount to about twenty three or four pounds.

I have the honour to remain your Ladyship's much obliged servant, JAMES WESTERN.

B

11 Gray's Inn Square,
December 15, 1806

DEAR MADAM,—The executors have not yet paid the costs incurred by filing the bill in Chancery but Mr. Haslewood has promised me they shall be paid. As soon as I have settled with him, I will send my account to Mr. Marsh.

Mr. Haslewood objects to executing the power of attorney to enable your bankers to receive the annuity, as the power would extend to enable them to receive the dividends upon all the stock in the Consols which might at any time be invested in the names of the executors. He promises instead to give an order to Mr. Davison to pay the annuity regularly to Mr. Marsh as the dividends are received which will answer the same purpose of securing to your Ladyship the punctual payment.

I have the honour to remain your Ladyship's obliged servant, JAMES WESTERN.

Lady Nelson's Dressmaker's Account, 1806 [1]

London.

VISCOUNTESS NELSON.

> Bought of E. Franks
> Milliner & Dress Maker, to their
> Royal Highnesses
> The Princess of Wales & Duchess of York
> St. James's Street.

		£	s.	d.
Dec. 13th	To Bill Delivered	1.	5.	0
Jan. 17th	A rich black silk gown made up compl. with body lining persian sleeve lining fine muslin weepers etc.	7.	17.	6
May 1st	A black crape bonnet	1.	16.	0
	A rich black twill sarsnet dress made up complete with body lining etc. etc. bound with crape.	6.	16.	6
	A black crape full dress gown made up complete with rope and tassel for the waist etc.	5.	15.	6
	Jet Ornaments	2.	12.	6
	A black sarsnet slip made up complete with body lining etc. etc.	4.	4.	0
	A fine muslin turban	1.	16.	0
	A black crape turban with Bugle, Bandeau	2.	12.	0
	A fine muslin Hand'f with frills	1.	11.	6
	A Do. Do.	1.	11.	6
	A black sarsnet Spanish cloak trimmed round with black crape	4.	4.	0
	A black twill sarsnet Spencer lin'd and made up complete	3.	10.	0
	A black crape hat and flowers	2.	2.	0
	A black crape veil	–.	14.	0
	Boxes	–.	8.	6
		48.	17.	0

Monmouth MSS., Nelson papers, Vol. V.

MADAM,—I forward this account to your Ladyship merely as a form which takes place at this period and am sorry to hear we are not to be favoured by your presence till late in the spring. I shall be happy to hear that its not want of health which has occasioned your removal to Clifton. Remaining Madam, your Ladyship's most obliged servant, E. FRANKS.

Viscountess Nelson & Bronte, Clifton near Bristol. 14 July 1806.

Mrs. Ricketts to Lady Nelson [1]

Bath,
Saturday, January 31, [1807]

MY DEAR LADY NELSON,—Lord St. Vincent desiring you might have a copy of his letter to me, my grand daughter has copied it; and he also says that when he has a little more leisure, he will select what other letters he had of Lord Nelson's that he thinks you may wish to be in possession of, and adds the rapid promotion of Captain Nisbet through all the grades are the best proofs of the anxiety of his Lordship and the solicitude of his commanding officer to that effect.

I expect to see him here the middle of next week. I hope you performed your journey without fatigue and are comfortably settled.

With great regard your Ladyship's affectionate friend, M. RICKETTS.

Copy

MY DEAR SISTER,—Upon reflection it appears best to send you the only letters I can find relative to Captain Nisbet and to authorise you to assert in my name that Lord Nelson assured me, that he owed his life to the resolution and admirable conduct of his son in law when wounded at Teneriffe, and that he had witnessed many instances of his courage and enterprise. Yours most affectionately. ST. VINCENT.

Mortimer Street, January 22nd, 1807.

To the Viscountess Nelson, Sidmouth.

[The letter has been forwarded by Lady Nelson to Dr. J. M'Arthur as follows:]

Exmouth,
February 28, 1807

DEAR SIR,—I think without exception Mr. Harris's Life of Lord Nelson[2] is the basest production that ever was offered to the public. It is replete

---

[1] Monmouth MSS., Nelson papers, Vol. V. This information was collected for Nelson's official biographers, the Rev. J. S. Clarke and Dr. J. M'Arthur.
[2] Mr. Harrison published his life of Nelson in 1806.

with untruths—in regards to my dear son and self—when my son was told what Mr. H. said in regard to his saving Lord Nelson's life at Tennereiffe, all the answer he made was 'God knows I saved Lord N.'s life at T. That's a pleasure no one can take from me.'[1]

Yours sincerely, F. H. N. & B.

Lord Nelson often said to me, 'it was not so much Josiah's tying up my arm' (Nisbet says a man in the boat, Lovel, assisted him) 'the grasp he gave it stopped the blood immediately, but his judgement in getting me to the ship.' By all account he rowed very very hard that night and steered well too under the batteries for which I am so thankful to Providence that I feel myself the humblest of God's creatures—for my son went to sea to oblige me.

This is a copy of Lord St. Vincent's letter to his sister Mrs. Ricketts when he sent me the two letters, which I got Lord Hood to frank to Dr. Clarke, requesting Dr. C. to forward them to me as soon as copied at Exmouth, Devonshire. As I promised Lord St. Vincent to return these letters soon, I am anxious to keep my word and I [have] been here five weeks. And as I am very nervous, pray send me the two letters, as I feel they ought to be returned besides my word. I went to the Post Office with the letter for I promised to do so.

This is a curious letter I did not intend writing two lines when I first began. My compliments to your family.

Lady Nelson to William Marsh [2]

Bath, 8 Russel Street,
January 29, 1810

MY DEAR SIR,—The vase the Patriotic Fund voted me is finished and I will thank you to direct Messrs. Rundle and Bridges to send it down to me taking care to have it insured if necessary.

More than a month since I enclosed to the house a letter my son had written to Mrs. Nisbet, directed to her at her brother's Mr. Parry, who resides in Berners St. and as he has no answer I fear it has not reached here, therefore will thank you to make some enquiries. The authors has sent me a presentation copy of my late Lord's life, which I hope will not only please, but give satisfaction. I desired Mr. McArthur to put me down for one copy which you will pay for and send me.

---

[1] James Harrison produced the first biography of Nelson, written with the patronage and help of Lady Hamilton. He made scant reference to Josiah's services on this occasion.
[2] N.M.M. 37 MS. 1254, Autograph collection.

The Earl, Countess, and Lady C. Nelson [1] came to Bath three weeks since, their good child not only sought me, but brought her father and mother to my house: I received them, they were much affected, and I think they have received some satisfaction from a shake of my hand.

I hope my god daughter and all your family are well make my kind regards to them. Bath is very gay—but not so full as last year—I hope if any part of your family comes here you will let me know. My son desires his best respects—And I remain Dear Sir

Your obliged and sincere FRANCES H. NELSON AND BRONTE.

Lady Nelson's Will [2]

April 18, 1831

I revoke all wills and give the *interest* of the two instalments of twelve hundred pounds each to Mrs. Nisbet [3] for her life the principal to my grand child Frances Herbert Nisbet—and in succession to the other two in case of death. If I live long enough to save any money I give the interest to Mrs. Nisbet and the principal as above mentioned. FRANCES NELSON AND BRONTE.

Witnessed ELLIN HOYE, 23 Harley Street.

FANNY FRANKLYN,[4] 26 Baker Street, Portman Square.

April 26, 1831

1st Codicil

I the right honourable Frances Viscountess Nelson, Duchess of Bronte hereby appoint Lord Bridport and General Egerton executors of my will hereunto annexed.

Witness to my hand the 26th April 1831. ELLIN HOYE.

May 3, 1831

2nd Codicil

It is my desire that the right honourable Lord Bridport gives one hundred pounds to Miss Locker immediately on my death. FRANCES NELSON AND BRONTE.[5]

---

[1] The Earl's son, Horatio, Viscount Trafalgar, had died in 1808. His daughter, Charlotte, married Lord Bridport and inherited the Duchy of Bronte together with all the manuscripts and other relics not entailed.

[2] Now preserved at Somerset House.

[3] Josiah, who had married Miss Frances Herbert Evans in 1819, had died in France in 1830.

[4] Lady Nelson's cousin. Mrs. Franklyn was with her when she died. Her son discovered Nelson's letters to his wife among Mrs. Franklyn's papers many years later.

[5] This signature is almost illegible. Lady Nelson died the next day, May 4. Her will was proved on May 13, the estate being under £4,000. The inscription on her tomb gives the date of her death as May 6.

ADDENDA

The text of the following letters from Nelson to Lady Nelson is taken from an article in *The Huntington Library Quarterly*, Vol. XI, no. 1, pp. 81–6 (November 1947), by Hardin Craig, Junior.

Southampton,
January 13, 1801

MY DEAR FANNY,—We are arrived and heartily tired, so tell Mrs. Nelson,[1] and with kindest regards to my father and all the family, Believe me your affectionate NELSON.

[Plymouth,]
5 o'clock, January 16, 1801

MY DEAR FANNY,—This moment of the posts departure we arrived. Your letters I received this morning at Tor Abbey[2] for which I thank you. I have only time to say God bless you and my dear father and believe me, your affectionate NELSON.

To Lady Nelson, 17 Dover Street, London.

[Plymouth,]
January 20, 1801

MY DEAR FANNY,—All my things are now breaking open for only one key can be found. My steward says I have no one thing for comfort come, but a load of useless articles from Burgess's and a large chest of green tea. I have been buying a few things just to make me *un*comfortable for in fact I have nothing useful but two chairs. £100 I have paid for carriage, £20 would have bought me more than I could want from Mr. Burgess. I know not where I shall be in a week, with my kindest regards to my father and Mrs. Nelson, I am your affectionate NELSON.

Plymouth Dock,
January 21, 1801

MY DEAR FANNY,—Half my wardrobe is left behind and that butler, a French rascal, ought to be hanged and I hope you will never lay out a farthing with Mr. Burgess. Had the waste of money been laid out in Wedgewood's ware, knives, forks for servants or cooking utensils it would

---

[1] Mrs. William Nelson, whose husband had gone to Plymouth with Nelson. See p. 573.
[2] Lord St. Vincent was staying at Tor Abbey, near Dartmouth.

have been well, but I am forced to buy every thing, even a little *tea* for who would open a large chest? In short I find myself without any thing comfortable or convenient. In glasses of some kind the steward tells me he finds a useless quantity of decanters, as yet not one can be found, and if he cannot find them today I must buy. In short I only regret that I desired any person to order things for me. I could have done all in ten minutes and for a 10th part of the expense, but never mind I can eat off a yellow ware plate. It is now too late to send my half wardrobe, as I know not what is to become of me, nor do I care. My brother[1] is very well and desires his regards, as I, to Mrs. Nelson. Yours truly, NELSON.

Captain B.[2] tells me you have changed your house.

To Lady Nelson, Dover Street, London.

San Josef, Torbay,
February 3, 1801

MY DEAR FANNY,—I received yesterday your letter from Brighton. It never was my intention to find [fault] but the fact is I have nothing and every thing. If I want a piece of pickle it must be put in saucer, if a piece of butter on an earthen plate, but I shall direct what things I want in future. The stands for the decanters I thought was to have been repaired and sent me, if they are not I shall desire Hancock to send me two. Not one thing that Mr. Dods sent but is ruined, large nails drove through the mahogany table and drawers to fasten the packing cases. If they had been sent so to a gentleman's house and new, of course they would have been returned. Mr. D. has only sent 3 keys, of the small table and chest of drawers not of the wardrobe, trunk, case of the Turkey cup[3] &c, &c. By the by the trident of Neptune is bent double from ill package. I have six silver bottle stands but not one decanter to fit them, you told me six of the house ones should be sent. I beg my kindest regards to Josiah and Miss Locker,[4] the Ellis's &c. and believe me your affectionate NELSON.

To Lady Nelson, Brighton, Sussex.

London,
February 24, 1801

As I am sent for to town on very particular business for a day or two I would not on any account have you come to London but rest quiet where

[1] The Rev. William Nelson.   [2] Captain Sir Edward Berry.
[3] The silver cup designed by Paul Storr presented to Nelson in 1799, 'by the Governor and company of the Merchants of England trading into the Levant Seas in commemoration of the glorious victory obtained by his Lordship at the mouth of the Nile', is now in the National Maritime Museum.
[4] The daughter of Captain William Locker, who was staying with Lady Nelson at Brighton.

you are. Nor would I have you come to Portsmouth for I never come on shore. The King is reported to be more than very ill, but I and every good subject must pray for his life. I hope Josiah may be able to get a ship now this change of ministers has taken place. As ever your affectionate NELSON.

Josiah is to have the *Thalia*, and I want to know from him two good Lieutenants, they must be of my approval. I wish Lieutenant Champion to be second, would he like Mr. Yule to be first, if I can induce him to quit the *St. George*?[1] He must return an answer by the post directed to me Lothians Hotel.[2]

To Lady Nelson, Brighton, Sussex.

[1] Nelson had transferred to the *St. George* on February 20. Lieutenant Yule was discharged from the *St. George* to the *Thalia* on March 8.
[2] The hotel where Nelson was staying in London.

INDEX

An Index of SHIPS follows this general index. Officers have been given the rank they held at the time of their death. Alternative spellings of proper names are given in brackets.

621

INDEX OF SHIPS

The following abbreviations are used to denote foreign ships: (Fr.) French; (Sp.) Spanish.